KB211214

# RGB ENGLISH BIBLE

이계양의 빨녹파특허영어 성경
# RGB ENGLISH BIBLE

2021년 12월 24일 초판 1쇄 발행

| | |
|---|---|
| 편역자 | 이계양 |
| 등록 | 제2016-000010호 (2016년 9월 20일) |
| 펴낸곳 | 한산(주) |
| 주소 | 17501 경기도 안성시 양성로 519-90번지 |
| | 519-90, Yangsung-Lo, Ansung City 17501 South Korea |
| Email | info@KnowSuperPower.com |
| Tel | +82) 10 9009 3594 |
| Fax | +82) 31 673 0686 |
| 편집&디자인 | 디자인비타 |

책값은 뒤표지에 있습니다.

본서의 본문은 특허 제10-2162109호(2020년 09월 25일) [색채구분에 의하여 쉽게 이해되는 영문이 포함된 인쇄물] (약칭, 빨녹파특허영어) 원리를 채용하고 있습니다.

영어 원문은 미국성서협회(American Bible Society)의 지식재산권 사용허가를 정식으로 취득하여 차용하고 있습니다.

본서의 편집내용은 특허법 및 관련 저작권법을 따르고 있으며, 본서의 특허원리나 원문을 서면허가 없이 채용할 경우 법적 제재를 받을 수 있습니다. 정식 사용권 취득과 관련된 사항은 출판사 한산주식회사로 문의바랍니다.

이계양의
빨녹파 특허영어 성경

# RGB

# ENGLISH
# BIBLE

Edited by Gheyang Lee

이계양 편역

# CONTENTS

# Acknowledgement
일러두기

**This GNT Bible was** printed according **to patented R**GB **English principles as** follows.

본 GNT영어성경은 **빨**녹피**특허영어** 원리를 적용하여 아래와 같이 인쇄되었다.

✔ **The verb of main clause was** printed **in red.**
주절의 동사는 **빨간색**으로 인쇄하였다.

✔ **The verb of subordinate clause was** painted **in green.**
종속절의 동사는 초록색으로 채색하였다.

✔ **In case the predicate part** was expressed **in progressive, passive voice and perfect tense, the first linking verb was** regarded **and** colored **as main verb.**
술어부가 진행형, 수동태, 완료시제로 표현된 경우에는 술어부의 첫째 요소를 본동사로 간주하여 색칠하였다.

✔ **Infinitive, gerund, participle and participial construction were** dyed **in** blue.
부정사, 동명사, 분사, 분사구문은 파란색으로 나타냈다.

✔ **In case of [preposition+noun] phrase, these phrases were** underlined.
[전치사+명사] 전명구의 경우에는 밑줄을 그었다.

기타 **빨**녹피**특허영어** 적용원리 및 영어문법은 이계양 저, [바로가능영어] 책을 참조 바란다.

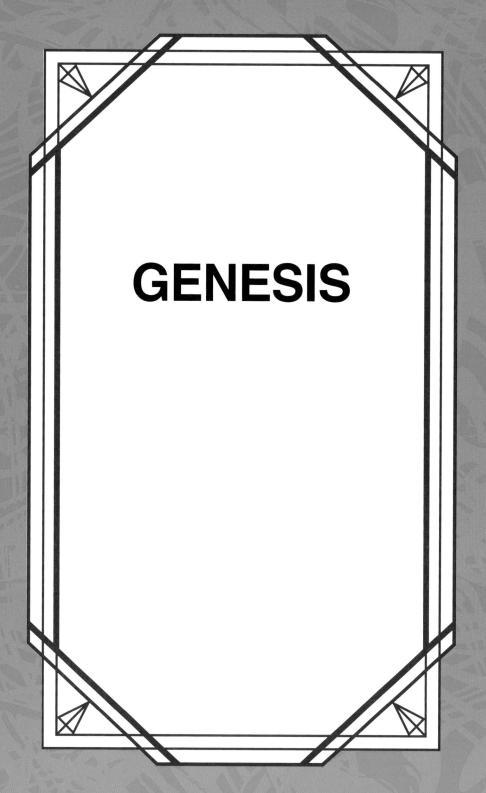

# GENESIS

# Genesis

1

<sup>1.1</sup> In the beginning, when God created the universe,
<sup>1.2</sup> the earth was formless and desolate. The raging ocean that covered everything was engulfed in total darkness, and the Spirit of God was moving over the water.
<sup>1.3</sup> Then God commanded, "Let there be light"—and light appeared.
<sup>1.4</sup> God was pleased with what he saw. Then he separated the light from the darkness,
<sup>1.5</sup> and he named the light "Day" and the darkness "Night." Evening passed and morning came—that was the first day.
<sup>1.6-7</sup> Then God commanded, "Let there be a dome to divide the water and to keep it in two separate places"—and it was done. So God made a dome, and it separated the water under it from the water above it.
<sup>1.8</sup> He named the dome "Sky." Evening passed and morning came—that was the second day.
<sup>1.9</sup> Then God commanded, "Let the water below the sky come together in one place, so that the land will appear"—and it was done.
<sup>1.10</sup> He named the land "Earth," and the water which had come together he named "Sea." And God was pleased with what he saw.
<sup>1.11</sup> Then he commanded, "Let the earth produce all kinds of plants, those that bear grain and those that bear fruit"—and it was done.
<sup>1.12</sup> So the earth produced all kinds of plants, and God was pleased with what he saw.
<sup>1.13</sup> Evening passed and morning came—that was the third day.
<sup>1.14</sup> Then God commanded, "Let lights appear in the sky to separate day from night and to show the time when days, years, and religious festivals begin;
<sup>1.15</sup> "they will shine in the sky to give light to the earth"—and it was done.
<sup>1.16</sup> So God made the two larger lights, the sun to rule over the day and the moon to rule over the night; he also made the stars.
<sup>1.17</sup> He placed the lights in the sky to shine on the earth,
<sup>1.18</sup> to rule over the day and the night, and to separate light from darkness. And God was pleased with what he saw.
<sup>1.19</sup> Evening passed and morning came—that was the fourth day.
<sup>1.20</sup> Then God commanded, "Let the water be filled with many kinds of living beings, and let the air be filled with birds."
<sup>1.21</sup> So God created the great sea monsters, all kinds of creatures that

live in the water, and all kinds of birds. And God was pleased with what he saw.

<sup>1.22</sup> He blessed them all and told the creatures that live in the water to reproduce and to fill the sea, and he told the birds to increase in number.

<sup>1.23</sup> Evening passed and morning came—that was the fifth day.

<sup>1.24</sup> Then God commanded, "Let the earth produce all kinds of animal life: domestic and wild, large and small"—and it was done.

<sup>1.25</sup> So God made them all, and he was pleased with what he saw.

<sup>1.26</sup> Then God said, "And now we will make human beings; they will be like us and resemble us. They will have power over the fish, the birds, and all animals, domestic and wild, large and small."

<sup>1.27</sup> So God created human beings, making them to be like himself. He created them male and female,

<sup>1.28</sup> blessed them, and said, "Have many children, so that your descendants will live all over the earth and bring it under their control. I am putting you in charge of the fish, the birds, and all the wild animals.

<sup>1.29</sup> "I have provided all kinds of grain and all kinds of fruit for you to eat;

<sup>1.30</sup> "but for all the wild animals and for all the birds I have provided grass and leafy plants for food"—and it was done .

<sup>1.31</sup> God looked at everything he had made, and he was very pleased. Evening passed and morning came—that was the sixth day.

# 2

<sup>2.1</sup> And so the whole universe was completed.

<sup>2.2</sup> By the seventh day God finished what he had been doing and stopped working.

<sup>2.3</sup> He blessed the seventh day and set it apart as a special day, because by that day he had completed his creation and stopped working.

<sup>2.4</sup> And that is how the universe was created.

When the Lord God made the universe,

<sup>2.5</sup> there were no plants on the earth and no seeds had sprouted, because he had not sent any rain, and there was no one to cultivate the land;

<sup>2.6</sup> but water would come up from beneath the surface and water the ground.

<sup>2.7</sup> Then the Lord God took some soil from the ground and formed a man out of it; he breathed life-giving breath into his nostrils and the

man began to live.

<sup></sup>^2.8 Then the Lord God planted a garden in Eden, in the East, and there he put the man he had formed.

^2.9 He made all kinds of beautiful trees grow there and produce good fruit. In the middle of the garden stood the tree that gives life and the tree that gives knowledge of what is good and what is bad.

^2.10 A stream flowed in Eden and watered the garden; beyond Eden it divided into four rivers.

^2.11 The first river is the Pishon; it flows around the country of Havilah.

^2.12 (Pure gold is found there and also rare perfume and precious stones.)

^2.13 The second river is the Gihon; it flows around the country of Cush.

^2.14 The third river is the Tigris, which flows east of Assyria, and the fourth river is the Euphrates.

^2.15 Then the Lord God placed the man in the Garden of Eden to cultivate it and guard it.

^2.16 He told him, "You may eat the fruit of any tree in the garden,

^2.17 "except the tree that gives knowledge of what is good and what is bad. You must not eat the fruit of that tree; if you do, you will die the same day."

^2.18 Then the Lord God said, "It is not good for the man to live alone. I will make a suitable companion to help him."

^2.19 So he took some soil from the ground and formed all the animals and all the birds. Then he brought them to the man to see what he would name them; and that is how they all got their names.

^2.20 So the man named all the birds and all the animals; but not one of them was a suitable companion to help him.

^2.21 Then the Lord God made the man fall into a deep sleep, and while he was sleeping, he took out one of the man's ribs and closed up the flesh.

^2.22 He formed a woman out of the rib and brought her to him.

^2.23 Then the man said, "At last, here is one of my own kind—Bone taken from my bone, and flesh from my flesh. 'Woman' is her name because she was taken out of man."

^2.24 That is why a man leaves his father and mother and is united with his wife, and they become one.

^2.25 The man and the woman were both naked, but they were not embarrassed.

3.1 Now the snake was the most cunning animal that the Lord God had made. The snake asked the woman, "Did God really tell you not to eat fruit from any tree in the garden?"

3.2 "We may eat the fruit of any tree in the garden," the woman answered,

3.3 "except the tree in the middle of it. God told us not to eat the fruit of that tree or even touch it; if we do, we will die."

3.4 The snake replied, "That's not true; you will not die.

3.5 "God said that because he knows that when you eat it, you will be like God and know what is good and what is bad."

3.6 The woman saw how beautiful the tree was and how good its fruit would be to eat, and she thought how wonderful it would be to become wise. So she took some of the fruit and ate it. Then she gave some to her husband, and he also ate it.

3.7 As soon as they had eaten it, they were given understanding and realized that they were naked; so they sewed fig leaves together and covered themselves.

3.8 That evening they heard the Lord God walking in the garden, and they hid from him among the trees.

3.9 But the Lord God called out to the man, "Where are you?"

3.10 He answered, "I heard you in the garden; I was afraid and hid from you, because I was naked."

3.11 "Who told you that you were naked?" God asked. "Did you eat the fruit that I told you not to eat?"

3.12 The man answered, "The woman you put here with me gave me the fruit, and I ate it."

3.13 The Lord God asked the woman, "Why did you do this?"

She replied, "The snake tricked me into eating it."

3.14 Then the Lord God said to the snake, "You will be punished for this; you alone of all the animals must bear this curse: From now on you will crawl on your belly, and you will have to eat dust as long as you live.

3.15 "I will make you and the woman hate each other; her offspring and yours will always be enemies. Her offspring will crush your head, and you will bite her offspring's heel."

3.16 And he said to the woman, "I will increase your trouble in pregnancy and your pain in giving birth. In spite of this, you will still have desire for your husband, yet you will be subject to him."

3.17 And he said to the man, "You listened to your wife and ate the fruit which I told you not to eat. Because of what you have done, the ground will be under a curse. You will have to work hard all your life to make it produce enough food for you.

3.18 "It will produce weeds and thorns, and you will have to eat wild plants.

3.19 "You will have to work hard and sweat to make the soil produce anything, until you go back to the soil from which you were formed. You were made from soil, and you will become soil again."

3.20 Adam named his wife Eve, because she was the mother of all human beings.

3.21 And the Lord God made clothes out of animal skins for Adam and his wife, and he clothed them.

3.22 Then the Lord God said, "Now these human beings have become like one of us and have knowledge of what is good and what is bad. They must not be allowed to take fruit from the tree that gives life, eat it, and live forever."

3.23 So the Lord God sent them out of the Garden of Eden and made them cultivate the soil from which they had been formed.

3.24 Then at the east side of the garden he put living creatures and a flaming sword which turned in all directions. This was to keep anyone from coming near the tree that gives life.

# 4

4.1 Then Adam had intercourse with his wife, and she became pregnant. She bore a son and said, "By the Lord's help I have gotten a son." So she named him Cain.

4.2 Later she gave birth to another son, Abel. Abel became a shepherd, but Cain was a farmer.

4.3 After some time Cain brought some of his harvest and gave it as an offering to the Lord.

4.4 Then Abel brought the first lamb born to one of his sheep, killed it, and gave the best parts of it as an offering. The Lord was pleased with Abel and his offering,

4.5 but he rejected Cain and his offering. Cain became furious, and he scowled in anger.

4.6 Then the Lord said to Cain, "Why are you angry? Why that scowl on your face?

4.7 "If you had done the right thing, you would be smiling; but because you have done evil, sin is crouching at your door. It wants to rule you, but you must overcome it."

4.8 Then Cain said to his brother Abel, "Let's go out in the fields." When they were out in the fields, Cain turned on his brother and killed him.

4.9 The Lord asked Cain, "Where is your brother Abel?"

He answered, "I don't know. Am I supposed to take care of my brother?"

4.10 Then the Lord said, "Why have you done this terrible thing? Your brother's blood is crying out to me from the ground, like a voice calling for revenge.

4.11 "You are placed under a curse and can no longer farm the soil. It has soaked up your brother's blood as if it had opened its mouth to receive it when you killed him.

4.12 "If you try to grow crops, the soil will not produce anything; you will be a homeless wanderer on the earth."

4.13 And Cain said to the Lord, "This punishment is too hard for me to bear.

4.14 "You are driving me off the land and away from your presence. I will be a homeless wanderer on the earth, and anyone who finds me will kill me."

4.15 But the Lord answered, "No. If anyone kills you, seven lives will be taken in revenge." So the Lord put a mark on Cain to warn anyone who met him not to kill him.

4.16 And Cain went away from the Lord's presence and lived in a land called "Wandering," which is east of Eden.

4.17 Cain and his wife had a son and named him Enoch. Then Cain built a city and named it after his son.

4.18 Enoch had a son named Irad, who was the father of Mehujael, and Mehujael had a son named Methushael, who was the father of Lamech.

4.19 Lamech had two wives, Adah and Zillah.

4.20 Adah gave birth to Jabal, who was the ancestor of those who raise livestock and live in tents.

4.21 His brother was Jubal, the ancestor of all musicians who play the harp and the flute.

4.22 Zillah gave birth to Tubal Cain, who made all kinds of tools out of bronze and iron. The sister of Tubal Cain was Naamah.

4.23 Lamech said to his wives, "Adah and Zillah, listen to me: I have killed a young man because he struck me.

4.24 "If seven lives are taken to pay for killing Cain, Seventy-seven will be taken if anyone kills me."

4.25 Adam and his wife had another son. She said, "God has given me a son to replace Abel, whom Cain killed." So she named him Seth.

4.26 Seth had a son whom he named Enosh. It was then that people began using the Lord's holy name in worship.

# 5

5.1 This is the list of the descendants of Adam. (When God created human beings, he made them like himself.
5.2 He created them male and female, blessed them, and named them "Human Beings.")
5.3 When Adam was 130 years old, he had a son who was like him, and he named him Seth.
5.4 After that, Adam lived another 800 years. He had other children
5.5 and died at the age of 930.
5.6 When Seth was 105, he had a son, Enosh,
5.7 and then lived another 807 years. He had other children
5.8 and died at the age of 912.
5.9 When Enosh was 90, he had a son, Kenan,
5.10 and then lived another 815 years. He had other children
5.11 and died at the age of 905.
5.12 When Kenan was 70, he had a son, Mahalalel,
5.13 and then lived another 840 years. He had other children
5.14 and died at the age of 910.
5.15 When Mahalalel was 65, he had a son, Jared,
5.16 and then lived another 830 years. He had other children
5.17 and died at the age of 895.
5.18 When Jared was 162, he had a son, Enoch,
5.19 and then lived another 800 years. He had other children
5.20 and died at the age of 962.
5.21 When Enoch was 65, he had a son, Methuselah.
5.22 After that, Enoch lived in fellowship with God for 300 years and had other children.
5.23 He lived to be 365 years old.
5.24 He spent his life in fellowship with God, and then he disappeared, because God took him away.
5.25 When Methuselah was 187, he had a son, Lamech,
5.26 and then lived another 782 years. He had other children
5.27 and died at the age of 969.
5.28 When Lamech was 182, he had a son
5.29 and said, "From the very ground on which the Lord put a curse, this child will bring us relief from all our hard work"; so he named him Noah.
5.30 Lamech lived another 595 years. He had other children
5.31 and died at the age of 777.

<sup>5.32</sup> After Noah was 500 years old, he had three sons, Shem, Ham, and Japheth.

<sup>6</sup>

<sup>6.1</sup> When people had spread all over the world, and daughters were being born,

<sup>6.2</sup> some of the heavenly beings saw that these young women were beautiful, so they took the ones they liked.

<sup>6.3</sup> Then the Lord said, "I will not allow people to live forever; they are mortal. From now on they will live no longer than 120 years."

<sup>6.4</sup> In those days, and even later, there were giants on the earth who were descendants of human women and the heavenly beings. They were the great heroes and famous men of long ago.

<sup>6.5</sup> When the Lord saw how wicked everyone on earth was and how evil their thoughts were all the time,

<sup>6.6</sup> he was sorry that he had ever made them and put them on the earth. He was so filled with regret

<sup>6.7</sup> that he said, "I will wipe out these people I have created, and also the animals and the birds, because I am sorry that I made any of them."

<sup>6.8</sup> But the Lord was pleased with Noah.

<sup>6.9-10</sup> This is the story of Noah. He had three sons, Shem, Ham, and Japheth. Noah had no faults and was the only good man of his time. He lived in fellowship with God,

<sup>6.11</sup> but everyone else was evil in God's sight, and violence had spread everywhere.

<sup>6.12</sup> God looked at the world and saw that it was evil, for the people were all living evil lives.

<sup>6.13</sup> God said to Noah, "I have decided to put an end to all people. I will destroy them completely, because the world is full of their violent deeds.

<sup>6.14</sup> "Build a boat for yourself out of good timber; make rooms in it and cover it with tar inside and out.

<sup>6.15</sup> "Make it 450 feet long, 75 feet wide, and 45 feet high.

<sup>6.16</sup> "Make a roof for the boat and leave a space of 18 inches between the roof and the sides. Build it with three decks and put a door in the side.

<sup>6.17</sup> "I am going to send a flood on the earth to destroy every living being. Everything on the earth will die,

<sup>6.18</sup> "but I will make a covenant with you. Go into the boat with your wife, your sons, and their wives.

6.19-20 "Take into the boat with you a male and a female of every kind of animal and of every kind of bird, in order to keep them alive.
6.21 "Take along all kinds of food for you and for them."
6.22 Noah did everything that God commanded.

# 7

7.1 The Lord said to Noah, "Go into the boat with your whole family; I have found that you are the only one in all the world who does what is right.
7.2 "Take with you seven pairs of each kind of ritually clean animal, but only one pair of each kind of unclean animal.
7.3 "Take also seven pairs of each kind of bird. Do this so that every kind of animal and bird will be kept alive to reproduce again on the earth.
7.4 "Seven days from now I am going to send rain that will fall for forty days and nights, in order to destroy all the living beings that I have made."
7.5 And Noah did everything that the Lord commanded.
7.6 Noah was six hundred years old when the flood came on the earth.
7.7 He and his wife, and his sons and their wives, went into the boat to escape the flood.
7.8 A male and a female of every kind of animal and bird, whether ritually clean or unclean,
7.9 went into the boat with Noah, as God had commanded.
7.10 Seven days later the flood came.
7.11 When Noah was six hundred years old, on the seventeenth day of the second month all the outlets of the vast body of water beneath the earth burst open, all the floodgates of the sky were opened,
7.12 and rain fell on the earth for forty days and nights.
7.13 On that same day Noah and his wife went into the boat with their three sons, Shem, Ham, and Japheth, and their wives.
7.14 With them went every kind of animal, domestic and wild, large and small, and every kind of bird.
7.15 A male and a female of each kind of living being went into the boat with Noah,
7.16 as God had commanded. Then the Lord shut the door behind Noah.
7.17 The flood continued for forty days, and the water became deep enough for the boat to float.
7.18 The water became deeper, and the boat drifted on the surface.

<sup>7.19</sup> It became so deep that it covered the highest mountains;
<sup>7.20</sup> it went on rising until it was <u>about twenty-five feet</u> <u>above the tops</u> <u>of the mountains.</u>
<sup>7.21</sup> Every living being <u>on the earth</u> died—every bird, every animal, and every person.
<sup>7.22</sup> Everything <u>on earth</u> that breathed died.
<sup>7.23</sup> The Lord destroyed all living beings <u>on the earth</u>—human beings, animals, and birds. The only ones left were Noah and those who were <u>with him</u> <u>in the boat.</u>
<sup>7.24</sup> The water did not start going down <u>for a hundred and fifty days.</u>

# 8

<sup>8.1</sup> God had not forgotten Noah and all the animals <u>with him</u> <u>in the boat;</u> he caused a wind to blow, and the water started going down.
<sup>8.2</sup> The outlets <u>of the water</u> <u>beneath the earth</u> and the floodgates <u>of the sky</u> were closed. The rain stopped,
<sup>8.3</sup> and the water gradually went down <u>for 150 days.</u>
<sup>8.4</sup> <u>On the seventeenth day</u> <u>of the seventh month</u> the boat came to rest <u>on a mountain</u> <u>in the Ararat range.</u>
<sup>8.5</sup> The water kept going down, and <u>on the first day</u> <u>of the tenth month</u> the tops <u>of the mountains</u> appeared.
<sup>8.6</sup> <u>After forty days</u> Noah opened a window
<sup>8.7</sup> and sent out a raven. It did not come back, but kept flying around until the water was completely gone.
<sup>8.8</sup> Meanwhile, Noah sent out a dove to see if the water had gone down,
<sup>8.9</sup> but since the water still covered all the land, the dove did not find a place to light. It flew back <u>to the boat</u>, and Noah reached out and took it in.
<sup>8.10</sup> He waited another seven days and sent out the dove again.
<sup>8.11</sup> It returned <u>to him</u> <u>in the evening</u> <u>with a fresh olive leaf</u> <u>in its beak.</u> So Noah knew that the water had gone down.
<sup>8.12</sup> Then he waited another seven days and sent out the dove once more; this time it did not come back.
<sup>8.13</sup> When Noah was 601 years old, <u>on the first day</u> <u>of the first month,</u> the water was gone. Noah removed the covering <u>of the boat,</u> looked around, and saw that the ground was getting dry.
<sup>8.14</sup> <u>By the twenty-seventh day</u> <u>of the second month</u> the earth was completely dry.
<sup>8.15</sup> God said <u>to Noah,</u>
<sup>8.16</sup> "Go <u>out of the boat</u> <u>with your wife, your sons, and their wives.</u>

<sup>8.17</sup> "Take all the birds and animals out <u>with you</u>, so that they may reproduce and spread <u>over all the earth</u>."

<sup>8.18</sup> So Noah went <u>out of the boat</u> <u>with his wife, his sons, and their wives</u>.

<sup>8.19</sup> All the animals and birds went <u>out of the boat</u> <u>in groups</u> <u>of their own kind</u>.

<sup>8.20</sup> Noah built an altar <u>to the Lord</u>; he took one <u>of each kind</u> of ritually <u>clean animal and bird</u>, and burned them whole <u>as a sacrifice</u> on the altar.

<sup>8.21</sup> The odor <u>of the sacrifice</u> pleased the Lord, and he said <u>to himself</u>, "Never again will I put the earth <u>under a curse</u> <u>because of what</u> people do; I know that <u>from the time</u> they are young their thoughts are evil. Never again will I destroy all living beings, as I have done this time.

<sup>8.22</sup> "As long as the world exists, there will be a time <u>for planting</u> and a time <u>for harvest</u>. There will always be cold and heat, summer and winter, day and night."

# 9

<sup>9.1</sup> God blessed Noah and his sons and said, "Have many children, so that your descendants will live all <u>over the earth</u>.

<sup>9.2</sup> "All the animals, birds, and fish will live <u>in fear</u> <u>of you</u>. They are all placed <u>under your power</u>.

<sup>9.3</sup> "Now you can eat them, as well <u>as green plants</u>; I give them all <u>to you</u> <u>for food</u>.

<sup>9.4</sup> "The one thing you must not eat is meat <u>with blood</u> still <u>in it</u>; I forbid this because the life is <u>in the blood</u>.

<sup>9.5</sup> "If anyone takes human life, he will be punished. I will punish <u>with death</u> any animal that takes a human life.

<sup>9.6</sup> "Human beings were made <u>like God</u>, so whoever murders one <u>of them</u> will be killed <u>by someone else</u>.

<sup>9.7</sup> "You must have many children, so that your descendants will live all <u>over the earth</u>."

<sup>9.8</sup> God said <u>to Noah and his sons</u>,

<sup>9.9</sup> "I am now making my covenant <u>with you</u> and <u>with your descendants</u>,

<sup>9.10</sup> "and <u>with all living beings</u>—all birds and all animals—everything that came <u>out of the boat</u> <u>with you</u>.

<sup>9.11</sup> "<u>With these words</u> I make my covenant <u>with you</u>: I promise that never again will all living beings be destroyed <u>by a flood</u>; never again will a flood destroy the earth.

<sup>9.12</sup> "As a sign of this everlasting covenant which I am making with you and with all living beings,

<sup>9.13</sup> "I am putting my bow in the clouds. It will be the sign of my covenant with the world.

<sup>9.14</sup> "Whenever I cover the sky with clouds and the rainbow appears,

<sup>9.15</sup> "I will remember my promise to you and to all the animals that a flood will never again destroy all living beings.

<sup>9.16</sup> "When the rainbow appears in the clouds, I will see it and remember the everlasting covenant between me and all living beings on earth.

<sup>9.17</sup> "That is the sign of the promise which I am making to all living beings."

<sup>9.18</sup> The sons of Noah who went out of the boat were Shem, Ham, and Japheth. (Ham was the father of Canaan.)

<sup>9.19</sup> These three sons of Noah were the ancestors of all the people on earth.

<sup>9.20</sup> Noah, who was a farmer, was the first man to plant a vineyard.

<sup>9.21</sup> After he drank some of the wine, he became drunk, took off his clothes, and lay naked in his tent.

<sup>9.22</sup> When Ham, the father of Canaan, saw that his father was naked, he went out and told his two brothers.

<sup>9.23</sup> Then Shem and Japheth took a robe and held it behind them on their shoulders. They walked backward into the tent and covered their father, keeping their faces turned away so as not to see him naked.

<sup>9.24</sup> When Noah sobered up and learned what his youngest son had done to him,

<sup>9.25</sup> he said, "A curse on Canaan! He will be a slave to his brothers.

<sup>9.26</sup> "Give praise to the Lord, the God of Shem! Canaan will be the slave of Shem.

<sup>9.27</sup> "May God cause Japheth to increase! May his descendants live with the people of Shem! Canaan will be the slave of Japheth."

<sup>9.28</sup> After the flood Noah lived 350 years

<sup>9.29</sup> and died at the age of 950.

# 10

<sup>10.1</sup> These are the descendants of Noah's sons, Shem, Ham, and Japheth. These three had sons after the flood.

<sup>10.2</sup> The sons of Japheth—Gomer, Magog, Madai, Javan, Tubal, Meshech, and Tiras—were the ancestors of the peoples who bear their names.

<sup>10.3</sup> The descendants of Gomer were the people of Ashkenaz, Riphath, and Togarmah.

<sup>10.4</sup> The descendants of Javan were the people of Elishah, Spain, Cyprus, and Rhodes;

<sup>10.5</sup> they were the ancestors of the people who live along the coast and on the islands. These are the descendants of Japheth, living in their different tribes and countries, each group speaking its own language.

<sup>10.6</sup> The sons of Ham—Cush, Egypt, Libya, and Canaan—were the ancestors of the peoples who bear their names.

<sup>10.7</sup> The descendants of Cush were the people of Seba, Havilah, Sabtah, Raamah, and Sabteca. The descendants of Raamah were the people of Sheba and Dedan.

<sup>10.8</sup> Cush had a son named Nimrod, who became the world's first great conqueror.

<sup>10.9</sup> By the Lord's help he was a great hunter, and that is why people say, "May the Lord make you as great a hunter as Nimrod!"

<sup>10.10</sup> At first his kingdom included Babylon, Erech, and Accad, all three of them in Babylonia.

<sup>10.11</sup> From that land he went to Assyria and built the cities of Nineveh, Rehoboth Ir, Calah,

<sup>10.12</sup> and Resen, which is between Nineveh and the great city of Calah.

<sup>10.13</sup> The descendants of Egypt were the people of Lydia, Anam, Lehab, Naphtuh,

<sup>10.14</sup> Pathrus, Casluh, and of Crete, from whom the Philistines are descended.

<sup>10.15</sup> Canaan's sons—Sidon, the oldest, and Heth—were the ancestors of the peoples who bear their names.

<sup>10.16</sup> Canaan was also the ancestor of the Jebusites, the Amorites, the Girgashites,

<sup>10.17</sup> the Hivites, the Arkites, the Sinites,

<sup>10.18</sup> the Arvadites, the Zemarites, and the Hamathites. The different tribes of the Canaanites spread out,

<sup>10.19</sup> until the Canaanite borders reached from Sidon southward to Gerar near Gaza, and eastward to Sodom, Gomorrah, Admah, and Zeboiim near Lasha.

<sup>10.20</sup> These are the descendants of Ham, living in their different tribes and countries, each group speaking its own language.

<sup>10.21</sup> Shem, the older brother of Japheth, was the ancestor of all the Hebrews.

<sup>10.22</sup> Shem's sons—Elam, Asshur, Arpachshad, Lud, and Aram—were the ancestors of the peoples who bear their names.

<sup>10.23</sup> The descendants of Aram were the people of Uz, Hul, Gether, and Meshek.

<sup>10.24</sup> Arpachshad was the father of Shelah, who was the father of Eber.

<sup>10.25</sup> Eber had two sons: one was named Peleg, because during his time the people of the world were divided; and the other was named Joktan.

<sup>10.26</sup> The descendants of Joktan were the people of Almodad, Sheleph, Hazarmaveth, Jerah,

<sup>10.27</sup> Hadoram, Uzal, Diklah,

<sup>10.28</sup> Obal, Abimael, Sheba,

<sup>10.29</sup> Ophir, Havilah, and Jobab. All of them were descended from Joktan.

<sup>10.30</sup> The land in which they lived extended from Mesha to Sephar in the eastern hill country.

<sup>10.31</sup> These are the descendants of Shem, living in their different tribes and countries, each group speaking its own language.

<sup>10.32</sup> All these peoples are the descendants of Noah, nation by nation, according to their different lines of descent. After the flood all the nations of the earth were descended from the sons of Noah.

# 11

<sup>11.1</sup> At first, the people of the whole world had only one language and used the same words.

<sup>11.2</sup> As they wandered about in the East, they came to a plain in Babylonia and settled there.

<sup>11.3</sup> They said to one another, "Come on! Let's make bricks and bake them hard." So they had bricks to build with and tar to hold them together.

<sup>11.4</sup> They said, "Now let's build a city with a tower that reaches the sky, so that we can make a name for ourselves and not be scattered all over the earth."

<sup>11.5</sup> Then the Lord came down to see the city and the tower which they had built,

<sup>11.6</sup> and he said, "Now then, these are all one people and they speak one language; this is just the beginning of what they are going to do. Soon they will be able to do anything they want!

<sup>11.7</sup> "Let us go down and mix up their language so that they will not understand each other."

<sup>11.8</sup> So the Lord scattered them all over the earth, and they stopped building the city.

<sup>11.9</sup> The city was called Babylon, because there the Lord mixed up the language of all the people, and from there he scattered them all over the earth.

<sup>11.10</sup> These are the descendants of Shem. Two years after the flood, when Shem was 100 years old, he had a son, Arpachshad.

<sup>11.11</sup> After that, he lived another 500 years and had other children.

<sup>11.12</sup> When Arpachshad was 35 years old, he had a son, Shelah; <sup>11.13</sup> after that, he lived another 403 years and had other children.

<sup>11.14</sup> When Shelah was 30 years old, he had a son, Eber; <sup>11.15</sup> after that, he lived another 403 years and had other children.

<sup>11.16</sup> When Eber was 34 years old, he had a son, Peleg; <sup>11.17</sup> after that, he lived another 430 years and had other children.

<sup>11.18</sup> When Peleg was 30 years old, he had a son, Reu; <sup>11.19</sup> after that, he lived another 209 years and had other children.

<sup>11.20</sup> When Reu was 32 years old, he had a son, Serug; <sup>11.21</sup> after that, he lived another 207 years and had other children.

<sup>11.22</sup> When Serug was 30 years old, he had a son, Nahor; <sup>11.23</sup> after that, he lived another 200 years and had other children.

<sup>11.24</sup> When Nahor was 29 years old, he had a son, Terah; <sup>11.25</sup> after that, he lived another 119 years and had other children.

<sup>11.26</sup> After Terah was 70 years old, he became the father of Abram, Nahor, and Haran.

<sup>11.27</sup> These are the descendants of Terah, who was the father of Abram, Nahor, and Haran. Haran was the father of Lot, <sup>11.28</sup> and Haran died in his hometown of Ur in Babylonia, while his father was still living.

<sup>11.29</sup> Abram married Sarai, and Nahor married Milcah, the daughter of Haran, who was also the father of Iscah.

<sup>11.30</sup> Sarai was not able to have children.

<sup>11.31</sup> Terah took his son Abram, his grandson Lot, who was the son of Haran, and his daughter-in-law Sarai, Abram's wife, and with them he left the city of Ur in Babylonia to go to the land of Canaan. They went as far as Haran and settled there.

<sup>11.32</sup> Terah died there at the age of 205.

# 12

<sup>12.1</sup> The Lord said to Abram, "Leave your country, your relatives, and your father's home, and go to a land that I am going to show you.

<sup>12.2</sup> "I will give you many descendants, and they will become a great

nation. I will bless you and make your name famous, so that you will be a blessing.

12.3 "I will bless those who bless you, but I will curse those who curse you. And through you I will bless all the nations."

12.4 When Abram was seventy-five years old, he started out from Haran, as the Lord had told him to do; and Lot went with him.

12.5 Abram took his wife Sarai, his nephew Lot, and all the wealth and all the slaves they had acquired in Haran, and they started out for the land of Canaan.

When they arrived in Canaan,

12.6 Abram traveled through the land until he came to the sacred tree of Moreh, the holy place at Shechem. (At that time the Canaanites were still living in the land.)

12.7 The Lord appeared to Abram and said to him, "This is the country that I am going to give to your descendants." Then Abram built an altar there to the Lord, who had appeared to him.

12.8 After that, he moved on south to the hill country east of the city of Bethel and set up his camp between Bethel on the west and Ai on the east. There also he built an altar and worshiped the Lord.

12.9 Then he moved on from place to place, going toward the southern part of Canaan.

12.10 But there was a famine in Canaan, and it was so bad that Abram went farther south to Egypt, to live there for a while.

12.11 When he was about to cross the border into Egypt, he said to his wife Sarai, "You are a beautiful woman.

12.12 "When the Egyptians see you, they will assume that you are my wife, and so they will kill me and let you live.

12.13 "Tell them that you are my sister; then because of you they will let me live and treat me well."

12.14 When he crossed the border into Egypt, the Egyptians did see that his wife was beautiful.

12.15 Some of the court officials saw her and told the king how beautiful she was; so she was taken to his palace.

12.16 Because of her the king treated Abram well and gave him flocks of sheep and goats, cattle, donkeys, slaves, and camels.

12.17 But because the king had taken Sarai, the Lord sent terrible diseases on him and on the people of his palace.

12.18 Then the king sent for Abram and asked him, "What have you done to me? Why didn't you tell me that she was your wife?

12.19 "Why did you say that she was your sister, and let me take her as my wife? Here is your wife; take her and get out!"

<sup>12.20</sup> The king gave orders to his men, so they took Abram and put him out of the country, together with his wife and everything he owned.

# 13

<sup>13.1</sup> Abram went north out of Egypt to the southern part of Canaan with his wife and everything he owned, and Lot went with him.
<sup>13.2</sup> Abram was a very rich man, with sheep, goats, and cattle, as well as silver and gold.
<sup>13.3</sup> Then he left there and moved from place to place, going toward Bethel. He reached the place between Bethel and Ai where he had camped before
<sup>13.4</sup> and had built an altar. There he worshiped the Lord.
<sup>13.5</sup> Lot also had sheep, goats, and cattle, as well as his own family and servants.
<sup>13.6</sup> And so there was not enough pasture land for the two of them to stay together, because they had too many animals.
<sup>13.7</sup> So quarrels broke out between the men who took care of Abram's animals and those who took care of Lot's animals. (At that time the Canaanites and the Perizzites were still living in the land.)
<sup>13.8</sup> Then Abram said to Lot, "We are relatives, and your men and my men shouldn't be quarreling.
<sup>13.9</sup> "So let's separate. Choose any part of the land you want. You go one way, and I'll go the other."
<sup>13.10</sup> Lot looked around and saw that the whole Jordan Valley, all the way to Zoar, had plenty of water, like the Garden of the Lord or like the land of Egypt. (This was before the Lord had destroyed the cities of Sodom and Gomorrah.)
<sup>13.11</sup> So Lot chose the whole Jordan Valley for himself and moved away toward the east. That is how the two men parted.
<sup>13.12</sup> Abram stayed in the land of Canaan, and Lot settled among the cities in the valley and camped near Sodom,
<sup>13.13</sup> whose people were wicked and sinned against the Lord.
<sup>13.14</sup> After Lot had left, the Lord said to Abram, "From where you are, look carefully in all directions.
<sup>13.15</sup> "I am going to give you and your descendants all the land that you see, and it will be yours forever.
<sup>13.16</sup> "I am going to give you so many descendants that no one will be able to count them all; it would be as easy to count all the specks of dust on earth!
<sup>13.17</sup> "Now, go and look over the whole land, because I am going to give

it all to you."

<sup>13.18</sup> So Abram moved his camp and settled near the sacred trees of Mamre at Hebron, and there he built an altar to the Lord.

<sup>14.1</sup> Four kings, Amraphel of Babylonia, Arioch of Ellasar, Chedorlaomer of Elam, and Tidal of Goiim,

<sup>14.2</sup> went to war against five other kings: Bera of Sodom, Birsha of Gomorrah, Shinab of Admah, Shemeber of Zeboiim, and the king of Bela (or Zoar).

<sup>14.3</sup> These five kings had formed an alliance and joined forces in Siddim Valley, which is now the Dead Sea.

<sup>14.4</sup> They had been under the control of Chedorlaomer for twelve years, but in the thirteenth year they rebelled against him.

<sup>14.5</sup> In the fourteenth year Chedorlaomer and his allies came with their armies and defeated the Rephaim in Ashteroth Karnaim, the Zuzim in Ham, the Emim in the plain of Kiriathaim,

<sup>14.6</sup> and the Horites in the mountains of Edom, pursuing them as far as Elparan on the edge of the desert.

<sup>14.7</sup> Then they turned around and came back to Kadesh (then known as Enmishpat). They conquered all the land of the Amalekites and defeated the Amorites who lived in Hazazon Tamar.

<sup>14.8</sup> Then the kings of Sodom, Gomorrah, Admah, Zeboiim, and Bela drew up their armies for battle in Siddim Valley and fought

<sup>14.9</sup> against the kings of Elam, Goiim, Babylonia, and Ellasar, five kings against four.

<sup>14.10</sup> The valley was full of tar pits, and when the kings of Sodom and Gomorrah tried to run away from the battle, they fell into the pits; but the other three kings escaped to the mountains.

<sup>14.11</sup> The four kings took everything in Sodom and Gomorrah, including the food, and went away.

<sup>14.12</sup> Lot, Abram's nephew, was living in Sodom, so they took him and all his possessions.

<sup>14.13</sup> But a man escaped and reported all this to Abram, the Hebrew, who was living near the sacred trees belonging to Mamre the Amorite. Mamre and his brothers Eshcol and Aner were Abram's allies.

<sup>14.14</sup> When Abram heard that his nephew had been captured, he called together all the fighting men in his camp, 318 in all, and pursued the four kings all the way to Dan.

<sup>14.15</sup> There he divided his men into groups, attacked the enemy by night, and defeated them. He chased them as far as Hobah, north of

Damascus,

<sup>14.16</sup> and got back all the loot that had been taken. He also brought back his nephew Lot and his possessions, together with the women and the other prisoners.

<sup>14.17</sup> When Abram came back from his victory over Chedorlaomer and the other kings, the king of Sodom went out to meet him in Shaveh Valley (also called King's Valley).

<sup>14.18</sup> And Melchizedek, who was king of Salem and also a priest of the Most High God, brought bread and wine to Abram,

<sup>14.19</sup> blessed him, and said, "May the Most High God, who made heaven and earth, bless Abram!

<sup>14.20</sup> "May the Most High God, who gave you victory over your enemies, be praised!" And Abram gave Melchizedek a tenth of all the loot he had recovered.

<sup>14.21</sup> The king of Sodom said to Abram, "Keep the loot, but give me back all my people."

<sup>14.22</sup> Abram answered, "I solemnly swear before the Lord, the Most High God, Maker of heaven and earth,

<sup>14.23</sup> "that I will not keep anything of yours, not even a thread or a sandal strap. Then you can never say, 'I am the one who made Abram rich.'

<sup>14.24</sup> "I will take nothing for myself. I will accept only what my men have used. But let my allies, Aner, Eshcol, and Mamre, take their share."

# 15

<sup>15.1</sup> After this, Abram had a vision and heard the Lord say to him, "Do not be afraid, Abram. I will shield you from danger and give you a great reward."

<sup>15.2</sup> But Abram answered, "Sovereign Lord, what good will your reward do me, since I have no children? My only heir is Eliezer of Damascus.

<sup>15.3</sup> "You have given me no children, and one of my slaves will inherit my property."

<sup>15.4</sup> Then he heard the Lord speaking to him again: "This slave Eliezer will not inherit your property; your own son will be your heir."

<sup>15.5</sup> The Lord took him outside and said, "Look at the sky and try to count the stars; you will have as many descendants as that."

<sup>15.6</sup> Abram put his trust in the Lord, and because of this the Lord was pleased with him and accepted him.

<sup>15.7</sup> Then the Lord said to him, "I am the Lord, who led you out of Ur in Babylonia, to give you this land as your own."

<sup>15.8</sup> But Abram asked, "Sovereign Lord, how can I know that it will be mine?"

<sup>15.9</sup> He answered, "Bring me a cow, a goat, and a ram, each of them three years old, and a dove and a pigeon."

<sup>15.10</sup> Abram brought the animals to God, cut them in half, and placed the halves opposite each other in two rows; but he did not cut up the birds.

<sup>15.11</sup> Vultures came down on the bodies, but Abram drove them off.

<sup>15.12</sup> When the sun was going down, Abram fell into a deep sleep, and fear and terror came over him.

<sup>15.13</sup> The Lord said to him, "Your descendants will be strangers in a foreign land; they will be slaves there and will be treated cruelly for four hundred years.

<sup>15.14</sup> "But I will punish the nation that enslaves them, and when they leave that foreign land, they will take great wealth with them.

<sup>15.15</sup> "You yourself will live to a ripe old age, die in peace, and be buried.

<sup>15.16</sup> "It will be four generations before your descendants come back here, because I will not drive out the Amorites until they become so wicked that they must be punished."

<sup>15.17</sup> When the sun had set and it was dark, a smoking fire pot and a flaming torch suddenly appeared and passed between the pieces of the animals.

<sup>15.18</sup> Then and there the Lord made a covenant with Abram. He said, "I promise to give your descendants all this land from the border of Egypt to the Euphrates River,

<sup>15.19</sup> "including the lands of the Kenites, the Kenizzites, the Kadmonites,

<sup>15.20</sup> "the Hittites, the Perizzites, the Rephaim,

<sup>15.21</sup> "the Amorites, the Canaanites, the Girgashites, and the Jebusites."

# 16

<sup>16.1</sup> Abram's wife Sarai had not borne him any children. But she had an Egyptian slave woman named Hagar,

<sup>16.2</sup> and so she said to Abram, "The Lord has kept me from having children. Why don't you sleep with my slave? Perhaps she can have a child for me." Abram agreed with what Sarai said.

<sup>16.3</sup> So she gave Hagar to him to be his concubine. (This happened af-

ter Abram had lived in Canaan for ten years.)

16.4 Abram had intercourse with Hagar, and she became pregnant. When she found out that she was pregnant, she became proud and despised Sarai.

16.5 Then Sarai said to Abram, "It's your fault that Hagar despises me. I myself gave her to you, and ever since she found out that she was pregnant, she has despised me. May the Lord judge which of us is right, you or me!"

16.6 Abram answered, "Very well, she is your slave and under your control; do whatever you want with her." Then Sarai treated Hagar so cruelly that she ran away.

16.7 The angel of the Lord met Hagar at a spring in the desert on the road to Shur

16.8 and said, "Hagar, slave of Sarai, where have you come from and where are you going?"

She answered, "I am running away from my mistress."

16.9 He said, "Go back to her and be her slave."

16.10 Then he said, "I will give you so many descendants that no one will be able to count them.

16.11 "You are going to have a son, and you will name him Ishmael, because the Lord has heard your cry of distress.

16.12 "But your son will live like a wild donkey; he will be against everyone, and everyone will be against him. He will live apart from all his relatives."

16.13 Hagar asked herself, "Have I really seen God and lived to tell about it?" So she called the Lord, who had spoken to her, "A God Who Sees."

16.14 That is why people call the well between Kadesh and Bered "The Well of the Living One Who Sees Me."

16.15 Hagar bore Abram a son, and he named him Ishmael.

16.16 Abram was eighty-six years old at the time.

# 17

17.1 When Abram was ninety-nine years old, the Lord appeared to him and said, "I am the Almighty God. Obey me and always do what is right.

17.2 "I will make my covenant with you and give you many descendants."

17.3 Abram bowed down with his face touching the ground, and God said,

17.4 "I make this covenant with you: I promise that you will be the ancestor of many nations.

17.5 "Your name will no longer be Abram, but Abraham, because I am making you the ancestor of many nations.

17.6 "I will give you many descendants, and some of them will be kings. You will have so many descendants that they will become nations.

17.7 "I will keep my promise to you and to your descendants in future generations as an everlasting covenant. I will be your God and the God of your descendants.

17.8 "I will give to you and to your descendants this land in which you are now a foreigner. The whole land of Canaan will belong to your descendants forever, and I will be their God."

17.9 God said to Abraham, "You also must agree to keep the covenant with me, both you and your descendants in future generations.

17.10 "You and your descendants must all agree to circumcise every male among you.

17.11-12 "From now on you must circumcise every baby boy when he is eight days old, including slaves born in your homes and slaves bought from foreigners. This will show that there is a covenant between you and me.

17.13 "Each one must be circumcised, and this will be a physical sign to show that my covenant with you is everlasting.

17.14 "Any male who has not been circumcised will no longer be considered one of my people, because he has not kept the covenant with me."

17.15 God said to Abraham, "You must no longer call your wife Sarai; from now on her name is Sarah.

17.16 "I will bless her, and I will give you a son by her. I will bless her, and she will become the mother of nations, and there will be kings among her descendants."

17.17 Abraham bowed down with his face touching the ground, but he began to laugh when he thought, "Can a man have a child when he is a hundred years old? Can Sarah have a child at ninety?"

17.18 He asked God, "Why not let Ishmael be my heir?"

17.19 But God said, "No. Your wife Sarah will bear you a son and you will name him Isaac. I will keep my covenant with him and with his descendants forever. It is an everlasting covenant.

17.20 "I have heard your request about Ishmael, so I will bless him and give him many children and many descendants. He will be the father of twelve princes, and I will make a great nation of his descendants.

<sup>17.21</sup> "But I will keep my covenant with your son Isaac, who will be born to Sarah about this time next year."

<sup>17.22</sup> When God finished speaking to Abraham, he left him.

<sup>17.23</sup> On that same day Abraham obeyed God and circumcised his son Ishmael and all the other males in his household, including the slaves born in his home and those he had bought.

<sup>17.24</sup> Abraham was ninety-nine years old when he was circumcised,

<sup>17.25</sup> and his son Ishmael was thirteen.

<sup>17.26</sup> They were both circumcised on the same day,

<sup>17.27</sup> together with all of Abraham's slaves.

# 18

<sup>18.1</sup> The Lord appeared to Abraham at the sacred trees of Mamre. As Abraham was sitting at the entrance of his tent during the hottest part of the day,

<sup>18.2</sup> he looked up and saw three men standing there. As soon as he saw them, he ran out to meet them. Bowing down with his face touching the ground,

<sup>18.3</sup> he said, "Sirs, please do not pass by my home without stopping; I am here to serve you.

<sup>18.4</sup> "Let me bring some water for you to wash your feet; you can rest here beneath this tree.

<sup>18.5</sup> "I will also bring a bit of food; it will give you strength to continue your journey. You have honored me by coming to my home, so let me serve you."

They replied, "Thank you; we accept."

<sup>18.6</sup> Abraham hurried into the tent and said to Sarah, "Quick, take a sack of your best flour, and bake some bread."

<sup>18.7</sup> Then he ran to the herd and picked out a calf that was tender and fat, and gave it to a servant, who hurried to get it ready.

<sup>18.8</sup> He took some cream, some milk, and the meat, and set the food before the men. There under the tree he served them himself, and they ate.

<sup>18.9</sup> Then they asked him, "Where is your wife Sarah?"

"She is there in the tent," he answered.

<sup>18.10</sup> One of them said, "Nine months from now I will come back, and your wife Sarah will have a son."

Sarah was behind him, at the door of the tent, listening.

<sup>18.11</sup> Abraham and Sarah were very old, and Sarah had stopped having her monthly periods.

<sup>18.12</sup> So Sarah laughed to herself and said, "Now that I am old and

worn out, can I still enjoy sex? And besides, my husband is old too."

<sup>18.13</sup> Then the Lord asked Abraham, "Why did Sarah laugh and say, 'Can I really have a child when I am so old?'

<sup>18.14</sup> "Is anything too hard for the Lord? As I said, nine months from now I will return, and Sarah will have a son."

<sup>18.15</sup> Because Sarah was afraid, she denied it. "I didn't laugh," she said.

"Yes, you did," he replied. "You laughed."

<sup>18.16</sup> Then the men left and went to a place where they could look down at Sodom, and Abraham went with them to send them on their way.

<sup>18.17</sup> And the Lord said to himself, "I will not hide from Abraham what I am going to do.

<sup>18.18</sup> "His descendants will become a great and mighty nation, and through him I will bless all the nations.

<sup>18.19</sup> "I have chosen him in order that he may command his sons and his descendants to obey me and to do what is right and just. If they do, I will do everything for him that I have promised."

<sup>18.20</sup> Then the Lord said to Abraham, "There are terrible accusations against Sodom and Gomorrah, and their sin is very great.

<sup>18.21</sup> "I must go down to find out whether or not the accusations which I have heard are true."

<sup>18.22</sup> Then the two men left and went on toward Sodom, but the Lord remained with Abraham.

<sup>18.23</sup> Abraham approached the Lord and asked, "Are you really going to destroy the innocent with the guilty?

<sup>18.24</sup> "If there are fifty innocent people in the city, will you destroy the whole city? Won't you spare it in order to save the fifty?

<sup>19.25</sup> "Surely you won't kill the innocent with the guilty. That's impossible! You can't do that. If you did, the innocent would be punished along with the guilty. That is impossible. The judge of all the earth has to act justly."

<sup>18.26</sup> The Lord answered, "If I find fifty innocent people in Sodom, I will spare the whole city for their sake."

<sup>18.27</sup> Abraham spoke again: "Please forgive my boldness in continuing to speak to you, Lord. I am only a man and have no right to say anything.

<sup>18.28</sup> "But perhaps there will be only forty-five innocent people instead of fifty. Will you destroy the whole city because there are five too few?"

The Lord answered, "I will not destroy the city if I find forty-five innocent people."

<sup>18.29</sup> Abraham spoke again: "Perhaps there will be only forty."

He replied, "I will not destroy it if there are forty."

<sup>18.30</sup> Abraham said, "Please don't be angry, Lord, but I must speak again. What if there are only thirty?"

He said, "I will not do it if I find thirty."

<sup>18.31</sup> Abraham said, "Please forgive my boldness in continuing to speak to you, Lord. Suppose that only twenty are found?"

He said, "I will not destroy the city if I find twenty."

<sup>18.32</sup> Abraham said, "Please don't be angry, Lord, and I will speak only once more. What if only ten are found?"

He said, "I will not destroy it if there are ten."

<sup>18.33</sup> After he had finished speaking with Abraham, the Lord went away, and Abraham returned home.

# 19

<sup>19.1</sup> When the two angels came to Sodom that evening, Lot was sitting at the city gate. As soon as he saw them, he got up and went to meet them. He bowed down before them

<sup>19.2</sup> and said, "Sirs, I am here to serve you. Please come to my house. You can wash your feet and spend the night. In the morning you can get up early and go on your way."

But they answered, "No, we will spend the night here in the city square."

<sup>19.3</sup> He kept on urging them, and finally they went with him to his house. Lot ordered his servants to bake some bread and prepare a fine meal for the guests. When it was ready, they ate it.

<sup>19.4</sup> Before the guests went to bed, the men of Sodom surrounded the house. All the men of the city, both young and old, were there.

<sup>19.5</sup> They called out to Lot and asked, "Where are the men who came to stay with you tonight? Bring them out to us!" The men of Sodom wanted to have sex with them.

<sup>19.6</sup> Lot went outside and closed the door behind him.

<sup>19.7</sup> He said to them, "Friends, I beg you, don't do such a wicked thing!

<sup>19.8</sup> "Look, I have two daughters who are still virgins. Let me bring them out to you, and you can do whatever you want with them. But don't do anything to these men; they are guests in my house, and I must protect them."

<sup>19.9</sup> But they said, "Get out of our way, you foreigner! Who are you to tell us what to do? Out of our way, or we will treat you worse than them." They pushed Lot back and moved up to break down the door.

<sup>19.10</sup> But the two men inside reached out, pulled Lot back into the house, and shut the door.

<sup>19.11</sup> Then they struck all the men outside with blindness, so that they couldn't find the door.

<sup>19.12</sup> The two men said to Lot, "If you have anyone else here—sons, daughters, sons-in-law, or any other relatives living in the city—get them out of here,

<sup>19.13</sup> "because we are going to destroy this place. The Lord has heard the terrible accusations against these people and has sent us to destroy Sodom."

<sup>19.14</sup> Then Lot went to the men that his daughters were going to marry, and said, "Hurry up and get out of here; the Lord is going to destroy this place." But they thought he was joking.

<sup>19.15</sup> At dawn the angels tried to make Lot hurry. "Quick!" they said. "Take your wife and your two daughters and get out, so that you will not lose your lives when the city is destroyed."

<sup>19.16</sup> Lot hesitated. The Lord, however, had pity on him; so the men took him, his wife, and his two daughters by the hand and led them out of the city.

<sup>19.17</sup> Then one of the angels said, "Run for your lives! Don't look back and don't stop in the valley. Run to the hills, so that you won't be killed."

<sup>19.18</sup> But Lot answered, "No, please don't make us do that, sir.

<sup>19.19</sup> "You have done me a great favor and saved my life. But the hills are too far away; the disaster will overtake me, and I will die before I get there.

<sup>19.20</sup> "Do you see that little town? It is near enough. Let me go over there—you can see it is just a small place—and I will be safe."

<sup>19.21</sup> He answered, "All right, I agree. I won't destroy that town.

<sup>19.22</sup> "Hurry! Run! I can't do anything until you get there."

Because Lot called it small, the town was named Zoar.

<sup>19.23</sup> The sun was rising when Lot reached Zoar.

<sup>19.24</sup> Suddenly the Lord rained burning sulfur on the cities of Sodom and Gomorrah

<sup>19.25</sup> and destroyed them and the whole valley, along with all the people there and everything that grew on the land.

<sup>19.26</sup> But Lot's wife looked back and was turned into a pillar of salt.

<sup>19.27</sup> Early the next morning Abraham hurried to the place where he had stood in the presence of the Lord.

<sup>19.28</sup> He looked down at Sodom and Gomorrah and the whole valley and saw smoke rising from the land, like smoke from a huge fur-

nace.

¹⁹·²⁹ But when God destroyed the cities of the valley where Lot was living, he kept Abraham in mind and allowed Lot to escape to safety.

¹⁹·³⁰ Because Lot was afraid to stay in Zoar, he and his two daughters moved up into the hills and lived in a cave.

¹⁹·³¹ The older daughter said to her sister, "Our father is getting old, and there are no men in the whole world to marry us so that we can have children.

¹⁹·³² "Come on, let's get our father drunk, so that we can sleep with him and have children by him."

¹⁹·³³ That night they gave him wine to drink, and the older daughter had intercourse with him. But he was so drunk that he didn't know it.

¹⁹·³⁴ The next day the older daughter said to her sister, "I slept with him last night; now let's get him drunk again tonight, and you sleep with him. Then each of us will have a child by our father."

¹⁹·³⁵ So that night they got him drunk, and the younger daughter had intercourse with him. Again he was so drunk that he didn't know it.

¹⁹·³⁶ In this way both of Lot's daughters became pregnant by their own father.

¹⁹·³⁷ The older daughter had a son, whom she named Moab. He was the ancestor of the present-day Moabites.

¹⁹·³⁸ The younger daughter also had a son, whom she named Benammi. He was the ancestor of the present-day Ammonites.

# 20

²⁰·¹ Abraham moved from Mamre to the southern part of Canaan and lived between Kadesh and Shur. Later, while he was living in Gerar,

²⁰·² he said that his wife Sarah was his sister. So King Abimelech of Gerar had Sarah brought to him.

²⁰·³ One night God appeared to him in a dream and said, "You are going to die, because you have taken this woman; she is already married."

²⁰·⁴ But Abimelech had not come near her, and he said, "Lord, I am innocent! Would you destroy me and my people?

²⁰·⁵ "Abraham himself said that she was his sister, and she said the same thing. I did this with a clear conscience, and I have done no wrong."

²⁰·⁶ God replied in the dream, "Yes, I know that you did it with a clear conscience; so I kept you from sinning against me and did not

let you touch her.

20.7 "But now, give the woman back to her husband. He is a prophet, and he will pray for you, so that you will not die. But if you do not give her back, I warn you that you are going to die, you and all your people."

20.8 Early the next morning Abimelech called all his officials and told them what had happened, and they were terrified.

20.9 Then Abimelech called Abraham and asked, "What have you done to us? What wrong have I done to you to make you bring this disaster on me and my kingdom? No one should ever do what you have done to me.

20.10 "Why did you do it?"

20.11 Abraham answered, "I thought that there would be no one here who has reverence for God and that they would kill me to get my wife.

20.12 "She really is my sister. She is the daughter of my father, but not of my mother, and I married her.

20.13 "So when God sent me from my father's house into foreign lands, I said to her, 'You can show how loyal you are to me by telling everyone that I am your brother.'"

20.14 Then Abimelech gave Sarah back to Abraham, and at the same time he gave him sheep, cattle, and slaves.

20.15 He said to Abraham, "Here is my whole land; live anywhere you like."

20.16 He said to Sarah, "I am giving your brother a thousand pieces of silver as proof to all who are with you that you are innocent; everyone will know that you have done no wrong."

20.17-18 Because of what had happened to Sarah, Abraham's wife, the Lord had made it impossible for any woman in Abimelech's palace to have children. So Abraham prayed for Abimelech, and God healed him. He also healed his wife and his slave women, so that they could have children.

# 21

21.1 The Lord blessed Sarah, as he had promised,

21.2 and she became pregnant and bore a son to Abraham when he was old. The boy was born at the time God had said he would be born.

21.3 Abraham named him Isaac,

21.4 and when Isaac was eight days old, Abraham circumcised him, as God had commanded.

<sup>21.5</sup> Abraham was a hundred years old when Isaac was born.

<sup>21.6</sup> Sarah said, "God has brought me joy and laughter. Everyone who hears about it will laugh with me."

<sup>21.7</sup> Then she added, "Who would have said to Abraham that Sarah would nurse children? Yet I have borne him a son in his old age."

<sup>21.8</sup> The child grew, and on the day that he was weaned, Abraham gave a great feast.

<sup>21.9</sup> One day Ishmael, whom Hagar the Egyptian had borne to Abraham, was playing with Sarah's son Isaac.

<sup>21.10</sup> Sarah saw them and said to Abraham, "Send this slave and her son away. The son of this woman must not get any part of your wealth, which my son Isaac should inherit."

<sup>21.11</sup> This troubled Abraham very much, because Ishmael also was his son.

<sup>21.12</sup> But God said to Abraham, "Don't be worried about the boy and your slave Hagar. Do whatever Sarah tells you, because it is through Isaac that you will have the descendants I have promised.

<sup>21.13</sup> "I will also give many children to the son of the slave woman, so that they will become a nation. He too is your son."

<sup>21.14</sup> Early the next morning Abraham gave Hagar some food and a leather bag full of water. He put the child on her back and sent her away. She left and wandered about in the wilderness of Beersheba.

<sup>21.15</sup> When the water was all gone, she left the child under a bush

<sup>21.16</sup> and sat down about a hundred yards away. She said to herself, "I can't bear to see my child die." While she was sitting there, she began to cry.

<sup>21.17</sup> God heard the boy crying, and from heaven the angel of God spoke to Hagar, "What are you troubled about, Hagar? Don't be afraid. God has heard the boy crying.

<sup>21.18</sup> "Get up, go and pick him up, and comfort him. I will make a great nation out of his descendants."

<sup>21.19</sup> Then God opened her eyes, and she saw a well. She went and filled the leather bag with water and gave some to the boy.

<sup>21.20</sup> God was with the boy as he grew up; he lived in the wilderness of Paran and became a skillful hunter.

<sup>21.21</sup> His mother got an Egyptian wife for him.

<sup>21.22</sup> At that time Abimelech went with Phicol, the commander of his army, and said to Abraham, "God is with you in everything you do.

<sup>21.23</sup> "So make a vow here in the presence of God that you will not deceive me, my children, or my descendants. I have been loyal to you, so promise that you will also be loyal to me and to this country in

which you are living."

<sup></sup>21.24 Abraham said, "I promise."

21.25 Abraham complained to Abimelech about a well which the servants of Abimelech had seized.

21.26 Abimelech said, "I don't know who did this. You didn't tell me about it, and this is the first I have heard of it."

21.27 Then Abraham gave some sheep and cattle to Abimelech, and the two of them made an agreement.

21.28 Abraham separated seven lambs from his flock,

21.29 and Abimelech asked him, "Why did you do that?"

21.30 Abraham answered, "Accept these seven lambs. By doing this, you admit that I am the one who dug this well."

21.31 And so the place was called Beersheba, because it was there that the two of them made a vow.

21.32 After they had made this agreement at Beersheba, Abimelech and Phicol went back to Philistia.

21.33 Then Abraham planted a tamarisk tree in Beersheba and worshiped the Lord, the Everlasting God.

21.34 Abraham lived in Philistia for a long time.

# 22

22.1 Some time later God tested Abraham; he called to him, "Abraham!" And Abraham answered, "Yes, here I am!"

22.2 "Take your son," God said, "your only son, Isaac, whom you love so much, and go to the land of Moriah. There on a mountain that I will show you, offer him as a sacrifice to me."

22.3 Early the next morning Abraham cut some wood for the sacrifice, loaded his donkey, and took Isaac and two servants with him. They started out for the place that God had told him about.

22.4 On the third day Abraham saw the place in the distance.

22.5 Then he said to the servants, "Stay here with the donkey. The boy and I will go over there and worship, and then we will come back to you."

22.6 Abraham made Isaac carry the wood for the sacrifice, and he himself carried a knife and live coals for starting the fire. As they walked along together,

22.7 Isaac spoke up, "Father!"

He answered, "Yes, my son?"

Isaac asked, "I see that you have the coals and the wood, but where is the lamb for the sacrifice?"

22.8 Abraham answered, "God himself will provide one." And the two of them walked on together.

<sup>22.9</sup> When they came to the place which God had told him about, Abraham built an altar and arranged the wood on it. He tied up his son and placed him on the altar, on top of the wood.

<sup>22.10</sup> Then he picked up the knife to kill him.

<sup>22.11</sup> But the angel of the Lord called to him from heaven, "Abraham, Abraham!"

He answered, "Yes, here I am."

<sup>22.12</sup> "Don't hurt the boy or do anything to him," he said. "Now I know that you honor and obey God, because you have not kept back your only son from him."

<sup>22.13</sup> Abraham looked around and saw a ram caught in a bush by its horns. He went and got it and offered it as a burnt offering instead of his son.

<sup>22.14</sup> Abraham named that place "The Lord Provides." And even today people say, "On the Lord's mountain he provides."

<sup>22.15</sup> The angel of the Lord called to Abraham from heaven a second time,

<sup>22.16</sup> "I make a vow by my own name—the Lord is speaking—that I will richly bless you. Because you did this and did not keep back your only son from me,

<sup>22.17</sup> "I promise that I will give you as many descendants as there are stars in the sky or grains of sand along the seashore. Your descendants will conquer their enemies.

<sup>22.18</sup> "All the nations will ask me to bless them as I have blessed your descendants—all because you obeyed my command."

<sup>22.19</sup> Abraham went back to his servants, and they went together to Beersheba, where Abraham settled.

<sup>22.20</sup> Some time later Abraham learned that Milcah had borne eight children to his brother Nahor:

<sup>22.21</sup> Uz the first-born, Buz his brother, Kemuel the father of Aram,

<sup>22.22</sup> Chesed, Hazo, Pildash, Jidlaph, and Bethuel,

<sup>22.23</sup> Rebecca's father. Milcah bore these eight sons to Nahor, Abraham's brother.

<sup>22.24</sup> Reumah, Nahor's concubine, bore Tebah, Gaham, Tahash, and Maacah.

# 23

<sup>23.1</sup> Sarah lived to be 127 years old.

<sup>23.2</sup> She died in Hebron in the land of Canaan, and Abraham mourned her death.

<sup></sup>²³·³ He left the place where his wife's body was lying, went to the Hittites, and said,

²³·⁴ "I am a foreigner living here among you; sell me some land, so that I can bury my wife."

²³·⁵ They answered,

²³·⁶ "Listen to us, sir. We look upon you as a mighty leader; bury your wife in the best grave that we have. Any of us would be glad to give you a grave, so that you can bury her."

²³·⁷ Then Abraham bowed before them

²³·⁸ and said, "If you are willing to let me bury my wife here, please ask Ephron son of Zohar

²³·⁹ "to sell me Machpelah Cave, which is near the edge of his field. Ask him to sell it to me for its full price, here in your presence, so that I can own it as a burial ground."

²³·¹⁰ Ephron himself was sitting with the other Hittites at the meeting place at the city gate; he answered in the hearing of everyone there,

²³·¹¹ "Listen, sir; I will give you the whole field and the cave that is in it. Here in the presence of my own people, I will give it to you, so that you can bury your wife."

²³·¹² But Abraham bowed before the Hittites

²³·¹³ and said to Ephron, so that everyone could hear, "May I ask you, please, to listen. I will buy the whole field. Accept my payment, and I will bury my wife there."

²³·¹⁴ Ephron answered,

²³·¹⁵ "Sir, land worth only four hundred pieces of silver—what is that between us? Bury your wife in it."

²³·¹⁶ Abraham agreed and weighed out the amount that Ephron had mentioned in the hearing of the people—four hundred pieces of silver, according to the standard weights used by the merchants.

²³·¹⁷ That is how the property which had belonged to Ephron at Machpelah east of Mamre, became Abraham's. It included the field, the cave which was in it, and all the trees in the field up to the edge of the property.

²³·¹⁸ It was recognized as Abraham's property by all the Hittites who were there at the meeting.

²³·¹⁹ Then Abraham buried his wife Sarah in that cave in the land of Canaan.

²³·²⁰ So the field which had belonged to the Hittites, and the cave in it, became the property of Abraham for a burial ground.

# 24

<sup>24.1</sup> Abraham was now very old, and the Lord had blessed him in everything he did.

<sup>24.2</sup> He said to his oldest servant, who was in charge of all that he had, "Place your hand between my thighs and make a vow.

<sup>24.3</sup> "I want you to make a vow in the name of the Lord, the God of heaven and earth, that you will not choose a wife for my son from the people here in Canaan.

<sup>24.4</sup> "You must go back to the country where I was born and get a wife for my son Isaac from among my relatives."

<sup>24.5</sup> But the servant asked, "What if the young woman will not leave home to come with me to this land? Shall I send your son back to the land you came from?"

<sup>24.6</sup> "Abraham answered, "Make sure that you don't send my son back there!

<sup>24.7</sup> "The Lord, the God of heaven, brought me from the home of my father and from the land of my relatives, and he solemnly promised me that he would give this land to my descendants. He will send his angel before you, so that you can get a wife there for my son.

<sup>24.8</sup> "If the young woman is not willing to come with you, you will be free from this promise. But you must not under any circumstances take my son back there."

<sup>24.9</sup> So the servant put his hand between the thighs of Abraham, his master, and made a vow to do what Abraham had asked.

<sup>24.10</sup> The servant, who was in charge of Abraham's property, took ten of his master's camels and went to the city where Nahor had lived in northern Mesopotamia.

<sup>24.11</sup> When he arrived, he made the camels kneel down at the well outside the city. It was late afternoon, the time when women came out to get water.

<sup>24.12</sup> He prayed, "Lord, God of my master Abraham, give me success today and keep your promise to my master.

<sup>24.13</sup> "Here I am at the well where the young women of the city will be coming to get water.

<sup>24.14</sup> "I will say to one of them, 'Please, lower your jar and let me have a drink.' If she says, 'Drink, and I will also bring water for your camels,' may she be the one that you have chosen for your servant Isaac. If this happens, I will know that you have kept your promise to my master."

<sup>24.15</sup> Before he had finished praying, Rebecca arrived with a water jar on her shoulder. She was the daughter of Bethuel, who was the son of Abraham's brother Nahor and his wife Milcah.

24.16 She was a very beautiful young woman and still a virgin. She went down to the well, filled her jar, and came back.

24.17 The servant ran to meet her and said, "Please give me a drink of water from your jar."

24.18 She said, "Drink, sir," and quickly lowered her jar from her shoulder and held it while he drank.

24.19 When he had finished, she said, "I will also bring water for your camels and let them have all they want."

24.20 She quickly emptied her jar into the animals' drinking trough and ran to the well to get more water, until she had watered all his camels.

24.21 The man kept watching her in silence, to see if the Lord had given him success.

24.22 When she had finished, the man took an expensive gold ring and put it in her nose and put two large gold bracelets on her arms.

24.23 He said, "Please tell me who your father is. Is there room in his house for my men and me to spend the night?"

24.24 "My father is Bethuel son of Nahor and Milcah," she answered.

24.25 "There is plenty of straw and fodder at our house, and there is a place for you to stay."

24.26 Then the man knelt down and worshiped the Lord.

24.27 He said, "Praise the Lord, the God of my master Abraham, who has faithfully kept his promise to my master. The Lord has led me straight to my master's relatives."

24.28 The young woman ran to her mother's house and told the whole story.

24.29 Now Rebecca had a brother named Laban, and he ran outside to go to the well where Abraham's servant was.

24.30 Laban had seen the nose ring and the bracelets on his sister's arms and had heard her say what the man had told her. He went to Abraham's servant, who was standing by his camels at the well,

24.31 and said, "Come home with me. You are a man whom the Lord has blessed. Why are you standing out here? I have a room ready for you in my house, and there is a place for your camels."

24.32 So the man went into the house, and Laban unloaded the camels and gave them straw and fodder. Then he brought water for Abraham's servant and his men to wash their feet.

24.33 When food was brought, the man said, "I will not eat until I have said what I have to say."

Laban said, "Go on and speak."

24.34 "I am the servant of Abraham," he began.

[24.35] "The Lord has greatly blessed my master and made him a rich man. He has given him flocks of sheep and goats, cattle, silver, gold, male and female slaves, camels, and donkeys.

[24.36] "Sarah, my master's wife, bore him a son when she was old, and my master has given everything he owns to him.

[24.37] "My master made me promise with a vow to obey his command. He said, 'Do not choose a wife for my son from the young women in the land of Canaan.

[24.38] "'Instead, go to my father's people, to my relatives, and choose a wife for him.'

[24.39] "And I asked my master, 'What if she will not come with me?'

[24.40] "He answered, 'The Lord, whom I have always obeyed, will send his angel with you and give you success. You will get for my son a wife from my own people, from my father's family.

[24.41] "'There is only one way for you to be free from your vow: if you go to my relatives and they refuse you, then you will be free.'

[24.42] "When I came to the well today, I prayed, 'Lord, God of my master Abraham, please give me success in what I am doing.

[24.43] "'Here I am at the well. When a young woman comes out to get water, I will ask her to give me a drink of water from her jar.

[24.44] "'If she agrees and also offers to bring water for my camels, may she be the one that you have chosen as the wife for my master's son.'

[24.45] "Before I had finished my silent prayer, Rebecca came with a water jar on her shoulder and went down to the well to get water. I said to her, 'Please give me a drink.'

[24.46] "She quickly lowered her jar from her shoulder and said, 'Drink, and I will also water your camels.' So I drank, and she watered the camels.

[24.47] "I asked her, 'Who is your father?' And she answered, 'My father is Bethuel son of Nahor and Milcah.' Then I put the ring in her nose and the bracelets on her arms.

[24.48] "I knelt down and worshiped the Lord. I praised the Lord, the God of my master Abraham, who had led me straight to my master's relative, where I found his daughter for my master's son.

[24.49] "Now, if you intend to fulfill your responsibility toward my master and treat him fairly, please tell me; if not, say so, and I will decide what to do."

[24.50] Laban and Bethuel answered, "Since this matter comes from the Lord, it is not for us to make a decision.

[24.51] "Here is Rebecca; take her and go. Let her become the wife of your master's son, as the Lord himself has said."

24.52 When the servant of Abraham heard this, he bowed down and worshiped the Lord.

24.53 Then he brought out clothing and silver and gold jewelry, and gave them to Rebecca. He also gave expensive gifts to her brother and to her mother.

24.54 Then Abraham's servant and the men with him ate and drank, and spent the night there. When they got up in the morning, he said, "Let me go back to my master."

24.55 But Rebecca's brother and her mother said, "Let her stay with us a week or ten days, and then she may go."

24.56 But he said, "Don't make us stay. The Lord has made my journey a success; let me go back to my master."

24.57 They answered, "Let's call her and find out what she has to say."

24.58 So they called Rebecca and asked, "Do you want to go with this man?"

"Yes," she answered.

24.59 So they let Rebecca and her old family servant go with Abraham's servant and his men.

24.60 And they gave Rebecca their blessing in these words:

"May you, sister, become the mother of millions!

May your descendants conquer the cities of their enemies!"

24.61 Then Rebecca and her young women got ready and mounted the camels to go with Abraham's servant, and they all started out.

24.62 Isaac had come into the wilderness of "The Well of the Living One Who Sees Me" and was staying in the southern part of Canaan.

24.63 He went out in the early evening to take a walk in the fields and saw camels coming.

24.64 When Rebecca saw Isaac, she got down from her camel

24.65 and asked Abraham's servant, "Who is that man walking toward us in the field?"

"He is my master," the servant answered. So she took her scarf and covered her face.

24.66 The servant told Isaac everything he had done.

24.67 Then Isaac brought Rebecca into the tent that his mother Sarah had lived in, and she became his wife. Isaac loved Rebecca, and so he was comforted for the loss of his mother.

# 25

25.1 Abraham married another woman, whose name was Keturah.

25.2 She bore him Zimran, Jokshan, Medan, Midian, Ishbak, and

Shuah.

²⁵·³ Jokshan was the father of Sheba and Dedan, and the descendants of Dedan were the Asshurim, the Letushim, and the Leummim.

²⁵·⁴ The sons of Midian were Ephah, Epher, Hanoch, Abida, and Eldaah. All these were Keturah's descendants.

²⁵·⁵ Abraham left everything he owned to Isaac; ²⁵·⁶ but while he was still alive, he gave presents to the sons his other wives had borne him. Then he sent these sons to the land of the East, away from his son Isaac.

²⁵·⁷⁻⁸ Abraham died at the ripe old age of 175.

²⁵·⁹ His sons Isaac and Ishmael buried him in Machpelah Cave, in the field east of Mamre that had belonged to Ephron son of Zohar the Hittite.

²⁵·¹⁰ It was the field that Abraham had bought from the Hittites; both Abraham and his wife Sarah were buried there.

²⁵·¹¹ After the death of Abraham, God blessed his son Isaac, who lived near "The Well of the Living One Who Sees Me."

²⁵·¹² Ishmael, whom Hagar, the Egyptian slave of Sarah, bore to Abraham,

²⁵·¹³ had the following sons, listed in the order of their birth: Nebaioth, Kedar, Adbeel, Mibsam,

²⁵·¹⁴ Mishma, Dumah, Massa,

²⁵·¹⁵ Hadad, Tema, Jetur, Naphish, and Kedemah.

²⁵·¹⁶ They were the ancestors of twelve tribes, and their names were given to their villages and camping places.

²⁵·¹⁷ Ishmael was 137 years old when he died.

²⁵·¹⁸ The descendants of Ishmael lived in the territory between Havilah and Shur, to the east of Egypt on the way to Assyria. They lived apart from the other descendants of Abraham.

²⁵·¹⁹ This is the story of Abraham's son Isaac.

²⁵·²⁰ Isaac was forty years old when he married Rebecca, the daughter of Bethuel (an Aramean from Mesopotamia) and sister of Laban.

²⁵·²¹ Because Rebecca had no children, Isaac prayed to the Lord for her. The Lord answered his prayer, and Rebecca became pregnant.

²⁵·²² She was going to have twins, and before they were born, they struggled against each other in her womb. She said, "Why should something like this happen to me?" So she went to ask the Lord for an answer.

²⁵·²³ The Lord said to her, "Two nations are within you; You will give birth to two rival peoples. One will be stronger than the other; The older will serve the younger."

<sup>25.24</sup> The time came for her to give birth, and she had twin sons.

<sup>25.25</sup> The first one was reddish, and his skin was like a hairy robe, so he was named Esau.

<sup>25.26</sup> The second one was born holding on tightly to the heel of Esau, so he was named Jacob. Isaac was sixty years old when they were born.

<sup>25.27</sup> The boys grew up, and Esau became a skilled hunter, a man who loved the outdoors, but Jacob was a quiet man who stayed at home.

<sup>25.28</sup> Isaac preferred Esau, because he enjoyed eating the animals Esau killed, but Rebecca preferred Jacob.

<sup>25.29</sup> One day while Jacob was cooking some bean soup, Esau came in from hunting. He was hungry

<sup>25.30</sup> and said to Jacob, "I'm starving; give me some of that red stuff." (That is why he was named Edom.)

<sup>25.31</sup> Jacob answered, "I will give it to you if you give me your rights as the first-born son."

<sup>25.32</sup> Esau said, "All right! I am about to die; what good will my rights do me?"

<sup>25.33</sup> Jacob answered, "First make a vow that you will give me your rights."

Esau made the vow and gave his rights to Jacob.

<sup>25.34</sup> Then Jacob gave him some bread and some of the soup. He ate and drank and then got up and left. That was all Esau cared about his rights as the first-born son.

# 26

<sup>26.1</sup> There was another famine in the land besides the earlier one during the time of Abraham. Isaac went to Abimelech, king of the Philistines, at Gerar.

<sup>26.2</sup> The Lord had appeared to Isaac and had said, "Do not go to Egypt; stay in this land, where I tell you to stay.

<sup>26.3</sup> "Live here, and I will be with you and bless you. I am going to give all this territory to you and to your descendants. I will keep the promise I made to your father Abraham.

<sup>26.4</sup> "I will give you as many descendants as there are stars in the sky, and I will give them all this territory. All the nations will ask me to bless them as I have blessed your descendants.

<sup>26.5</sup> "I will bless you, because Abraham obeyed me and kept all my laws and commands."

<sup>26.6</sup> So Isaac lived at Gerar.

<sup>26.7</sup> When the men there asked about his wife, he said that she was his sister. He would not admit that she was his wife, because he was afraid that the men there would kill him to get Rebecca, who was very beautiful.

<sup>26.8</sup> When Isaac had been there for some time, King Abimelech looked down from his window and saw Isaac and Rebecca making love.

<sup>26.9</sup> Abimelech sent for Isaac and said, "So she is your wife! Why did you say she was your sister?"

He answered, "I thought I would be killed if I said she was my wife."

<sup>26.10</sup> "What have you done to us?" Abimelech said. "One of my men might easily have slept with your wife, and you would have been responsible for our guilt."

<sup>26.11</sup> Abimelech warned all the people: "Anyone who mistreats this man or his wife will be put to death."

<sup>26.12</sup> Isaac sowed crops in that land, and that year he harvested a hundred times as much as he had sown, because the Lord blessed him.

<sup>26.13</sup> He continued to prosper and became a very rich man.

<sup>26.14</sup> Because he had many herds of sheep and cattle and many servants, the Philistines were jealous of him.

<sup>26.15</sup> So they filled in all the wells which the servants of his father Abraham had dug while Abraham was alive.

<sup>26.16</sup> Then Abimelech said to Isaac, "Leave our country. You have become more powerful than we are."

<sup>26.17</sup> So Isaac left and set up his camp in Gerar Valley, where he stayed for some time.

<sup>26.18</sup> He dug once again the wells which had been dug during the time of Abraham and which the Philistines had stopped up after Abraham's death. Isaac gave the wells the same names that his father had given them.

<sup>26.19</sup> Isaac's servants dug a well in the valley and found water.

<sup>26.20</sup> The shepherds of Gerar quarreled with Isaac's shepherds and said, "This water belongs to us." So Isaac named the well "Quarrel."

<sup>26.21</sup> Isaac's servants dug another well, and there was a quarrel about that one also, so he named it "Enmity."

<sup>26.22</sup> He moved away from there and dug another well. There was no dispute about this one, so he named it "Freedom." He said, "Now the Lord has given us freedom to live in the land, and we will be prosperous here."

<sup>26.23</sup> Isaac left and went to Beersheba.

<sup>26.24</sup> That night the Lord appeared to him and said, "I am the God of your father Abraham. Do not be afraid; I am with you. I will bless you and give you many descendants because of my promise to my servant Abraham."

<sup>26.25</sup> Isaac built an altar there and worshiped the Lord. Then he set up his camp there, and his servants dug another well.

<sup>26.26</sup> Abimelech came from Gerar with Ahuzzath his adviser and Phicol the commander of his army to see Isaac.

<sup>26.27</sup> So Isaac asked, "Why have you now come to see me, when you were so unfriendly to me before and made me leave your country?"

<sup>26.28</sup> They answered, "Now we know that the Lord is with you, and we think that there should be a solemn agreement between us. We want you to promise

<sup>26.29</sup> "that you will not harm us, just as we did not harm you. We were kind to you and let you go peacefully. Now it is clear that the Lord has blessed you."

<sup>26.30</sup> Isaac prepared a feast for them, and they ate and drank.

<sup>26.31</sup> Early next morning each man made his promise and sealed it with a vow. Isaac said good-bye to them, and they parted as friends.

<sup>26.32</sup> On that day Isaac's servants came and told him about the well which they had dug. They said, "We have found water."

<sup>26.33</sup> He named the well "Vow." That is how the city of Beersheba got its name.

<sup>26.34</sup> When Esau was forty years old, he married two Hittites, Judith the daughter of Beeri, and Basemath the daughter of Elon.

<sup>26.35</sup> They made life miserable for Isaac and Rebecca.

# 27

<sup>27.1</sup> Isaac was now old and had become blind. He sent for his older son Esau and said to him, "Son!" "Yes," he answered.

<sup>27.2</sup> Isaac said, "You see that I am old and may die soon.

<sup>27.3</sup> "Take your bow and arrows, go out into the country, and kill an animal for me.

<sup>27.4</sup> "Cook me some of that tasty food that I like, and bring it to me. After I have eaten it, I will give you my final blessing before I die."

<sup>27.5</sup> While Isaac was talking to Esau, Rebecca was listening. So when Esau went out to hunt,

<sup>27.6</sup> she said to Jacob, "I have just heard your father say to Esau,

<sup>27.7</sup> "'Bring me an animal and cook it for me. After I have eaten it, I will give you my blessing in the presence of the Lord before I die.'

<sup>27.8</sup> "Now, son," Rebecca continued, "listen to me and do what I say.

<sup>27.9</sup> "Go to the flock and pick out two fat young goats, so that I can cook them and make some of that food your father likes so much.

<sup>27.10</sup> "You can take it to him to eat, and he will give you his blessing before he dies."

<sup>27.11</sup> But Jacob said to his mother, "You know that Esau is a hairy man, but I have smooth skin.

<sup>27.12</sup> "Perhaps my father will touch me and find out that I am deceiving him; in this way, I will bring a curse on myself instead of a blessing."

<sup>27.13</sup> His mother answered, "Let any curse against you fall on me, my son; just do as I say, and go and get the goats for me."

<sup>27.14</sup> So he went to get them and brought them to her, and she cooked the kind of food that his father liked.

<sup>27.15</sup> Then she took Esau's best clothes, which she kept in the house, and put them on Jacob.

<sup>27.16</sup> She put the skins of the goats on his arms and on the hairless part of his neck.

<sup>27.17</sup> She handed him the tasty food, along with the bread she had baked.

<sup>27.18</sup> Then Jacob went to his father and said, "Father!"

"Yes," he answered. "Which of my sons are you?"

<sup>27.19</sup> Jacob answered, "I am your older son Esau; I have done as you told me. Please sit up and eat some of the meat that I have brought you, so that you can give me your blessing."

<sup>27.20</sup> Isaac said, "How did you find it so quickly, son?"

Jacob answered, "The Lord your God helped me find it."

<sup>27.21</sup> Isaac said to Jacob, "Please come closer so that I can touch you. Are you really Esau?"

<sup>27.22</sup> Jacob moved closer to his father, who felt him and said, "Your voice sounds like Jacob's voice, but your arms feel like Esau's arms."

<sup>27.23</sup> He did not recognize Jacob, because his arms were hairy like Esau's. He was about to give him his blessing,

<sup>27.24</sup> but asked again, "Are you really Esau?"

"I am," he answered.

<sup>27.25</sup> Isaac said, "Bring me some of the meat. After I eat it, I will give you my blessing." Jacob brought it to him, and he also brought him some wine to drink.

<sup>27.26</sup> Then his father said to him, "Come closer and kiss me, son."

<sup>27.27</sup> As he came up to kiss him, Isaac smelled his clothes—so he gave him his blessing. He said, "The pleasant smell of my son is like the smell of a field which the Lord has blessed.

<sup>27.28</sup> "May God give you dew from heaven and make your fields fertile! May he give you plenty of grain and wine!

<sup>27.29</sup> "May nations be your servants, and may peoples bow down before you. May you rule over all your relatives, and may your mother's descendants bow down before you. May those who curse you be cursed, and may those who bless you be blessed."

<sup>27.30</sup> Isaac finished giving his blessing, and as soon as Jacob left, his brother Esau came in from hunting.

<sup>27.31</sup> He also cooked some tasty food and took it to his father. He said, "Please, father, sit up and eat some of the meat that I have brought you, so that you can give me your blessing."

<sup>27.32</sup> "Who are you?" Isaac asked.

"Your older son Esau," he answered.

<sup>27.33</sup> Isaac began to tremble and shake all over, and he asked, "Who was it, then, who killed an animal and brought it to me? I ate it just before you came. I gave him my final blessing, and so it is his forever."

<sup>27.34</sup> When Esau heard this, he cried out loudly and bitterly and said, "Give me your blessing also, father!"

<sup>27.35</sup> Isaac answered, "Your brother came and deceived me. He has taken away your blessing."

<sup>27.36</sup> Esau said, "This is the second time that he has cheated me. No wonder his name is Jacob. He took my rights as the first-born son, and now he has taken away my blessing. Haven't you saved a blessing for me?"

<sup>27.37</sup> Isaac answered, "I have already made him master over you, and I have made all his relatives his slaves. I have given him grain and wine. Now there is nothing that I can do for you, son!"

<sup>27.38</sup> Esau continued to plead with his father: "Do you have only one blessing, father? Bless me too, father!" He began to cry.

<sup>27.39</sup> Then Isaac said to him, "No dew from heaven for you, no fertile fields for you.

<sup>27.40</sup> "You will live by your sword, but be your brother's slave. Yet when you rebel, you will break away from his control."

<sup>27.41</sup> Esau hated Jacob, because his father had given Jacob the blessing. He thought, "The time to mourn my father's death is near; then I will kill Jacob."

<sup>27.42</sup> But when Rebecca heard about Esau's plan, she sent for Jacob and said, "Listen, your brother Esau is planning to get even with you and kill you.

<sup>27.43</sup> "Now, son, do what I say. Go at once to my brother Laban in Ha-

ran,

<sup>27.44</sup> "and stay with him for a while, until your brother's anger cools down

<sup>27.45</sup> "and he forgets what you have done to him. Then I will send someone to bring you back. Why should I lose both of my sons on the same day?"

<sup>27.46</sup> Rebecca said to Isaac, "I am sick and tired of Esau's foreign wives. If Jacob also marries one of these Hittites, I might as well die."

# 28

<sup>28.1</sup> Isaac called Jacob, greeted him, and told him, "Don't marry a Canaanite.

<sup>28.2</sup> "Go instead to Mesopotamia, to the home of your grandfather Bethuel, and marry one of the young women there, one of your uncle Laban's daughters.

<sup>28.3</sup> "May Almighty God bless your marriage and give you many children, so that you will become the father of many nations!

<sup>28.4</sup> "May he bless you and your descendants as he blessed Abraham, and may you take possession of this land, in which you have lived and which God gave to Abraham!"

<sup>28.5</sup> Isaac sent Jacob away to Mesopotamia, to Laban, who was the son of Bethuel the Aramean and the brother of Rebecca, the mother of Jacob and Esau.

<sup>28.6</sup> Esau learned that Isaac had blessed Jacob and sent him away to Mesopotamia to find a wife. He also learned that when Isaac blessed him, he commanded him not to marry a Canaanite woman.

<sup>28.7</sup> He found out that Jacob had obeyed his father and mother and had gone to Mesopotamia.

<sup>28.8</sup> Esau then understood that his father Isaac did not approve of Canaanite women.

<sup>28.9</sup> So he went to Ishmael son of Abraham and married his daughter Mahalath, who was the sister of Nebaioth.

<sup>28.10</sup> Jacob left Beersheba and started toward Haran.

<sup>28.11</sup> At sunset he came to a holy place and camped there. He lay down to sleep, resting his head on a stone.

<sup>28.12</sup> He dreamed that he saw a stairway reaching from earth to heaven, with angels going up and coming down on it.

<sup>28.13</sup> And there was the Lord standing beside him. "I am the Lord, the God of Abraham and Isaac," he said. "I will give to you and to your descendants this land on which you are lying.

<sup>28.14</sup> "They will be as numerous as the specks of dust on the earth. They will extend their territory in all directions, and through you and your descendants I will bless all the nations.

<sup>28.15</sup> "Remember, I will be with you and protect you wherever you go, and I will bring you back to this land. I will not leave you until I have done all that I have promised you."

<sup>28.16</sup> Jacob woke up and said, "The Lord is here! He is in this place, and I didn't know it!"

<sup>28.17</sup> He was afraid and said, "What a terrifying place this is! It must be the house of God; it must be the gate that opens into heaven."

<sup>28.18</sup> Jacob got up early next morning, took the stone that was under his head, and set it up as a memorial. Then he poured olive oil on it to dedicate it to God.

<sup>28.19</sup> He named the place Bethel. (The town there was once known as Luz.)

<sup>28.20</sup> Then Jacob made a vow to the Lord: "If you will be with me and protect me on the journey I am making and give me food and clothing,

<sup>28.21</sup> "and if I return safely to my father's home, then you will be my God.

<sup>28.22</sup> "This memorial stone which I have set up will be the place where you are worshiped, and I will give you a tenth of everything you give me."

# 29

<sup>29.1</sup> Jacob continued on his way and went toward the land of the East.

<sup>29.2</sup> Suddenly he came upon a well out in the fields with three flocks of sheep lying around it. The flocks were watered from this well, which had a large stone over the opening.

<sup>29.3</sup> Whenever all the flocks came together there, the shepherds would roll the stone back and water them. Then they would put the stone back in place.

<sup>29.4</sup> Jacob asked the shepherds, "My friends, where are you from?"

"From Haran," they answered.

<sup>29.5</sup> He asked, "Do you know Laban, grandson of Nahor?"

"Yes, we do," they answered.

<sup>29.6</sup> "Is he well?" he asked.

"He is well," they answered. "Look, here comes his daughter Rachel with his flock."

<sup>29.7</sup> Jacob said, "Since it is still broad daylight and not yet time to

bring the flocks in, why don't you water them and take them back to pasture?"

<sup></sup>²⁹·⁸ They answered, "We can't do that until all the flocks are here and the stone has been rolled back; then we will water the flocks."

²⁹·⁹ While Jacob was still talking with them, Rachel arrived with the flock.

²⁹·¹⁰ When Jacob saw Rachel with his uncle Laban's flock, he went to the well, rolled the stone back, and watered the sheep.

²⁹·¹¹ Then he kissed her and began to cry for joy.

²⁹·¹² He told her, "I am your father's relative, the son of Rebecca."

She ran to tell her father;

²⁹·¹³ and when he heard the news about his nephew Jacob, he ran to meet him, hugged him and kissed him, and brought him into the house. When Jacob told Laban everything that had happened,

²⁹·¹⁴ Laban said, "Yes, indeed, you are my own flesh and blood." Jacob stayed there a whole month.

²⁹·¹⁵ Laban said to Jacob, "You shouldn't work for me for nothing just because you are my relative. How much pay do you want?"

²⁹·¹⁶ Laban had two daughters; the older was named Leah, and the younger Rachel.

²⁹·¹⁷ Leah had lovely eyes, but Rachel was shapely and beautiful.

²⁹·¹⁸ Jacob was in love with Rachel, so he said, "I will work seven years for you, if you will let me marry Rachel."

²⁹·¹⁹ Laban answered, "I would rather give her to you than to anyone else; stay here with me."

²⁹·²⁰ Jacob worked seven years so that he could have Rachel, and the time seemed like only a few days to him, because he loved her.

²⁹·²¹ Then Jacob said to Laban, "The time is up; let me marry your daughter."

²⁹·²² So Laban gave a wedding feast and invited everyone.

²⁹·²³ But that night, instead of Rachel, he took Leah to Jacob, and Jacob had intercourse with her.

²⁹·²⁴ (Laban gave his slave woman Zilpah to his daughter Leah as her maid.)

²⁹·²⁵ Not until the next morning did Jacob discover that it was Leah. He went to Laban and said, "Why did you do this to me? I worked to get Rachel. Why have you tricked me?"

²⁹·²⁶ Laban answered, "It is not the custom here to give the younger daughter in marriage before the older.

²⁹·²⁷ "Wait until the week's marriage celebrations are over, and I will give you Rachel, if you will work for me another seven years."

<sup>29.28</sup> Jacob agreed, and when the week of marriage celebrations was over, Laban gave him his daughter Rachel as his wife.

<sup>29.29</sup> (Laban gave his slave woman Bilhah to his daughter Rachel as her maid.)

<sup>29.30</sup> Jacob had intercourse with Rachel also, and he loved her more than Leah. Then he worked for Laban another seven years.

<sup>29.31</sup> When the Lord saw that Leah was loved less than Rachel, he made it possible for her to have children, but Rachel remained childless.

<sup>29.32</sup> Leah became pregnant and gave birth to a son. She said, "The Lord has seen my trouble, and now my husband will love me"; so she named him Reuben.

<sup>29.33</sup> She became pregnant again and gave birth to another son. She said, "The Lord has given me this son also, because he heard that I was not loved"; so she named him Simeon.

<sup>29.34</sup> Once again she became pregnant and gave birth to another son. She said, "Now my husband will be bound more tightly to me, because I have borne him three sons"; so she named him Levi.

<sup>29.35</sup> Then she became pregnant again and gave birth to another son. She said, "This time I will praise the Lord"; so she named him Judah. Then she stopped having children.

# 30

<sup>30.1</sup> But Rachel had not borne Jacob any children, and so she became jealous of her sister and said to Jacob, "Give me children, or I will die."

<sup>30.2</sup> Jacob became angry with Rachel and said, "I can't take the place of God. He is the one who keeps you from having children."

<sup>30.3</sup> She said, "Here is my slave Bilhah; sleep with her, so that she can have a child for me. In this way I can become a mother through her."

<sup>30.4</sup> So she gave Bilhah to her husband, and he had intercourse with her.

<sup>30.5</sup> Bilhah became pregnant and bore Jacob a son.

<sup>30.6</sup> Rachel said, "God has judged in my favor. He has heard my prayer and has given me a son"; so she named him Dan.

<sup>30.7</sup> Bilhah became pregnant again and bore Jacob a second son.

<sup>30.8</sup> Rachel said, "I have fought a hard fight with my sister, but I have won"; so she named him Naphtali.

<sup>30.9</sup> When Leah realized that she had stopped having children, she gave her slave Zilpah to Jacob as his wife.

<sup>30.10</sup> Then Zilpah bore Jacob a son.

<sup>30.11</sup> Leah said, "I have been lucky"; so she named him Gad.

<sup>30.12</sup> Zilpah bore Jacob another son,

<sup>30.13</sup> and Leah said, "How happy I am! Now women will call me happy"; so she named him Asher.

<sup>30.14</sup> During the wheat harvest Reuben went into the fields and found mandrakes, which he brought to his mother Leah. Rachel said to Leah, "Please give me some of your son's mandrakes."

<sup>30.15</sup> Leah answered, "Isn't it enough that you have taken away my husband? Now you are even trying to take away my son's mandrakes."

Rachel said, "If you will give me your son's mandrakes, you can sleep with Jacob tonight."

<sup>30.16</sup> When Jacob came in from the fields in the evening, Leah went out to meet him and said, "You are going to sleep with me tonight, because I have paid for you with my son's mandrakes." So he had intercourse with her that night.

<sup>30.17</sup> God answered Leah's prayer, and she became pregnant and bore Jacob a fifth son.

<sup>30.18</sup> Leah said, "God has given me my reward, because I gave my slave to my husband"; so she named her son Issachar.

<sup>30.19</sup> Leah became pregnant again and bore Jacob a sixth son.

<sup>30.20</sup> She said, "God has given me a fine gift. Now my husband will accept me, because I have borne him six sons"; so she named him Zebulun.

<sup>30.21</sup> Later she bore a daughter, whom she named Dinah.

<sup>30.22</sup> Then God remembered Rachel; he answered her prayer and made it possible for her to have children.

<sup>30.23</sup> She became pregnant and gave birth to a son. She said, "God has taken away my disgrace by giving me a son.

<sup>30.24</sup> "May the Lord give me another son"; so she named him Joseph.

<sup>30.25</sup> After the birth of Joseph, Jacob said to Laban, "Let me go, so that I can return home.

<sup>30.26</sup> "Give me my wives and children that I have earned by working for you, and I will leave. You know how well I have served you."

<sup>30.27</sup> Laban said to him, "Let me say this: I have learned by divination that the Lord has blessed me because of you.

<sup>30.28</sup> "Name your wages, and I will pay them."

<sup>30.29</sup> Jacob answered, "You know how I have worked for you and how your flocks have prospered under my care.

<sup>30.30</sup> "The little you had before I came has grown enormously, and the

Lord has blessed you wherever I went. Now it is time for me to look out for my own interests."

<sup>30.31</sup> "What shall I pay you?" Laban asked.

Jacob answered, "I don't want any wages. I will continue to take care of your flocks if you agree to this suggestion:

<sup>30.32</sup> "Let me go through all your flocks today and take every black lamb and every spotted or speckled young goat. That is all the wages I want.

<sup>30.33</sup> "In the future you can easily find out if I have been honest. When you come to check up on my wages, if I have any goat that isn't speckled or spotted or any sheep that isn't black, you will know that it has been stolen."

<sup>30.34</sup> Laban answered, "Agreed. We will do as you suggest."

<sup>30.35</sup> But that day Laban removed the male goats that had stripes or spots and all the females that were speckled and spotted or which had white on them; he also removed all the black sheep. He put his sons in charge of them,

<sup>30.36</sup> and then went away from Jacob with this flock as far as he could travel in three days. Jacob took care of the rest of Laban's flocks.

<sup>30.37</sup> Jacob got green branches of poplar, almond, and plane trees and stripped off some of the bark so that the branches had white stripes on them.

<sup>30.38</sup> He placed these branches in front of the flocks at their drinking troughs. He put them there, because the animals mated when they came to drink.

<sup>30.39</sup> So when the goats bred in front of the branches, they produced young that were streaked, speckled, and spotted.

<sup>30.40</sup> Jacob kept the sheep separate from the goats and made them face in the direction of the streaked and black animals of Laban's flock. In this way he built up his own flock and kept it apart from Laban's.

<sup>30.41</sup> When the healthy animals were mating, Jacob put the branches in front of them at the drinking troughs, so that they would breed among the branches.

<sup>30.42</sup> But he did not put the branches in front of the weak animals. Soon Laban had all the weak animals, and Jacob all the healthy ones.

<sup>30.43</sup> In this way Jacob became very wealthy. He had many flocks, slaves, camels, and donkeys.

# 31

<sup>31.1</sup> Jacob heard that Laban's sons were saying, "Jacob has taken everything that belonged to our father. He got all his wealth from what our father owned."

<sup>31.2</sup> He also saw that Laban was no longer as friendly as he had been earlier.

<sup>31.3</sup> Then the Lord said to him, "Go back to the land of your fathers and to your relatives. I will be with you."

<sup>31.4</sup> So Jacob sent word to Rachel and Leah to meet him in the field where his flocks were.

<sup>31.5</sup> He said to them, "I have noticed that your father is not as friendly toward me as he used to be; but my father's God has been with me.

<sup>31.6</sup> "You both know that I have worked for your father with all my strength.

<sup>31.7</sup> "Yet he has cheated me and changed my wages ten times. But God did not let him harm me.

<sup>31.8</sup> "Whenever Laban said, 'The speckled goats shall be your wages,' all the flocks produced speckled young. When he said, 'The striped goats shall be your wages,' all the flocks produced striped young.

<sup>31.9</sup> "God has taken flocks away from your father and given them to me.

<sup>31.10</sup> "During the breeding season I had a dream, and I saw that the male goats that were mating were striped, spotted, and speckled.

<sup>31.11</sup> "The angel of God spoke to me in the dream and said, 'Jacob!' 'Yes,' I answered.

<sup>31.12</sup> "'Look,' he continued, 'all the male goats that are mating are striped, spotted, and speckled. I am making this happen because I have seen all that Laban is doing to you.

<sup>31.13</sup> "'I am the God who appeared to you at Bethel, where you dedicated a stone as a memorial by pouring olive oil on it and where you made a vow to me. Now get ready and go back to the land where you were born.'"

<sup>31.14</sup> Rachel and Leah answered Jacob, "There is nothing left for us to inherit from our father.

<sup>31.15</sup> "He treats us like foreigners. He sold us, and now he has spent all the money he was paid for us.

<sup>31.16</sup> "All this wealth which God has taken from our father belongs to us and to our children. Do whatever God has told you."

<sup>31.17-18</sup> So Jacob got ready to go back to his father in the land of Canaan. He put his children and his wives on the camels, and drove all his flocks ahead of him, with everything that he had gotten in Mesopotamia.

31.19 Laban had gone to shear his sheep, and during his absence Rachel stole the household gods that belonged to her father.

31.20 Jacob deceived Laban by not letting him know that he was leaving.

31.21 He took everything he owned and left in a hurry. He crossed the Euphrates River and started for the hill country of Gilead.

31.22 Three days later Laban was told that Jacob had fled.

31.23 He took his men with him and pursued Jacob for seven days until he caught up with him in the hill country of Gilead.

31.24 In a dream that night God came to Laban and said to him, "Be careful not to threaten Jacob in any way."

31.25 Jacob had set up his camp on a mountain, and Laban set up his camp with his relatives in the hill country of Gilead.

31.26 Laban said to Jacob, "Why did you deceive me and carry off my daughters like women captured in war?

31.27 "Why did you deceive me and slip away without telling me? If you had told me, I would have sent you on your way with rejoicing and singing to the music of tambourines and harps.

31.28 "You did not even let me kiss my grandchildren and my daughters good-bye. That was a foolish thing to do!

31.29 "I have the power to do you harm, but last night the God of your father warned me not to threaten you in any way.

31.30 "I know that you left because you were so anxious to get back home, but why did you steal my household gods?"

31.31 Jacob answered, "I was afraid, because I thought that you might take your daughters away from me.

31.32 "But if you find that anyone here has your gods, he will be put to death. Here, with our men as witnesses, look for anything that belongs to you and take what is yours." Jacob did not know that Rachel had stolen Laban's gods.

31.33 Laban went and searched Jacob's tent; then he went into Leah's tent, and the tent of the two slave women, but he did not find his gods. Then he went into Rachel's tent.

31.34 Rachel had taken the household gods and put them in a camel's saddlebag and was sitting on them. Laban searched through the whole tent, but did not find them.

31.35 Rachel said to her father, "Do not be angry with me, sir, but I am not able to stand up in your presence; I am having my monthly period." Laban searched but did not find his household gods.

31.36 Then Jacob lost his temper. "What crime have I committed?" he asked angrily. "What law have I broken that gives you the right to hunt me down?

<sup>31.37</sup> "Now that you have searched through all my belongings, what household article have you found that belongs to you? Put it out here where your men and mine can see it, and let them decide which one of us is right.

<sup>31.38</sup> "I have been with you now for twenty years; your sheep and your goats have not failed to reproduce, and I have not eaten any rams from your flocks.

<sup>31.39</sup> "Whenever a sheep was killed by wild animals, I always bore the loss myself. I didn't take it to you to show that it was not my fault. You demanded that I make good anything that was stolen during the day or during the night.

<sup>31.40</sup> "Many times I suffered from the heat during the day and from the cold at night. I was not able to sleep.

<sup>31.41</sup> "It was like that for the whole twenty years I was with you. For fourteen years I worked to win your two daughters—and six years for your flocks. And even then, you changed my wages ten times.

<sup>31.42</sup> "If the God of my fathers, the God of Abraham and Isaac, had not been with me, you would have already sent me away empty-handed. But God has seen my trouble and the work I have done, and last night he gave his judgment."

<sup>31.43</sup> Laban answered Jacob, "These young women are my daughters; their children belong to me, and these flocks are mine. In fact, everything you see here belongs to me. But since I can do nothing to keep my daughters and their children,

<sup>31.44</sup> "I am ready to make an agreement with you. Let us make a pile of stones to remind us of our agreement."

<sup>31.45</sup> So Jacob got a stone and set it up as a memorial.

<sup>31.46</sup> He told his men to gather some rocks and pile them up. Then they ate a meal beside the pile of rocks.

<sup>31.47</sup> Laban named it Jegar Sahadutha, while Jacob named it Galeed.

<sup>31.48</sup> Laban said to Jacob, "This pile of rocks will be a reminder for both of us." That is why that place was named Galeed.

<sup>31.49</sup> Laban also said, "May the Lord keep an eye on us while we are separated from each other." So the place was also named Mizpah.

<sup>31.50</sup> Laban went on, "If you mistreat my daughters or if you marry other women, even though I don't know about it, remember that God is watching us.

<sup>31.51</sup> "Here are the rocks that I have piled up between us, and here is the memorial stone.

<sup>31.52</sup> "Both this pile and this memorial stone are reminders. I will

never go beyond this pile to attack you, and you must never go beyond it or beyond this memorial stone to attack me.

³¹·⁵³ "The God of Abraham and the God of Nahor will judge between us." Then, in the name of the God whom his father Isaac worshiped, Jacob solemnly vowed to keep this promise.

³¹·⁵⁴ He killed an animal, which he offered as a sacrifice on the mountain, and he invited his men to the meal. After they had eaten, they spent the night on the mountain.

³¹·⁵⁵ Early the next morning Laban kissed his grandchildren and his daughters good-bye, and left to go back home.

# 32

³²·¹ As Jacob went on his way, some angels met him.

³²·² When he saw them, he said, "This is God's camp"; so he named the place Mahanaim.

³²·³ Jacob sent messengers ahead of him to his brother Esau in the country of Edom.

³²·⁴ He instructed them to say: "I, Jacob, your obedient servant, report to my master Esau that I have been staying with Laban and that I have delayed my return until now.

³²·⁵ "I own cattle, donkeys, sheep, goats, and slaves. I am sending you word, sir, in the hope of gaining your favor."

³²·⁶ When the messengers came back to Jacob, they said, "We went to your brother Esau, and he is already on his way to meet you. He has four hundred men with him."

³²·⁷ Jacob was frightened and worried. He divided into two groups the people who were with him, and also his sheep, goats, cattle, and camels.

³²·⁸ He thought, "If Esau comes and attacks the first group, the other may be able to escape."

³²·⁹ Then Jacob prayed, "God of my grandfather Abraham and God of my father Isaac, hear me! You told me, Lord, to go back to my land and to my relatives, and you would make everything go well for me.

³²·¹⁰ "I am not worth all the kindness and faithfulness that you have shown me, your servant. I crossed the Jordan with nothing but a walking stick, and now I have come back with these two groups.

³²·¹¹ "Save me, I pray, from my brother Esau. I am afraid—afraid that he is coming to attack us and destroy us all, even the women and children.

³²·¹² "Remember that you promised to make everything go well for me and to give me more descendants than anyone could count, as many

as the grains of sand along the seashore."

[32.13-15] After spending the night there, Jacob chose from his livestock as a present for his brother Esau: 200 female goats and 20 males, 200 female sheep and 20 males, 30 milk camels with their young, 40 cows and 10 bulls, 20 female donkeys and 10 males.

[32.16] He divided them into herds and put one of his servants in charge of each herd. He said to them, "Go ahead of me, and leave a space between each herd and the one behind it."

[32.17] He ordered the first servant, "When my brother Esau meets you and asks, 'Who is your master? Where are you going? Who owns these animals in front of you?'

[32.18] "you must answer, 'They belong to your servant Jacob. He sends them as a present to his master Esau. Jacob himself is right behind us.'"

[32.19] He gave the same order to the second, the third, and to all the others who were in charge of the herds: "This is what you must say to Esau when you meet him.

[32.20] "You must say, 'Yes, your servant Jacob is right behind us.'" Jacob was thinking, "I will win him over with the gifts, and when I meet him, perhaps he will forgive me."

[32.21] He sent the gifts on ahead of him and spent that night in camp.

[32.22] That same night Jacob got up, took his two wives, his two concubines, and his eleven children, and crossed the Jabbok River.

[32.23] After he had sent them across, he also sent across all that he owned,

[32.24] but he stayed behind, alone.

Then a man came and wrestled with him until just before daybreak.

[32.25] When the man saw that he was not winning the struggle, he hit Jacob on the hip, and it was thrown out of joint.

[32.26] The man said, "Let me go; daylight is coming."

"I won't, unless you bless me," Jacob answered.

[32.27] "What is your name?" the man asked.

"Jacob," he answered.

[32.28] The man said, "Your name will no longer be Jacob. You have struggled with God and with men, and you have won; so your name will be Israel."

[32.29] Jacob said, "Now tell me your name."

But he answered, "Why do you want to know my name?" Then he blessed Jacob.

[32.30] Jacob said, "I have seen God face-to-face, and I am still alive";

so he named the place Peniel.

<sup>32.31</sup> The sun rose as Jacob was leaving Peniel, and he was limping because of his hip.

<sup>32.32</sup> Even today the descendants of Israel do not eat the muscle which is on the hip joint, because it was on this muscle that Jacob was hit.

# 33

<sup>33.1</sup> Jacob saw Esau coming with his four hundred men, so he divided the children among Leah, Rachel, and the two concubines.

<sup>33.2</sup> He put the concubines and their children first, then Leah and her children, and finally Rachel and Joseph at the rear.

<sup>33.3</sup> Jacob went ahead of them and bowed down to the ground seven times as he approached his brother.

<sup>33.4</sup> But Esau ran to meet him, threw his arms around him, and kissed him. They were both crying.

<sup>33.5</sup> When Esau looked around and saw the women and the children, he asked, "Who are these people with you?"

"These, sir, are the children whom God has been good enough to give me," Jacob answered.

<sup>33.6</sup> Then the concubines came up with their children and bowed down;

<sup>33.7</sup> then Leah and her children came, and last of all Joseph and Rachel came and bowed down.

<sup>33.8</sup> Esau asked, "What about that other group I met? What did that mean?"

Jacob answered, "It was to gain your favor."

<sup>33.9</sup> But Esau said, "I have enough, my brother; keep what you have."

<sup>33.10</sup> Jacob said, "No, please, if I have gained your favor, accept my gift. To see your face is for me like seeing the face of God, now that you have been so friendly to me.

<sup>33.11</sup> "Please accept this gift which I have brought for you; God has been kind to me and given me everything I need." Jacob kept on urging him until he accepted.

<sup>33.12</sup> Esau said, "Let's get ready and leave. I will go ahead of you."

<sup>33.13</sup> Jacob answered, "You know that the children are weak, and I must think of the sheep and livestock with their young. If they are driven hard for even one day, the whole herd will die.

<sup>33.14</sup> "Please go on ahead of me, and I will follow slowly, going as fast as I can with the livestock and the children until I catch up with you in Edom."

<sup>33.15</sup> Esau said, "Then let me leave some of my men with you."

But Jacob answered, "There is no need for that for I only want to gain your favor."

<sup>33.16</sup> So that day Esau started on his way back to Edom.

<sup>33.17</sup> But Jacob went to Sukkoth, where he built a house for himself and shelters for his livestock. That is why the place was named Sukkoth.

<sup>33.18</sup> On his return from Mesopotamia Jacob arrived safely at the city of Shechem in the land of Canaan and set up his camp in a field near the city.

<sup>33.19</sup> He bought that part of the field from the descendants of Hamor father of Shechem for a hundred pieces of silver.

<sup>33.20</sup> He put up an altar there and named it for El, the God of Israel.

# 34

<sup>34.1</sup> One day Dinah, the daughter of Jacob and Leah, went to visit some of the Canaanite women.

<sup>34.2</sup> When Shechem son of Hamor the Hivite, who was chief of that region, saw her, he took her and raped her.

<sup>34.3</sup> But he found the young woman so attractive that he fell in love with her and tried to win her affection.

<sup>34.4</sup> He told his father, "I want you to get Dinah for me as my wife."

<sup>34.5</sup> Jacob learned that his daughter had been disgraced, but because his sons were out in the fields with his livestock, he did nothing until they came back.

<sup>34.6</sup> Shechem's father Hamor went out to talk with Jacob,

<sup>34.7</sup> just as Jacob's sons were coming in from the fields. When they heard about it, they were shocked and furious that Shechem had done such a thing and had insulted the people of Israel by raping Jacob's daughter.

<sup>34.8</sup> Hamor said to him, "My son Shechem has fallen in love with your daughter; please let him marry her.

<sup>34.9</sup> "Let us make an agreement that there will be intermarriage between our people and yours.

<sup>34.10</sup> "Then you may stay here in our country with us; you may live anywhere you wish, trade freely, and own property."

<sup>34.11</sup> Then Shechem said to Dinah's father and brothers, "Do me this favor, and I will give you whatever you want.

<sup>34.12</sup> "Tell me what presents you want, and set the payment for the bride as high as you wish; I will give you whatever you ask, if you will only let me marry her."

<sup>34.13</sup> Because Shechem had disgraced their sister Dinah, Jacob's

sons answered Shechem and his father Hamor in a deceitful way.

<sup>34.14</sup> They said to him, "We cannot let our sister marry a man who is not circumcised; that would be a disgrace for us.

<sup>34.15</sup> "We can agree only on the condition that you become like us by circumcising all your males.

<sup>34.16</sup> "Then we will agree to intermarriage. We will settle among you and become one people with you.

<sup>34.17</sup> "But if you will not accept our terms and be circumcised, we will take her and leave."

<sup>34.18</sup> These terms seemed fair to Hamor and his son Shechem,

<sup>34.19</sup> and the young man lost no time in doing what was suggested, because he was in love with Jacob's daughter. He was the most important member of his family.

<sup>34.20</sup> Hamor and his son Shechem went to the meeting place at the city gate and spoke to the people of the town:

<sup>34.21</sup> "These men are friendly; let them live in the land with us and travel freely. The land is large enough for them also. Let us marry their daughters and give them ours in marriage.

<sup>34.22</sup> "But these men will agree to live among us and be one people with us only on the condition that we circumcise all our males, as they are circumcised.

<sup>34.23</sup> "Won't all their livestock and everything else they own be ours? So let us agree that they can live among us."

<sup>34.24</sup> All the citizens of the city agreed with what Hamor and Shechem proposed, and all the males were circumcised.

<sup>34.25</sup> Three days later, when the men were still sore from their circumcision, two of Jacob's sons, Simeon and Levi, the brothers of Dinah, took their swords, went into the city without arousing suspicion, and killed all the men,

<sup>34.26</sup> including Hamor and his son Shechem. Then they took Dinah from Shechem's house and left.

<sup>34.27</sup> After the slaughter Jacob's other sons looted the town to take revenge for their sister's disgrace.

<sup>34.28</sup> They took the flocks, the cattle, the donkeys, and everything else in the city and in the fields.

<sup>34.29</sup> They took everything of value, captured all the women and children, and carried off everything in the houses.

<sup>34.30</sup> Jacob said to Simeon and Levi, "You have gotten me into trouble; now the Canaanites, the Perizzites, and everybody else in the land will hate me. I do not have many men; if they all band together against me and attack me, our whole family will be destroyed."

<sup>34.31</sup> But they answered, "We cannot let our sister be treated like a common whore."

# 35

<sup>35.1</sup> God said to Jacob, "Go to Bethel at once, and live there. Build an altar there to me, the God who appeared to you when you were running away from your brother Esau."

<sup>35.2</sup> So Jacob said to his family and to all who were with him, "Get rid of the foreign gods that you have; purify yourselves and put on clean clothes.

<sup>35.3</sup> "We are going to leave here and go to Bethel, where I will build an altar to the God who helped me in the time of my trouble and who has been with me everywhere I have gone."

<sup>35.4</sup> So they gave Jacob all the foreign gods that they had and also the earrings that they were wearing. He buried them beneath the oak tree near Shechem.

<sup>35.5</sup> When Jacob and his sons started to leave, great fear fell on the people of the nearby towns, and they did not pursue them.

<sup>35.6</sup> Jacob came with all his people to Luz, which is now known as Bethel, in the land of Canaan.

<sup>35.7</sup> He built an altar there and named the place for the God of Bethel, because God had revealed himself to him there when he was running away from his brother.

<sup>35.8</sup> Rebecca's nurse Deborah died and was buried beneath the oak south of Bethel. So it was named "Oak of Weeping."

<sup>35.9</sup> When Jacob returned from Mesopotamia, God appeared to him again and blessed him.

<sup>35.10</sup> God said to him, "Your name is Jacob, but from now on it will be Israel." So God named him Israel.

<sup>35.11</sup> And God said to him, "I am Almighty God. Have many children. Nations will be descended from you, and you will be the ancestor of kings.

<sup>35.12</sup> "I will give you the land which I gave to Abraham and to Isaac, and I will also give it to your descendants after you."

<sup>35.13</sup> Then God left him.

<sup>35.14</sup> There, where God had spoken to him, Jacob set up a memorial stone and consecrated it by pouring wine and olive oil on it.

<sup>35.15</sup> He named the place Bethel.

<sup>35.16</sup> Jacob and his family left Bethel, and when they were still some distance from Ephrath, the time came for Rachel to have her baby, and she was having difficult labor.

<sup>35.17</sup> When her labor pains were at their worst, the midwife said to her, "Don't be afraid, Rachel; it's another boy."

<sup>35.18</sup> But she was dying, and as she breathed her last, she named her son Benoni, but his father named him Benjamin.

<sup>35.19</sup> When Rachel died, she was buried beside the road to Ephrath, now known as Bethlehem.

<sup>35.20</sup> Jacob set up a memorial stone there, and it still marks Rachel's grave to this day.

<sup>35.21</sup> Jacob moved on and set up his camp on the other side of the tower of Eder.

<sup>35.22</sup> While Jacob was living in that land, Reuben had sexual intercourse with Bilhah, one of his father's concubines; Jacob heard about it and was furious.

Jacob had twelve sons.

<sup>35.23</sup> The sons of Leah were Reuben (Jacob's oldest son), Simeon, Levi, Judah, Issachar, and Zebulun.

<sup>35.24</sup> The sons of Rachel were Joseph and Benjamin.

<sup>35.25</sup> The sons of Rachel's slave Bilhah were Dan and Naphtali.

<sup>35.26</sup> The sons of Leah's slave Zilpah were Gad and Asher. These sons were born in Mesopotamia.

<sup>35.27</sup> Jacob went to his father Isaac at Mamre, near Hebron, where Abraham and Isaac had lived.

<sup>35.28</sup> Isaac lived to be a hundred and eighty years old

<sup>35.29</sup> and died at a ripe old age; and his sons Esau and Jacob buried him.

# 36

<sup>36.1</sup> These are the descendants of Esau, also called Edom.

<sup>36.2</sup> Esau married Canaanite women: Adah, the daughter of Elon the Hittite; Oholibamah, the daughter of Anah son of Zibeon the Hivite;

<sup>36.3</sup> and Basemath, the daughter of Ishmael and sister of Nebaioth.

<sup>36.4</sup> Adah bore Eliphaz; Basemath bore Reuel;

<sup>36.5</sup> and Oholibamah bore Jeush, Jalam, and Korah. All these sons were born to Esau in the land of Canaan.

<sup>36.6</sup> Then Esau took his wives, his sons, his daughters, and all the people of his house, along with all his livestock and all the possessions he had gotten in the land of Canaan, and went away from his brother Jacob to another land.

<sup>36.7</sup> He left because the land where he and Jacob were living was not able to support them; they had too much livestock and could no longer stay together.

<sup>36.8</sup> So Esau lived in the hill country of Edom.

<sup>36.9</sup> These are the descendants of Esau, the ancestor of the Edomites.

<sup>36.10-13</sup> Esau's wife Adah bore him one son, Eliphaz, and Eliphaz had five sons: Teman, Omar, Zepho, Gatam, and Kenaz. And by another wife, Timna, he had one more son, Amalek.

Esau's wife Basemath bore him one son, Reuel, and Reuel had four sons: Nahath, Zerah, Shammah, and Mizzah.

<sup>36.14</sup> Esau's wife Oholibamah, the daughter of Anah son of Zibeon, bore him three sons: Jeush, Jalam, and Korah.

<sup>36.15</sup> These are the tribes descended from Esau. Esau's first son Eliphaz was the ancestor of the following tribes: Teman, Omar, Zepho, Kenaz,

<sup>36.16</sup> Korah, Gatam, and Amalek. These were all descendants of Esau's wife Adah.

<sup>36.17</sup> Esau's son Reuel was the ancestor of the following tribes: Nahath, Zerah, Shammah, and Mizzah. These were all descendants of Esau's wife Basemath.

<sup>36.18</sup> The following tribes were descended from Esau by his wife Oholibamah, the daughter of Anah: Jeush, Jalam, and Korah.

<sup>36.19</sup> All these tribes were descended from Esau.

<sup>36.20-21</sup> The original inhabitants of the land of Edom were divided into tribes which traced their ancestry to the following descendants of Seir, a Horite: Lotan, Shobal, Zibeon, Anah, Dishon, Ezer, and Dishan.

<sup>36.22</sup> Lotan was the ancestor of the clans of Hori and Heman. (Lotan had a sister named Timna.)

<sup>36.23</sup> Shobal was the ancestor of the clans of Alvan, Manahath, Ebal, Shepho, and Onam.

<sup>36.24</sup> Zibeon had two sons, Aiah and Anah. (This is the Anah who found the hot springs in the wilderness when he was taking care of his father's donkeys.)

<sup>36.25-26</sup> Anah was the father of Dishon, who was the ancestor of the clans of Hemdan, Eshban, Ithran, and Cheran. Anah also had a daughter named Oholibamah.

<sup>36.27</sup> Ezer was the ancestor of the clans of Bilhan, Zaavan, and Akan.

<sup>36.28</sup> Dishan was the ancestor of the clans of Uz and Aran.

<sup>36.29-30</sup> These are the Horite tribes in the land of Edom: Lotan, Shobal, Zibeon, Anah, Dishon, Ezer, and Dishan.

<sup>36.31-39</sup> Before there were any kings in Israel, the following kings

ruled the land of Edom in succession:

Bela son of Beor from Dinhabah

Jobab son of Zerah from Bozrah

Husham from the region of Teman

Hadad son of Bedad from Avith (he defeated the Midianites in a battle in the country of Moab)

Samlah from Masrekah

Shaul from Rehoboth-on-the-River

Baal Hanan son of Achbor

Hadad from Pau (his wife was Mehetabel, the daughter of Matred and granddaughter of Mezahab)

36.40-43 Esau was the ancestor of the following Edomite tribes: Timna, Alvah, Jetheth, Oholibamah, Elah, Pinon, Kenaz, Teman, Mibzar, Magdiel, and Iram. The area where each of these tribes lived was known by the name of the tribe.

# 37

37.1 Jacob continued to live in the land of Canaan, where his father had lived,

37.2 and this is the story of Jacob's family.

Joseph, a young man of seventeen, took care of the sheep and goats with his brothers, the sons of Bilhah and Zilpah, his father's concubines. He brought bad reports to his father about what his brothers were doing.

37.3 Jacob loved Joseph more than all his other sons, because he had been born to him when he was old. He made a long robe with full sleeves for him.

37.4 When his brothers saw that their father loved Joseph more than he loved them, they hated their brother so much that they would not speak to him in a friendly manner.

37.5 One time Joseph had a dream, and when he told his brothers about it, they hated him even more.

37.6 He said, "Listen to the dream I had.

37.7 "We were all in the field tying up sheaves of wheat, when my sheaf got up and stood up straight. Yours formed a circle around mine and bowed down to it."

37.8 "Do you think you are going to be a king and rule over us?" his brothers asked. So they hated him even more because of his dreams and because of what he said about them.

37.9 Then Joseph had another dream and told his brothers, "I had another dream, in which I saw the sun, the moon, and eleven stars bowing **down** <u>to me</u>."

<sup>37.10</sup> He also told the dream <u>to his father</u>, and his father scolded him: "What kind <u>of a dream</u> is that? Do you think that your mother, your brothers, and I are going to come and bow **down** <u>to you</u>?"

<sup>37.11</sup> Joseph's brothers were jealous <u>of him</u>, but his father kept thinking <u>about the whole matter</u>.

<sup>37.12</sup> One day when Joseph's brothers had gone <u>to Shechem</u> to take care <u>of their father's flock</u>,

<sup>37.13</sup> Jacob said <u>to Joseph</u>, "I want you to go <u>to Shechem</u>, where your brothers are taking care <u>of the flock</u>."

Joseph answered, "I am ready."

<sup>37.14</sup> His father told him, "Go and see if your brothers are safe and if the flock is all right; then come back and tell me." So his father sent him <u>on his way</u> <u>from Hebron Valley</u>.

Joseph arrived <u>at Shechem</u>

<sup>37.15</sup> and was wandering around <u>in the country</u> when a man saw him and asked him, "What are you looking for?"

<sup>37.16</sup> "I am looking <u>for my brothers</u>, who are taking care <u>of their flock</u>," he answered. "Can you tell me where they are?"

<sup>37.17</sup> The man said, "They have already left. I heard them say that they were going <u>to Dothan</u>." So Joseph went <u>after his brothers</u> and found them <u>at Dothan</u>.

<sup>37.18</sup> They saw him <u>in the distance</u>, and before he reached them, they plotted <u>against him</u> and decided to kill him.

<sup>37.19</sup> They said <u>to one another</u>, "Here comes that dreamer.

<sup>37.20</sup> "Come on now, let's kill him and throw his body <u>into one</u> <u>of the dry wells</u>. We can say that a wild animal killed him. Then we will see what becomes <u>of his dreams</u>."

<sup>37.21</sup> Reuben heard them and tried to save Joseph. "Let's not kill him," he said.

<sup>37.22</sup> "Just throw him <u>into this well</u> <u>in the wilderness</u>, but don't hurt him." He said this, planning to save him <u>from them</u> and send him back <u>to his father</u>.

<sup>37.23</sup> When Joseph came up <u>to his brothers</u>, they ripped off his long robe <u>with full sleeves</u>.

<sup>37.24</sup> Then they took him and threw him <u>into the well</u>, which was dry.

<sup>37.25</sup> While they were eating, they suddenly saw a group <u>of Ishmaelites</u> traveling <u>from Gilead</u> <u>to Egypt</u>. Their camels were loaded <u>with spices and resins</u>.

<sup>37.26</sup> Judah said <u>to his brothers</u>, "What will we gain <u>by</u> killing our brother <u>and</u> covering up the murder?

<sup>37.27</sup> "Let's sell him to these Ishmaelites. Then we won't have to hurt him; after all, he is our brother, our own flesh and blood." His brothers agreed,

<sup>37.28</sup> and when some Midianite traders came by, the brothers pulled Joseph out of the well and sold him for twenty pieces of silver to the Ishmaelites, who took him to Egypt.

<sup>37.29</sup> When Reuben came back to the well and found that Joseph was not there, he tore his clothes in sorrow.

<sup>37.30</sup> He returned to his brothers and said, "The boy is not there! What am I going to do?"

<sup>37.31</sup> Then they killed a goat and dipped Joseph's robe in its blood.

<sup>37.32</sup> They took the robe to their father and said, "We found this. Does it belong to your son?"

<sup>37.33</sup> He recognized it and said, "Yes, it is his! Some wild animal has killed him. My son Joseph has been torn to pieces!"

<sup>37.34</sup> Jacob tore his clothes in sorrow and put on sackcloth. He mourned for his son a long time.

<sup>37.35</sup> All his sons and daughters came to comfort him, but he refused to be comforted and said, "I will go down to the world of the dead still mourning for my son." So he continued to mourn for his son Joseph.

<sup>37.36</sup> Meanwhile, in Egypt the Midianites had sold Joseph to Potiphar, one of the king's officers, who was the captain of the palace guard.

# 38

<sup>38.1</sup> About that time Judah left his brothers and went to stay with a man named Hirah, who was from the town of Adullam.

<sup>38.2</sup> There Judah met a young Canaanite woman whose father was named Shua. He married her,

<sup>38.3</sup> and she bore him a son, whom he named Er.

<sup>38.4</sup> She became pregnant again and bore another son and named him Onan.

<sup>38.5</sup> Again she had a son and named him Shelah. Judah was at Achzib when the boy was born.

<sup>38.6</sup> For his first son Er, Judah got a wife whose name was Tamar.

<sup>38.7</sup> Er's conduct was evil, and it displeased the Lord, so the Lord killed him.

<sup>38.8</sup> Then Judah said to Er's brother Onan, "Go and sleep with your brother's widow. Fulfill your obligation to her as her husband's brother, so that your brother may have descendants."

<sup>38.9</sup> But Onan knew that the children would not belong to him, so when he had intercourse with his brother's widow, he let the semen spill on the ground, so that there would be no children for his brother.

<sup>38.10</sup> What he did displeased the Lord, and the Lord killed him also.

<sup>38.11</sup> Then Judah said to his daughter-in-law Tamar, "Return to your father's house and remain a widow until my son Shelah grows up." He said this because he was afraid that Shelah would be killed, as his brothers had been. So Tamar went back home.

<sup>38.12</sup> After some time Judah's wife died. When he had finished the time of mourning, he and his friend Hirah of Adullam went to Timnah, where his sheep were being sheared.

<sup>38.13</sup> Someone told Tamar that her father-in-law was going to Timnah to shear his sheep.

<sup>38.14</sup> So she changed from the widow's clothes she had been wearing, covered her face with a veil, and sat down at the entrance to Enaim, a town on the road to Timnah. As she well knew, Judah's youngest son Shelah was now grown up, and yet she had not been given to him in marriage.

<sup>38.15</sup> When Judah saw her, he thought that she was a prostitute, because she had her face covered.

<sup>38.16</sup> He went over to her at the side of the road and said, "All right, how much do you charge?" (He did not know that she was his daughter-in-law.)

She said, "What will you give me?"

<sup>38.17</sup> He answered, "I will send you a young goat from my flock."

She said, "All right, if you will give me something to keep as a pledge until you send the goat."

<sup>38.18</sup> "What shall I give you as a pledge?" he asked.

She answered, "Your seal with its cord and the walking stick you are carrying." He gave them to her. Then they had intercourse, and she became pregnant.

<sup>38.19</sup> Tamar went home, took off her veil, and put her widow's clothes back on.

<sup>38.20</sup> Judah sent his friend Hirah to take the goat and get back from the woman the articles he had pledged, but Hirah could not find her.

<sup>38.21</sup> He asked some men at Enaim, "Where is the prostitute who was here by the road?"

"There has never been a prostitute here," they answered.

<sup>38.22</sup> He returned to Judah and said, "I couldn't find her. The men of the place said that there had never been a prostitute there."

$^{38.23}$ Judah said, "Let her keep the things. We don't want people to laugh at us. I did try to pay her, but you couldn't find her."

$^{38.24}$ About three months later someone told Judah, "Your daughter-in-law Tamar has been acting like a whore, and now she is pregnant."

Judah ordered, "Take her out and burn her to death."

$^{38.25}$ As she was being taken out, she sent word to her father-in-law: "I am pregnant by the man who owns these things. Look at them and see whose they are—this seal with its cord and this walking stick."

$^{38.26}$ Judah recognized them and said, "She is in the right. I have failed in my obligation to her—I should have given her to my son Shelah in marriage." And Judah never had intercourse with her again.

$^{38.27}$ When the time came for her to give birth, it was discovered that she was going to have twins.

$^{38.28}$ While she was in labor, one of them put out an arm; the midwife caught it, tied a red thread around it, and said, "This one was born first."

$^{38.29}$ But he pulled his arm back, and his brother was born first. Then the midwife said, "So this is how you break your way out!" So he was named Perez.

$^{38.30}$ Then his brother was born with the red thread on his arm, and he was named Zerah.

# 39

$^{39.1}$ Now the Ishmaelites had taken Joseph to Egypt and sold him to Potiphar, one of the king's officers, who was the captain of the palace guard.

$^{39.2}$ The Lord was with Joseph and made him successful. He lived in the house of his Egyptian master,

$^{39.3}$ who saw that the Lord was with Joseph and had made him successful in everything he did.

$^{39.4}$ Potiphar was pleased with him and made him his personal servant; so he put him in charge of his house and everything he owned.

$^{39.5}$ From then on, because of Joseph the Lord blessed the household of the Egyptian and everything that he had in his house and in his fields.

$^{39.6}$ Potiphar turned over everything he had to the care of Joseph and did not concern himself with anything except the food he ate.

Joseph was well-built and good-looking,

$^{39.7}$ and after a while his master's wife began to desire Joseph and asked him to go to bed with her.

<sup>39.8</sup> He refused and said to her, "Look, my master does not have to concern himself with anything in the house, because I am here. He has put me in charge of everything he has.

<sup>39.9</sup> "I have as much authority in this house as he has, and he has not kept back anything from me except you. How then could I do such an immoral thing and sin against God?"

<sup>39.10</sup> Although she asked Joseph day after day, he would not go to bed with her.

<sup>39.11</sup> But one day when Joseph went into the house to do his work, none of the house servants was there.

<sup>39.12</sup> She caught him by his robe and said, "Come to bed with me." But he escaped and ran outside, leaving his robe in her hand.

<sup>39.13</sup> When she saw that he had left his robe and had run out of the house,

<sup>39.14</sup> she called to her house servants and said, "Look at this! This Hebrew that my husband brought to the house is insulting us. He came into my room and tried to rape me, but I screamed as loud as I could.

<sup>39.15</sup> "When he heard me scream, he ran outside, leaving his robe beside me."

<sup>39.16</sup> She kept his robe with her until Joseph's master came home.

<sup>39.17</sup> Then she told him the same story: "That Hebrew slave that you brought here came into my room and insulted me.

<sup>39.18</sup> "But when I screamed, he ran outside, leaving his robe beside me."

<sup>39.19</sup> Joseph's master was furious

<sup>39.20</sup> and had Joseph arrested and put in the prison where the king's prisoners were kept, and there he stayed.

<sup>39.21</sup> But the Lord was with Joseph and blessed him, so that the jailer was pleased with him.

<sup>39.22</sup> He put Joseph in charge of all the other prisoners and made him responsible for everything that was done in the prison.

<sup>39.23</sup> The jailer did not have to look after anything for which Joseph was responsible, because the Lord was with Joseph and made him succeed in everything he did.

# 40

<sup>40.1</sup> Some time later the king of Egypt's wine steward and his chief baker offended the king.

<sup>40.2</sup> He was angry with these two officials

<sup>40.3</sup> and put them in prison in the house of the captain of the guard,

in the same place where Joseph was being kept.

<sup>40.4</sup> They spent a long time in prison, and the captain assigned Joseph as their servant.

<sup>40.5</sup> One night there in prison the wine steward and the chief baker each had a dream, and the dreams had different meanings.

<sup>40.6</sup> When Joseph came to them in the morning, he saw that they were upset.

<sup>40.7</sup> He asked them, "Why do you look so worried today?"

<sup>40.8</sup> They answered, "Each of us had a dream, and there is no one here to explain what the dreams mean."

"It is God who gives the ability to interpret dreams," Joseph said. "Tell me your dreams."

<sup>40.9</sup> So the wine steward said, "In my dream there was a grapevine in front of me

<sup>40.10</sup> "with three branches on it. As soon as the leaves came out, the blossoms appeared, and the grapes ripened.

<sup>40.11</sup> "I was holding the king's cup; so I took the grapes and squeezed them into the cup and gave it to him."

<sup>40.12</sup> Joseph said, "This is what it means: the three branches are three days.

<sup>40.13</sup> "In three days the king will release you, pardon you, and restore you to your position. You will give him his cup as you did before when you were his wine steward.

<sup>40.14</sup> "But please remember me when everything is going well for you, and please be kind enough to mention me to the king and help me get out of this prison.

<sup>40.15</sup> "After all, I was kidnapped from the land of the Hebrews, and even here in Egypt I didn't do anything to deserve being put in prison."

<sup>40.16</sup> When the chief baker saw that the interpretation of the wine steward's dream was favorable, he said to Joseph, "I had a dream too; I was carrying three breadbaskets on my head.

<sup>40.17</sup> "In the top basket there were all kinds of baked goods for the king, and the birds were eating them."

<sup>40.18</sup> Joseph answered, "This is what it means: the three baskets are three days.

<sup>40.19</sup> "In three days the king will release you—and have your head cut off! Then he will hang your body on a pole, and the birds will eat your flesh."

<sup>40.20</sup> On his birthday three days later the king gave a banquet for all his officials; he released his wine steward and his chief baker and

brought them before his officials. ⁴⁰·²¹ He restored the wine steward to his former position, ⁴⁰·²² but he executed the chief baker. It all happened just as Joseph had said.

⁴⁰·²³ But the wine steward never gave Joseph another thought—he forgot all about him.

# 41

⁴¹·¹ After two years had passed, the king of Egypt dreamed that he was standing by the Nile River, ⁴¹·² when seven cows, fat and sleek, came up out of the river and began to feed on the grass. ⁴¹·³ Then seven other cows came up; they were thin and bony. They came and stood by the other cows on the riverbank, ⁴¹·⁴ and the thin cows ate up the fat cows. Then the king woke up.

⁴¹·⁵ He fell asleep again and had another dream. Seven heads of grain, full and ripe, were growing on one stalk. ⁴¹·⁶ Then seven other heads of grain sprouted, thin and scorched by the desert wind, ⁴¹·⁷ and the thin heads of grain swallowed the full ones. The king woke up and realized that he had been dreaming.

⁴¹·⁸ In the morning he was worried, so he sent for all the magicians and wise men of Egypt. He told them his dreams, but no one could explain them to him.

⁴¹·⁹ Then the wine steward said to the king, "I must confess today that I have done wrong. ⁴¹·¹⁰ "You were angry with the chief baker and me, and you put us in prison in the house of the captain of the guard. ⁴¹·¹¹ "One night each of us had a dream, and the dreams had different meanings. ⁴¹·¹² "A young Hebrew was there with us, a slave of the captain of the guard. We told him our dreams, and he interpreted them for us. ⁴¹·¹³ "Things turned out just as he said: you restored me to my position, but you executed the baker."

⁴¹·¹⁴ The king sent for Joseph, and he was immediately brought from the prison. After he had shaved and changed his clothes, he came into the king's presence. ⁴¹·¹⁵ The king said to him, "I have had a dream, and no one can explain it. I have been told that you can interpret dreams."

⁴¹·¹⁶ Joseph answered, "I cannot, Your Majesty, but God will give a favorable interpretation."

<sup>41.17</sup> The king said, "I dreamed that I was standing on the bank of the Nile,

<sup>41.18</sup> "when seven cows, fat and sleek, came up out of the river and began feeding on the grass.

<sup>41.19</sup> "Then seven other cows came up which were thin and bony. They were the poorest cows I have ever seen anywhere in Egypt.

<sup>41.20</sup> "The thin cows ate up the fat ones,

<sup>41.21</sup> "but no one would have known it, because they looked just as bad as before. Then I woke up.

<sup>41.22</sup> "I also dreamed that I saw seven heads of grain which were full and ripe, growing on one stalk.

<sup>41.23</sup> "Then seven heads of grain sprouted, thin and scorched by the desert wind,

<sup>41.24</sup> "and the thin heads of grain swallowed the full ones. I told the dreams to the magicians, but none of them could explain them to me."

<sup>41.25</sup> Joseph said to the king, "The two dreams mean the same thing; God has told you what he is going to do.

<sup>41.26</sup> "The seven fat cows are seven years, and the seven full heads of grain are also seven years; they have the same meaning.

<sup>41.27</sup> "The seven thin cows which came up later and the seven thin heads of grain scorched by the desert wind are seven years of famine.

<sup>41.28</sup> "It is just as I told you—God has shown you what he is going to do.

<sup>41.29</sup> "There will be seven years of great plenty in all the land of Egypt.

<sup>41.30</sup> "After that, there will be seven years of famine, and all the good years will be forgotten, because the famine will ruin the country.

<sup>41.31</sup> "The time of plenty will be entirely forgotten, because the famine which follows will be so terrible.

<sup>41.32</sup> "The repetition of your dream means that the matter is fixed by God and that he will make it happen in the near future.

<sup>41.33</sup> "Now you should choose some man with wisdom and insight and put him in charge of the country.

<sup>41.34</sup> "You must also appoint other officials and take a fifth of the crops during the seven years of plenty.

<sup>41.35</sup> "Order them to collect all the food during the good years that are coming, and give them authority to store up grain in the cities and guard it.

<sup>41.36</sup> "The food will be a reserve supply for the country during the

seven years of famine which are going to come on Egypt. In this way the people will not starve."

⁴¹·³⁷ The king and his officials approved this plan, ⁴¹·³⁸ and he said to them, "We will never find a better man than Joseph, a man who has God's spirit in him."

⁴¹·³⁹ The king said to Joseph, "God has shown you all this, so it is obvious that you have greater wisdom and insight than anyone else. ⁴¹·⁴⁰ "I will put you in charge of my country, and all my people will obey your orders. Your authority will be second only to mine. ⁴¹·⁴¹ "I now appoint you governor over all Egypt."

⁴¹·⁴² The king removed from his finger the ring engraved with the royal seal and put it on Joseph's finger. He put a fine linen robe on him, and placed a gold chain around his neck. ⁴¹·⁴³ He gave him the second royal chariot to ride in, and his guard of honor went ahead of him and cried out, "Make way! Make way!" And so Joseph was appointed governor over all Egypt. ⁴¹·⁴⁴ The king said to him, "I am the king—and no one in all Egypt shall so much as lift a hand or a foot without your permission."

⁴¹·⁴⁵⁻⁴⁶ He gave Joseph the Egyptian name Zaphenath Paneah, and he gave him a wife, Asenath, the daughter of Potiphera, a priest in the city of Heliopolis.

Joseph was thirty years old when he began to serve the king of Egypt. He left the king's court and traveled all over the land. ⁴¹·⁴⁷ During the seven years of plenty the land produced abundant crops, ⁴¹·⁴⁸ all of which Joseph collected and stored in the cities. In each city he stored the food from the fields around it. ⁴¹·⁴⁹ There was so much grain that Joseph stopped measuring it—it was like the sand of the sea.

⁴¹·⁵⁰ Before the years of famine came, Joseph had two sons by Asenath. ⁴¹·⁵¹ He said, "God has made me forget all my sufferings and all my father's family"; so he named his first son Manasseh. ⁴¹·⁵² He also said, "God has given me children in the land of my trouble"; so he named his second son Ephraim.

⁴¹·⁵³ The seven years of plenty that the land of Egypt had enjoyed came to an end, ⁴¹·⁵⁴ and the seven years of famine began, just as Joseph had said. There was famine in every other country, but there was food throughout Egypt. ⁴¹·⁵⁵ When the Egyptians began to be hungry, they cried out to the

king for food. So he ordered them to go to Joseph and do what he told them.

⁴¹·⁵⁶ The famine grew worse and spread over the whole country, so Joseph opened all the storehouses and sold grain to the Egyptians.

⁴¹·⁵⁷ People came to Egypt from all over the world to buy grain from Joseph, because the famine was severe everywhere.

# 42

⁴²·¹ When Jacob learned that there was grain in Egypt, he said to his sons, "Why don't you do something?

⁴²·² "I hear that there is grain in Egypt; go there and buy some to keep us from starving to death."

⁴²·³ So Joseph's ten half brothers went to buy grain in Egypt,

⁴²·⁴ but Jacob did not send Joseph's full brother Benjamin with them, because he was afraid that something might happen to him.

⁴²·⁵ The sons of Jacob came with others to buy grain, because there was famine in the land of Canaan.

⁴²·⁶ Joseph, as governor of the land of Egypt, was selling grain to people from all over the world. So Joseph's brothers came and bowed down before him with their faces to the ground.

⁴²·⁷ When Joseph saw his brothers, he recognized them, but he acted as if he did not know them. He asked them harshly, "Where do you come from?"

"We have come from Canaan to buy food," they answered.

⁴²·⁸ Although Joseph recognized his brothers, they did not recognize him.

⁴²·⁹ He remembered the dreams he had dreamed about them and said, "You are spies; you have come to find out where our country is weak."

⁴²·¹⁰ "No, sir," they answered. "We have come as your slaves, to buy food.

⁴²·¹¹ "We are all brothers. We are not spies, sir, we are honest men."

⁴²·¹² Joseph said to them, "No! You have come to find out where our country is weak."

⁴²·¹³ They said, "We were twelve brothers in all, sir, sons of the same man in the land of Canaan. One brother is dead, and the youngest is now with our father."

⁴²·¹⁴ "It is just as I said," Joseph answered. "You are spies.

⁴²·¹⁵ "This is how you will be tested: I swear by the name of the king that you will never leave unless your youngest brother comes here.

⁴²·¹⁶ "One of you must go and get him. The rest of you will be kept un-

der guard until the truth of what you say can be tested. Otherwise, as sure as the king lives, you are spies."

42.17 With that, he put them in prison for three days.

42.18 On the third day Joseph said to them, "I am a God-fearing man, and I will spare your lives on one condition.

42.19 "To prove that you are honest, one of you will stay in the prison where you have been kept; the rest of you may go and take back to your starving families the grain that you have bought.

42.20 "Then you must bring your youngest brother to me. This will prove that you have been telling the truth, and I will not put you to death."

They agreed to this

42.21 and said to one another, "Yes, now we are suffering the consequences of what we did to our brother; we saw the great trouble he was in when he begged for help, but we would not listen. That is why we are in this trouble now."

42.22 Reuben said, "I told you not to harm the boy, but you wouldn't listen. And now we are being paid back for his death."

42.23 Joseph understood what they said, but they did not know it, because they had been speaking to him through an interpreter.

42.24 Joseph left them and began to cry. When he was able to speak again, he came back, picked out Simeon, and had him tied up in front of them.

42.25 Joseph gave orders to fill his brothers' packs with grain, to put each man's money back in his sack, and to give them food for the trip. This was done.

42.26 The brothers loaded their donkeys with the grain they had bought, and then they left.

42.27 At the place where they spent the night, one of them opened his sack to feed his donkey and found his money at the top of the sack.

42.28 "My money has been returned to me," he called to his brothers. "Here it is in my sack!" Their hearts sank, and in fear they asked one another, "What has God done to us?"

42.29 When they came to their father Jacob in Canaan, they told him all that had happened to them:

42.30 "The governor of Egypt spoke harshly to us and accused us of spying against his country.

42.31 "'We are not spies,' we answered, 'we are honest men.

42.32 "'We were twelve brothers in all, sons of the same father. One brother is dead, and the youngest is still in Canaan with our father.'

42.33 "The man answered, 'This is how I will find out if you are honest men: One of you will stay with me; the rest will take grain for your starving families and leave.

⁴²·³⁴ "'Bring your youngest brother to me. Then I will know that you are not spies, but honest men; I will give your brother back to you, and you can stay here and trade.'"

⁴²·³⁵ Then when they emptied out their sacks, every one of them found his bag of money; and when they saw the money, they and their father Jacob were afraid.

⁴²·³⁶ Their father said to them, "Do you want to make me lose all my children? Joseph is gone; Simeon is gone; and now you want to take away Benjamin. I am the one who suffers!"

⁴²·³⁷ Reuben said to his father, "If I do not bring Benjamin back to you, you can kill my two sons. Put him in my care, and I will bring him back."

⁴²·³⁸ But Jacob said, "My son cannot go with you; his brother is dead, and he is the only one left. Something might happen to him on the way. I am an old man, and the sorrow you would cause me would kill me."

# 43

⁴³·¹ The famine in Canaan got worse,

⁴³·² and when the family of Jacob had eaten all the grain which had been brought from Egypt, Jacob said to his sons, "Go back and buy a little food for us."

⁴³·³ Judah said to him, "The man sternly warned us that we would not be admitted to his presence unless we had our brother with us.

⁴³·⁴ "If you are willing to send our brother with us, we will go and buy food for you.

⁴³·⁵ "If you are not willing, we will not go, because the man told us we would not be admitted to his presence unless our brother was with us."

⁴³·⁶ Jacob said, "Why did you cause me so much trouble by telling the man that you had another brother?"

⁴³·⁷ They answered, "The man kept asking about us and our family, 'Is your father still living? Do you have another brother?' We had to answer his questions. How could we know that he would tell us to bring our brother with us?"

⁴³·⁸ Judah said to his father, "Send the boy with me, and we will leave at once. Then none of us will starve to death.

⁴³·⁹ "I will pledge my own life, and you can hold me responsible for him. If I do not bring him back to you safe and sound, I will always

bear the blame.

<sup>43.10</sup> "If we had not waited so long, we could have been there and back twice by now."

<sup>43.11</sup> Their father said to them, "If that is how it has to be, then take the best products of the land in your packs as a present for the governor: a little resin, a little honey, spices, pistachio nuts, and almonds.

<sup>43.12</sup> "Take with you also twice as much money, because you must take back the money that was returned in the top of your sacks. Maybe it was a mistake.

<sup>43.13</sup> "Take your brother and return at once.

<sup>43.14</sup> "May Almighty God cause the man to have pity on you, so that he will give Benjamin and your other brother back to you. As for me, if I must lose my children, I must lose them."

<sup>43.15</sup> So the brothers took the gifts and twice as much money, and set out for Egypt with Benjamin. There they presented themselves to Joseph.

<sup>43.16</sup> When Joseph saw Benjamin with them, he said to the servant in charge of his house, "Take these men to my house. They are going to eat with me at noon, so kill an animal and prepare it."

<sup>43.17</sup> The servant did as he was commanded and took the brothers to Joseph's house.

<sup>43.18</sup> As they were being brought to the house, they were afraid and thought, "We are being brought here because of the money that was returned in our sacks the first time. They will suddenly attack us, take our donkeys, and make us his slaves."

<sup>43.19</sup> So at the door of the house, they said to the servant in charge,

<sup>43.20</sup> "If you please, sir, we came here once before to buy food.

<sup>43.21</sup> "When we set up camp on the way home, we opened our sacks, and each man found his money in the top of his sack—every bit of it. We have brought it back to you.

<sup>43.22</sup> "We have also brought some more money with us to buy more food. We do not know who put our money back in our sacks."

<sup>43.23</sup> The servant said, "Don't worry. Don't be afraid. Your God, the God of your father, must have put the money in your sacks for you. I received your payment." Then he brought Simeon to them.

<sup>43.24</sup> The servant took the brothers into the house. He gave them water so that they could wash their feet, and he fed their donkeys.

<sup>43.25</sup> They got their gifts ready to present to Joseph when he arrived at noon, because they had been told that they were to eat with him.

<sup>43.26</sup> When Joseph got home, they took the gifts into the house to him and bowed down to the ground before him.

<sup>43.27</sup> He asked about their health and then said, "You told me about your old father—how is he? Is he still alive and well?"

<sup>43.28</sup> They answered, "Your humble servant, our father, is still alive and well." And they knelt and bowed down before him.

<sup>43.29</sup> When Joseph saw his brother Benjamin, he said, "So this is your youngest brother, the one you told me about. God bless you, my son."

<sup>43.30</sup> Then Joseph left suddenly, because his heart was full of tender feelings for his brother. He was about to break down, so he went to his room and cried.

<sup>43.31</sup> After he had washed his face, he came out, and controlling himself, he ordered the meal to be served.

<sup>43.32</sup> Joseph was served at one table and his brothers at another. The Egyptians who were eating there were served separately, because they considered it beneath their dignity to eat with Hebrews.

<sup>43.33</sup> The brothers had been seated at the table, facing Joseph, in the order of their age from the oldest to the youngest. When they saw how they had been seated, they looked at one another in amazement.

<sup>43.34</sup> Food was served to them from Joseph's table, and Benjamin was served five times as much as the rest of them. So they ate and drank with Joseph until they were drunk.

# 44

<sup>44.1</sup> Joseph commanded the servant in charge of his house, "Fill the men's sacks with as much food as they can carry, and put each man's money in the top of his sack.

<sup>44.2</sup> "Put my silver cup in the top of the youngest brother's sack, together with the money for his grain." He did as he was told.

<sup>44.3</sup> Early in the morning the brothers were sent on their way with their donkeys.

<sup>44.4</sup> When they had gone only a short distance from the city, Joseph said to the servant in charge of his house, "Hurry after those men. When you catch up with them, ask them, 'Why have you paid back evil for good?

<sup>44.5</sup> "'Why did you steal my master's silver cup? It is the one he drinks from, the one he uses for divination. You have committed a serious crime!'"

<sup>44.6</sup> When the servant caught up with them, he repeated these words.

<sup>44.7</sup> They answered him, "What do you mean, sir, by talking like this? We swear that we have done no such thing.

[44.8] "You know that we brought back to you from the land of Canaan the money we found in the top of our sacks. Why then should we steal silver or gold from your master's house?

[44.9] "Sir, if any one of us is found to have it, he will be put to death, and the rest of us will become your slaves."

[44.10] He said, "I agree; but only the one who has taken the cup will become my slave, and the rest of you can go free."

[44.11] So they quickly lowered their sacks to the ground, and each man opened his sack.

[44.12] Joseph's servant searched carefully, beginning with the oldest and ending with the youngest, and the cup was found in Benjamin's sack.

[44.13] The brothers tore their clothes in sorrow, loaded their donkeys, and returned to the city.

[44.14] When Judah and his brothers came to Joseph's house, he was still there. They bowed down before him,

[44.15] and Joseph said, "What have you done? Didn't you know that a man in my position could find you out by practicing divination?"

[44.16] "What can we say to you, sir?" Judah answered. "How can we argue? How can we clear ourselves? God has uncovered our guilt. All of us are now your slaves and not just the one with whom the cup was found."

[44.17] Joseph said, "Oh, no! I would never do that! Only the one who had the cup will be my slave. The rest of you may go back safe and sound to your father."

[44.18] Judah went up to Joseph and said, "Please, sir, allow me to speak with you freely. Don't be angry with me; you are like the king himself.

[44.19] "Sir, you asked us, 'Do you have a father or another brother?'

[44.20] "We answered, 'We have a father who is old and a younger brother, born to him in his old age. The boy's brother is dead, and he is the only one of his mother's children still alive; his father loves him very much.'

[44.21] "Sir, you told us to bring him here, so that you could see him,

[44.22] "and we answered that the boy could not leave his father; if he did, his father would die.

[44.23] "Then you said, 'You will not be admitted to my presence again unless your youngest brother comes with you.'

[44.24] "When we went back to our father, we told him what you had said.

[44.25] "Then he told us to return and buy a little food.

<sup>44.26</sup> "We answered, 'We cannot go; we will not be admitted to the man's presence unless our youngest brother is with us. We can go only if our youngest brother goes also.'

<sup>44.27</sup> "Our father said to us, 'You know that my wife Rachel bore me only two sons.

<sup>44.28</sup> "'One of them has already left me. He must have been torn to pieces by wild animals, because I have not seen him since he left.

<sup>44.29</sup> "'If you take this one from me now and something happens to him, the sorrow you would cause me would kill me, as old as I am.'

<sup>44.30-31</sup> "And now, sir," Judah continued, "if I go back to my father without the boy, as soon as he sees that the boy is not with me, he will die. His life is wrapped up with the life of the boy, and he is so old that the sorrow we would cause him would kill him.

<sup>44.32</sup> "What is more, I pledged my life to my father for the boy. I told him that if I did not bring the boy back to him, I would bear the blame all my life.

<sup>44.33</sup> "And now, sir, I will stay here as your slave in place of the boy; let him go back with his brothers.

<sup>44.34</sup> "How can I go back to my father if the boy is not with me? I cannot bear to see this disaster come upon my father."

# 45

<sup>45.1</sup> Joseph was no longer able to control his feelings in front of his servants, so he ordered them all to leave the room. No one else was with him when Joseph told his brothers who he was.

<sup>45.2</sup> He cried with such loud sobs that the Egyptians heard it, and the news was taken to the king's palace.

<sup>45.3</sup> Joseph said to his brothers, "I am Joseph. Is my father still alive?" But when his brothers heard this, they were so terrified that they could not answer.

<sup>45.4</sup> Then Joseph said to them, "Please come closer." They did, and he said, "I am your brother Joseph, whom you sold into Egypt.

<sup>45.5</sup> "Now do not be upset or blame yourselves because you sold me here. It was really God who sent me ahead of you to save people's lives.

<sup>45.6</sup> "This is only the second year of famine in the land; there will be five more years in which there will be neither plowing nor reaping.

<sup>45.7</sup> "God sent me ahead of you to rescue you in this amazing way and to make sure that you and your descendants survive.

<sup>45.8</sup> "So it was not really you who sent me here, but God. He has made me the king's highest official. I am in charge of his whole country; I

am the ruler of all Egypt.

<sup>45.9</sup> "Now hurry back to my father and tell him that this is what his son Joseph says: 'God has made me ruler of all Egypt; come to me without delay.

<sup>45.10</sup> "'You can live in the region of Goshen, where you can be near me—you, your children, your grandchildren, your sheep, your goats, your cattle, and everything else that you have.

<sup>45.11</sup> "'If you are in Goshen, I can take care of you. There will still be five years of famine; and I do not want you, your family, and your livestock to starve.'"

<sup>45.12</sup> Joseph continued, "Now all of you, and you too, Benjamin, can see that I am really Joseph.

<sup>45.13</sup> "Tell my father how powerful I am here in Egypt and tell him about everything that you have seen. Then hurry and bring him here."

<sup>45.14</sup> He threw his arms around his brother Benjamin and began to cry; Benjamin also cried as he hugged him.

<sup>45.15</sup> Then, still weeping, he embraced each of his brothers and kissed them. After that, his brothers began to talk with him.

<sup>45.16</sup> When the news reached the palace that Joseph's brothers had come, the king and his officials were pleased.

<sup>45.17</sup> He said to Joseph, "Tell your brothers to load their animals and to return to the land of Canaan.

<sup>45.18</sup> "Let them get their father and their families and come back here. I will give them the best land in Egypt, and they will have more than enough to live on.

<sup>45.19</sup> "Tell them also to take wagons with them from Egypt for their wives and small children and to bring their father with them.

<sup>45.20</sup> "They are not to worry about leaving their possessions behind; the best in the whole land of Egypt will be theirs."

<sup>45.21</sup> Jacob's sons did as they were told. Joseph gave them wagons, as the king had ordered, and food for the trip.

<sup>45.22</sup> He also gave each of them a change of clothes, but he gave Benjamin three hundred pieces of silver and five changes of clothes.

<sup>45.23</sup> He sent his father ten donkeys loaded with the best Egyptian goods and ten donkeys loaded with grain, bread, and other food for the trip.

<sup>45.24</sup> He sent his brothers off and as they left, he said to them, "Don't quarrel on the way."

<sup>45.25</sup> They left Egypt and went back home to their father Jacob in Canaan.

<sup>45.26</sup> "Joseph is still alive!" they told him. "He is the ruler of all Egypt!" Jacob was stunned and could not believe them.

<sup>45.27</sup> But when they told him all that Joseph had said to them, and when he saw the wagons which Joseph had sent to take him to Egypt, he recovered from the shock.

<sup>45.28</sup> "My son Joseph is still alive!" he said. "This is all I could ask for! I must go and see him before I die."

# 46

<sup>46.1</sup> Jacob packed up all he had and went to Beersheba, where he offered sacrifices to the God of his father Isaac.

<sup>46.2</sup> God spoke to him in a vision at night and called, "Jacob, Jacob!"

"Yes, here I am," he answered.

<sup>46.3</sup> "I am God, the God of your father," he said. "Do not be afraid to go to Egypt; I will make your descendants a great nation there.

<sup>46.4</sup> "I will go with you to Egypt, and I will bring your descendants back to this land. Joseph will be with you when you die."

<sup>46.5</sup> Jacob set out from Beersheba. His sons put him, their small children, and their wives in the wagons which the king of Egypt had sent.

<sup>46.6</sup> They took their livestock and the possessions they had acquired in Canaan and went to Egypt. Jacob took all his descendants with him:

<sup>46.7</sup> his sons, his grandsons, his daughters, and his granddaughters.

<sup>46.8</sup> The members of Jacob's family who went to Egypt with him were his oldest son Reuben

<sup>46.9</sup> and Reuben's sons: Hanoch, Pallu, Hezron, and Carmi.

<sup>46.10</sup> Simeon and his sons: Jemuel, Jamin, Ohad, Jachin, Zohar, and Shaul, the son of a Canaanite woman.

<sup>46.11</sup> Levi and his sons: Gershon, Kohath, and Merari.

<sup>46.12</sup> Judah and his sons: Shelah, Perez, and Zerah. (Judah's other sons, Er and Onan, had died in Canaan.) Perez' sons were Hezron and Hamul.

<sup>46.13</sup> Issachar and his sons: Tola, Puah, Jashub, and Shimron.

<sup>46.14</sup> Zebulun and his sons: Sered, Elon, and Jahleel.

<sup>46.15</sup> These are the sons that Leah had borne to Jacob in Mesopotamia, besides his daughter Dinah. In all, his descendants by Leah numbered thirty-three.

<sup>46.16</sup> Gad and his sons: Zephon, Haggi, Shuni, Ezbon, Eri, Arod, and Areli.

<sup>46.17</sup> Asher and his sons: Imnah, Ishvah, Ishvi, Beriah, and their sis-

ter Serah. Beriah's sons were Heber and Malchiel.

<sup>46.18</sup> These sixteen are the descendants of Jacob by Zilpah, the slave woman whom Laban gave to his daughter Leah.

<sup>46.19</sup> Jacob's wife Rachel bore him two sons: Joseph and Benjamin.

<sup>46.20</sup> In Egypt Joseph had two sons, Manasseh and Ephraim, by Asenath, the daughter of Potiphera, a priest in Heliopolis.

<sup>46.21</sup> Benjamin's sons were Bela, Becher, Ashbel, Gera, Naaman, Ehi, Rosh, Muppim, Huppim, and Ard.

<sup>46.22</sup> These fourteen are the descendants of Jacob by Rachel.

<sup>46.23</sup> Dan and his son Hushim.

<sup>46.24</sup> Naphtali and his sons: Jahzeel, Guni, Jezer, and Shillem.

<sup>46.25</sup> These seven are the descendants of Jacob by Bilhah, the slave woman whom Laban gave to his daughter Rachel.

<sup>46.26</sup> The total number of the direct descendants of Jacob who went to Egypt was sixty-six, not including his sons' wives.

<sup>46.27</sup> Two sons were born to Joseph in Egypt, bringing to seventy the total number of Jacob's family who went there.

<sup>46.28</sup> Jacob sent Judah ahead to ask Joseph to meet them in Goshen. When they arrived,

<sup>46.29</sup> Joseph got in his chariot and went to Goshen to meet his father. When they met, Joseph threw his arms around his father's neck and cried for a long time.

<sup>46.30</sup> Jacob said to Joseph, "I am ready to die, now that I have seen you and know that you are still alive."

<sup>46.31</sup> Then Joseph said to his brothers and the rest of his father's family, "I must go and tell the king that my brothers and all my father's family, who were living in Canaan, have come to me.

<sup>46.32</sup> "I will tell him that you are shepherds and take care of livestock and that you have brought your flocks and herds and everything else that belongs to you.

<sup>46.33</sup> "When the king calls for you and asks what your occupation is,

<sup>46.34</sup> "be sure to tell him that you have taken care of livestock all your lives, just as your ancestors did. In this way he will let you live in the region of Goshen." Joseph said this because Egyptians will have nothing to do with shepherds.

# 47

<sup>47.1</sup> So Joseph took five of his brothers and went to the king. He told him, "My father and my brothers have come from Canaan with their flocks, their herds, and all that they own. They are now in the region of Goshen."

<sup>47.2</sup> He then presented his brothers to the king.

<sup>47.3</sup> The king asked them, "What is your occupation?"

"We are shepherds, sir, just as our ancestors were," they answered.

<sup>47.4</sup> "We have come to live in this country, because in the land of Canaan the famine is so severe that there is no pasture for our flocks. Please give us permission to live in the region of Goshen."

<sup>47.5</sup> The king said to Joseph, "Now that your father and your brothers have arrived,

<sup>47.6</sup> "the land of Egypt is theirs. Let them settle in the region of Goshen, the best part of the land. And if there are any capable men among them, put them in charge of my own livestock."

<sup>47.7</sup> Then Joseph brought his father Jacob and presented him to the king. Jacob gave the king his blessing,

<sup>47.8</sup> and the king asked him, "How old are you?"

<sup>47.9</sup> Jacob answered, "My life of wandering has lasted a hundred and thirty years. Those years have been few and difficult, unlike the long years of my ancestors in their wanderings."

<sup>47.10</sup> Jacob gave the king a farewell blessing and left.

<sup>47.11</sup> Then Joseph settled his father and his brothers in Egypt, giving them property in the best of the land near the city of Rameses, as the king had commanded.

<sup>47.12</sup> Joseph provided food for his father, his brothers, and all the rest of his father's family, including the very youngest.

<sup>47.13</sup> The famine was so severe that there was no food anywhere, and the people of Egypt and Canaan became weak with hunger.

<sup>47.14</sup> As they bought grain, Joseph collected all the money and took it to the palace.

<sup>47.15</sup> When all the money in Egypt and Canaan was spent, the Egyptians came to Joseph and said, "Give us food! Don't let us die. Do something! Our money is all gone."

<sup>47.16</sup> Joseph answered, "Bring your livestock; I will give you food in exchange for it if your money is all gone."

<sup>47.17</sup> So they brought their livestock to Joseph, and he gave them food in exchange for their horses, sheep, goats, cattle, and donkeys. That year he supplied them with food in exchange for all their livestock.

<sup>47.18</sup> The following year they came to him and said, "We will not hide the fact from you, sir, that our money is all gone and our livestock belongs to you. There is nothing left to give you except our bodies and our lands.

<sup>47.19</sup> "Don't let us die. Do something! Don't let our fields be deserted. Buy us and our land in exchange for food. We will be the king's

slaves, and he will own our land. Give us grain to keep us alive and seed so that we can plant our fields."

<sup>47.20</sup> Joseph bought all the land in Egypt for the king. Every Egyptian was forced to sell his land, because the famine was so severe; and all the land became the king's property.

<sup>47.21</sup> Joseph made slaves of the people from one end of Egypt to the other.

<sup>47.22</sup> The only land he did not buy was the land that belonged to the priests. They did not have to sell their lands, because the king gave them an allowance to live on.

<sup>47.23</sup> Joseph said to the people, "You see, I have now bought you and your lands for the king. Here is seed for you to sow in your fields.

<sup>47.24</sup> "At the time of harvest you must give one-fifth to the king. You can use the rest for seed and for food for yourselves and your families."

<sup>47.25</sup> They answered, "You have saved our lives; you have been good to us, sir, and we will be the king's slaves."

<sup>47.26</sup> So Joseph made it a law for the land of Egypt that one-fifth of the harvest should belong to the king. This law still remains in force today. Only the lands of the priests did not become the king's property.

<sup>47.27</sup> The Israelites lived in Egypt in the region of Goshen, where they became rich and had many children.

<sup>47.28</sup> Jacob lived in Egypt seventeen years, until he was a hundred and forty-seven years old.

<sup>47.29</sup> When the time drew near for him to die, he called for his son Joseph and said to him, "Place your hand between my thighs and make a solemn vow that you will not bury me in Egypt.

<sup>47.30</sup> "I want to be buried where my fathers are; carry me out of Egypt and bury me where they are buried."

Joseph answered, "I will do as you say."

<sup>47.31</sup> Jacob said, "Make a vow that you will." Joseph made the vow, and Jacob gave thanks there on his bed.

# 48

<sup>48.1</sup> Some time later Joseph was told that his father was ill. So he took his two sons, Manasseh and Ephraim, and went to see Jacob.

<sup>48.2</sup> When Jacob was told that his son Joseph had come to see him, he gathered his strength and sat up in bed.

<sup>48.3</sup> Jacob said to Joseph, "Almighty God appeared to me at Luz in the land of Canaan and blessed me.

<sup>48.4</sup> "He said to me, 'I will give you many children, so that your de-

scendants will become many nations; I will give this land to your descendants as their possession forever.' "

48.5 Jacob continued, "Joseph, your two sons, who were born to you in Egypt before I came here, belong to me; Ephraim and Manasseh are just as much my sons as Reuben and Simeon.

48.6 "If you have any more sons, they will not be considered mine; the inheritance they get will come through Ephraim and Manasseh.

48.7 "I am doing this because of your mother Rachel. To my great sorrow she died in the land of Canaan, not far from Ephrath, as I was returning from Mesopotamia. I buried her there beside the road to Ephrath." (Ephrath is now known as Bethlehem.)

48.8 When Jacob saw Joseph's sons, he asked, "Who are these boys?"

48.9 Joseph answered, "These are my sons, whom God has given me here in Egypt."

Jacob said, "Bring them to me so that I may bless them."

48.10 Jacob's eyesight was failing because of his age, and he could not see very well. Joseph brought the boys to him, and he hugged them and kissed them.

48.11 Jacob said to Joseph, "I never expected to see you again, and now God has even let me see your children."

48.12 Then Joseph took them from Jacob's lap and bowed down before him with his face to the ground.

48.13 Joseph put Ephraim at Jacob's left and Manasseh at his right.

48.14 But Jacob crossed his hands, and put his right hand on the head of Ephraim, even though he was the younger, and his left hand on the head of Manasseh, who was the older.

48.15 Then he blessed Joseph:

"May God, whom my fathers Abraham and Isaac served, bless these boys!

May God, who has led me to this very day, bless them!

48.16 "May the angel, who has rescued me from all harm, bless them!

May my name and the name of my fathers Abraham and Isaac live on through these boys!

May they have many children, many descendants!"

48.17 Joseph was upset when he saw that his father had put his right hand on Ephraim's head; so he took his father's hand to move it from Ephraim's head to the head of Manasseh.

48.18 He said to his father, "Not that way, father. This is the older boy; put your right hand on his head."

48.19 His father refused, saying, "I know, son, I know. Manasseh's descendants will also become a great people. But his younger brother will be greater than he, and his descendants will become great nations."

<sup>48.20</sup> So he blessed them that day, saying, "The Israelites will use your names when they pronounce blessings. They will say, 'May God make you like Ephraim and Manasseh.'" In this way Jacob put Ephraim before Manasseh.

<sup>48.21</sup> Then Jacob said to Joseph, "As you see, I am about to die, but God will be with you and will take you back to the land of your ancestors.

<sup>48.22</sup> "It is to you and not to your brothers that I am giving Shechem, that fertile region which I took from the Amorites with my sword and my bow."

# 49

<sup>49.1</sup> Jacob called for his sons and said, "Gather around, and I will tell you what will happen to you in the future:

<sup>49.2</sup> "Come together and listen, sons of Jacob. Listen to your father Israel.

<sup>49.3</sup> "Reuben, my first-born, you are my strength and the first child of my manhood, the proudest and strongest of all my sons.

<sup>49.4</sup> "You are like a raging flood, but you will not be the most important, for you slept with my concubine and dishonored your father's bed.

<sup>49.5</sup> "Simeon and Levi are brothers. They use their weapons to commit violence.

<sup>49.6</sup> "I will not join in their secret talks, nor will I take part in their meetings, for they killed people in anger and they crippled bulls for sport.

<sup>49.7</sup> "A curse be on their anger, because it is so fierce, and on their fury, because it is so cruel. I will scatter them throughout the land of Israel. I will disperse them among its people.

<sup>49.8</sup> "Judah, your brothers will praise you. You hold your enemies by the neck. Your brothers will bow down before you.

<sup>49.9</sup> "Judah is like a lion, killing his victim and returning to his den, stretching out and lying down. No one dares disturb him.

<sup>49.10</sup> "Judah will hold the royal scepter, and his descendants will always rule. Nations will bring him tribute and bow in obedience before him.

<sup>49.11</sup> "He ties his young donkey to a grapevine, to the very best of the vines. He washes his clothes in blood-red wine.

<sup>49.12</sup> "His eyes are bloodshot from drinking wine, his teeth white

from drinking milk.

<sup>49.13</sup>"Zebulun will live beside the sea. His shore will be a haven for ships. His territory will reach as far as Sidon.

<sup>49.14</sup>"Issachar is no better than a donkey that lies stretched out between its saddlebags.

<sup>49.15</sup>"But he sees that the resting place is good and that the land is delightful. So he bends his back to carry the load and is forced to work as a slave.

<sup>49.16</sup>"Dan will be a ruler for his people. They will be like the other tribes of Israel.

<sup>49.17</sup>"Dan will be a snake at the side of the road, a poisonous snake beside the path, that strikes at the horse's heel, so that the rider is thrown off backward.

<sup>49.18</sup>"I wait for your deliverance, Lord.

<sup>49.19</sup>"Gad will be attacked by a band of robbers, but he will turn and pursue them.

<sup>49.20</sup>"Asher's land will produce rich food. He will provide food fit for a king.

<sup>49.21</sup>"Naphtali is a deer that runs free, who bears lovely fawns.

<sup>49.22</sup>"Joseph is like a wild donkey by a spring, a wild colt on a hill-side.

<sup>49.23</sup>"His enemies attack him fiercely and pursue him with their bows and arrows.

<sup>49.24</sup>"But his bow remains steady, and his arms are made strong by the power of the Mighty God of Jacob, by the Shepherd, the Protector of Israel.

<sup>49.25</sup>"It is your father's God who helps you, the Almighty God who blesses you with blessings of rain from above and of deep waters from beneath the ground, blessings of many cattle and children,

<sup>49.26</sup>"blessings of grain and flowers, blessings of ancient mountains, delightful things from everlasting hills. May these blessings rest on the head of Joseph, on the brow of the one set apart from his brothers.

<sup>49.27</sup>"Benjamin is like a vicious wolf. Morning and evening he kills and devours."

<sup>49.28</sup>These are the twelve tribes of Israel, and this is what their father said as he spoke a suitable word of farewell to each son.

<sup>49.29</sup>Then Jacob commanded his sons, "Now that I am going to join my people in death, bury me with my fathers in the cave that is in the field of Ephron the Hittite,

<sup>49.30</sup>"at Machpelah east of Mamre in the land of Canaan. Abraham

bought this cave and field from Ephron for a burial ground.

<sup>49.31</sup> "That is where they buried Abraham and his wife Sarah; that is where they buried Isaac and his wife Rebecca; and that is where I buried Leah.

<sup>49.32</sup> "The field and the cave in it were bought from the Hittites. Bury me there."

<sup>49.33</sup> When Jacob had finished giving instructions to his sons, he lay back down and died.

# 50

<sup>50.1</sup> Joseph threw himself on his father, crying and kissing his face.

<sup>50.2</sup> Then Joseph gave orders to embalm his father's body.

<sup>50.3</sup> It took forty days, the normal time for embalming. The Egyptians mourned for him seventy days.

<sup>50.4</sup> When the time of mourning was over, Joseph said to the king's officials, "Please take this message to the king:

<sup>50.5</sup> "'When my father was about to die, he made me promise him that I would bury him in the tomb which he had prepared in the land of Canaan. So please let me go and bury my father, and then I will come back.'"

<sup>50.6</sup> The king answered, "Go and bury your father, as you promised you would."

<sup>50.7</sup> So Joseph went to bury his father. All the king's officials, the senior men of his court, and all the leading men of Egypt went with Joseph.

<sup>50.8</sup> His family, his brothers, and the rest of his father's family all went with him. Only their small children and their sheep, goats, and cattle stayed in the region of Goshen.

<sup>50.9</sup> Men in chariots and men on horseback also went with him; it was a huge group.

<sup>50.10</sup> When they came to the threshing place at Atad east of the Jordan, they mourned loudly for a long time, and Joseph performed mourning ceremonies for seven days.

<sup>50.11</sup> When the citizens of Canaan saw those people mourning at Atad, they said, "What a solemn ceremony of mourning the Egyptians are holding!" That is why the place was named Abel Mizraim.

<sup>50.12</sup> So Jacob's sons did as he had commanded them;

<sup>50.13</sup> they carried his body to Canaan and buried it in the cave at Machpelah east of Mamre in the field which Abraham had bought from Ephron the Hittite for a burial ground.

<sup>50.14</sup> After Joseph had buried his father, he returned to Egypt with

his brothers and all who had gone with him for the funeral.

⁵⁰·¹⁵ After the death of their father, Joseph's brothers said, "What if Joseph still hates us and plans to pay us back for all the harm we did to him?"

⁵⁰·¹⁶ So they sent a message to Joseph: "Before our father died,

⁵⁰·¹⁷ "he told us to ask you, 'Please forgive the crime your brothers committed when they wronged you.' Now please forgive us the wrong that we, the servants of your father's God, have done." Joseph cried when he received this message.

⁵⁰·¹⁸ Then his brothers themselves came and bowed down before him. "Here we are before you as your slaves," they said.

⁵⁰·¹⁹ But Joseph said to them, "Don't be afraid; I can't put myself in the place of God.

⁵⁰·²⁰ "You plotted evil against me, but God turned it into good, in order to preserve the lives of many people who are alive today because of what happened.

⁵⁰·²¹ "You have nothing to fear. I will take care of you and your children." So he reassured them with kind words that touched their hearts.

⁵⁰·²² Joseph continued to live in Egypt with his father's family; he was a hundred and ten years old when he died.

⁵⁰·²³ He lived to see Ephraim's children and grandchildren. He also lived to receive the children of Machir son of Manasseh into the family.

⁵⁰·²⁴ He said to his brothers, "I am about to die, but God will certainly take care of you and lead you out of this land to the land he solemnly promised to Abraham, Isaac, and Jacob."

⁵⁰·²⁵ Then Joseph asked his people to make a vow. "Promise me," he said, "that when God leads you to that land, you will take my body with you."

⁵⁰·²⁶ So Joseph died in Egypt at the age of a hundred and ten. They embalmed his body and put it in a coffin.

# EXODUS

# Exodus

# 1

<sup>1.1</sup> The sons of Jacob who went to Egypt with him, each with his family, were

<sup>1.2</sup> Reuben, Simeon, Levi, Judah,

<sup>1.3</sup> Issachar, Zebulun, Benjamin,

<sup>1.4</sup> Dan, Naphtali, Gad, and Asher.

<sup>1.5</sup> The total number of these people directly descended from Jacob was seventy. His son Joseph was already in Egypt.

<sup>1.6</sup> In the course of time Joseph, his brothers, and all the rest of that generation died,

<sup>1.7</sup> but their descendants, the Israelites, had many children and became so numerous and strong that Egypt was filled with them.

<sup>1.8</sup> Then, a new king, who knew nothing about Joseph, came to power in Egypt.

<sup>1.9</sup> He said to his people, "These Israelites are so numerous and strong that they are a threat to us.

<sup>1.10</sup> "In case of war they might join our enemies in order to fight against us, and might escape from the country. We must find some way to keep them from becoming even more numerous."

<sup>1.11</sup> So the Egyptians put slave drivers over them to crush their spirits with hard labor. The Israelites built the cities of Pithom and Rameses to serve as supply centers for the king.

<sup>1.12</sup> But the more the Egyptians oppressed the Israelites, the more they increased in number and the farther they spread through the land. The Egyptians came to fear the Israelites

<sup>1.13-14</sup> and made their lives miserable by forcing them into cruel slavery. They made them work on their building projects and in their fields, and they had no pity on them.

<sup>1.15</sup> Then the king of Egypt spoke to Shiphrah and Puah, the two midwives who helped the Hebrew women.

<sup>1.16</sup> "When you help the Hebrew women give birth," he said to them, "kill the baby if it is a boy; but if it is a girl, let it live."

<sup>1.17</sup> But the midwives were God-fearing and so did not obey the king; instead, they let the boys live.

<sup>1.18</sup> So the king sent for the midwives and asked them, "Why are you doing this? Why are you letting the boys live?"

<sup>1.19</sup> They answered, "The Hebrew women are not like Egyptian women; they give birth easily, and their babies are born before ei-

ther of us gets there."

<sup>1.20-21</sup> Because the midwives were God-fearing, God was good to them and gave them families of their own. And the Israelites continued to increase and become strong.

<sup>1.22</sup> Finally the king issued a command to all his people: "Take every newborn Hebrew boy and throw him into the Nile, but let all the girls live."

# 2

<sup>2.1</sup> During this time a man from the tribe of Levi married a woman of his own tribe,

<sup>2.2</sup> and she bore him a son. When she saw what a fine baby he was, she hid him for three months.

<sup>2.3</sup> But when she could not hide him any longer, she took a basket made of reeds and covered it with tar to make it watertight. She put the baby in it and then placed it in the tall grass at the edge of the river.

<sup>2.4</sup> The baby's sister stood some distance away to see what would happen to him.

<sup>2.5</sup> The king's daughter came down to the river to bathe, while her servants walked along the bank. Suddenly she noticed the basket in the tall grass and sent a slave woman to get it.

<sup>2.6</sup> The princess opened it and saw a baby boy. He was crying, and she felt sorry for him. "This is one of the Hebrew babies," she said.

<sup>2.7</sup> Then his sister asked her, "Shall I go and call a Hebrew woman to nurse the baby for you?"

<sup>2.8</sup> "Please do," she answered. So the girl went and brought the baby's own mother.

<sup>2.9</sup> The princess told the woman, "Take this baby and nurse him for me, and I will pay you." So she took the baby and nursed him.

<sup>2.10</sup> Later, when the child was old enough, she took him to the king's daughter, who adopted him as her own son. She said to herself, "I pulled him out of the water, and so I name him Moses."

<sup>2.11</sup> When Moses had grown up, he went out to visit his people, the Hebrews, and he saw how they were forced to do hard labor. He even saw an Egyptian kill a Hebrew, one of Moses' own people.

<sup>2.12</sup> Moses looked all around, and when he saw that no one was watching, he killed the Egyptian and hid his body in the sand.

<sup>2.13</sup> The next day he went back and saw two Hebrew men fighting. He said to the one who was in the wrong, "Why are you beating up a fellow Hebrew?"

<sup>2.14</sup> The man answered, "Who made you our ruler and judge? Are you going to kill me just as you killed that Egyptian?" Then Moses was afraid and said to himself, "People have found out what I have done."

<sup>2.15-16</sup> When the king heard about what had happened, he tried to have Moses killed, but Moses fled and went to live in the land of Midian.

One day, when Moses was sitting by a well, seven daughters of Jethro, the priest of Midian, came to draw water and fill the troughs for their father's sheep and goats.

<sup>2.17</sup> But some shepherds drove Jethro's daughters away. Then Moses went to their rescue and watered their animals for them.

<sup>2.18</sup> When they returned to their father, he asked, "Why have you come back so early today?"

<sup>2.19</sup> "An Egyptian rescued us from the shepherds," they answered, "and he even drew water for us and watered our animals."

<sup>2.20</sup> "Where is he?" he asked his daughters. "Why did you leave the man out there? Go and invite him to eat with us."

<sup>2.21</sup> So Moses decided to live there, and Jethro gave him his daughter Zipporah in marriage,

<sup>2.22</sup> who bore him a son. Moses said to himself, "I am a foreigner in this land, and so I name him Gershom."

<sup>2.23</sup> Years later the king of Egypt died, but the Israelites were still groaning under their slavery and cried out for help. Their cry went up to God,

<sup>2.24</sup> who heard their groaning and remembered his covenant with Abraham, Isaac, and Jacob.

<sup>2.25</sup> He saw the slavery of the Israelites and was concerned for them.

# 3

<sup>3.1</sup> One day while Moses was taking care of the sheep and goats of his father-in-law Jethro, the priest of Midian, he led the flock across the desert and came to Sinai, the holy mountain.

<sup>3.2</sup> There the angel of the Lord appeared to him as a flame coming from the middle of a bush. Moses saw that the bush was on fire but that it was not burning up.

<sup>3.3</sup> "This is strange," he thought. "Why isn't the bush burning up? I will go closer and see."

<sup>3.4</sup> When the Lord saw that Moses was coming closer, he called to him from the middle of the bush and said, "Moses! Moses!"

He answered, "Yes, here I am."

<sup>3.5</sup> God said, "Do not come any closer. Take off your sandals, because you are standing on holy ground.

<sup>3.6</sup> "I am the God of your ancestors, the God of Abraham, Isaac, and Jacob." So Moses covered his face, because he was afraid to look at God.

<sup>3.7</sup> Then the Lord said, "I have seen how cruelly my people are being treated in Egypt; I have heard them cry out to be rescued from their slave drivers. I know all about their sufferings,

<sup>3.8</sup> "and so I have come down to rescue them from the Egyptians and to bring them out of Egypt to a spacious land, one which is rich and fertile and in which the Canaanites, the Hittites, the Amorites, the Perizzites, the Hivites, and the Jebusites now live.

<sup>3.9</sup> "I have indeed heard the cry of my people, and I see how the Egyptians are oppressing them.

<sup>3.10</sup> "Now I am sending you to the king of Egypt so that you can lead my people out of his country."

<sup>3.11</sup> But Moses said to God, "I am nobody. How can I go to the king and bring the Israelites out of Egypt?"

<sup>3.12</sup> God answered, "I will be with you, and when you bring the people out of Egypt, you will worship me on this mountain. That will be the proof that I have sent you."

<sup>3.13</sup> But Moses replied, "When I go to the Israelites and say to them, 'The God of your ancestors sent me to you,' they will ask me, 'What is his name?' So what can I tell them?"

<sup>3.14</sup> God said, "I am who I am. You must tell them: 'The one who is called I AM has sent me to you.'

<sup>3.15</sup> "Tell the Israelites that I, the Lord, the God of their ancestors, the God of Abraham, Isaac, and Jacob, have sent you to them. This is my name forever; this is what all future generations are to call me.

<sup>3.16</sup> "Go and gather the leaders of Israel together and tell them that I, the Lord, the God of their ancestors, the God of Abraham, Isaac, and Jacob, appeared to you. Tell them that I have come to them and have seen what the Egyptians are doing to them.

<sup>3.17</sup> "I have decided that I will bring them out of Egypt, where they are being treated cruelly, and will take them to a rich and fertile land—the land of the Canaanites, the Hittites, the Amorites, the Perizzites, the Hivites, and the Jebusites.

<sup>3.18</sup> "My people will listen to what you say to them. Then you must go with the leaders of Israel to the king of Egypt and say to him,

'The Lord, the God of the Hebrews, has revealed himself to us. Now allow us to travel three days into the desert to offer sacrifices to the Lord, our God.'

3.19 "I know that the king of Egypt will not let you go unless he is forced to do so.

3.20 "But I will use my power and will punish Egypt by doing terrifying things there. After that he will let you go.

3.21 "I will make the Egyptians respect you so that when my people leave, they will not go empty-handed.

3.22 "Every Israelite woman will go to her Egyptian neighbors and to any Egyptian woman living in her house and will ask for clothing and for gold and silver jewelry. The Israelites will put these things on their sons and daughters and carry away the wealth of the Egyptians."

# 4

4.1 Then Moses answered the Lord, "But suppose the Israelites do not believe me and will not listen to what I say. What shall I do if they say that you did not appear to me?"

4.2 So the Lord asked him, "What are you holding?"

"A walking stick," he answered.

4.3 The Lord said, "Throw it on the ground." When Moses threw it down, it turned into a snake, and he ran away from it.

4.4 Then the Lord said to Moses, "Reach down and pick it up by the tail." So Moses reached down and caught it, and it became a walking stick again.

4.5 The Lord said, "Do this to prove to the Israelites that the Lord, the God of their ancestors, the God of Abraham, Isaac, and Jacob, has appeared to you."

4.6 The Lord spoke to Moses again, "Put your hand inside your robe." Moses obeyed; and when he took his hand out, it was diseased, covered with white spots, like snow.

4.7 Then the Lord said, "Put your hand inside your robe again." He did so, and when he took it out this time, it was healthy, just like the rest of his body.

4.8 The Lord said, "If they will not believe you or be convinced by the first miracle, then this one will convince them.

4.9 "If in spite of these two miracles they still will not believe you, and if they refuse to listen to what you say, take some water from the Nile and pour it on the ground. The water will turn into blood."

<sup>4.10</sup> But Moses said, "No, Lord, don't send me. I have never been a good speaker, and I haven't become one since you began to speak to me. I am a poor speaker, slow and hesitant."

<sup>4.11</sup> The Lord said to him, "Who gives man his mouth? Who makes him deaf or dumb? Who gives him sight or makes him blind? It is I, the Lord.

<sup>4.12</sup> "Now, go! I will help you to speak, and I will tell you what to say."

<sup>4.13</sup> But Moses answered, "No, Lord, please send someone else."

<sup>4.14</sup> At this the Lord became angry with Moses and said, "What about your brother Aaron, the Levite? I know that he can speak well. In fact, he is now coming to meet you and will be glad to see you.

<sup>4.15</sup> "You can speak to him and tell him what to say. I will help both of you to speak, and I will tell you both what to do.

<sup>4.16</sup> "He will be your spokesman and speak to the people for you. Then you will be like God, telling him what to say.

<sup>4.17</sup> "Take this walking stick with you; for with it you will perform miracles."

<sup>4.18</sup> Then Moses went back to Jethro, his father-in-law, and said to him, "Please let me go back to my relatives in Egypt to see if they are still alive." Jethro agreed and told him good-bye.

<sup>4.19</sup> While Moses was still in Midian, the Lord said to him, "Go back to Egypt, for all those who wanted to kill you are dead."

<sup>4.20</sup> So Moses took his wife and his sons, put them on a donkey, and set out with them for Egypt, carrying the walking stick that God had told him to take.

<sup>4.21</sup> Again the Lord said to Moses, "Now that you are going back to Egypt, be sure to perform before the king all the miracles which I have given you the power to do. But I will make the king stubborn, and he will not let the people go.

<sup>4.22</sup> "Then you must tell him that I, the Lord, say, 'Israel is my first-born son.

<sup>4.23</sup> "'I told you to let my son go, so that he might worship me, but you refused. Now I am going to kill your first-born son.'"

<sup>4.24</sup> At a camping place on the way to Egypt, the Lord met Moses and tried to kill him.

<sup>4.25-26</sup> Then Zipporah, his wife, took a sharp stone, cut off the foreskin of her son, and touched Moses' feet with it. Because of the rite of circumcision she said to Moses, "You are a husband of blood to me." And so the Lord spared Moses' life.

<sup>4.27</sup> Meanwhile the Lord had said to Aaron, "Go into the desert to meet Moses." So he went to meet him at the holy mountain; and when he met him, he kissed him.

<sup>4.28</sup> Then Moses told Aaron everything that the Lord had said when he told him to return to Egypt; he also told him about the miracles which the Lord had ordered him to perform.

<sup>4.29</sup> So Moses and Aaron went to Egypt and gathered all the Israelite leaders together.

<sup>4.30</sup> Aaron told them everything that the Lord had said to Moses, and then Moses performed all the miracles in front of the people.

<sup>4.31</sup> They believed, and when they heard that the Lord had come to them and had seen how they were being treated cruelly, they bowed down and worshiped.

# 5

<sup>5.1</sup> Then Moses and Aaron went to the king of Egypt and said, "The Lord, the God of Israel, says, 'Let my people go, so that they can hold a festival in the desert to honor me.'"

<sup>5.2</sup> "Who is the Lord?" the king demanded. "Why should I listen to him and let Israel go? I do not know the Lord; and I will not let Israel go."

<sup>5.3</sup> Moses and Aaron replied, "The God of the Hebrews has revealed himself to us. Allow us to travel three days into the desert to offer sacrifices to the Lord our God. If we don't do so, he will kill us with disease or by war."

<sup>5.4</sup> The king said to Moses and Aaron, "What do you mean by making the people neglect their work? Get those slaves back to work!

<sup>5.5</sup> "You people have become more numerous than the Egyptians. And now you want to stop working!"

<sup>5.6</sup> That same day the king commanded the Egyptian slave drivers and the Israelite foremen:

<sup>5.7</sup> "Stop giving the people straw for making bricks. Make them go and find it for themselves.

<sup>5.8</sup> "But still require them to make the same number of bricks as before, not one brick less. They don't have enough work to do, and that is why they keep asking me to let them go and offer sacrifices to their God!

<sup>5.9</sup> "Make them work harder and keep them busy, so that they won't have time to listen to a pack of lies."

<sup>5.10</sup> The slave drivers and the Israelite foremen went out and said

to the Israelites, "The king has said that he will not supply you with any more straw.

<sup>5.11</sup> "He says that you must go and get it for yourselves wherever you can find it, but you must still make the same number of bricks."

<sup>5.12</sup> So the people went all over Egypt looking for straw.

<sup>5.13</sup> The slave drivers kept trying to force them to make the same number of bricks every day as they had made when they were given straw.

<sup>5.14</sup> The Egyptian slave drivers beat the Israelite foremen, whom they had put in charge of the work. They demanded, "Why aren't you people making the same number of bricks that you made before?"

<sup>5.15</sup> Then the foremen went to the king and complained, "Why do you do this to us, Your Majesty?

<sup>5.16</sup> "We are given no straw, but we are still ordered to make bricks! And now we are being beaten. It is your people that are at fault."

<sup>5.17</sup> The king answered, "You are lazy and don't want to work, and that is why you ask me to let you go and offer sacrifices to the Lord.

<sup>5.18</sup> "Now get back to work! You will not be given any straw, but you must still make the same number of bricks."

<sup>5.19</sup> The foremen realized that they were in trouble when they were told that they had to make the same number of bricks every day as they had made before.

<sup>5.20</sup> As they were leaving, they met Moses and Aaron, who were waiting for them.

<sup>5.21</sup> They said to Moses and Aaron, "The Lord has seen what you have done and will punish you for making the king and his officers hate us. You have given them an excuse to kill us."

<sup>5.22</sup> Then Moses turned to the Lord again and said, "Lord, why do you mistreat your people? Why did you send me here?

<sup>5.23</sup> "Ever since I went to the king to speak for you, he has treated them cruelly. And you have done nothing to help them!"

# 6

<sup>6.1</sup> Then the Lord said to Moses, "Now you are going to see what I will do to the king. I will force him to let my people go. In fact, I will force him to drive them out of his land."

<sup>6.2</sup> God spoke to Moses and said, "I am the Lord.

<sup>6.3</sup> "I appeared to Abraham, to Isaac, and to Jacob as Almighty God,

but I did not make myself known to them by my holy name, the Lord.

⁶·⁴ "I also made my covenant with them, promising to give them the land of Canaan, the land in which they had lived as foreigners.

⁶·⁵ "Now I have heard the groaning of the Israelites, whom the Egyptians have enslaved, and I have remembered my covenant.

⁶·⁶ "So tell the Israelites that I say to them, 'I am the Lord; I will rescue you and set you free from your slavery to the Egyptians. I will raise my mighty arm to bring terrible punishment upon them, and I will save you.

⁶·⁷ "'I will make you my own people, and I will be your God. You will know that I am the Lord your God when I set you free from slavery in Egypt.

⁶·⁸ "'I will bring you to the land that I solemnly promised to give to Abraham, Isaac, and Jacob; and I will give it to you as your own possession. I am the Lord.'"

⁶·⁹ Moses told this to the Israelites, but they would not listen to him, because their spirit had been broken by their cruel slavery.

⁶·¹⁰ Then the Lord said to Moses,

⁶·¹¹ "Go and tell the king of Egypt that he must let the Israelites leave his land."

⁶·¹² But Moses replied, "Even the Israelites will not listen to me, so why should the king? I am such a poor speaker."

⁶·¹³ The Lord commanded Moses and Aaron: "Tell the Israelites and the king of Egypt that I have ordered you to lead the Israelites out of Egypt."

⁶·¹⁴ Reuben, Jacob's first-born, had four sons: Hanoch, Pallu, Hezron, and Carmi; they were the ancestors of the clans that bear their names.

⁶·¹⁵ Simeon had six sons: Jemuel, Jamin, Ohad, Jachin, Zohar, and Shaul, the son of a Canaanite woman; they were the ancestors of the clans that bear their names.

⁶·¹⁶ Levi had three sons: Gershon, Kohath, and Merari; they were the ancestors of the clans that bear their names. Levi lived 137 years.

⁶·¹⁷ Gershon had two sons: Libni and Shimei, and they had many descendants.

⁶·¹⁸ Kohath had four sons: Amram, Izhar, Hebron, and Uzziel. Kohath lived 133 years.

⁶·¹⁹ Merari had two sons: Mahli and Mushi. These are the clans of Levi with their descendants.

<sup>6.20</sup> Amram married his father's sister Jochebed, who bore him Aaron and Moses. Amram lived 137 years.

<sup>6.21</sup> Izhar had three sons: Korah, Nepheg, and Zichri.

<sup>6.22</sup> Uzziel also had three sons: Mishael, Elzaphan, and Sithri.

<sup>6.23</sup> Aaron married Elisheba, the daughter of Amminadab and sister of Nahshon; she bore him Nadab, Abihu, Eleazar, and Ithamar.

<sup>6.24</sup> Korah had three sons: Assir, Elkanah, and Abiasaph; they were the ancestors of the divisions of the clan of Korah.

<sup>6.25</sup> Eleazar, Aaron's son, married one of Putiel's daughters, who bore him Phinehas. These were the heads of the families and the clans of the tribe of Levi.

<sup>6.26</sup> Aaron and Moses were the ones to whom the Lord said, "Lead the tribes of Israel out of Egypt."

<sup>6.27</sup> They were the men who told the king of Egypt to free the Israelites.

<sup>6.28</sup> When the Lord spoke to Moses in the land of Egypt,

<sup>6.29</sup> he said, "I am the Lord. Tell the king of Egypt everything I tell you."

<sup>6.30</sup> But Moses answered, "You know that I am such a poor speaker; why should the king listen to me?"

# 7

<sup>7.1</sup> The Lord said, "I am going to make you like God to the king, and your brother Aaron will speak to him as your prophet.

<sup>7.2</sup> "Tell Aaron everything I command you, and he will tell the king to let the Israelites leave his country.

<sup>7.3-4</sup> "But I will make the king stubborn, and he will not listen to you, no matter how many terrifying things I do in Egypt. Then I will bring severe punishment on Egypt and lead the tribes of my people out of the land.

<sup>7.5</sup> "The Egyptians will then know that I am the Lord, when I raise my hand against them and bring the Israelites out of their country."

<sup>7.6</sup> Moses and Aaron did what the Lord commanded.

<sup>7.7</sup> At the time when they spoke to the king, Moses was eighty years old, and Aaron was eighty-three.

<sup>7.8</sup> The Lord said to Moses and Aaron,

<sup>7.9</sup> "If the king demands that you prove yourselves by performing a miracle, tell Aaron to take his walking stick and throw it down in front of the king, and it will turn into a snake."

<sup>7.10</sup> So Moses and Aaron went to the king and did as the Lord had

commanded. Aaron threw his walking stick down in front of the king and his officers, and it turned into a snake.

<sup>7.11</sup> Then the king called for his wise men and magicians, and by their magic they did the same thing.

<sup>7.12</sup> They threw down their walking sticks, and the sticks turned into snakes. But Aaron's stick swallowed theirs.

<sup>7.13</sup> The king, however, remained stubborn and, just as the Lord had said, the king would not listen to Moses and Aaron.

<sup>7.14</sup> Then the Lord said to Moses, "The king is very stubborn and refuses to let the people go.

<sup>7.15</sup> "So go and meet him in the morning when he goes down to the Nile. Take with you the walking stick that was turned into a snake, and wait for him on the riverbank.

<sup>7.16</sup> "Then say to the king, 'The Lord, the God of the Hebrews, sent me to tell you to let his people go, so that they can worship him in the desert. But until now you have not listened.

<sup>7.17</sup> "'Now, Your Majesty, the Lord says that you will find out who he is by what he is going to do. Look, I am going to strike the surface of the river with this stick, and the water will be turned into blood.

<sup>7.18</sup> "'The fish will die, and the river will stink so much that the Egyptians will not be able to drink from it.'"

<sup>7.19</sup> The Lord said to Moses, "Tell Aaron to take his stick and hold it out over all the rivers, canals, and pools in Egypt. The water will become blood, and all over the land there will be blood, even in the wooden tubs and stone jars."

<sup>7.20</sup> Then Moses and Aaron did as the Lord commanded. In the presence of the king and his officers, Aaron raised his stick and struck the surface of the river, and all the water in it was turned into blood.

<sup>7.21</sup> The fish in the river died, and it smelled so bad that the Egyptians could not drink from it. There was blood everywhere in Egypt.

<sup>7.22</sup> Then the king's magicians did the same thing by means of their magic, and the king was as stubborn as ever. Just as the Lord had said, the king refused to listen to Moses and Aaron.

<sup>7.23</sup> Instead, he turned and went back to his palace without paying any attention even to this.

<sup>7.24</sup> All the Egyptians dug along the bank of the river for drinking water, because they were not able to drink water from the river.

<sup>7.25</sup> Seven days passed after the Lord struck the river.

<sup>8.1</sup> Then the Lord said to Moses, "Go to the king and tell him that the Lord says, 'Let my people go, so that they can worship me.

<sup>8.2</sup> "'If you refuse, I will punish your country by covering it with frogs.

<sup>8.3</sup> "'The Nile will be so full of frogs that they will leave it and go into your palace, your bedroom, your bed, the houses of your officials and your people, and even into your ovens and baking pans.

<sup>8.4</sup> "'They will jump up on you, your people, and all your officials.'"

<sup>8.5</sup> The Lord said to Moses, "Tell Aaron to hold out his walking stick over the rivers, the canals, and the pools, and make frogs come up and cover the land of Egypt."

<sup>8.6</sup> So Aaron held it out over all the water, and the frogs came out and covered the land.

<sup>8.7</sup> But the magicians used magic, and they also made frogs come up on the land.

<sup>8.8</sup> The king called for Moses and Aaron and said, "Pray to the Lord to take away these frogs, and I will let your people go, so that they can offer sacrifices to the Lord."

<sup>8.9</sup> Moses replied, "I will be glad to pray for you. Just set the time when I am to pray for you, your officers, and your people. Then you will be rid of the frogs, and there will be none left except in the Nile."

<sup>8.10</sup> The king answered, "Pray for me tomorrow."

Moses said, "I will do as you ask, and then you will know that there is no other god like the Lord, our God.

<sup>8.11</sup> "You, your officials, and your people will be rid of the frogs, and there will be none left except in the Nile."

<sup>8.12</sup> Then Moses and Aaron left the king, and Moses prayed to the Lord to take away the frogs which he had brought on the king.

<sup>8.13</sup> The Lord did as Moses asked, and the frogs in the houses, the courtyards, and the fields died.

<sup>8.14</sup> The Egyptians piled them up in great heaps, until the land stank with them.

<sup>8.15</sup> When the king saw that the frogs were dead, he became stubborn again and, just as the Lord had said, the king would not listen to Moses and Aaron.

<sup>8.16</sup> The Lord said to Moses, "Tell Aaron to strike the ground with his stick, and all over the land of Egypt the dust will change into gnats."

<sup>8.17</sup> So Aaron struck the ground with his stick, and all the dust in Egypt was turned into gnats, which covered the people and the

<sup>8</sup>

animals.

<sup>8.18</sup> The magicians tried to use their magic to make gnats appear, but they failed. There were gnats everywhere,

<sup>8.19</sup> and the magicians said to the king, "God has done this!" But the king was stubborn and, just as the Lord had said, the king would not listen to Moses and Aaron.

<sup>8.20</sup> The Lord said to Moses, "Early tomorrow morning go and meet the king as he goes to the river, and tell him that the Lord says, 'Let my people go, so that they can worship me.

<sup>8.21</sup> "'I warn you that if you refuse, I will punish you by sending flies on you, your officials, and your people. The houses of the Egyptians will be full of flies, and the ground will be covered with them.

<sup>8.22</sup> "'But I will spare the region of Goshen, where my people live, so that there will be no flies there. I will do this so that you will know that I, the Lord, am at work in this land.

<sup>8.23</sup> "'I will make a distinction between my people and your people. This miracle will take place tomorrow.'"

<sup>8.24</sup> The Lord sent great swarms of flies into the king's palace and the houses of his officials. The whole land of Egypt was brought to ruin by the flies.

<sup>8.25</sup> Then the king called for Moses and Aaron and said, "Go and offer sacrifices to your God here in this country."

<sup>8.26</sup> "It would not be right to do that," Moses answered, "because the Egyptians would be offended by our sacrificing the animals that we offer to the Lord our God. If we use these animals and offend the Egyptians by sacrificing them where they can see us, they will stone us to death.

<sup>8.27</sup> "We must travel three days into the desert to offer sacrifices to the Lord our God, just as he commanded us."

<sup>8.28</sup> The king said, "I will let you go to sacrifice to the Lord, your God, in the desert, if you do not go very far. Pray for me."

<sup>8.29</sup> Moses answered, "As soon as I leave, I will pray to the Lord that tomorrow the flies will leave you, your officials, and your people. But you must not deceive us again and prevent the people from going to sacrifice to the Lord."

<sup>8.30</sup> Moses left the king and prayed to the Lord,

<sup>8.31</sup> and the Lord did as Moses asked. The flies left the king, his officials, and his people; not one fly remained.

<sup>8.32</sup> But even this time the king became stubborn, and again he would not let the people go.

<sup>9.1</sup> The Lord said to Moses, "Go to the king and tell him that the Lord, the God of the Hebrews, says, 'Let my people go, so that they may worship me.

<sup>9.2</sup> "'If you again refuse to let them go,

<sup>9.3</sup> "'I will punish you by sending a terrible disease on all your animals—your horses, donkeys, camels, cattle, sheep, and goats.

<sup>9.4</sup> "'I will make a distinction between the animals of the Israelites and those of the Egyptians, and no animal that belongs to the Israelites will die.

<sup>9.5</sup> "'I, the Lord, have set tomorrow as the time when I will do this.'"

<sup>9.6</sup> The next day the Lord did as he had said, and all the animals of the Egyptians died, but not one of the animals of the Israelites died.

<sup>9.7</sup> The king asked what had happened and was told that none of the animals of the Israelites had died. But he was stubborn and would not let the people go.

<sup>9.8</sup> Then the Lord said to Moses and Aaron, "Take a few handfuls of ashes from a furnace; Moses is to throw them into the air in front of the king.

<sup>9.9</sup> "They will spread out like fine dust over all the land of Egypt, and everywhere they will produce boils that become open sores on the people and the animals."

<sup>9.10</sup> So they got some ashes and stood before the king; Moses threw them into the air, and they produced boils that became open sores on the people and the animals.

<sup>9.11</sup> The magicians were not able to appear before Moses, because they were covered with boils, like all the other Egyptians.

<sup>9.12</sup> But the Lord made the king stubborn and, just as the Lord had said, the king would not listen to Moses and Aaron.

<sup>9.13</sup> The Lord then said to Moses, "Early tomorrow morning meet with the king and tell him that the Lord, the God of the Hebrews, says, 'Let my people go, so that they may worship me.

<sup>9.14</sup> "'This time I will punish not only your officials and your people, but I will punish you as well, so that you may know that there is no one like me in all the world.

<sup>9.15</sup> "'If I had raised my hand to strike you and your people with disease, you would have been completely destroyed.

<sup>9.16</sup> "'But to show you my power I have let you live so that my fame might spread over the whole world.

<sup>9.17</sup> "'Yet you are still arrogant and refuse to let my people go.

<sup>9.18</sup> "'This time tomorrow I will cause a heavy hailstorm, such as

Egypt has never known in all its history.

<sup>9.19</sup> "Now give orders for your livestock and everything else you have in the open to be put under shelter. Hail will fall on the people and animals left outside unprotected, and they will all die.'"

<sup>9.20</sup> Some of the king's officials were afraid because of what the Lord had said, and they brought their slaves and animals indoors for shelter.

<sup>9.21</sup> Others, however, paid no attention to the Lord's warning and left their slaves and animals out in the open.

<sup>9.22</sup> Then the Lord said to Moses, "Raise your hand toward the sky, and hail will fall over the whole land of Egypt—on the people, the animals, and all the plants in the fields."

<sup>9.23</sup> So Moses raised his stick toward the sky, and the Lord sent thunder and hail, and lightning struck the ground. The Lord sent <sup>9.24</sup> a heavy hailstorm, with lightning flashing back and forth. It was the worst storm that Egypt had ever known in all its history.

<sup>9.25</sup> All over Egypt the hail struck down everything in the open, including all the people and all the animals. It beat down all the plants in the fields and broke all the trees.

<sup>9.26</sup> The region of Goshen, where the Israelites lived, was the only place where there was no hail.

<sup>9.27</sup> The king sent for Moses and Aaron and said, "This time I have sinned; the Lord is in the right, and my people and I are in the wrong.

<sup>9.28</sup> "Pray to the Lord! We have had enough of this thunder and hail! I promise to let you go; you don't have to stay here any longer."

<sup>9.29</sup> Moses said to him, "As soon as I go out of the city, I will lift up my hands in prayer to the Lord. The thunder will stop, and there will be no more hail, so that you may know that the earth belongs to the Lord.

<sup>9.30</sup> "But I know that you and your officials do not yet fear the Lord God."

<sup>9.31</sup> The flax and the barley were ruined, because the barley was ripe, and the flax was budding.

<sup>9.32</sup> But none of the wheat was ruined, because it ripens later.

<sup>9.33</sup> Moses left the king, went out of the city, and lifted up his hands in prayer to the Lord. The thunder, the hail, and the rain all stopped.

<sup>9.34</sup> When the king saw what had happened, he sinned again. He and his officials remained as stubborn as ever

9.35 and, just as the Lord had foretold through Moses, the king
would not let the Israelites go.

# 10

10.1 Then the Lord said to Moses, "Go and see the king. I have
made him and his officials stubborn, in order that I may perform
these miracles among them
10.2 "and in order that you may be able to tell your children and
grandchildren how I made fools of the Egyptians when I performed the miracles. All of you will know that I am the Lord."
10.3 So Moses and Aaron went to the king and said to him, "The
Lord, the God of the Hebrews, says, 'How much longer will you refuse to submit to me? Let my people go, so that they may worship
me.
10.4 "'If you keep on refusing, then I will bring locusts into your
country tomorrow.
10.5 "'There will be so many that they will completely cover the
ground. They will eat everything that the hail did not destroy,
even the trees that are left.
10.6 "'They will fill your palaces and the houses of all your officials
and all your people. They will be worse than anything your ancestors ever saw.'" Then Moses turned and left.
10.7 The king's officials said to him, "How long is this man going to
give us trouble? Let the Israelite men go, so that they can worship
the Lord their God. Don't you realize that Egypt is ruined?"
10.8 So Moses and Aaron were brought back to the king, and he
said to them, "You may go and worship the Lord your God. But exactly who will go?"
10.9 Moses answered, "We will all go, including our children and
our old people. We will take our sons and daughters, our sheep
and goats, and our cattle, because we must hold a festival to honor
the Lord."
10.10 The king said, "I swear by the Lord that I will never let you
take your women and children! It is clear that you are plotting to
revolt.
10.11 "No! Only the men may go and worship the Lord if that is what
you want." With that, Moses and Aaron were driven out of the
king's presence.
10.12 Then the Lord said to Moses, "Raise your hand over the land
of Egypt to bring the locusts. They will come and eat everything
that grows, everything that has survived the hail."

<sup>10.13</sup> So Moses raised his stick, and the Lord caused a wind from the east to blow on the land all that day and all that night. By morning it had brought the locusts.

<sup>10.14</sup> They came in swarms and settled over the whole country. It was the largest swarm of locusts that had ever been seen or that ever would be seen again.

<sup>10.15</sup> They covered the ground until it was black with them; they ate everything that the hail had left, including all the fruit on the trees. Not a green thing was left on any tree or plant in all the land of Egypt.

<sup>10.16</sup> Then the king hurriedly called Moses and Aaron and said, "I have sinned against the Lord your God and against you.

<sup>10.17</sup> "Now forgive my sin this one time and pray to the Lord your God to take away this fatal punishment from me."

<sup>10.18</sup> Moses left the king and prayed to the Lord.

<sup>10.19</sup> And the Lord changed the east wind into a very strong west wind, which picked up the locusts and blew them into the Gulf of Suez. Not one locust was left in all of Egypt.

<sup>10.20</sup> But the Lord made the king stubborn, and he did not let the Israelites go.

<sup>10.21</sup> The Lord then said to Moses, "Raise your hand toward the sky, and a darkness thick enough to be felt will cover the land of Egypt."

<sup>10.22</sup> Moses raised his hand toward the sky, and there was total darkness throughout Egypt for three days.

<sup>10.23</sup> The Egyptians could not see each other, and no one left his house during that time. But the Israelites had light where they were living.

<sup>10.24</sup> The king called Moses and said, "You may go and worship the Lord; even your women and children may go with you. But your sheep, goats, and cattle must stay here."

<sup>10.25</sup> Moses answered, "Then you would have to provide us with animals for sacrifices and burnt offerings to offer to the Lord our God.

<sup>10.26</sup> "No, we will take our animals with us; not one will be left behind. We ourselves must select the animals with which to worship the Lord our God. And until we get there, we will not know what animals to sacrifice to him."

<sup>10.27</sup> The Lord made the king stubborn, and he would not let them go.

<sup>10.28</sup> He said to Moses, "Get out of my sight! Don't let me ever see

you again! On the day I do, you will die!"

<sup>10.29</sup> "You are right," Moses answered. "You will never see me again."

# 11

<sup>11.1</sup> Then the Lord said to Moses, "I will send only one more punishment on the king of Egypt and his people. After that he will let you leave. In fact, he will drive all of you out of here.

<sup>11.2</sup> "Now speak to the people of Israel and tell all of them to ask their neighbors for gold and silver jewelry."

<sup>11.3</sup> The Lord made the Egyptians respect the Israelites. Indeed, the officials and all the people considered Moses to be a very great man.

<sup>11.4</sup> Moses then said to the king, "The Lord says, 'At about midnight I will go through Egypt,

<sup>11.5</sup> "and every first-born son in Egypt will die, from the king's son, who is heir to the throne, to the son of the slave woman who grinds grain. The first-born of all the cattle will die also.

<sup>11.6</sup> "There will be loud crying all over Egypt, such as there has never been before or ever will be again.

<sup>11.7</sup> "But not even a dog will bark at the Israelites or their animals. Then you will know that I, the Lord, make a distinction between the Egyptians and the Israelites.'"

<sup>11.8</sup> Moses concluded by saying, "All your officials will come to me and bow down before me, and they will beg me to take all my people and go away. After that, I will leave." Then in great anger Moses left the king.

<sup>11.9</sup> The Lord had said to Moses, "The king will continue to refuse to listen to you, in order that I may do more of my miracles in Egypt."

<sup>11.10</sup> Moses and Aaron performed all these miracles before the king, but the Lord made him stubborn, and he would not let the Israelites leave his country.

# 12

<sup>12.1</sup> The Lord spoke to Moses and Aaron in Egypt:

<sup>12.2</sup> "This month is to be the first month of the year for you.

<sup>12.3</sup> "Give these instructions to the whole community of Israel: On the tenth day of this month each man must choose either a lamb or a young goat for his household.

<sup>12.4</sup> "If his family is too small to eat a whole animal, he and his

next-door neighbor may share an animal, in proportion to the number of people and the amount that each person can eat.

<sup>12.5</sup> "You may choose either a sheep or a goat, but it must be a one-year-old male without any defects.

<sup>12.6</sup> "Then, on the evening of the fourteenth day of the month, the whole community of Israel will kill the animals.

<sup>12.7</sup> "The people are to take some of the blood and put it on the door-posts and above the doors of the houses in which the animals are to be eaten.

<sup>12.8</sup> "That night the meat is to be roasted, and eaten with bitter herbs and with bread made without yeast.

<sup>12.9</sup> "Do not eat any of it raw or boiled, but eat it roasted whole, including the head, the legs, and the internal organs.

<sup>12.10</sup> "You must not leave any of it until morning; if any is left over, it must be burned.

<sup>12.11</sup> "You are to eat it quickly, for you are to be dressed for travel, with your sandals on your feet and your walking stick in your hand. It is the Passover Festival to honor me, the Lord.

<sup>12.12</sup> "On that night I will go through the land of Egypt, killing every first-born male, both human and animal, and punishing all the gods of Egypt. I am the Lord.

<sup>12.13</sup> "The blood on the doorposts will be a sign to mark the houses in which you live. When I see the blood, I will pass over you and will not harm you when I punish the Egyptians.

<sup>12.14</sup> "You must celebrate this day as a religious festival to remind you of what I, the Lord, have done. Celebrate it for all time to come."

<sup>12.15</sup> The Lord said, "For seven days you must not eat any bread made with yeast—eat only unleavened bread. On the first day you are to get rid of all the yeast in your houses, for if anyone during those seven days eats bread made with yeast, he shall no longer be considered one of my people.

<sup>12.16</sup> "On the first day and again on the seventh day you are to meet for worship. No work is to be done on those days, but you may prepare food.

<sup>12.17</sup> "Keep this festival, because it was on this day that I brought your tribes out of Egypt. For all time to come you must celebrate this day as a festival.

<sup>12.18</sup> "From the evening of the fourteenth day of the first month to the evening of the twenty-first day, you must not eat any bread made with yeast.

<sup>12.19-20</sup> "For seven days no yeast must be found in your houses, for if anyone, native-born or foreign, eats bread made with yeast, he shall no longer be considered one of my people."

<sup>12.21</sup> Moses called for all the leaders of Israel and said to them, "Each of you is to choose a lamb or a young goat and kill it, so that your families can celebrate Passover.

<sup>12.22</sup> "Take a sprig of hyssop, dip it in the bowl containing the animal's blood, and wipe the blood on the doorposts and the beam above the door of your house. Not one of you is to leave the house until morning.

<sup>12.23</sup> "When the Lord goes through Egypt to kill the Egyptians, he will see the blood on the beams and the doorposts and will not let the Angel of Death enter your houses and kill you.

<sup>12.24</sup> "You and your children must obey these rules forever.

<sup>12.25</sup> "When you enter the land that the Lord has promised to give you, you must perform this ritual.

<sup>12.26</sup> "When your children ask you, 'What does this ritual mean?'

<sup>12.27</sup> "you will answer, 'It is the sacrifice of Passover to honor the Lord, because he passed over the houses of the Israelites in Egypt. He killed the Egyptians, but spared us.'"

The Israelites knelt down and worshiped.

<sup>12.28</sup> Then they went and did what the Lord had commanded Moses and Aaron.

<sup>12.29</sup> At midnight the Lord killed all the first-born sons in Egypt, from the king's son, who was heir to the throne, to the son of the prisoner in the dungeon; all the first-born of the animals were also killed.

<sup>12.30</sup> That night, the king, his officials, and all the other Egyptians were awakened. There was loud crying throughout Egypt, because there was not one home in which there was not a dead son.

<sup>12.31</sup> That same night the king sent for Moses and Aaron and said, "Get out, you and your Israelites! Leave my country; go and worship the Lord, as you asked.

<sup>12.32</sup> "Take your sheep, goats, and cattle, and leave. Also pray for a blessing on me."

<sup>12.33</sup> The Egyptians urged the people to hurry and leave the country; they said, "We will all be dead if you don't leave."

<sup>12.34</sup> So the people filled their baking pans with unleavened dough, wrapped them in clothing, and carried them on their shoulders.

<sup>12.35</sup> The Israelites had done as Moses had said, and had asked the Egyptians for gold and silver jewelry and for clothes.

<sup>12.36</sup> The Lord made the Egyptians respect the people and give them what they asked for. In this way the Israelites carried away the wealth of the Egyptians.

<sup>12.37</sup> The Israelites set out on foot from Rameses for Sukkoth. There were about 600,000 men, not counting women and children. <sup>12.38</sup> A large number of other people and many sheep, goats, and cattle also went with them. <sup>12.39</sup> They baked unleavened bread from the dough that they had brought out of Egypt, for they had been driven out of Egypt so suddenly that they did not have time to get their food ready or to prepare leavened dough.

<sup>12.40</sup> The Israelites had lived in Egypt for 430 years. <sup>12.41</sup> On the day the 430 years ended, all the tribes of the Lord's people left Egypt.

<sup>12.42</sup> It was a night when the Lord kept watch to bring them out of Egypt; this same night is dedicated to the Lord for all time to come as a night when the Israelites must keep watch.

<sup>12.43</sup> The Lord said to Moses and Aaron, "These are the Passover regulations: No foreigner shall eat the Passover meal, <sup>12.44</sup> "but any slave that you have bought may eat it if you circumcise him first. <sup>12.45</sup> "No temporary resident or hired worker may eat it. <sup>12.46</sup> "The whole meal must be eaten in the house in which it was prepared; it must not be taken outside. And do not break any of the animal's bones. <sup>12.47</sup> "The whole community of Israel must celebrate this festival, <sup>12.48</sup> "but no uncircumcised man may eat it. If a foreigner has settled among you and wants to celebrate Passover to honor the Lord, you must first circumcise all the males of his household. He is then to be treated like a native-born Israelite and may join in the festival. <sup>12.49</sup> "The same regulations apply to native-born Israelites and to foreigners who settle among you."

<sup>12.50</sup> All the Israelites obeyed and did what the Lord had commanded Moses and Aaron. <sup>12.51</sup> On that day the Lord brought the Israelite tribes out of Egypt.

# 13

<sup>13.1</sup> The Lord said to Moses, <sup>13.2</sup> "Dedicate all the first-born males to me, for every first-born male Israelite and every first-born male animal belongs to me."

<sup>13.3</sup> Moses said to the people, "Remember this day—the day on which you left Egypt, the place where you were slaves. This is the day the Lord brought you out by his great power. No leavened bread is to be eaten.

<sup>13.4</sup> "You are leaving Egypt on this day in the first month, the month of Abib.

<sup>13.5</sup> "The Lord solemnly promised your ancestors to give you the land of the Canaanites, the Hittites, the Amorites, the Hivites, and the Jebusites. When he brings you into that rich and fertile land, you must celebrate this festival in the first month of every year.

<sup>13.6</sup> "For seven days you must eat unleavened bread and on the seventh day there is to be a festival to honor the Lord.

<sup>13.7</sup> "For seven days you must not eat any bread made with yeast; there must be no yeast or leavened bread anywhere in your land.

<sup>13.8</sup> "When the festival begins, explain to your sons that you do all this because of what the Lord did for you when you left Egypt.

<sup>13.9</sup> "This observance will be a reminder, like something tied on your hand or on your forehead; it will remind you to continue to recite and study the Law of the Lord, because the Lord brought you out of Egypt by his great power.

<sup>13.10</sup> "Celebrate this festival at the appointed time each year.

<sup>13.11</sup> "The Lord will bring you into the land of the Canaanites, which he solemnly promised to you and your ancestors. When he gives it to you,

<sup>13.12</sup> "you must offer every first-born male to the Lord. Every first-born male of your animals belongs to the Lord,

<sup>13.13</sup> "but you must buy back from him every first-born male donkey by offering a lamb in its place. If you do not want to buy back the donkey, break its neck. You must buy back every first-born male child of yours.

<sup>13.14</sup> "In the future, when your son asks what this observance means, you will answer him, 'By using great power the Lord brought us out of Egypt, the place where we were slaves.

<sup>13.15</sup> "When the king of Egypt was stubborn and refused to let us go, the Lord killed every first-born male in the land of Egypt, both human and animal. That is why we sacrifice every first-born male animal to the Lord, but buy back our first-born sons.

<sup>13.16</sup> "This observance will be a reminder, like something tied on our hands or on our foreheads; it will remind us that the Lord brought us out of Egypt by his great power.'"

¹³·¹⁷ When the king of Egypt let the people go, God did not take them by the road that goes up the coast to Philistia, although it was the shortest way. God thought, "I do not want the people to change their minds and return to Egypt when they see that they are going to have to fight."

¹³·¹⁸ Instead, he led them in a roundabout way through the desert toward the Red Sea. The Israelites were armed for battle.

¹³·¹⁹ Moses took the body of Joseph with him, as Joseph had made the Israelites solemnly promise to do. Joseph had said, "When God rescues you, you must carry my body with you from this place."

¹³·²⁰ The Israelites left Sukkoth and camped at Etham on the edge of the desert.

¹³·²¹ During the day the Lord went in front of them in a pillar of cloud to show them the way, and during the night he went in front of them in a pillar of fire to give them light, so that they could travel night and day.

¹³·²² The pillar of cloud was always in front of the people during the day, and the pillar of fire at night.

# 14

¹⁴·¹ Then the Lord said to Moses,

¹⁴·² "Tell the Israelites to turn back and camp in front of Pi Hahiroth, between Migdol and the Red Sea, near Baal Zephon.

¹⁴·³ "The king will think that the Israelites are wandering around in the country and are closed in by the desert.

¹⁴·⁴ "I will make him stubborn, and he will pursue you, and my victory over the king and his army will bring me honor. Then the Egyptians will know that I am the Lord." The Israelites did as they were told.

¹⁴·⁵ When the king of Egypt was told that the people had escaped, he and his officials changed their minds and said, "What have we done? We have let the Israelites escape, and we have lost them as our slaves!"

¹⁴·⁶ The king got his war chariot and his army ready.

¹⁴·⁷ He set out with all his chariots, including the six hundred finest, commanded by their officers.

¹⁴·⁸ The Lord made the king stubborn, and he pursued the Israelites, who were leaving triumphantly.

¹⁴·⁹ The Egyptian army, with all the horses, chariots, and drivers, pursued them and caught up with them where they were camped by the Red Sea near Pi Hahiroth and Baal Zephon.

¹⁴·¹⁰ When the Israelites saw the king and his army marching against them, they were terrified and cried out to the Lord for help.

¹⁴·¹¹ They said to Moses, "Weren't there any graves in Egypt? Did you have to bring us out here in the desert to die? Look what you have done by bringing us out of Egypt!

¹⁴·¹² "Didn't we tell you before we left that this would happen? We told you to leave us alone and let us go on being slaves of the Egyptians. It would be better to be slaves there than to die here in the desert."

¹⁴·¹³ Moses answered, "Don't be afraid! Stand your ground, and you will see what the Lord will do to save you today; you will never see these Egyptians again.

¹⁴·¹⁴ "The Lord will fight for you, and all you have to do is keep still."

¹⁴·¹⁵ The Lord said to Moses, "Why are you crying out for help? Tell the people to move forward.

¹⁴·¹⁶ "Lift up your walking stick and hold it out over the sea. The water will divide, and the Israelites will be able to walk through the sea on dry ground.

¹⁴·¹⁷ "I will make the Egyptians so stubborn that they will go in after them, and I will gain honor by my victory over the king, his army, his chariots, and his drivers.

¹⁴·¹⁸ "When I defeat them, the Egyptians will know that I am the Lord."

¹⁴·¹⁹ The angel of God, who had been in front of the army of Israel, moved and went to the rear. The pillar of cloud also moved until it was

¹⁴·²⁰ between the Egyptians and the Israelites. The cloud made it dark for the Egyptians, but gave light to the people of Israel, and so the armies could not come near each other all night.

¹⁴·²¹ Moses held out his hand over the sea, and the Lord drove the sea back with a strong east wind. It blew all night and turned the sea into dry land. The water was divided,

¹⁴·²² and the Israelites went through the sea on dry ground, with walls of water on both sides.

¹⁴·²³ The Egyptians pursued them and went after them into the sea with all their horses, chariots, and drivers.

¹⁴·²⁴ Just before dawn the Lord looked down from the pillar of fire and cloud at the Egyptian army and threw them into a panic.

¹⁴·²⁵ He made the wheels of their chariots get stuck, so that they

moved with great difficulty. The Egyptians said, "The Lord is fighting for the Israelites against us. Let's get out of here!"

<sup>14.26</sup> The Lord said to Moses, "Hold out your hand over the sea, and the water will come back over the Egyptians and their chariots and drivers."

<sup>14.27</sup> So Moses held out his hand over the sea, and at daybreak the water returned to its normal level. The Egyptians tried to escape from the water, but the Lord threw them into the sea. <sup>14.28</sup> The water returned and covered the chariots, the drivers, and all the Egyptian army that had followed the Israelites into the sea; not one of them was left. <sup>14.29</sup> But the Israelites walked through the sea on dry ground, with walls of water on both sides.

<sup>14.30</sup> On that day the Lord saved the people of Israel from the Egyptians, and the Israelites saw them lying dead on the seashore. <sup>14.31</sup> When the Israelites saw the great power with which the Lord had defeated the Egyptians, they stood in awe of the Lord; and they had faith in the Lord and in his servant Moses.

# 15

<sup>15.1</sup> Then Moses and the Israelites sang this song to the Lord:
"I will sing to the Lord, because he has won a glorious victory;
he has thrown the horses and their riders into the sea.
<sup>15.2</sup> "The Lord is my strong defender;
he is the one who has saved me.
He is my God, and I will praise him, my father's God, and I will sing about his greatness.
<sup>15.3</sup> "The Lord is a warrior; the Lord is his name.
<sup>15.4</sup> "He threw Egypt's army and its chariots into the sea;
the best of its officers were drowned in the Red Sea.
<sup>15.5</sup> "The deep sea covered them;
they sank to the bottom like a stone.
<sup>15.6</sup> "Your right hand, Lord, is awesome in power;
it breaks the enemy in pieces.
<sup>15.7</sup> "In majestic triumph you overthrow your foes;
your anger blazes out and burns them up like straw.
<sup>15.8</sup> "You blew on the sea and the water piled up high;
it stood up straight like a wall;
the deepest part of the sea became solid.
<sup>15.9</sup> "The enemy said, 'I will pursue them and catch them;

I will divide their wealth and take all I want;
I will draw my sword and take all they have.'
15.10 "But one breath from you, Lord, and the Egyptians were drowned;
they sank like lead in the terrible water.
15.11 "Lord, who among the gods is like you?
Who is like you, wonderful in holiness?
Who can work miracles and mighty acts like yours?
15.12 "You stretched out your right hand, and the earth swallowed our enemies.
15.13 "Faithful to your promise, you led the people you had rescued;
by your strength you guided them to your sacred land.
15.14 "The nations have heard, and they tremble with fear;
the Philistines are seized with terror.
15.15 "The leaders of Edom are terrified;
Moab's mighty men are trembling;
the people of Canaan lose their courage.
15.16 "Terror and dread fall upon them.
They see your strength, O Lord, and stand helpless with fear until your people have marched past—the people you set free from slavery.
15.17 "You bring them in and plant them on your mountain, the place that you, Lord, have chosen for your home, the Temple that you yourself have built.
15.18 "You, Lord, will be king forever and ever."

15.19 The Israelites walked through the sea on dry ground. But when the Egyptian chariots with their horses and drivers went into the sea, the Lord brought the water back, and it covered them.

15.20 The prophet Miriam, Aaron's sister, took her tambourine, and all the women followed her, playing tambourines and dancing. 15.21 Miriam sang for them:

"Sing to the Lord, because he has won a glorious victory;
he has thrown the horses and their riders into the sea."

15.22 Then Moses led the people of Israel away from the Red Sea into the desert of Shur. For three days they walked through the desert, but found no water. 15.23 Then they came to a place called Marah, but the water there was so bitter that they could not drink it. That is why it was named Marah.

15.24 The people complained to Moses and asked, "What are we going to drink?"

15.25 Moses prayed earnestly to the Lord, and the Lord showed him a piece of wood, which he threw into the water; and the water became fit to drink.

There the Lord gave them laws to live by, and there he also tested them.

15.26 He said, "If you will obey me completely by doing what I consider right and by keeping my commands, I will not punish you with any of the diseases that I brought on the Egyptians. I am the Lord, the one who heals you."

15.27 Next they came to Elim, where there were twelve springs and seventy palm trees; there they camped by the water.

# 16

16.1 The whole Israelite community set out from Elim, and on the fifteenth day of the second month after they had left Egypt, they came to the desert of Sin, which is between Elim and Sinai.

16.2 There in the desert they all complained to Moses and Aaron

16.3 and said to them, "We wish that the Lord had killed us in Egypt. There we could at least sit down and eat meat and as much other food as we wanted. But you have brought us out into this desert to starve us all to death."

16.4 The Lord said to Moses, "Now I am going to cause food to rain down from the sky for all of you. The people must go out every day and gather enough for that day. In this way I can test them to find out if they will follow my instructions.

16.5 "On the sixth day they are to bring in twice as much as usual and prepare it."

16.6 So Moses and Aaron said to all the Israelites, "This evening you will know that it was the Lord who brought you out of Egypt.

16.7 "In the morning you will see the dazzling light of the Lord's presence. He has heard your complaints against him—yes, against him, because we are only carrying out his instructions."

16.8 Then Moses said, "It is the Lord who will give you meat to eat in the evening and as much bread as you want in the morning, because he has heard how much you have complained against him. When you complain against us, you are really complaining against the Lord."

16.9 Moses said to Aaron, "Tell the whole community to come and stand before the Lord, because he has heard their complaints."

<sup>16.10</sup> As Aaron spoke to the whole community, they turned toward the desert, and suddenly the dazzling light of the Lord appeared in a cloud.

<sup>16.11</sup> The Lord said to Moses,

<sup>16.12</sup> "I have heard the complaints of the Israelites. Tell them that at twilight they will have meat to eat, and in the morning they will have all the bread they want. Then they will know that I, the Lord, am their God."

<sup>16.13</sup> In the evening a large flock of quails flew in, enough to cover the camp, and in the morning there was dew all around the camp.

<sup>16.14</sup> When the dew evaporated, there was something thin and flaky on the surface of the desert. It was as delicate as frost.

<sup>16.15</sup> When the Israelites saw it, they didn't know what it was and asked each other, "What is it?"

Moses said to them, "This is the food that the Lord has given you to eat.

<sup>16.16</sup> "The Lord has commanded that each of you is to gather as much of it as he needs, two quarts for each member of his household."

<sup>16.17</sup> The Israelites did this, some gathering more, others less.

<sup>16.18</sup> When they measured it, those who gathered much did not have too much, and those who gathered less did not have too little. Each had gathered just what he needed.

<sup>16.19</sup> Moses said to them, "No one is to keep any of it for tomorrow."

<sup>16.20</sup> But some of them did not listen to Moses and saved part of it. The next morning it was full of worms and smelled rotten, and Moses was angry with them.

<sup>16.21</sup> Every morning each one gathered as much as he needed; and when the sun grew hot, what was left on the ground melted.

<sup>16.22</sup> On the sixth day they gathered twice as much food, four quarts for each person. All the leaders of the community came and told Moses about it,

<sup>16.23</sup> and he said to them, "The Lord has commanded that tomorrow is a holy day of rest, dedicated to him. Bake today what you want to bake and boil what you want to boil. Whatever is left should be put aside and kept for tomorrow."

<sup>16.24</sup> As Moses had commanded, they kept what was left until the next day; it did not spoil or get worms in it.

<sup>16.25</sup> Moses said, "Eat this today, because today is the Sabbath, a day of rest dedicated to the Lord, and you will not find any food outside the camp.

16.26 "You must gather food for six days, but on the seventh day, the day of rest, there will be none."

16.27 On the seventh day some of the people went out to gather food, but they did not find any.

16.28 Then the Lord said to Moses, "How much longer will you people refuse to obey my commands?

16.29 "Remember that I, the Lord, have given you a day of rest, and that is why on the sixth day I will always give you enough food for two days. Everyone is to stay where he is on the seventh day and not leave his home."

16.30 So the people did no work on the seventh day.

16.31 The people of Israel called the food manna. It was like a small white seed, and tasted like thin cakes made with honey.

16.32 Moses said, "The Lord has commanded us to save some manna, to be kept for our descendants, so that they can see the food which he gave us to eat in the desert when he brought us out of Egypt."

16.33 Moses said to Aaron, "Take a jar, put two quarts of manna in it, and place it in the Lord's presence to be kept for our descendants."

16.34 As the Lord had commanded Moses, Aaron put it in front of the Covenant Box, so that it could be kept.

16.35 The Israelites ate manna for the next forty years, until they reached the land of Canaan, where they settled.

16.36 (The standard dry measure then in use equaled twenty quarts.)

# 17

17.1 The whole Israelite community left the desert of Sin, moving from one place to another at the command of the Lord. They camped at Rephidim, but there was no water there to drink.

17.2 They complained to Moses and said, "Give us water to drink."

Moses answered, "Why are you complaining? Why are you putting the Lord to the test?"

17.3 But the people were very thirsty and continued to complain to Moses. They said, "Why did you bring us out of Egypt? To kill us and our children and our livestock with thirst?"

17.4 Moses prayed earnestly to the Lord and said, "What can I do with these people? They are almost ready to stone me."

17.5 The Lord said to Moses, "Take some of the leaders of Israel with you, and go on ahead of the people. Take along the stick with which you struck the Nile.

17.6 "I will stand before you on a rock at Mount Sinai. Strike the rock, and water will come out of it for the people to drink." Moses did so in the presence of the leaders of Israel.

<sup>17.7</sup> "The place was named Massah and Meribah, because the Israelites complained and put the Lord to the test when they asked, "Is the Lord with us or not?"

<sup>17.8</sup> The Amalekites came and attacked the Israelites at Rephidim.

<sup>17.9</sup> Moses said to Joshua, "Pick out some men to go and fight the Amalekites tomorrow. I will stand on top of the hill holding the stick that God told me to carry."

<sup>17.10</sup> Joshua did as Moses commanded him and went out to fight the Amalekites, while Moses, Aaron, and Hur went up to the top of the hill.

<sup>17.11</sup> As long as Moses held up his arms, the Israelites won, but when he put his arms down, the Amalekites started winning.

<sup>17.12</sup> When Moses' arms grew tired, Aaron and Hur brought a stone for him to sit on, while they stood beside him and held up his arms, holding them steady until the sun went down.

<sup>17.13</sup> In this way Joshua totally defeated the Amalekites.

<sup>17.14</sup> Then the Lord said to Moses, "Write an account of this victory, so that it will be remembered. Tell Joshua that I will completely destroy the Amalekites."

<sup>17.15</sup> Moses built an altar and named it "The Lord is my Banner."

<sup>17.16</sup> He said, "Hold high the banner of the Lord! The Lord will continue to fight against the Amalekites forever!"

# 18

<sup>18.1</sup> Moses' father-in-law Jethro, the priest of Midian, heard about everything that God had done for Moses and the people of Israel when he led them out of Egypt.

<sup>18.2</sup> So he came to Moses, bringing with him Moses' wife Zipporah, who had been left behind,

<sup>18.3</sup> and Gershom and Eliezer, her two sons. (Moses had said, "I have been a foreigner in a strange land"; so he had named one son Gershom.

<sup>18.4</sup> He had also said, "The God of my father helped me and saved me from being killed by the king of Egypt"; so he had named the other son Eliezer.)

<sup>18.5</sup> Jethro came with Moses' wife and her two sons into the desert where Moses was camped at the holy mountain.

<sup>18.6</sup> He had sent word to Moses that they were coming,

<sup>18.7</sup> so Moses went out to meet him, bowed before him, and kissed

him. They asked about each other's health and then went into Moses' tent.

¹⁸·⁸ Moses told Jethro everything that the Lord had done to the king and the people of Egypt in order to rescue the Israelites. He also told him about the hardships the people had faced on the way and how the Lord had saved them.

¹⁸·⁹ When Jethro heard all this, he was happy

¹⁸·¹⁰ and said, "Praise the Lord, who saved you from the king and the people of Egypt! Praise the Lord, who saved his people from slavery!

¹⁸·¹¹ "Now I know that the Lord is greater than all the gods, because he did this when the Egyptians treated the Israelites with such contempt."

¹⁸·¹² Then Jethro brought an offering to be burned whole and other sacrifices to be offered to God; and Aaron and all the leaders of Israel went with him to eat the sacred meal as an act of worship.

¹⁸·¹³ The next day Moses was settling disputes among the people, and he was kept busy from morning till night.

¹⁸·¹⁴ When Jethro saw everything that Moses had to do, he asked, "What is all this that you are doing for the people? Why are you doing this all alone, with people standing here from morning till night to consult you?"

¹⁸·¹⁵ Moses answered, "I must do this because the people come to me to learn God's will.

¹⁸·¹⁶ "When two people have a dispute, they come to me, and I decide which one of them is right, and I tell them God's commands and laws."

¹⁸·¹⁷ Then Jethro said, "You are not doing this right.

¹⁸·¹⁸ "You will wear yourself out and these people as well. This is too much for you to do alone.

¹⁸·¹⁹ "Now let me give you some good advice, and God will be with you. It is right for you to represent the people before God and bring their disputes to him.

¹⁸·²⁰ "You should teach them God's commands and explain to them how they should live and what they should do.

¹⁸·²¹ "But in addition, you should choose some capable men and appoint them as leaders of the people: leaders of thousands, hundreds, fifties, and tens. They must be God-fearing men who can be trusted and who cannot be bribed.

¹⁸·²² "Let them serve as judges for the people on a permanent basis. They can bring all the difficult cases to you, but they themselves

can decide all the smaller disputes. That will make it easier for you, as they share your burden.

<sup>18.23</sup> "If you do this, as God commands, you will not wear yourself out, and all these people can go home with their disputes settled."

<sup>18.24</sup> Moses took Jethro's advice

<sup>18.25</sup> and chose capable men from among all the Israelites. He appointed them as leaders of thousands, hundreds, fifties, and tens.

<sup>18.26</sup> They served as judges for the people on a permanent basis, bringing the difficult cases to Moses but deciding the smaller disputes themselves.

<sup>18.27</sup> Then Moses said good-bye to Jethro, and Jethro went back home.

# 19

<sup>19.1-2</sup> The people of Israel left Rephidim, and on the first day of the third month after they had left Egypt they came to the desert of Sinai. There they set up camp at the foot of Mount Sinai,

<sup>19.3</sup> and Moses went up the mountain to meet with God.

The Lord called to him from the mountain and told him to say to the Israelites, Jacob's descendants:

<sup>19.4</sup> "You saw what I, the Lord, did to the Egyptians and how I carried you as an eagle carries her young on her wings, and brought you here to me.

<sup>19.5</sup> "Now, if you will obey me and keep my covenant, you will be my own people. The whole earth is mine, but you will be my chosen people,

<sup>19.6</sup> "a people dedicated to me alone, and you will serve me as priests."

<sup>19.7</sup> So Moses went down and called the leaders of the people together and told them everything that the Lord had commanded him.

<sup>19.8</sup> Then all the people answered together, "We will do everything that the Lord has said," and Moses reported this to the Lord.

<sup>19.9</sup> The Lord said to Moses, "I will come to you in a thick cloud, so that the people will hear me speaking with you and will believe you from now on."

Moses told the Lord what the people had answered,

<sup>19.10</sup> and the Lord said to him, "Go to the people and tell them to spend today and tomorrow purifying themselves for worship. They must wash their clothes

<sup>19.11</sup> "and be ready the day after tomorrow. On that day I will come

down on Mount Sinai, where all the people can see me.

<sup>19.12</sup> "Mark a boundary around the mountain that the people must not cross, and tell them not to go up the mountain or even get near it. If any of you set foot on it, you are to be put to death;

<sup>19.13</sup> "you must either be stoned or shot with arrows, without anyone touching you. This applies to both people and animals; they must be put to death. But when the trumpet is blown, then the people are to go up to the mountain."

<sup>19.14</sup> Then Moses came down the mountain and told the people to get ready for worship. So they washed their clothes,

<sup>19.15</sup> and Moses told them, "Be ready by the day after tomorrow and don't have sexual intercourse in the meantime."

<sup>19.16</sup> On the morning of the third day there was thunder and lightning, a thick cloud appeared on the mountain, and a very loud trumpet blast was heard. All the people in the camp trembled with fear.

<sup>19.17</sup> Moses led them out of the camp to meet God, and they stood at the foot of the mountain.

<sup>19.18</sup> All of Mount Sinai was covered with smoke, because the Lord had come down on it in fire. The smoke went up like the smoke of a furnace, and all the people trembled violently.

<sup>19.19</sup> The sound of the trumpet became louder and louder. Moses spoke, and God answered him with thunder.

<sup>19.20</sup> The Lord came down on the top of Mount Sinai and called Moses to the top of the mountain. Moses went up

<sup>19.21</sup> and the Lord said to him, "Go down and warn the people not to cross the boundary to come and look at me; if they do, many of them will die.

<sup>19.22</sup> "Even the priests who come near me must purify themselves, or I will punish them."

<sup>19.23</sup> Moses said to the Lord, "The people cannot come up, because you commanded us to consider the mountain sacred and to mark a boundary around it."

<sup>19.24</sup> The Lord replied, "Go down and bring Aaron back with you. But the priests and the people must not cross the boundary to come up to me, or I will punish them."

<sup>19.25</sup> Moses then went down to the people and told them what the Lord had said.

# 20

<sup>20.1</sup> God spoke, and these were his words:

20.2 "I am the Lord your God who brought you out of Egypt, where you were slaves.

20.3 "Worship no god but me.

20.4 "Do not make for yourselves images of anything in heaven or on earth or in the water under the earth.

20.5 "Do not bow down to any idol or worship it, because I am the Lord your God and I tolerate no rivals. I bring punishment on those who hate me and on their descendants down to the third and fourth generation.

20.6 "But I show my love to thousands of generations of those who love me and obey my laws.

20.7 "Do not use my name for evil purposes, for I, the Lord your God, will punish anyone who misuses my name.

20.8 "Observe the Sabbath and keep it holy.

20.9 "You have six days in which to do your work,

20.10 "but the seventh day is a day of rest dedicated to me. On that day no one is to work—neither you, your children, your slaves, your animals, nor the foreigners who live in your country.

20.11 "In six days I, the Lord, made the earth, the sky, the seas, and everything in them, but on the seventh day I rested. That is why I, the Lord, blessed the Sabbath and made it holy.

20.12 "Respect your father and your mother, so that you may live a long time in the land that I am giving you.

20.13 "Do not commit murder.

20.14 "Do not commit adultery.

20.15 "Do not steal.

20.16 "Do not accuse anyone falsely.

20.17 "Do not desire another man's house; do not desire his wife, his slaves, his cattle, his donkeys, or anything else that he owns."

20.18 When the people heard the thunder and the trumpet blast and saw the lightning and the smoking mountain, they trembled with fear and stood a long way off.

20.19 They said to Moses, "If you speak to us, we will listen; but we are afraid that if God speaks to us, we will die."

20.20 Moses replied, "Don't be afraid; God has only come to test you and make you keep on obeying him, so that you will not sin."

20.21 But the people continued to stand a long way off, and only Moses went near the dark cloud where God was.

20.22 The Lord commanded Moses to tell the Israelites: "You have seen how I, the Lord, have spoken to you from heaven.

20.23 "Do not make for yourselves gods of silver or gold to be worshiped in addition to me.

20.24 "Make an altar of earth for me, and on it sacrifice your sheep and your cattle as offerings to be completely burned and as fellowship offerings. In every place that I set aside for you to worship me, I will come to you and bless you.

20.25 "If you make an altar of stone for me, do not build it out of cut stones, because when you use a chisel on stones, you make them unfit for my use.

20.26 "Do not build an altar for me with steps leading up to it; if you do, you will expose yourselves as you go up the steps.

# 21

21.1 "Give the Israelites the following laws:

21.2 "If you buy a Hebrew slave, he shall serve you for six years. In the seventh year he is to be set free without having to pay anything.

21.3 "If he was unmarried when he became your slave, he is not to take a wife with him when he leaves; but if he was married when he became your slave, he may take his wife with him.

21.4 "If his master gave him a wife and she bore him sons or daughters, the woman and her children belong to the master, and the man is to leave by himself.

21.5 "But if the slave declares that he loves his master, his wife, and his children and does not want to be set free,

21.6 "then his master shall take him to the place of worship. There he is to make him stand against the door or the doorpost and put a hole through his ear. Then he will be his slave for life.

21.7 "If a man sells his daughter as a slave, she is not to be set free, as male slaves are.

21.8 "If she is sold to someone who intends to make her his wife, but he doesn't like her, then she is to be sold back to her father; her master cannot sell her to foreigners, because he has treated her unfairly.

21.9 "If a man buys a female slave to give to his son, he is to treat her like a daughter.

21.10 "If a man takes a second wife, he must continue to give his first wife the same amount of food and clothing and the same rights that she had before.

21.11 "If he does not fulfill these duties to her, he must set her free and not receive any payment.

21.12 "Whoever hits someone and kills him is to be put to death.

21.13 "But if it was an accident and he did not mean to kill him, he can escape to a place which I will choose for you, and there he will be safe.

21.14 "But when someone gets angry and deliberately kills someone else, he is to be put to death, even if he has run to my altar for safety.

21.15 "Whoever hits his father or his mother is to be put to death.

21.16 "Whoever kidnaps someone, either to sell him or to keep him as a slave, is to be put to death.

21.17 "Whoever curses his father or his mother is to be put to death.

21.18-19 "If there is a fight and someone hits someone else with a stone or with his fist, but does not kill him, he is not to be punished. If the one who was hit has to stay in bed, but later is able to get up and walk outside with the help of a cane, the one who hit him is to pay for his lost time and take care of him until he gets well.

21.20 "If a slave owner takes a stick and beats his slave, whether male or female, and the slave dies on the spot, the owner is to be punished.

21.21 "But if the slave does not die for a day or two, the master is not to be punished. The loss of his property is punishment enough.

21.22 "If some men are fighting and hurt a pregnant woman so that she loses her child, but she is not injured in any other way, the one who hurt her is to be fined whatever amount the woman's husband demands, subject to the approval of the judges.

21.23 "But if the woman herself is injured, the punishment shall be life for life,

21.24 "eye for eye, tooth for tooth, hand for hand, foot for foot,

21.25 "burn for burn, wound for wound, bruise for bruise.

21.26 "If someone hits his male or female slave in the eye and puts it out, he is to free the slave as payment for the eye.

21.27 "If he knocks out a tooth, he is to free the slave as payment for the tooth.

21.28 "If a bull gores someone to death, it is to be stoned, and its flesh shall not be eaten; but its owner is not to be punished.

21.29 "But if the bull had been in the habit of attacking people and its owner had been warned, but did not keep it penned up—then if it gores someone to death, it is to be stoned, and its owner is to be put to death also.

21.30 "However, if the owner is allowed to pay a fine to save his life, he must pay the full amount required.

<sup>21.31</sup> "If the bull kills a boy or a girl, the same rule applies.

<sup>21.32</sup> "If the bull kills a male or female slave, its owner shall pay the owner of the slave thirty pieces of silver, and the bull shall be stoned to death.

<sup>21.33</sup> "If someone takes the cover off a pit or if he digs one and does not cover it, and a bull or a donkey falls into it,

<sup>21.34</sup> "he must pay for the animal. He is to pay the money to the owner and may keep the dead animal.

<sup>21.35</sup> "If someone's bull kills someone else's bull, the two of them shall sell the live bull and divide the money; they shall also divide up the meat from the dead animal.

<sup>21.36</sup> "But if it was known that the bull had been in the habit of attacking and its owner did not keep it penned up, he must make good the loss by giving the other man a live bull, but he may keep the dead animal.

# 22

<sup>22.1</sup> "If someone steals a cow or a sheep and kills it or sells it, he must pay five cows for one cow and four sheep for one sheep.

<sup>22.2-4</sup> "He must pay for what he stole. If he owns nothing, he shall be sold as a slave to pay for what he has stolen. If the stolen animal, whether a cow, a donkey, or a sheep, is found alive in his possession, he shall pay two for one.

"If a thief is caught breaking into a house at night and is killed, the one who killed him is not guilty of murder. But if it happens during the day, he is guilty of murder.

<sup>22.5</sup> "If someone lets his animals graze in a field or a vineyard and they stray away and eat up the crops growing in someone else's field, he must make good the loss with the crops from his own fields or vineyards.

<sup>22.6</sup> "If someone starts a fire in his own field and it spreads through the weeds to someone else's field and burns up grain that is growing or that has been cut and stacked, the one who started the fire is to pay for the damage.

<sup>22.7</sup> "If anyone agrees to keep someone else's money or other valuables for him and they are stolen from his house, the thief, if found, shall repay double.

<sup>22.8</sup> "But if the thief is not found, the one who was keeping the valuables is to be brought to the place of worship and there he must take an oath that he has not stolen the other one's property.

<sup>22.9</sup> "In every case of a dispute about property, whether it involves cattle, donkeys, sheep, clothing, or any other lost object, the two people claiming the property shall be taken to the place of worship. The one whom God declares to be guilty shall pay double to the other one.

<sup>22.10</sup> "If anyone agrees to keep someone else's donkey, cow, sheep, or other animal for him, and the animal dies or is injured or is carried off in a raid, and if there was no witness,

<sup>22.11</sup> "the man must go to the place of worship and take an oath that he has not stolen the other man's animal. If the animal was not stolen, the owner shall accept the loss, and the other man need not repay him;

<sup>22.22</sup> "but if the animal was stolen, the man must repay the owner.

<sup>22.13</sup> "If it was killed by wild animals, the man is to bring the remains as evidence; he need not pay for what has been killed by wild animals.

<sup>22.14</sup> "If anyone borrows an animal from someone else and it is injured or dies when its owner is not present, he must pay for it.

<sup>22.15</sup> "But if that happens when the owner is present, he need not repay. If it is a rented animal, the loss is covered by the rental price.

<sup>22.16</sup> "If a man seduces a virgin who is not engaged, he must pay the bride price for her and marry her.

<sup>22.17</sup> "But if her father refuses to let him marry her, he must pay the father a sum of money equal to the bride price for a virgin.

<sup>22.18</sup> "Put to death any woman who practices magic.

<sup>22.19</sup> "Put to death any man who has sexual relations with an animal.

<sup>22.20</sup> "Condemn to death anyone who offers sacrifices to any god except to me, the Lord.

<sup>22.21</sup> "Do not mistreat or oppress a foreigner; remember that you were foreigners in Egypt.

<sup>22.22</sup> "Do not mistreat any widow or orphan.

<sup>22.23</sup> "If you do, I, the Lord, will answer them when they cry out to me for help,

<sup>22.24</sup> "and I will become angry and kill you in war. Your wives will become widows, and your children will be fatherless.

<sup>22.25</sup> "If you lend money to any of my people who are poor, do not act like a moneylender and require him to pay interest.

<sup>22.26</sup> "If you take someone's cloak as a pledge that he will pay you, you must give it back to him before the sun sets,

<sup>22.27</sup> "because it is the only covering he has to keep him warm. What else can he sleep in? When he cries out to me for help, I will answer him because I am merciful.

<sup>22.28</sup> "Do not speak evil of God, and do not curse a leader of your people.

<sup>22.29</sup> "Give me the offerings from your grain, your wine, and your olive oil when they are due.

"Give me your first-born sons.

<sup>22.30</sup> "Give me the first-born of your cattle and your sheep. Let the first-born male stay with its mother for seven days, and on the eighth day offer it to me.

<sup>22.31</sup> "You are my people, so you must not eat the meat of any animal that has been killed by wild animals; instead, give it to the dogs.

# 23

<sup>23.1</sup> "Do not spread false rumors, and do not help a guilty person by giving false testimony.

<sup>23.2</sup> "Do not follow the majority when they do wrong or when they give testimony that perverts justice.

<sup>23.3</sup> "Do not show partiality to a poor person at his trial.

<sup>23.4</sup> "If you happen to see your enemy's cow or donkey running loose, take it back to him.

<sup>23.5</sup> "If his donkey has fallen under its load, help him get the donkey to its feet again; don't just walk off.

<sup>23.6</sup> "Do not deny justice to a poor person when he appears in court.

<sup>23.7</sup> "Do not make false accusations, and do not put an innocent person to death, for I will condemn anyone who does such an evil thing.

<sup>23.8</sup> "Do not accept a bribe, for a bribe makes people blind to what is right and ruins the cause of those who are innocent.

<sup>23.9</sup> "Do not mistreat a foreigner; you know how it feels to be a foreigner, because you were foreigners in Egypt.

<sup>23.10</sup> "For six years plant your land and gather in what it produces.

<sup>23.11</sup> "But in the seventh year let it rest, and do not harvest anything that grows on it. The poor may eat what grows there, and the wild animals can have what is left. Do the same with your vineyards and your olive trees.

<sup>23.12</sup> "Work six days a week, but do no work on the seventh day,

so that your slaves and the foreigners who work for you and even your animals can rest.

23.13 "Listen to everything that I, the Lord, have said to you. Do not pray to other gods; do not even mention their names.

23.14 "Celebrate three festivals a year to honor me.

23.15 "In the month of Abib, the month in which you left Egypt, celebrate the Festival of Unleavened Bread in the way that I commanded you. Do not eat any bread made with yeast during the seven days of this festival. Never come to worship me without bringing an offering.

23.16 "Celebrate the Harvest Festival when you begin to harvest your crops.

"Celebrate the Festival of Shelters in the autumn, when you gather the fruit from your vineyards and orchards.

23.17 "Every year at these three festivals all your men must come to worship me, the Lord your God.

23.18 "Do not offer bread made with yeast when you sacrifice an animal to me. The fat of animals sacrificed to me during these festivals is not to be left until the following morning.

23.19 "Each year bring to the house of the Lord your God the first grain that you harvest.

"Do not cook a young sheep or goat in its mother's milk.

23.20 "I will send an angel ahead of you to protect you as you travel and to bring you to the place which I have prepared.

23.21 "Pay attention to him and obey him. Do not rebel against him, for I have sent him, and he will not pardon such rebellion.

23.22 "But if you obey him and do everything I command, I will fight against all your enemies.

23.23 "My angel will go ahead of you and take you into the land of the Amorites, the Hittites, the Perizzites, the Canaanites, the Hivites, and the Jebusites, and I will destroy them.

23.24 "Do not bow down to their gods or worship them, and do not adopt their religious practices. Destroy their gods and break down their sacred stone pillars.

23.25 "If you worship me, the Lord your God, I will bless you with food and water and take away all your sicknesses.

23.26 "In your land no woman will have a miscarriage or be without children. I will give you long lives.

23.27 "I will make the people who oppose you afraid of me; I will bring confusion among the people against whom you fight, and I will make all your enemies turn and run from you.

²³·²⁸ "I will throw your enemies into panic; I will drive out the Hivites, the Canaanites, and the Hittites as you advance.
²³·²⁹ "I will not drive them out within a year's time; if I did, the land would become deserted, and the wild animals would be too many for you.
²³·³⁰ "Instead, I will drive them out little by little, until there are enough of you to take possession of the land.
²³·³¹ "I will make the borders of your land extend from the Gulf of Aqaba to the Mediterranean Sea and from the desert to the Euphrates River. I will give you power over the inhabitants of the land, and you will drive them out as you advance.
²³·³² "Do not make any agreement with them or with their gods.
²³·³³ "Do not let those people live in your country; if you do, they will make you sin against me. If you worship their gods, it will be a fatal trap for you."

# 24

²⁴·¹ The Lord said to Moses, "Come up the mountain to me, you and Aaron, Nadab, Abihu, and seventy of the leaders of Israel; and while you are still some distance away, bow down in worship.
²⁴·² "You alone, and none of the others, are to come near me. The people are not even to come up the mountain."
²⁴·³ Moses went and told the people all the Lord's commands and all the ordinances, and all the people answered together, "We will do everything that the Lord has said."
²⁴·⁴ Moses wrote down all the Lord's commands. Early the next morning he built an altar at the foot of the mountain and set up twelve stones, one for each of the twelve tribes of Israel.
²⁴·⁵ Then he sent young men, and they burned sacrifices to the Lord and sacrificed some cattle as fellowship offerings.
²⁴·⁶ Moses took half of the blood of the animals and put it in bowls; and the other half he threw against the altar.
²⁴·⁷ Then he took the book of the Covenant, in which the Lord's commands were written, and read it aloud to the people. They said, "We will obey the Lord and do everything that he has commanded."
²⁴·⁸ Then Moses took the blood in the bowls and threw it on the people. He said, "This is the blood that seals the covenant which the Lord made with you when he gave all these commands."
²⁴·⁹ Moses, Aaron, Nadab, Abihu, and seventy of the leaders of Israel went up the mountain

<sup>24.10</sup> and they saw the God of Israel. Beneath his feet was what looked like a pavement of sapphire, as blue as the sky.

<sup>24.11</sup> God did not harm these leading men of Israel; they saw God, and then they ate and drank together.

<sup>24.12</sup> The Lord said to Moses, "Come up the mountain to me, and while you are here, I will give you two stone tablets which contain all the laws that I have written for the instruction of the people."

<sup>24.13</sup> Moses and his helper Joshua got ready, and Moses began to go up the holy mountain.

<sup>24.14</sup> Moses said to the leaders, "Wait here in the camp for us until we come back. Aaron and Hur are here with you; and so whoever has a dispute to settle can go to them."

<sup>24.15</sup> Moses went up Mount Sinai, and a cloud covered it.

<sup>24.16-17</sup> The dazzling light of the Lord's presence came down on the mountain. To the Israelites the light looked like a fire burning on top of the mountain. The cloud covered the mountain for six days, and on the seventh day the Lord called to Moses from the cloud.

<sup>24.18</sup> Moses went on up the mountain into the cloud. There he stayed for forty days and nights.

# 25

<sup>25.1</sup> The Lord said to Moses,

<sup>25.2</sup> "Tell the Israelites to make an offering to me. Receive whatever offerings anyone wishes to give.

<sup>25.3</sup> "These offerings are to be: gold, silver, and bronze;

<sup>25.4</sup> "fine linen; blue, purple, and red wool; cloth made of goats' hair;

<sup>25.5</sup> "rams' skin dyed red; fine leather; acacia wood;

<sup>25.6</sup> "oil for the lamps; spices for the anointing oil and for the sweet-smelling incense;

<sup>25.7</sup> "carnelians and other jewels to be set in the ephod of the High Priest and in his breastpiece.

<sup>25.8</sup> "The people must make a sacred Tent for me, so that I may live among them.

<sup>25.9</sup> "Make it and all its furnishings according to the plan that I will show you.

<sup>25.10</sup> "Make a Box out of acacia wood, 45 inches long, 27 inches wide, and 27 inches high.

<sup>25.11</sup> "Cover it with pure gold inside and out and put a gold border all around it.

<sup>25.12</sup> "Make four carrying rings of gold for it and attach them to its four legs, with two rings on each side.

25.13 "Make carrying poles of acacia wood and cover them with gold
25.14 "and put them through the rings on each side of the Box.
25.15 "The poles are to be left in the rings and must not be taken out.
25.16 "Then put in the Box the two stone tablets that I will give you, on which the commandments are written.
25.17 "Make a lid of pure gold, 45 inches long and 27 inches wide.
25.18 "Make two winged creatures of hammered gold,
25.19 "one for each end of the lid. Make them so that they form one piece with the lid.
25.20 "The winged creatures are to face each other across the lid, and their outspread wings are to cover it.
25.21 "Put the two stone tablets inside the Box and put the lid on top of it.
25.22 "I will meet you there, and from above the lid between the two winged creatures I will give you all my laws for the people of Israel.
25.23 "Make a table out of acacia wood, 36 inches long, 18 inches wide, and 27 inches high.
25.24 "Cover it with pure gold and put a gold border around it.
25.25 "Make a rim 3 inches wide around it and a gold border around the rim.
25.26 "Make four carrying rings of gold for it and put them at the four corners, where the legs are.
25.27 "The rings to hold the poles for carrying the table are to be placed near the rim.
25.28 "Make the poles of acacia wood and cover them with gold.
25.29 "Make plates, cups, jars, and bowls to be used for the wine offerings. All of these are to be made of pure gold.
25.30 "The table is to be placed in front of the Covenant Box, and on the table there is always to be the sacred bread offered to me.
25.31 "Make a lampstand of pure gold. Make its base and its shaft of hammered gold; its decorative flowers, including buds and petals, are to form one piece with it.
25.32 "Six branches shall extend from its sides, three from each side.
25.33 "Each of the six branches is to have three decorative flowers shaped like almond blossoms with buds and petals.
25.34 "The shaft of the lampstand is to have four decorative flowers shaped like almond blossoms with buds and petals.
25.35 "There is to be one bud below each of the three pairs of branches.

<sup>25.36</sup> "The buds, the branches, and the lampstand are to be a single piece of pure hammered gold.

<sup>25.37</sup> "Make seven lamps for the lampstand and set them up so that they shine toward the front.

<sup>25.38</sup> "Make its tongs and trays of pure gold.

<sup>25.39</sup> "Use seventy-five pounds of pure gold to make the lampstand and all this equipment.

<sup>25.40</sup> "Take care to make them according to the plan that I showed you on the mountain.

# 26

<sup>26.1</sup> "Make the interior of the sacred Tent, the Tent of my presence, out of ten pieces of fine linen woven with blue, purple, and red wool. Embroider them with figures of winged creatures.

<sup>26.2</sup> "Make each piece the same size, 14 yards long and 2 yards wide.

<sup>26.3</sup> "Sew five of them together in one set, and do the same with the other five.

<sup>26.4</sup> "Make loops of blue cloth on the edge of the outside piece in each set.

<sup>26.5</sup> "Put fifty loops on the first piece of the first set and fifty loops matching them on the last piece of the second set.

<sup>26.6</sup> "Make fifty gold hooks with which to join the two sets into one piece.

<sup>26.7</sup> "Make a cover for the Tent out of eleven pieces of cloth made of goats' hair.

<sup>26.8</sup> "Make them all the same size, 15 yards long and 2 yards wide.

<sup>26.9</sup> "Sew five of them together in one set, and the other six in another set. Fold the sixth piece double over the front of the Tent.

<sup>26.10</sup> "Put fifty loops on the edge of the last piece of one set, and fifty loops on the edge of the other set.

<sup>26.11</sup> "Make fifty bronze hooks and put them in the loops to join the two sets so as to form one cover.

<sup>26.12</sup> "Hang the extra half piece over the back of the Tent.

<sup>26.13</sup> "The extra half yard on each side of the length is to hang over the sides of the Tent to cover it.

<sup>26.14</sup> "Make two more coverings, one of rams' skin dyed red and the other of fine leather, to serve as the outer cover.

<sup>26.15</sup> "Make upright frames for the Tent out of acacia wood.

<sup>26.16</sup> "Each frame is to be 15 feet long and 27 inches wide,

<sup>26.17</sup> "with two matching projections, so that the frames can be

joined together. All the frames are to have these projections.

26.18 "Make twenty frames for the south side

26.19 "and forty silver bases to go under them, two bases under each frame to hold its two projections.

26.20 "Make twenty frames for the north side of the Tent

26.21 "and forty silver bases, two under each frame.

26.22 "For the back of the Tent on the west, make six frames,

26.23 "and two frames for the corners.

26.24 "These corner frames are to be joined at the bottom and connected all the way to the top. The two frames that form the two corners are to be made in this way.

26.25 "So there will be eight frames with their sixteen silver bases, two under each frame.

26.26 "Make fifteen crossbars of acacia wood, five for the frames on one side of the Tent,

26.27 "five for the frames on the other side, and five for the frames on the west end, at the back.

26.28 "The middle crossbar, set halfway up the frames, is to extend from one end of the Tent to the other.

26.29 "Cover the frames with gold and fit them with gold rings to hold the crossbars, which are also to be covered with gold.

26.30 "Set up the Tent according to the plan that I showed you on the mountain.

26.31 "Make a curtain of fine linen woven with blue, purple, and red wool. Embroider it with figures of winged creatures.

26.32 "Hang it on four posts of acacia wood covered with gold, fitted with hooks, and set in four silver bases.

26.33 "Place the curtain under the row of hooks in the roof of the Tent, and put behind the curtain the Covenant Box containing the two stone tablets. The curtain will separate the Holy Place from the Most Holy Place.

26.34 "Put the lid on the Covenant Box.

26.35 "Outside the Most Holy Place put the table against the north side of the Tent and the lampstand against the south side.

26.36 "For the entrance of the Tent make a curtain of fine linen woven with blue, purple, and red wool and decorated with embroidery.

26.37 "For this curtain make five posts of acacia wood covered with gold and fitted with gold hooks; make five bronze bases for these posts.

# 27

27.1 "Make an altar out of acacia wood. It is to be square, 7½ feet long and 7½ feet wide, and it is to be 4½ feet high.

27.2 "Make projections at the top of the four corners. They are to form one piece with the altar, and the whole is to be covered with bronze.

27.3 "Make pans for the greasy ashes, and make shovels, bowls, hooks, and fire pans. All this equipment is to be made of bronze.

27.4 "Make a bronze grating and put four bronze carrying rings on its corners.

27.5 "Put the grating under the rim of the altar, so that it reaches halfway up the altar.

27.6 "Make carrying poles of acacia wood, cover them with bronze,

27.7 "and put them in the rings on each side of the altar when it is carried.

27.8 "Make the altar out of boards and leave it hollow, according to the plan that I showed you on the mountain.

27.9 "For the Tent of my presence make an enclosure out of fine linen curtains. On the south side the curtains are to be 50 yards long,

27.10 "supported by twenty bronze posts in twenty bronze bases, with hooks and rods made of silver.

27.11 "Do the same on the north side of the enclosure.

27.12 "On the west side there are to be curtains 25 yards long, with ten posts and ten bases.

27.13 "On the east side, where the entrance is, the enclosure is also to be 25 yards wide.

27.14-15 "On each side of the entrance there are to be 7½ yards of curtains, with three posts and three bases.

27.16 "For the entrance itself there is to be a curtain 10 yards long made of fine linen woven with blue, purple, and red wool, and decorated with embroidery. It is to be supported by four posts in four bases.

27.17 "All the posts around the enclosure are to be connected with silver rods, and their hooks are to be made of silver and their bases of bronze.

27.18 "The enclosure is to be 50 yards long, 25 yards wide, and 2½ yards high. The curtains are to be made of fine linen and the bases of bronze.

27.19 "All the equipment that is used in the Tent and all the pegs for the Tent and for the enclosure are to be made of bronze.

27.20 "Command the people of Israel to bring you the best olive oil for the lamp, so that it can be lit each evening.

<sup>27.21</sup> "Aaron and his sons are to set up the lamp in the Tent of my presence outside the curtain which is in front of the Covenant Box. There in my presence it is to burn from evening until morning. This command is to be kept forever by the Israelites and their descendants.

# 28

<sup>28.1</sup> "Summon your brother Aaron and his sons, Nadab, Abihu, Eleazar, and Ithamar. Separate them from the people of Israel, so that they may serve me as priests.

<sup>28.2</sup> "Make priestly garments for your brother Aaron, to provide him with dignity and beauty.

<sup>28.3</sup> "Call all the skilled workers to whom I have given ability, and tell them to make Aaron's clothes, so that he may be dedicated as a priest in my service.

<sup>28.4</sup> "Tell them to make a breastpiece, an ephod, a robe, an embroidered shirt, a turban, and a sash. They are to make these priestly garments for your brother Aaron and his sons, so that they can serve me as priests.

<sup>28.5</sup> "The skilled workers are to use blue, purple, and red wool, gold thread, and fine linen.

<sup>28.6</sup> "They are to make the ephod of blue, purple, and red wool, gold thread, and fine linen, decorated with embroidery.

<sup>28.7</sup> "Two shoulder straps, by which it can be fastened, are to be attached to the sides.

<sup>28.8</sup> "A finely woven belt made of the same materials is to be attached to the ephod so as to form one piece with it.

<sup>28.9</sup> "Take two carnelian stones and engrave on them the names of the twelve sons of Jacob,

<sup>28.10</sup> "in the order of their birth, with six on one stone and six on the other.

<sup>28.11</sup> "Have a skillful jeweler engrave on the two stones the names of the sons of Jacob, and mount the stones in gold settings.

<sup>28.12</sup> "Put them on the shoulder straps of the ephod to represent the twelve tribes of Israel. In this way Aaron will carry their names on his shoulders, so that I, the Lord, will always remember my people.

<sup>28.13</sup> "Make two gold settings

<sup>28.14</sup> "and two chains of pure gold twisted like cords, and attach them to the settings.

<sup>28.15</sup> "Make a breastpiece for the High Priest to use in determining God's will. It is to be made of the same materials as the ephod and with similar embroidery.

<sup>28.16</sup> "It is to be square and folded double, 9 inches long and 9 inches wide.

<sup>28.17</sup> "Mount four rows of precious stones on it; in the first row mount a ruby, a topaz, and a garnet;

<sup>28.18</sup> "in the second row, an emerald, a sapphire, and a diamond;

<sup>28.19</sup> "in the third row, a turquoise, an agate, and an amethyst;

<sup>28.20</sup> "and in the fourth row, a beryl, a carnelian, and a jasper. These are to be mounted in gold settings.

<sup>28.21</sup> "Each of these twelve stones is to have engraved on it the name of one of the sons of Jacob, to represent the tribes of Israel.

<sup>28.22</sup> "For the breastpiece make chains of pure gold, twisted like cords.

<sup>28.23</sup> "Make two gold rings and attach them to the upper corners of the breastpiece,

<sup>28.24</sup> "and fasten the two gold cords to the two rings.

<sup>28.25</sup> "Fasten the other two ends of the cords to the two settings, and in this way attach them in front to the shoulder straps of the ephod.

<sup>28.26</sup> "Then make two rings of gold and attach them to the lower corners of the breastpiece on the inside edge next to the ephod.

<sup>28.27</sup> "Make two more gold rings and attach them to the lower part of the front of the two shoulder straps of the ephod, near the seam and above the finely woven belt.

<sup>28.28</sup> "Tie the rings of the breastpiece to the rings of the ephod with a blue cord, so that the breastpiece rests above the belt and does not come loose.

<sup>28.29</sup> "When Aaron enters the Holy Place, he will wear this breastpiece engraved with the names of the tribes of Israel, so that I, the Lord, will always remember my people.

<sup>28.30</sup> "Put the Urim and Thummim in the breastpiece, so that Aaron will carry them when he comes into my holy presence. At such times he must always wear this breastpiece, so that he can determine my will for the people of Israel.

<sup>28.31</sup> "The robe that goes under the ephod is to be made entirely of blue wool.

<sup>28.32</sup> "It is to have a hole for the head, and this hole is to be reinforced with a woven binding to keep it from tearing.

<sup>28.33-34</sup> "All around its lower hem put pomegranates of blue, purple,

and red wool, alternating with gold bells.

[28.35] "Aaron is to wear this robe when he serves as priest. When he comes into my presence in the Holy Place or when he leaves it, the sound of the bells will be heard, and he will not be killed.

[28.36] "Make an ornament of pure gold and engrave on it 'Dedicated to the Lord.'

[28.37] "Tie it to the front of the turban with a blue cord.

[28.38] "Aaron is to wear it on his forehead, so that I, the Lord, will accept all the offerings that the Israelites dedicate to me, even if the people commit some error in offering them.

[28.39] "Weave Aaron's shirt of fine linen and make a turban of fine linen and also a sash decorated with embroidery.

[28.40] "Make shirts, sashes, and caps for Aaron's sons, to provide them with dignity and beauty.

[28.41] "Put these clothes on your brother Aaron and his sons. Then ordain them and dedicate them by anointing them with olive oil, so that they may serve me as priests.

[28.42] "Make linen shorts for them, reaching from the waist to the thighs, so that they will not expose themselves.

[28.43] "Aaron and his sons must always wear them when they go into the Tent of my presence or approach the altar to serve as priests in the Holy Place, so that they will not be killed for exposing themselves. This is a permanent rule for Aaron and his descendants.

# 29

[29.1] "This is what you are to do to Aaron and his sons to dedicate them as priests in my service. Take one young bull and two rams without any defects.

[29.2] "Use the best wheat flour, but no yeast, and make some bread with olive oil, some without it, and some in the form of thin cakes brushed with oil.

[29.3] "Put them in a basket and offer them to me when you sacrifice the bull and the two rams.

[29.4] "Bring Aaron and his sons to the entrance of the Tent of my presence, and have them take a ritual bath.

[29.5] "Then dress Aaron in the priestly garments—the shirt, the robe that goes under the ephod, the ephod, the breastpiece, and the belt.

[29.6] "Put the turban on him and tie on it the sacred sign of dedication engraved 'Dedicated to the Lord.'

[29.7] "Then take the anointing oil, pour it on his head, and anoint him.

<sup>29.8</sup> "Bring his sons and put shirts on them;

<sup>29.9</sup> "put sashes around their waists and tie caps on their heads. That is how you are to ordain Aaron and his sons. They and their descendants are to serve me as priests forever.

<sup>29.10</sup> "Bring the bull to the front of the Tent of my presence and tell Aaron and his sons to put their hands on its head.

<sup>29.11</sup> "Kill the bull there in my holy presence at the entrance of the Tent.

<sup>29.12</sup> "Take some of the bull's blood and with your finger put it on the projections of the altar. Then pour out the rest of the blood at the base of the altar.

<sup>29.13</sup> "Next, take all the fat which covers the internal organs, the best part of the liver, and the two kidneys with the fat on them, and burn them on the altar as an offering to me.

<sup>29.14</sup> "But burn the bull's flesh, its skin, and its intestines outside the camp. This is an offering to take away the sins of the priests.

<sup>29.15</sup> "Take one of the rams and tell Aaron and his sons to put their hands on its head.

<sup>29.16</sup> "Kill it, and take its blood and throw it against all four sides of the altar.

<sup>29.17</sup> "Cut the ram in pieces; wash its internal organs and its hind legs, and put them on top of the head and the other pieces.

<sup>29.18</sup> "Burn the whole ram on the altar as a food offering. The odor of this offering pleases me.

<sup>29.19</sup> "Take the other ram—the ram used for dedication—and tell Aaron and his sons to put their hands on its head.

<sup>29.20</sup> "Kill it, and take some of its blood and put it on the lobes of the right ears of Aaron and his sons, on the thumbs of their right hands and on the big toes of their right feet. Throw the rest of the blood against all four sides of the altar.

<sup>29.21</sup> "Take some of the blood that is on the altar and some of the anointing oil, and sprinkle it on Aaron and his clothes and on his sons and their clothes. He, his sons, and their clothes will then be dedicated to me.

<sup>29.22</sup> "Cut away the ram's fat, the fat tail, the fat covering the internal organs, the best part of the liver, the two kidneys with the fat on them, and the right thigh.

<sup>29.23</sup> "From the basket of bread which has been offered to me, take one loaf of each kind: one loaf made with olive oil and one made without it and one thin cake.

29.24 "Put all this food in the hands of Aaron and his sons and have them dedicate it to me as a special gift.

29.25 "Then take it from them and burn it on the altar, on top of the burnt offering, as a food offering to me. The odor of this offering pleases me.

29.26 "Take the breast of this ram and dedicate it to me as a special gift. This part of the animal will be yours.

29.27 "When a priest is ordained, the breast and the thigh of the ram being used for the ordination are to be dedicated to me as a special gift and set aside for the priests.

29.28 "It is my unchanging decision that when my people make their fellowship offerings, the breast and the thigh of the animal belong to the priests. This is the people's gift to me, the Lord.

29.29 "Aaron's priestly garments are to be handed on to his sons after his death, for them to wear when they are ordained.

29.30 "The son of Aaron who succeeds him as priest and who goes into the Tent of my presence to serve in the Holy Place is to wear these garments for seven days.

29.31 "Take the meat of the ram used for the ordination of Aaron and his sons and boil it in a holy place.

29.32 "At the entrance of the Tent of my presence they are to eat it along with the bread left in the basket.

29.33 "They shall eat what was used in the ritual of forgiveness at their ordination. Only priests may eat this food, because it is sacred.

29.34 "If some of the meat or some of the bread is not eaten by morning, it is to be burned; it is not to be eaten, for it is sacred.

29.35 "Perform the rites of ordination for Aaron and his sons for seven days exactly as I have commanded you.

29.36 "Each day you must offer a bull as a sacrifice, so that sin may be forgiven. This will purify the altar. Then anoint it with olive oil to make it holy.

29.37 "Do this every day for seven days. Then the altar will be completely holy, and anyone or anything that touches it will be harmed by the power of its holiness.

29.38 "Every day for all time to come, sacrifice on the altar two one-year-old lambs.

29.39 "Sacrifice one of the lambs in the morning and the other in the evening.

29.40 "With the first lamb offer two pounds of fine wheat flour mixed with one quart of pure olive oil. Pour out one quart of wine as an offering.

<sup>29.41</sup> "Sacrifice the second lamb in the evening, and offer with it the same amounts of flour, olive oil, and wine as in the morning. This is a food offering to me, the Lord, and its odor pleases me.

<sup>29.42</sup> "For all time to come, this burnt offering is to be offered in my presence at the entrance of the Tent of my presence. That is where I will meet my people and speak to you.

<sup>29.43</sup> "There I will meet the people of Israel, and the dazzling light of my presence will make the place holy.

<sup>29.44</sup> "I will make the Tent and the altar holy, and I will set Aaron and his sons apart to serve me as priests.

<sup>29.45</sup> "I will live among the people of Israel, and I will be their God.

<sup>29.46</sup> "They will know that I am the Lord their God who brought them out of Egypt so that I could live among them. I am the Lord their God.

# 30

<sup>30.1</sup> "Make an altar out of acacia wood, for burning incense.

<sup>30.2</sup> "It is to be square, 18 inches long and 18 inches wide, and it is to be 36 inches high. Its projections at the four corners are to form one piece with it.

<sup>30.3</sup> "Cover its top, all four sides, and its projections with pure gold, and put a gold border around it.

<sup>30.4</sup> "Make two gold carrying rings for it and attach them below the border on two sides to hold the poles with which it is to be carried.

<sup>30.5</sup> "Make these poles of acacia wood and cover them with gold.

<sup>30.6</sup> "Put this altar outside the curtain which hangs in front of the Covenant Box. That is the place where I will meet you.

<sup>30.7</sup> "Every morning when Aaron comes to take care of the lamps, he is to burn sweet-smelling incense on it.

<sup>30.8</sup> "He must do the same when he lights the lamps in the evening. This offering of incense is to continue without interruption for all time to come.

<sup>30.9</sup> "Do not offer on this altar any forbidden incense, any animal offering, or any grain offering, and do not pour out any wine offering on it.

<sup>30.10</sup> "Once a year Aaron is to perform the ritual for purifying the altar by putting on its four projections the blood of the animal sacrificed for sin. This is to be done every year for all time to come. This altar is to be completely holy, dedicated to me, the Lord."

<sup>30.11</sup> "The Lord said to Moses,

<sup>30.12</sup> "When you take a census of the people of Israel, each man is to pay me a price for his life, so that no disaster will come on him while the census is being taken.

<sup>30.13</sup> "Everyone included in the census must pay the required amount of money, weighed according to the official standard. Everyone must pay this as an offering to me.

<sup>30.14</sup> "Everyone being counted in the census, that is, every man twenty years old or older, is to pay me this amount.

<sup>30.15</sup> "The rich man is not to pay more, nor the poor man less, when they pay this amount for their lives.

<sup>30.16</sup> "Collect this money from the people of Israel and spend it for the upkeep of the Tent of my presence. This tax will be the payment for their lives, and I will remember to protect them."

<sup>30.17</sup> The Lord said to Moses,

<sup>30.18</sup> "Make a bronze basin with a bronze base. Place it between the Tent and the altar, and put water in it.

<sup>30.19</sup> "Aaron and his sons are to use the water to wash their hands and feet

<sup>30.20</sup> "before they go into the Tent or approach the altar to offer the food offering. Then they will not be killed.

<sup>30.21</sup> "They must wash their hands and feet, so that they will not die. This is a rule which they and their descendants are to observe forever."

<sup>30.22</sup> The Lord said to Moses,

<sup>30.23</sup> "Take the finest spices—12 pounds of liquid myrrh, 6 pounds of sweet-smelling cinnamon, 6 pounds of sweet-smelling cane,

<sup>30.24</sup> "and 12 pounds of cassia (all weighed according to the official standard). Add one gallon of olive oil,

<sup>30.25</sup> "and make a sacred anointing oil, mixed like perfume.

<sup>30.26</sup> "Use it to anoint the Tent of my presence, the Covenant Box,

<sup>30.27</sup> "the table and all its equipment, the lampstand and its equipment, the altar for burning incense,

<sup>30.28</sup> "the altar for burning offerings, together with all its equipment, and the washbasin with its base.

<sup>30.29</sup> "Dedicate these things in this way, and they will be completely holy, and anyone or anything that touches them will be harmed by the power of its holiness.

<sup>30.30</sup> "Then anoint Aaron and his sons, and ordain them as priests in my service.

<sup>30.31</sup> "Say to the people of Israel, 'This holy anointing oil is to be used in my service for all time to come.

30.32 "It must not be poured on ordinary men, and you must not use the same formula to make any mixture like it. It is holy, and you must treat it as holy.

30.33 "'Whoever makes any like it or uses any of it on anyone who is not a priest will no longer be considered one of my people.'"

30.34 The Lord said to Moses, "Take an equal part of each of the following sweet spices—stacte, onycha, galbanum, and pure frankincense.

30.35 "Use them to make incense, mixed like perfume. Add salt to keep it pure and holy.

30.36 "Beat part of it into a fine powder, take it into the Tent of my presence, and sprinkle it in front of the Covenant Box. Treat this incense as completely holy.

30.37 "Do not use the same formula to make any incense like it for yourselves. Treat it as a holy thing dedicated to me.

30.38 "If anyone makes any like it for use as perfume, he will no longer be considered one of my people."

# 31

31.1 The Lord said to Moses,

31.2 "I have chosen Bezalel, the son of Uri and grandson of Hur, from the tribe of Judah,

31.3 "and I have filled him with my power. I have given him understanding, skill, and ability for every kind of artistic work—

31.4 "for planning skillful designs and working them in gold, silver, and bronze;

31.5 "for cutting jewels to be set; for carving wood; and for every other kind of artistic work.

31.6 "I have also selected Oholiab son of Ahisamach, from the tribe of Dan, to work with him. I have also given great ability to all the other skilled workers, so that they can make everything I have commanded to be made:

31.7 "the Tent of my presence, the Covenant Box and its lid, all the furnishings of the Tent,

31.8 "the table and its equipment, the lampstand of pure gold and all its equipment, the altar for burning incense,

31.9 "the altar for burnt offerings and all its equipment, the washbasin and its base,

31.10 "the magnificent priestly garments for Aaron and his sons to use when they serve as priests,

31.11 "the anointing oil, and the sweet-smelling incense for the Holy

Place. In making all these things, they are to do exactly as I have commanded you."

31.12 The Lord commanded Moses

31.13 to tell the people of Israel, "Keep the Sabbath, my day of rest, because it is a sign between you and me for all time to come, to show that I, the Lord, have made you my own people.

31.14 "You must keep the day of rest, because it is sacred. Whoever does not keep it, but works on that day, is to be put to death.

31.15 "You have six days in which to do your work, but the seventh day is a solemn day of rest dedicated to me. Whoever does any work on that day is to be put to death.

31.16 "The people of Israel are to keep this day as a sign of the covenant.

31.17 "It is a permanent sign between the people of Israel and me, because I, the Lord, made heaven and earth in six days, and on the seventh day I stopped working and rested."

31.18 When God had finished speaking to Moses on Mount Sinai, he gave him the two stone tablets on which God himself had written the commandments.

# 32

32.1 When the people saw that Moses had not come down from the mountain but was staying there a long time, they gathered around Aaron and said to him, "We do not know what has happened to this man Moses, who led us out of Egypt; so make us a god to lead us."

32.2 Aaron said to them, "Take off the gold earrings which your wives, your sons, and your daughters are wearing, and bring them to me."

32.3 So all the people took off their gold earrings and brought them to Aaron.

32.4 He took the earrings, melted them, poured the gold into a mold, and made a gold bull-calf.

The people said, "Israel, this is our god, who led us out of Egypt!"

32.5 Then Aaron built an altar in front of the gold bull-calf and announced, "Tomorrow there will be a festival to honor the Lord."

32.6 Early the next morning they brought some animals to burn as sacrifices and others to eat as fellowship offerings. The people sat down to a feast, which turned into an orgy of drinking and sex.

32.7 The Lord said to Moses, "Hurry and go back down, because your people, whom you led out of Egypt, have sinned and rejected me.

³²·⁸ "They have already left the way that I commanded them to follow; they have made a bull-calf out of melted gold and have worshiped it and offered sacrifices to it. They are saying that this is their god, who led them out of Egypt.

³²·⁹ "I know how stubborn these people are.

³²·¹⁰ "Now, don't try to stop me. I am angry with them, and I am going to destroy them. Then I will make you and your descendants into a great nation."

³²·¹¹ But Moses pleaded with the Lord his God and said, "Lord, why should you be so angry with your people, whom you rescued from Egypt with great might and power?

³²·¹² "Why should the Egyptians be able to say that you led your people out of Egypt, planning to kill them in the mountains and destroy them completely? Stop being angry; change your mind and do not bring this disaster on your people.

³²·¹³ "Remember your servants Abraham, Isaac, and Jacob. Remember the solemn promise you made to them to give them as many descendants as there are stars in the sky and to give their descendants all that land you promised would be their possession forever."

³²·¹⁴ So the Lord changed his mind and did not bring on his people the disaster he had threatened.

³²·¹⁵ Moses went back down the mountain, carrying the two stone tablets with the commandments written on both sides.

³²·¹⁶ God himself had made the tablets and had engraved the commandments on them.

³²·¹⁷ Joshua heard the people shouting and said to Moses, "I hear the sound of battle in the camp."

³²·¹⁸ Moses said, "That doesn't sound like a shout of victory or a cry of defeat; it's the sound of singing."

³²·¹⁹ When Moses came close enough to the camp to see the bull-calf and to see the people dancing, he became furious. There at the foot of the mountain, he threw down the tablets he was carrying and broke them.

³²·²⁰ He took the bull-calf which they had made, melted it, ground it into fine powder, and mixed it with water. Then he made the people of Israel drink it.

³²·²¹ He said to Aaron, "What did these people do to you, that you have made them commit such a terrible sin?"

³²·²² Aaron answered, "Don't be angry with me; you know how de-

termined these people are to do evil.

<sup>32.23</sup> "They said to me, 'We don't know what has happened to this man Moses, who brought us out of Egypt; so make us a god to lead us.'

<sup>32.24</sup> "I asked them to bring me their gold ornaments, and those who had any took them off and gave them to me. I threw the ornaments into the fire and out came this bull-calf!"

<sup>32.25</sup> Moses saw that Aaron had let the people get out of control and make fools of themselves in front of their enemies.

<sup>32.26</sup> So he stood at the gate of the camp and shouted, "Everyone who is on the Lord's side come over here!" So all the Levites gathered around him,

<sup>32.27</sup> and he said to them, "The Lord God of Israel commands every one of you to put on your sword and go through the camp from this gate to the other and kill your brothers, your friends, and your neighbors."

<sup>32.28</sup> The Levites obeyed, and killed about three thousand men that day.

<sup>32.29</sup> Moses said to the Levites, "Today you have consecrated yourselves as priests in the service of the Lord by killing your sons and brothers, so the Lord has given you his blessing."

<sup>32.30</sup> The next day Moses said to the people, "You have committed a terrible sin. But now I will again go up the mountain to the Lord; perhaps I can obtain forgiveness for your sin."

<sup>32.31</sup> Moses then returned to the Lord and said, "These people have committed a terrible sin. They have made a god out of gold and worshiped it.

<sup>32.32</sup> "Please forgive their sin; but if you won't, then remove my name from the book in which you have written the names of your people."

<sup>32.33</sup> The Lord answered, "It is those who have sinned against me whose names I will remove from my book.

<sup>32.34</sup> "Now go, lead the people to the place I told you about. Remember that my angel will guide you, but the time is coming when I will punish these people for their sin."

<sup>32.35</sup> So the Lord sent a disease on the people, because they had caused Aaron to make the gold bull-calf.

# 33

<sup>33.1</sup> The Lord said to Moses, "Leave this place, you and the people you brought out of Egypt, and go to the land that I promised to

give to Abraham, Isaac, and Jacob and to their descendants.

<sup>33.2</sup> "I will send an angel to guide you, and I will drive out the Canaanites, the Amorites, the Hittites, the Perizzites, the Hivites, and the Jebusites.

<sup>33.3</sup> "You are going to a rich and fertile land. But I will not go with you myself, because you are a stubborn people, and I might destroy you on the way."

<sup>33.4</sup> When the people heard this, they began to mourn and did not wear jewelry any more.

<sup>33.5</sup> For the Lord had commanded Moses to tell them, "You are a stubborn people. If I were to go with you even for a moment, I would completely destroy you. Now take off your jewelry, and I will decide what to do with you."

<sup>33.6</sup> So after they left Mount Sinai, the people of Israel no longer wore jewelry.

<sup>33.7</sup> Whenever the people of Israel set up camp, Moses would take the sacred Tent and put it up some distance outside the camp. It was called the Tent of the Lord's presence, and anyone who wanted to consult the Lord would go out to it.

<sup>33.8</sup> Whenever Moses went out there, the people would stand at the door of their tents and watch Moses until he entered it.

<sup>33.9</sup> After Moses had gone in, the pillar of cloud would come down and stay at the door of the Tent, and the Lord would speak to Moses from the cloud.

<sup>33.10</sup> As soon as the people saw the pillar of cloud at the door of the Tent, they would bow down.

<sup>33.11</sup> The Lord would speak with Moses face-to-face, just as someone speaks with a friend. Then Moses would return to the camp. But the young man who was his helper, Joshua son of Nun, stayed in the Tent.

<sup>33.12</sup> Moses said to the Lord, "It is true that you have told me to lead these people to that land, but you did not tell me whom you would send with me. You have said that you know me well and are pleased with me.

<sup>33.13</sup> "Now if you are, tell me your plans, so that I may serve you and continue to please you. Remember also that you have chosen this nation to be your own."

<sup>33.14</sup> The Lord said, "I will go with you, and I will give you victory."

<sup>33.15</sup> Moses replied, "If you do not go with us, don't make us leave this place.

<sup>33.16</sup> "How will anyone know that you are pleased with your people

and <u>with me</u> if you do not go <u>with us</u>? Your presence <u>with us</u> will distinguish us <u>from any other people</u> on earth."

<sup>33.17</sup> The Lord said <u>to Moses</u>, "I will do just as you have asked, because I know you very well and I am pleased <u>with you</u>."

<sup>33.18</sup> Then Moses requested, "Please, let me see the dazzling light <u>of your presence</u>."

<sup>33.19</sup> The Lord answered, "I will make all my splendor pass <u>before</u> <u>you</u> and <u>in your presence</u> I will pronounce my sacred name. I am the Lord, and I show compassion and pity <u>on those</u> I choose.

<sup>33.20</sup> "I will not let you see my face, because no one can see me and stay alive,

<sup>33.21</sup> "but here is a place <u>beside me</u> where you can stand <u>on a rock</u>.

<sup>33.22</sup> "When the dazzling light <u>of my presence</u> passes by, I will put you <u>in an opening</u> <u>in the rock</u> and cover you <u>with my hand</u> until I have passed by.

<sup>33.23</sup> "Then I will take my hand away, and you will see my back but not my face."

# 34

<sup>34.1</sup> The Lord said <u>to Moses</u>, "Cut two stone tablets <u>like the first</u> <u>ones</u>, and I will write <u>on them</u> the words that were <u>on the first tab-</u> <u>lets</u>, which you broke.

<sup>34.2</sup> "Get ready tomorrow morning, and come up Mount Sinai to meet me there <u>at the top</u>.

<sup>34.3</sup> "No one is to come up <u>with you</u>; no one is to be seen <u>on any part</u> <u>of the mountain</u>; and no sheep or cattle are to graze <u>at the foot</u> of <u>the mountain</u>."

<sup>34.4</sup> So Moses cut two more stone tablets, and early the next morning he carried them up Mount Sinai, just as the Lord had commanded.

<sup>34.5</sup> The Lord came down <u>in a cloud</u>, stood <u>with him</u> there, and pronounced his holy name, the Lord.

<sup>34.6</sup> The Lord then passed <u>in front</u> <u>of him</u> and called out, "I, the Lord, am a God who is full <u>of compassion and pity</u>, who is not easily angered and who shows great love and faithfulness.

<sup>34.7</sup> "I keep my promise <u>for thousands</u> <u>of generations</u> and forgive evil and sin; but I will not fail to punish children and grandchildren <u>to the third and fourth generation</u> <u>for the sins</u> <u>of their par-</u> <u>ents</u>."

<sup>34.8</sup> Moses quickly bowed down <u>to the ground</u> and worshiped.

<sup>34.9</sup> He said, "Lord, if you really are pleased <u>with me</u>, I ask you to

go with us. These people are stubborn, but forgive our evil and our sin, and accept us as your own people."

<sup>34.10</sup> The Lord said to Moses, "I now make a covenant with the people of Israel. In their presence I will do great things such as have never been done anywhere on earth among any of the nations. All the people will see what great things I, the Lord, can do, because I am going to do an awesome thing for you.

<sup>34.11</sup> "Obey the laws that I am giving you today. I will drive out the Amorites, the Canaanites, the Hittites, the Perizzites, the Hivites, and the Jebusites, as you advance.

<sup>34.12</sup> "Do not make any treaties with the people of the country into which you are going, because this could be a fatal trap for you.

<sup>34.13</sup> "Instead, tear down their altars, destroy their sacred pillars, and cut down their symbols of the goddess Asherah.

<sup>34.14</sup> "Do not worship any other god, because I, the Lord, tolerate no rivals.

<sup>34.15</sup> "Do not make any treaties with the people of the country, because when they worship their pagan gods and sacrifice to them, they will invite you to join them, and you will be tempted to eat the food they offer to their gods.

<sup>34.16</sup> "Your sons might marry those foreign women, who would lead them to be unfaithful to me and to worship their pagan gods.

<sup>34.17</sup> "Do not make gods of metal and worship them.

<sup>34.18</sup> "Keep the Festival of Unleavened Bread. As I have commanded you, eat unleavened bread for seven days in the month of Abib, because it was in that month that you left Egypt.

<sup>34.19</sup> "Every first-born son and first-born male domestic animal belongs to me,

<sup>34.20</sup> "but you are to buy back every first-born donkey by offering a lamb in its place. If you do not buy it back, break its neck. Buy back every first-born son.

"No one is to appear before me without an offering.

<sup>34.21</sup> "You have six days in which to do your work, but do not work on the seventh day, not even during plowing time or harvest.

<sup>34.22</sup> "Keep the Harvest Festival when you begin to harvest the first crop of your wheat, and keep the Festival of Shelters in the autumn when you gather your fruit.

<sup>34.23</sup> "Three times a year all of your men must come to worship me, the Lord, the God of Israel.

<sup>34.24</sup> "After I have driven out the nations before you and extended your territory, no one will try to conquer your country during the

three festivals.

<sup>34.25</sup> "Do not offer bread made with yeast when you sacrifice an animal to me. Do not keep until the following morning any part of the animal killed at the Passover Festival.

<sup>34.26</sup> "Each year bring to the house of the Lord the first grain that you harvest.

"Do not cook a young sheep or goat in its mother's milk."

<sup>34.27</sup> The Lord said to Moses, "Write these words down, because it is on the basis of these words that I am making a covenant with you and with Israel."

<sup>34.28</sup> Moses stayed there with the Lord forty days and nights, eating and drinking nothing. He wrote on the tablets the words of the covenant—the Ten Commandments.

<sup>34.29</sup> When Moses went down from Mount Sinai carrying the Ten Commandments, his face was shining because he had been speaking with the Lord; but he did not know it.

<sup>34.30</sup> Aaron and all the people looked at Moses and saw that his face was shining, and they were afraid to go near him.

<sup>34.31</sup> But Moses called them, and Aaron and all the leaders of the community went to him, and Moses spoke with them.

<sup>34.32</sup> After that, all the people of Israel gathered around him, and Moses gave them all the laws that the Lord had given him on Mount Sinai.

<sup>34.33</sup> When Moses had finished speaking with them, he covered his face with a veil.

<sup>34.34</sup> Whenever Moses went into the Tent of the Lord's presence to speak to the Lord, he would take the veil off. When he came out, he would tell the people of Israel everything that he had been commanded to say,

<sup>34.35</sup> and they would see that his face was shining. Then he would put the veil back on until the next time he went to speak with the Lord.

# 35

<sup>35.1</sup> Moses called together the whole community of the people of Israel and said to them, "This is what the Lord has commanded you to do:

<sup>35.2</sup> "You have six days in which to do your work, but the seventh day is to be sacred, a solemn day of rest dedicated to me, the Lord. Anyone who does any work on that day is to be put to death.

<sup>35.3</sup> "Do not even light a fire in your homes on the Sabbath."

<sup>35.4</sup> Moses said to all the people of Israel, "This is what the Lord has commanded:

<sup>35.5</sup> "Make an offering to the Lord. Everyone who wishes to do so is to bring an offering of gold, silver, or bronze;

<sup>35.6</sup> "fine linen; blue, purple, and red wool; cloth made of goats' hair;

<sup>35.7</sup> "rams' skin dyed red; fine leather; acacia wood;

<sup>35.8</sup> "oil for the lamps; spices for the anointing oil and for the sweet-smelling incense;

<sup>35.9</sup> "carnelians and other jewels to be set in the High Priest's ephod and in his breastpiece.

<sup>35.10</sup> "All the skilled workers among you are to come and make everything that the Lord commanded:

<sup>35.11</sup> "the Tent, its covering and its outer covering, its hooks and its frames, its crossbars, its posts, and its bases;

<sup>35.12</sup> "the Covenant Box, its poles, its lid, and the curtain to screen it off;

<sup>35.13</sup> "the table, its poles, and all its equipment; the bread offered to God;

<sup>35.14</sup> "the lampstand for the light and its equipment; the lamps with their oil;

<sup>35.15</sup> "the altar for burning incense and its poles; the anointing oil; the sweet-smelling incense; the curtain for the entrance of the Tent;

<sup>35.16</sup> "the altar on which to burn offerings, with its bronze grating attached, its poles, and all its equipment; the washbasin and its base;

<sup>35.17</sup> "the curtains for the enclosure, its posts and bases; the curtain for the entrance of the enclosure;

<sup>35.18</sup> "Tent pegs and ropes for the Tent and the enclosure;

<sup>35.19</sup> "and the magnificent garments the priests are to wear when they serve in the Holy Place—the sacred clothes for Aaron the priest and for his sons."

<sup>35.20</sup> All the people of Israel left,

<sup>35.21</sup> and everyone who wished to do so brought an offering to the Lord for making the Tent of the Lord's presence. They brought everything needed for use in worship and for making the priestly garments.

<sup>35.22</sup> All who wanted to, both men and women, brought decorative pins, earrings, rings, necklaces, and all kinds of gold jewelry and dedicated them to the Lord.

<sup>35.23</sup> Everyone who had fine linen; blue, purple, or red wool; cloth of

goats' hair; rams' skin dyed red; or fine leather, brought it.

<sup>35.24</sup> All who were able to contribute silver or bronze brought their offering for the Lord, and all who had acacia wood which could be used for any of the work brought it.

<sup>35.25</sup> All the skilled women brought fine linen thread and thread of blue, purple, and red wool, which they had made.

<sup>35.26</sup> They also made thread of goats' hair.

<sup>35.27</sup> The leaders brought carnelians and other jewels to be set in the ephod and the breastpiece

<sup>35.28</sup> and spices and oil for the lamps, for the anointing oil, and for the sweet-smelling incense.

<sup>35.29</sup> All the people of Israel who wanted to brought their offering to the Lord for the work which he had commanded Moses to do.

<sup>35.30</sup> Moses said to the Israelites, "The Lord has chosen Bezalel, the son of Uri and grandson of Hur from the tribe of Judah.

<sup>35.31</sup> "God has filled him with his power and given him skill, ability, and understanding for every kind of artistic work,

<sup>35.32</sup> "for planning skillful designs and working them in gold, silver, and bronze;

<sup>35.33</sup> "cutting jewels to be set; for carving wood; and for every other kind of artistic work.

<sup>35.34</sup> "The Lord has given to him and to Oholiab son of Ahisamach, from the tribe of Dan, the ability to teach their crafts to others.

<sup>35.35</sup> "He has given them skill in all kinds of work done by engravers, designers, and weavers of fine linen; blue, purple, and red wool; and other cloth. They are able to do all kinds of work and are skillful designers.

# 36

<sup>36.1</sup> "Bezalel, Oholiab, and all the other workers to whom the Lord has given skill and understanding, who know how to make everything needed to build the sacred Tent, are to make everything just as the Lord has commanded."

<sup>36.2</sup> Moses called Bezalel, Oholiab, and all the other skilled men to whom the Lord had given ability and who were willing to help, and Moses told them to start working.

<sup>36.3</sup> They received from him all the offerings which the Israelites had brought for constructing the sacred Tent. But the people of Israel continued to bring Moses their offerings every morning.

<sup>36.4</sup> Then the skilled men who were doing the work went

<sup>36.5</sup> and told Moses, "The people are bringing more than is needed

for the work which the Lord commanded to be done."

<sup>36.6</sup> So Moses sent a command throughout the camp that no one was to make any further contribution for the sacred Tent; so the people did not bring any more.

<sup>36.7</sup> What had already been brought was more than enough to finish all the work.

<sup>36.8</sup> The most skilled men among those doing the work made the Tent of the Lord's presence. They made it out of ten pieces of fine linen woven with blue, purple, and red wool and embroidered with figures of winged creatures.

<sup>36.9</sup> Each piece was the same size, 14 yards long and 2 yards wide.

<sup>36.10</sup> They sewed five of them together in one set and did the same with the other five.

<sup>36.11</sup> They made loops of blue cloth on the edge of the outside piece in each set.

<sup>36.12</sup> They put fifty loops on the first piece of the first set and fifty loops matching them on the last piece of the second set.

<sup>36.13</sup> They made fifty gold hooks, with which to join the two sets into one piece.

<sup>36.14</sup> Then they made a cover for the Tent out of eleven pieces of cloth made of goats' hair.

<sup>36.15</sup> They made them all the same size, 15 yards long and 2 yards wide.

<sup>36.16</sup> They sewed five of them together in one set and the other six in another set.

<sup>36.17</sup> They put fifty loops on the edge of the last piece of one set and fifty loops on the edge of the other set.

<sup>36.18</sup> They made fifty bronze hooks to join the two sets, so as to form one cover.

<sup>36.19</sup> They made two more coverings, one of rams' skin dyed red and the other of fine leather, to serve as an outer cover.

<sup>36.20</sup> They made upright frames of acacia wood for the Tent.

<sup>36.21</sup> Each frame was 15 feet tall and 27 inches wide,

<sup>36.22</sup> with two matching projections, so that the frames could be joined together. All the frames had these projections.

<sup>36.23</sup> They made twenty frames for the south side

<sup>36.24</sup> and forty silver bases to go under them, two bases under each frame to hold its two projections.

<sup>36.25</sup> They made twenty frames for the north side of the Tent

<sup>36.26</sup> and forty silver bases, two under each frame.

<sup>36.27</sup> For the back of the Tent, on the west, they made six frames

<sup>36.28</sup> and two frames for the corners.

<sup>36.29</sup> These corner frames were joined at the bottom and connected all the way to the top. The two frames that formed the two corners were made in this way.

<sup>36.30</sup> So there were eight frames and sixteen silver bases, two under each frame.

<sup>36.31</sup> They made fifteen crossbars of acacia wood, five for the frames on one side of the Tent,

<sup>36.32</sup> five for the frames on the other side, and five for the frames on the west end, at the back.

<sup>36.33</sup> The middle crossbar, set halfway up the frames, extended from one end of the Tent to the other.

<sup>36.34</sup> They covered the frames with gold and fitted them with gold rings to hold the crossbars, which were also covered with gold.

<sup>36.35</sup> They made a curtain of fine linen, woven with blue, purple, and red wool and embroidered it with figures of winged creatures.

<sup>36.36</sup> They made four posts of acacia wood to hold the curtain, covered them with gold, and fitted them with gold hooks. Then they made four silver bases to hold the posts.

<sup>36.37</sup> For the entrance of the Tent they made a curtain of fine linen woven with blue, purple, and red wool and decorated with embroidery.

<sup>36.38</sup> For this curtain they made five posts fitted with hooks, covered their tops and their rods with gold, and made five bronze bases for the posts.

# 37

<sup>37.1</sup> Bezalel made the Covenant Box out of acacia wood, 45 inches long, 27 inches wide, and 27 inches high.

<sup>37.2</sup> He covered it with pure gold inside and out and put a gold border all around it.

<sup>37.3</sup> He made four carrying rings of gold for it and attached them to its four feet, with two rings on each side.

<sup>37.4</sup> He made carrying poles of acacia wood, covered them with gold,

<sup>37.5</sup> and put them through the rings on each side of the Box.

<sup>37.6</sup> He made a lid of pure gold, 45 inches long and 27 inches wide.

<sup>37.7</sup> He made two winged creatures of hammered gold,

<sup>37.8</sup> one for each end of the lid. He made them so that they formed one piece with the lid.

<sup>37.9</sup> The winged creatures faced each other across the lid, and their outspread wings covered it.

<sup>37.10</sup> He made the table out of acacia wood, 36 inches long, 18 inches wide, and 27 inches high.

<sup>37.11</sup> He covered it with pure gold and put a gold border around it.

<sup>37.12</sup> He made a rim 3 inches wide around it and put a gold border around the rim.

<sup>37.13</sup> He made four carrying rings of gold for it and put them at the four corners, where the legs were.

<sup>37.14</sup> The rings to hold the poles for carrying the table were placed near the rim.

<sup>37.15</sup> He made the poles of acacia wood and covered them with gold.

<sup>37.16</sup> He made the dishes of pure gold for the table: the plates, the cups, the jars, and the bowls to be used for the wine offering.

<sup>37.17</sup> He made the lampstand of pure gold. He made its base and its shaft of hammered gold; its decorative flowers, including buds and petals, formed one piece with it.

<sup>37.18</sup> Six branches extended from its sides, three from each side.

<sup>37.19</sup> Each of the six branches had three decorative flowers shaped like almond blossoms with buds and petals.

<sup>37.20</sup> The shaft of the lampstand had four decorative flowers shaped like almond blossoms with buds and petals.

<sup>37.21</sup> There was one bud below each of the three pairs of branches.

<sup>37.22</sup> The buds, the branches, and the lampstand were a single piece of pure hammered gold.

<sup>37.23</sup> He made seven lamps for the lampstand, and he made its tongs and trays of pure gold.

<sup>37.24</sup> He used seventy-five pounds of pure gold to make the lampstand and all its equipment.

<sup>37.25</sup> He made an altar out of acacia wood, for burning incense. It was square, 18 inches long and 18 inches wide, and it was 36 inches high. Its projections at the four corners formed one piece with it.

<sup>37.26</sup> He covered its top, all four sides, and its projections with pure gold and put a gold border around it.

<sup>37.27</sup> He made two gold carrying rings for it and attached them below the border on the two sides, to hold the poles with which it was to be carried.

<sup>37.28</sup> He made the poles of acacia wood and covered them with gold.

<sup>37.29</sup> He also made the sacred anointing oil and the pure sweet-smelling incense, mixed like perfume.

# 38

<sup>38.1</sup> For burning offerings, he made an altar out of acacia wood. It was square, 7½ feet long and 7½ feet wide, and it was 4½ feet high. <sup>38.2</sup> He made the projections at the top of the four corners, so that they formed one piece with the altar. He covered it all with bronze. <sup>38.3</sup> He also made all the equipment for the altar: the pans, the shovels, the bowls, the hooks, and the fire pans. All this equipment was made of bronze. <sup>38.4</sup> He made a bronze grating and put it under the rim of the altar, so that it reached halfway up the altar. <sup>38.5</sup> He made four carrying rings and put them on the four corners. <sup>38.6</sup> He made carrying poles of acacia wood, covered them with bronze, <sup>38.7</sup> and put them in the rings on each side of the altar. The altar was made of boards and was hollow.

<sup>38.8</sup> He made the bronze basin and its bronze base out of the mirrors belonging to the women who served at the entrance of the Tent of the Lord's presence.

<sup>38.9</sup> For the Tent of the Lord's presence he made the enclosure out of fine linen curtains. On the south side the curtains were 50 yards long, <sup>38.10</sup> supported by twenty bronze posts in twenty bronze bases, with hooks and rods made of silver. <sup>38.11</sup> The enclosure was the same on the north side. <sup>38.12</sup> On the west side there were curtains 25 yards long, with ten posts and ten bases and with hooks and rods made of silver. <sup>38.13</sup> On the east side, where the entrance was, the enclosure was also 25 yards wide. <sup>38.14-15</sup> On each side of the entrance there were 7½ yards of curtains, with three posts and three bases. <sup>38.16</sup> All the curtains around the enclosure were made of fine linen. <sup>38.17</sup> The bases for the posts were made of bronze, and the hooks, the rods, and the covering of the tops of the posts were made of silver. All the posts around the enclosure were connected with silver rods. <sup>38.18</sup> The curtain for the entrance of the enclosure was made of fine linen woven with blue, purple, and red wool and decorated with embroidery. It was 10 yards long and 2½ yards high, like the curtains of the enclosure. <sup>38.19</sup> It was supported by four posts in four bronze bases. Their hooks, the covering of their tops, and their rods were made of sil-

ver.

<sup>38.20</sup> All the pegs for the Tent and for the surrounding enclosure were made of bronze.

<sup>38.21</sup> Here is a list of the amounts of the metals used in the Tent of the Lord's presence, where the two stone tablets were kept on which the Ten Commandments were written. The list was ordered by Moses and made by the Levites who worked under the direction of Ithamar son of Aaron the priest.

<sup>38.22</sup> Bezalel, the son of Uri and grandson of Hur from the tribe of Judah, made everything that the Lord had commanded.

<sup>38.23</sup> His helper, Oholiab son of Ahisamach, from the tribe of Dan, was an engraver, a designer, and a weaver of fine linen and of blue, purple, and red wool.

<sup>38.24</sup> All the gold that had been dedicated to the Lord for the sacred Tent weighed 2,195 pounds, weighed according to the official standard.

<sup>38.25</sup> The silver from the census of the community weighed 7,550 pounds, weighed according to the official standard.

<sup>38.26</sup> This amount equaled the total paid by all persons enrolled in the census, each one paying the required amount, weighed according to the official standard. There were 603,550 men twenty years old or older enrolled in the census.

<sup>38.27</sup> Of the silver, 7,500 pounds were used to make the hundred bases for the sacred Tent and for the curtain, 75 pounds for each base.

<sup>38.28</sup> With the remaining 50 pounds of silver Bezalel made the rods, the hooks for the posts, and the covering for their tops.

<sup>38.29</sup> The bronze which was dedicated to the Lord amounted to 5,310 pounds.

<sup>38.30</sup> With it he made the bases for the entrance of the Tent of the Lord's presence, the bronze altar with its bronze grating, all the equipment for the altar,

<sup>38.31</sup> the bases for the surrounding enclosure and for the entrance of the enclosure, and all the pegs for the Tent and the surrounding enclosure.

# 39

<sup>39.1</sup> With the blue, purple, and red wool they made the magnificent garments which the priests were to wear when they served in the Holy Place. They made the priestly garments for Aaron, as the Lord had commanded Moses.

<sup>39.2</sup> They made the ephod of fine linen; blue, purple, and red wool; and gold thread.
<sup>39.3</sup> They hammered out sheets of gold and cut them into thin strips to be worked into the fine linen and into the blue, purple, and red wool.
<sup>39.4</sup> They made two shoulder straps for the ephod and attached them to its sides, so that it could be fastened.
<sup>39.5</sup> The finely woven belt, made of the same materials, was attached to the ephod so as to form one piece with it, as the Lord had commanded Moses.
<sup>39.6</sup> They prepared the carnelians and mounted them in gold settings; they were skillfully engraved with the names of the twelve sons of Jacob.
<sup>39.7</sup> They put them on the shoulder straps of the ephod to represent the twelve tribes of Israel, just as the Lord had commanded Moses.
<sup>39.8</sup> They made the breastpiece of the same materials as the ephod and with similar embroidery.
<sup>39.9</sup> It was square and folded double, 9 inches long and 9 inches wide.
<sup>39.10</sup> They mounted four rows of precious stones on it: in the first row they mounted a ruby, a topaz, and a garnet;
<sup>39.11</sup> in the second row, an emerald, a sapphire, and a diamond;
<sup>39.12</sup> in the third row, a turquoise, an agate, and an amethyst;
<sup>39.13</sup> and in the fourth row, a beryl, a carnelian, and a jasper. These were mounted in gold settings.
<sup>39.14</sup> Each of the twelve stones had engraved on it the name of one of the sons of Jacob, in order to represent the twelve tribes of Israel.
<sup>39.15</sup> For the breastpiece they made chains of pure gold, twisted like cords.
<sup>39.16</sup> They made two gold settings and two gold rings and attached the two rings to the upper corners of the breastpiece.
<sup>39.17</sup> They fastened the two gold cords to the two rings
<sup>39.18</sup> and fastened the other two ends of the cords to the two settings and in this way attached them in front to the shoulder straps of the ephod.
<sup>39.19</sup> They made two rings of gold and attached them to the lower corners of the breastpiece, on the inside edge next to the ephod.
<sup>39.20</sup> They made two more gold rings and attached them to the lower part of the front of the two shoulder straps of the ephod, near

the seam and above the finely woven belt.

<sup>39.21</sup> Just as the Lord had commanded Moses, they tied the rings of the breastpiece to the rings of the ephod with a blue cord, so that the breastpiece rested above the belt and did not come loose.

<sup>39.22</sup> The robe that goes under the ephod was made entirely of blue wool.

<sup>39.23</sup> The hole for the head was reinforced with a woven binding to keep it from tearing.

<sup>39.24-26</sup> All around its lower hem they put pomegranates of fine linen and of blue, purple, and red wool, alternating with bells of pure gold, just as the Lord had commanded Moses.

<sup>39.27</sup> They made the shirts for Aaron and his sons,

<sup>39.28</sup> and the turban, the caps, the linen shorts,

<sup>39.29</sup> and the sash of fine linen and of blue, purple, and red wool, decorated with embroidery, as the Lord had commanded Moses.

<sup>39.30</sup> They made the ornament, the sacred sign of dedication, out of pure gold, and they engraved on it "Dedicated to the Lord."

<sup>39.31</sup> They tied it to the front of the turban with a blue cord, just as the Lord had commanded Moses.

<sup>39.32</sup> All the work on the Tent of the Lord's presence was finally completed. The Israelites made everything just as the Lord had commanded Moses.

<sup>39.33</sup> They brought to Moses the Tent and all its equipment, its hooks, its frames, its crossbars, its posts, and its bases;

<sup>39.34</sup> the covering of rams' skin dyed red; the covering of fine leather; the curtain;

<sup>39.35</sup> the Covenant Box containing the stone tablets, its poles, and its lid;

<sup>39.36</sup> the table and all its equipment, and the bread offered to God;

<sup>39.37</sup> the lampstand of pure gold, its lamps, all its equipment, and the oil for the lamps;

<sup>39.38</sup> the gold altar; the anointing oil; the sweet-smelling incense; the curtain for the entrance of the Tent;

<sup>39.39</sup> the bronze altar with its bronze grating, its poles, and all its equipment; the washbasin and its base;

<sup>39.40</sup> the curtains for the enclosure and its posts and bases; the curtain for the entrance of the enclosure and its ropes; the Tent pegs; all the equipment to be used in the Tent;

<sup>39.41</sup> and the magnificent garments the priests were to wear in the Holy Place—the sacred clothes for Aaron the priest and for his sons.

<sup>39.42</sup> The Israelites had done all the work just as the Lord had commanded Moses.

<sup>39.43</sup> Moses examined everything and saw that they had made it all just as the Lord had commanded. So Moses blessed them.

# 40

<sup>40.1</sup> The Lord said to Moses,

<sup>40.2</sup> "On the first day of the first month set up the Tent of the Lord's presence.

<sup>40.3</sup> "Place in it the Covenant Box containing the Ten Commandments and put the curtain in front of it.

<sup>40.4</sup> "Bring in the table and place the equipment on it. Also bring in the lampstand and set up the lamps on it.

<sup>40.5</sup> "Put the gold altar for burning incense in front of the Covenant Box and hang the curtain at the entrance of the Tent.

<sup>40.6</sup> "Put in front of the Tent the altar for burning offerings.

<sup>40.7</sup> "Put the washbasin between the Tent and the altar and fill it with water.

<sup>40.8</sup> "Put up the surrounding enclosure and hang the curtain at its entrance.

<sup>40.9</sup> "Then dedicate the Tent and all its equipment by anointing it with the sacred oil, and it will be holy.

<sup>40.10</sup> "Next, dedicate the altar and all its equipment by anointing it, and it will be completely holy.

<sup>40.11</sup> "Also dedicate the washbasin and its base in the same way.

<sup>40.12</sup> "Bring Aaron and his sons to the entrance of the Tent, and have them take a ritual bath.

<sup>40.13</sup> "Dress Aaron in the priestly garments, anoint him, and in this way consecrate him, so that he can serve me as priest.

<sup>40.14</sup> "Bring his sons and put the shirts on them.

<sup>40.15</sup> "Then anoint them, just as you anointed their father, so that they can serve me as priests. This anointing will make them priests for all time to come."

<sup>40.16</sup> Moses did everything just as the Lord had commanded.

<sup>40.17</sup> So on the first day of the first month of the second year after they left Egypt, the Tent of the Lord's presence was set up.

<sup>40.18</sup> Moses put down its bases, set up its frames, attached its crossbars, and put up its posts.

<sup>40.19</sup> He spread out the covering over the Tent and put the outer covering over it, just as the Lord had commanded.

<sup>40.20</sup> Then he took the two stone tablets and put them in the Cove-

nant Box. He put the poles in the rings of the Box and put the lid on it.

⁴⁰·²¹ Then he put the Box in the Tent and hung up the curtain. In this way he screened off the Covenant Box, just as the Lord had commanded.

⁴⁰·²² He put the table in the Tent, on the north side outside the curtain,

⁴⁰·²³ and placed on it the bread offered to the Lord, just as the Lord had commanded.

⁴⁰·²⁴ He put the lampstand in the Tent, on the south side, opposite the table,

⁴⁰·²⁵ and there in the Lord's presence he lit the lamps, just as the Lord had commanded.

⁴⁰·²⁶ He put the gold altar in the Tent, in front of the curtain,

⁴⁰·²⁷ and burned the sweet-smelling incense, just as the Lord had commanded.

⁴⁰·²⁸ He hung the curtain at the entrance of the Tent,

⁴⁰·²⁹ and there in front of the curtain he placed the altar for burning offerings. On it he sacrificed the burnt offering and the grain offering, just as the Lord had commanded.

⁴⁰·³⁰ He put the washbasin between the Tent and the altar and filled it with water.

⁴⁰·³¹ Moses, Aaron, and his sons washed their hands and their feet there

⁴⁰·³² whenever they went into the Tent or to the altar, just as the Lord had commanded.

⁴⁰·³³ Moses set up the enclosure around the Tent and the altar and hung the curtain at the entrance of the enclosure. So he finished all the work.

⁴⁰·³⁴ Then the cloud covered the Tent and the dazzling light of the Lord's presence filled it.

⁴⁰·³⁵ Because of this, Moses could not go into the Tent.

⁴⁰·³⁶ The Israelites moved their camp to another place only when the cloud lifted from the Tent.

⁴⁰·³⁷ As long as the cloud stayed there, they did not move their camp.

⁴⁰·³⁸ During all their wanderings they could see the cloud of the Lord's presence over the Tent during the day and a fire burning above it during the night.

# MATTHEW

# Matthew

# 1

<sup>1.1</sup> This is the list of the ancestors of Jesus Christ, a descendant of David, who was a descendant of Abraham.

<sup>1.2-6a</sup> From Abraham to King David, the following ancestors are listed: Abraham, Isaac, Jacob, Judah and his brothers; then Perez and Zerah (their mother was Tamar), Hezron, Ram, Amminadab, Nahshon, Salmon, Boaz (his mother was Rahab), Obed (his mother was Ruth), Jesse, and King David.

<sup>1.6b-11</sup> From David to the time when the people of Israel were taken into exile in Babylon, the following ancestors are listed: David, Solomon (his mother was the woman who had been Uriah's wife), Rehoboam, Abijah, Asa, Jehoshaphat, Jehoram, Uzziah, Jotham, Ahaz, Hezekiah, Manasseh, Amon, Josiah, and Jehoiachin and his brothers.

<sup>1.12-16</sup> From the time after the exile in Babylon to the birth of Jesus, the following ancestors are listed: Jehoiachin, Shealtiel, Zerubbabel, Abiud, Eliakim, Azor, Zadok, Achim, Eliud, Eleazar, Matthan, Jacob, and Joseph, who married Mary, the mother of Jesus, who was called the Messiah.

<sup>1.17</sup> So then, there were fourteen generations from Abraham to David, and fourteen from David to the exile in Babylon, and fourteen from then to the birth of the Messiah.

<sup>1.18</sup> This was how the birth of Jesus Christ took place. His mother Mary was engaged to Joseph, but before they were married, she found out that she was going to have a baby by the Holy Spirit.

<sup>1.19</sup> Joseph was a man who always did what was right, but he did not want to disgrace Mary publicly; so he made plans to break the engagement privately.

<sup>1.20</sup> While he was thinking about this, an angel of the Lord appeared to him in a dream and said, "Joseph, descendant of David, do not be afraid to take Mary to be your wife. For it is by the Holy Spirit that she has conceived.

<sup>1.21</sup> "She will have a son, and you will name him Jesus — because he will save his people from their sins."

<sup>1.22</sup> Now all this happened in order to make come true what the Lord had said through the prophet,

<sup>1.23</sup> "A virgin will become pregnant and have a son, and he will be called Immanuel" (which means, "God is with us").

<sup>1.24</sup> So when Joseph woke up, he married Mary, as the angel of the

Lord had told him to.
<sup></sup> But he had no sexual relations with her before she gave birth to her son. And Joseph named him Jesus.

2

2.1 Jesus was born in the town of Bethlehem in Judea, during the time when Herod was king. Soon afterward, some men who studied the stars came from the East to Jerusalem
2.2 and asked, "Where is the baby born to be the king of the Jews? We saw his star when it came up in the east, and we have come to worship him."
2.3 When King Herod heard about this, he was very upset, and so was everyone else in Jerusalem.
2.4 He called together all the chief priests and the teachers of the Law and asked them, "Where will the Messiah be born?"
2.5 "In the town of Bethlehem in Judea," they answered. "For this is what the prophet wrote:
2.6 'Bethlehem in the land of Judah, you are by no means the least of the leading cities of Judah; for from you will come a leader who will guide my people Israel.'"
2.7 So Herod called the visitors from the East to a secret meeting and found out from them the exact time the star had appeared.
2.8 Then he sent them to Bethlehem with these instructions: "Go and make a careful search for the child; and when you find him, let me know, so that I too may go and worship him."
2.9-10 And so they left, and on their way they saw the same star they had seen in the East. When they saw it, how happy they were, what joy was theirs! It went ahead of them until it stopped over the place where the child was.
2.11 They went into the house, and when they saw the child with his mother Mary, they knelt down and worshiped him. They brought out their gifts of gold, frankincense, and myrrh, and presented them to him.
2.12 Then they returned to their country by another road, since God had warned them in a dream not to go back to Herod.
2.13 After they had left, an angel of the Lord appeared in a dream to Joseph and said, "Herod will be looking for the child in order to kill him. So get up, take the child and his mother and escape to Egypt, and stay there until I tell you to leave."
2.14 Joseph got up, took the child and his mother, and left during the night for Egypt,

2.15 where he stayed until Herod died. This was done to make come true what the Lord had said through the prophet, "I called my Son out of Egypt."

2.16 When Herod realized that the visitors from the East had tricked him, he was furious. He gave orders to kill all the boys in Bethlehem and its neighborhood who were two years old and younger — this was done in accordance with what he had learned from the visitors about the time when the star had appeared.

2.17 In this way what the prophet Jeremiah had said came true:

2.18 "A sound is heard in Ramah, the sound of bitter weeping. Rachel is crying for her children; she refuses to be comforted, for they are dead."

2.19 After Herod died, an angel of the Lord appeared in a dream to Joseph in Egypt

2.20 and said, "Get up, take the child and his mother, and go back to the land of Israel, because those who tried to kill the child are dead."

2.21 So Joseph got up, took the child and his mother, and went back to Israel.

2.22 But when Joseph heard that Archelaus had succeeded his father Herod as king of Judea, he was afraid to go there. He was given more instructions in a dream, so he went to the province of Galilee

2.23 and made his home in a town named Nazareth. And so what the prophets had said came true: "He will be called a Nazarene."

# 3

3.1 At that time John the Baptist came to the desert of Judea and started preaching.

3.2 "Turn away from your sins," he said, "because the Kingdom of heaven is near!"

3.3 John was the man the prophet Isaiah was talking about when he said,

"Someone is shouting in the desert, 'Prepare a road for the Lord; make a straight path for him to travel!'"

3.4 John's clothes were made of camel's hair; he wore a leather belt around his waist, and his food was locusts and wild honey.

3.5 People came to him from Jerusalem, from the whole province of Judea, and from all over the country near the Jordan River.

3.6 They confessed their sins, and he baptized them in the Jordan.

3.7 When John saw many Pharisees and Sadducees coming to him to be baptized, he said to them, "You snakes — who told you that you could escape from the punishment God is about to send?

<sup>3.8</sup> "Do those things that will show that you have turned from your sins.

<sup>3.9</sup> "And don't think you can escape punishment by saying that Abraham is your ancestor. I tell you that God can take these rocks and make descendants for Abraham!

<sup>3.10</sup> "The ax is ready to cut down the trees at the roots; every tree that does not bear good fruit will be cut down and thrown in the fire.

<sup>3.11</sup> "I baptize you with water to show that you have repented, but the one who will come after me will baptize you with the Holy Spirit and fire. He is much greater than I am; and I am not good enough even to carry his sandals.

<sup>3.12</sup> "He has his winnowing shovel with him to thresh out all the grain. He will gather his wheat into his barn, but he will burn the chaff in a fire that never goes out."

<sup>3.13</sup> At that time Jesus arrived from Galilee and came to John at the Jordan to be baptized by him.

<sup>3.14</sup> But John tried to make him change his mind. "I ought to be baptized by you," John said, "and yet you have come to me!"

<sup>3.15</sup> But Jesus answered him, "Let it be so for now. For in this way we shall do all that God requires." So John agreed.

<sup>3.16</sup> As soon as Jesus was baptized, he came up out of the water. Then heaven was opened to him, and he saw the Spirit of God coming down like a dove and lighting on him.

<sup>3.17</sup> Then a voice said from heaven, "This is my own dear Son, with whom I am pleased."

# 4

<sup>4.1</sup> Then the Spirit led Jesus into the desert to be tempted by the Devil.

<sup>4.2</sup> After spending forty days and nights without food, Jesus was hungry.

<sup>4.3</sup> Then the Devil came to him and said, "If you are God's Son, order these stones to turn into bread."

<sup>4.4</sup> But Jesus answered, "The scripture says, 'Human beings cannot live on bread alone, but need every word that God speaks.'"

<sup>4.5</sup> Then the Devil took Jesus to Jerusalem, the Holy City, set him on the highest point of the Temple,

<sup>4.6</sup> and said to him, "If you are God's Son, throw yourself down, for the scripture says, 'God will give orders to his angels about you; they will hold you up with their hands, so that not even your feet will be hurt on the stones.'"

4.7 Jesus answered, "But the scripture also says, 'Do not put the Lord your God to the test.'"

4.8 Then the Devil took Jesus to a very high mountain and showed him all the kingdoms of the world in all their greatness.

4.9 "All this I will give you," the Devil said, "if you kneel down and worship me."

4.10 Then Jesus answered, "Go away, Satan! The scripture says, 'Worship the Lord your God and serve only him!'"

4.11 Then the Devil left Jesus; and angels came and helped him.

4.12 When Jesus heard that John had been put in prison, he went away to Galilee.

4.13 He did not stay in Nazareth, but went to live in Capernaum, a town by Lake Galilee, in the territory of Zebulun and Naphtali.

4.14 This was done to make come true what the prophet Isaiah had said,

4.15 "Land of Zebulun and land of Naphtali, on the road to the sea, on the other side of the Jordan, Galilee, land of the Gentiles!

4.16 "The people who live in darkness will see a great light. On those who live in the dark land of death the light will shine."

4.17 From that time Jesus began to preach his message: "Turn away from your sins, because the Kingdom of heaven is near!"

4.18 As Jesus walked along the shore of Lake Galilee, he saw two brothers who were fishermen, Simon (called Peter) and his brother Andrew, catching fish in the lake with a net.

4.19 Jesus said to them, "Come with me, and I will teach you to catch people."

4.20 At once they left their nets and went with him.

4.21 He went on and saw two other brothers, James and John, the sons of Zebedee. They were in their boat with their father Zebedee, getting their nets ready. Jesus called them,

4.22 and at once they left the boat and their father, and went with him.

4.23 Jesus went all over Galilee, teaching in the synagogues, preaching the Good News about the Kingdom, and healing people who had all kinds of disease and sickness.

4.24 The news about him spread through the whole country of Syria, so that people brought to him all those who were sick, suffering from all kinds of diseases and disorders: people with demons, and epileptics, and paralytics - and Jesus healed them all.

4.25 Large crowds followed him from Galilee and the Ten Towns, from Jerusalem, Judea, and the land on the other side of the Jordan.

<sup>5.1</sup> Jesus saw the crowds and went up a hill, where he sat down. His disciples gathered around him, **5**

<sup>5.2</sup> and he began to teach them:

<sup>5.3</sup> "Happy are those who know they are spiritually poor; the Kingdom of heaven belongs to them!

<sup>5.4</sup> "Happy are those who mourn; God will comfort them!

<sup>5.5</sup> "Happy are those who are humble; they will receive what God has promised!

<sup>5.6</sup> "Happy are those whose greatest desire is to do what God requires; God will satisfy them fully!

<sup>5.7</sup> "Happy are those who are merciful to others; God will be merciful to them!

<sup>5.8</sup> "Happy are the pure in heart; they will see God!

<sup>5.9</sup> "Happy are those who work for peace; God will call them his children!

<sup>5.10</sup> "Happy are those who are persecuted because they do what God requires; the Kingdom of heaven belongs to them!

<sup>5.11</sup> "Happy are you when people insult you and persecute you and tell all kinds of evil lies against you because you are my followers.

<sup>5.12</sup> "Be happy and glad, for a great reward is kept for you in heaven. This is how the prophets who lived before you were persecuted.

<sup>5.13</sup> "You are like salt for the whole human race. But if salt loses its saltiness, there is no way to make it salty again. It has become worthless, so it is thrown out and people trample on it.

<sup>5.14</sup> "You are like light for the whole world. A city built on a hill cannot be hid.

<sup>5.15</sup> "No one lights a lamp and puts it under a bowl; instead it is put on the lampstand, where it gives light for everyone in the house.

<sup>5.16</sup> "In the same way your light must shine before people, so that they will see the good things you do and praise your Father in heaven.

<sup>5.17</sup> "Do not think that I have come to do away with the Law of Moses and the teachings of the prophets. I have not come to do away with them, but to make their teachings come true.

<sup>5.18</sup> "Remember that as long as heaven and earth last, not the least point nor the smallest detail of the Law will be done away with — not until the end of all things.

<sup>5.19</sup> "So then, whoever disobeys even the least important of the commandments and teaches others to do the same, will be least in the Kingdom of heaven. On the other hand, whoever obeys the Law and teaches others to do the same, will be great in the Kingdom of heav-

en.

<sup>5.20</sup> "I tell you, then, that you will be able to enter the Kingdom of heaven only if you are more faithful than the teachers of the Law and the Pharisees in doing what God requires.

<sup>5.21</sup> "You have heard that people were told in the past, 'Do not commit murder; anyone who does will be brought to trial.'

<sup>5.22</sup> "But now I tell you: if you are angry with your brother you will be brought to trial, if you call your brother 'You good-for-nothing!' you will be brought before the Council, and if you call your brother a worthless fool you will be in danger of going to the fire of hell.

<sup>5.23</sup> "So if you are about to offer your gift to God at the altar and there you remember that your brother has something against you,

<sup>5.24</sup> "leave your gift there in front of the altar, go at once and make peace with your brother, and then come back and offer your gift to God.

<sup>5.25</sup> "If someone brings a lawsuit against you and takes you to court, settle the dispute while there is time, before you get to court. Once you are there, you will be turned over to the judge, who will hand you over to the police, and you will be put in jail.

<sup>5.26</sup> "There you will stay, I tell you, until you pay the last penny of your fine.

<sup>5.27</sup> "You have heard that it was said, 'Do not commit adultery.'

<sup>5.28</sup> "But now I tell you: anyone who looks at a woman and wants to possess her is guilty of committing adultery with her in his heart.

<sup>5.29</sup> "So if your right eye causes you to sin, take it out and throw it away! It is much better for you to lose a part of your body than to have your whole body thrown into hell.

<sup>5.30</sup> "If your right hand causes you to sin, cut it off and throw it away! It is much better for you to lose one of your limbs than to have your whole body go off to hell.

<sup>5.31</sup> "It was also said, 'Anyone who divorces his wife must give her a written notice of divorce.'

<sup>5.32</sup> "But now I tell you: if a man divorces his wife for any cause other than her unfaithfulness, then he is guilty of making her commit adultery if she marries again; and the man who marries her commits adultery also.

<sup>5.33</sup> "You have also heard that people were told in the past, 'Do not break your promise, but do what you have vowed to the Lord to do.'

<sup>5.34</sup> "But now I tell you: do not use any vow when you make a promise. Do not swear by heaven, for it is God's throne;

<sup>5.35</sup> "nor by earth, for it is the resting place for his feet; nor by Jerusa-

lem, for it is the city of the great King.

5.36 "Do not even swear by your head, because you cannot make a single hair white or black.

5.37 "Just say 'Yes' or 'No' — anything else you say comes from the Evil One.

5.38 "You have heard that it was said, 'An eye for an eye, and a tooth for a tooth.'

5.39 "But now I tell you: do not take revenge on someone who wrongs you. If anyone slaps you on the right cheek, let him slap your left cheek too.

5.40 "And if someone takes you to court to sue you for your shirt, let him have your coat as well.

5.41 "And if one of the occupation troops forces you to carry his pack one mile, carry it two miles.

5.42 "When someone asks you for something, give it to him; when someone wants to borrow something, lend it to him.

5.43 "You have heard that it was said, 'Love your friends, hate your enemies.'

5.44 "But now I tell you: love your enemies and pray for those who persecute you,

5.45 "so that you may become the children of your Father in heaven. For he makes his sun to shine on bad and good people alike, and gives rain to those who do good and to those who do evil.

5.46 "Why should God reward you if you love only the people who love you? Even the tax collectors do that!

out of the ordinary? Even the pagans do that!

5.48 "You must be perfect — just as your Father in heaven is perfect.

# 6

6.1 "Make certain you do not perform your religious duties in public so that people will see what you do. If you do these things publicly, you will not have any reward from your Father in heaven.

6.2 "So when you give something to a needy person, do not make a big show of it, as the hypocrites do in the houses of worship and on the streets. They do it so that people will praise them. I assure you, they have already been paid in full.

6.3 "But when you help a needy person, do it in such a way that even your closest friend will not know about it.

6.4 "Then it will be a private matter. And your Father, who sees what you do in private, will reward you.

6.5 "When you pray, do not be like the hypocrites! They love to stand up and pray in the houses of worship and on the street corners, so that everyone will see them. I assure you, they have already been paid in full.

6.6 "But when you pray, go to your room, close the door, and pray to your Father, who is unseen. And your Father, who sees what you do in private, will reward you.

6.7 "When you pray, do not use a lot of meaningless words, as the pagans do, who think that their gods will hear them because their prayers are long.

6.8 "Do not be like them. Your Father already knows what you need before you ask him.

6.9 "This, then, is how you should pray: 'Our Father in heaven: May your holy name be honored;

6.10 " 'may your Kingdom come; may your will be done on earth as it is in heaven.

6.11 " 'Give us today the food we need.

6.12 " 'Forgive us the wrongs we have done, as we forgive the wrongs that others have done to us.

6.13 " 'Do not bring us to hard testing, but keep us safe from the Evil One.' "

6.14 "If you forgive others the wrongs they have done to you, your Father in heaven will also forgive you.

6.15 "But if you do not forgive others, then your Father will not forgive the wrongs you have done.

6.16 "And when you fast, do not put on a sad face as the hypocrites do. They neglect their appearance so that everyone will see that they are fasting. I assure you, they have already been paid in full.

6.17 "When you go without food, wash your face and comb your hair,

6.18 "so that others cannot know that you are fasting — only your Father, who is unseen, will know. And your Father, who sees what you do in private, will reward you.

6.19 "Do not store up riches for yourselves here on earth, where moths and rust destroy, and robbers break in and steal.

6.20 "Instead, store up riches for yourselves in heaven, where moths and rust cannot destroy, and robbers cannot break in and steal.

6.21 "For your heart will always be where your riches are.

6.22 "The eyes are like a lamp for the body. If your eyes are sound, your whole body will be full of light;

6.23 "but if your eyes are no good, your body will be in darkness. So if the light in you is darkness, how terribly dark it will be!

6.24 "You cannot be a slave of two masters; you will hate one and love the other; you will be loyal to one and despise the other. You cannot serve both God and money. <sup>6.25</sup> "This is why I tell you: do not be worried about the food and drink you need in order to stay alive, or about clothes for your body. After all, isn't life worth more than food? And isn't the body worth more than clothes?

<sup>6.26</sup> "Look at the birds: they do not plant seeds, gather a harvest and put it in barns; yet your Father in heaven takes care of them! Aren't you worth much more than birds?

<sup>6.27</sup> "Can any of you live a bit longer by worrying about it?

<sup>6.28</sup> "And why worry about clothes? Look how the wild flowers grow: they do not work or make clothes for themselves.

<sup>6.29</sup> "But I tell you that not even King Solomon with all his wealth had clothes as beautiful as one of these flowers.

<sup>6.30</sup> "It is God who clothes the wild grass — grass that is here today and gone tomorrow, burned up in the oven. Won't he be all the more sure to clothe you? What little faith you have!

<sup>6.31</sup> "So do not start worrying: 'Where will my food come from? or my drink? or my clothes?'

<sup>6.32</sup> "(These are the things the pagans are always concerned about.) Your Father in heaven knows that you need all these things.

<sup>6.33</sup> "Instead, be concerned above everything else with the Kingdom of God and with what he requires of you, and he will provide you with all these other things.

<sup>6.34</sup> "So do not worry about tomorrow; it will have enough worries of its own. There is no need to add to the troubles each day brings.

# 7

<sup>7.1</sup> "Do not judge others, so that God will not judge you,

<sup>7.2</sup> "for God will judge you in the same way you judge others, and he will apply to you the same rules you apply to others.

<sup>7.3</sup> "Why, then, do you look at the speck in your brother's eye and pay no attention to the log in your own eye?

<sup>7.4</sup> "How dare you say to your brother, 'Please, let me take that speck out of your eye,' when you have a log in your own eye?

<sup>7.5</sup> "You hypocrite! First take the log out of your own eye, and then you will be able to see clearly to take the speck out of your brother's eye.

<sup>7.6</sup> "Do not give what is holy to dogs — they will only turn and attack you. Do not throw your pearls in front of pigs — they will only trample them underfoot.

<sup>7.7</sup> "Ask, and you will receive; seek, and you will find; knock, and the door will be opened to you.
<sup>7.8</sup> "For everyone who asks will receive, and anyone who seeks will find, and the door will be opened to those who knock.
<sup>7.9</sup> "Would any of you who are fathers give your son a stone when he asks for bread?
<sup>7.10</sup> "Or would you give him a snake when he asks for a fish?
<sup>7.11</sup> "As bad as you are, you know how to give good things to your children. How much more, then, will your Father in heaven give good things to those who ask him!
<sup>7.12</sup> "Do for others what you want them to do for you: this is the meaning of the Law of Moses and of the teachings of the prophets.
<sup>7.13</sup> "Go in through the narrow gate, because the gate to hell is wide and the road that leads to it is easy, and there are many who travel it.
<sup>7.14</sup> "But the gate to life is narrow and the way that leads to it is hard, and there are few people who find it.
<sup>7.15</sup> "Be on your guard against false prophets; they come to you looking like sheep on the outside, but on the inside they are really like wild wolves.
<sup>7.16</sup> "You will know them by what they do. Thorn bushes do not bear grapes, and briers do not bear figs.
<sup>7.17</sup> "A healthy tree bears good fruit, but a poor tree bears bad fruit.
<sup>7.18</sup> "A healthy tree cannot bear bad fruit, and a poor tree cannot bear good fruit.
<sup>7.19</sup> "And any tree that does not bear good fruit is cut down and thrown in the fire.
<sup>7.20</sup> "So then, you will know the false prophets by what they do.
<sup>7.21</sup> "Not everyone who calls me 'Lord, Lord' will enter the Kingdom of heaven, but only those who do what my Father in heaven wants them to do.
<sup>7.22</sup> "When the Judgment Day comes, many will say to me, 'Lord, Lord! In your name we spoke God's message, by your name we drove out many demons and performed many miracles!'
<sup>7.23</sup> "Then I will say to them, 'I never knew you. Get away from me, you wicked people!'
<sup>7.24</sup> "So then, anyone who hears these words of mine and obeys them is like a wise man who built his house on rock.
<sup>7.25</sup> "The rain poured down, the rivers flooded over, and the wind blew hard against that house. But it did not fall, because it was built on rock.

<sup>7.26</sup> "But anyone who hears these words of mine and does not obey them is like a foolish man who built his house on sand.

<sup>7.27</sup> "The rain poured down, the rivers flooded over, the wind blew hard against that house, and it fell. And what a terrible fall that was!"

<sup>7.28</sup> When Jesus finished saying these things, the crowd was amazed at the way he taught.

<sup>7.29</sup> He wasn't like the teachers of the Law; instead, he taught with authority.

# 8

<sup>8.1</sup> When Jesus came down from the hill, large crowds followed him.

<sup>8.2</sup> Then a man suffering from a dreaded skin disease came to him, knelt down before him, and said, "Sir, if you want to, you can make me clean."

<sup>8.3</sup> Jesus reached out and touched him. "I do want to," he answered. "Be clean!" At once the man was healed of his disease.

<sup>8.4</sup> Then Jesus said to him, "Listen! Don't tell anyone, but go straight to the priest and let him examine you; then in order to prove to everyone that you are cured, offer the sacrifice that Moses ordered."

<sup>8.5</sup> When Jesus entered Capernaum, a Roman officer met him and begged for help:

<sup>8.6</sup> "Sir, my servant is sick in bed at home, unable to move and suffering terribly."

<sup>8.7</sup> "I will go and make him well," Jesus said.

<sup>8.8</sup> "Oh no, sir," answered the officer. "I do not deserve to have you come into my house. Just give the order, and my servant will get well.

<sup>8.9</sup> "I, too, am a man under the authority of superior officers, and I have soldiers under me. I order this one, 'Go!' and he goes; and I order that one, 'Come!' and he comes; and I order my slave, 'Do this!' and he does it."

<sup>8.10</sup> When Jesus heard this, he was surprised and said to the people following him, "I tell you, I have never found anyone in Israel with faith like this.

<sup>8.11</sup> "I assure you that many will come from the east and the west and sit down with Abraham, Isaac, and Jacob at the feast in the Kingdom of heaven.

<sup>8.12</sup> "But those who should be in the Kingdom will be thrown out into the darkness, where they will cry and gnash their teeth."

<sup>8.13</sup> Then Jesus said to the officer, "Go home, and what you believe

will be done for you." And the officer's servant was healed that very moment.

<sup>8.14</sup> Jesus went to Peter's home, and there he saw Peter's mother-in-law sick in bed with a fever. <sup>8.15</sup> He touched her hand; the fever left her, and she got up and began to wait on him.

<sup>8.16</sup> When evening came, people brought to Jesus many who had demons in them. Jesus drove out the evil spirits with a word and healed all who were sick. <sup>8.17</sup> He did this to make come true what the prophet Isaiah had said, "He himself took our sickness and carried away our diseases."

<sup>8.18</sup> When Jesus noticed the crowd around him, he ordered his disciples to go to the other side of the lake. <sup>8.19</sup> A teacher of the Law came to him. "Teacher," he said, "I am ready to go with you wherever you go."

<sup>8.20</sup> Jesus answered him, "Foxes have holes, and birds have nests, but the Son of Man has no place to lie down and rest."

<sup>8.21</sup> Another man, who was a disciple, said, "Sir, first let me go back and bury my father."

<sup>8.22</sup> "Follow me," Jesus answered, "and let the dead bury their own dead."

<sup>8.23</sup> Jesus got into a boat, and his disciples went with him. <sup>8.24</sup> Suddenly a fierce storm hit the lake, and the boat was in danger of sinking. But Jesus was asleep. <sup>8.25</sup> The disciples went to him and woke him up. "Save us, Lord!" they said. "We are about to die!"

<sup>8.26</sup> "Why are you so frightened?" Jesus answered. "What little faith you have!" Then he got up and ordered the winds and the waves to stop, and there was a great calm.

<sup>8.27</sup> Everyone was amazed. "What kind of man is this?" they said. "Even the winds and the waves obey him!"

<sup>8.28</sup> When Jesus came to the territory of Gadara on the other side of the lake, he was met by two men who came out of the burial caves there. These men had demons in them and were so fierce that no one dared travel on that road. <sup>8.29</sup> At once they screamed, "What do you want with us, you Son of God? Have you come to punish us before the right time?"

<sup>8.30</sup> Not far away there was a large herd of pigs feeding. <sup>8.31</sup> So the demons begged Jesus, "If you are going to drive us out, send us into that herd of pigs."

<sup>8.32</sup> "Go," Jesus told them; so they left and went off into the pigs. The

whole herd rushed down the side of the cliff into the lake and was drowned.

8.33 The men who had been taking care of the pigs ran away and went into the town, where they told the whole story and what had happened to the men with the demons.

8.34 So everyone from the town went out to meet Jesus; and when they saw him, they begged him to leave their territory.

# 9

9.1 Jesus got into the boat and went back across the lake to his own town,

9.2 where some people brought to him a paralyzed man, lying on a bed. When Jesus saw how much faith they had, he said to the paralyzed man, "Courage, my son! Your sins are forgiven."

9.3 Then some teachers of the Law said to themselves, "This man is speaking blasphemy!"

9.4 Jesus perceived what they were thinking, and so he said, "Why are you thinking such evil things?

9.5 "Is it easier to say, 'Your sins are forgiven,' or to say, 'Get up and walk'?

9.6 "I will prove to you, then, that the Son of Man has authority on earth to forgive sins." So he said to the paralyzed man, "Get up, pick up your bed, and go home!"

9.7 The man got up and went home.

9.8 When the people saw it, they were afraid, and praised God for giving such authority to people.

9.9 Jesus left that place, and as he walked along, he saw a tax collector, named Matthew, sitting in his office. He said to him, "Follow me." Matthew got up and followed him.

9.10 While Jesus was having a meal in Matthew's house, many tax collectors and other outcasts came and joined Jesus and his disciples at the table.

9.11 Some Pharisees saw this and asked his disciples, "Why does your teacher eat with such people?"

9.12 Jesus heard them and answered, "People who are well do not need a doctor, but only those who are sick.

9.13 "Go and find out what is meant by the scripture that says: 'It is kindness that I want, not animal sacrifices.' I have not come to call respectable people, but outcasts."

9.14 Then the followers of John the Baptist came to Jesus, asking, "Why is it that we and the Pharisees fast often, but your disciples don't fast at all?"

9.15 Jesus answered, "Do you expect the guests at a wedding party to be sad as long as the bridegroom is with them? Of course not! But the day will come when the bridegroom will be taken away from them, and then they will fast.

9.16 "No one patches up an old coat with a piece of new cloth, for the new patch will shrink and make an even bigger hole in the coat.

9.17 "Nor does anyone pour new wine into used wineskins, for the skins will burst, the wine will pour out, and the skins will be ruined. Instead, new wine is poured into fresh wineskins, and both will keep in good condition."

9.18 While Jesus was saying this, a Jewish official came to him, knelt down before him, and said, "My daughter has just died; but come and place your hands on her, and she will live."

9.19 So Jesus got up and followed him, and his disciples went along with him.

9.20 A woman who had suffered from severe bleeding for twelve years came up behind Jesus and touched the edge of his cloak.

9.21 She said to herself, "If only I touch his cloak, I will get well."

9.22 Jesus turned around and saw her, and said, "Courage, my daughter! Your faith has made you well." At that very moment the woman became well.

9.23 Then Jesus went into the official's house. When he saw the musicians for the funeral and the people all stirred up,

9.24 he said, "Get out, everybody! The little girl is not dead - she is only sleeping!" Then they all started making fun of him.

9.25 But as soon as the people had been put out, Jesus went into the girl's room and took hold of her hand, and she got up.

9.26 The news about this spread all over that part of the country.

9.27 Jesus left that place, and as he walked along, two blind men started following him. "Have mercy on us, Son of David!" they shouted.

9.28 When Jesus had gone indoors, the two blind men came to him, and he asked them, "Do you believe that I can heal you?" "Yes, sir!" they answered.

9.29 Then Jesus touched their eyes and said, "Let it happen, then, just as you believe!"

9.30 and their sight was restored. Jesus spoke sternly to them, "Don't tell this to anyone!"

9.31 But they left and spread the news about Jesus all over that part of the country.

9.32 As the men were leaving, some people brought to Jesus a man who could not talk because he had a demon.
9.33 But as soon as the demon was driven out, the man started talking, and everyone was amazed. "We have never seen anything like this in Israel!" they exclaimed.
9.34 But the Pharisees said, "It is the chief of the demons who gives Jesus the power to drive out demons."
9.35 Jesus went around visiting all the towns and villages. He taught in the synagogues, preached the Good News about the Kingdom, and healed people with every kind of disease and sickness.
9.36 As he saw the crowds, his heart was filled with pity for them, because they were worried and helpless, like sheep without a shepherd.
9.37 So he said to his disciples, "The harvest is large, but there are few workers to gather it in.
9.38 "Pray to the owner of the harvest that he will send out workers to gather in his harvest."

# 10

10.1 Jesus called his twelve disciples together and gave them authority to drive out evil spirits and to heal every disease and every sickness.
10.2 These are the names of the twelve apostles: first, Simon (called Peter) and his brother Andrew; James and his brother John, the sons of Zebedee;
10.3 Philip and Bartholomew; Thomas and Matthew, the tax collector; James son of Alphaeus, and Thaddaeus;
10.4 Simon the Patriot, and Judas Iscariot, who betrayed Jesus.
10.5 These twelve men were sent out by Jesus with the following instructions: "Do not go to any Gentile territory or any Samaritan towns.
10.6 "Instead, you are to go to the lost sheep of the people of Israel.
10.7 "Go and preach, 'The Kingdom of heaven is near!'
10.8 "Heal the sick, bring the dead back to life, heal those who suffer from dreaded skin diseases, and drive out demons. You have received without paying, so give without being paid.
10.9 "Do not carry any gold, silver, or copper money in your pockets;
10.10 "do not carry a beggar's bag for the trip or an extra shirt or shoes or a walking stick. Workers should be given what they need.
10.11 "When you come to a town or village, go in and look for someone who is willing to welcome you, and stay with him until you leave that place.
10.12 "When you go into a house, say, 'Peace be with you.'

10.13 "If the people in that house welcome you, let your greeting of peace remain; but if they do not welcome you, then take back your greeting.

10.14 "And if some home or town will not welcome you or listen to you, then leave that place and shake the dust off your feet.

10.15 "I assure you that on the Judgment Day God will show more mercy to the people of Sodom and Gomorrah than to the people of that town!

10.16 "Listen! I am sending you out just like sheep to a pack of wolves. You must be as cautious as snakes and as gentle as doves.

10.17 "Watch out, for there will be those who will arrest you and take you to court, and they will whip you in the synagogues.

10.18 "For my sake you will be brought to trial before rulers and kings, to tell the Good News to them and to the Gentiles.

10.19 "When they bring you to trial, do not worry about what you are going to say or how you will say it; when the time comes, you will be given what you will say.

10.20 "For the words you will speak will not be yours; they will come from the Spirit of your Father speaking through you.

10.21 "People will hand over their own brothers to be put to death, and fathers will do the same to their children; children will turn against their parents and have them put to death.

10.22 "Everyone will hate you because of me. But whoever holds out to the end will be saved.

10.23 "When they persecute you in one town, run away to another one. I assure you that you will not finish your work in all the towns of Israel before the Son of Man comes.

10.24 "No pupil is greater than his teacher; no slave is greater than his master.

10.25 "So a pupil should be satisfied to become like his teacher, and a slave like his master. If the head of the family is called Beelzebul, the members of the family will be called even worse names!

10.26 "So do not be afraid of people. Whatever is now covered up will be uncovered, and every secret will be made known.

10.27 "What I am telling you in the dark you must repeat in broad daylight, and what you have heard in private you must announce from the housetops.

10.28 "Do not be afraid of those who kill the body but cannot kill the soul; rather be afraid of God, who can destroy both body and soul in hell.

10.29 "For only a penny you can buy two sparrows, yet not one sparrow falls to the ground without your Father's consent.

[10.30] "As for you, even the hairs of your head have all been counted.

[10.31] "So do not be afraid; you are worth much more than many sparrows!

[10.32] "Those who declare publicly that they belong to me, I will do the same for them before my Father in heaven.

[10.33] "But those who reject me publicly, I will reject before my Father in heaven.

[10.34] "Do not think that I have come to bring peace to the world. No, I did not come to bring peace, but a sword.

[10.35] "I came to set sons against their fathers, daughters against their mothers, daughters-in-law against their mothers-in-law;

[10.36] "your worst enemies will be the members of your own family.

[10.37] "Those who love their father or mother more than me are not fit to be my disciples; those who love their son or daughter more than me are not fit to be my disciples.

[10.38] "Those who do not take up their cross and follow in my steps are not fit to be my disciples.

[10.39] "Those who try to gain their own life will lose it; but those who lose their life for my sake will gain it.

[10.40] "Whoever welcomes you welcomes me; and whoever welcomes me welcomes the one who sent me.

[10.41] "Whoever welcomes God's messenger because he is God's messenger, will share in his reward. And whoever welcomes a good man because he is good, will share in his reward.

[10.42] "You can be sure that whoever gives even a drink of cold water to one of the least of these my followers because he is my follower, will certainly receive a reward."

# 11

[11.1] When Jesus finished giving these instructions to his twelve disciples, he left that place and went off to teach and preach in the towns near there.

[11.2] When John the Baptist heard in prison about the things that Christ was doing, he sent some of his disciples to him.

[11.3] "Tell us," they asked Jesus, "are you the one John said was going to come, or should we expect someone else?"

[11.4] Jesus answered, "Go back and tell John what you are hearing and seeing:

[11.5] "the blind can see, the lame can walk, those who suffer from dreaded skin diseases are made clean, the deaf hear, the dead are brought back to life, and the Good News is preached to the poor.

11.6 "How happy are those who have no doubts about me!"

11.7 While John's disciples were leaving, Jesus spoke about him to the crowds: "When you went out to John in the desert, what did you expect to see? A blade of grass bending in the wind?."

11.8 "What did you go out to see? A man dressed up in fancy clothes? People who dress like that live in palaces!

11.9 "Tell me, what did you go out to see? A prophet? Yes indeed, but you saw much more than a prophet.

11.10 "For John is the one of whom the scripture says: 'God said, I will send my messenger ahead of you to open the way for you.'

11.11 "I assure you that John the Baptist is greater than anyone who has ever lived. But the one who is least in the Kingdom of heaven is greater than John.

11.12 "From the time John preached his message until this very day the Kingdom of heaven has suffered violent attacks, and violent men try to seize it.

11.13 "Until the time of John all the prophets and the Law of Moses spoke about the Kingdom;

11.14 "and if you are willing to believe their message, John is Elijah, whose coming was predicted.

11.15 "Listen, then, if you have ears!

11.16 "Now, to what can I compare the people of this day? They are like children sitting in the marketplace. One group shouts to the other,

11.17 " 'We played wedding music for you, but you wouldn't dance! We sang funeral songs, but you wouldn't cry!' "

11.18 "When John came, he fasted and drank no wine, and everyone said, 'He has a demon in him!'

11.19 "When the Son of Man came, he ate and drank, and everyone said, 'Look at this man! He is a glutton and wine drinker, a friend of tax collectors and other outcasts!' God's wisdom, however, is shown to be true by its results."

11.20 The people in the towns where Jesus had performed most of his miracles did not turn from their sins, so he reproached those towns.

11.21 "How terrible it will be for you, Chorazin! How terrible for you too, Bethsaida! If the miracles which were performed in you had been performed in Tyre and Sidon, the people there would have long ago put on sackcloth and sprinkled ashes on themselves, to show that they had turned from their sins!

11.22 "I assure you that on the Judgment Day God will show more mercy to the people of Tyre and Sidon than to you!

11.23 "And as for you, Capernaum! Did you want to lift yourself up to heaven? You will be thrown down to hell! If the miracles which were performed in you had been performed in Sodom, it would still be in existence today!

11.24 "You can be sure that on the Judgment Day God will show more mercy to Sodom than to you!"

11.25 At that time Jesus said, "Father, Lord of heaven and earth! I thank you because you have shown to the unlearned what you have hidden from the wise and learned.

11.26 "Yes, Father, this was how you were pleased to have it happen.

11.27 "My Father has given me all things. No one knows the Son except the Father, and no one knows the Father except the Son and those to whom the Son chooses to reveal him.

11.28 "Come to me, all of you who are tired from carrying heavy loads, and I will give you rest.

11.29 "Take my yoke and put it on you, and learn from me, because I am gentle and humble in spirit; and you will find rest.

11.30 "For the yoke I will give you is easy, and the load I will put on you is light."

# 12

12.1 Not long afterward Jesus was walking through some wheat fields on a Sabbath. His disciples were hungry, so they began to pick heads of wheat and eat the grain.

12.2 When the Pharisees saw this, they said to Jesus, "Look, it is against our Law for your disciples to do this on the Sabbath!"

12.3 Jesus answered, "Have you never read what David did that time when he and his men were hungry?

12.4 "He went into the house of God, and he and his men ate the bread offered to God, even though it was against the Law for them to eat it — only the priests were allowed to eat that bread.

12.5 "Or have you not read in the Law of Moses that every Sabbath the priests in the Temple actually break the Sabbath law, yet they are not guilty?

12.6 "I tell you that there is something here greater than the Temple.

12.7 "The scripture says, 'It is kindness that I want, not animal sacrifices.' If you really knew what this means, you would not condemn people who are not guilty;

12.8 "for the Son of Man is Lord of the Sabbath."

12.9 Jesus left that place and went to a synagogue,

<sup></sup> 12.10 where there was a man who had a paralyzed hand. Some people were there who wanted to accuse Jesus of doing wrong, so they asked him, "Is it against our Law to heal on the Sabbath?"

12.11 Jesus answered, "What if one of you has a sheep and it falls into a deep hole on the Sabbath? Will you not take hold of it and lift it out?

12.12 "And a human being is worth much more than a sheep! So then, our Law does allow us to help someone on the Sabbath."

12.13 Then he said to the man with the paralyzed hand, "Stretch out your hand." He stretched it out, and it became well again, just like the other one.

12.14 Then the Pharisees left and made plans to kill Jesus.

12.15 When Jesus heard about the plot against him, he went away from that place; and large crowds followed him. He healed all the sick

12.16 and gave them orders not to tell others about him.

12.17 He did this so as to make come true what God had said through the prophet Isaiah:

12.18 "Here is my servant, whom I have chosen, the one I love, and with whom I am pleased. I will send my Spirit upon him, and he will announce my judgment to the nations.

12.19 "He will not argue or shout, or make loud speeches in the streets.

12.20 "He will not break off a bent reed, nor put out a flickering lamp. He will persist until he causes justice to triumph,

12.21 "and on him all peoples will put their hope."

12.22 Then some people brought to Jesus a man who was blind and could not talk because he had a demon. Jesus healed the man, so that he was able to talk and see.

12.23 The crowds were all amazed at what Jesus had done. "Could he be the Son of David?" they asked.

12.24 When the Pharisees heard this, they replied, "He drives out demons only because their ruler Beelzebul gives him power to do so."

12.25 Jesus knew what they were thinking, and so he said to them, "Any country that divides itself into groups which fight each other will not last very long. And any town or family that divides itself into groups which fight each other will fall apart.

12.26 "So if one group is fighting another in Satan's kingdom, this means that it is already divided into groups and will soon fall apart!

12.27 "You say that I drive out demons because Beelzebul gives me the power to do so. Well, then, who gives your followers the power to drive them out? What your own followers do proves that you are wrong!

<sup>12.28</sup> "No, it is not Beelzebul, but God's Spirit, who gives me the power to drive out demons, which proves that the Kingdom of God has already come upon you.

<sup>12.29</sup> "No one can break into a strong man's house and take away his belongings unless he first ties up the strong man; then he can plunder his house.

<sup>12.30</sup> "Anyone who is not for me is really against me; anyone who does not help me gather is really scattering.

<sup>12.31</sup> "For this reason I tell you: people can be forgiven any sin and any evil thing they say; but whoever says evil things against the Holy Spirit will not be forgiven.

<sup>12.32</sup> "Anyone who says something against the Son of Man can be forgiven; but whoever says something against the Holy Spirit will not be forgiven — now or ever.

<sup>12.33</sup> "To have good fruit you must have a healthy tree; if you have a poor tree, you will have bad fruit. A tree is known by the kind of fruit it bears.

<sup>12.34</sup> "You snakes — how can you say good things when you are evil? For the mouth speaks what the heart is full of.

<sup>12.35</sup> "A good person brings good things out of a treasure of good things; a bad person brings bad things out of a treasure of bad things.

<sup>12.36</sup> "You can be sure that on the Judgment Day you will have to give account of every useless word you have ever spoken.

<sup>12.37</sup> "Your words will be used to judge you — to declare you either innocent or guilty."

<sup>12.38</sup> Then some teachers of the Law and some Pharisees spoke up. "Teacher," they said, "we want to see you perform a miracle."

<sup>12.39</sup> "How evil and godless are the people of this day!" Jesus exclaimed. "You ask me for a miracle? No! The only miracle you will be given is the miracle of the prophet Jonah.

<sup>12.40</sup> "In the same way that Jonah spent three days and nights in the big fish, so will the Son of Man spend three days and nights in the depths of the earth.

<sup>12.41</sup> "On the Judgment Day the people of Nineveh will stand up and accuse you, because they turned from their sins when they heard Jonah preach; and I tell you that there is something here greater than Jonah!

<sup>12.42</sup> "On the Judgment Day the Queen of Sheba will stand up and accuse you, because she traveled all the way from her country to lis-

ten to King Solomon's wise teaching; and I assure you that there is something here greater than Solomon!

<sup>12.43</sup> "When an evil spirit goes out of a person, it travels over dry country looking for a place to rest. If it can't find one,

<sup>12.44</sup> "it says to itself, 'I will go back to my house.' So it goes back and finds the house empty, clean, and all fixed up.

<sup>12.45</sup> "Then it goes out and brings along seven other spirits even worse than itself, and they come and live there. So when it is all over, that person is in worse shape than at the beginning. This is what will happen to the evil people of this day."

<sup>12.46</sup> Jesus was still talking to the people when his mother and brothers arrived. They stood outside, asking to speak with him.

<sup>12.47</sup> So one of the people there said to him, "Look, your mother and brothers are standing outside, and they want to speak with you."

<sup>12.48</sup> Jesus answered, "Who is my mother? Who are my brothers?"

<sup>12.49</sup> Then he pointed to his disciples and said, "Look! Here are my mother and my brothers!

<sup>12.50</sup> "Whoever does what my Father in heaven wants is my brother, my sister, and my mother."

# 13

<sup>13.1</sup> That same day Jesus left the house and went to the lakeside, where he sat down to teach.

<sup>13.2</sup> The crowd that gathered around him was so large that he got into a boat and sat in it, while the crowd stood on the shore.

<sup>13.3</sup> He used parables to tell them many things. "Once there was a man who went out to sow grain.

<sup>13.4</sup> "As he scattered the seed in the field, some of it fell along the path, and the birds came and ate it up.

<sup>13.5</sup> "Some of it fell on rocky ground, where there was little soil. The seeds soon sprouted, because the soil wasn't deep.

<sup>13.6</sup> "But when the sun came up, it burned the young plants; and because the roots had not grown deep enough, the plants soon dried up.

<sup>13.7</sup> "Some of the seed fell among thorn bushes, which grew up and choked the plants.

<sup>13.8</sup> "But some seeds fell in good soil, and the plants bore grain: some had one hundred grains, others sixty, and others thirty."

<sup>13.9</sup> And Jesus concluded, "Listen, then, if you have ears!"

<sup>13.10</sup> Then the disciples came to Jesus and asked him, "Why do you use parables when you talk to the people?"

<sup>13.11</sup> Jesus answered, "The knowledge about the secrets of the Kingdom of heaven has been given to you, but not to them.

<sup>13.12</sup> "For the person who has something will be given more, so that he will have more than enough; but the person who has nothing will have taken away from him even the little he has.

<sup>13.13</sup> "The reason I use parables in talking to them is that they look, but do not see, and they listen, but do not hear or understand.

<sup>13.14</sup> "So the prophecy of Isaiah applies to them: 'This people will listen and listen, but not understand; they will look and look, but not see,

<sup>13.15</sup> " 'because their minds are dull, and they have stopped up their ears and have closed their eyes. Otherwise, their eyes would see, their ears would hear, their minds would understand, and they would turn to me, says God, and I would heal them.' "

<sup>13.16</sup> "As for you, how fortunate you are! Your eyes see and your ears hear.

<sup>13.17</sup> "I assure you that many prophets and many of God's people wanted very much to see what you see, but they could not, and to hear what you hear, but they did not.

<sup>13.18</sup> "Listen, then, and learn what the parable of the sower means.

<sup>13.19</sup> "Those who hear the message about the Kingdom but do not understand it are like the seeds that fell along the path. The Evil One comes and snatches away what was sown in them.

<sup>13.20</sup> "The seeds that fell on rocky ground stand for those who receive the message gladly as soon as they hear it.

<sup>13.21</sup> "But it does not sink deep into them, and they don't last long. So when trouble or persecution comes because of the message, they give up at once.

<sup>13.22</sup> "The seeds that fell among thorn bushes stand for those who hear the message; but the worries about this life and the love for riches choke the message, and they don't bear fruit.

<sup>13.23</sup> "And the seeds sown in the good soil stand for those who hear the message and understand it: they bear fruit, some as much as one hundred, others sixty, and others thirty."

<sup>13.24</sup> Jesus told them another parable: "The Kingdom of heaven is like this. A man sowed good seed in his field.

<sup>13.25</sup> "One night, when everyone was asleep, an enemy came and sowed weeds among the wheat and went away.

<sup>13.26</sup> "When the plants grew and the heads of grain began to form, then the weeds showed up.

<sup>13.27</sup> "The man's servants came to him and said, 'Sir, it was good seed

you sowed in your field; where did the weeds come from?'

13.28 " 'It was some enemy who did this,' he answered. 'Do you want us to go and pull up the weeds?' they asked him.

13.29 " 'No,' he answered, 'because as you gather the weeds you might pull up some of the wheat along with them.

13.30 " 'Let the wheat and the weeds both grow together until harvest. Then I will tell the harvest workers to pull up the weeds first, tie them in bundles and burn them, and then to gather in the wheat and put it in my barn.' "

13.31 Jesus told them another parable: "The Kingdom of heaven is like this. A man takes a mustard seed and sows it in his field.

13.32 "It is the smallest of all seeds, but when it grows up, it is the biggest of all plants. It becomes a tree, so that birds come and make their nests in its branches."

13.33 Jesus told them still another parable: "The Kingdom of heaven is like this. A woman takes some yeast and mixes it with a bushel of flour until the whole batch of dough rises."

13.34 Jesus used parables to tell all these things to the crowds; he would not say a thing to them without using a parable.

13.35 He did this to make come true what the prophet had said, "I will use parables when I speak to them; I will tell them things unknown since the creation of the world."

13.36 When Jesus had left the crowd and gone indoors, his disciples came to him and said, "Tell us what the parable about the weeds in the field means."

13.37 Jesus answered, "The man who sowed the good seed is the Son of Man;

13.38 "the field is the world; the good seed is the people who belong to the Kingdom; the weeds are the people who belong to the Evil One;

13.39 "and the enemy who sowed the weeds is the Devil. The harvest is the end of the age, and the harvest workers are angels.

13.40 "Just as the weeds are gathered up and burned in the fire, so the same thing will happen at the end of the age:

13.41 "the Son of Man will send out his angels to gather up out of his Kingdom all those who cause people to sin and all others who do evil things,

13.42 "and they will throw them into the fiery furnace, where they will cry and gnash their teeth.

13.43 "Then God's people will shine like the sun in their Father's King-dom. Listen, then, if you have ears!

13.44 "The Kingdom of heaven is like this. A man happens to find a treasure hidden in a field. He covers it up again, and is so happy that he goes and sells everything he has, and then goes back and buys that field.

<sup>13.45</sup> "Also, the Kingdom of heaven is like this. A man is looking for fine pearls,

<sup>13.46</sup> "and when he finds one that is unusually fine, he goes and sells everything he has, and buys that pearl.

<sup>13.47</sup> "Also, the Kingdom of heaven is like this. Some fishermen throw their net out in the lake and catch all kinds of fish.

<sup>13.48</sup> "When the net is full, they pull it to shore and sit down to divide the fish: the good ones go into the buckets, the worthless ones are thrown away.

<sup>13.49</sup> "It will be like this at the end of the age: the angels will go out and gather up the evil people from among the good

<sup>13.50</sup> "and will throw them into the fiery furnace, where they will cry and gnash their teeth.

<sup>13.51</sup> "Do you understand these things?" Jesus asked them. "Yes," they answered.

<sup>13.52</sup> So he replied, "This means, then, that every teacher of the Law who becomes a disciple in the Kingdom of heaven is like a homeowner who takes new and old things out of his storage room."

<sup>13.53</sup> When Jesus finished telling these parables, he left that place

<sup>13.54</sup> and went back to his hometown. He taught in the synagogue, and those who heard him were amazed. "Where did he get such wisdom?" they asked. "And what about his miracles?

<sup>13.55</sup> "Isn't he the carpenter's son? Isn't Mary his mother, and aren't James, Joseph, Simon, and Judas his brothers?

<sup>13.56</sup> "Aren't all his sisters living here? Where did he get all this?"

<sup>13.57</sup> And so they rejected him. Jesus said to them, "A prophet is respected everywhere except in his hometown and by his own family."

<sup>13.58</sup> Because they did not have faith, he did not perform many miracles there.

# 14

<sup>14.1</sup> At that time Herod, the ruler of Galilee, heard about Jesus.

<sup>14.2</sup> "He is really John the Baptist, who has come back to life," he told his officials. "That is why he has this power to perform miracles."

<sup>14.3</sup> For Herod had earlier ordered John's arrest, and he had him tied up and put in prison. He had done this because of Herodias, his brother Philip's wife.

<sup>14.4</sup> For some time John the Baptist had told Herod, "It isn't right for

you to be married to Herodias!"

<sup>14.5</sup> Herod wanted to kill him, but he was afraid of the Jewish people, because they considered John to be a prophet.

<sup>14.6</sup> On Herod's birthday the daughter of Herodias danced in front of the whole group. Herod was so pleased

<sup>14.7</sup> that he promised her, "I swear that I will give you anything you ask for!"

<sup>14.8</sup> At her mother's suggestion she asked him, "Give me here and now the head of John the Baptist on a plate!"

<sup>14.9</sup> The king was sad, but because of the promise he had made in front of all his guests he gave orders that her wish be granted.

<sup>14.10</sup> So he had John beheaded in prison.

<sup>14.11</sup> The head was brought in on a plate and given to the girl, who took it to her mother.

<sup>14.12</sup> John's disciples came, carried away his body, and buried it; then they went and told Jesus.

<sup>14.13</sup> When Jesus heard the news about John, he left there in a boat and went to a lonely place by himself. The people heard about it, and so they left their towns and followed him by land.

<sup>14.14</sup> Jesus got out of the boat, and when he saw the large crowd, his heart was filled with pity for them, and he healed their sick.

<sup>14.15</sup> That evening his disciples came to him and said, "It is already very late, and this is a lonely place. Send the people away and let them go to the villages to buy food for themselves."

<sup>14.16</sup> "They don't have to leave," answered Jesus. "You yourselves give them something to eat!"

<sup>14.17</sup> "All we have here are five loaves and two fish," they replied.

<sup>14.18</sup> "Then bring them here to me," Jesus said.

<sup>14.19</sup> He ordered the people to sit down on the grass; then he took the five loaves and the two fish, looked up to heaven, and gave thanks to God. He broke the loaves and gave them to the disciples, and the disciples gave them to the people.

<sup>14.20</sup> Everyone ate and had enough. Then the disciples took up twelve baskets full of what was left over.

<sup>14.21</sup> The number of men who ate was about five thousand, not counting the women and children.

<sup>14.22</sup> Then Jesus made the disciples get into the boat and go on ahead to the other side of the lake, while he sent the people away.

<sup>14.23</sup> After sending the people away, he went up a hill by himself to pray. When evening came, Jesus was there alone;

<sup>14.24</sup> and by this time the boat was far out in the lake, tossed about by

the waves, because the wind was blowing against it.
<sup>14.25</sup> Between three and six o'clock in the morning Jesus came to the disciples, walking on the water.
<sup>14.26</sup> When they saw him walking on the water, they were terrified. "It's a ghost!" they said, and screamed with fear.
<sup>14.27</sup> Jesus spoke to them at once. "Courage!" he said. "It is I. Don't be afraid!"
<sup>14.28</sup> Then Peter spoke up. "Lord, if it is really you, order me to come out on the water to you."
<sup>14.29</sup> "Come!" answered Jesus. So Peter got out of the boat and started walking on the water to Jesus.
<sup>14.30</sup> But when he noticed the strong wind, he was afraid and started to sink down in the water. "Save me, Lord!" he cried.
<sup>14.31</sup> At once Jesus reached out and grabbed hold of him and said, "What little faith you have! Why did you doubt?"
<sup>14.32</sup> They both got into the boat, and the wind died down.
<sup>14.33</sup> Then the disciples in the boat worshiped Jesus. "Truly you are the Son of God!" they exclaimed.
<sup>14.34</sup> They crossed the lake and came to land at Gennesaret,
<sup>14.35</sup> where the people recognized Jesus. So they sent for the sick people in all the surrounding country and brought them to Jesus.
<sup>14.36</sup> They begged him to let the sick at least touch the edge of his cloak; and all who touched it were made well.

# 15

<sup>15.1</sup> Then some Pharisees and teachers of the Law came from Jerusalem to Jesus and asked him,
<sup>15.2</sup> "Why is it that your disciples disobey the teaching handed down by our ancestors? They don't wash their hands in the proper way before they eat!"
<sup>15.3</sup> Jesus answered, "And why do you disobey God's command and follow your own teaching?
<sup>15.4</sup> "For God said, 'Respect your father and your mother,' and 'If you curse your father or your mother, you are to be put to death.'
<sup>15.5</sup> "But you teach that if people have something they could use to help their father or mother, but say, 'This belongs to God,'
<sup>15.6</sup> "they do not need to honor their father. In this way you disregard God's command, in order to follow your own teaching.
<sup>15.7</sup> "You hypocrites! How right Isaiah was when he prophesied about you!
<sup>15.8</sup> " 'These people, says God, honor me with their words, but their

heart is really far away from me.
15.9 " 'It is no use for them to worship me, because they teach human rules as though they were my laws!' "

15.10 Then Jesus called the crowd to him and said to them, "Listen and understand!

15.11 "It is not what goes into your mouth that makes you ritually unclean; rather, what comes out of it makes you unclean."

15.12 Then the disciples came to him and said, "Do you know that the Pharisees had their feelings hurt by what you said?"

15.13 "Every plant which my Father in heaven did not plant will be pulled up," answered Jesus.

15.14 "Don't worry about them! They are blind leaders of the blind; and when one blind man leads another, both fall into a ditch."

15.15 Peter spoke up, "Explain this saying to us."

15.16 Jesus said to them, "You are still no more intelligent than the others.

15.17 "Don't you understand? Anything that goes into your mouth goes into your stomach and then on out of your body.

15.18 "But the things that come out of the mouth come from the heart, and these are the things that make you ritually unclean.

15.19 "For from your heart come the evil ideas which lead you to kill, commit adultery, and do other immoral things; to rob, lie, and slander others.

15.20 "These are the things that make you unclean. But to eat without washing your hands as they say you should — this doesn't make you unclean."

15.21 Jesus left that place and went off to the territory near the cities of Tyre and Sidon.

15.22 A Canaanite woman who lived in that region came to him. "Son of David!" she cried out. "Have mercy on me, sir! My daughter has a demon and is in a terrible condition."

15.23 But Jesus did not say a word to her. His disciples came to him and begged him, "Send her away! She is following us and making all this noise!"

15.24 Then Jesus replied, "I have been sent only to the lost sheep of the people of Israel."

15.25 At this the woman came and fell at his feet. "Help me, sir!" she said.

15.26 Jesus answered, "It isn't right to take the children's food and throw it to the dogs."

15.27 "That's true, sir," she answered, "but even the dogs eat the leftovers that fall from their masters' table."

15.28 So Jesus answered her, "You are a woman of great faith! What you want will be done for you." And at that very moment her daughter was healed.

15.29 Jesus left there and went along by Lake Galilee. He climbed a hill and sat down.

15.30 Large crowds came to him, bringing with them the lame, the blind, the crippled, the dumb, and many other sick people, whom they placed at Jesus' feet; and he healed them.

15.31 The people were amazed as they saw the dumb speaking, the crippled made whole, the lame walking, and the blind seeing; and they praised the God of Israel.

15.32 Jesus called his disciples to him and said, "I feel sorry for these people, because they have been with me for three days and now have nothing to eat. I don't want to send them away without feeding them, for they might faint on their way home."

15.33 The disciples asked him, "Where will we find enough food in this desert to feed this crowd?"

15.34 "How much bread do you have?" Jesus asked. "Seven loaves," they answered, "and a few small fish."

15.35 So Jesus ordered the crowd to sit down on the ground.

15.36 Then he took the seven loaves and the fish, gave thanks to God, broke them, and gave them to the disciples; and the disciples gave them to the people.

15.37 They all ate and had enough. Then the disciples took up seven baskets full of pieces left over.

15.38 The number of men who ate was four thousand, not counting the women and children.

15.39 Then Jesus sent the people away, got into a boat, and went to the territory of Magadan.

# 16

16.1 Some Pharisees and Sadducees who came to Jesus wanted to trap him, so they asked him to perform a miracle for them, to show that God approved of him.

16.2 But Jesus answered, "When the sun is setting, you say, 'We are going to have fine weather, because the sky is red.'

16.3 "And early in the morning you say, 'It is going to rain, because the sky is red and dark.' You can predict the weather by looking at the sky, but you cannot interpret the signs concerning these times!

16.4 "How evil and godless are the people of this day! You ask me for a miracle? No! The only miracle you will be given is the miracle of Jonah." So he left them and went away.

16.5 When the disciples crossed over to the other side of the lake, they forgot to take any bread.

16.6 Jesus said to them, "Take care; be on your guard against the yeast of the Pharisees and Sadducees."

16.7 They started discussing among themselves, "He says this because we didn't bring any bread."

16.8 Jesus knew what they were saying, so he asked them, "Why are you discussing among yourselves about not having any bread? What little faith you have!

16.9 "Don't you understand yet? Don't you remember when I broke the five loaves for the five thousand men? How many baskets did you fill?

16.10 "And what about the seven loaves for the four thousand men? How many baskets did you fill?

16.11 "How is it that you don't understand that I was not talking to you about bread? Guard yourselves from the yeast of the Pharisees and Sadducees!"

16.12 Then the disciples understood that he was not warning them to guard themselves from the yeast used in bread but from the teaching of the Pharisees and Sadducees.

16.13 Jesus went to the territory near the town of Caesarea Philippi, where he asked his disciples, "Who do people say the Son of Man is?"

16.14 "Some say John the Baptist," they answered. "Others say Elijah, while others say Jeremiah or some other prophet."

16.15 "What about you?" he asked them. "Who do you say I am?"

16.16 Simon Peter answered, "You are the Messiah, the Son of the living God."

16.17 "Good for you, Simon son of John!" answered Jesus. "For this truth did not come to you from any human being, but it was given to you directly by my Father in heaven.

16.18 "And so I tell you, Peter: you are a rock, and on this rock foundation I will build my church, and not even death will ever be able to overcome it.

16.19 "I will give you the keys of the Kingdom of heaven; what you prohibit on earth will be prohibited in heaven, and what you permit on earth will be permitted in heaven."

16.20 Then Jesus ordered his disciples not to tell anyone that he was the Messiah.

16.21 From that time on Jesus began to say plainly to his disciples, "I must go to Jerusalem and suffer much from the elders, the chief priests, and the teachers of the Law. I will be put to death, but three days later I will be raised to life."

<sup>16.22</sup> Peter took him aside and began to rebuke him. "God forbid it, Lord!" he said. "That must never happen to you!"

<sup>16.23</sup> Jesus turned around and said to Peter, "Get away from me, Satan! You are an obstacle in my way, because these thoughts of yours don't come from God, but from human nature."

<sup>16.24</sup> Then Jesus said to his disciples, "If any of you want to come with me, you must forget yourself, carry your cross, and follow me.

<sup>16.25</sup> "For if you want to save your own life, you will lose it; but if you lose your life for my sake, you will find it.

<sup>16.26</sup> "Will you gain anything if you win the whole world but lose your life? Of course not! There is nothing you can give to regain your life.

<sup>16.27</sup> "For the Son of Man is about to come in the glory of his Father with his angels, and then he will reward each one according to his deeds.

<sup>16.28</sup> "I assure you that there are some here who will not die until they have seen the Son of Man come as King."

# 17

<sup>17.1</sup> Six days later Jesus took with him Peter and the brothers James and John and led them up a high mountain where they were alone.

<sup>17.2</sup> As they looked on, a change came over Jesus: his face was shining like the sun, and his clothes were dazzling white.

<sup>17.3</sup> Then the three disciples saw Moses and Elijah talking with Jesus.

<sup>17.4</sup> So Peter spoke up and said to Jesus, "Lord, how good it is that we are here! If you wish, I will make three tents here, one for you, one for Moses, and one for Elijah."

<sup>17.5</sup> While he was talking, a shining cloud came over them, and a voice from the cloud said, "This is my own dear Son, with whom I am pleased - listen to him!"

<sup>17.6</sup> When the disciples heard the voice, they were so terrified that they threw themselves face downward on the ground.

<sup>17.7</sup> Jesus came to them and touched them. "Get up," he said. "Don't be afraid!"

<sup>17.8</sup> So they looked up and saw no one there but Jesus.

<sup>17.9</sup> As they came down the mountain, Jesus ordered them, "Don't tell anyone about this vision you have seen until the Son of Man has been raised from death."

<sup>17.10</sup> Then the disciples asked Jesus, "Why do the teachers of the Law

say that Elijah has to come first?"

<sup>17.11</sup> "Elijah is indeed coming first," answered Jesus, "and he will get everything ready.

<sup>17.12</sup> "But I tell you that Elijah has already come and people did not recognize him, but treated him just as they pleased. In the same way they will also mistreat the Son of Man."

<sup>17.13</sup> Then the disciples understood that he was talking to them about John the Baptist.

<sup>17.14</sup> When they returned to the crowd, a man came to Jesus, knelt before him,

<sup>17.15</sup> and said, "Sir, have mercy on my son! He is an epileptic and has such terrible attacks that he often falls in the fire or into water.

<sup>17.16</sup> "I brought him to your disciples, but they could not heal him."

<sup>17.17</sup> Jesus answered, "How unbelieving and wrong you people are! How long must I stay with you? How long do I have to put up with you? Bring the boy here to me!"

<sup>17.18</sup> Jesus gave a command to the demon, and it went out of the boy, and at that very moment he was healed.

<sup>17.19</sup> Then the disciples came to Jesus in private and asked him, "Why couldn't we drive the demon out?"

<sup>17.20</sup> "It was because you do not have enough faith," answered Jesus. "I assure you that if you have faith as big as a mustard seed, you can say to this hill, 'Go from here to there!' and it will go. You could do anything!"

<sup>17.21</sup> (But only prayer and fasting can drive this kind out; nothing else can.

<sup>17.22</sup> When the disciples all came together in Galilee, Jesus said to them, "The Son of Man is about to be handed over to those

<sup>17.23</sup> "who will kill him; but three days later he will be raised to life." The disciples became very sad.

<sup>17.24</sup> When Jesus and his disciples came to Capernaum, the collectors of the Temple tax came to Peter and asked, "Does your teacher pay the Temple tax?"

<sup>17.25</sup> "Of course," Peter answered. When Peter went into the house, Jesus spoke up first, "Simon, what is your opinion? Who pays duties or taxes to the kings of this world? The citizens of the country or the foreigners?"

<sup>17.26</sup> "The foreigners," answered Peter. "Well, then," replied Jesus, "that means that the citizens don't have to pay.

<sup>17.27</sup> "But we don't want to offend these people. So go to the lake and drop in a line. Pull up the first fish you hook, and in its mouth you

will find a coin worth enough for my Temple tax and yours. Take it and pay them our taxes."

# 18

<sup>18.1</sup> At that time the disciples came to Jesus, asking, "Who is the greatest in the Kingdom of heaven?"

<sup>18.2</sup> So Jesus called a child to come and stand in front of them,

<sup>18.3</sup> and said, "I assure you that unless you change and become like children, you will never enter the Kingdom of heaven.

<sup>18.4</sup> "The greatest in the Kingdom of heaven is the one who humbles himself and becomes like this child.

<sup>18.5</sup> "And whoever welcomes in my name one such child as this, welcomes me.

<sup>18.6</sup> "If anyone should cause one of these little ones to lose his faith in me, it would be better for that person to have a large millstone tied around his neck and be drowned in the deep sea.

<sup>18.7</sup> "How terrible for the world that there are things that make people lose their faith! Such things will always happen — but how terrible for the one who causes them!

<sup>18.8</sup> "If your hand or your foot makes you lose your faith, cut it off and throw it away! It is better for you to enter life without a hand or a foot than to keep both hands and both feet and be thrown into the eternal fire.

<sup>18.9</sup> "And if your eye makes you lose your faith, take it out and throw it away! It is better for you to enter life with only one eye than to keep both eyes and be thrown into the fire of hell.

<sup>18.10</sup> "See that you don't despise any of these little ones. Their angels in heaven, I tell you, are always in the presence of my Father in heaven.

<sup>18.11</sup> (For the Son of Man came to save the lost.)

<sup>18.12</sup> "What do you think a man does who has one hundred sheep and one of them gets lost? He will leave the other ninety-nine grazing on the hillside and go and look for the lost sheep.

<sup>18.13</sup> "When he finds it, I tell you, he feels far happier over this one sheep than over the ninety-nine that did not get lost.

<sup>18.14</sup> "In just the same way your Father in heaven does not want any of these little ones to be lost.

<sup>18.15</sup> "If your brother sins against you, go to him and show him his fault. But do it privately, just between yourselves. If he listens to you, you have won your brother back.

<sup>18.16</sup> "But if he will not listen to you, take one or two other persons

with you, so that 'every accusation may be upheld by the testimony of two or more witnesses,' as the scripture says.

18.17 "And if he will not listen to them, then tell the whole thing to the church. Finally, if he will not listen to the church, treat him as though he were a pagan or a tax collector.

18.18 "And so I tell all of you: what you prohibit on earth will be prohibited in heaven, and what you permit on earth will be permitted in heaven.

18.19 "And I tell you more: whenever two of you on earth agree about anything you pray for, it will be done for you by my Father in heaven.

18.20 "For where two or three come together in my name, I am there with them."

18.21 Then Peter came to Jesus and asked, "Lord, if my brother keeps on sinning against me, how many times do I have to forgive him? Seven times?"

18.22 "No, not seven times," answered Jesus, "but seventy times seven, 18.23 "because the Kingdom of heaven is like this. Once there was a king who decided to check on his servants' accounts.

18.24 "He had just begun to do so when one of them was brought in who owed him millions of dollars.

18.25 "The servant did not have enough to pay his debt, so the king ordered him to be sold as a slave, with his wife and his children and all that he had, in order to pay the debt.

18.26 "The servant fell on his knees before the king. 'Be patient with me,' he begged, 'and I will pay you everything!'

18.27 "The king felt sorry for him, so he forgave him the debt and let him go.

18.28 "Then the man went out and met one of his fellow servants who owed him a few dollars. He grabbed him and started choking him. 'Pay back what you owe me!' he said.

18.29 "His fellow servant fell down and begged him, 'Be patient with me, and I will pay you back!'

18.30 "But he refused; instead, he had him thrown into jail until he should pay the debt.

18.31 "When the other servants saw what had happened, they were very upset and went to the king and told him everything.

18.32 "So he called the servant in. 'You worthless slave!' he said. 'I forgave you the whole amount you owed me, just because you asked me to.

18.33 " 'You should have had mercy on your fellow servant, just as I had mercy on you.' "

<sup>18.34</sup> "The king was very angry, and he sent the servant to jail to be punished until he should pay back the whole amount."

<sup>18.35</sup> And Jesus concluded, "That is how my Father in heaven will treat every one of you unless you forgive your brother from your heart."

# 19

<sup>19.1</sup> When Jesus finished saying these things, he left Galilee and went to the territory of Judea on the other side of the Jordan River.

<sup>19.2</sup> Large crowds followed him, and he healed them there.

<sup>19.3</sup> Some Pharisees came to him and tried to trap him by asking, "Does our Law allow a man to divorce his wife for whatever reason he wishes?"

<sup>19.4</sup> Jesus answered, "Haven't you read the scripture that says that in the beginning the Creator made people male and female?

<sup>19.5</sup> "And God said, 'For this reason a man will leave his father and mother and unite with his wife, and the two will become one.'

<sup>19.6</sup> "So they are no longer two, but one. No human being must separate, then, what God has joined together."

<sup>19.7</sup> The Pharisees asked him, "Why, then, did Moses give the law for a man to hand his wife a divorce notice and send her away?"

<sup>19.8</sup> Jesus answered, "Moses gave you permission to divorce your wives because you are so hard to teach. But it was not like that at the time of creation.

<sup>19.9</sup> "I tell you, then, that any man who divorces his wife for any cause other than her unfaithfulness, commits adultery if he marries some other woman."

<sup>19.10</sup> His disciples said to him, "If this is how it is between a man and his wife, it is better not to marry."

<sup>19.11</sup> Jesus answered, "This teaching does not apply to everyone, but only to those to whom God has given it.

<sup>19.12</sup> "For there are different reasons why men cannot marry: some, because they were born that way; others, because men made them that way; and others do not marry for the sake of the Kingdom of heaven. Let him who can accept this teaching do so."

<sup>19.13</sup> Some people brought children to Jesus for him to place his hands on them and to pray for them, but the disciples scolded the people.

<sup>19.14</sup> Jesus said, "Let the children come to me and do not stop them, because the Kingdom of heaven belongs to such as these."

<sup>19.15</sup> He placed his hands on them and then went away.

¹⁹·¹⁶ Once a man came to Jesus. "Teacher," he asked, "what good thing must I do to receive eternal life?"

¹⁹·¹⁷ "Why do you ask me concerning what is good?" answered Jesus. "There is only One who is good. Keep the commandments if you want to enter life."

¹⁹·¹⁸ "What commandments?" he asked. Jesus answered, "Do not commit murder; do not commit adultery; do not steal; do not accuse anyone falsely;

¹⁹·¹⁹ "respect your father and your mother; and love your neighbor as you love yourself."

¹⁹·²⁰ "I have obeyed all these commandments," the young man replied. "What else do I need to do?"

¹⁹·²¹ Jesus said to him, "If you want to be perfect, go and sell all you have and give the money to the poor, and you will have riches in heaven; then come and follow me."

¹⁹·²² When the young man heard this, he went away sad, because he was very rich.

¹⁹·²³ Jesus then said to his disciples, "I assure you: it will be very hard for rich people to enter the Kingdom of heaven.

¹⁹·²⁴ "I repeat: it is much harder for a rich person to enter the Kingdom of God than for a camel to go through the eye of a needle."

¹⁹·²⁵ When the disciples heard this, they were completely amazed. "Who, then, can be saved?" they asked.

¹⁹·²⁶ Jesus looked straight at them and answered, "This is impossible for human beings, but for God everything is possible."

¹⁹·²⁷ Then Peter spoke up. "Look," he said, "we have left everything and followed you. What will we have?"

¹⁹·²⁸ Jesus said to them, "You can be sure that when the Son of Man sits on his glorious throne in the New Age, then you twelve followers of mine will also sit on thrones, to rule the twelve tribes of Israel.

¹⁹·²⁹ "And everyone who has left houses or brothers or sisters or father or mother or children or fields for my sake, will receive a hundred times more and will be given eternal life.

¹⁹·³⁰ "But many who now are first will be last, and many who now are last will be first.

# 20

²⁰·¹ "The Kingdom of heaven is like this. Once there was a man who went out early in the morning to hire some men to work in his vineyard.

²⁰·² "He agreed to pay them the regular wage, a silver coin a day, and

sent them to work in his vineyard.

20.3 "He went out again to the marketplace at nine o'clock and saw some men standing there doing nothing,

20.4 "so he told them, 'You also go and work in the vineyard, and I will pay you a fair wage.'

20.5 "So they went. Then at twelve o'clock and again at three o'clock he did the same thing.

20.6 "It was nearly five o'clock when he went to the marketplace and saw some other men still standing there. 'Why are you wasting the whole day here doing nothing?' he asked them.

20.7 " 'No one hired us,' they answered. 'Well, then, you go and work in the vineyard,' he told them."

20.8 "When evening came, the owner told his foreman, 'Call the workers and pay them their wages, starting with those who were hired last and ending with those who were hired first.'

20.9 "The men who had begun to work at five o'clock were paid a silver coin each.

20.10 "So when the men who were the first to be hired came to be paid, they thought they would get more; but they too were given a silver coin each.

20.11 "They took their money and started grumbling against the employer.

20.12 " 'These men who were hired last worked only one hour,' they said, 'while we put up with a whole day's work in the hot sun — yet you paid them the same as you paid us!'

20.13 " 'Listen, friend,' the owner answered one of them, 'I have not cheated you. After all, you agreed to do a day's work for one silver coin.

20.14 " 'Now take your pay and go home. I want to give this man who was hired last as much as I gave you.

20.15 " 'Don't I have the right to do as I wish with my own money? Or are you jealous because I am generous?' "

20.16 And Jesus concluded, "So those who are last will be first, and those who are first will be last."

20.17 As Jesus was going up to Jerusalem, he took the twelve disciples aside and spoke to them privately, as they walked along.

20.18 "Listen," he told them, "we are going up to Jerusalem, where the Son of Man will be handed over to the chief priests and the teachers of the Law. They will condemn him to death

20.19 "and then hand him over to the Gentiles, who will make fun of him, whip him, and crucify him; but three days later he will be raised to life."

20.20 Then the wife of Zebedee came to Jesus with her two sons, bowed before him, and asked him for a favor.

20.21 "What do you want?" Jesus asked her. She answered, "Promise me that these two sons of mine will sit at your right and your left when you are King."

20.22 "You don't know what you are asking for," Jesus answered the sons. "Can you drink the cup of suffering that I am about to drink?" "We can," they answered.

20.23 "You will indeed drink from my cup," Jesus told them, "but I do not have the right to choose who will sit at my right and my left. These places belong to those for whom my Father has prepared them."

20.24 When the other ten disciples heard about this, they became angry with the two brothers.

20.25 So Jesus called them all together and said, "You know that the rulers of the heathen have power over them, and the leaders have complete authority.

20.26 "This, however, is not the way it shall be among you. If one of you wants to be great, you must be the servant of the rest;

20.27 "and if one of you wants to be first, you must be the slave of the others

20.28 "like the Son of Man, who did not come to be served, but to serve and to give his life to redeem many people."

20.29 As Jesus and his disciples were leaving Jericho, a large crowd was following.

20.30 Two blind men who were sitting by the road heard that Jesus was passing by, so they began to shout, "Son of David! Have mercy on us, sir!"

20.31 The crowd scolded them and told them to be quiet. But they shouted even more loudly, "Son of David! Have mercy on us, sir!"

20.32 Jesus stopped and called them. "What do you want me to do for you?" he asked them.

20.33 "Sir," they answered, "we want you to give us our sight!"

20.34 Jesus had pity on them and touched their eyes; at once they were able to see, and they followed him.

# 21

21.1 As Jesus and his disciples approached Jerusalem, they came to Bethphage at the Mount of Olives. There Jesus sent two of the disciples on ahead

21.2 with these instructions: "Go to the village there ahead of you, and at once you will find a donkey tied up with her colt beside her. Untie them and bring them to me.

21.3 And if anyone says anything, tell him, 'The Master needs them'; and then he will let them go at once."

21.4 This happened in order to make come true what the prophet had said:

21.5 "Tell the city of Zion, Look, your king is coming to you! He is humble and rides on a donkey and on a colt, the foal of a donkey."

21.6 So the disciples went and did what Jesus had told them to do:

21.7 they brought the donkey and the colt, threw their cloaks over them, and Jesus got on.

21.8 A large crowd of people spread their cloaks on the road while others cut branches from the trees and spread them on the road.

21.9 The crowds walking in front of Jesus and those walking behind began to shout, "Praise to David's Son! God bless him who comes in the name of the Lord! Praise be to God!"

21.10 When Jesus entered Jerusalem, the whole city was thrown into an uproar. "Who is he?" the people asked.

21.11 "This is the prophet Jesus, from Nazareth in Galilee," the crowds answered.

21.12 Jesus went into the Temple and drove out all those who were buying and selling there. He overturned the tables of the money-changers and the stools of those who sold pigeons,

21.13 and said to them, "It is written in the Scriptures that God said, 'My Temple will be called a house of prayer.' But you are making it a hideout for thieves!"

21.14 The blind and the crippled came to him in the Temple, and he healed them.

21.15 The chief priests and the teachers of the Law became angry when they saw the wonderful things he was doing and the children shouting in the Temple, "Praise to David's Son!"

21.16 So they asked Jesus, "Do you hear what they are saying?" "Indeed I do," answered Jesus. "Haven't you ever read this scripture? 'You have trained children and babies to offer perfect praise.'"

21.17 Jesus left them and went out of the city to Bethany, where he spent the night.

21.18 On his way back to the city early next morning, Jesus was hungry.

21.19 He saw a fig tree by the side of the road and went to it, but found nothing on it except leaves. So he said to the tree, "You will never again bear fruit!" At once the fig tree dried up.

21.20 The disciples saw this and were astounded. "How did the fig tree dry up so quickly?" they asked.

21.21 Jesus answered, "I assure you that if you believe and do not doubt, you will be able to do what I have done to this fig tree. And not only this, but you will even be able to say to this hill, 'Get up and throw yourself in the sea,' and it will.

21.22 "If you believe, you will receive whatever you ask for in prayer."

21.23 Jesus came back to the Temple; and as he taught, the chief priests and the elders came to him and asked, "What right do you have to do these things? Who gave you such right?"

21.24 Jesus answered them, "I will ask you just one question, and if you give me an answer, I will tell you what right I have to do these things.

21.25 "Where did John's right to baptize come from: was it from God or from human beings?" They started to argue among themselves, "What shall we say? If we answer, 'From God,' he will say to us, 'Why, then, did you not believe John?'

21.26 "But if we say, 'From human beings,' we are afraid of what the people might do, because they are all convinced that John was a prophet."

21.27 So they answered Jesus, "We don't know." And he said to them, "Neither will I tell you, then, by what right I do these things.

21.28 "Now, what do you think? There was once a man who had two sons. He went to the older one and said, 'Son, go and work in the vineyard today.'

21.29 " 'I don't want to,' he answered, but later he changed his mind and went.' "

21.30 "Then the father went to the other son and said the same thing. 'Yes, sir,' he answered, but he did not go.

21.31 "Which one of the two did what his father wanted?" "The older one," they answered. So Jesus said to them, "I tell you: the tax collectors and the prostitutes are going into the Kingdom of God ahead of you.

21.32 "For John the Baptist came to you showing you the right path to take, and you would not believe him; but the tax collectors and the prostitutes believed him. Even when you saw this, you did not later change your minds and believe him."

21.33 "Listen to another parable," Jesus said. "There was once a land-owner who planted a vineyard, put a fence around it, dug a hole for the wine press, and built a watchtower. Then he rented the vineyard to tenants and left home on a trip.

<sup>21.34</sup> "When the time came to gather the grapes, he sent his slaves to the tenants to receive his share of the harvest.

<sup>21.35</sup> "The tenants grabbed his slaves, beat one, killed another, and stoned another.

<sup>21.36</sup> "Again the man sent other slaves, more than the first time, and the tenants treated them the same way.

<sup>21.37</sup> "Last of all he sent his son to them. 'Surely they will respect my son,' he said.

<sup>21.38</sup> "But when the tenants saw the son, they said to themselves, 'This is the owner's son. Come on, let's kill him, and we will get his property!'

<sup>21.39</sup> "So they grabbed him, threw him out of the vineyard, and killed him.

<sup>21.40</sup> "Now, when the owner of the vineyard comes, what will he do to those tenants?" Jesus asked.

<sup>21.41</sup> "He will certainly kill those evil men," they answered, "and rent the vineyard out to other tenants, who will give him his share of the harvest at the right time."

<sup>21.42</sup> Jesus said to them, "Haven't you ever read what the Scriptures say? 'The stone which the builders rejected as worthless turned out to be the most important of all. This was done by the Lord; what a wonderful sight it is!'

<sup>21.43</sup> "And so I tell you," added Jesus, "the Kingdom of God will be taken away from you and given to a people who will produce the proper fruits."

<sup>21.44</sup> ("Whoever falls on this stone will be cut to pieces; and if the stone falls on someone, it will crush him to dust.")

<sup>21.45</sup> The chief priests and the Pharisees heard Jesus' parables and knew that he was talking about them,

<sup>21.46</sup> so they tried to arrest him. But they were afraid of the crowds, who considered Jesus to be a prophet.

# 22

<sup>22.1</sup> Jesus again used parables in talking to the people.

<sup>22.2</sup> "The Kingdom of heaven is like this. Once there was a king who prepared a wedding feast for his son.

<sup>22.3</sup> "He sent his servants to tell the invited guests to come to the feast, but they did not want to come.

<sup>22.4</sup> "So he sent other servants with this message for the guests: 'My feast is ready now; my steers and prize calves have been butchered,

and everything is ready. Come to the wedding feast!'

<sup>22.5</sup> "But the invited guests paid no attention and went about their business: one went to his farm, another to his store,

<sup>22.6</sup> "while others grabbed the servants, beat them, and killed them.

<sup>22.7</sup> "The king was very angry; so he sent his soldiers, who killed those murderers and burned down their city.

<sup>22.8</sup> "Then he called his servants and said to them, 'My wedding feast is ready, but the people I invited did not deserve it.

<sup>22.9</sup> " 'Now go to the main streets and invite to the feast as many people as you find.' "

<sup>22.10</sup> "So the servants went out into the streets and gathered all the people they could find, good and bad alike; and the wedding hall was filled with people.

<sup>22.11</sup> "The king went in to look at the guests and saw a man who was not wearing wedding clothes.

<sup>22.12</sup> " 'Friend, how did you get in here without wedding clothes?' the king asked him. But the man said nothing.' "

<sup>22.13</sup> "Then the king told the servants, 'Tie him up hand and foot, and throw him outside in the dark. There he will cry and gnash his teeth.'"

<sup>22.14</sup> And Jesus concluded, "Many are invited, but few are chosen."

<sup>22.15</sup> The Pharisees went off and made a plan to trap Jesus with questions.

<sup>22.16</sup> Then they sent to him some of their disciples and some members of Herod's party. "Teacher," they said, "we know that you tell the truth. You teach the truth about God's will for people, without worrying about what others think, because you pay no attention to anyone's status.

<sup>22.17</sup> "Tell us, then, what do you think? Is it against our Law to pay taxes to the Roman Emperor, or not?"

<sup>22.18</sup> Jesus, however, was aware of their evil plan, and so he said, "You hypocrites! Why are you trying to trap me?

<sup>22.19</sup> "Show me the coin for paying the tax!" They brought him the coin,

<sup>22.20</sup> and he asked them, "Whose face and name are these?"

<sup>22.21</sup> "The Emperor's," they answered. So Jesus said to them, "Well, then, pay to the Emperor what belongs to the Emperor, and pay to God what belongs to God."

<sup>22.22</sup> When they heard this, they were amazed; and they left him and went away.

<sup>22.23</sup> That same day some Sadducees came to Jesus and claimed that

people will not rise from death.

<sup></sup>22.24 "Teacher," they said, "Moses said that if a man who has no children dies, his brother must marry the widow so that they can have children who will be considered the dead man's children.

22.25 "Now, there were seven brothers who used to live here. The oldest got married and died without having children, so he left his widow to his brother.

22.26 "The same thing happened to the second brother, to the third, and finally to all seven.

22.27 "Last of all, the woman died.

22.28 "Now, on the day when the dead rise to life, whose wife will she be? All of them had married her."

22.29 Jesus answered them, "How wrong you are! It is because you don't know the Scriptures or God's power.

22.30 "For when the dead rise to life, they will be like the angels in heaven and will not marry.

22.31 "Now, as for the dead rising to life: haven't you ever read what God has told you? He said,

22.32 " 'I am the God of Abraham, the God of Isaac, and the God of Jacob.' He is the God of the living, not of the dead."

22.33 When the crowds heard this, they were amazed at his teaching.

22.34 When the Pharisees heard that Jesus had silenced the Sadducees, they came together,

22.35 and one of them, a teacher of the Law, tried to trap him with a question.

22.36 "Teacher," he asked, "which is the greatest commandment in the Law?"

22.37 Jesus answered, " 'Love the Lord your God with all your heart, with all your soul, and with all your mind.' "

22.38 "This is the greatest and the most important commandment.

22.39 "The second most important commandment is like it: 'Love your neighbor as you love yourself.'

22.40 "The whole Law of Moses and the teachings of the prophets depend on these two commandments."

22.41 When some Pharisees gathered together, Jesus asked them,

22.42 "What do you think about the Messiah? Whose descendant is he?"

"He is David's descendant," they answered.

22.43 "Why, then," Jesus asked, "did the Spirit inspire David to call him 'Lord'? David said,

22.44 " 'The Lord said to my Lord: Sit here at my right side until I put your enemies under your feet.'"

<sup>22.45</sup> "If, then, David called him 'Lord,' how can the Messiah be David's descendant?"

<sup>22.46</sup> No one was able to give Jesus any answer, and from that day on no one dared to ask him any more questions.

# 23

<sup>23.1</sup> Then Jesus spoke to the crowds and to his disciples.

<sup>23.2</sup> "The teachers of the Law and the Pharisees are the authorized interpreters of Moses' Law.

<sup>23.3</sup> "So you must obey and follow everything they tell you to do; do not, however, imitate their actions, because they don't practice what they preach.

<sup>23.4</sup> "They tie onto people's backs loads that are heavy and hard to carry, yet they aren't willing even to lift a finger to help them carry those loads.

<sup>23.5</sup> "They do everything so that people will see them. Look at the straps with scripture verses on them which they wear on their foreheads and arms, and notice how large they are! Notice also how long are the tassels on their cloaks!

<sup>23.6</sup> "They love the best places at feasts and the reserved seats in the synagogues;

<sup>23.7</sup> " 'they love to be greeted with respect in the marketplaces and to have people call them 'Teacher.' "

<sup>23.8</sup> "You must not be called 'Teacher,' because you are all equal and have only one Teacher.

<sup>23.9</sup> "And you must not call anyone here on earth 'Father,' because you have only the one Father in heaven.

<sup>23.10</sup> "Nor should you be called 'Leader,' because your one and only leader is the Messiah.

<sup>23.11</sup> "The greatest one among you must be your servant.

<sup>23.12</sup> "Whoever makes himself great will be humbled, and whoever humbles himself will be made great.

<sup>23.13</sup> "How terrible for you, teachers of the Law and Pharisees! You hypocrites! You lock the door to the Kingdom of heaven in people's faces, but you yourselves don't go in, nor do you allow in those who are trying to enter!

<sup>23.14</sup> ("How terrible for you, teachers of the Law and Pharisees! You hypocrites! You take advantage of widows and rob them of their homes, and then make a show of saying long prayers! Because of this your punishment will be all the worse!)

<sup>23.15</sup> "How terrible for you, teachers of the Law and Pharisees! You hypocrites! You sail the seas and cross whole countries to win one convert; and when you succeed, you make him twice as deserving of going to hell as you yourselves are!

<sup>23.16</sup> "How terrible for you, blind guides! You teach, 'If someone swears by the Temple, he isn't bound by his vow; but if he swears by the gold in the Temple, he is bound.'

<sup>23.17</sup> "Blind fools! Which is more important, the gold or the Temple which makes the gold holy?

<sup>23.18</sup> "You also teach, 'If someone swears by the altar, he isn't bound by his vow; but if he swears by the gift on the altar, he is bound.'

<sup>23.19</sup> "How blind you are! Which is the more important, the gift or the altar which makes the gift holy?

<sup>23.20</sup> "So then, when a person swears by the altar, he is swearing by it and by all the gifts on it;

<sup>23.21</sup> "and when he swears by the Temple, he is swearing by it and by God, who lives there;

<sup>23.22</sup> "and when someone swears by heaven, he is swearing by God's throne and by him who sits on it.

<sup>23.23</sup> "How terrible for you, teachers of the Law and Pharisees! You hypocrites! You give to God one tenth even of the seasoning herbs, such as mint, dill, and cumin, but you neglect to obey the really important teachings of the Law, such as justice and mercy and honesty. These you should practice, without neglecting the others.

<sup>23.24</sup> "Blind guides! You strain a fly out of your drink, but swallow a camel!

<sup>23.25</sup> "How terrible for you, teachers of the Law and Pharisees! You hypocrites! You clean the outside of your cup and plate, while the inside is full of what you have gotten by violence and selfishness.

<sup>23.26</sup> "Blind Pharisee! Clean what is inside the cup first, and then the outside will be clean too!

<sup>23.27</sup> "How terrible for you, teachers of the Law and Pharisees! You hypocrites! You are like whitewashed tombs, which look fine on the outside but are full of bones and decaying corpses on the inside.

<sup>23.28</sup> "In the same way, on the outside you appear good to everybody, but inside you are full of hypocrisy and sins.

<sup>23.29</sup> "How terrible for you, teachers of the Law and Pharisees! You hypocrites! You make fine tombs for the prophets and decorate the monuments of those who lived good lives;

<sup>23.30</sup> "and you claim that if you had lived during the time of your ancestors, you would not have done what they did and killed the proph-

ets.

<sup>23.31</sup> "So you actually admit that you are the descendants of those who murdered the prophets!

<sup>23.32</sup> "Go on, then, and finish up what your ancestors started!

<sup>23.33</sup> "You snakes and children of snakes! How do you expect to escape from being condemned to hell?

<sup>23.34</sup> "And so I tell you that I will send you prophets and wise men and teachers; you will kill some of them, crucify others, and whip others in the synagogues and chase them from town to town.

<sup>23.35</sup> "As a result, the punishment for the murder of all innocent people will fall on you, from the murder of innocent Abel to the murder of Zechariah son of Berechiah, whom you murdered between the Temple and the altar.

<sup>23.36</sup> "I tell you indeed: the punishment for all these murders will fall on the people of this day!

<sup>23.37</sup> "Jerusalem, Jerusalem! You kill the prophets and stone the messengers God has sent you! How many times I wanted to put my arms around all your people, just as a hen gathers her chicks under her wings, but you would not let me!

<sup>23.38</sup> "And so your Temple will be abandoned and empty.

<sup>23.39</sup> "From now on, I tell you, you will never see me again until you say, 'God bless him who comes in the name of the Lord.'"

# 24

<sup>24.1</sup> Jesus left and was going away from the Temple when his disciples came to him to call his attention to its buildings.

<sup>24.2</sup> "Yes," he said, "you may well look at all these. I tell you this: not a single stone here will be left in its place; every one of them will be thrown down."

<sup>24.3</sup> As Jesus sat on the Mount of Olives, the disciples came to him in private. "Tell us when all this will be," they asked, "and what will happen to show that it is the time for your coming and the end of the age."

<sup>24.4</sup> Jesus answered, "Watch out, and do not let anyone fool you.

<sup>24.5</sup> "Many men, claiming to speak for me, will come and say, 'I am the Messiah!' and they will fool many people.

<sup>24.6</sup> "You are going to hear the noise of battles close by and the news of battles far away; but do not be troubled. Such things must happen, but they do not mean that the end has come.

<sup>24.7</sup> "Countries will fight each other; kingdoms will attack one another. There will be famines and earthquakes everywhere.

[24.8] "All these things are like the first pains of childbirth.

[24.9] "Then you will be arrested and handed over to be punished and be put to death. Everyone will hate you because of me.

[24.10] "Many will give up their faith at that time; they will betray one another and hate one another.

[24.11] "Then many false prophets will appear and fool many people.

[24.12] "Such will be the spread of evil that many people's love will grow cold.

[24.13] "But whoever holds out to the end will be saved.

[24.14] "And this Good News about the Kingdom will be preached through all the world for a witness to all people; and then the end will come.

[24.15] "You will see 'The Awful Horror' of which the prophet Daniel spoke. It will be standing in the holy place." (Note to the reader: understand what this means!)

[24.16] "Then those who are in Judea must run away to the hills.

[24.17] "Someone who is on the roof of a house must not take the time to go down and get any belongings from the house.

[24.18] "Someone who is in the field must not go back to get a cloak.

[24.19] "How terrible it will be in those days for women who are pregnant and for mothers with little babies!

[24.20] "Pray to God that you will not have to run away during the winter or on a Sabbath!

[24.21] "For the trouble at that time will be far more terrible than any there has ever been, from the beginning of the world to this very day. Nor will there ever be anything like it again.

[24.22] "But God has already reduced the number of days; had he not done so, nobody would survive. For the sake of his chosen people, however, God will reduce the days.

[24.23] "Then, if anyone says to you, 'Look, here is the Messiah!' or 'There he is!' — do not believe it.

[24.24] "For false Messiahs and false prophets will appear; they will perform great miracles and wonders in order to deceive even God's chosen people, if possible.

[24.25] "Listen! I have told you this ahead of time.

[24.26] "Or, if people should tell you, 'Look, he is out in the desert!' - don't go there; or if they say, 'Look, he is hiding here!' — don't believe it.

[24.27] "For the Son of Man will come like the lightning which flashes across the whole sky from the east to the west.

[24.28] "Wherever there is a dead body, the vultures will gather.

24.29 "Soon after the trouble of those days, the sun will grow dark, the moon will no longer shine, the stars will fall from heaven, and the powers in space will be driven from their courses.

24.30 "Then the sign of the Son of Man will appear in the sky; and all the peoples of earth will weep as they see the Son of Man coming on the clouds of heaven with power and great glory.

24.31 "The great trumpet will sound, and he will send out his angels to the four corners of the earth, and they will gather his chosen people from one end of the world to the other.

24.32 "Let the fig tree teach you a lesson. When its branches become green and tender and it starts putting out leaves, you know that summer is near.

24.33 "In the same way, when you see all these things, you will know that the time is near, ready to begin.

24.34 "Remember that all these things will happen before the people now living have all died.

24.35 "Heaven and earth will pass away, but my words will never pass away.

24.36 "No one knows, however, when that day and hour will come — neither the angels in heaven nor the Son; the Father alone knows.

24.37 "The coming of the Son of Man will be like what happened in the time of Noah.

24.38 "In the days before the flood people ate and drank, men and women married, up to the very day Noah went into the boat;

24.39 "yet they did not realize what was happening until the flood came and swept them all away. That is how it will be when the Son of Man comes.

24.40 "At that time two men will be working in a field: one will be taken away, the other will be left behind.

24.41 "Two women will be at a mill grinding meal: one will be taken away, the other will be left behind.

24.42 "Watch out, then, because you do not know what day your Lord will come.

24.43 "If the owner of a house knew the time when the thief would come, you can be sure that he would stay awake and not let the thief break into his house.

24.44 "So then, you also must always be ready, because the Son of Man will come at an hour when you are not expecting him.

24.45 "Who, then, is a faithful and wise servant? It is the one that his master has placed in charge of the other servants to give them their food at the proper time.

<sup>24.46</sup> "How happy that servant is if his master finds him doing this when he comes home!

<sup>24.47</sup> "Indeed, I tell you, the master will put that servant in charge of all his property.

<sup>24.48</sup> "But if he is a bad servant, he will tell himself that his master will not come back for a long time,

<sup>24.49</sup> "and he will begin to beat his fellow servants and to eat and drink with drunkards.

<sup>24.50</sup> "Then that servant's master will come back one day when the servant does not expect him and at a time he does not know.

<sup>24.51</sup> "The master will cut him in pieces and make him share the fate of the hypocrites. There he will cry and gnash his teeth.

# 25

<sup>25.1</sup> "At that time the Kingdom of heaven will be like this. Once there were ten young women who took their oil lamps and went out to meet the bridegroom.

<sup>25.2</sup> "Five of them were foolish, and the other five were wise.

<sup>25.3</sup> "The foolish ones took their lamps but did not take any extra oil with them,

<sup>25.4</sup> "while the wise ones took containers full of oil for their lamps.

<sup>25.5</sup> "The bridegroom was late in coming, so they began to nod and fall asleep.

<sup>25.6</sup> "It was already midnight when the cry rang out, 'Here is the bridegroom! Come and meet him!'

<sup>25.7</sup> "The ten young women woke up and trimmed their lamps.

<sup>25.8</sup> "Then the foolish ones said to the wise ones, 'Let us have some of your oil, because our lamps are going out.'

<sup>25.9</sup> " 'No, indeed,' the wise ones answered, 'there is not enough for you and for us. Go to the store and buy some for yourselves.'

<sup>25.10</sup> "So the foolish ones went off to buy some oil; and while they were gone, the bridegroom arrived. The five who were ready went in with him to the wedding feast, and the door was closed.

<sup>25.11</sup> "Later the others arrived. 'Sir, sir! Let us in!' they cried out.

<sup>25.12</sup> "'Certainly not! I don't know you,' the bridegroom answered."

<sup>25.13</sup> And Jesus concluded, "Watch out, then, because you do not know the day or the hour.

<sup>25.14</sup> "At that time the Kingdom of heaven will be like this. Once there was a man who was about to leave home on a trip; he called his servants and put them in charge of his property.

<sup>25.15</sup> "He gave to each one according to his ability: to one he gave five

thousand gold coins, to another he gave two thousand, and to another he gave one thousand. Then he left on his trip.

25.16 "The servant who had received five thousand coins went at once and invested his money and earned another five thousand.

25.17 "In the same way the servant who had received two thousand coins earned another two thousand.

25.18 "But the servant who had received one thousand coins went off, dug a hole in the ground, and hid his master's money.

25.19 "After a long time the master of those servants came back and settled accounts with them.

25.20 "The servant who had received five thousand coins came in and handed over the other five thousand. 'You gave me five thousand coins, sir,' he said. 'Look! Here are another five thousand that I have earned.'

25.21 "'Well done, you good and faithful servant!' said his master. 'You have been faithful in managing small amounts, so I will put you in charge of large amounts. Come on in and share my happiness!'

25.22 "Then the servant who had been given two thousand coins came in and said, 'You gave me two thousand coins, sir. Look! Here are another two thousand that I have earned.'

25.23 "'Well done, you good and faithful servant!' said his master. 'You have been faithful in managing small amounts, so I will put you in charge of large amounts. Come on in and share my happiness!'

25.24 "Then the servant who had received one thousand coins came in and said, 'Sir, I know you are a hard man; you reap harvests where you did not plant, and you gather crops where you did not scatter seed.

25.25 " 'I was afraid, so I went off and hid your money in the ground. Look! Here is what belongs to you.'

25.26 " 'You bad and lazy servant!' his master said. 'You knew, did you, that I reap harvests where I did not plant, and gather crops where I did not scatter seed?

25.27 " 'Well, then, you should have deposited my money in the bank, and I would have received it all back with interest when I returned.

25.28 " 'Now, take the money away from him and give it to the one who has ten thousand coins.

25.29 " 'For to every person who has something, even more will be given, and he will have more than enough; but the person who has nothing, even the little that he has will be taken away from him.

25.30 " 'As for this useless servant — throw him outside in the darkness; there he will cry and gnash his teeth.'

[25.31] "When the Son of Man comes as King and all the angels with him, he will sit on his royal throne,

[25.32] "and the people of all the nations will be gathered before him. Then he will divide them into two groups, just as a shepherd separates the sheep from the goats.

[25.33] "He will put the righteous people at his right and the others at his left.

[25.34] "Then the King will say to the people on his right, 'Come, you that are blessed by my Father! Come and possess the kingdom which has been prepared for you ever since the creation of the world.

[25.35] " 'I was hungry and you fed me, thirsty and you gave me a drink; I was a stranger and you received me in your homes,

[25.36] " 'naked and you clothed me; I was sick and you took care of me, in prison and you visited me.'

[25.37] "The righteous will then answer him, 'When, Lord, did we ever see you hungry and feed you, or thirsty and give you a drink?

[25.38] " 'When did we ever see you a stranger and welcome you in our homes, or naked and clothe you?

[25.39] " 'When did we ever see you sick or in prison, and visit you?'

[25.40] "The King will reply, 'I tell you, whenever you did this for one of the least important of these followers of mine, you did it for me!'

[25.41] "Then he will say to those on his left, 'Away from me, you that are under God's curse! Away to the eternal fire which has been prepared for the Devil and his angels!

[25.42] " 'I was hungry but you would not feed me, thirsty but you would not give me a drink;

[25.43] " 'I was a stranger but you would not welcome me in your homes, naked but you would not clothe me; I was sick and in prison but you would not take care of me.'

[25.44] "Then they will answer him, 'When, Lord, did we ever see you hungry or thirsty or a stranger or naked or sick or in prison, and we would not help you?'

[25.45] "The King will reply, 'I tell you, whenever you refused to help one of these least important ones, you refused to help me.'

[25.46] "These, then, will be sent off to eternal punishment, but the righteous will go to eternal life."

# 26

[26.1] When Jesus had finished teaching all these things, he said to his disciples,

[26.2] "In two days, as you know, it will be the Passover Festival, and the Son of Man will be handed over to be crucified."

26.3 Then the chief priests and the elders met together in the palace of Caiaphas, the High Priest,

26.4 and made plans to arrest Jesus secretly and put him to death.

26.5 "We must not do it during the festival," they said, "or the people will riot."

26.6 Jesus was in Bethany at the house of Simon, a man who had suffered from a dreaded skin disease.

26.7 While Jesus was eating, a woman came to him with an alabaster jar filled with an expensive perfume, which she poured on his head.

26.8 The disciples saw this and became angry. "Why all this waste?" they asked.

26.9 "This perfume could have been sold for a large amount and the money given to the poor!"

26.10 Jesus knew what they were saying, and so he said to them, "Why are you bothering this woman? It is a fine and beautiful thing that she has done for me.

26.11 "You will always have poor people with you, but you will not always have me.

26.12 "What she did was to pour this perfume on my body to get me ready for burial.

26.13 "Now, I assure you that wherever this gospel is preached all over the world, what she has done will be told in memory of her."

26.14 Then one of the twelve disciples — the one named Judas Iscariot — went to the chief priests

26.15 and asked, "What will you give me if I betray Jesus to you?" They counted out thirty silver coins and gave them to him.

26.16 From then on Judas was looking for a good chance to hand Jesus over to them.

26.17 On the first day of the Festival of Unleavened Bread the disciples came to Jesus and asked him, "Where do you want us to get the Passover meal ready for you?"

26.18 "Go to a certain man in the city," he said to them, "and tell him: 'The Teacher says, My hour has come; my disciples and I will celebrate the Passover at your house.'"

26.19 The disciples did as Jesus had told them and prepared the Passover meal.

26.20 When it was evening, Jesus and the twelve disciples sat down to eat.

26.21 During the meal Jesus said, "I tell you, one of you will betray me."

$^{26.22}$ The disciples were very upset and began to ask him, one after the other, "Surely, Lord, you don't mean me?"

$^{26.23}$ Jesus answered, "One who dips his bread in the dish with me will betray me.

$^{26.24}$ "The Son of Man will die as the Scriptures say he will, but how terrible for that man who will betray the Son of Man! It would have been better for that man if he had never been born!"

$^{26.25}$ Judas, the traitor, spoke up. "Surely, Teacher, you don't mean me?" he asked. Jesus answered, "So you say."

$^{26.26}$ While they were eating, Jesus took a piece of bread, gave a prayer of thanks, broke it, and gave it to his disciples. "Take and eat it," he said; "this is my body."

$^{26.27}$ Then he took a cup, gave thanks to God, and gave it to them. "Drink it, all of you," he said;

$^{26.28}$ "this is my blood, which seals God's covenant, my blood poured out for many for the forgiveness of sins.

$^{26.29}$ "I tell you, I will never again drink this wine until the day I drink the new wine with you in my Father's Kingdom."

$^{26.30}$ Then they sang a hymn and went out to the Mount of Olives.

$^{26.31}$ Then Jesus said to them, "This very night all of you will run away and leave me, for the scripture says, 'God will kill the shepherd, and the sheep of the flock will be scattered.'

$^{26.32}$ "But after I am raised to life, I will go to Galilee ahead of you."

$^{26.33}$ Peter spoke up and said to Jesus, "I will never leave you, even though all the rest do!"

$^{26.34}$ Jesus said to Peter, "I tell you that before the rooster crows tonight, you will say three times that you do not know me."

$^{26.35}$ Peter answered, "I will never say that, even if I have to die with you!" And all the other disciples said the same thing.

$^{26.36}$ Then Jesus went with his disciples to a place called Gethsemane, and he said to them, "Sit here while I go over there and pray."

$^{26.37}$ He took with him Peter and the two sons of Zebedee. Grief and anguish came over him,

$^{26.38}$ and he said to them, "The sorrow in my heart is so great that it almost crushes me. Stay here and keep watch with me."

$^{26.39}$ He went a little farther on, threw himself face downward on the ground, and prayed, "My Father, if it is possible, take this cup of suffering from me! Yet not what I want, but what you want."

$^{26.40}$ Then he returned to the three disciples and found them asleep; and he said to Peter, "How is it that you three were not able to keep watch with me for even one hour?

26.41 "Keep watch and pray that you will not fall into temptation. The spirit is willing, but the flesh is weak."

26.42 Once more Jesus went away and prayed, "My Father, if this cup of suffering cannot be taken away unless I drink it, your will be done."

26.43 He returned once more and found the disciples asleep; they could not keep their eyes open.

26.44 Again Jesus left them, went away, and prayed the third time, saying the same words.

26.45 Then he returned to the disciples and said, "Are you still sleeping and resting? Look! The hour has come for the Son of Man to be handed over to the power of sinners.

26.46 "Get up, let us go. Look, here is the man who is betraying me!"

26.47 Jesus was still speaking when Judas, one of the twelve disciples, arrived. With him was a large crowd armed with swords and clubs and sent by the chief priests and the elders.

26.48 The traitor had given the crowd a signal: "The man I kiss is the one you want. Arrest him!"

26.49 Judas went straight to Jesus and said, "Peace be with you, Teacher," and kissed him.

26.50 Jesus answered, "Be quick about it, friend!" Then they came up, arrested Jesus, and held him tight.

26.51 One of those who were with Jesus drew his sword and struck at the High Priest's slave, cutting off his ear.

26.52 "Put your sword back in its place," Jesus said to him. "All who take the sword will die by the sword.

26.53 "Don't you know that I could call on my Father for help, and at once he would send me more than twelve armies of angels?

26.54 "But in that case, how could the Scriptures come true which say that this is what must happen?"

26.55 Then Jesus spoke to the crowd, "Did you have to come with swords and clubs to capture me, as though I were an outlaw? Every day I sat down and taught in the Temple, and you did not arrest me.

26.56 "But all this has happened in order to make come true what the prophets wrote in the Scriptures." Then all the disciples left him and ran away.

26.57 Those who had arrested Jesus took him to the house of Caiaphas, the High Priest, where the teachers of the Law and the elders had gathered together.

26.58 Peter followed from a distance, as far as the courtyard of the High Priest's house. He went into the courtyard and sat down with the guards to see how it would all come out.

<sup>26.59</sup> The chief priests and the whole Council tried to find some false evidence against Jesus to put him to death;

<sup>26.60</sup> but they could not find any, even though many people came forward and told lies about him. Finally two men stepped up

<sup>26.61</sup> and said, "This man said, 'I am able to tear down God's Temple and three days later build it back up.'"

<sup>26.62</sup> The High Priest stood up and said to Jesus, "Have you no answer to give to this accusation against you?"

<sup>26.63</sup> But Jesus kept quiet. Again the High Priest spoke to him, "In the name of the living God I now put you under oath: tell us if you are the Messiah, the Son of God."

<sup>26.64</sup> Jesus answered him, "So you say. But I tell all of you: from this time on you will see the Son of Man sitting at the right side of the Almighty and coming on the clouds of heaven!"

<sup>26.65</sup> At this the High Priest tore his clothes and said, "Blasphemy! We don't need any more witnesses! You have just heard his blasphemy!

<sup>26.66</sup> "What do you think?" They answered, "He is guilty and must die."

<sup>26.67</sup> Then they spat in his face and beat him; and those who slapped him

<sup>26.68</sup> said, "Prophesy for us, Messiah! Guess who hit you!"

<sup>26.69</sup> Peter was sitting outside in the courtyard when one of the High Priest's servant women came to him and said, "You, too, were with Jesus of Galilee."

<sup>26.70</sup> But he denied it in front of them all. "I don't know what you are talking about," he answered,

<sup>26.71</sup> and went on out to the entrance of the courtyard. Another servant woman saw him and said to the men there, "He was with Jesus of Nazareth."

<sup>26.72</sup> Again Peter denied it and answered, "I swear that I don't know that man!"

<sup>26.73</sup> After a little while the men standing there came to Peter. "Of course you are one of them," they said. "After all, the way you speak gives you away!"

<sup>26.74</sup> Then Peter said, "I swear that I am telling the truth! May God punish me if I am not! I do not know that man!" Just then a rooster crowed,

<sup>26.75</sup> and Peter remembered what Jesus had told him: "Before the rooster crows, you will say three times that you do not know me." He went out and wept bitterly.

**27** <sup>27.1</sup> Early in the morning all the chief priests and the elders made their plans against Jesus to put him to death.

<sup>27.2</sup> They put him in chains, led him off, and handed him over to Pilate, the Roman governor.

<sup>27.3</sup> When Judas, the traitor, learned that Jesus had been condemned, he repented and took back the thirty silver coins to the chief priests and the elders.

<sup>27.4</sup> "I have sinned by betraying an innocent man to death!" he said. "What do we care about that?" they answered. "That is your business!"

<sup>27.5</sup> Judas threw the coins down in the Temple and left; then he went off and hanged himself.

<sup>27.6</sup> The chief priests picked up the coins and said, "This is blood money, and it is against our Law to put it in the Temple treasury."

<sup>27.7</sup> After reaching an agreement about it, they used the money to buy Potter's Field, as a cemetery for foreigners.

<sup>27.8</sup> That is why that field is called "Field of Blood" to this very day.

<sup>27.9</sup> Then what the prophet Jeremiah had said came true: "They took the thirty silver coins, the amount the people of Israel had agreed to pay for him,

<sup>27.10</sup> "and used the money to buy the potter's field, as the Lord had commanded me."

<sup>27.11</sup> Jesus stood before the Roman governor, who questioned him. "Are you the king of the Jews?" he asked. "So you say," answered Jesus.

<sup>27.12</sup> But he said nothing in response to the accusations of the chief priests and elders.

<sup>27.13</sup> So Pilate said to him, "Don't you hear all these things they accuse you of?"

<sup>27.14</sup> But Jesus refused to answer a single word, with the result that the Governor was greatly surprised.

<sup>27.15</sup> At every Passover Festival the Roman governor was in the habit of setting free any one prisoner the crowd asked for.

<sup>27.16</sup> At that time there was a well-known prisoner named Jesus Barabbas.

<sup>27.17</sup> So when the crowd gathered, Pilate asked them, "Which one do you want me to set free for you? Jesus Barabbas or Jesus called the Messiah?"

<sup>27.18</sup> He knew very well that the Jewish authorities had handed Jesus over to him because they were jealous.

<sup>27.19</sup> While Pilate was sitting in the judgment hall, his wife sent him a message: "Have nothing to do with that innocent man, because in

a dream last night I suffered much on account of him."

<sup>27.20</sup> The chief priests and the elders persuaded the crowd to ask Pilate to set Barabbas free and have Jesus put to death.

<sup>27.21</sup> But Pilate asked the crowd, "Which one of these two do you want me to set free for you?" "Barabbas!" they answered.

<sup>27.22</sup> "What, then, shall I do with Jesus called the Messiah?" Pilate asked them. "Crucify him!" they all answered.

<sup>27.23</sup> But Pilate asked, "What crime has he committed?" Then they started shouting at the top of their voices: "Crucify him!"

<sup>27.24</sup> When Pilate saw that it was no use to go on, but that a riot might break out, he took some water, washed his hands in front of the crowd, and said, "I am not responsible for the death of this man! This is your doing!"

<sup>27.25</sup> The whole crowd answered, "Let the responsibility for his death fall on us and on our children!"

<sup>27.26</sup> Then Pilate set Barabbas free for them; and after he had Jesus whipped, he handed him over to be crucified.

<sup>27.27</sup> Then Pilate's soldiers took Jesus into the governor's palace, and the whole company gathered around him.

<sup>27.28</sup> They stripped off his clothes and put a scarlet robe on him.

<sup>27.29</sup> Then they made a crown out of thorny branches and placed it on his head, and put a stick in his right hand; then they knelt before him and made fun of him. "Long live the King of the Jews!" they said.

<sup>27.30</sup> They spat on him, and took the stick and hit him over the head.

<sup>27.31</sup> When they had finished making fun of him, they took the robe off and put his own clothes back on him. Then they led him out to crucify him.

<sup>27.32</sup> As they were going out, they met a man from Cyrene named Simon, and the soldiers forced him to carry Jesus' cross.

<sup>27.33</sup> They came to a place called Golgotha, which means, "The Place of the Skull."

<sup>27.34</sup> There they offered Jesus wine mixed with a bitter substance; but after tasting it, he would not drink it.

<sup>27.35</sup> They crucified him and then divided his clothes among them by throwing dice.

<sup>27.36</sup> After that they sat there and watched him.

<sup>27.37</sup> Above his head they put the written notice of the accusation against him: "This is Jesus, the King of the Jews."

<sup>27.38</sup> Then they crucified two bandits with Jesus, one on his right and the other on his left.

<sup>27.39</sup> People passing by shook their heads and hurled insults at Jesus: <sup>27.40</sup> "You were going to tear down the Temple and build it back up in three days! Save yourself if you are God's Son! Come on down from the cross!"

<sup>27.41</sup> In the same way the chief priests and the teachers of the Law and the elders made fun of him: <sup>27.42</sup> "He saved others, but he cannot save himself! Isn't he the king of Israel? If he will come down off the cross now, we will believe in him! <sup>27.43</sup> "He trusts in God and claims to be God's Son. Well, then, let us see if God wants to save him now!"

<sup>27.44</sup> Even the bandits who had been crucified with him insulted him in the same way.

<sup>27.45</sup> At noon the whole country was covered with darkness, which lasted for three hours.

<sup>27.46</sup> At about three o'clock Jesus cried out with a loud shout, "Eli, Eli, lema sabachthani?" which means, "My God, my God, why did you abandon me?"

<sup>27.47</sup> Some of the people standing there heard him and said, "He is calling for Elijah!"

<sup>27.48</sup> One of them ran up at once, took a sponge, soaked it in cheap wine, put it on the end of a stick, and tried to make him drink it.

<sup>27.49</sup> But the others said, "Wait, let us see if Elijah is coming to save him!"

<sup>27.50</sup> Jesus again gave a loud cry and breathed his last.

<sup>27.51</sup> Then the curtain hanging in the Temple was torn in two from top to bottom. The earth shook, the rocks split apart, <sup>27.52</sup> the graves broke open, and many of God's people who had died were raised to life.

<sup>27.53</sup> They left the graves, and after Jesus rose from death, they went into the Holy City, where many people saw them.

<sup>27.54</sup> When the army officer and the soldiers with him who were watching Jesus saw the earthquake and everything else that happened, they were terrified and said, "He really was the Son of God!"

<sup>27.55</sup> There were many women there, looking on from a distance, who had followed Jesus from Galilee and helped him.

<sup>27.56</sup> Among them were Mary Magdalene, Mary the mother of James and Joseph, and the wife of Zebedee.

<sup>27.57</sup> When it was evening, a rich man from Arimathea arrived; his name was Joseph, and he also was a disciple of Jesus.

<sup>27.58</sup> He went into the presence of Pilate and asked for the body of Jesus. Pilate gave orders for the body to be given to Joseph.

<sup>27.59</sup> So Joseph took it, wrapped it in a new linen sheet, <sup>27.60</sup> and placed it in his own tomb, which he had just recently dug out of solid rock. Then he rolled a large stone across the entrance to the tomb and went away.

<sup>27.61</sup> Mary Magdalene and the other Mary were sitting there, facing the tomb.

<sup>27.62</sup> The next day, which was a Sabbath, the chief priests and the Pharisees met with Pilate <sup>27.63</sup> and said, "Sir, we remember that while that liar was still alive he said, 'I will be raised to life three days later.' <sup>27.64</sup> "Give orders, then, for his tomb to be carefully guarded until the third day, so that his disciples will not be able to go and steal the body, and then tell the people that he was raised from death. This last lie would be even worse than the first one."

<sup>27.65</sup> "Take a guard," Pilate told them; "go and make the tomb as secure as you can." <sup>27.66</sup> So they left and made the tomb secure by putting a seal on the stone and leaving the guard on watch.

# 28

<sup>28.1</sup> After the Sabbath, as Sunday morning was dawning, Mary Magdalene and the other Mary went to look at the tomb. <sup>28.2</sup> Suddenly there was a violent earthquake; an angel of the Lord came down from heaven, rolled the stone away, and sat on it. <sup>28.3</sup> His appearance was like lightning, and his clothes were white as snow. <sup>28.4</sup> The guards were so afraid that they trembled and became like dead men.

<sup>28.5</sup> The angel spoke to the women. "You must not be afraid," he said. "I know you are looking for Jesus, who was crucified. <sup>28.6</sup> "He is not here; he has been raised, just as he said. Come here and see the place where he was lying. <sup>28.7</sup> "Go quickly now, and tell his disciples, 'He has been raised from death, and now he is going to Galilee ahead of you; there you will see him!' Remember what I have told you."

<sup>28.8</sup> So they left the tomb in a hurry, afraid and yet filled with joy, and ran to tell his disciples. <sup>28.9</sup> Suddenly Jesus met them and said, "Peace be with you." They came up to him, took hold of his feet, and worshiped him. <sup>28.10</sup> "Do not be afraid," Jesus said to them. "Go and tell my brothers to go to Galilee, and there they will see me."

<sup>28.11</sup> While the women went on their way, some of the soldiers guarding the tomb went back to the city and told the chief priests everything that had happened.

<sup>28.12</sup> The chief priests met with the elders and made their plan; they gave a large sum of money to the soldiers

<sup>28.13</sup> and said, "You are to say that his disciples came during the night and stole his body while you were asleep.

<sup>28.14</sup> "And if the Governor should hear of this, we will convince him that you are innocent, and you will have nothing to worry about."

<sup>28.15</sup> The guards took the money and did what they were told to do. And so that is the report spread around by the Jews to this very day.

<sup>28.16</sup> The eleven disciples went to the hill in Galilee where Jesus had told them to go.

<sup>28.17</sup> When they saw him, they worshiped him, even though some of them doubted.

<sup>28.18</sup> Jesus drew near and said to them, "I have been given all authority in heaven and on earth.

<sup>28.19</sup> "Go, then, to all peoples everywhere and make them my disciples: baptize them in the name of the Father, the Son, and the Holy Spirit,

<sup>28.20</sup> "and teach them to obey everything I have commanded you. And I will be with you always, to the end of the age."

# MARK

# Mark

## 1

<sup>1.1</sup> This is the Good News about Jesus Christ, the Son of God.

<sup>1.2</sup> It began as the prophet Isaiah had written: "God said, 'I will send my messenger ahead of you to open the way for you.'

<sup>1.3</sup> " 'Someone is shouting in the desert, 'Get the road ready for the Lord; make a straight path for him to travel!' "

<sup>1.4</sup> So John appeared in the desert, baptizing and preaching. "Turn away from your sins and be baptized," he told the people, "and God will forgive your sins."

<sup>1.5</sup> Many people from the province of Judea and the city of Jerusalem went out to hear John. They confessed their sins, and he baptized them in the Jordan River.

<sup>1.6</sup> John wore clothes made of camel's hair, with a leather belt around his waist, and his food was locusts and wild honey.

<sup>1.7</sup> He announced to the people, "The man who will come after me is much greater than I am. I am not good enough even to bend down and untie his sandals.

<sup>1.8</sup> "I baptize you with water, but he will baptize you with the Holy Spirit."

<sup>1.9</sup> Not long afterward Jesus came from Nazareth in the province of Galilee, and was baptized by John in the Jordan.

<sup>1.10</sup> As soon as Jesus came up out of the water, he saw heaven opening and the Spirit coming down on him like a dove.

<sup>1.11</sup> And a voice came from heaven, "You are my own dear Son. I am pleased with you."

<sup>1.12</sup> At once the Spirit made him go into the desert,

<sup>1.13</sup> where he stayed forty days, being tempted by Satan. Wild animals were there also, but angels came and helped him.

<sup>1.14</sup> After John had been put in prison, Jesus went to Galilee and preached the Good News from God.

<sup>1.15</sup> "The right time has come," he said, "and the Kingdom of God is near! Turn away from your sins and believe the Good News!"

<sup>1.16</sup> As Jesus walked along the shore of Lake Galilee, he saw two fishermen, Simon and his brother Andrew, catching fish with a net.

<sup>1.17</sup> Jesus said to them, "Come with me, and I will teach you to catch people."

<sup>1.18</sup> At once they left their nets and went with him.

<sup>1.19</sup> He went a little farther on and saw two other brothers, James

and John, the sons of Zebedee. They were in their boat getting their nets ready.

1.20 As soon as Jesus saw them, he called them; they left their father Zebedee in the boat with the hired men and went with Jesus.

1.21 Jesus and his disciples came to the town of Capernaum, and on the next Sabbath Jesus went to the synagogue and began to teach.

1.22 The people who heard him were amazed at the way he taught, for he wasn't like the teachers of the Law; instead, he taught with authority.

1.23 Just then a man with an evil spirit came into the synagogue and screamed,

1.24 "What do you want with us, Jesus of Nazareth? Are you here to destroy us? I know who you are - you are God's holy messenger!"

1.25 Jesus ordered the spirit, "Be quiet, and come out of the man!"

1.26 The evil spirit shook the man hard, gave a loud scream, and came out of him.

1.27 The people were all so amazed that they started saying to one another, "What is this? Is it some kind of new teaching? This man has authority to give orders to the evil spirits, and they obey him!"

1.28 And so the news about Jesus spread quickly everywhere in the province of Galilee.

1.29 Jesus and his disciples, including James and John, left the synagogue and went straight to the home of Simon and Andrew.

1.30 Simon's mother-in-law was sick in bed with a fever, and as soon as Jesus arrived, he was told about her.

1.31 He went to her, took her by the hand, and helped her up. The fever left her, and she began to wait on them.

1.32 After the sun had set and evening had come, people brought to Jesus all the sick and those who had demons.

1.33 All the people of the town gathered in front of the house.

1.34 Jesus healed many who were sick with all kinds of diseases and drove out many demons. He would not let the demons say anything, because they knew who he was.

1.35 Very early the next morning, long before daylight, Jesus got up and left the house. He went out of town to a lonely place, where he prayed.

1.36 But Simon and his companions went out searching for him,

1.37 and when they found him, they said, "Everyone is looking for you."

1.38 But Jesus answered, "We must go on to the other villages around here. I have to preach in them also, because that is why I came."

<sup>1.39</sup> So he traveled all <u>over Galilee</u>, preaching <u>in the synagogues</u> and driving out demons.

<sup>1.40</sup> A man suffering <u>from a dreaded skin disease</u> came <u>to Jesus</u>, knelt down, and begged him <u>for help</u>. "If you want to," he said, "you can make me clean."

<sup>1.41</sup> Jesus was filled <u>with pity</u>, and reached out and touched him. "I do want to," he answered. "Be clean!"

<sup>1.42</sup> <u>At once</u> the disease left the man, and he was clean.

<sup>1.43</sup> Then Jesus spoke sternly <u>to him</u> and sent him away <u>at once</u>,

<sup>1.44</sup> after saying <u>to him</u>, "Listen, don't tell anyone <u>about this</u>. But go straight <u>to the priest</u> and let him examine you; then <u>in order</u> to prove <u>to everyone</u> that you are cured, offer the sacrifice that Moses ordered."

<sup>1.45</sup> But the man went away and began to spread the news everywhere. Indeed, he talked so much that Jesus could not go <u>into a town</u> publicly. Instead, he stayed out <u>in lonely places</u>, and people came <u>to him</u> <u>from everywhere</u>.

# 2

<sup>2.1</sup> A few days later Jesus went back <u>to Capernaum</u>, and the news spread that he was <u>at home</u>.

<sup>2.2</sup> So many people came together that there was no room left, not even <u>out in front</u> <u>of the door</u>. Jesus was preaching the message <u>to them</u>

<sup>2.3</sup> when four men arrived, carrying a paralyzed man <u>to Jesus</u>.

<sup>2.4</sup> <u>Because of the crowd</u>, however, they could not get the man <u>to him</u>. So they made a hole <u>in the roof</u> right <u>above the place</u> where Jesus was. When they had made an opening, they let the man down, lying <u>on his mat</u>.

<sup>2.5</sup> Seeing how much faith they had, Jesus said <u>to the paralyzed man</u>, "My son, your sins are forgiven."

<sup>2.6</sup> Some teachers <u>of the Law</u> who were sitting there thought <u>to themselves</u>,

<sup>2.7</sup> "How does he dare talk <u>like this</u>? This is blasphemy! God is the only one who can forgive sins!"

<sup>2.8</sup> <u>At once</u> Jesus knew what they were thinking, so he said <u>to them</u>, "Why do you think such things?

<sup>2.9</sup> "Is it easier to say <u>to this paralyzed man</u>, 'Your sins are forgiven,' or to say, 'Get up, pick up your mat, and walk'?

<sup>2.10</sup> "I will prove <u>to you</u>, then, that the Son <u>of Man</u> has authority <u>on earth</u> to forgive sins." So he said <u>to the paralyzed man</u>,

2.11 "I tell you, get up, pick up your mat, and go home!"

2.12 While they all watched, the man got up, picked up his mat, and hurried away. They were all completely amazed and praised God, saying, "We have never seen anything like this!"

2.13 Jesus went back again to the shore of Lake Galilee. A crowd came to him, and he started teaching them.

2.14 As he walked along, he saw a tax collector, Levi son of Alphaeus, sitting in his office. Jesus said to him, "Follow me." Levi got up and followed him.

2.15 Later on Jesus was having a meal in Levi's house. A large number of tax collectors and other outcasts was following Jesus, and many of them joined him and his disciples at the table.

2.16 Some teachers of the Law, who were Pharisees, saw that Jesus was eating with these outcasts and tax collectors, so they asked his disciples, "Why does he eat with such people?"

2.17 Jesus heard them and answered, "People who are well do not need a doctor, but only those who are sick. I have not come to call respectable people, but outcasts."

2.18 On one occasion the followers of John the Baptist and the Pharisees were fasting. Some people came to Jesus and asked him, "Why is it that the disciples of John the Baptist and the disciples of the Pharisees fast, but yours do not?"

2.19 Jesus answered, "Do you expect the guests at a wedding party to go without food? Of course not! As long as the bridegroom is with them, they will not do that.

2.20 "But the day will come when the bridegroom will be taken away from them, and then they will fast.

2.21 "No one uses a piece of new cloth to patch up an old coat, because the new patch will shrink and tear off some of the old cloth, making an even bigger hole.

2.22 "Nor does anyone pour new wine into used wineskins, because the wine will burst the skins, and both the wine and the skins will be ruined. Instead, new wine must be poured into fresh wineskins."

2.23 Jesus was walking through some wheat fields on a Sabbath. As his disciples walked along with him, they began to pick the heads of wheat.

2.24 So the Pharisees said to Jesus, "Look, it is against our Law for your disciples to do that on the Sabbath!"

2.25 Jesus answered, "Have you never read what David did that time when he needed something to eat? He and his men were hungry,

2.26 "so he went into the house of God and ate the bread offered to

God. This happened when Abiathar was the High Priest. According to our Law only the priests may eat this bread — but David ate it and even gave it to his men."

2.27 And Jesus concluded, "The Sabbath was made for the good of human beings; they were not made for the Sabbath.

2.28 "So the Son of Man is Lord even of the Sabbath."

# 3

3.1 Then Jesus went back to the synagogue, where there was a man who had a paralyzed hand.

3.2 Some people were there who wanted to accuse Jesus of doing wrong; so they watched him closely to see whether he would cure the man on the Sabbath.

3.3 Jesus said to the man, "Come up here to the front."

3.4 Then he asked the people, "What does our Law allow us to do on the Sabbath? To help or to harm? To save someone's life or to destroy it?" But they did not say a thing.

3.5 Jesus was angry as he looked around at them, but at the same time he felt sorry for them, because they were so stubborn and wrong. Then he said to the man, "Stretch out your hand." He stretched it out, and it became well again.

3.6 So the Pharisees left the synagogue and met at once with some members of Herod's party, and they made plans to kill Jesus.

3.7 Jesus and his disciples went away to Lake Galilee, and a large crowd followed him. They had come from Galilee, from Judea,

3.8 from Jerusalem, from the territory of Idumea, from the territory on the east side of the Jordan, and from the region around the cities of Tyre and Sidon. All these people came to Jesus because they had heard of the things he was doing.

3.9 The crowd was so large that Jesus told his disciples to get a boat ready for him, so that the people would not crush him.

3.10 He had healed many people, and all the sick kept pushing their way to him in order to touch him.

3.11 And whenever the people who had evil spirits in them saw him, they would fall down before him and scream, "You are the Son of God!"

3.12 Jesus sternly ordered the evil spirits not to tell anyone who he was.

3.13 Then Jesus went up a hill and called to himself the men he wanted. They came to him,

3.14 and he chose twelve, whom he named apostles. "I have chosen you to be with me," he told them. "I will also send you out to preach, 3.15 "and you will have authority to drive out demons."

3.16 These are the twelve he chose: Simon (Jesus gave him the name Peter);

3.17 James and his brother John, the sons of Zebedee (Jesus gave them the name Boanerges, which means "Men of Thunder");

3.18 Andrew, Philip, Bartholomew, Matthew, Thomas, James son of Alphaeus, Thaddaeus, Simon the Patriot, 3.19 and Judas Iscariot, who betrayed Jesus.

3.20 Then Jesus went home. Again such a large crowd gathered that Jesus and his disciples had no time to eat.

3.21 When his family heard about it, they set out to take charge of him, because people were saying, "He's gone mad!"

3.22 Some teachers of the Law who had come from Jerusalem were saying, "He has Beelzebul in him! It is the chief of the demons who gives him the power to drive them out."

3.23 So Jesus called them to him and spoke to them in parables: "How can Satan drive out Satan?

3.24 "If a country divides itself into groups which fight each other, that country will fall apart.

3.25 "If a family divides itself into groups which fight each other, that family will fall apart.

3.26 "So if Satan's kingdom divides into groups, it cannot last, but will fall apart and come to an end.

3.27 "No one can break into a strong man's house and take away his belongings unless he first ties up the strong man; then he can plunder his house.

3.28 "I assure you that people can be forgiven all their sins and all the evil things they may say.

3.29 "But whoever says evil things against the Holy Spirit will never be forgiven, because he has committed an eternal sin."

3.30 (Jesus said this because some people were saying, "He has an evil spirit in him.")

3.31 Then Jesus' mother and brothers arrived. They stood outside the house and sent in a message, asking for him.

3.32 A crowd was sitting around Jesus, and they said to him, "Look, your mother and your brothers and sisters are outside, and they want you."

3.33 Jesus answered, "Who is my mother? Who are my brothers?"

3.34 He looked at the people sitting around him and said, "Look! Here are my mother and my brothers!

<sup></sup>3.35 "Whoever does what God wants is my brother, my sister, my mother."

# 4

4.1 Again Jesus began to teach beside Lake Galilee. The crowd that gathered around him was so large that he got into a boat and sat in it. The boat was out in the water, and the crowd stood on the shore at the water's edge.
4.2 He used parables to teach them many things, saying to them:
4.3 "Listen! Once there was a man who went out to sow grain.
4.4 "As he scattered the seed in the field, some of it fell along the path, and the birds came and ate it up.
4.5 "Some of it fell on rocky ground, where there was little soil. The seeds soon sprouted, because the soil wasn't deep.
4.6 "Then, when the sun came up, it burned the young plants; and because the roots had not grown deep enough, the plants soon dried up.
4.7 "Some of the seed fell among thorn bushes, which grew up and choked the plants, and they didn't bear grain.
4.8 "But some seeds fell in good soil, and the plants sprouted, grew, and bore grain: some had thirty grains, others sixty, and others one hundred."
4.9 And Jesus concluded, "Listen, then, if you have ears!"
4.10 When Jesus was alone, some of those who had heard him came to him with the twelve disciples and asked him to explain the parables.
4.11 "You have been given the secret of the Kingdom of God," Jesus answered. "But the others, who are on the outside, hear all things by means of parables,
4.12 "so that, 'They may look and look, yet not see; they may listen and listen, yet not understand. For if they did, they would turn to God, and he would forgive them.'"
4.13 Then Jesus asked them, "Don't you understand this parable? How, then, will you ever understand any parable?
4.14 "The sower sows God's message.
4.15 "Some people are like the seeds that fall along the path; as soon as they hear the message, Satan comes and takes it away.
4.16 "Other people are like the seeds that fall on rocky ground. As soon as they hear the message, they receive it gladly.
4.17 "But it does not sink deep into them, and they don't last long. So when trouble or persecution comes because of the message, they give up at once.

<sup></sup>4.18 "Other people are like the seeds sown among the thorn bushes. These are the ones who hear the message,

4.19 "but the worries about this life, the love for riches, and all other kinds of desires crowd in and choke the message, and they don't bear fruit.

4.20 "But other people are like seeds sown in good soil. They hear the message, accept it, and bear fruit: some thirty, some sixty, and some one hundred."

4.21 Jesus continued, "Does anyone ever bring in a lamp and put it under a bowl or under the bed? Isn't it put on the lampstand?

4.22 "Whatever is hidden away will be brought out into the open, and whatever is covered up will be uncovered.

4.23 "Listen, then, if you have ears!"

4.24 He also said to them, "Pay attention to what you hear! The same rules you use to judge others will be used by God to judge you — but with even greater severity.

4.25 "Those who have something will be given more, and those who have nothing will have taken away from them even the little they have."

4.26 Jesus went on to say, "The Kingdom of God is like this. A man scatters seed in his field.

4.27 "He sleeps at night, is up and about during the day, and all the while the seeds are sprouting and growing. Yet he does not know how it happens.

4.28 "The soil itself makes the plants grow and bear fruit; first the tender stalk appears, then the head, and finally the head full of grain.

4.29 "When the grain is ripe, the man starts cutting it with his sickle, because harvest time has come.

4.30 "What shall we say the Kingdom of God is like?" asked Jesus. "What parable shall we use to explain it?

4.31 "It is like this. A man takes a mustard seed, the smallest seed in the world, and plants it in the ground.

4.32 "After a while it grows up and becomes the biggest of all plants. It puts out such large branches that the birds come and make their nests in its shade."

4.33 Jesus preached his message to the people, using many other parables like these; he told them as much as they could understand.

4.34 He would not speak to them without using parables, but when he was alone with his disciples, he would explain everything to them.

4.35 On the evening of that same day Jesus said to his disciples, "Let us go across to the other side of the lake."

[4.36] So they left the crowd; the disciples got into the boat in which Jesus was already sitting, and they took him with them. Other boats were there too.

[4.37] Suddenly a strong wind blew up, and the waves began to spill over into the boat, so that it was about to fill with water.

[4.38] Jesus was in the back of the boat, sleeping with his head on a pillow. The disciples woke him up and said, "Teacher, don't you care that we are about to die?"

[4.39] Jesus stood up and commanded the wind, "Be quiet!" and he said to the waves, "Be still!" The wind died down, and there was a great calm.

[4.40] Then Jesus said to his disciples, "Why are you frightened? Do you still have no faith?"

[4.41] But they were terribly afraid and began to say to one another, "Who is this man? Even the wind and the waves obey him!"

# 5

[5.1] Jesus and his disciples arrived on the other side of Lake Galilee, in the territory of Gerasa.

[5.2] As soon as Jesus got out of the boat, he was met by a man who came out of the burial caves there. This man had an evil spirit in him

[5.3] and lived among the tombs. Nobody could keep him tied with chains any more;

[5.4] many times his feet and his hands had been tied, but every time he broke the chains and smashed the irons on his feet. He was too strong for anyone to control him.

[5.5] Day and night he wandered among the tombs and through the hills, screaming and cutting himself with stones.

[5.6] He was some distance away when he saw Jesus; so he ran, fell on his knees before him,

[5.7] and screamed in a loud voice, "Jesus, Son of the Most High God! What do you want with me? For God's sake, I beg you, don't punish me!"

[5.8] (He said this because Jesus was saying, "Evil spirit, come out of this man!")

[5.9] So Jesus asked him, "What is your name!" The man answered, "My name is 'Mob' — there are so many of us!"

[5.10] And he kept begging Jesus not to send the evil spirits out of that region.

5.11 There was a large herd of pigs near by, feeding on a hillside.
5.12 So the spirits begged Jesus, "Send us to the pigs, and let us go into them."
5.13 He let them go, and the evil spirits went out of the man and entered the pigs. The whole herd — about two thousand pigs in all — rushed down the side of the cliff into the lake and was drowned.
5.14 The men who had been taking care of the pigs ran away and spread the news in the town and among the farms. People went out to see what had happened,
5.15 and when they came to Jesus, they saw the man who used to have the mob of demons in him. He was sitting there, clothed and in his right mind; and they were all afraid.
5.16 Those who had seen it told the people what had happened to the man with the demons, and about the pigs.
5.17 So they asked Jesus to leave their territory.
5.18 As Jesus was getting into the boat, the man who had had the demons begged him, "Let me go with you!"
5.19 But Jesus would not let him. Instead, he told him, "Go back home to your family and tell them how much the Lord has done for you and how kind he has been to you."
5.20 So the man left and went all through the Ten Towns, telling what Jesus had done for him. And all who heard it were amazed.
5.21 Jesus went back across to the other side of the lake. There at the lakeside a large crowd gathered around him.
5.22 Jairus, an official of the local synagogue, arrived, and when he saw Jesus, he threw himself down at his feet
5.23 and begged him earnestly, "My little daughter is very sick. Please come and place your hands on her, so that she will get well and live!"
5.24 Then Jesus started off with him. So many people were going along with Jesus that they were crowding him from every side.
5.25 There was a woman who had suffered terribly from severe bleeding for twelve years,
5.26 even though she had been treated by many doctors. She had spent all her money, but instead of getting better she got worse all the time.
5.27 She had heard about Jesus, so she came in the crowd behind him,
5.28 saying to herself, "If I just touch his clothes, I will get well."
5.29 She touched his cloak, and her bleeding stopped at once; and she had the feeling inside herself that she was healed of her trouble.
5.30 At once Jesus knew that power had gone out of him, so he turned around in the crowd and asked, "Who touched my clothes?"

<sup>5.31</sup> His disciples answered, "You see how the people are crowding you; why do you ask who touched you?"

<sup>5.32</sup> But Jesus kept looking around to see who had done it.

<sup>5.33</sup> The woman realized what had happened to her, so she came, trembling with fear, knelt at his feet, and told him the whole truth.

<sup>5.34</sup> Jesus said to her, "My daughter, your faith has made you well. Go in peace, and be healed of your trouble."

<sup>5.35</sup> While Jesus was saying this, some messengers came from Jairus' house and told him, "Your daughter has died. Why bother the Teacher any longer?"

<sup>5.36</sup> Jesus paid no attention to what they said, but told him, "Don't be afraid, only believe."

<sup>5.37</sup> Then he did not let anyone else go on with him except Peter and James and his brother John.

<sup>5.38</sup> They arrived at Jairus' house, where Jesus saw the confusion and heard all the loud crying and wailing.

<sup>5.39</sup> He went in and said to them, "Why all this confusion? Why are you crying? The child is not dead — she is only sleeping!"

<sup>5.40</sup> They started making fun of him, so he put them all out, took the child's father and mother and his three disciples, and went into the room where the child was lying.

<sup>5.41</sup> He took her by the hand and said to her, "Talitha, koum," which means, "Little girl, I tell you to get up!"

<sup>5.42</sup> She got up at once and started walking around. (She was twelve years old.) When this happened, they were completely amazed.

<sup>5.43</sup> But Jesus gave them strict orders not to tell anyone, and he said, "Give her something to eat."

# 6

<sup>6.1</sup> Jesus left that place and went back to his hometown, followed by his disciples.

<sup>6.2</sup> On the Sabbath he began to teach in the synagogue. Many people were there; and when they heard him, they were all amazed. "Where did he get all this?" they asked. "What wisdom is this that has been given him? How does he perform miracles?

<sup>6.3</sup> "Isn't he the carpenter, the son of Mary, and the brother of James, Joseph, Judas, and Simon? Aren't his sisters living here?" And so they rejected him.

<sup>6.4</sup> Jesus said to them, "Prophets are respected everywhere except in their own hometown and by their relatives and their family."

<sup>6.5</sup> He was not able to perform any miracles there, except that he

placed his hands on a few sick people and healed them.

⁶·⁶ He was greatly surprised, because the people did not have faith. Then Jesus went to the villages around there, teaching the people.

⁶·⁷ He called the twelve disciples together and sent them out two by two. He gave them authority over the evil spirits

⁶·⁸ and ordered them, "Don't take anything with you on the trip except a walking stick - no bread, no beggar's bag, no money in your pockets.

⁶·⁹ "Wear sandals, but don't carry an extra shirt."

⁶·¹⁰ He also told them, "Wherever you are welcomed, stay in the same house until you leave that place.

⁶·¹¹ "If you come to a town where people do not welcome you or will not listen to you, leave it and shake the dust off your feet. That will be a warning to them!"

⁶·¹² So they went out and preached that people should turn away from their sins.

⁶·¹³ They drove out many demons, and rubbed olive oil on many sick people and healed them.

⁶·¹⁴ Now King Herod heard about all this, because Jesus' reputation had spread everywhere. Some people were saying, "John the Baptist has come back to life! That is why he has this power to perform miracles."

⁶·¹⁵ Others, however, said, "He is Elijah." Others said, "He is a prophet, like one of the prophets of long ago."

⁶·¹⁶ When Herod heard it, he said, "He is John the Baptist! I had his head cut off, but he has come back to life!"

⁶·¹⁷ Herod himself had ordered John's arrest, and he had him tied up and put in prison. Herod did this because of Herodias, whom he had married, even though she was the wife of his brother Philip.

⁶·¹⁸ John the Baptist kept telling Herod, "It isn't right for you to marry your brother's wife!"

⁶·¹⁹ So Herodias held a grudge against John and wanted to kill him, but she could not because of Herod.

⁶·²⁰ Herod was afraid of John because he knew that John was a good and holy man, and so he kept him safe. He liked to listen to him, even though he became greatly disturbed every time he heard him.

⁶·²¹ Finally Herodias got her chance. It was on Herod's birthday, when he gave a feast for all the top government officials, the military chiefs, and the leading citizens of Galilee.

⁶·²² The daughter of Herodias came in and danced, and pleased Herod and his guests. So the king said to the girl, "What would you

like to have? I will give you anything you want."

<sup>6.23</sup> With many vows he said to her, "I swear that I will give you anything you ask for, even as much as half my kingdom!"

<sup>6.24</sup> So the girl went out and asked her mother, "What shall I ask for?" "The head of John the Baptist," she answered.

<sup>6.25</sup> The girl hurried back at once to the king and demanded, "I want you to give me here and now the head of John the Baptist on a plate!"

<sup>6.26</sup> This made the king very sad, but he could not refuse her because of the vows he had made in front of all his guests.

<sup>6.27</sup> So he sent off a guard at once with orders to bring John's head. The guard left, went to the prison, and cut John's head off;

<sup>6.28</sup> then he brought it on a plate and gave it to the girl, who gave it to her mother.

<sup>6.29</sup> When John's disciples heard about this, they came and got his body, and buried it.

<sup>6.30</sup> The apostles returned and met with Jesus, and told him all they had done and taught.

<sup>6.31</sup> There were so many people coming and going that Jesus and his disciples didn't even have time to eat. So he said to them, "Let us go off by ourselves to some place where we will be alone and you can rest a while."

<sup>6.32</sup> So they started out in a boat by themselves to a lonely place.

<sup>6.33</sup> Many people, however, saw them leave and knew at once who they were; so they went from all the towns and ran ahead by land and arrived at the place ahead of Jesus and his disciples.

<sup>6.34</sup> When Jesus got out of the boat, he saw this large crowd, and his heart was filled with pity for them, because they were like sheep without a shepherd. So he began to teach them many things.

<sup>6.35</sup> When it was getting late, his disciples came to him and said, "It is already very late, and this is a lonely place.

<sup>6.36</sup> "Send the people away, and let them go to the nearby farms and villages in order to buy themselves something to eat."

<sup>6.37</sup> "You yourselves give them something to eat," Jesus answered. They asked, "Do you want us to go and spend two hundred silver coins on bread in order to feed them?"

<sup>6.38</sup> So Jesus asked them, "How much bread do you have? Go and see." When they found out, they told him, "Five loaves and also two fish."

<sup>6.39</sup> Jesus then told his disciples to make all the people divide into groups and sit down on the green grass.

<sup>6.40</sup> So the people sat down in rows, in groups of a hundred and groups of fifty.

<sup>6.41</sup> Then Jesus took the five loaves and the two fish, looked up to heaven, and gave thanks to God. He broke the loaves and gave them to his disciples to distribute to the people. He also divided the two fish among them all.

<sup>6.42</sup> Everyone ate and had enough.

<sup>6.43</sup> Then the disciples took up twelve baskets full of what was left of the bread and the fish.

<sup>6.44</sup> The number of men who were fed was five thousand.

<sup>6.45</sup> At once Jesus made his disciples get into the boat and go ahead of him to Bethsaida, on the other side of the lake, while he sent the crowd away.

<sup>6.46</sup> After saying good-bye to the people, he went away to a hill to pray.

<sup>6.47</sup> When evening came, the boat was in the middle of the lake, while Jesus was alone on land.

<sup>6.48</sup> He saw that his disciples were straining at the oars, because they were rowing against the wind; so sometime between three and six o'clock in the morning, he came to them, walking on the water. He was going to pass them by,

<sup>6.49</sup> but they saw him walking on the water. "It's a ghost!" they thought, and screamed.

<sup>6.50</sup> They were all terrified when they saw him. Jesus spoke to them at once, "Courage!" he said. "It is I. Don't be afraid!"

<sup>6.51</sup> Then he got into the boat with them, and the wind died down. The disciples were completely amazed,

<sup>6.52</sup> because they had not understood the real meaning of the feeding of the five thousand; their minds could not grasp it.

<sup>6.53</sup> They crossed the lake and came to land at Gennesaret, where they tied up the boat.

<sup>6.54</sup> As they left the boat, people recognized Jesus at once.

<sup>6.55</sup> So they ran throughout the whole region; and wherever they heard he was, they brought to him the sick lying on their mats.

<sup>6.56</sup> And everywhere Jesus went, to villages, towns, or farms, people would take their sick to the marketplaces and beg him to let the sick at least touch the edge of his cloak. And all who touched it were made well.

# 7

<sup>7.1</sup> Some Pharisees and teachers of the Law who had come from Jeru-

salem gathered around Jesus.
<sup></sup>7.2 They noticed that some of his disciples were eating their food with hands that were ritually unclean - that is, they had not washed them in the way the Pharisees said people should.
7.3 (For the Pharisees, as well as the rest of the Jews, follow the teaching they received from their ancestors: they do not eat unless they wash their hands in the proper way;
7.4 nor do they eat anything that comes from the market unless they wash it first. And they follow many other rules which they have received, such as the proper way to wash cups, pots, copper bowls, and beds.)
7.5 So the Pharisees and the teachers of the Law asked Jesus, "Why is it that your disciples do not follow the teaching handed down by our ancestors, but instead eat with ritually unclean hands?"
7.6 Jesus answered them, "How right Isaiah was when he prophesied about you! You are hypocrites, just as he wrote: 'These people, says God, honor me with their words, but their heart is really far away from me.
7.7 " 'It is no use for them to worship me, because they teach human rules as though they were my laws!'
7.8 "You put aside God's command and obey human teachings."
7.9 And Jesus continued, "You have a clever way of rejecting God's law in order to uphold your own teaching.
7.10 "For Moses commanded, 'Respect your father and your mother,' and, 'If you curse your father or your mother, you are to be put to death.'
7.11 "But you teach that if people have something they could use to help their father or mother, but say, 'This is Corban' (which means, it belongs to God),
7.12 "they are excused from helping their father or mother.
7.13 "In this way the teaching you pass on to others cancels out the word of God. And there are many other things like this that you do."
7.14 Then Jesus called the crowd to him once more and said to them, "Listen to me, all of you, and understand.
7.15 "There is nothing that goes into you from the outside which can make you ritually unclean. Rather, it is what comes out of you that makes you unclean."
7.16 ("Listen, then, if you have ears!")
7.17 When he left the crowd and went into the house, his disciples asked him to explain this saying.
7.18 "You are no more intelligent than the others," Jesus said to them.

"Don't you understand? Nothing that goes into you from the outside can really make you unclean,

7.19 "because it does not go into your heart but into your stomach and then goes on out of the body." (In saying this, Jesus declared that all foods are fit to be eaten.)

7.20 And he went on to say, "It is what comes out of you that makes you unclean.

7.21 "For from the inside, from your heart, come the evil ideas which lead you to do immoral things, to rob, kill,

7.22 "commit adultery, be greedy, and do all sorts of evil things; deceit, indecency, jealousy, slander, pride, and folly —

7.23 "all these evil things come from inside you and make you unclean."

7.24 Then Jesus left and went away to the territory near the city of Tyre. He went into a house and did not want anyone to know he was there, but he could not stay hidden.

7.25 A woman, whose daughter had an evil spirit in her, heard about Jesus and came to him at once and fell at his feet.

7.26 The woman was a Gentile, born in the region of Phoenicia in Syria. She begged Jesus to drive the demon out of her daughter.

7.27 But Jesus answered, "Let us first feed the children. It isn't right to take the children's food and throw it to the dogs."

7.28 "Sir," she answered, "even the dogs under the table eat the children's leftovers!"

7.29 So Jesus said to her, "Because of that answer, go back home, where you will find that the demon has gone out of your daughter!"

7.30 She went home and found her child lying on the bed; the demon had indeed gone out of her.

7.31 Jesus then left the neighborhood of Tyre and went on through Sidon to Lake Galilee, going by way of the territory of the Ten Towns.

7.32 Some people brought him a man who was deaf and could hardly speak, and they begged Jesus to place his hands on him.

7.33 So Jesus took him off alone, away from the crowd, put his fingers in the man's ears, spat, and touched the man's tongue.

7.34 Then Jesus looked up to heaven, gave a deep groan, and said to the man, "Ephphatha," which means, "Open up!"

7.35 At once the man was able to hear, his speech impediment was removed, and he began to talk without any trouble.

7.36 Then Jesus ordered the people not to speak of it to anyone; but the more he ordered them not to, the more they told it.

<sup>7.37</sup> And all who heard were completely amazed. "How well he does everything!" they exclaimed. "He even causes the deaf to hear and the dumb to speak!"

# 8

<sup>8.1</sup> Not long afterward another large crowd came together. When the people had nothing left to eat, Jesus called the disciples to him and said,
<sup>8.2</sup> "I feel sorry for these people, because they have been with me for three days and now have nothing to eat.
<sup>8.3</sup> "If I send them home without feeding them, they will faint as they go, because some of them have come a long way."
<sup>8.4</sup> His disciples asked him, "Where in this desert can anyone find enough food to feed all these people?"
<sup>8.5</sup> "How much bread do you have?" Jesus asked. "Seven loaves," they answered.
<sup>8.6</sup> He ordered the crowd to sit down on the ground. Then he took the seven loaves, gave thanks to God, broke them, and gave them to his disciples to distribute to the crowd; and the disciples did so.
<sup>8.7</sup> They also had a few small fish. Jesus gave thanks for these and told the disciples to distribute them too.
<sup>8.8-9</sup> Everybody ate and had enough — there were about four thousand people. Then the disciples took up seven baskets full of pieces left over. Jesus sent the people away
<sup>8.10</sup> and at once got into a boat with his disciples and went to the district of Dalmanutha.
<sup>8.11</sup> Some Pharisees came to Jesus and started to argue with him. They wanted to trap him, so they asked him to perform a miracle to show that God approved of him.
<sup>8.12</sup> But Jesus gave a deep groan and said, "Why do the people of this day ask for a miracle? No, I tell you! No such proof will be given to these people!"
<sup>8.13</sup> He left them, got back into the boat, and started across to the other side of the lake.
<sup>8.14</sup> The disciples had forgotten to bring enough bread and had only one loaf with them in the boat.
<sup>8.15</sup> "Take care," Jesus warned them, "and be on your guard against the yeast of the Pharisees and the yeast of Herod."
<sup>8.16</sup> They started discussing among themselves: "He says this because we don't have any bread."
<sup>8.17</sup> Jesus knew what they were saying, so he asked them, "Why are

you discussing about not having any bread? Don't you know or understand yet? Are your minds so dull?

8.18 "You have eyes — can't you see? You have ears — can't you hear? Don't you remember

8.19 "when I broke the five loaves for the five thousand people? How many baskets full of leftover pieces did you take up?" "Twelve," they answered.

8.20 "And when I broke the seven loaves for the four thousand people," asked Jesus, "how many baskets full of leftover pieces did you take up?" "Seven," they answered.

8.21 "And you still don't understand?" he asked them.

8.22 They came to Bethsaida, where some people brought a blind man to Jesus and begged him to touch him.

8.23 Jesus took the blind man by the hand and led him out of the village. After spitting on the man's eyes, Jesus placed his hands on him and asked him, "Can you see anything?"

8.24 The man looked up and said, "Yes, I can see people, but they look like trees walking around."

8.25 Jesus again placed his hands on the man's eyes. This time the man looked intently, his eyesight returned, and he saw everything clearly.

8.26 Jesus then sent him home with the order, "Don't go back into the village."

8.27 Then Jesus and his disciples went away to the villages near Caesarea Philippi. On the way he asked them, "Tell me, who do people say I am?"

8.28 "Some say that you are John the Baptist," they answered; "others say that you are Elijah, while others say that you are one of the prophets."

8.29 "What about you?" he asked them. "Who do you say I am?"
Peter answered, "You are the Messiah."

8.30 Then Jesus ordered them, "Do not tell anyone about me."

8.31 Then Jesus began to teach his disciples: "The Son of Man must suffer much and be rejected by the elders, the chief priests, and the teachers of the Law. He will be put to death, but three days later he will rise to life."

8.32 He made this very clear to them. So Peter took him aside and began to rebuke him.

8.33 But Jesus turned around, looked at his disciples, and rebuked Peter. "Get away from me, Satan," he said. "Your thoughts don't come from God but from human nature!"

<sup>8.34</sup> Then Jesus called the crowd and his disciples to him. "If any of you want to come with me," he told them, "you must forget yourself, carry your cross, and follow me.

<sup>8.35</sup> "For if you want to save your own life, you will lose it; but if you lose your life for me and for the gospel, you will save it.

<sup>8.36</sup> "Do you gain anything if you win the whole world but lose your life? Of course not!

<sup>8.37</sup> "There is nothing you can give to regain your life.

<sup>8.38</sup> "If you are ashamed of me and of my teaching in this godless and wicked day, then the Son of Man will be ashamed of you when he comes in the glory of his Father with the holy angels."

# 9

<sup>9.1</sup> And he went on to say, "I tell you, there are some here who will not die until they have seen the Kingdom of God come with power."

<sup>9.2</sup> Six days later Jesus took with him Peter, James, and John, and led them up a high mountain, where they were alone. As they looked on, a change came over Jesus,

<sup>9.3</sup> and his clothes became shining white — whiter than anyone in the world could wash them.

<sup>9.4</sup> Then the three disciples saw Elijah and Moses talking with Jesus.

<sup>9.5</sup> Peter spoke up and said to Jesus, "Teacher, how good it is that we are here! We will make three tents, one for you, one for Moses, and one for Elijah."

<sup>9.6</sup> He and the others were so frightened that he did not know what to say.

<sup>9.7</sup> Then a cloud appeared and covered them with its shadow, and a voice came from the cloud, "This is my own dear Son — listen to him!"

<sup>9.8</sup> They took a quick look around but did not see anyone else; only Jesus was with them.

<sup>9.9</sup> As they came down the mountain, Jesus ordered them, "Don't tell anyone what you have seen, until the Son of Man has risen from death."

<sup>9.10</sup> They obeyed his order, but among themselves they started discussing the matter, "What does this 'rising from death' mean?"

<sup>9.11</sup> And they asked Jesus, "Why do the teachers of the Law say that Elijah has to come first?"

<sup>9.12</sup> His answer was, "Elijah is indeed coming first in order to get everything ready. Yet why do the Scriptures say that the Son of Man will suffer much and be rejected?

<sup>9.13</sup> "I tell you, however, that Elijah has already come and that people

treated him just as they pleased, as the Scriptures say about him."

9.14 When they joined the rest of the disciples, they saw a large crowd around them and some teachers of the Law arguing with them.

9.15 When the people saw Jesus, they were greatly surprised, and ran to him and greeted him.

9.16 Jesus asked his disciples, "What are you arguing with them about?"

9.17 A man in the crowd answered, "Teacher, I brought my son to you, because he has an evil spirit in him and cannot talk.

9.18 "Whenever the spirit attacks him, it throws him to the ground, and he foams at the mouth, grits his teeth, and becomes stiff all over. I asked your disciples to drive the spirit out, but they could not."

9.19 Jesus said to them, "How unbelieving you people are! How long must I stay with you? How long do I have to put up with you? Bring the boy to me!"

9.20 They brought him to Jesus. As soon as the spirit saw Jesus, it threw the boy into a fit, so that he fell on the ground and rolled around, foaming at the mouth.

9.21 "How long has he been like this?" Jesus asked the father. "Ever since he was a child," he replied.

9.22 "Many times the evil spirit has tried to kill him by throwing him in the fire and into water. Have pity on us and help us, if you possibly can!"

9.23 "Yes," said Jesus, "if you yourself can! Everything is possible for the person who has faith."

9.24 The father at once cried out, "I do have faith, but not enough. Help me have more!"

9.25 Jesus noticed that the crowd was closing in on them, so he gave a command to the evil spirit. "Deaf and dumb spirit," he said, "I order you to come out of the boy and never go into him again!"

9.26 The spirit screamed, threw the boy into a bad fit, and came out. The boy looked like a corpse, and everyone said, "He is dead!"

9.27 But Jesus took the boy by the hand and helped him rise, and he stood up.

9.28 After Jesus had gone indoors, his disciples asked him privately, "Why couldn't we drive the spirit out?"

9.29 "Only prayer can drive this kind out," answered Jesus; "nothing else can."

9.30 Jesus and his disciples left that place and went on through Galilee. Jesus did not want anyone to know where he was,

<sup>9.31</sup> because he was teaching his disciples: "The Son of Man will be handed over to those who will kill him. Three days later, however, he will rise to life."

<sup>9.32</sup> But they did not understand what this teaching meant, and they were afraid to ask him.

<sup>9.33</sup> They came to Capernaum, and after going indoors Jesus asked his disciples, "What were you arguing about on the road?"

<sup>9.34</sup> But they would not answer him, because on the road they had been arguing among themselves about who was the greatest.

<sup>9.35</sup> Jesus sat down, called the twelve disciples, and said to them, "Whoever wants to be first must place himself last of all and be the servant of all."

<sup>9.36</sup> Then he took a child and had him stand in front of them. He put his arms around him and said to them,

<sup>9.37</sup> "Whoever welcomes in my name one of these children, welcomes me; and whoever welcomes me, welcomes not only me but also the one who sent me."

<sup>9.38</sup> John said to him, "Teacher, we saw a man who was driving out demons in your name, and we told him to stop, because he doesn't belong to our group."

<sup>9.39</sup> "Do not try to stop him," Jesus told them, "because no one who performs a miracle in my name will be able soon afterward to say evil things about me.

<sup>9.40</sup> "For whoever is not against us is for us.

<sup>9.41</sup> "I assure you that anyone who gives you a drink of water because you belong to me will certainly receive a reward.

<sup>9.42</sup> "If anyone should cause one of these little ones to lose faith in me, it would be better for that person to have a large millstone tied around the neck and be thrown into the sea.

<sup>9.43</sup> "So if your hand makes you lose your faith, cut it off! It is better for you to enter life without a hand than to keep both hands and go off to hell, to the fire that never goes out.

<sup>9.44</sup> ("There 'the worms that eat them never die, and the fire that burns them is never put out.')

<sup>9.45</sup> "And if your foot makes you lose your faith, cut it off! It is better for you to enter life without a foot than to keep both feet and be thrown into hell.

<sup>9.46</sup> ("There 'the worms that eat them never die, and the fire that burns them is never put out.')

<sup>9.47</sup> "And if your eye makes you lose your faith, take it out! It is better for you to enter the Kingdom of God with only one eye than to keep

both eyes and be thrown into hell.
<sup>9.48</sup> "There 'the worms that eat them never die, and the fire that burns them is never put out.'
<sup>9.49</sup> "Everyone will be purified by fire as a sacrifice is purified by salt.
<sup>9.50</sup> "Salt is good; but if it loses its saltiness, how can you make it salty again? Have the salt of friendship among yourselves, and live in peace with one another."

# 10

<sup>10.1</sup> Then Jesus left that place, went to the province of Judea, and crossed the Jordan River. Crowds came flocking to him again, and he taught them, as he always did.
<sup>10.2</sup> Some Pharisees came to him and tried to trap him. "Tell us," they asked, "does our Law allow a man to divorce his wife?"
<sup>10.3</sup> Jesus answered with a question, "What law did Moses give you?"
<sup>10.4</sup> Their answer was, "Moses gave permission for a man to write a divorce notice and send his wife away."
<sup>10.5</sup> Jesus said to them, "Moses wrote this law for you because you are so hard to teach.
<sup>10.6</sup> "But in the beginning, at the time of creation, 'God made them male and female,' as the scripture says.
<sup>10.7</sup> " 'And for this reason a man will leave his father and mother and unite with his wife,
<sup>10.8</sup> " 'and the two will become one.' So they are no longer two, but one.
<sup>10.9</sup> "No human being must separate, then, what God has joined together."
<sup>10.10</sup> When they went back into the house, the disciples asked Jesus about this matter.
<sup>10.11</sup> He said to them, "A man who divorces his wife and marries another woman commits adultery against his wife.
<sup>10.12</sup> "In the same way, a woman who divorces her husband and marries another man commits adultery."
<sup>10.13</sup> Some people brought children to Jesus for him to place his hands on them, but the disciples scolded the people.
<sup>10.14</sup> When Jesus noticed this, he was angry and said to his disciples, "Let the children come to me, and do not stop them, because the Kingdom of God belongs to such as these.
<sup>10.15</sup> "I assure you that whoever does not receive the Kingdom of God like a child will never enter it."
<sup>10.16</sup> Then he took the children in his arms, placed his hands on each of them, and blessed them.

<sup>10.17</sup> As Jesus was starting on his way again, a man ran up, knelt before him, and asked him, "Good Teacher, what must I do to receive eternal life?"

<sup>10.18</sup> "Why do you call me good?" Jesus asked him. "No one is good except God alone.

<sup>10.19</sup> "You know the commandments: 'Do not commit murder; do not commit adultery; do not steal; do not accuse anyone falsely; do not cheat; respect your father and your mother.'"

<sup>10.20</sup> "Teacher," the man said, "ever since I was young, I have obeyed all these commandments."

<sup>10.21</sup> Jesus looked straight at him with love and said, "You need only one thing. Go and sell all you have and give the money to the poor, and you will have riches in heaven; then come and follow me."

<sup>10.22</sup> When the man heard this, gloom spread over his face, and he went away sad, because he was very rich.

<sup>10.23</sup> Jesus looked around at his disciples and said to them, "How hard it will be for rich people to enter the Kingdom of God!"

<sup>10.24</sup> The disciples were shocked at these words, but Jesus went on to say, "My children, how hard it is to enter the Kingdom of God!

<sup>10.25</sup> "It is much harder for a rich person to enter the Kingdom of God than for a camel to go through the eye of a needle."

<sup>10.26</sup> At this the disciples were completely amazed and asked one another, "Who, then, can be saved?"

<sup>10.27</sup> Jesus looked straight at them and answered, "This is impossible for human beings but not for God; everything is possible for God."

<sup>10.28</sup> Then Peter spoke up, "Look, we have left everything and followed you."

<sup>10.29</sup> "Yes," Jesus said to them, "and I tell you that those who leave home or brothers or sisters or mother or father or children or fields for me and for the gospel,

<sup>10.30</sup> "will receive much more in this present age. They will receive a hundred times more houses, brothers, sisters, mothers, children, and fields — and persecutions as well; and in the age to come they will receive eternal life.

<sup>10.31</sup> "But many who are now first will be last, and many who are now last will be first."

<sup>10.32</sup> Jesus and his disciples were now on the road going up to Jerusalem. Jesus was going ahead of the disciples, who were filled with alarm; the people who followed behind were afraid. Once again Jesus took the twelve disciples aside and spoke of the things that were going to happen to him.

¹⁰·³³ "Listen," he told them, "we are going up to Jerusalem where the Son of Man will be handed over to the chief priests and the teachers of the Law. They will condemn him to death and then hand him over to the Gentiles,

¹⁰·³⁴ "who will make fun of him, spit on him, whip him, and kill him; but three days later he will rise to life."

¹⁰·³⁵ Then James and John, the sons of Zebedee, came to Jesus. "Teacher," they said, "there is something we want you to do for us."

¹⁰·³⁶ "What is it?" Jesus asked them.

¹⁰·³⁷ They answered, "When you sit on your throne in your glorious Kingdom, we want you to let us sit with you, one at your right and one at your left."

¹⁰·³⁸ Jesus said to them, "You don't know what you are asking for. Can you drink the cup of suffering that I must drink? Can you be baptized in the way I must be baptized?"

¹⁰·³⁹ "We can," they answered. Jesus said to them, "You will indeed drink the cup I must drink and be baptized in the way I must be baptized.

¹⁰·⁴⁰ "But I do not have the right to choose who will sit at my right and my left. It is God who will give these places to those for whom he has prepared them."

¹⁰·⁴¹ When the other ten disciples heard about it, they became angry with James and John.

¹⁰·⁴² So Jesus called them all together to him and said, "You know that those who are considered rulers of the heathen have power over them, and the leaders have complete authority.

¹⁰·⁴³ "This, however, is not the way it is among you. If one of you wants to be great, you must be the servant of the rest;

¹⁰·⁴⁴ "and if one of you wants to be first, you must be the slave of all.

¹⁰·⁴⁵ "For even the Son of Man did not come to be served; he came to serve and to give his life to redeem many people."

¹⁰·⁴⁶ They came to Jericho, and as Jesus was leaving with his disciples and a large crowd, a blind beggar named Bartimaeus son of Timaeus was sitting by the road.

¹⁰·⁴⁷ When he heard that it was Jesus of Nazareth, he began to shout, "Jesus! Son of David! Have mercy on me!"

¹⁰·⁴⁸ Many of the people scolded him and told him to be quiet. But he shouted even more loudly, "Son of David, have mercy on me!"

¹⁰·⁴⁹ Jesus stopped and said, "Call him." So they called the blind man. "Cheer up!" they said. "Get up, he is calling you."

¹⁰·⁵⁰ So he threw off his cloak, jumped up, and came to Jesus.

<sup>10.51</sup> "What do you want me to do for you?" Jesus asked him. "Teacher," the blind man answered, "I want to see again."

<sup>10.52</sup> "Go," Jesus told him, "your faith has made you well." At once he was able to see and followed Jesus on the road.

# 11

<sup>11.1</sup> As they approached Jerusalem, near the towns of Bethphage and Bethany, they came to the Mount of Olives. Jesus sent two of his disciples on ahead

<sup>11.2</sup> with these instructions: "Go to the village there ahead of you. As soon as you get there, you will find a colt tied up that has never been ridden. Untie it and bring it here.

<sup>11.3</sup> "And if someone asks you why you are doing that, say that the Master needs it and will send it back at once."

<sup>11.4</sup> So they went and found a colt out in the street, tied to the door of a house. As they were untying it,

<sup>11.5</sup> some of the bystanders asked them, "What are you doing, untying that colt?"

<sup>11.6</sup> They answered just as Jesus had told them, and the crowd let them go.

<sup>11.7</sup> They brought the colt to Jesus, threw their cloaks over the animal, and Jesus got on.

<sup>11.8</sup> Many people spread their cloaks on the road, while others cut branches in the field and spread them on the road.

<sup>11.9</sup> The people who were in front and those who followed behind began to shout, "Praise God! God bless him who comes in the name of the Lord!

<sup>11.10</sup> "God bless the coming kingdom of King David, our father! Praise be to God!"

<sup>11.11</sup> Jesus entered Jerusalem, went into the Temple, and looked around at everything. But since it was already late in the day, he went out to Bethany with the twelve disciples.

<sup>11.12</sup> The next day, as they were coming back from Bethany, Jesus was hungry.

<sup>11.13</sup> He saw in the distance a fig tree covered with leaves, so he went to see if he could find any figs on it. But when he came to it, he found only leaves, because it was not the right time for figs.

<sup>11.14</sup> Jesus said to the fig tree, "No one shall ever eat figs from you again!" And his disciples heard him.

<sup>11.15</sup> When they arrived in Jerusalem, Jesus went to the Temple and began to drive out all those who were buying and selling. He over-

turned the tables of the moneychangers and the stools of those who sold pigeons,

<sup>11.16</sup> and he would not let anyone carry anything through the Temple courtyards.

<sup>11.17</sup> He then taught the people: "It is written in the Scriptures that God said, 'My Temple will be called a house of prayer for the people of all nations.' But you have turned it into a hideout for thieves!"

<sup>11.18</sup> The chief priests and the teachers of the Law heard of this, so they began looking for some way to kill Jesus. They were afraid of him, because the whole crowd was amazed at his teaching.

<sup>11.19</sup> When evening came, Jesus and his disciples left the city.

<sup>11.20</sup> Early next morning, as they walked along the road, they saw the fig tree. It was dead all the way down to its roots.

<sup>11.21</sup> Peter remembered what had happened and said to Jesus, "Look, Teacher, the fig tree you cursed has died!"

<sup>11.22</sup> Jesus answered them, "Have faith in God.

<sup>11.23</sup> "I assure you that whoever tells this hill to get up and throw itself in the sea and does not doubt in his heart, but believes that what he says will happen, it will be done for him.

<sup>11.24</sup> "For this reason I tell you: When you pray and ask for something, believe that you have received it, and you will be given whatever you ask for.

<sup>11.25</sup> "And when you stand and pray, forgive anything you may have against anyone, so that your Father in heaven will forgive the wrongs you have done."

<sup>11.26</sup> ("If you do not forgive others, your Father in heaven will not forgive the wrongs you have done.")

<sup>11.27</sup> They arrived once again in Jerusalem. As Jesus was walking in the Temple, the chief priests, the teachers of the Law, and the elders came to him

<sup>11.28</sup> and asked him, "What right do you have to do these things? Who gave you such right?"

<sup>11.29</sup> Jesus answered them, "I will ask you just one question, and if you give me an answer, I will tell you what right I have to do these things.

<sup>11.30</sup> "Tell me, where did John's right to baptize come from: was it from God or from human beings?"

<sup>11.31</sup> They started to argue among themselves: "What shall we say? If we answer, 'From God,' he will say, 'Why, then, did you not believe John?'

<sup>11.32</sup> "But if we say, 'From human beings ...'" (They were afraid of the

people, because everyone was convinced that John had been a prophet.)

<sup>11.33</sup> So their answer to Jesus was, "We don't know." Jesus said to them, "Neither will I tell you, then, by what right I do these things."

# 12

<sup>12.1</sup> Then Jesus spoke to them in parables: "Once there was a man who planted a vineyard, put a fence around it, dug a hole for the wine press, and built a watchtower. Then he rented the vineyard to tenants and left home on a trip.

<sup>12.2</sup> "When the time came to gather the grapes, he sent a slave to the tenants to receive from them his share of the harvest.

<sup>12.3</sup> "The tenants grabbed the slave, beat him, and sent him back without a thing.

<sup>12.4</sup> "Then the owner sent another slave; the tenants beat him over the head and treated him shamefully.

<sup>12.5</sup> "The owner sent another slave, and they killed him; and they treated many others the same way, beating some and killing others.

<sup>12.6</sup> "The only one left to send was the man's own dear son. Last of all, then, he sent his son to the tenants. 'I am sure they will respect my son,' he said.

<sup>12.7</sup> "But those tenants said to one another, 'This is the owner's son. Come on, let's kill him, and his property will be ours!'

<sup>12.8</sup> "So they grabbed the son and killed him and threw his body out of the vineyard.

<sup>12.9</sup> "What, then, will the owner of the vineyard do?" asked Jesus. "He will come and kill those tenants and turn the vineyard over to others.

<sup>12.10</sup> "Surely you have read this scripture? 'The stone which the builders rejected as worthless turned out to be the most important of all.

<sup>12.11</sup> " 'This was done by the Lord; what a wonderful sight it is!'"

<sup>12.12</sup> The Jewish leaders tried to arrest Jesus, because they knew that he had told this parable against them. But they were afraid of the crowd, so they left him and went away.

<sup>12.13</sup> Some Pharisees and some members of Herod's party were sent to Jesus to trap him with questions.

<sup>12.14</sup> They came to him and said, "Teacher, we know that you tell the truth, without worrying about what people think. You pay no attention to anyone's status, but teach the truth about God's will for people. Tell us, is it against our Law to pay taxes to the Roman Emperor? Should we pay them or not?"

¹²·¹⁵ But Jesus saw through their trick and answered, "Why are you trying to trap me? Bring a silver coin, and let me see it."

¹²·¹⁶ They brought him one, and he asked, "Whose face and name are these?" "The Emperor's," they answered.

¹²·¹⁷ So Jesus said, "Well, then, pay to the Emperor what belongs to the Emperor, and pay to God what belongs to God." And they were amazed at Jesus.

¹²·¹⁸ Then some Sadducees, who say that people will not rise from death, came to Jesus and said,

¹²·¹⁹ "Teacher, Moses wrote this law for us: 'If a man dies and leaves a wife but no children, that man's brother must marry the widow so that they can have children who will be considered the dead man's children.'

¹²·²⁰ "Once there were seven brothers; the oldest got married and died without having children.

¹²·²¹ "Then the second one married the woman, and he also died without having children. The same thing happened to the third brother,

¹²·²² "and then to the rest: all seven brothers married the woman and died without having children. Last of all, the woman died.

¹²·²³ "Now, when all the dead rise to life on the day of resurrection, whose wife will she be? All seven of them had married her."

¹²·²⁴ Jesus answered them, "How wrong you are! And do you know why? It is because you don't know the Scriptures or God's power.

¹²·²⁵ "For when the dead rise to life, they will be like the angels in heaven and will not marry.

¹²·²⁶ "Now, as for the dead being raised: haven't you ever read in the Book of Moses the passage about the burning bush? There it is written that God said to Moses, 'I am the God of Abraham, the God of Isaac, and the God of Jacob.'

¹²·²⁷ "He is the God of the living, not of the dead. You are completely wrong!"

¹²·²⁸ A teacher of the Law was there who heard the discussion. He saw that Jesus had given the Sadducees a good answer, so he came to him with a question: "Which commandment is the most important of all?"

¹²·²⁹ Jesus replied, "The most important one is this: 'Listen, Israel! The Lord our God is the only Lord.

¹²·³⁰ " 'Love the Lord your God with all your heart, with all your soul, with all your mind, and with all your strength.'

¹²·³¹ "The second most important commandment is this: 'Love your neighbor as you love yourself.' There is no other commandment more

important than these two."

12.32 The teacher of the Law said to Jesus, "Well done, Teacher! It is true, as you say, that only the Lord is God and that there is no other god but he.

12.33 "And you must love God with all your heart and with all your mind and with all your strength; and you must love your neighbor as you love yourself. It is more important to obey these two commandments than to offer on the altar animals and other sacrifices to God."

12.34 Jesus noticed how wise his answer was, and so he told him, "You are not far from the Kingdom of God." After this nobody dared to ask Jesus any more questions.

12.35 As Jesus was teaching in the Temple, he asked the question, "How can the teachers of the Law say that the Messiah will be the descendant of David?

12.36 "The Holy Spirit inspired David to say: 'The Lord said to my Lord: Sit here at my right side until I put your enemies under your feet.'

12.37 "David himself called him 'Lord'; so how can the Messiah be David's descendant?" A large crowd was listening to Jesus gladly.

12.38 As he taught them, he said, "Watch out for the teachers of the Law, who like to walk around in their long robes and be greeted with respect in the marketplace,

12.39 "who choose the reserved seats in the synagogues and the best places at feasts.

12.40 "They take advantage of widows and rob them of their homes, and then make a show of saying long prayers. Their punishment will be all the worse!"

12.41 As Jesus sat near the Temple treasury, he watched the people as they dropped in their money. Many rich men dropped in a lot of money;

12.42 then a poor widow came along and dropped in two little copper coins, worth about a penny.

12.43 He called his disciples together and said to them, "I tell you that this poor widow put more in the offering box than all the others.

12.44 "For the others put in what they had to spare of their riches; but she, poor as she is, put in all she had — she gave all she had to live on."

# 13

13.1 As Jesus was leaving the Temple, one of his disciples said, "Look, Teacher! What wonderful stones and buildings!"

<sup>13.2</sup> Jesus answered, "You see these great buildings? Not a single stone here will be left in its place; every one of them will be thrown down."

<sup>13.3</sup> Jesus was sitting on the Mount of Olives, across from the Temple, when Peter, James, John, and Andrew came to him in private.

<sup>13.4</sup> "Tell us when this will be," they said, "and tell us what will happen to show that the time has come for all these things to take place."

<sup>13.5</sup> Jesus said to them, "Watch out, and don't let anyone fool you.

<sup>13.6</sup> "Many men, claiming to speak for me, will come and say, 'I am he!' and they will fool many people.

<sup>13.7</sup> "And don't be troubled when you hear the noise of battles close by and news of battles far away. Such things must happen, but they do not mean that the end has come.

<sup>13.8</sup> "Countries will fight each other; kingdoms will attack one another. There will be earthquakes everywhere, and there will be famines. These things are like the first pains of childbirth.

<sup>13.9</sup> "You yourselves must watch out. You will be arrested and taken to court. You will be beaten in the synagogues; you will stand before rulers and kings for my sake to tell them the Good News.

<sup>13.10</sup> "But before the end comes, the gospel must be preached to all peoples.

<sup>13.11</sup> "And when you are arrested and taken to court, do not worry ahead of time about what you are going to say; when the time comes, say whatever is then given to you. For the words you speak will not be yours; they will come from the Holy Spirit.

<sup>13.12</sup> "Men will hand over their own brothers to be put to death, and fathers will do the same to their children. Children will turn against their parents and have them put to death.

<sup>13.13</sup> "Everyone will hate you because of me. But whoever holds out to the end will be saved.

<sup>13.14</sup> "You will see 'The Awful Horror' standing in the place where he should not be." (Note to the reader: understand what this means!) "Then those who are in Judea must run away to the hills.

<sup>13.15</sup> "Someone who is on the roof of a house must not lose time by going down into the house to get anything to take along.

<sup>13.16</sup> "Someone who is in the field must not go back to the house for a cloak.

<sup>13.17</sup> "How terrible it will be in those days for women who are pregnant and for mothers with little babies!

<sup>13.18</sup> "Pray to God that these things will not happen in the winter!

<sup>13.19</sup> "For the trouble of those days will be far worse than any the world has ever known from the very beginning when God created the world until the present time. Nor will there ever be anything like it again.

<sup>13.20</sup> "But the Lord has reduced the number of those days; if he had not, nobody would survive. For the sake of his chosen people, however, he has reduced those days.

<sup>13.21</sup> "Then, if anyone says to you, 'Look, here is the Messiah!' or, 'Look, there he is!' — do not believe it.

<sup>13.22</sup> "For false Messiahs and false prophets will appear. They will perform miracles and wonders in order to deceive even God's chosen people, if possible.

<sup>13.23</sup> "Be on your guard! I have told you everything ahead of time.

<sup>13.24</sup> "In the days after that time of trouble the sun will grow dark, the moon will no longer shine,

<sup>13.25</sup> "the stars will fall from heaven, and the powers in space will be driven from their courses.

<sup>13.26</sup> "Then the Son of Man will appear, coming in the clouds with great power and glory.

<sup>13.27</sup> "He will send the angels out to the four corners of the earth to gather God's chosen people from one end of the world to the other.

<sup>13.28</sup> "Let the fig tree teach you a lesson. When its branches become green and tender and it starts putting out leaves, you know that summer is near.

<sup>13.29</sup> "In the same way, when you see these things happening, you will know that the time is near, ready to begin.

<sup>13.30</sup> "Remember that all these things will happen before the people now living have all died.

<sup>13.31</sup> "Heaven and earth will pass away, but my words will never pass away.

<sup>13.32</sup> "No one knows, however, when that day or hour will come — neither the angels in heaven, nor the Son; only the Father knows.

<sup>13.33</sup> "Be on watch, be alert, for you do not know when the time will come.

<sup>13.34</sup> "It will be like a man who goes away from home on a trip and leaves his servants in charge, after giving to each one his own work to do and after telling the doorkeeper to keep watch.

<sup>13.35</sup> "Watch, then, because you do not know when the master of the house is coming — it might be in the evening or at midnight or before dawn or at sunrise.

<sup>13.36</sup> "If he comes suddenly, he must not find you asleep.

<sup>13.37</sup> "What I say to you, then, I say to all: Watch!"

# 14

<sup>14.1</sup> It was now two days before the Festival of Passover and Unleavened Bread. The chief priests and the teachers of the Law were looking for a way to arrest Jesus secretly and put him to death.
<sup>14.2</sup> "We must not do it during the festival," they said, "or the people might riot."
<sup>14.3</sup> Jesus was in Bethany at the house of Simon, a man who had suffered from a dreaded skin disease. While Jesus was eating, a woman came in with an alabaster jar full of a very expensive perfume made of pure nard. She broke the jar and poured the perfume on Jesus' head.
<sup>14.4</sup> Some of the people there became angry and said to one another, "What was the use of wasting the perfume?
<sup>14.5</sup> "It could have been sold for more than three hundred silver coins and the money given to the poor!" And they criticized her harshly.
<sup>14.6</sup> But Jesus said, "Leave her alone! Why are you bothering her? She has done a fine and beautiful thing for me.
<sup>14.7</sup> "You will always have poor people with you, and any time you want to, you can help them. But you will not always have me.
<sup>14.8</sup> "She did what she could; she poured perfume on my body to prepare it ahead of time for burial.
<sup>14.9</sup> "Now, I assure you that wherever the gospel is preached all over the world, what she has done will be told in memory of her."
<sup>14.10</sup> Then Judas Iscariot, one of the twelve disciples, went off to the chief priests in order to betray Jesus to them.
<sup>14.11</sup> They were pleased to hear what he had to say, and promised to give him money. So Judas started looking for a good chance to hand Jesus over to them.
<sup>14.12</sup> On the first day of the Festival of Unleavened Bread, the day the lambs for the Passover meal were killed, Jesus' disciples asked him, "Where do you want us to go and get the Passover meal ready for you?"
<sup>14.13</sup> Then Jesus sent two of them with these instructions: "Go into the city, and a man carrying a jar of water will meet you. Follow him
<sup>14.14</sup> "to the house he enters, and say to the owner of the house: 'The Teacher says, Where is the room where my disciples and I will eat the Passover meal?'
<sup>14.15</sup> "Then he will show you a large upstairs room, fixed up and furnished, where you will get everything ready for us."

14.16 The disciples left, went to the city, and found everything just as Jesus had told them; and they prepared the Passover meal.

14.17 When it was evening, Jesus came with the twelve disciples.

14.18 While they were at the table eating, Jesus said, "I tell you that one of you will betray me — one who is eating with me."

14.19 The disciples were upset and began to ask him, one after the other, "Surely you don't mean me, do you?"

14.20 Jesus answered, "It will be one of you twelve, one who dips his bread in the dish with me.

14.21 "The Son of Man will die as the Scriptures say he will; but how terrible for that man who will betray the Son of Man! It would have been better for that man if he had never been born!"

14.22 While they were eating, Jesus took a piece of bread, gave a prayer of thanks, broke it, and gave it to his disciples. "Take it," he said, "this is my body."

14.23 Then he took a cup, gave thanks to God, and handed it to them; and they all drank from it.

14.24 Jesus said, "This is my blood which is poured out for many, my blood which seals God's covenant.

14.25 "I tell you, I will never again drink this wine until the day I drink the new wine in the Kingdom of God."

14.26 Then they sang a hymn and went out to the Mount of Olives.

14.27 Jesus said to them, "All of you will run away and leave me, for the scripture says, 'God will kill the shepherd, and the sheep will all be scattered.'

14.28 "But after I am raised to life, I will go to Galilee ahead of you."

14.29 Peter answered, "I will never leave you, even though all the rest do!"

14.30 Jesus said to Peter, "I tell you that before the rooster crows two times tonight, you will say three times that you do not know me."

14.31 Peter answered even more strongly, "I will never say that, even if I have to die with you!" And all the other disciples said the same thing.

14.32 They came to a place called Gethsemane, and Jesus said to his disciples, "Sit here while I pray."

14.33 He took Peter, James, and John with him. Distress and anguish came over him,

14.34 and he said to them, "The sorrow in my heart is so great that it almost crushes me. Stay here and keep watch."

14.35 He went a little farther on, threw himself on the ground, and prayed that, if possible, he might not have to go through that time of suffering.

14.36 "Father," he prayed, "my Father! All things are possible for you. Take this cup of suffering away from me. Yet not what I want, but what you want."

14.37 Then he returned and found the three disciples asleep. He said to Peter, "Simon, are you asleep? Weren't you able to stay awake for even one hour?"

14.38 And he said to them, "Keep watch, and pray that you will not fall into temptation. The spirit is willing, but the flesh is weak."

14.39 He went away once more and prayed, saying the same words.

14.40 Then he came back to the disciples and found them asleep; they could not keep their eyes open. And they did not know what to say to him.

14.41 When he came back the third time, he said to them, "Are you still sleeping and resting? Enough! The hour has come! Look, the Son of Man is now being handed over to the power of sinners.

14.42 "Get up, let us go. Look, here is the man who is betraying me!"

14.43 Jesus was still speaking when Judas, one of the twelve disciples, arrived. With him was a crowd armed with swords and clubs and sent by the chief priests, the teachers of the Law, and the elders.

14.44 The traitor had given the crowd a signal: "The man I kiss is the one you want. Arrest him and take him away under guard."

14.45 As soon as Judas arrived, he went up to Jesus and said, "Teacher!" and kissed him.

14.46 So they arrested Jesus and held him tight.

14.47 But one of those standing there drew his sword and struck at the High Priest's slave, cutting off his ear.

14.48 Then Jesus spoke up and said to them, "Did you have to come with swords and clubs to capture me, as though I were an outlaw?

14.49 "Day after day I was with you teaching in the Temple, and you did not arrest me. But the Scriptures must come true."

14.50 Then all the disciples left him and ran away.

14.51 A certain young man, dressed only in a linen cloth, was following Jesus. They tried to arrest him,

14.52 but he ran away naked, leaving the cloth behind.

14.53 Then Jesus was taken to the High Priest's house, where all the chief priests, the elders, and the teachers of the Law were gathering.

14.54 Peter followed from a distance and went into the courtyard of the High Priest's house. There he sat down with the guards, keeping himself warm by the fire.

14.55 The chief priests and the whole Council tried to find some evidence against Jesus in order to put him to death, but they could not find any.

<sup>14.56</sup> Many witnesses told lies against Jesus, but their stories did not agree.

<sup>14.57</sup> Then some men stood up and told this lie against Jesus:

<sup>14.58</sup> "We heard him say, 'I will tear down this Temple which men have made, and after three days I will build one that is not made by men.'"

<sup>14.59</sup> Not even they, however, could make their stories agree.

<sup>14.60</sup> The High Priest stood up in front of them all and questioned Jesus, "Have you no answer to the accusation they bring against you?"

<sup>14.61</sup> But Jesus kept quiet and would not say a word. Again the High Priest questioned him, "Are you the Messiah, the Son of the Blessed God?"

<sup>14.62</sup> "I am," answered Jesus, "and you will all see the Son of Man seated at the right side of the Almighty and coming with the clouds of heaven!"

<sup>14.63</sup> The High Priest tore his robes and said, "We don't need any more witnesses!

<sup>14.64</sup> "You heard his blasphemy. What is your decision?" They all voted against him: he was guilty and should be put to death.

<sup>14.65</sup> Some of them began to spit on Jesus, and they blindfolded him and hit him. "Guess who hit you!" they said. And the guards took him and slapped him.

<sup>14.66</sup> Peter was still down in the courtyard when one of the High Priest's servant women came by.

<sup>14.67</sup> When she saw Peter warming himself, she looked straight at him and said, "You, too, were with Jesus of Nazareth."

<sup>14.68</sup> But he denied it. "I don't know ... I don't understand what you are talking about," he answered, and went out into the passageway. Just then a rooster crowed.

<sup>14.69</sup> The servant woman saw him there and began to repeat to the bystanders, "He is one of them!"

<sup>14.70</sup> But Peter denied it again. A little while later the bystanders accused Peter again, "You can't deny that you are one of them, because you, too, are from Galilee."

<sup>14.71</sup> Then Peter said, "I swear that I am telling the truth! May God punish me if I am not! I do not know the man you are talking about!"

<sup>14.72</sup> Just then a rooster crowed a second time, and Peter remembered how Jesus had said to him, "Before the rooster crows two times, you will say three times that you do not know me." And he broke down

and cried.

15.1 Early in the morning the chief priests met hurriedly with the elders, the teachers of the Law, and the whole Council, and made their plans. They put Jesus in chains, led him away, and handed him over to Pilate.
15.2 Pilate questioned him, "Are you the king of the Jews?" Jesus answered, "So you say."
15.3 The chief priests were accusing Jesus of many things,
15.4 so Pilate questioned him again, "Aren't you going to answer? Listen to all their accusations!"
15.5 Again Jesus refused to say a word, and Pilate was amazed.
15.6 At every Passover Festival Pilate was in the habit of setting free any one prisoner the people asked for.
15.7 At that time a man named Barabbas was in prison with the rebels who had committed murder in the riot.
15.8 When the crowd gathered and began to ask Pilate for the usual favor,
15.9 he asked them, "Do you want me to set free for you the king of the Jews?"
15.10 He knew very well that the chief priests had handed Jesus over to him because they were jealous.
15.11 But the chief priests stirred up the crowd to ask, instead, that Pilate set Barabbas free for them.
15.12 Pilate spoke again to the crowd, "What, then, do you want me to do with the one you call the king of the Jews?"
15.13 They shouted back, "Crucify him!"
15.14 "But what crime has he committed?" Pilate asked. They shouted all the louder, "Crucify him!"
15.15 Pilate wanted to please the crowd, so he set Barabbas free for them. Then he had Jesus whipped and handed him over to be crucified.
15.16 The soldiers took Jesus inside to the courtyard of the governor's palace and called together the rest of the company.
15.17 They put a purple robe on Jesus, made a crown out of thorny branches, and put it on his head.
15.18 Then they began to salute him: "Long live the King of the Jews!"
15.19 They beat him over the head with a stick, spat on him, fell on their knees, and bowed down to him.
15.20 When they had finished making fun of him, they took off the

purple robe and put his own clothes back on him. Then they led him out to crucify him.

<sup></sup>15.21 On the way they met a man named Simon, who was coming into the city from the country, and the soldiers forced him to carry Jesus' cross. (Simon was from Cyrene and was the father of Alexander and Rufus.)

15.22 They took Jesus to a place called Golgotha, which means "The Place of the Skull."

15.23 There they tried to give him wine mixed with a drug called myrrh, but Jesus would not drink it.

15.24 Then they crucified him and divided his clothes among themselves, throwing dice to see who would get which piece of clothing.

15.25 It was nine o'clock in the morning when they crucified him.

15.26 The notice of the accusation against him said: "The King of the Jews."

15.27 They also crucified two bandits with Jesus, one on his right and the other on his left.

15.28 In this way the scripture came true which says, "He shared the fate of criminals."

15.29 People passing by shook their heads and hurled insults at Jesus: "Aha! You were going to tear down the Temple and build it back up in three days!

15.30 "Now come down from the cross and save yourself!"

15.31 In the same way the chief priests and the teachers of the Law made fun of Jesus, saying to one another, "He saved others, but he cannot save himself!

15.32 "Let us see the Messiah, the king of Israel, come down from the cross now, and we will believe in him!" And the two who were crucified with Jesus insulted him also.

15.33 At noon the whole country was covered with darkness, which lasted for three hours.

15.34 At three o'clock Jesus cried out with a loud shout, "Eloi, Eloi, lema sabachthani?" which means, "My God, my God, why did you abandon me?"

15.35 Some of the people there heard him and said, "Listen, he is calling for Elijah!"

15.36 One of them ran up with a sponge, soaked it in cheap wine, and put it on the end of a stick. Then he held it up to Jesus' lips and said, "Wait! Let us see if Elijah is coming to bring him down from the cross!"

15.37 With a loud cry Jesus died.

<sup>15.38</sup> The curtain hanging in the Temple was torn in two, from top to bottom.

<sup>15.39</sup> The army officer who was standing there in front of the cross saw how Jesus had died. "This man was really the Son of God!" he said.

<sup>15.40</sup> Some women were there, looking on from a distance. Among them were Mary Magdalene, Mary the mother of the younger James and of Joseph, and Salome.

<sup>15.41</sup> They had followed Jesus while he was in Galilee and had helped him. Many other women who had come to Jerusalem with him were there also.

<sup>15.42-43</sup> It was toward evening when Joseph of Arimathea arrived. He was a respected member of the Council, who was waiting for the coming of the Kingdom of God. It was Preparation day (that is, the day before the Sabbath), so Joseph went boldly into the presence of Pilate and asked him for the body of Jesus.

<sup>15.44</sup> Pilate was surprised to hear that Jesus was already dead. He called the army officer and asked him if Jesus had been dead a long time.

<sup>15.45</sup> After hearing the officer's report, Pilate told Joseph he could have the body.

<sup>15.46</sup> Joseph bought a linen sheet, took the body down, wrapped it in the sheet, and placed it in a tomb which had been dug out of solid rock. Then he rolled a large stone across the entrance to the tomb.

<sup>15.47</sup> Mary Magdalene and Mary the mother of Joseph were watching and saw where the body of Jesus was placed.

# 16

<sup>16.1</sup> After the Sabbath was over, Mary Magdalene, Mary the mother of James, and Salome bought spices to go and anoint the body of Jesus.

<sup>16.2</sup> Very early on Sunday morning, at sunrise, they went to the tomb.

<sup>16.3-4</sup> On the way they said to one another, "Who will roll away the stone for us from the entrance to the tomb?" (It was a very large stone.) Then they looked up and saw that the stone had already been rolled back.

<sup>16.5</sup> So they entered the tomb, where they saw a young man sitting at the right, wearing a white robe — and they were alarmed.

<sup>16.6</sup> "Don't be alarmed," he said. "I know you are looking for Jesus of Nazareth, who was crucified. He is not here — he has been raised! Look, here is the place where he was placed.

<sup>16.7</sup> "Now go and give this message to his disciples, including Peter: 'He is going to Galilee ahead of you; there you will see him, just as he told you.'"

<sup>16.8</sup> So they went out and ran from the tomb, distressed and terrified. They said nothing to anyone, because they were afraid.

<sup>16.9</sup> After Jesus rose from death early on Sunday, he appeared first to Mary Magdalene, from whom he had driven out seven demons.

<sup>16.10</sup> She went and told his companions. They were mourning and crying;

<sup>16.11</sup> and when they heard her say that Jesus was alive and that she had seen him, they did not believe her.

<sup>16.12</sup> After this, Jesus appeared in a different manner to two of them while they were on their way to the country.

<sup>16.13</sup> They returned and told the others, but these would not believe it.

<sup>16.14</sup> Last of all, Jesus appeared to the eleven disciples as they were eating. He scolded them, because they did not have faith and because they were too stubborn to believe those who had seen him alive.

<sup>16.15</sup> He said to them, "Go throughout the whole world and preach the gospel to all people.

<sup>16.16</sup> "Whoever believes and is baptized will be saved; whoever does not believe will be condemned.

<sup>16.17</sup> "Believers will be given the power to perform miracles: they will drive out demons in my name; they will speak in strange tongues;

<sup>16.18</sup> "if they pick up snakes or drink any poison, they will not be harmed; they will place their hands on sick people, and these will get well."

<sup>16.19</sup> After the Lord Jesus had talked with them, he was taken up to heaven and sat at the right side of God.

<sup>16.20</sup> The disciples went and preached everywhere, and the Lord worked with them and proved that their preaching was true by the miracles that were performed.

# LUKE

# Luke

# 1

<sup>1.1</sup> Dear Theophilus: Many people have done their best to write a report of the things that have taken place among us. <sup>1.2</sup> They wrote what we have been told by those who saw these things from the beginning and who proclaimed the message. <sup>1.3</sup> And so, Your Excellency, because I have carefully studied all these matters from their beginning, I thought it would be good to write an orderly account for you. <sup>1.4</sup> I do this so that you will know the full truth about everything which you have been taught.

<sup>1.5</sup> During the time when Herod was king of Judea, there was a priest named Zechariah, who belonged to the priestly order of Abijah. His wife's name was Elizabeth; she also belonged to a priestly family. <sub>1.6</sub> They both lived good lives in God's sight and obeyed fully all the Lord's laws and commands. <sup>1.7</sup> They had no children because Elizabeth could not have any, and she and Zechariah were both very old.

<sup>1.8</sup> One day Zechariah was doing his work as a priest in the Temple, taking his turn in the daily service. <sup>1.9</sup> According to the custom followed by the priests, he was chosen by lot to burn incense on the altar. So he went into the Temple of the Lord, <sup>1.10</sup> while the crowd of people outside prayed during the hour when the incense was burned. <sup>1.11</sup> An angel of the Lord appeared to him, standing at the right side of the altar where the incense was burned. <sup>1.12</sup> When Zechariah saw him, he was alarmed and felt afraid. <sup>1.13</sup> But the angel said to him, "Don't be afraid, Zechariah! God has heard your prayer, and your wife Elizabeth will bear you a son. You are to name him John. <sup>1.14</sup> "How glad and happy you will be, and how happy many others will be when he is born! <sup>1.15</sup> "John will be great in the Lord's sight. He must not drink any wine or strong drink. From his very birth he will be filled with the Holy Spirit, <sup>1.16</sup> "and he will bring back many of the people of Israel to the Lord their God. <sup>1.17</sup> "He will go ahead of the Lord, strong and mighty like the proph-

et Elijah. He will bring fathers and children together again; he will turn disobedient people back to the way of thinking of the righteous; he will get the Lord's people ready for him."

1.18 Zechariah said to the angel, "How shall I know if this is so? I am an old man, and my wife is old also."

1.19 "I am Gabriel," the angel answered. "I stand in the presence of God, who sent me to speak to you and tell you this good news.

1.20 "But you have not believed my message, which will come true at the right time. Because you have not believed, you will be unable to speak; you will remain silent until the day my promise to you comes true."

1.21 In the meantime the people were waiting for Zechariah and wondering why he was spending such a long time in the Temple.

1.22 When he came out, he could not speak to them, and so they knew that he had seen a vision in the Temple. Unable to say a word, he made signs to them with his hands.

1.23 When his period of service in the Temple was over, Zechariah went back home.

1.24 Some time later his wife Elizabeth became pregnant and did not leave the house for five months.

1.25 "Now at last the Lord has helped me," she said. "He has taken away my public disgrace!"

1.26 In the sixth month of Elizabeth's pregnancy God sent the angel Gabriel to a town in Galilee named Nazareth.

1.27 He had a message for a young woman promised in marriage to a man named Joseph, who was a descendant of King David. Her name was Mary.

1.28 The angel came to her and said, "Peace be with you! The Lord is with you and has greatly blessed you!"

1.29 Mary was deeply troubled by the angel's message, and she wondered what his words meant.

1.30 The angel said to her, "Don't be afraid, Mary; God has been gracious to you.

1.31 "You will become pregnant and give birth to a son, and you will name him Jesus.

1.32 "He will be great and will be called the Son of the Most High God. The Lord God will make him a king, as his ancestor David was,

1.33 "and he will be the king of the descendants of Jacob forever; his kingdom will never end!"

1.34 Mary said to the angel, "I am a virgin. How, then, can this be?"

[1.35] The angel answered, "The Holy Spirit will come on you, and God's power will rest upon you. For this reason the holy child will be called the Son of God.

[1.36] "Remember your relative Elizabeth. It is said that she cannot have children, but she herself is now six months pregnant, even though she is very old.

[1.37] "For there is nothing that God cannot do."

[1.38] "I am the Lord's servant," said Mary; "may it happen to me as you have said." And the angel left her.

[1.39] Soon afterward Mary got ready and hurried off to a town in the hill country of Judea.

[1.40] She went into Zechariah's house and greeted Elizabeth.

[1.41] When Elizabeth heard Mary's greeting, the baby moved within her. Elizabeth was filled with the Holy Spirit

[1.42] and said in a loud voice, "You are the most blessed of all women, and blessed is the child you will bear!

[1.43] "Why should this great thing happen to me, that my Lord's mother comes to visit me?

[1.44] "For as soon as I heard your greeting, the baby within me jumped with gladness.

[1.45] "How happy you are to believe that the Lord's message to you will come true!"

[1.46] Mary said, "My heart praises the Lord;

[1.47] "my soul is glad because of God my Savior,

[1.48] "for he has remembered me, his lowly servant! From now on all people will call me happy,

[1.49] "because of the great things the Mighty God has done for me. His name is holy;

[1.50] "from one generation to another he shows mercy to those who honor him.

[1.51] "He has stretched out his mighty arm and scattered the proud with all their plans.

[1.52] "He has brought down mighty kings from their thrones, and lifted up the lowly.

[1.53] "He has filled the hungry with good things, and sent the rich away with empty hands.

[1.54] "He has kept the promise he made to our ancestors, and has come to the help of his servant Israel.

[1.55] "He has remembered to show mercy to Abraham and to all his descendants forever!"

[1.56] Mary stayed about three months with Elizabeth and then went back home. <sup></sup>

1.57 The time came for Elizabeth to have her baby, and she gave birth to a son.

1.58 Her neighbors and relatives heard how wonderfully good the Lord had been to her, and they all rejoiced with her.

1.59 When the baby was a week old, they came to circumcise him, and they were going to name him Zechariah, after his father.

1.60 But his mother said, "No! His name is to be John."

1.61 They said to her, "But you don't have any relative with that name!"

1.62 Then they made signs to his father, asking him what name he would like the boy to have.

1.63 Zechariah asked for a writing pad and wrote, "His name is John." How surprised they all were!

1.64 At that moment Zechariah was able to speak again, and he started praising God.

1.65 The neighbors were all filled with fear, and the news about these things spread through all the hill country of Judea.

1.66 Everyone who heard of it thought about it and asked, "What is this child going to be?" For it was plain that the Lord's power was upon him.

1.67 John's father Zechariah was filled with the Holy Spirit, and he spoke God's message:

1.68 "Let us praise the Lord, the God of Israel! He has come to the help of his people and has set them free.

1.69 "He has provided for us a mighty Savior, a descendant of his servant David.

1.70 "He promised through his holy prophets long ago

1.71 "that he would save us from our enemies, from the power of all those who hate us.

1.72 "He said he would show mercy to our ancestors and remember his sacred covenant.

1.73-74 "With a solemn oath to our ancestor Abraham he promised to rescue us from our enemies and allow us to serve him without fear,

1.75 "so that we might be holy and righteous before him all the days of our life.

1.76 "You, my child, will be called a prophet of the Most High God. You will go ahead of the Lord to prepare his road for him,

1.77 "to tell his people that they will be saved by having their sins forgiven.

1.78 "Our God is merciful and tender. He will cause the bright dawn

of salvation to rise on us
<sup></sup>1.79 "and to shine from heaven on all those who live in the dark shadow of death, to guide our steps into the path of peace."
1.80 The child grew and developed in body and spirit. He lived in the desert until the day when he appeared publicly to the people of Israel.

# 2

2.1 At that time Emperor Augustus ordered a census to be taken throughout the Roman Empire.
2.2 When this first census took place, Quirinius was the governor of Syria.
2.3 Everyone, then, went to register himself, each to his own hometown.
2.4 Joseph went from the town of Nazareth in Galilee to the town of Bethlehem in Judea, the birthplace of King David. Joseph went there because he was a descendant of David.
2.5 He went to register with Mary, who was promised in marriage to him. She was pregnant,
2.6 and while they were in Bethlehem, the time came for her to have her baby.
2.7 She gave birth to her first son, wrapped him in cloths and laid him in a manger — there was no room for them to stay in the inn.
2.8 There were some shepherds in that part of the country who were spending the night in the fields, taking care of their flocks.
2.9 An angel of the Lord appeared to them, and the glory of the Lord shone over them. They were terribly afraid,
2.10 but the angel said to them, "Don't be afraid! I am here with good news for you, which will bring great joy to all the people.
2.11 "This very day in David's town your Savior was born — Christ the Lord!
2.12 "And this is what will prove it to you: you will find a baby wrapped in cloths and lying in a manger."
2.13 Suddenly a great army of heaven's angels appeared with the angel, singing praises to God:
2.14 "Glory to God in the highest heaven, and peace on earth to those with whom he is pleased!"
2.15 When the angels went away from them back into heaven, the shepherds said to one another, "Let's go to Bethlehem and see this thing that has happened, which the Lord has told us."
2.16 So they hurried off and found Mary and Joseph and saw the baby

lying in the manger.

<sup>2.17</sup> When the shepherds saw him, they told them what the angel had said about the child.

<sup>2.18</sup> All who heard it were amazed at what the shepherds said.

<sup>2.19</sup> Mary remembered all these things and thought deeply about them.

<sup>2.20</sup> The shepherds went back, singing praises to God for all they had heard and seen; it had been just as the angel had told them.

<sup>2.21</sup> A week later, when the time came for the baby to be circumcised, he was named Jesus, the name which the angel had given him before he had been conceived.

<sup>2.22</sup> The time came for Joseph and Mary to perform the ceremony of purification, as the Law of Moses commanded. So they took the child to Jerusalem to present him to the Lord,

<sup>2.23</sup> as it is written in the law of the Lord: "Every first-born male is to be dedicated to the Lord."

<sup>2.24</sup> They also went to offer a sacrifice of a pair of doves or two young pigeons, as required by the law of the Lord.

<sup>2.25</sup> At that time there was a man named Simeon living in Jerusalem. He was a good, God-fearing man and was waiting for Israel to be saved. The Holy Spirit was with him

<sup>2.26</sup> and had assured him that he would not die before he had seen the Lord's promised Messiah.

<sup>2.27</sup> Led by the Spirit, Simeon went into the Temple. When the parents brought the child Jesus into the Temple to do for him what the Law required,

<sup>2.28</sup> Simeon took the child in his arms and gave thanks to God:

<sup>2.29</sup> "Now, Lord, you have kept your promise, and you may let your servant go in peace.

<sup>2.30</sup> "With my own eyes I have seen your salvation,

<sup>2.31</sup> "which you have prepared in the presence of all peoples:

<sup>2.32</sup> "A light to reveal your will to the Gentiles and bring glory to your people Israel."

<sup>2.33</sup> The child's father and mother were amazed at the things Simeon said about him.

<sup>2.34</sup> Simeon blessed them and said to Mary, his mother, "This child is chosen by God for the destruction and the salvation of many in Israel. He will be a sign from God which many people will speak against

<sup>2.35</sup> "and so reveal their secret thoughts. And sorrow, like a sharp sword, will break your own heart."

<sup>2.36-37</sup> There was a very old prophet, a widow named Anna, daughter

of Phanuel of the tribe of Asher. She had been married for only seven years and was now eighty-four years old. She never left the Temple; day and night she worshiped God, fasting and praying.

2.38 That very same hour she arrived and gave thanks to God and spoke about the child to all who were waiting for God to set Jerusalem free.

2.39 When Joseph and Mary had finished doing all that was required by the Law of the Lord, they returned to their hometown of Nazareth in Galilee.

2.40 The child grew and became strong; he was full of wisdom, and God's blessings were upon him.

2.41 Every year the parents of Jesus went to Jerusalem for the Passover Festival.

2.42 When Jesus was twelve years old, they went to the festival as usual.

2.43 When the festival was over, they started back home, but the boy Jesus stayed in Jerusalem. His parents did not know this;

2.44 they thought that he was with the group, so they traveled a whole day and then started looking for him among their relatives and friends.

2.45 They did not find him, so they went back to Jerusalem looking for him.

2.46 On the third day they found him in the Temple, sitting with the Jewish teachers, listening to them and asking questions.

2.47 All who heard him were amazed at his intelligent answers.

2.48 His parents were astonished when they saw him, and his mother said to him, "Son, why have you done this to us? Your father and I have been terribly worried trying to find you."

2.49 He answered them, "Why did you have to look for me? Didn't you know that I had to be in my Father's house?"

2.50 But they did not understand his answer.

2.51 So Jesus went back with them to Nazareth, where he was obedient to them. His mother treasured all these things in her heart.

2.52 Jesus grew both in body and in wisdom, gaining favor with God and people.

# 3

3.1 It was the fifteenth year of the rule of Emperor Tiberius; Pontius Pilate was governor of Judea, Herod was ruler of Galilee, and his brother Philip was ruler of the territory of Iturea and Trachonitis; Lysanias was ruler of Abilene,

<sup>3.2</sup> and Annas and Caiaphas were High Priests. At that time the word of God came to John son of Zechariah in the desert.

<sup>3.3</sup> So John went throughout the whole territory of the Jordan River, preaching, "Turn away from your sins and be baptized, and God will forgive your sins."

<sup>3.4</sup> As it is written in the book of the prophet Isaiah: "Someone is shouting in the desert: 'Get the road ready for the Lord; make a straight path for him to travel!

<sup>3.5</sup> " 'Every valley must be filled up, every hill and mountain leveled off. The winding roads must be made straight, and the rough paths made smooth.

<sup>3.6</sup> " 'The whole human race will see God's salvation!' "

<sup>3.7</sup> Crowds of people came out to John to be baptized by him. "You snakes!" he said to them. "Who told you that you could escape from the punishment God is about to send?

<sup>3.8</sup> "Do those things that will show that you have turned from your sins. And don't start saying among yourselves that Abraham is your ancestor. I tell you that God can take these rocks and make descendants for Abraham!

<sup>3.9</sup> "The ax is ready to cut down the trees at the roots; every tree that does not bear good fruit will be cut down and thrown in the fire."

<sup>3.10</sup> The people asked him, "What are we to do, then?"

<sup>3.11</sup> He answered, "Whoever has two shirts must give one to the man who has none, and whoever has food must share it."

<sup>3.12</sup> Some tax collectors came to be baptized, and they asked him, "Teacher, what are we to do?"

<sup>3.13</sup> "Don't collect more than is legal," he told them.

<sup>3.14</sup> Some soldiers also asked him, "What about us? What are we to do?" He said to them, "Don't take money from anyone by force or accuse anyone falsely. Be content with your pay."

<sup>3.15</sup> People's hopes began to rise, and they began to wonder whether John perhaps might be the Messiah.

<sup>3.16</sup> So John said to all of them, "I baptize you with water, but someone is coming who is much greater than I am. I am not good enough even to untie his sandals. He will baptize you with the Holy Spirit and fire.

<sup>3.17</sup> "He has his winnowing shovel with him, to thresh out all the grain and gather the wheat into his barn; but he will burn the chaff in a fire that never goes out."

<sup>3.18</sup> In many different ways John preached the Good News to the people and urged them to change their ways.

<sup>3.19</sup> But John reprimanded Governor Herod, because he had married Herodias, his brother's wife, and had done many other evil things. <sup>3.20</sup> Then Herod did an even worse thing by putting John in prison. <sup>3.21</sup> After all the people had been baptized, Jesus also was baptized. While he was praying, heaven was opened, <sup>3.22</sup> and the Holy Spirit came down upon him in bodily form like a dove. And a voice came from heaven, "You are my own dear Son. I am pleased with you."

<sup>3.23</sup> When Jesus began his work, he was about thirty years old. He was the son, so people thought, of Joseph, who was the son of Heli, <sup>3.24</sup> the son of Matthat, the son of Levi, the son of Melchi, the son of Jannai, the son of Joseph, <sup>3.25</sup> the son of Mattathias, the son of Amos, the son of Nahum, the son of Esli, the son of Naggai, <sup>3.26</sup> the son of Maath, the son of Mattathias, the son of Semein, the son of Josech, the son of Joda, <sup>3.27</sup> the son of Joanan, the son of Rhesa, the son of Zerubbabel, the son of Shealtiel, the son of Neri, <sup>3.28</sup> the son of Melchi, the son of Addi, the son of Cosam, the son of Elmadam, the son of Er, <sup>3.29</sup> the son of Joshua, the son of Eliezer, the son of Jorim, the son of Matthat, the son of Levi, <sup>3.30</sup> the son of Simeon, the son of Judah, the son of Joseph, the son of Jonam, the son of Eliakim, <sup>3.31</sup> the son of Melea, the son of Menna, the son of Mattatha, the son of Nathan, the son of David, <sup>3.32</sup> the son of Jesse, the son of Obed, the son of Boaz, the son of Salmon, the son of Nahshon, <sup>3.33</sup> the son of Amminadab, the son of Admin, the son of Arni, the son of Hezron, the son of Perez, the son of Judah, <sup>3.34</sup> the son of Jacob, the son of Isaac, the son of Abraham, the son of Terah, the son of Nahor, <sup>3.35</sup> the son of Serug, the son of Reu, the son of Peleg, the son of Eber, the son of Shelah, <sup>3.36</sup> the son of Cainan, the son of Arphaxad, the son of Shem, the son of Noah, the son of Lamech, <sup>3.37</sup> the son of Methuselah, the son of Enoch, the son of Jared, the son of Mahalaleel, the son of Kenan, <sup>3.38</sup> the son of Enosh, the son of Seth, the son of Adam, the son of God.

<sup>4.1</sup> Jesus returned from the Jordan full of the Holy Spirit and was led by the Spirit into the desert,

<sup>4.2</sup> where he was tempted by the Devil for forty days. In all that time he ate nothing, so that he was hungry when it was over.

<sup>4.3</sup> The Devil said to him, "If you are God's Son, order this stone to turn into bread."

<sup>4.4</sup> But Jesus answered, "The scripture says, 'Human beings cannot live on bread alone.'"

<sup>4.5</sup> Then the Devil took him up and showed him in a second all the kingdoms of the world.

<sup>4.6</sup> "I will give you all this power and all this wealth," the Devil told him. "It has all been handed over to me, and I can give it to anyone I choose.

<sup>4.7</sup> "All this will be yours, then, if you worship me."

<sup>4.8</sup> Jesus answered, "The scripture says, 'Worship the Lord your God and serve only him!'"

<sup>4.9</sup> Then the Devil took him to Jerusalem and set him on the highest point of the Temple, and said to him, "If you are God's Son, throw yourself down from here.

<sup>4.10</sup> "For the scripture says, 'God will order his angels to take good care of you.'

<sup>4.11</sup> "It also says, 'They will hold you up with their hands so that not even your feet will be hurt on the stones.'"

<sup>4.12</sup> But Jesus answered, "The scripture says, 'Do not put the Lord your God to the test.'"

<sup>4.13</sup> When the Devil finished tempting Jesus in every way, he left him for a while.

<sup>4.14</sup> Then Jesus returned to Galilee, and the power of the Holy Spirit was with him. The news about him spread throughout all that territory.

<sup>4.15</sup> He taught in the synagogues and was praised by everyone.

<sup>4.16</sup> Then Jesus went to Nazareth, where he had been brought up, and on the Sabbath he went as usual to the synagogue. He stood up to read the Scriptures

<sup>4.17</sup> and was handed the book of the prophet Isaiah. He unrolled the scroll and found the place where it is written,

<sup>4.18</sup> "The Spirit of the Lord is upon me, because he has chosen me to bring good news to the poor. He has sent me to proclaim liberty to the captives and recovery of sight to the blind, to set free the oppressed

<sup>4.19</sup> "and announce that the time has come when the Lord will save

his people."

<sup>4.20</sup> Jesus rolled up the scroll, gave it back to the attendant, and sat down. All the people in the synagogue had their eyes fixed on him, <sup>4.21</sup> as he said to them, "This passage of scripture has come true today, as you heard it being read."

<sup>4.22</sup> They were all well impressed with him and marveled at the eloquent words that he spoke. They said, "Isn't he the son of Joseph?"

<sup>4.23</sup> He said to them, "I am sure that you will quote this proverb to me, 'Doctor, heal yourself.' You will also tell me to do here in my hometown the same things you heard were done in Capernaum.

<sup>4.24</sup> "I tell you this," Jesus added, "prophets are never welcomed in their hometown.

<sup>4.25</sup> "Listen to me: it is true that there were many widows in Israel during the time of Elijah, when there was no rain for three and a half years and a severe famine spread throughout the whole land.

<sup>4.26</sup> "Yet Elijah was not sent to anyone in Israel, but only to a widow living in Zarephath in the territory of Sidon.

<sup>4.27</sup> "And there were many people suffering from a dreaded skin disease who lived in Israel during the time of the prophet Elisha; yet not one of them was healed, but only Naaman the Syrian."

<sup>4.28</sup> When the people in the synagogue heard this, they were filled with anger.

<sup>4.29</sup> They rose up, dragged Jesus out of town, and took him to the top of the hill on which their town was built. They meant to throw him over the cliff,

<sup>4.30</sup> but he walked through the middle of the crowd and went his way.

<sup>4.31</sup> Then Jesus went to Capernaum, a town in Galilee, where he taught the people on the Sabbath.

<sup>4.32</sup> They were all amazed at the way he taught, because he spoke with authority.

<sup>4.33</sup> In the synagogue was a man who had the spirit of an evil demon in him; he screamed out in a loud voice,

<sup>4.34</sup> "Ah! What do you want with us, Jesus of Nazareth? Are you here to destroy us? I know who you are: you are God's holy messenger!"

<sup>4.35</sup> Jesus ordered the spirit, "Be quiet and come out of the man!" The demon threw the man down in front of them and went out of him without doing him any harm.

<sup>4.36</sup> The people were all amazed and said to one another, "What kind of words are these? With authority and power this man gives orders to the evil spirits, and they come out!"

<sup>4.37</sup> And the report about Jesus spread everywhere in that region.

<sup>4.38</sup> Jesus left the synagogue and went to Simon's home. Simon's mother-in-law was sick with a high fever, and they spoke to Jesus about her.

<sup>4.39</sup> He went and stood at her bedside and ordered the fever to leave her. The fever left her, and she got up at once and began to wait on them.

<sup>4.40</sup> After sunset all who had friends who were sick with various diseases brought them to Jesus; he placed his hands on every one of them and healed them all.

<sup>4.41</sup> Demons also went out from many people, screaming, "You are the Son of God!" Jesus gave the demons an order and would not let them speak, because they knew he was the Messiah.

<sup>4.42</sup> At daybreak Jesus left the town and went off to a lonely place. The people started looking for him, and when they found him, they tried to keep him from leaving.

<sup>4.43</sup> But he said to them, "I must preach the Good News about the Kingdom of God in other towns also, because that is what God sent me to do."

<sup>4.44</sup> So he preached in the synagogues throughout the country.

# 5

<sup>5.1</sup> One day Jesus was standing on the shore of Lake Gennesaret while the people pushed their way up to him to listen to the word of God.

<sup>5.2</sup> He saw two boats pulled up on the beach; the fishermen had left them and were washing the nets.

<sup>5.3</sup> Jesus got into one of the boats — it belonged to Simon — and asked him to push off a little from the shore. Jesus sat in the boat and taught the crowd.

<sup>5.4</sup> When he finished speaking, he said to Simon, "Push the boat out further to the deep water, and you and your partners let down your nets for a catch."

<sup>5.5</sup> "Master," Simon answered, "we worked hard all night long and caught nothing. But if you say so, I will let down the nets."

<sup>5.6</sup> They let them down and caught such a large number of fish that the nets were about to break.

<sup>5.7</sup> So they motioned to their partners in the other boat to come and help them. They came and filled both boats so full of fish that the boats were about to sink.

<sup>5.8</sup> When Simon Peter saw what had happened, he fell on his knees before Jesus and said, "Go away from me, Lord! I am a sinful man!"

$^{5.9}$ He and the others with him were all amazed at the large number of fish they had caught.

$^{5.10}$ The same was true of Simon's partners, James and John, the sons of Zebedee. Jesus said to Simon, "Don't be afraid; from now on you will be catching people."

$^{5.11}$ They pulled the boats up on the beach, left everything, and followed Jesus.

$^{5.12}$ Once Jesus was in a town where there was a man who was suffering from a dreaded skin disease. When he saw Jesus, he threw himself down and begged him, "Sir, if you want to, you can make me clean!"

$^{5.13}$ Jesus reached out and touched him. "I do want to," he answered. "Be clean!" At once the disease left the man.

$^{5.14}$ Jesus ordered him, "Don't tell anyone, but go straight to the priest and let him examine you; then to prove to everyone that you are cured, offer the sacrifice as Moses ordered."

$^{5.15}$ But the news about Jesus spread all the more widely, and crowds of people came to hear him and be healed from their diseases.

$^{5.16}$ But he would go away to lonely places, where he prayed.

$^{5.17}$ One day when Jesus was teaching, some Pharisees and teachers of the Law were sitting there who had come from every town in Galilee and Judea and from Jerusalem. The power of the Lord was present for Jesus to heal the sick.

$^{5.18}$ Some men came carrying a paralyzed man on a bed, and they tried to carry him into the house and put him in front of Jesus.

$^{5.19}$ Because of the crowd, however, they could find no way to take him in. So they carried him up on the roof, made an opening in the tiles, and let him down on his bed into the middle of the group in front of Jesus.

$^{5.20}$ When Jesus saw how much faith they had, he said to the man, "Your sins are forgiven, my friend."

$^{5.21}$ The teachers of the Law and the Pharisees began to say to themselves, "Who is this man who speaks such blasphemy! God is the only one who can forgive sins!"

$^{5.22}$ Jesus knew their thoughts and said to them, "Why do you think such things?

$^{5.23}$ "Is it easier to say, 'Your sins are forgiven you,' or to say, 'Get up and walk'?

$^{5.24}$ "I will prove to you, then, that the Son of Man has authority on earth to forgive sins." So he said to the paralyzed man, "I tell you, get up, pick up your bed, and go home!"

5.25 At once the man got up in front of them all, took the bed he had been lying on, and went home, praising God.

5.26 They were all completely amazed! Full of fear, they praised God, saying, "What marvelous things we have seen today!"

5.27 After this, Jesus went out and saw a tax collector named Levi, sitting in his office. Jesus said to him, "Follow me."

5.28 Levi got up, left everything, and followed him.

5.29 Then Levi had a big feast in his house for Jesus, and among the guests was a large number of tax collectors and other people.

5.30 Some Pharisees and some teachers of the Law who belonged to their group complained to Jesus' disciples. "Why do you eat and drink with tax collectors and other outcasts?" they asked.

5.31 Jesus answered them, "People who are well do not need a doctor, but only those who are sick.

5.32 "I have not come to call respectable people to repent, but outcasts."

5.33 Some people said to Jesus, "The disciples of John fast frequently and offer prayers, and the disciples of the Pharisees do the same; but your disciples eat and drink."

5.34 Jesus answered, "Do you think you can make the guests at a wedding party go without food as long as the bridegroom is with them? Of course not!

5.35 "But the day will come when the bridegroom will be taken away from them, and then they will fast."

5.36 Jesus also told them this parable: "You don't tear a piece off a new coat to patch up an old coat. If you do, you will have torn the new coat, and the piece of new cloth will not match the old.

5.37 "Nor do you pour new wine into used wineskins, because the new wine will burst the skins, the wine will pour out, and the skins will be ruined.

5.38 "Instead, new wine must be poured into fresh wineskins!

5.39 "And you don't want new wine after drinking old wine. 'The old is better,' you say."

# 6

6.1 Jesus was walking through some wheat fields on a Sabbath. His disciples began to pick the heads of wheat, rub them in their hands, and eat the grain.

6.2 Some Pharisees asked, "Why are you doing what our Law says you cannot do on the Sabbath?"

6.3 Jesus answered them, "Haven't you read what David did when he and his men were hungry?

6.4 "He went into the house of God, took the bread offered to God, ate it, and gave it also to his men. Yet it is against our Law for anyone except the priests to eat that bread."

6.5 And Jesus concluded, "The Son of Man is Lord of the Sabbath."

6.6 On another Sabbath Jesus went into a synagogue and taught. A man was there whose right hand was paralyzed.

6.7 Some teachers of the Law and some Pharisees wanted a reason to accuse Jesus of doing wrong, so they watched him closely to see if he would heal on the Sabbath.

6.8 But Jesus knew their thoughts and said to the man, "Stand up and come here to the front." The man got up and stood there.

6.9 Then Jesus said to them, "I ask you: What does our Law allow us to do on the Sabbath? To help or to harm? To save someone's life or destroy it?"

6.10 He looked around at them all; then he said to the man, "Stretch out your hand." He did so, and his hand became well again.

6.11 They were filled with rage and began to discuss among themselves what they could do to Jesus.

6.12 At that time Jesus went up a hill to pray and spent the whole night there praying to God.

6.13 When day came, he called his disciples to him and chose twelve of them, whom he named apostles:

6.14 Simon (whom he named Peter) and his brother Andrew; James and John, Philip and Bartholomew,

6.15 Matthew and Thomas, James son of Alphaeus, and Simon (who was called the Patriot),

6.16 Judas son of James, and Judas Iscariot, who became the traitor.

6.17 When Jesus had come down from the hill with the apostles, he stood on a level place with a large number of his disciples. A large crowd of people was there from all over Judea and from Jerusalem and from the coast cities of Tyre and Sidon;

6.18 they had come to hear him and to be healed of their diseases. Those who were troubled by evil spirits also came and were healed.

6.19 All the people tried to touch him, for power was going out from him and healing them all.

6.20 Jesus looked at his disciples and said, "Happy are you poor; the Kingdom of God is yours!

6.21 "Happy are you who are hungry now; you will be filled! Happy are you who weep now; you will laugh!

6.22 "Happy are you when people hate you, reject you, insult you, and say that you are evil, all because of the Son of Man!

<sup>6.23</sup> "Be glad when that happens and dance for joy, because a great reward is kept for you in heaven. For their ancestors did the very same things to the prophets.

<sup>6.24</sup> "But how terrible for you who are rich now; you have had your easy life!

<sup>6.25</sup> "How terrible for you who are full now; you will go hungry! How terrible for you who laugh now; you will mourn and weep!

<sup>6.26</sup> "How terrible when all people speak well of you; their ancestors said the very same things about the false prophets.

<sup>6.27</sup> "But I tell you who hear me: Love your enemies, do good to those who hate you,

<sup>6.28</sup> "bless those who curse you, and pray for those who mistreat you.

<sup>6.29</sup> "If anyone hits you on one cheek, let him hit the other one too; if someone takes your coat, let him have your shirt as well.

<sup>6.30</sup> "Give to everyone who asks you for something, and when someone takes what is yours, do not ask for it back.

<sup>6.31</sup> "Do for others just what you want them to do for you.

<sup>6.32</sup> "If you love only the people who love you, why should you receive a blessing? Even sinners love those who love them!

<sup>6.33</sup> "And if you do good only to those who do good to you, why should you receive a blessing? Even sinners do that!

<sup>6.34</sup> "And if you lend only to those from whom you hope to get it back, why should you receive a blessing? Even sinners lend to sinners, to get back the same amount!

<sup>6.35</sup> "No! Love your enemies and do good to them; lend and expect nothing back. You will then have a great reward, and you will be children of the Most High God. For he is good to the ungrateful and the wicked.

<sup>6.36</sup> "Be merciful just as your Father is merciful.

<sup>6.37</sup> "Do not judge others, and God will not judge you; do not condemn others, and God will not condemn you; forgive others, and God will forgive you.

<sup>6.38</sup> "Give to others, and God will give to you. Indeed, you will receive a full measure, a generous helping, poured into your hands — all that you can hold. The measure you use for others is the one that God will use for you."

<sup>6.39</sup> And Jesus told them this parable: "One blind man cannot lead another one; if he does, both will fall into a ditch.

<sup>6.40</sup> "No pupils are greater than their teacher; but all pupils, when they have completed their training, will be like their teacher.

6.41 "Why do you look at the speck in your brother's eye, but pay no attention to the log in your own eye?

6.42 "How can you say to your brother, 'Please, brother, let me take that speck out of your eye,' yet cannot even see the log in your own eye? You hypocrite! First take the log out of your own eye, and then you will be able to see clearly to take the speck out of your brother's eye.

6.43 "A healthy tree does not bear bad fruit, nor does a poor tree bear good fruit.

6.44 "Every tree is known by the fruit it bears; you do not pick figs from thorn bushes or gather grapes from bramble bushes.

6.45 "A good person brings good out of the treasure of good things in his heart; a bad person brings bad out of his treasure of bad things. For the mouth speaks what the heart is full of.

6.46 "Why do you call me, 'Lord, Lord,' and yet don't do what I tell you?

6.47 "Anyone who comes to me and listens to my words and obeys them — I will show you what he is like.

6.48 "He is like a man who, in building his house, dug deep and laid the foundation on rock. The river flooded over and hit that house but could not shake it, because it was well built.

6.49 "But anyone who hears my words and does not obey them is like a man who built his house without laying a foundation; when the flood hit that house it fell at once - and what a terrible crash that was!"

# 7

7.1 When Jesus had finished saying all these things to the people, he went to Capernaum.

7.2 A Roman officer there had a servant who was very dear to him; the man was sick and about to die.

7.3 When the officer heard about Jesus, he sent some Jewish elders to ask him to come and heal his servant.

7.4 They came to Jesus and begged him earnestly, "This man really deserves your help.

7.5 "He loves our people and he himself built a synagogue for us."

7.6 So Jesus went with them. He was not far from the house when the officer sent friends to tell him, "Sir, don't trouble yourself. I do not deserve to have you come into my house,

7.7 "neither do I consider myself worthy to come to you in person. Just give the order, and my servant will get well.

7.8 "I, too, am a man placed under the authority of superior officers, and I have soldiers under me. I order this one, 'Go!' and he goes; I order that one, 'Come!' and he comes; and I order my slave, 'Do this!' and he does it."

7.9 Jesus was surprised when he heard this; he turned around and said to the crowd following him, "I tell you, I have never found faith like this, not even in Israel!"

7.10 The messengers went back to the officer's house and found his servant well.

7.11 Soon afterward Jesus went to a town named Nain, accompanied by his disciples and a large crowd.

7.12 Just as he arrived at the gate of the town, a funeral procession was coming out. The dead man was the only son of a woman who was a widow, and a large crowd from the town was with her.

7.13 When the Lord saw her, his heart was filled with pity for her, and he said to her, "Don't cry."

7.14 Then he walked over and touched the coffin, and the men carrying it stopped. Jesus said, "Young man! Get up, I tell you!"

7.15 The dead man sat up and began to talk, and Jesus gave him back to his mother.

7.16 They all were filled with fear and praised God. "A great prophet has appeared among us!" they said; "God has come to save his people!"

7.17 This news about Jesus went out through all the country and the surrounding territory.

7.18 When John's disciples told him about all these things, he called two of them

7.19 and sent them to the Lord to ask him, "Are you the one John said was going to come, or should we expect someone else?"

7.20 When they came to Jesus, they said, "John the Baptist sent us to ask if you are the one he said was going to come, or should we expect someone else?"

7.21 At that very time Jesus healed many people from their sicknesses, diseases, and evil spirits, and gave sight to many blind people.

7.22 He answered John's messengers, "Go back and tell John what you have seen and heard: the blind can see, the lame can walk, those who suffer from dreaded skin diseases are made clean, the deaf can hear, the dead are raised to life, and the Good News is preached to the poor.

7.23 "How happy are those who have no doubts about me!"

7.24 After John's messengers had left, Jesus began to speak about him to the crowds: "When you went out to John in the desert, what did

you expect to see? A blade of grass bending in the wind?
<sup>7.25</sup> "What did you go out to see? A man dressed up in fancy clothes? People who dress like that and live in luxury are found in palaces!
<sup>7.26</sup> "Tell me, what did you go out to see? A prophet? Yes indeed, but you saw much more than a prophet.
<sup>7.27</sup> "For John is the one of whom the scripture says: 'God said, I will send my messenger ahead of you to open the way for you.'
<sup>7.28</sup> "I tell you," Jesus added, "John is greater than anyone who has ever lived. But the one who is least in the Kingdom of God is greater than John."
<sup>7.29</sup> All the people heard him; they and especially the tax collectors were the ones who had obeyed God's righteous demands and had been baptized by John.
<sup>7.30</sup> But the Pharisees and the teachers of the Law rejected God's purpose for themselves and refused to be baptized by John.
<sup>7.31</sup> Jesus continued, "Now to what can I compare the people of this day? What are they like?
<sup>7.32</sup> "They are like children sitting in the marketplace. One group shouts to the other, 'We played wedding music for you, but you wouldn't dance! We sang funeral songs, but you wouldn't cry!'
<sup>7.33</sup> "John the Baptist came, and he fasted and drank no wine, and you said, 'He has a demon in him!'
<sup>7.34</sup> "The Son of Man came, and he ate and drank, and you said, 'Look at this man! He is a glutton and wine drinker, a friend of tax collectors and other outcasts!'
<sup>7.35</sup> "God's wisdom, however, is shown to be true by all who accept it."
<sup>7.36</sup> A Pharisee invited Jesus to have dinner with him, and Jesus went to his house and sat down to eat.
<sup>7.37</sup> In that town was a woman who lived a sinful life. She heard that Jesus was eating in the Pharisee's house, so she brought an alabaster jar full of perfume
<sup>7.38</sup> and stood behind Jesus, by his feet, crying and wetting his feet with her tears. Then she dried his feet with her hair, kissed them, and poured the perfume on them.
<sup>7.39</sup> When the Pharisee saw this, he said to himself, "If this man really were a prophet, he would know who this woman is who is touching him; he would know what kind of sinful life she lives!"
<sup>7.40</sup> Jesus spoke up and said to him, "Simon, I have something to tell you." "Yes, Teacher," he said, "tell me."
<sup>7.41</sup> "There were two men who owed money to a moneylender," Jesus began. "One owed him five hundred silver coins, and the other owed

him fifty.

7.42 "Neither of them could pay him back, so he canceled the debts of both. Which one, then, will love him more?"

7.43 "I suppose," answered Simon, "that it would be the one who was forgiven more." "You are right," said Jesus.

7.44 Then he turned to the woman and said to Simon, "Do you see this woman? I came into your home, and you gave me no water for my feet, but she has washed my feet with her tears and dried them with her hair.

7.45 "You did not welcome me with a kiss, but she has not stopped kissing my feet since I came.

7.46 "You provided no olive oil for my head, but she has covered my feet with perfume.

7.47 "I tell you, then, the great love she has shown proves that her many sins have been forgiven. But whoever has been forgiven little shows only a little love."

7.48 Then Jesus said to the woman, "Your sins are forgiven."

7.49 The others sitting at the table began to say to themselves, "Who is this, who even forgives sins?"

7.50 But Jesus said to the woman, "Your faith has saved you; go in peace."

# 8

8.1 Some time later Jesus traveled through towns and villages, preaching the Good News about the Kingdom of God. The twelve disciples went with him,

8.2 and so did some women who had been healed of evil spirits and diseases: Mary (who was called Magdalene), from whom seven demons had been driven out;

8.3 Joanna, whose husband Chuza was an officer in Herod's court; and Susanna, and many other women who used their own resources to help Jesus and his disciples.

8.4 People kept coming to Jesus from one town after another; and when a great crowd gathered, Jesus told this parable:

8.5 "Once there was a man who went out to sow grain. As he scattered the seed in the field, some of it fell along the path, where it was stepped on, and the birds ate it up.

8.6 "Some of it fell on rocky ground, and when the plants sprouted, they dried up because the soil had no moisture.

8.7 "Some of the seed fell among thorn bushes, which grew up with the plants and choked them.

8.8 "And some seeds fell in good soil; the plants grew and bore grain, one hundred grains each." And Jesus concluded, "Listen, then, if you have ears!"

8.9 His disciples asked Jesus what this parable meant,

8.10 and he answered, "The knowledge of the secrets of the Kingdom of God has been given to you, but to the rest it comes by means of parables, so that they may look but not see, and listen but not understand.

8.11 "This is what the parable means: the seed is the word of God.

8.12 "The seeds that fell along the path stand for those who hear; but the Devil comes and takes the message away from their hearts in order to keep them from believing and being saved.

8.13 "The seeds that fell on rocky ground stand for those who hear the message and receive it gladly. But it does not sink deep into them; they believe only for a while but when the time of testing comes, they fall away.

8.14 "The seeds that fell among thorn bushes stand for those who hear; but the worries and riches and pleasures of this life crowd in and choke them, and their fruit never ripens.

8.15 "The seeds that fell in good soil stand for those who hear the message and retain it in a good and obedient heart, and they persist until they bear fruit.

8.16 "No one lights a lamp and covers it with a bowl or puts it under a bed. Instead, it is put on the lampstand, so that people will see the light as they come in.

8.17 "Whatever is hidden away will be brought out into the open, and whatever is covered up will be found and brought to light.

8.18 "Be careful, then, how you listen; because those who have something will be given more, but whoever has nothing will have taken away from them even the little they think they have."

8.19 Jesus' mother and brothers came to him, but were unable to join him because of the crowd.

8.20 Someone said to Jesus, "Your mother and brothers are standing outside and want to see you."

8.21 Jesus said to them all, "My mother and brothers are those who hear the word of God and obey it."

8.22 One day Jesus got into a boat with his disciples and said to them, "Let us go across to the other side of the lake." So they started out.

8.23 As they were sailing, Jesus fell asleep. Suddenly a strong wind blew down on the lake, and the boat began to fill with water, so that they were all in great danger.

$^{8.24}$ The disciples went to Jesus and woke him up, saying, "Master, Master! We are about to die!" Jesus got up and gave an order to the wind and to the stormy water; they quieted down, and there was a great calm.

$^{8.25}$ Then he said to the disciples, "Where is your faith?" But they were amazed and afraid, and said to one another, "Who is this man? He gives orders to the winds and waves, and they obey him!"

$^{8.26}$ Jesus and his disciples sailed on over to the territory of Gerasa, which is across the lake from Galilee.

$^{8.27}$ As Jesus stepped ashore, he was met by a man from the town who had demons in him. For a long time this man had gone without clothes and would not stay at home, but spent his time in the burial caves.

$^{8.28}$ When he saw Jesus, he gave a loud cry, threw himself down at his feet, and shouted, "Jesus, Son of the Most High God! What do you want with me? I beg you, don't punish me!"

$^{8.29}$ He said this because Jesus had ordered the evil spirit to go out of him. Many times it had seized him, and even though he was kept a prisoner, his hands and feet tied with chains, he would break the chains and be driven by the demon out into the desert.

$^{8.30}$ Jesus asked him, "What is your name?" "My name is 'Mob,'" he answered — because many demons had gone into him.

$^{8.31}$ The demons begged Jesus not to send them into the abyss.

$^{8.32}$ There was a large herd of pigs near by, feeding on a hillside. So the demons begged Jesus to let them go into the pigs, and he let them.

$^{8.33}$ They went out of the man and into the pigs. The whole herd rushed down the side of the cliff into the lake and was drowned.

$^{8.34}$ The men who had been taking care of the pigs saw what happened, so they ran off and spread the news in the town and among the farms.

$^{8.35}$ People went out to see what had happened, and when they came to Jesus, they found the man from whom the demons had gone out sitting at the feet of Jesus, clothed and in his right mind; and they were all afraid.

$^{8.36}$ Those who had seen it told the people how the man had been cured.

$^{8.37}$ Then all the people from that territory asked Jesus to go away, because they were terribly afraid. So Jesus got into the boat and left.

$^{8.38}$ The man from whom the demons had gone out begged Jesus, "Let me go with you." But Jesus sent him away, saying,

<sup>8.39</sup> "Go back home and tell what God has done for you." The man went through the town, telling what Jesus had done for him.

<sup>8.40</sup> When Jesus returned to the other side of the lake, the people welcomed him, because they had all been waiting for him.

<sup>8.41</sup> Then a man named Jairus arrived; he was an official in the local synagogue. He threw himself down at Jesus' feet and begged him to go to his home,

<sup>8.42</sup> because his only daughter, who was twelve years old, was dying. As Jesus went along, the people were crowding him from every side.

<sup>8.43</sup> Among them was a woman who had suffered from severe bleeding for twelve years; she had spent all she had on doctors, but no one had been able to cure her.

<sup>8.44</sup> She came up in the crowd behind Jesus and touched the edge of his cloak, and her bleeding stopped at once.

<sup>8.45</sup> Jesus asked, "Who touched me?" Everyone denied it, and Peter said, "Master, the people are all around you and crowding in on you."

<sup>8.46</sup> But Jesus said, "Someone touched me, for I knew it when power went out of me."

<sup>8.47</sup> The woman saw that she had been found out, so she came trembling and threw herself at Jesus' feet. There in front of everybody, she told him why she had touched him and how she had been healed at once.

<sup>8.48</sup> Jesus said to her, "My daughter, your faith has made you well. Go in peace."

<sup>8.49</sup> While Jesus was saying this, a messenger came from the official's house. "Your daughter has died," he told Jairus; "don't bother the Teacher any longer."

<sup>8.50</sup> But Jesus heard it and said to Jairus, "Don't be afraid; only believe, and she will be well."

<sup>8.51</sup> When he arrived at the house, he would not let anyone go in with him except Peter, John, and James, and the child's father and mother.

<sup>8.52</sup> Everyone there was crying and mourning for the child. Jesus said, "Don't cry; the child is not dead — she is only sleeping!"

<sup>8.53</sup> They all made fun of him, because they knew that she was dead.

<sup>8.54</sup> But Jesus took her by the hand and called out, "Get up, child!"

<sup>8.55</sup> Her life returned, and she got up at once, and Jesus ordered them to give her something to eat.

<sup>8.56</sup> Her parents were astounded, but Jesus commanded them not to tell anyone what had happened.

<sup>9.1</sup> Jesus called the twelve disciples together and gave them power and authority to drive out all demons and to cure diseases.
<sup>9.2</sup> Then he sent them out to preach the Kingdom <u>of God</u> and to heal the sick,
<sup>9.3</sup> <u>after</u> saying <u>to them,</u> "Take nothing <u>with you</u> <u>for the trip</u>: no walking stick, no beggar's bag, no food, no money, not even an extra shirt.
<sup>9.4</sup> "Wherever you are welcomed, stay <u>in the same house</u> until you leave that town;
<sup>9.5</sup> "wherever people don't welcome you, leave that town and shake the dust <u>off your feet</u> <u>as a warning</u> <u>to them.</u>"
<sup>9.6</sup> The disciples left and traveled <u>through all the villages,</u> preaching the Good News and healing people everywhere.
<sup>9.7</sup> When Herod, the ruler <u>of Galilee,</u> heard <u>about all the things</u> that were happening, he was very confused, because some people were saying that John the Baptist had come back <u>to life.</u>
<sup>9.8</sup> Others were saying that Elijah had appeared, and still others that one <u>of the prophets</u> <u>of long ago</u> had come back <u>to life.</u>
<sup>9.9</sup> Herod said, "I had John's head cut off; but who is this man I hear these things about?" And he kept trying to see Jesus.
<sup>9.10</sup> The apostles came back and told Jesus everything they had done. He took them <u>with him,</u> and they went off <u>by themselves</u> <u>to a town</u> named Bethsaida.
<sup>9.11</sup> When the crowds heard <u>about it,</u> they followed him. He welcomed them, spoke <u>to them</u> <u>about the Kingdom</u> <u>of God,</u> and healed those who needed it.
<sup>9.12</sup> When the sun was beginning to set, the twelve disciples came <u>to him</u> and said, "Send the people away so that they can go <u>to the villages and farms</u> <u>around here</u> and find food and lodging, because this is a lonely place."
<sup>9.13</sup> But Jesus said <u>to them,</u> "You yourselves give them something to eat." They answered, "All we have are five loaves and two fish. Do you want us to go and buy food <u>for this whole crowd?</u>"
<sup>9.14</sup> (There were about five thousand men there.) Jesus said <u>to his disciples,</u> "Make the people sit down <u>in groups</u> <u>of about fifty</u> each."
<sup>9.15</sup> After the disciples had done so,
<sup>9.16</sup> Jesus took the five loaves and two fish, looked up <u>to heaven,</u> thanked God <u>for them,</u> broke them, and gave them <u>to the disciples</u> to distribute <u>to the people.</u>
<sup>9.17</sup> They all ate and had enough, and the disciples took up twelve baskets of what was left over.
<sup>9.18</sup> One day when Jesus was praying alone, the disciples came <u>to</u>

him. "Who do the crowds say I am?" he asked them.

9.19 "Some say that you are John the Baptist," they answered. "Others say that you are Elijah, while others say that one of the prophets of long ago has come back to life."

9.20 "What about you?" he asked them. "Who do you say I am?" Peter answered, "You are God's Messiah."

9.21 Then Jesus gave them strict orders not to tell this to anyone.

9.22 He also told them, "The Son of Man must suffer much and be rejected by the elders, the chief priests, and the teachers of the Law. He will be put to death, but three days later he will be raised to life."

9.23 And he said to them all, "If you want to come with me, you must forget yourself, take up your cross every day, and follow me.

9.24 "For if you want to save your own life, you will lose it, but if you lose your life for my sake, you will save it.

9.25 "Will you gain anything if you win the whole world but are yourself lost or defeated? Of course not!

9.26 "If you are ashamed of me and of my teaching, then the Son of Man will be ashamed of you when he comes in his glory and in the glory of the Father and of the holy angels.

9.27 "I assure you that there are some here who will not die until they have seen the Kingdom of God."

9.28 About a week after he had said these things, Jesus took Peter, John, and James with him and went up a hill to pray.

9.29 While he was praying, his face changed its appearance, and his clothes became dazzling white.

9.30 Suddenly two men were there talking with him. They were Moses and Elijah,

9.31 who appeared in heavenly glory and talked with Jesus about the way in which he would soon fulfill God's purpose by dying in Jerusalem.

9.32 Peter and his companions were sound asleep, but they woke up and saw Jesus' glory and the two men who were standing with him.

9.33 As the men were leaving Jesus, Peter said to him, "Master, how good it is that we are here! We will make three tents, one for you, one for Moses, and one for Elijah." (He did not really know what he was saying.)

9.34 While he was still speaking, a cloud appeared and covered them with its shadow; and the disciples were afraid as the cloud came over them.

9.35 A voice said from the cloud, "This is my Son, whom I have chosen — listen to him!"

9.36 When the voice stopped, there was Jesus all alone. The disciples kept quiet about all this and told no one at that time anything they had seen.

9.37 The next day Jesus and the three disciples went down from the hill, and a large crowd met Jesus.

9.38 A man shouted from the crowd, "Teacher! I beg you, look at my son — my only son!

9.39 "A spirit attacks him with a sudden shout and throws him into a fit, so that he foams at the mouth; it keeps on hurting him and will hardly let him go!

9.40 "I begged your disciples to drive it out, but they couldn't."

9.41 Jesus answered, "How unbelieving and wrong you people are! How long must I stay with you? How long do I have to put up with you?" Then he said to the man, "Bring your son here."

9.42 As the boy was coming, the demon knocked him to the ground and threw him into a fit. Jesus gave a command to the evil spirit, healed the boy, and gave him back to his father.

9.43 All the people were amazed at the mighty power of God. The people were still marveling at everything Jesus was doing, when he said to his disciples,

9.44 "Don't forget what I am about to tell you! The Son of Man is going to be handed over to the power of human beings."

9.45 But the disciples did not know what this meant. It had been hidden from them so that they could not understand it, and they were afraid to ask him about the matter.

9.46 An argument broke out among the disciples as to which one of them was the greatest.

9.47 Jesus knew what they were thinking, so he took a child, stood him by his side,

9.48 and said to them, "Whoever welcomes this child in my name, welcomes me; and whoever welcomes me, also welcomes the one who sent me. For the one who is least among you all is the greatest."

9.49 John spoke up, "Master, we saw a man driving out demons in your name, and we told him to stop, because he doesn't belong to our group."

9.50 "Do not try to stop him," Jesus said to him and to the other disciples, "because whoever is not against you is for you."

9.51 As the time drew near when Jesus would be taken up to heaven, he made up his mind and set out on his way to Jerusalem.

9.52 He sent messengers ahead of him, who went into a village in Samaria to get everything ready for him.

<sup>9.53</sup> But the people there would not receive him, because it was clear that he was on his way to Jerusalem.

<sup>9.54</sup> When the disciples James and John saw this, they said, "Lord, do you want us to call fire down from heaven to destroy them?"

<sup>9.55</sup> Jesus turned and rebuked them.

<sup>9.56</sup> Then Jesus and his disciples went on to another village.

<sup>9.57</sup> As they went on their way, a man said to Jesus, "I will follow you wherever you go."

<sup>9.58</sup> Jesus said to him, "Foxes have holes, and birds have nests, but the Son of Man has no place to lie down and rest."

<sup>9.59</sup> He said to another man, "Follow me." But that man said, "Sir, first let me go back and bury my father."

<sup>9.60</sup> Jesus answered, "Let the dead bury their own dead. You go and proclaim the Kingdom of God."

<sup>9.61</sup> Someone else said, "I will follow you, sir; but first let me go and say good-bye to my family."

<sup>9.62</sup> Jesus said to him, "Anyone who starts to plow and then keeps looking back is of no use for the Kingdom of God."

# 10

<sup>10.1</sup> After this the Lord chose another seventy-two men and sent them out two by two, to go ahead of him to every town and place where he himself was about to go.

<sup>10.2</sup> He said to them, "There is a large harvest, but few workers to gather it in. Pray to the owner of the harvest that he will send out workers to gather in his harvest.

<sup>10.3</sup> "Go! I am sending you like lambs among wolves.

<sup>10.4</sup> "Don't take a purse or a beggar's bag or shoes; don't stop to greet anyone on the road.

<sup>10.5</sup> "Whenever you go into a house, first say, 'Peace be with this house.'

<sup>10.6</sup> "If someone who is peace-loving lives there, let your greeting of peace remain on that person; if not, take back your greeting of peace.

<sup>10.7</sup> "Stay in that same house, eating and drinking whatever they offer you, for workers should be given their pay. Don't move around from one house to another.

<sup>10.8</sup> "Whenever you go into a town and are made welcome, eat what is set before you,

<sup>10.9</sup> "heal the sick in that town, and say to the people there, 'The Kingdom of God has come near you.'

10.10 "But whenever you go into a town and are not welcomed, go out in the streets and say,

10.11 " 'Even the dust from your town that sticks to our feet we wipe off against you. But remember that the Kingdom of God has come near you!'

10.12 "I assure you that on the Judgment Day God will show more mercy to Sodom than to that town!

10.13 "How terrible it will be for you, Chorazin! How terrible for you too, Bethsaida! If the miracles which were performed in you had been performed in Tyre and Sidon, the people there would have long ago sat down, put on sackcloth, and sprinkled ashes on themselves, to show that they had turned from their sins!

10.14 "God will show more mercy on the Judgment Day to Tyre and Sidon than to you.

10.15 "And as for you, Capernaum! Did you want to lift yourself up to heaven? You will be thrown down to hell!"

10.16 Jesus said to his disciples, "Whoever listens to you listens to me; whoever rejects you rejects me; and whoever rejects me rejects the one who sent me."

10.17 The seventy-two men came back in great joy. "Lord," they said, "even the demons obeyed us when we gave them a command in your name!"

10.18 Jesus answered them, "I saw Satan fall like lightning from heaven.

10.19 "Listen! I have given you authority, so that you can walk on snakes and scorpions and overcome all the power of the Enemy, and nothing will hurt you.

10.20 "But don't be glad because the evil spirits obey you; rather be glad because your names are written in heaven."

10.21 At that time Jesus was filled with joy by the Holy Spirit and said, "Father, Lord of heaven and earth! I thank you because you have shown to the unlearned what you have hidden from the wise and learned. Yes, Father, this was how you were pleased to have it happen.

10.22 "My Father has given me all things. No one knows who the Son is except the Father, and no one knows who the Father is except the Son and those to whom the Son chooses to reveal him."

10.23 Then Jesus turned to the disciples and said to them privately, "How fortunate you are to see the things you see!

10.24 "I tell you that many prophets and kings wanted to see what you see, but they could not, and to hear what you hear, but they did not."

<sup>10.25</sup> A teacher of the Law came up and tried to trap Jesus. "Teacher," he asked, "what must I do to receive eternal life?"

<sup>10.26</sup> Jesus answered him, "What do the Scriptures say? How do you interpret them?"

<sup>10.27</sup> The man answered, "'Love the Lord your God with all your heart, with all your soul, with all your strength, and with all your mind'; and 'Love your neighbor as you love yourself.'"

<sup>10.28</sup> "You are right," Jesus replied; "do this and you will live."

<sup>10.29</sup> But the teacher of the Law wanted to justify himself, so he asked Jesus, "Who is my neighbor?"

<sup>10.30</sup> Jesus answered, "There was once a man who was going down from Jerusalem to Jericho when robbers attacked him, stripped him, and beat him up, leaving him half dead.

<sup>10.31</sup> "It so happened that a priest was going down that road; but when he saw the man, he walked on by on the other side.

<sup>10.32</sup> "In the same way a Levite also came there, went over and looked at the man, and then walked on by on the other side.

<sup>10.33</sup> "But a Samaritan who was traveling that way came upon the man, and when he saw him, his heart was filled with pity.

<sup>10.34</sup> "He went over to him, poured oil and wine on his wounds and bandaged them; then he put the man on his own animal and took him to an inn, where he took care of him.

<sup>10.35</sup> "The next day he took out two silver coins and gave them to the innkeeper. 'Take care of him,' he told the innkeeper, 'and when I come back this way, I will pay you whatever else you spend on him.'"

<sup>10.36</sup> And Jesus concluded, "In your opinion, which one of these three acted like a neighbor toward the man attacked by the robbers?"

<sup>10.37</sup> The teacher of the Law answered, "The one who was kind to him." Jesus replied, "You go, then, and do the same."

<sup>10.38</sup> As Jesus and his disciples went on their way, he came to a village where a woman named Martha welcomed him in her home.

<sup>10.39</sup> She had a sister named Mary, who sat down at the feet of the Lord and listened to his teaching.

<sup>10.40</sup> Martha was upset over all the work she had to do, so she came and said, "Lord, don't you care that my sister has left me to do all the work by myself? Tell her to come and help me!"

<sup>10.41</sup> The Lord answered her, "Martha, Martha! You are worried and troubled over so many things.

<sup>10.42</sup> "but just one is needed. Mary has chosen the right thing, and it will not be taken away from her."

<sup>11.1</sup> One day Jesus was praying in a certain place. When he had finished, one of his disciples said to him, "Lord, teach us to pray, just as John taught his disciples."

<sup>11.2</sup> Jesus said to them, "When you pray, say this: 'Father: May your holy name be honored; may your Kingdom come.

<sup>11.3</sup> " 'Give us day by day the food we need.

<sup>11.4</sup> " 'Forgive us our sins, for we forgive everyone who does us wrong. And do not bring us to hard testing.' "

<sup>11.5</sup> And Jesus said to his disciples, "Suppose one of you should go to a friend's house at midnight and say, 'Friend, let me borrow three loaves of bread.

<sup>11.6</sup> " 'A friend of mine who is on a trip has just come to my house, and I don't have any food for him!'

<sup>11.7</sup> "And suppose your friend should answer from inside, 'Don't bother me! The door is already locked, and my children and I are in bed. I can't get up and give you anything.'

<sup>11.8</sup> "Well, what then? I tell you that even if he will not get up and give you the bread because you are his friend, yet he will get up and give you everything you need because you are not ashamed to keep on asking.

<sup>11.9</sup> "And so I say to you: Ask, and you will receive; seek, and you will find; knock, and the door will be opened to you.

<sup>11.10</sup> "For those who ask will receive, and those who seek will find, and the door will be opened to anyone who knocks.

<sup>11.11</sup> "Would any of you who are fathers give your son a snake when he asks for fish?

<sup>11.12</sup> "Or would you give him a scorpion when he asks for an egg?

<sup>11.13</sup> "As bad as you are, you know how to give good things to your children. How much more, then, will the Father in heaven give the Holy Spirit to those who ask him!"

<sup>11.14</sup> " 'Jesus was driving out a demon that could not talk; and when the demon went out, the man began to talk. The crowds were amazed,

<sup>11.15</sup> but some of the people said, "It is Beelzebul, the chief of the demons, who gives him the power to drive them out."

<sup>11.16</sup> Others wanted to trap Jesus, so they asked him to perform a miracle to show that God approved of him.

<sup>11.17</sup> But Jesus knew what they were thinking, so he said to them, "Any country that divides itself into groups which fight each other will not last very long; a family divided against itself falls apart.

<sup>11.18</sup> "So if Satan's kingdom has groups fighting each other, how can it

last? You say that I drive out demons because Beelzebul gives me the power to do so.

<sup>11.19</sup> "If this is how I drive them out, how do your followers drive them out? Your own followers prove that you are wrong!

<sup>11.20</sup> "No, it is rather by means of God's power that I drive out demons, and this proves that the Kingdom of God has already come to you.

<sup>11.21</sup> "When a strong man, with all his weapons ready, guards his own house, all his belongings are safe.

<sup>11.22</sup> "But when a stronger man attacks him and defeats him, he carries away all the weapons the owner was depending on and divides up what he stole.

<sup>11.23</sup> "Anyone who is not for me is really against me; anyone who does not help me gather is really scattering.

<sup>11.24</sup> "When an evil spirit goes out of a person, it travels over dry country looking for a place to rest. If it can't find one, it says to itself, 'I will go back to my house.'

<sup>11.25</sup> "So it goes back and finds the house clean and all fixed up.

<sup>11.26</sup> "Then it goes out and brings seven other spirits even worse than itself, and they come and live there. So when it is all over, that person is in worse shape than at the beginning."

<sup>11.27</sup> When Jesus had said this, a woman spoke up from the crowd and said to him, "How happy is the woman who bore you and nursed you!"

<sup>11.28</sup> But Jesus answered, "Rather, how happy are those who hear the word of God and obey it!"

<sup>11.29</sup> As the people crowded around Jesus, he went on to say, "How evil are the people of this day! They ask for a miracle, but none will be given them except the miracle of Jonah.

<sup>11.30</sup> "In the same way that the prophet Jonah was a sign for the people of Nineveh, so the Son of Man will be a sign for the people of this day.

<sup>11.31</sup> "On the Judgment Day the Queen of Sheba will stand up and accuse the people of today, because she traveled all the way from her country to listen to King Solomon's wise teaching; and there is something here, I tell you, greater than Solomon.

<sup>11.32</sup> "On the Judgment Day the people of Nineveh will stand up and accuse you, because they turned from their sins when they heard Jonah preach; and I assure you that there is something here greater than Jonah!

<sup>11.33</sup> "No one lights a lamp and then hides it or puts it under a bowl;

instead, it is put on the lampstand, so that people may see the light as they come in.

<sup>11.34</sup> "Your eyes are like a lamp for the body. When your eyes are sound, your whole body is full of light; but when your eyes are no good, your whole body will be in darkness.

<sup>11.35</sup> "Make certain, then, that the light in you is not darkness.

<sup>11.36</sup> "If your whole body is full of light, with no part of it in darkness, it will be bright all over, as when a lamp shines on you with its brightness."

<sup>11.37</sup> When Jesus finished speaking, a Pharisee invited him to eat with him; so he went in and sat down to eat.

<sup>11.38</sup> The Pharisee was surprised when he noticed that Jesus had not washed before eating.

<sup>11.39</sup> So the Lord said to him, "Now then, you Pharisees clean the outside of your cup and plate, but inside you are full of violence and evil.

<sup>11.40</sup> "Fools! Did not God, who made the outside, also make the inside?

<sup>11.41</sup> "But give what is in your cups and plates to the poor, and everything will be ritually clean for you.

<sup>11.42</sup> "How terrible for you Pharisees! You give to God one tenth of the seasoning herbs, such as mint and rue and all the other herbs, but you neglect justice and love for God. These you should practice, without neglecting the others.

<sup>11.43</sup> "How terrible for you Pharisees! You love the reserved seats in the synagogues and to be greeted with respect in the marketplaces.

<sup>11.44</sup> "How terrible for you! You are like unmarked graves which people walk on without knowing it."

<sup>11.45</sup> One of the teachers of the Law said to him, "Teacher, when you say this, you insult us too!"

<sup>11.46</sup> Jesus answered, "How terrible also for you teachers of the Law! You put onto people's backs loads which are hard to carry, but you yourselves will not stretch out a finger to help them carry those loads.

<sup>11.47</sup> "How terrible for you! You make fine tombs for the prophets — the very prophets your ancestors murdered.

<sup>11.48</sup> "You yourselves admit, then, that you approve of what your ancestors did; they murdered the prophets, and you build their tombs.

<sup>11.49</sup> "For this reason the Wisdom of God said, 'I will send them prophets and messengers; they will kill some of them and persecute others.'

<sup>11.50</sup> "So the people of this time will be punished for the murder of all the prophets killed since the creation of the world,

11.51 "from the murder of Abel to the murder of Zechariah, who was killed between the altar and the Holy Place. Yes, I tell you, the people of this time will be punished for them all!

11.52 "How terrible for you teachers of the Law! You have kept the key that opens the door to the house of knowledge; you yourselves will not go in, and you stop those who are trying to go in!"

11.53 When Jesus left that place, the teachers of the Law and the Pharisees began to criticize him bitterly and ask him questions about many things,

11.54 trying to lay traps for him and catch him saying something wrong.

# 12

12.1 As thousands of people crowded together, so that they were stepping on each other, Jesus said first to his disciples, "Be on guard against the yeast of the Pharisees — I mean their hypocrisy.

12.2 "Whatever is covered up will be uncovered, and every secret will be made known.

12.3 "So then, whatever you have said in the dark will be heard in broad daylight, and whatever you have whispered in private in a closed room will be shouted from the housetops.

12.4 "I tell you, my friends, do not be afraid of those who kill the body but cannot afterward do anything worse.

12.5 "I will show you whom to fear: fear God, who, after killing, has the authority to throw into hell. Believe me, he is the one you must fear!

12.6 "Aren't five sparrows sold for two pennies? Yet not one sparrow is forgotten by God.

12.7 "Even the hairs of your head have all been counted. So do not be afraid; you are worth much more than many sparrows!

12.8 "I assure you that those who declare publicly that they belong to me, the Son of Man will do the same for them before the angels of God.

12.9 "But those who reject me publicly, the Son of Man will also reject them before the angels of God.

12.10 "Whoever says a word against the Son of Man can be forgiven; but whoever says evil things against the Holy Spirit will not be forgiven.

12.11 "When they bring you to be tried in the synagogues or before governors or rulers, do not be worried about how you will defend yourself or what you will say.

<sup>12.12</sup> "For the Holy Spirit will teach you at that time what you should say."

<sup>12.13</sup> A man in the crowd said to Jesus, "Teacher, tell my brother to divide with me the property our father left us."

<sup>12.14</sup> Jesus answered him, "Friend, who gave me the right to judge or to divide the property between you two?"

<sup>12.15</sup> And he went on to say to them all, "Watch out and guard yourselves from every kind of greed; because your true life is not made up of the things you own, no matter how rich you may be."

<sup>12.16</sup> Then Jesus told them this parable: "There was once a rich man who had land which bore good crops.

<sup>12.17</sup> "He began to think to himself, 'I don't have a place to keep all my crops. What can I do?

<sup>12.18</sup> " 'This is what I will do,' he told himself; 'I will tear down my barns and build bigger ones, where I will store the grain and all my other goods.

<sup>12.19</sup> " 'Then I will say to myself, Lucky man! You have all the good things you need for many years. Take life easy, eat, drink, and enjoy yourself!'

<sup>12.20</sup> "But God said to him, 'You fool! This very night you will have to give up your life; then who will get all these things you have kept for yourself?' "

<sup>12.21</sup> And Jesus concluded, "This is how it is with those who pile up riches for themselves but are not rich in God's sight."

<sup>12.22</sup> Then Jesus said to the disciples, "And so I tell you not to worry about the food you need to stay alive or about the clothes you need for your body.

<sup>12.23</sup> "Life is much more important than food, and the body much more important than clothes.

<sup>12.24</sup> "Look at the crows: they don't plant seeds or gather a harvest; they don't have storage rooms or barns; God feeds them! You are worth so much more than birds!

<sup>12.25</sup> "Can any of you live a bit longer by worrying about it?

<sup>12.26</sup> "If you can't manage even such a small thing, why worry about the other things?

<sup>12.27</sup> "Look how the wild flowers grow: they don't work or make clothes for themselves. But I tell you that not even King Solomon with all his wealth had clothes as beautiful as one of these flowers.

<sup>12.28</sup> "It is God who clothes the wild grass — grass that is here today and gone tomorrow, burned up in the oven. Won't he be all the more sure to clothe you? What little faith you have!

<sup>12.29</sup> "So don't be all upset, always concerned about what you will eat and drink.

<sup>12.30</sup> "(For the pagans of this world are always concerned about all these things.) Your Father knows that you need these things.

<sup>12.31</sup> "Instead, be concerned with his Kingdom, and he will provide you with these things.

<sup>12.32</sup> "Do not be afraid, little flock, for your Father is pleased to give you the Kingdom.

<sup>12.33</sup> "Sell all your belongings and give the money to the poor. Provide for yourselves purses that don't wear out, and save your riches in heaven, where they will never decrease, because no thief can get to them, and no moth can destroy them.

<sup>12.34</sup> "For your heart will always be where your riches are.

<sup>12.35</sup> "Be ready for whatever comes, dressed for action and with your lamps lit,

<sup>12.36</sup> "like servants who are waiting for their master to come back from a wedding feast. When he comes and knocks, they will open the door for him at once.

<sup>12.37</sup> "How happy are those servants whose master finds them awake and ready when he returns! I tell you, he will take off his coat, have them sit down, and will wait on them.

<sup>12.38</sup> "How happy they are if he finds them ready, even if he should come at midnight or even later!

<sup>12.39</sup> "And you can be sure that if the owner of a house knew the time when the thief would come, he would not let the thief break into his house.

<sup>12.40</sup> "And you, too, must be ready, because the Son of Man will come at an hour when you are not expecting him."

<sup>12.41</sup> Peter said, "Lord, does this parable apply to us, or do you mean it for everyone?"

<sup>12.42</sup> The Lord answered, "Who, then, is the faithful and wise servant? He is the one that his master will put in charge, to run the household and give the other servants their share of the food at the proper time.

<sup>12.43</sup> "How happy that servant is if his master finds him doing this when he comes home!

<sup>12.44</sup> "Indeed, I tell you, the master will put that servant in charge of all his property.

<sup>12.45</sup> "But if that servant says to himself that his master is taking a long time to come back and if he begins to beat the other servants, both the men and the women, and eats and drinks and gets drunk,

12.46 "then the master will come back one day when the servant does not expect him and at a time he does not know. The master will cut him in pieces and make him share the fate of the disobedient.
12.47 "The servant who knows what his master wants him to do, but does not get himself ready and do it, will be punished with a heavy whipping.
12.48 "But the servant who does not know what his master wants, and yet does something for which he deserves a whipping, will be punished with a light whipping. Much is required from the person to whom much is given; much more is required from the person to whom much more is given.
12.49 "I came to set the earth on fire, and how I wish it were already kindled!
12.50 "I have a baptism to receive, and how distressed I am until it is over!
12.51 "Do you suppose that I came to bring peace to the world? No, not peace, but division.
12.52 "From now on a family of five will be divided, three against two and two against three.
12.53 "Fathers will be against their sons, and sons against their fathers; mothers will be against their daughters, and daughters against their mothers; mothers-in-law will be against their daughters-in-law, and daughters-in-law against their mothers-in-law."
12.54 Jesus said also to the people, "When you see a cloud coming up in the west, at once you say that it is going to rain — and it does.
12.55 "And when you feel the south wind blowing, you say that it is going to get hot — and it does.
12.56 "Hypocrites! You can look at the earth and the sky and predict the weather; why, then, don't you know the meaning of this present time?
12.57 "Why do you not judge for yourselves the right thing to do?
12.58 "If someone brings a lawsuit against you and takes you to court, do your best to settle the dispute before you get to court. If you don't, you will be dragged before the judge, who will hand you over to the police, and you will be put in jail.
12.59 "There you will stay, I tell you, until you pay the last penny of your fine."

# 13

13.1 At that time some people were there who told Jesus about the Galileans whom Pilate had killed while they were offering sacrifices to God.

<sup>13.2</sup> Jesus answered them, "Because those Galileans were killed in that way, do you think it proves that they were worse sinners than all other Galileans?

<sup>13.3</sup> "No indeed! And I tell you that if you do not turn from your sins, you will all die as they did.

<sup>13.4</sup> "What about those eighteen people in Siloam who were killed when the tower fell on them? Do you suppose this proves that they were worse than all the other people living in Jerusalem?

<sup>13.5</sup> "No indeed! And I tell you that if you do not turn from your sins, you will all die as they did."

<sup>13.6</sup> Then Jesus told them this parable: "There was once a man who had a fig tree growing in his vineyard. He went looking for figs on it but found none.

<sup>13.7</sup> "So he said to his gardener, 'Look, for three years I have been coming here looking for figs on this fig tree, and I haven't found any. Cut it down! Why should it go on using up the soil?'

<sup>13.8</sup> "But the gardener answered, 'Leave it alone, sir, just one more year; I will dig around it and put in some fertilizer.

<sup>13.9</sup> " 'Then if the tree bears figs next year, so much the better; if not, then you can have it cut down.'"

<sup>13.10</sup> One Sabbath Jesus was teaching in a synagogue.

<sup>13.11</sup> A woman there had an evil spirit that had kept her sick for eighteen years; she was bent over and could not straighten up at all.

<sup>13.12</sup> When Jesus saw her, he called out to her, "Woman, you are free from your sickness!"

<sup>13.13</sup> He placed his hands on her, and at once she straightened herself up and praised God.

<sup>13.14</sup> The official of the synagogue was angry that Jesus had healed on the Sabbath, so he spoke up and said to the people, "There are six days in which we should work; so come during those days and be healed, but not on the Sabbath!"

<sup>13.15</sup> The Lord answered him, "You hypocrites! Any one of you would untie your ox or your donkey from the stall and take it out to give it water on the Sabbath.

<sup>13.16</sup> "Now here is this descendant of Abraham whom Satan has kept in bonds for eighteen years; should she not be released on the Sabbath?"

<sup>13.17</sup> His answer made his enemies ashamed of themselves, while the people rejoiced over all the wonderful things that he did.

<sup>13.18</sup> Jesus asked, "What is the Kingdom of God like? What shall I

compare it with?

<sup>13.19</sup> "It is like this. A man takes a mustard seed and plants it in his field. The plant grows and becomes a tree, and the birds make their nests in its branches."

<sup>13.20</sup> Again Jesus asked, "What shall I compare the Kingdom of God with?

<sup>13.21</sup> "It is like this. A woman takes some yeast and mixes it with a bushel of flour until the whole batch of dough rises."

<sup>13.22</sup> Jesus went through towns and villages, teaching the people and making his way toward Jerusalem.

<sup>13.23</sup> Someone asked him, "Sir, will just a few people be saved?"Jesus answered them,

<sup>13.24</sup> "Do your best to go in through the narrow door; because many people will surely try to go in but will not be able.

<sup>13.25</sup> "The master of the house will get up and close the door; then when you stand outside and begin to knock on the door and say, 'Open the door for us, sir!' he will answer you, 'I don't know where you come from!'

<sup>13.26</sup> "Then you will answer, 'We ate and drank with you; you taught in our town!'

<sup>13.27</sup> "But he will say again, 'I don't know where you come from. Get away from me, all you wicked people!'

<sup>13.28</sup> "How you will cry and gnash your teeth when you see Abraham, Isaac, and Jacob, and all the prophets in the Kingdom of God, while you are thrown out!

<sup>13.29</sup> "People will come from the east and the west, from the north and the south, and sit down at the feast in the Kingdom of God.

<sup>13.30</sup> "Then those who are now last will be first, and those who are now first will be last."

<sup>13.31</sup> At that same time some Pharisees came to Jesus and said to him, "You must get out of here and go somewhere else, because Herod wants to kill you."

<sup>13.32</sup> Jesus answered them, "Go and tell that fox: 'I am driving out demons and performing cures today and tomorrow, and on the third day I shall finish my work.'

<sup>13.33</sup> "Yet I must be on my way today, tomorrow, and the next day; it is not right for a prophet to be killed anywhere except in Jerusalem.

<sup>13.34</sup> "Jerusalem, Jerusalem! You kill the prophets, you stone the messengers God has sent you! How many times I wanted to put my arms around all your people, just as a hen gathers her chicks under her wings, but you would not let me!

<sup></sup>13.35 "And so your Temple will be abandoned. I assure you that you will not see me until the time comes when you say, 'God bless him who comes in the name of the Lord.'"

# 14

14.1 One Sabbath Jesus went to eat a meal at the home of one of the leading Pharisees; and people were watching Jesus closely.

14.2 A man whose legs and arms were swollen came to Jesus,

14.3 and Jesus spoke up and asked the teachers of the Law and the Pharisees, "Does our Law allow healing on the Sabbath or not?"

14.4 But they would not say a thing. Jesus took the man, healed him, and sent him away.

14.5 Then he said to them, "If any one of you had a child or an ox that happened to fall in a well on a Sabbath, would you not pull it out at once on the Sabbath itself?"

14.6 But they were not able to answer him about this.

14.7 Jesus noticed how some of the guests were choosing the best places, so he told this parable to all of them:

14.8 "When someone invites you to a wedding feast, do not sit down in the best place. It could happen that someone more important than you has been invited,

14.9 and your host, who invited both of you, would have to come and say to you, 'Let him have this place.' Then you would be embarrassed and have to sit in the lowest place.

14.10 "Instead, when you are invited, go and sit in the lowest place, so that your host will come to you and say, 'Come on up, my friend, to a better place.' This will bring you honor in the presence of all the other guests.

14.11 "For those who make themselves great will be humbled, and those who humble themselves will be made great."

14.12 Then Jesus said to his host, "When you give a lunch or a dinner, do not invite your friends or your brothers or your relatives or your rich neighbors — for they will invite you back, and in this way you will be paid for what you did.

14.13 "When you give a feast, invite the poor, the crippled, the lame, and the blind;

14.14 "and you will be blessed, because they are not able to pay you back. God will repay you on the day the good people rise from death."

14.15 When one of the guests sitting at the table heard this, he said to Jesus, "How happy are those who will sit down at the feast in the Kingdom of God!"

<sup>14.16</sup> Jesus said to him, "There was once a man who was giving a great feast to which he invited many people.

<sup>14.17</sup> "When it was time for the feast, he sent his servant to tell his guests, 'Come, everything is ready!'

<sup>14.18</sup> "But they all began, one after another, to make excuses. The first one told the servant, 'I have bought a field and must go and look at it; please accept my apologies.'

<sup>14.19</sup> "Another one said, 'I have bought five pairs of oxen and am on my way to try them out; please accept my apologies.'

<sup>14.20</sup> "Another one said, 'I have just gotten married, and for that reason I cannot come.'

<sup>14.21</sup> "The servant went back and told all this to his master. The master was furious and said to his servant, 'Hurry out to the streets and alleys of the town, and bring back the poor, the crippled, the blind, and the lame.'

<sup>14.22</sup> "Soon the servant said, 'Your order has been carried out, sir, but there is room for more.'

<sup>14.23</sup> "So the master said to the servant, 'Go out to the country roads and lanes and make people come in, so that my house will be full.

<sup>14.24</sup> " 'I tell you all that none of those who were invited will taste my dinner!'"

<sup>14.25</sup> Once when large crowds of people were going along with Jesus, he turned and said to them,

<sup>14.26</sup> "Those who come to me cannot be my disciples unless they love me more than they love father and mother, wife and children, brothers and sisters, and themselves as well.

<sup>14.27</sup> "Those who do not carry their own cross and come after me cannot be my disciples.

<sup>14.28</sup> "If one of you is planning to build a tower, you sit down first and figure out what it will cost, to see if you have enough money to finish the job.

<sup>14.29</sup> "If you don't, you will not be able to finish the tower after laying the foundation; and all who see what happened will make fun of you.

<sup>14.30</sup> " 'You began to build but can't finish the job!' they will say.

<sup>14.31</sup> "If a king goes out with ten thousand men to fight another king who comes against him with twenty thousand men, he will sit down first and decide if he is strong enough to face that other king.

<sup>14.32</sup> "If he isn't, he will send messengers to meet the other king to ask for terms of peace while he is still a long way off.

<sup>14.33</sup> "In the same way," concluded Jesus, "none of you can be my disciple unless you give up everything you have.

<sup></sup>14.34 "Salt is good, but if it loses its saltiness, there is no way to make it salty again.

14.35 "It is no good for the soil or for the manure pile; it is thrown away. Listen, then, if you have ears!"

# 15

15.1 One day when many tax collectors and other outcasts came to listen to Jesus,

15.2 the Pharisees and the teachers of the Law started grumbling, "This man welcomes outcasts and even eats with them!"

15.3 So Jesus told them this parable:

15.4 "Suppose one of you has a hundred sheep and loses one of them —what do you do? You leave the other ninety-nine sheep in the pasture and go looking for the one that got lost until you find it.

15.5 "When you find it, you are so happy that you put it on your shoulders

15.6 "and carry it back home. Then you call your friends and neighbors together and say to them, 'I am so happy I found my lost sheep. Let us celebrate!'

15.7 "In the same way, I tell you, there will be more joy in heaven over one sinner who repents than over ninety-nine respectable people who do not need to repent.

15.8 "Or suppose a woman who has ten silver coins loses one of them — what does she do? She lights a lamp, sweeps her house, and looks carefully everywhere until she finds it.

15.9 "When she finds it, she calls her friends and neighbors together, and says to them, 'I am so happy I found the coin I lost. Let us celebrate!'

15.10 "In the same way, I tell you, the angels of God rejoice over one sinner who repents."

15.11 Jesus went on to say, "There was once a man who had two sons.

15.12 "The younger one said to him, 'Father, give me my share of the property now.' So the man divided his property between his two sons.

15.13 "After a few days the younger son sold his part of the property and left home with the money. He went to a country far away, where he wasted his money in reckless living.

15.14 "He spent everything he had. Then a severe famine spread over that country, and he was left without a thing.

15.15 "So he went to work for one of the citizens of that country, who sent him out to his farm to take care of the pigs.

15.16 "He wished he could fill himself with the bean pods the pigs ate, but no one gave him anything to eat.

15.17 "At last he came to his senses and said, 'All my father's hired workers have more than they can eat, and here I am about to starve! 15.18 " 'I will get up and go to my father and say, "Father, I have sinned against God and against you. 15.19 " ' "I am no longer fit to be called your son; treat me as one of your hired workers." '

15.20 "So he got up and started back to his father. He was still a long way from home when his father saw him; his heart was filled with pity, and he ran, threw his arms around his son, and kissed him. 15.21 " 'Father,' the son said, 'I have sinned against God and against you. I am no longer fit to be called your son.'

15.22 "But the father called to his servants. 'Hurry!' he said. 'Bring the best robe and put it on him. Put a ring on his finger and shoes on his feet. 15.23 " 'Then go and get the prize calf and kill it, and let us celebrate with a feast! 15.24 " 'For this son of mine was dead, but now he is alive; he was lost, but now he has been found.' And so the feasting began.

15.25 "In the meantime the older son was out in the field. On his way back, when he came close to the house, he heard the music and dancing. 15.26 "So he called one of the servants and asked him, 'What's going on?' 15.27 " 'Your brother has come back home,' the servant answered, 'and your father has killed the prize calf, because he got him back safe and sound.'

15.28 "The older brother was so angry that he would not go into the house; so his father came out and begged him to come in. 15.29 "But he spoke back to his father, 'Look, all these years I have worked for you like a slave, and I have never disobeyed your orders. What have you given me? Not even a goat for me to have a feast with my friends! 15.30 " 'But this son of yours wasted all your property on prostitutes, and when he comes back home, you kill the prize calf for him!' 15.31 " 'My son,' the father answered, 'you are always here with me, and everything I have is yours. 15.32 " 'But we had to celebrate and be happy, because your brother was dead, but now he is alive; he was lost, but now he has been found.' "

**16** ¹⁶·¹ Jesus said to his disciples, "There was once a rich man who had a servant who managed his property. The rich man was told that the manager was wasting his master's money,

¹⁶·² "so he called him in and said, 'What is this I hear about you? Turn in a complete account of your handling of my property, because you cannot be my manager any longer.'

¹⁶·³ "The servant said to himself, 'My master is going to dismiss me from my job. What shall I do? I am not strong enough to dig ditches, and I am ashamed to beg.

¹⁶·⁴ " 'Now I know what I will do! Then when my job is gone, I shall have friends who will welcome me in their homes.'

¹⁶·⁵ "So he called in all the people who were in debt to his master. He asked the first one, 'How much do you owe my master?'

¹⁶·⁶ " 'One hundred barrels of olive oil,' he answered. 'Here is your account,' the manager told him; 'sit down and write fifty.'

¹⁶·⁷ "Then he asked another one, 'And you - how much do you owe?' 'A thousand bushels of wheat,' he answered. 'Here is your account,' the manager told him; 'write eight hundred.'

¹⁶·⁸ "As a result the master of this dishonest manager praised him for doing such a shrewd thing; because the people of this world are much more shrewd in handling their affairs than the people who belong to the light."

¹⁶·⁹ And Jesus went on to say, "And so I tell you: make friends for yourselves with worldly wealth, so that when it gives out, you will be welcomed in the eternal home.

¹⁶·¹⁰ "Whoever is faithful in small matters will be faithful in large ones; whoever is dishonest in small matters will be dishonest in large ones.

¹⁶·¹¹ "If, then, you have not been faithful in handling worldly wealth, how can you be trusted with true wealth?

¹⁶·¹² "And if you have not been faithful with what belongs to someone else, who will give you what belongs to you?

¹⁶·¹³ "No servant can be the slave of two masters; such a slave will hate one and love the other or will be loyal to one and despise the other. You cannot serve both God and money."

¹⁶·¹⁴ When the Pharisees heard all this, they made fun of Jesus, because they loved money.

¹⁶·¹⁵ Jesus said to them, "You are the ones who make yourselves look right in other people's sight, but God knows your hearts. For the things that are considered of great value by people are worth nothing in God's sight.

16.16 "The Law of Moses and the writings of the prophets were in effect up to the time of John the Baptist; since then the Good News about the Kingdom of God is being told, and everyone forces their way in.

16.17 "But it is easier for heaven and earth to disappear than for the smallest detail of the Law to be done away with.

16.18 "Any man who divorces his wife and marries another woman commits adultery; and the man who marries a divorced woman commits adultery.

16.19 "There was once a rich man who dressed in the most expensive clothes and lived in great luxury every day.

16.20 "There was also a poor man named Lazarus, covered with sores, who used to be brought to the rich man's door,

16.21 "hoping to eat the bits of food that fell from the rich man's table. Even the dogs would come and lick his sores.

16.22 "The poor man died and was carried by the angels to sit beside Abraham at the feast in heaven. The rich man died and was buried,

16.23 "and in Hades, where he was in great pain, he looked up and saw Abraham, far away, with Lazarus at his side.

16.24 "So he called out, 'Father Abraham! Take pity on me, and send Lazarus to dip his finger in some water and cool off my tongue, because I am in great pain in this fire!'

16.25 "But Abraham said, 'Remember, my son, that in your lifetime you were given all the good things, while Lazarus got all the bad things. But now he is enjoying himself here, while you are in pain.

16.26 " 'Besides all that, there is a deep pit lying between us, so that those who want to cross over from here to you cannot do so, nor can anyone cross over to us from where you are.'

16.27 "The rich man said, 'Then I beg you, father Abraham, send Lazarus to my father's house,

16.28 " 'where I have five brothers. Let him go and warn them so that they, at least, will not come to this place of pain.'

16.29 "Abraham said, 'Your brothers have Moses and the prophets to warn them; your brothers should listen to what they say.'

16.30 "The rich man answered, 'That is not enough, father Abraham! But if someone were to rise from death and go to them, then they would turn from their sins.'

16.31 "But Abraham said, 'If they will not listen to Moses and the prophets, they will not be convinced even if someone were to rise from death.'"

**17** <sup>17.1</sup> Jesus said to his disciples, "Things that make people fall into sin are bound to happen, but how terrible for the one who makes them happen!

<sup>17.2</sup> "It would be better for him if a large millstone were tied around his neck and he were thrown into the sea than for him to cause one of these little ones to sin.

<sup>17.3</sup> "So watch what you do! If your brother sins, rebuke him, and if he repents, forgive him.

<sup>17.4</sup> "If he sins against you seven times in one day, and each time he comes to you saying, 'I repent,' you must forgive him."

<sup>17.5</sup> The apostles said to the Lord, "Make our faith greater."

<sup>17.6</sup> The Lord answered, "If you had faith as big as a mustard seed, you could say to this mulberry tree, 'Pull yourself up by the roots and plant yourself in the sea!' and it would obey you.

<sup>17.7</sup> "Suppose one of you has a servant who is plowing or looking after the sheep. When he comes in from the field, do you tell him to hurry along and eat his meal?

<sup>17.8</sup> "Of course not! Instead, you say to him, 'Get my supper ready, then put on your apron and wait on me while I eat and drink; after that you may have your meal.'

<sup>17.9</sup> "The servant does not deserve thanks for obeying orders, does he?

<sup>17.10</sup> "It is the same with you; when you have done all you have been told to do, say, 'We are ordinary servants; we have only done our duty.'"

<sup>17.11</sup> As Jesus made his way to Jerusalem, he went along the border between Samaria and Galilee.

<sup>17.12</sup> He was going into a village when he was met by ten men suffering from a dreaded skin disease. They stood at a distance

<sup>17.13</sup> and shouted, "Jesus! Master! Have pity on us!"

<sup>17.14</sup> Jesus saw them and said to them, "Go and let the priests examine you." On the way they were made clean.

<sup>17.15</sup> When one of them saw that he was healed, he came back, praising God in a loud voice.

<sup>17.16</sup> He threw himself to the ground at Jesus' feet and thanked him. The man was a Samaritan.

<sup>17.17</sup> Jesus spoke up, "There were ten who were healed; where are the other nine?

<sup>17.18</sup> "Why is this foreigner the only one who came back to give thanks to God?"

<sup>17.19</sup> And Jesus said to him, "Get up and go; your faith has made you well."

<sup>17.20</sup> Some Pharisees asked Jesus when the Kingdom of God would come. His answer was, "The Kingdom of God does not come in such a way as to be seen.

<sup>17.21</sup> "No one will say, 'Look, here it is!' or, 'There it is!'; because the Kingdom of God is within you."

<sup>17.22</sup> Then he said to the disciples, "The time will come when you will wish you could see one of the days of the Son of Man, but you will not see it.

<sup>17.23</sup> "There will be those who will say to you, 'Look, over there!' or, 'Look, over here!' But don't go out looking for it.

<sup>17.24</sup> "As the lightning flashes across the sky and lights it up from one side to the other, so will the Son of Man be in his day.

<sup>17.25</sup> "But first he must suffer much and be rejected by the people of this day.

<sup>17.26</sup> "As it was in the time of Noah so shall it be in the days of the Son of Man.

<sup>17.27</sup> "Everybody kept on eating and drinking, and men and women married, up to the very day Noah went into the boat and the flood came and killed them all.

<sup>17.28</sup> "It will be as it was in the time of Lot. Everybody kept on eating and drinking, buying and selling, planting and building.

<sup>17.29</sup> "On the day Lot left Sodom, fire and sulfur rained down from heaven and killed them all.

<sup>17.30</sup> "That is how it will be on the day the Son of Man is revealed.

<sup>17.31</sup> "On that day someone who is on the roof of a house must not go down into the house to get any belongings; in the same way anyone who is out in the field must not go back to the house.

<sup>17.32</sup> "Remember Lot's wife!

<sup>17.33</sup> "Those who try to save their own life will lose it; those who lose their life will save it.

<sup>17.34</sup> "On that night, I tell you, there will be two people sleeping in the same bed: one will be taken away, the other will be left behind.

<sup>17.35</sup> "Two women will be grinding meal together: one will be taken away, the other will be left behind."

<sup>17.36</sup> ("Two men will be working meal together: one will be taken away, the other will be left behind.")

<sup>17.37</sup> The disciples asked him, "Where, Lord?" Jesus answered, "Wherever there is a dead body, the vultures will gather."

# 18

<sup>18.1</sup> Then Jesus told his disciples a parable to teach them that they

should always pray and never become discouraged.

18.2 "In a certain town there was a judge who neither feared God nor respected people.

18.3 "And there was a widow in that same town who kept coming to him and pleading for her rights, saying, 'Help me against my opponent!'

18.4 "For a long time the judge refused to act, but at last he said to himself, 'Even though I don't fear God or respect people,

18.5 " 'yet because of all the trouble this widow is giving me, I will see to it that she gets her rights. If I don't, she will keep on coming and finally wear me out!'"

18.6 And the Lord continued, "Listen to what that corrupt judge said.

18.7 "Now, will God not judge in favor of his own people who cry to him day and night for help? Will he be slow to help them?

18.8 "I tell you, he will judge in their favor and do it quickly. But will the Son of Man find faith on earth when he comes?"

18.9 Jesus also told this parable to people who were sure of their own goodness and despised everybody else.

18.10 "Once there were two men who went up to the Temple to pray: one was a Pharisee, the other a tax collector.

18.11 "The Pharisee stood apart by himself and prayed, 'I thank you, God, that I am not greedy, dishonest, or an adulterer, like everybody else. I thank you that I am not like that tax collector over there.

18.12 " 'I fast two days a week, and I give you one tenth of all my income.'

18.13 "But the tax collector stood at a distance and would not even raise his face to heaven, but beat on his breast and said, 'God, have pity on me, a sinner!'

18.14 "I tell you," said Jesus, "the tax collector, and not the Pharisee, was in the right with God when he went home. For those who make themselves great will be humbled, and those who humble themselves will be made great."

18.15 Some people brought their babies to Jesus for him to place his hands on them. The disciples saw them and scolded them for doing so,

18.16 but Jesus called the children to him and said, "Let the children come to me and do not stop them, because the Kingdom of God belongs to such as these.

18.17 "Remember this! Whoever does not receive the Kingdom of God like a child will never enter it."

18.18 A Jewish leader asked Jesus, "Good Teacher, what must I do to receive eternal life?"

18.19 "Why do you call me good?" Jesus asked him. "No one is good except God alone.

18.20 "You know the commandments: 'Do not commit adultery; do not commit murder; do not steal; do not accuse anyone falsely; respect your father and your mother.'"

18.21 The man replied, "Ever since I was young, I have obeyed all these commandments."

18.22 When Jesus heard this, he said to him, "There is still one more thing you need to do. Sell all you have and give the money to the poor, and you will have riches in heaven; then come and follow me."

18.23 But when the man heard this, he became very sad, because he was very rich.

18.24 Jesus saw that he was sad and said, "How hard it is for rich people to enter the Kingdom of God!

18.25 "It is much harder for a rich person to enter the Kingdom of God than for a camel to go through the eye of a needle."

18.26 The people who heard him asked, "Who, then, can be saved?"

18.27 Jesus answered, "What is humanly impossible is possible for God."

18.28 Then Peter said, "Look! We have left our homes to follow you."

18.29 "Yes," Jesus said to them, "and I assure you that anyone who leaves home or wife or brothers or parents or children for the sake of the Kingdom of God

18.30 "will receive much more in this present age and eternal life in the age to come."

18.31 Jesus took the twelve disciples aside and said to them, "Listen! We are going to Jerusalem where everything the prophets wrote about the Son of Man will come true.

18.32 "He will be handed over to the Gentiles, who will make fun of him, insult him, and spit on him.

18.33 "They will whip him and kill him, but three days later he will rise to life."

18.34 But the disciples did not understand any of these things; the meaning of the words was hidden from them, and they did not know what Jesus was talking about.

18.35 As Jesus was coming near Jericho, there was a blind man sitting by the road, begging.

18.36 When he heard the crowd passing by, he asked, "What is this?"

18.37 "Jesus of Nazareth is passing by," they told him.

18.38 He cried out, "Jesus! Son of David! Have mercy on me!"

<sup>18.39</sup> The people in front scolded him and told him to be quiet. But he shouted even more loudly, "Son of David! Have mercy on me!"

<sup>18.40</sup> So Jesus stopped and ordered the blind man to be brought to him. When he came near, Jesus asked him,

<sup>18.41</sup> "What do you want me to do for you?" "Sir," he answered, "I want to see again."

<sup>18.42</sup> Jesus said to him, "Then see! Your faith has made you well."

<sup>18.43</sup> At once he was able to see, and he followed Jesus, giving thanks to God. When the crowd saw it, they all praised God.

# 19

<sup>19.1</sup> Jesus went on into Jericho and was passing through.

<sup>19.2</sup> There was a chief tax collector there named Zacchaeus, who was rich.

<sup>19.3</sup> He was trying to see who Jesus was, but he was a little man and could not see Jesus because of the crowd.

<sup>19.4</sup> So he ran ahead of the crowd and climbed a sycamore tree to see Jesus, who was going to pass that way.

<sup>19.5</sup> When Jesus came to that place, he looked up and said to Zacchaeus, "Hurry down, Zacchaeus, because I must stay in your house today."

<sup>19.6</sup> Zacchaeus hurried down and welcomed him with great joy.

<sup>19.7</sup> All the people who saw it started grumbling, "This man has gone as a guest to the home of a sinner!"

<sup>19.8</sup> Zacchaeus stood up and said to the Lord, "Listen, sir! I will give half my belongings to the poor, and if I have cheated anyone, I will pay back four times as much."

<sup>19.9</sup> Jesus said to him, "Salvation has come to this house today, for this man, also, is a descendant of Abraham.

<sup>19.10</sup> "The Son of Man came to seek and to save the lost."

<sup>19.11</sup> While the people were listening to this, Jesus continued and told them a parable. He was now almost at Jerusalem, and they supposed that the Kingdom of God was just about to appear.

<sup>19.12</sup> So he said, "There was once a man of high rank who was going to a country far away to be made king, after which he planned to come back home.

<sup>19.13</sup> "Before he left, he called his ten servants and gave them each a gold coin and told them, 'See what you can earn with this while I am gone.'

<sup>19.14</sup> "Now, his own people hated him, and so they sent messengers after him to say, 'We don't want this man to be our king.'

19.15 "The man was made king and came back. At once he ordered his servants to appear before him, in order to find out how much they had earned.

19.16 "The first one came and said, 'Sir, I have earned ten gold coins with the one you gave me.'

19.17 " 'Well done,' he said; 'you are a good servant! Since you were faithful in small matters, I will put you in charge of ten cities.'

19.18 "The second servant came and said, 'Sir, I have earned five gold coins with the one you gave me.'

19.19 "To this one he said, 'You will be in charge of five cities.'

19.20 "Another servant came and said, 'Sir, here is your gold coin; I kept it hidden in a handkerchief.

19.21 " 'I was afraid of you, because you are a hard man. You take what is not yours and reap what you did not plant.'

19.22 "He said to him, 'You bad servant! I will use your own words to condemn you! You know that I am a hard man, taking what is not mine and reaping what I have not planted.

19.23 " 'Well, then, why didn't you put my money in the bank? Then I would have received it back with interest when I returned.'

19.24 "Then he said to those who were standing there, 'Take the gold coin away from him and give it to the servant who has ten coins.'

19.25 But they said to him, 'Sir, he already has ten coins!'

19.26 " 'I tell you,' he replied, 'that to those who have something, even more will be given; but those who have nothing, even the little that they have will be taken away from them.

19.27 " 'Now, as for those enemies of mine who did not want me to be their king, bring them here and kill them in my presence!'"

19.28 After Jesus said this, he went on in front of them toward Jerusalem.

19.29 As he came near Bethphage and Bethany at the Mount of Olives, he sent two disciples ahead

19.30 with these instructions: "Go to the village there ahead of you; as you go in, you will find a colt tied up that has never been ridden. Untie it and bring it here.

19.31 "If someone asks you why you are untying it, tell him that the Master needs it."

19.32 They went on their way and found everything just as Jesus had told them.

19.33 As they were untying the colt, its owners said to them, "Why are you untying it?"

19.34 "The Master needs it," they answered,

<sup>19.35</sup> and they took the colt to Jesus. Then they threw their cloaks over the animal and helped Jesus get on.

<sup>19.36</sup> As he rode on, people spread their cloaks on the road.

<sup>19.37</sup> When he came near Jerusalem, at the place where the road went down the Mount of Olives, the large crowd of his disciples began to thank God and praise him in loud voices for all the great things that they had seen:

<sup>19.38</sup> "God bless the king who comes in the name of the Lord! Peace in heaven and glory to God!"

<sup>19.39</sup> Then some of the Pharisees in the crowd spoke to Jesus. "Teacher," they said, "command your disciples to be quiet!"

<sup>19.40</sup> Jesus answered, "I tell you that if they keep quiet, the stones themselves will start shouting."

<sup>19.41</sup> He came closer to the city, and when he saw it, he wept over it,

<sup>19.42</sup> saying, "If you only knew today what is needed for peace! But now you cannot see it!

<sup>19.43</sup> "The time will come when your enemies will surround you with barricades, blockade you, and close in on you from every side.

<sup>19.44</sup> "They will completely destroy you and the people within your walls; not a single stone will they leave in its place, because you did not recognize the time when God came to save you!"

<sup>19.45</sup> Then Jesus went into the Temple and began to drive out the merchants,

<sup>19.46</sup> saying to them, "It is written in the Scriptures that God said, 'My Temple will be a house of prayer.' But you have turned it into a hideout for thieves!"

<sup>19.47</sup> Every day Jesus taught in the Temple. The chief priests, the teachers of the Law, and the leaders of the people wanted to kill him,

<sup>19.48</sup> but they could not find a way to do it, because all the people kept listening to him, not wanting to miss a single word.

# 20

<sup>20.1</sup> One day when Jesus was in the Temple teaching the people and preaching the Good News, the chief priests and the teachers of the Law, together with the elders, came

<sup>20.2</sup> and said to him, "Tell us, what right do you have to do these things? Who gave you such right?"

<sup>20.3</sup> Jesus answered them, "Now let me ask you a question. Tell me,

<sup>20.4</sup> "did John's right to baptize come from God or from human beings?"

<sup>20.5</sup> They started to argue among themselves, "What shall we say?

If we say, 'From God,' he will say, 'Why, then, did you not believe John?'

20.6 "But if we say, 'From human beings,' this whole crowd here will stone us, because they are convinced that John was a prophet."

20.7 So they answered, "We don't know where it came from."

20.8 And Jesus said to them, "Neither will I tell you, then, by what right I do these things."

20.9 Then Jesus told the people this parable: "There was once a man who planted a vineyard, rented it out to tenants, and then left home for a long time.

20.10 "When the time came to gather the grapes, he sent a slave to the tenants to receive from them his share of the harvest. But the tenants beat the slave and sent him back without a thing.

20.11 "So he sent another slave; but the tenants beat him also, treated him shamefully, and sent him back without a thing.

20.12 "Then he sent a third slave; the tenants wounded him, too, and threw him out.

20.13 "Then the owner of the vineyard said, 'What shall I do? I will send my own dear son; surely they will respect him!'

20.14 "But when the tenants saw him, they said to one another, 'This is the owner's son. Let's kill him, and his property will be ours!'

20.15 "So they threw him out of the vineyard and killed him. What, then, will the owner of the vineyard do to the tenants?" Jesus asked.

20.16 "He will come and kill those men, and turn the vineyard over to other tenants." When the people heard this, they said, "Surely not!"

20.17 Jesus looked at them and asked, "What, then, does this scripture mean? 'The stone which the builders rejected as worthless turned out to be the most important of all.'

20.18 "Everyone who falls on that stone will be cut to pieces; and if that stone falls on someone, that person will be crushed to dust."

20.19 The teachers of the Law and the chief priests tried to arrest Jesus on the spot, because they knew that he had told this parable against them; but they were afraid of the people.

20.20 So they looked for an opportunity. They bribed some men to pretend they were sincere, and they sent them to trap Jesus with questions, so that they could hand him over to the authority and power of the Roman Governor.

20.21 These spies said to Jesus, "Teacher, we know that what you say and teach is right. We know that you pay no attention to anyone's status, but teach the truth about God's will for people.

20.22 "Tell us, is it against our Law for us to pay taxes to the Roman

Emperor, or not?"

20.23 But Jesus saw through their trick and said to them,

20.24 "Show me a silver coin. Whose face and name are these on it?" "The Emperor's," they answered.

20.25 So Jesus said, "Well, then, pay to the Emperor what belongs to the Emperor, and pay to God what belongs to God."

20.26 There before the people they could not catch him in a thing, so they kept quiet, amazed at his answer.

20.27 Then some Sadducees, who say that people will not rise from death, came to Jesus and said,

20.28 "Teacher, Moses wrote this law for us: 'If a man dies and leaves a wife but no children, that man's brother must marry the widow so that they can have children who will be considered the dead man's children.'

20.29 "Once there were seven brothers; the oldest got married and died without having children.

20.30 "Then the second one married the woman,

20.31 "and then the third. The same thing happened to all seven — they died without having children.

20.32 "Last of all, the woman died.

20.33 "Now, on the day when the dead rise to life, whose wife will she be? All seven of them had married her."

20.34 Jesus answered them, "The men and women of this age marry,

20.35 "but the men and women who are worthy to rise from death and live in the age to come will not then marry.

20.36 "They will be like angels and cannot die. They are the children of God, because they have risen from death.

20.37 "And Moses clearly proves that the dead are raised to life. In the passage about the burning bush he speaks of the Lord as 'the God of Abraham, the God of Isaac, and the God of Jacob.'

20.38 "He is the God of the living, not of the dead, for to him all are alive."

20.39 Some of the teachers of the Law spoke up, "A good answer, Teacher!"

20.40 For they did not dare ask him any more questions.

20.41 Jesus asked them, "How can it be said that the Messiah will be the descendant of David?

20.42 "For David himself says in the book of Psalms, 'The Lord said to my Lord: Sit here at my right side

20.43 until I put your enemies as a footstool under your feet.'

20.44 "David called him 'Lord'; how, then, can the Messiah be David's descendant?"

<sup>20.45</sup> As all the people listened to him, Jesus said to his disciples,

<sup>20.46</sup> "Be on your guard against the teachers of the Law, who like to walk around in their long robes and love to be greeted with respect in the marketplace; who choose the reserved seats in the synagogues and the best places at feasts;

<sup>20.47</sup> "who take advantage of widows and rob them of their homes, and then make a show of saying long prayers! Their punishment will be all the worse!"

# 21

<sup>21.1</sup> Jesus looked around and saw rich people dropping their gifts in the Temple treasury,

<sup>21.2</sup> and he also saw a very poor widow dropping in two little copper coins.

<sup>21.3</sup> He said, "I tell you that this poor widow put in more than all the others.

<sup>21.4</sup> "For the others offered their gifts from what they had to spare of their riches; but she, poor as she is, gave all she had to live on."

<sup>21.5</sup> Some of the disciples were talking about the Temple, how beautiful it looked with its fine stones and the gifts offered to God. Jesus said,

<sup>21.6</sup> "All this you see — the time will come when not a single stone here will be left in its place; every one will be thrown down."

<sup>21.7</sup> "Teacher," they asked, "when will this be? And what will happen in order to show that the time has come for it to take place?"

<sup>21.8</sup> Jesus said, "Watch out; don't be fooled. Many men, claiming to speak for me, will come and say, 'I am he!' and, 'The time has come!' But don't follow them.

<sup>21.9</sup> "Don't be afraid when you hear of wars and revolutions; such things must happen first, but they do not mean that the end is near."

<sup>21.10</sup> He went on to say, "Countries will fight each other; kingdoms will attack one another.

<sup>21.11</sup> "There will be terrible earthquakes, famines, and plagues everywhere; there will be strange and terrifying things coming from the sky.

<sup>21.12</sup> "Before all these things take place, however, you will be arrested and persecuted; you will be handed over to be tried in synagogues and be put in prison; you will be brought before kings and rulers for my sake.

<sup>21.13</sup> "This will be your chance to tell the Good News.

21.14 "Make up your minds ahead of time not to worry about how you will defend yourselves,

21.15 "because I will give you such words and wisdom that none of your enemies will be able to refute or contradict what you say.

21.16 "You will be handed over by your parents, your brothers, your relatives, and your friends; and some of you will be put to death.

21.17 "Everyone will hate you because of me.

21.18 "But not a single hair from your heads will be lost.

21.19 "Stand firm, and you will save yourselves.

21.20 "When you see Jerusalem surrounded by armies, then you will know that it will soon be destroyed.

21.21 "Then those who are in Judea must run away to the hills; those who are in the city must leave, and those who are out in the country must not go into the city.

21.22 "For those will be 'The Days of Punishment,' to make come true all that the Scriptures say.

21.23 "How terrible it will be in those days for women who are pregnant and for mothers with little babies! Terrible distress will come upon this land, and God's punishment will fall on this people.

21.24 "Some will be killed by the sword, and others will be taken as prisoners to all countries; and the heathen will trample over Jerusalem until their time is up.

21.25 "There will be strange things happening to the sun, the moon, and the stars. On earth whole countries will be in despair, afraid of the roar of the sea and the raging tides.

21.26 "People will faint from fear as they wait for what is coming over the whole earth, for the powers in space will be driven from their courses.

21.27 "Then the Son of Man will appear, coming in a cloud with great power and glory.

21.28 "When these things begin to happen, stand up and raise your heads, because your salvation is near."

21.29 Then Jesus told them this parable: "Think of the fig tree and all the other trees.

21.30 "When you see their leaves beginning to appear, you know that summer is near.

21.31 "In the same way, when you see these things happening, you will know that the Kingdom of God is about to come.

21.32 "Remember that all these things will take place before the people now living have all died.

21.33 "Heaven and earth will pass away, but my words will never pass away.

<sup>21.34</sup> "Be careful not to let yourselves become occupied with too much feasting and drinking and with the worries of this life, or that Day may suddenly catch you

<sup>21.35</sup> "like a trap. For it will come upon all people everywhere on earth.

<sup>21.36</sup> "Be on watch and pray always that you will have the strength to go safely through all those things that will happen and to stand before the Son of Man."

<sup>21.37</sup> Jesus spent those days teaching in the Temple, and when evening came, he would go out and spend the night on the Mount of Olives.

<sup>21.38</sup> Early each morning all the people went to the Temple to listen to him.

# 22

<sup>22.1</sup> The time was near for the Festival of Unleavened Bread, which is called the Passover.

<sup>22.2</sup> The chief priests and the teachers of the Law were afraid of the people, and so they were trying to find a way of putting Jesus to death secretly.

<sup>22.3</sup> Then Satan entered into Judas, called Iscariot, who was one of the twelve disciples.

<sup>22.4</sup> So Judas went off and spoke with the chief priests and the officers of the Temple guard about how he could betray Jesus to them.

<sup>22.5</sup> They were pleased and offered to pay him money.

<sup>22.6</sup> Judas agreed to it and started looking for a good chance to hand Jesus over to them without the people knowing about it.

<sup>22.7</sup> The day came during the Festival of Unleavened Bread when the lambs for the Passover meal were to be killed.

<sup>22.8</sup> Jesus sent Peter and John with these instructions: "Go and get the Passover meal ready for us to eat."

<sup>22.9</sup> "Where do you want us to get it ready?" they asked him.

<sup>22.10</sup> He answered, "As you go into the city, a man carrying a jar of water will meet you. Follow him into the house that he enters,

<sup>22.11</sup> "and say to the owner of the house: 'The Teacher says to you, Where is the room where my disciples and I will eat the Passover meal?'

<sup>22.12</sup> "He will show you a large furnished room upstairs, where you will get everything ready."

<sup>22.13</sup> They went off and found everything just as Jesus had told them,

and they prepared the Passover meal.

<sup>22.14</sup> When the hour came, Jesus took his place at the table with the apostles.

<sup>22.15</sup> He said to them, "I have wanted so much to eat this Passover meal with you before I suffer!

<sup>22.16</sup> "For I tell you, I will never eat it until it is given its full meaning in the Kingdom of God."

<sup>22.17</sup> Then Jesus took a cup, gave thanks to God, and said, "Take this and share it among yourselves.

<sup>22.18</sup> "I tell you that from now on I will not drink this wine until the Kingdom of God comes."

<sup>22.19</sup> Then he took a piece of bread, gave thanks to God, broke it, and gave it to them, saying, "This is my body, which is given for you. Do this in memory of me."

<sup>22.20</sup> In the same way, he gave them the cup after the supper, saying, "This cup is God's new covenant sealed with my blood, which is poured out for you.

<sup>22.21</sup> "But, look! The one who betrays me is here at the table with me!

<sup>22.22</sup> "The Son of Man will die as God has decided, but how terrible for that man who betrays him!"

<sup>22.23</sup> Then they began to ask among themselves which one of them it could be who was going to do this.

<sup>22.24</sup> An argument broke out among the disciples as to which one of them should be thought of as the greatest.

<sup>22.25</sup> Jesus said to them, "The kings of the pagans have power over their people, and the rulers claim the title 'Friends of the People.'

<sup>22.26</sup> "But this is not the way it is with you; rather, the greatest one among you must be like the youngest, and the leader must be like the servant.

<sup>22.27</sup> "Who is greater, the one who sits down to eat or the one who serves? The one who sits down, of course. But I am among you as one who serves.

<sup>22.28</sup> "You have stayed with me all through my trials;

<sup>22.29</sup> "and just as my Father has given me the right to rule, so I will give you the same right.

<sup>22.30</sup> "You will eat and drink at my table in my Kingdom, and you will sit on thrones to rule over the twelve tribes of Israel.

<sup>22.31</sup> "Simon, Simon! Listen! Satan has received permission to test all of you, to separate the good from the bad, as a farmer separates the wheat from the chaff.

<sup>22.32</sup> "But I have prayed for you, Simon, that your faith will not fail.

And when you turn back to me, you must strengthen your brothers."
22.33 Peter answered, "Lord, I am ready to go to prison with you and to die with you!"

22.34 "I tell you, Peter," Jesus said, "the rooster will not crow tonight until you have said three times that you do not know me."

22.35 Then Jesus asked his disciples, "When I sent you out that time without purse, bag, or shoes, did you lack anything?" "Not a thing," they answered.

22.36 "But now," Jesus said, "whoever has a purse or a bag must take it; and whoever does not have a sword must sell his coat and buy one.

22.37 "For I tell you that the scripture which says, 'He shared the fate of criminals,' must come true about me, because what was written about me is coming true."

22.38 The disciples said, "Look! Here are two swords, Lord!" "That is enough!" he replied.

22.39 Jesus left the city and went, as he usually did, to the Mount of Olives; and the disciples went with him.

22.40 When he arrived at the place, he said to them, "Pray that you will not fall into temptation."

22.41 Then he went off from them about the distance of a stone's throw and knelt down and prayed.

22.42 "Father," he said, "if you will, take this cup of suffering away from me. Not my will, however, but your will be done."

22.43 An angel from heaven appeared to him and strengthened him.

22.44 In great anguish he prayed even more fervently; his sweat was like drops of blood falling to the ground.

22.45 Rising from his prayer, he went back to the disciples and found them asleep, worn out by their grief.

22.46 He said to them, "Why are you sleeping? Get up and pray that you will not fall into temptation."

22.47 Jesus was still speaking when a crowd arrived, led by Judas, one of the twelve disciples. He came up to Jesus to kiss him.

22.48 But Jesus said, "Judas, is it with a kiss that you betray the Son of Man?"

22.49 When the disciples who were with Jesus saw what was going to happen, they asked, "Shall we use our swords, Lord?"

22.50 And one of them struck the High Priest's slave and cut off his right ear.

22.51 But Jesus said, "Enough of this!" He touched the man's ear and healed him.

<sup>22.52</sup> Then Jesus said to the chief priests and the officers of the Temple guard and the elders who had come there to get him, "Did you have to come with swords and clubs, as though I were an outlaw? <sup>22.53</sup> "I was with you in the Temple every day, and you did not try to arrest me. But this is your hour to act, when the power of darkness rules."

<sup>22.54</sup> They arrested Jesus and took him away into the house of the High Priest; and Peter followed at a distance.

<sup>22.55</sup> A fire had been lit in the center of the courtyard, and Peter joined those who were sitting around it.

<sup>22.56</sup> When one of the servant women saw him sitting there at the fire, she looked straight at him and said, "This man too was with Jesus!"

<sup>22.57</sup> But Peter denied it, "Woman, I don't even know him!"

<sup>22.58</sup> After a little while a man noticed Peter and said, "You are one of them, too!" But Peter answered, "Man, I am not!"

<sup>22.59</sup> And about an hour later another man insisted strongly, "There isn't any doubt that this man was with Jesus, because he also is a Galilean!"

<sup>22.60</sup> But Peter answered, "Man, I don't know what you are talking about!" At once, while he was still speaking, a rooster crowed.

<sup>22.61</sup> The Lord turned around and looked straight at Peter, and Peter remembered that the Lord had said to him, "Before the rooster crows tonight, you will say three times that you do not know me."

<sup>22.62</sup> Peter went out and wept bitterly.

<sup>22.63</sup> The men who were guarding Jesus made fun of him and beat him.

<sup>22.64</sup> They blindfolded him and asked him, "Who hit you? Guess!"

<sup>22.65</sup> And they said many other insulting things to him.

<sup>22.66</sup> When day came, the elders, the chief priests, and the teachers of the Law met together, and Jesus was brought before the Council.

<sup>22.67</sup> "Tell us," they said, "are you the Messiah?" He answered, "If I tell you, you will not believe me;

<sup>22.68</sup> "and if I ask you a question, you will not answer.

<sup>22.69</sup> "But from now on the Son of Man will be seated at the right side of Almighty God."

<sup>22.70</sup> They all said, "Are you, then, the Son of God?" He answered them, "You say that I am."

<sup>22.71</sup> And they said, "We don't need any witnesses! We ourselves have heard what he said!"

23.1 The whole group rose up and took Jesus before Pilate,

23.2 where they began to accuse him: "We caught this man misleading our people, telling them not to pay taxes to the Emperor and claiming that he himself is the Messiah, a king."

23.3 Pilate asked him, "Are you the king of the Jews?" "So you say," answered Jesus.

23.4 Then Pilate said to the chief priests and the crowds, "I find no reason to condemn this man."

23.5 But they insisted even more strongly, "With his teaching he is starting a riot among the people all through Judea. He began in Galilee and now has come here."

23.6 When Pilate heard this, he asked, "Is this man a Galilean?"

23.7 When he learned that Jesus was from the region ruled by Herod, he sent him to Herod, who was also in Jerusalem at that time.

23.8 Herod was very pleased when he saw Jesus, because he had heard about him and had been wanting to see him for a long time. He was hoping to see Jesus perform some miracle.

23.9 So Herod asked Jesus many questions, but Jesus made no answer.

23.10 The chief priests and the teachers of the Law stepped forward and made strong accusations against Jesus.

23.11 Herod and his soldiers made fun of Jesus and treated him with contempt; then they put a fine robe on him and sent him back to Pilate.

23.12 On that very day Herod and Pilate became friends; before this they had been enemies.

23.13 Pilate called together the chief priests, the leaders, and the people,

23.14 and said to them, "You brought this man to me and said that he was misleading the people. Now, I have examined him here in your presence, and I have not found him guilty of any of the crimes you accuse him of.

23.15 "Nor did Herod find him guilty, for he sent him back to us. There is nothing this man has done to deserve death.

23.16 "So I will have him whipped and let him go."

23.17 (At every Passover Festival Pilate had to set free one prisoner for them.)

23.18 The whole crowd cried out, "Kill him! Set Barabbas free for us!"

23.19 (Barabbas had been put in prison for a riot that had taken place in the city, and for murder.)

23.20 Pilate wanted to set Jesus free, so he appealed to the crowd again.

23.21 But they shouted back, "Crucify him! Crucify him!"

23.22 Pilate said to them the third time, "But what crime has he committed? I cannot find anything he has done to deserve death! I will have him whipped and set him free."

23.23 But they kept on shouting at the top of their voices that Jesus should be crucified, and finally their shouting succeeded.

23.24 So Pilate passed the sentence on Jesus that they were asking for.

23.25 He set free the man they wanted, the one who had been put in prison for riot and murder, and he handed Jesus over for them to do as they wished.

23.26 The soldiers led Jesus away, and as they were going, they met a man from Cyrene named Simon who was coming into the city from the country. They seized him, put the cross on him, and made him carry it behind Jesus.

23.27 A large crowd of people followed him; among them were some women who were weeping and wailing for him.

23.28 Jesus turned to them and said, "Women of Jerusalem! Don't cry for me, but for yourselves and your children.

23.29 "For the days are coming when people will say, 'How lucky are the women who never had children, who never bore babies, who never nursed them!'

23.30 "That will be the time when people will say to the mountains, 'Fall on us!' and to the hills, 'Hide us!'

23.31 "For if such things as these are done when the wood is green, what will happen when it is dry?"

23.32 Two other men, both of them criminals, were also led out to be put to death with Jesus.

23.33 When they came to the place called "The Skull," they crucified Jesus there, and the two criminals, one on his right and the other on his left.

23.34 Jesus said, "Forgive them, Father! They don't know what they are doing." They divided his clothes among themselves by throwing dice.

23.35 The people stood there watching while the Jewish leaders made fun of him: "He saved others; let him save himself if he is the Messiah whom God has chosen!"

23.36 The soldiers also made fun of him: they came up to him and offered him cheap wine,

23.37 and said, "Save yourself if you are the king of the Jews!"

23.38 Above him were written these words: "This is the King of the

Jews."

<sup>23.39</sup> One of the criminals hanging there hurled insults at him: "Aren't you the Messiah? Save yourself and us!"

<sup>23.40</sup> The other one, however, rebuked him, saying, "Don't you fear God? You received the same sentence he did.

<sup>23.41</sup> "Ours, however, is only right, because we are getting what we deserve for what we did; but he has done no wrong."

<sup>23.42</sup> And he said to Jesus, "Remember me, Jesus, when you come as King!"

<sup>23.43</sup> Jesus said to him, "I promise you that today you will be in Paradise with me."

<sup>23.44-45</sup> It was about twelve o'clock when the sun stopped shining and darkness covered the whole country until three o'clock; and the curtain hanging in the Temple was torn in two.

<sup>23.46</sup> Jesus cried out in a loud voice, "Father! In your hands I place my spirit!" He said this and died.

<sup>23.47</sup> The army officer saw what had happened, and he praised God, saying, "Certainly he was a good man!"

<sup>23.48</sup> When the people who had gathered there to watch the spectacle saw what happened, they all went back home, beating their breasts in sorrow.

<sup>23.49</sup> All those who knew Jesus personally, including the women who had followed him from Galilee, stood at a distance to watch.

<sup>23.50-51</sup> There was a man named Joseph from Arimathea, a town in Judea. He was a good and honorable man, who was waiting for the coming of the Kingdom of God. Although he was a member of the Council, he had not agreed with their decision and action.

<sup>23.52</sup> He went into the presence of Pilate and asked for the body of Jesus.

<sup>23.53</sup> Then he took the body down, wrapped it in a linen sheet, and placed it in a tomb which had been dug out of solid rock and which had never been used.

<sup>23.54</sup> It was Friday, and the Sabbath was about to begin.

<sup>23.55</sup> The women who had followed Jesus from Galilee went with Joseph and saw the tomb and how Jesus' body was placed in it.

<sup>23.56</sup> Then they went back home and prepared the spices and perfumes for the body. On the Sabbath they rested, as the Law commanded.

# 24

<sup>24.1</sup> Very early on Sunday morning the women went to the tomb, car-

rying the spices they had prepared.
24.2 They found the stone rolled away from the entrance to the tomb,
24.3 so they went in; but they did not find the body of the Lord Jesus.
24.4 They stood there puzzled about this, when suddenly two men in bright shining clothes stood by them.
24.5 Full of fear, the women bowed down to the ground, as the men said to them, "Why are you looking among the dead for one who is alive?
24.6 "He is not here; he has been raised. Remember what he said to you while he was in Galilee:
24.7 " 'The Son of Man must be handed over to sinners, be crucified, and three days later rise to life.'"
24.8 Then the women remembered his words,
24.9 returned from the tomb, and told all these things to the eleven disciples and all the rest.
24.10 The women were Mary Magdalene, Joanna, and Mary the mother of James; they and the other women with them told these things to the apostles.
24.11 But the apostles thought that what the women said was nonsense, and they did not believe them.
24.12 But Peter got up and ran to the tomb; he bent down and saw the grave cloths but nothing else. Then he went back home amazed at what had happened.
24.13 On that same day two of Jesus' followers were going to a village named Emmaus, about seven miles from Jerusalem,
24.14 and they were talking to each other about all the things that had happened.
24.15 As they talked and discussed, Jesus himself drew near and walked along with them;
24.16 they saw him, but somehow did not recognize him.
24.17 Jesus said to them, "What are you talking about to each other, as you walk along?" They stood still, with sad faces.
24.18 One of them, named Cleopas, asked him, "Are you the only visitor in Jerusalem who doesn't know the things that have been happening there these last few days?"
24.19 "What things?" he asked. "The things that happened to Jesus of Nazareth," they answered. "This man was a prophet and was considered by God and by all the people to be powerful in everything he said and did.
24.20 "Our chief priests and rulers handed him over to be sentenced to death, and he was crucified.

24.21 "And we had hoped that he would be the one who was going to set Israel free! Besides all that, this is now the third day since it happened.

24.22 "Some of the women of our group surprised us; they went at dawn to the tomb,

24.23 "but could not find his body. They came back saying they had seen a vision of angels who told them that he is alive.

24.24 "Some of our group went to the tomb and found it exactly as the women had said, but they did not see him."

24.25 Then Jesus said to them, "How foolish you are, how slow you are to believe everything the prophets said!

24.26 "Was it not necessary for the Messiah to suffer these things and then to enter his glory?"

24.27 And Jesus explained to them what was said about himself in all the Scriptures, beginning with the books of Moses and the writings of all the prophets.

24.28 As they came near the village to which they were going, Jesus acted as if he were going farther;

24.29 but they held him back, saying, "Stay with us; the day is almost over and it is getting dark." So he went in to stay with them.

24.30 He sat down to eat with them, took the bread, and said the blessing; then he broke the bread and gave it to them.

24.31 Then their eyes were opened and they recognized him, but he disappeared from their sight.

24.32 They said to each other, "Wasn't it like a fire burning in us when he talked to us on the road and explained the Scriptures to us?"

24.33 They got up at once and went back to Jerusalem, where they found the eleven disciples gathered together with the others

24.34 and saying, "The Lord is risen indeed! He has appeared to Simon!"

24.35 The two then explained to them what had happened on the road, and how they had recognized the Lord when he broke the bread.

24.36 While the two were telling them this, suddenly the Lord himself stood among them and said to them, "Peace be with you."

24.37 They were terrified, thinking that they were seeing a ghost.

24.38 But he said to them, "Why are you alarmed? Why are these doubts coming up in your minds?

24.39 "Look at my hands and my feet, and see that it is I myself. Feel me, and you will know, for a ghost doesn't have flesh and bones, as you can see I have."

24.40 He said this and showed them his hands and his feet.

[24.41] They still could not believe, they were so full of joy and wonder; so he asked them, "Do you have anything here to eat?"
[24.42] They gave him a piece of cooked fish,
[24.43] which he took and ate in their presence.
[24.44] Then he said to them, "These are the very things I told you about while I was still with you: everything written about me in the Law of Moses, the writings of the prophets, and the Psalms had to come true."
[24.45] Then he opened their minds to understand the Scriptures,
[24.46] and said to them, "This is what is written: the Messiah must suffer and must rise from death three days later,
[24.47] "and in his name the message about repentance and the forgiveness of sins must be preached to all nations, beginning in Jerusalem.
[24.48] "You are witnesses of these things.
[24.49] "And I myself will send upon you what my Father has promised. But you must wait in the city until the power from above comes down upon you."
[24.50] Then he led them out of the city as far as Bethany, where he raised his hands and blessed them.
[24.51] As he was blessing them, he departed from them and was taken up into heaven.
[24.52] They worshiped him and went back into Jerusalem, filled with great joy,
[24.53] and spent all their time in the Temple giving thanks to God.

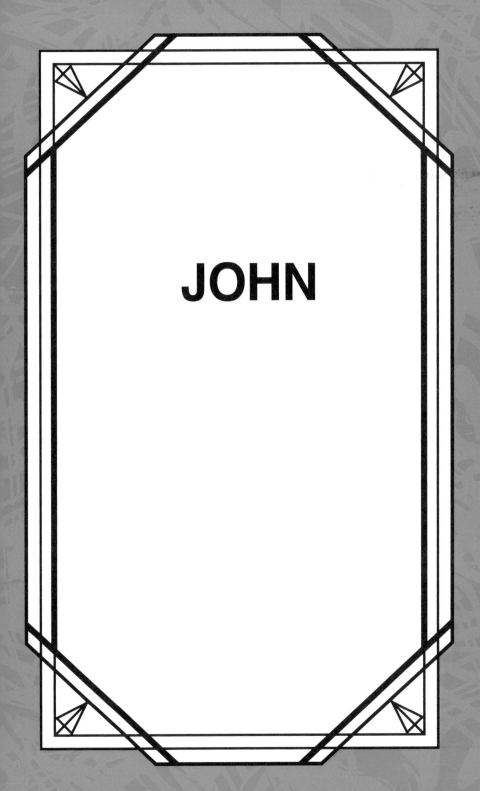

# JOHN

# John

## 1

<sup>1.1</sup> In the beginning the Word already existed; the Word was <u>with God</u>, and the Word was God.

<sup>1.2</sup> From the very beginning the Word was <u>with God</u>.

<sup>1.3</sup> <u>Through him</u> God made all the things; not one thing <u>in all creation</u> was made <u>without him</u>.

<sup>1.4</sup> The Word was the source <u>of life</u>, and this life brought light <u>to people</u>.

<sup>1.5</sup> The light shines <u>in the darkness</u>, and the darkness has never put it out.

<sup>1.6</sup> God sent his messenger, a man named John,

<sup>1.7</sup> who came to tell people <u>about the light</u>, so that all should hear the message and believe.

<sup>1.8</sup> He himself was not the light; he came to tell <u>about the light</u>.

<sup>1.9</sup> This was the real light – the light that comes <u>into the world</u> and shines <u>on all people</u>.

<sup>1.10</sup> The Word was <u>in the world</u>, and though God made the world <u>through him</u>, yet the world did not recognize him.

<sup>1.11</sup> He came <u>to his own country</u>, but his own people did not receive him.

<sup>1.12</sup> Some, however, did receive him and believed <u>in him</u>; so he gave them the right to become God's children.

<sup>1.13</sup> They did not become God's children <u>by natural means</u>, that is, by being born <u>as the children of a human father</u>; God himself was their Father.

<sup>1.14</sup> The Word became a human being and full <u>of grace and truth</u>, lived <u>among us</u>. We saw his glory, the glory which he received <u>as the Father's only son</u>.

<sup>1.15</sup> John spoke <u>about him</u>. He cried out, "This is the one I was talking about when I said, 'He comes <u>after me</u>, but he is greater than I am, because he existed before I was born.'"

<sup>1.16</sup> <u>Out of the fullness of his grace</u> he has blessed us all, giving us one blessing <u>after another</u>.

<sup>1.17</sup> God gave the Law <u>through Moses</u>, but grace and truth came <u>through Jesus Christ</u>.

<sup>1.18</sup> No one has ever seen God. The only Son, who is the same <u>as God</u> and is <u>at the Father's side</u>, he has made him known.

<sup>1.19</sup> The Jewish authorities <u>in Jerusalem</u> sent some priests and Lev-

ites to John to ask him, "Who are you?"

1.20 John did not refuse to answer, but spoke out openly and clearly, saying; "I am not the Messiah."

1.21 "Who are you, then?" they asked. "Are you Elijah?" "No, I am not," John answered. "Are you the Prophet?" they asked. "No" he replied.

1.22 "Then tell us who you are," they said. "We have to take an answer back to those who sent us. What do you say about yourself?"

1.23 John answered by quoting the prophet Isaiah: "I am 'the voice of someone shouting in the desert: Make a straight path for the Lord to travel!'"

1.24 The messengers, who had been sent by the Pharisees,

1.25 then asked John, "If you are not the Messiah nor Elijah nor the Prophet, why do you baptize?"

1.26 John answered, "I baptize with water, but among you stands the one you do not know.

1.27 "He is coming after me, but I am not good enough even to untie his sandals."

1.28 All this happened in Bethany on the east side of the Jordan River, where John was baptizing.

1.29 The next day John saw Jesus coming to him, and said, "There is the Lamb of God, who takes away the sin of the world!

1.30 "This is the one I was talking about when I said, 'A man is coming after me, but he is greater than I am, because he existed before I was born.'

1.31 "I did not know who he would be, but I came baptizing with water in order to make him known to the people of Israel."

1.32 And John gave this testimony: "I saw the Spirit come down like a dove from heaven and stay on him.

1.33 "I still did not know that he was the one, but God, who sent me to baptize with water, had said to me, 'You will see the Spirit come down and stay on a man; he is the one who baptizes with the Holy Spirit.'

1.34 "I have seen it," said John, "and I tell you that he is the Son of God."

1.35 The next day John was standing there again with two of his disciples,

1.36 when he saw Jesus walking by, "There is the Lamb of God!" he said.

1.37 The two disciples heard him say this and went with Jesus.

1.38 Jesus turned, saw them following him, and asked, "What are you looking for?" They answered, "Where do you live, Rabbi?" (This word means "Teacher.")

<sup>1.39</sup> "Come and see," he answered. (It was then about four o'clock in the afternoon.) So they went with him and saw where he lived, and spent the rest of that day with him.

<sup>1.40</sup> One of them was Andrew, Simon Peter's brother.

<sup>1.41</sup> At once he found his brother Simon and told him, "We have found the Messiah." (This word means "Christ.")

<sup>1.42</sup> Then he took Simon to Jesus. Jesus looked at him and said, "Your name is Simon son of John, but you will be called Cephas." (This is the same as Peter and means "a rock.")

<sup>1.43</sup> The next day Jesus decided to go to Galilee. He found Philip and said to him, "Come with me!"

<sup>1.44</sup> (Philip was from Bethsaida, the town where Andrew and Peter lived.)

<sup>1.45</sup> Philip found Nathanael and told him, "We have found the one whom Moses wrote about in the book of the Law and whom the prophets also wrote about. He is Jesus son of Joseph, from Nazareth."

<sup>1.46</sup> "Can anything good come from Nazareth?" Nathanael asked. "Come and see," answered Philip.

<sup>1.47</sup> When Jesus saw Nathanael coming to him, he said about him, "Here is a real Israelite; there is nothing false in him!"

<sup>1.48</sup> Nathanael asked him, "How do you know me?" Jesus answered, "I saw you when you were under the fig tree before Philip called you."

<sup>1.49</sup> "Teacher," answered Nathanael, "you are the Son of God! You are the King of Israel!"

<sup>1.50</sup> Jesus said, "Do you believe just because I told you I saw you when you were under the fig tree? You will see much greater things than this!"

<sup>1.51</sup> And he said to them, "I am telling you the truth: you will see heaven open and God's angels going up and coming down on the Son of Man."

# 2

<sup>2.1</sup> Two days later there was a wedding in the town of Cana in Galilee. Jesus' mother was there,

<sup>2.2</sup> and Jesus and his disciples had also been invited to the wedding.

<sup>2.3</sup> When the wine had given out, Jesus' mother said to him, "They are out of wine."

<sup>2.4</sup> "You must not tell me what to do," Jesus replied. "My time has not

yet come."

<sup>2.5</sup> Jesus' mother then told the servants, "Do whatever he tells you."

<sup>2.6</sup> The Jews have rules about ritual washing, and for this purpose six stone water jars were there, each one large enough to hold between twenty and thirty gallons.

<sup>2.7</sup> Jesus said to the servants, "Fill these jars with water." They filled them to the brim,

<sup>2.8</sup> and then he told them, "Now draw some water out and take it to the man in charge of the feast." They took him the water,

<sup>2.9</sup> which now had turned into wine, and he tasted it. He did not know where this wine had come from (but, of course, the servants who had drawn out the water knew); so he called the bridegroom

<sup>2.10</sup> and said to him, "Everyone else serves the best wine first, and after the guests have drunk a lot, he serves the ordinary wine. But you have kept the best wine until now!"

<sup>2.11</sup> Jesus performed this first miracle in Cana in Galilee; there he revealed his glory, and his disciples believed in him.

<sup>2.12</sup> After this, Jesus and his mother, brothers, and disciples went to Capernaum and stayed there a few days.

<sup>2.13</sup> It was almost time for the Passover Festival, so Jesus went to Jerusalem.

<sup>2.14</sup> There in the Temple he found people selling cattle, sheep, and pigeons, and also the moneychangers sitting at their tables.

<sup>2.15</sup> So he made a whip from cords and drove all the animals out of the Temple, both the sheep and the cattle; he overturned the tables of the moneychangers and scattered their coins;

<sup>2.16</sup> and he ordered those who sold the pigeons, "Take them out of here! Stop making my Father's house a marketplace!"

<sup>2.17</sup> His disciples remembered that the scripture says, "My devotion to your house, O God, burns in me like a fire."

<sup>2.18</sup> The Jewish authorities came back at him with a question, "What miracle can you perform to show us that you have the right to do this?"

<sup>2.19</sup> Jesus answered, "Tear down this Temple, and in three days I will build it again."

<sup>2.20</sup> "Are you going to build it again in three days?" they asked him. "It has taken forty-six years to build this Temple!"

<sup>2.21</sup> But the temple Jesus was speaking about was his body.

<sup>2.22</sup> So when he was raised from death, his disciples remembered that he had said this, and they believed the scripture and what Jesus had said.

2.23 While Jesus was in Jerusalem during the Passover Festival, many believed in him as they saw the miracles he performed.
2.24 But Jesus did not trust himself to them, because he knew them all.
2.25 There was no need for anyone to tell him about them, because he himself knew what was in their hearts.

# 3

3.1 There was a Jewish leader named Nicodemus, who belonged to the party of the Pharisees.
3.2 One night he went to Jesus and said to him, "Rabbi, we know that you are a teacher sent by God. No one could perform the miracles you are doing unless God were with him."
3.3 Jesus answered, "I am telling you the truth: no one can see the Kingdom of God without being born again."
3.4 "How can a grown man be born again?" Nicodemus asked. "He certainly cannot enter his mother's womb and be born a second time!"
3.5 "I am telling you the truth," replied Jesus, "that no one can enter the Kingdom of God without being born of water and the Spirit.
3.6 "A person is born physically of human parents, but is born spiritually of the Spirit.
3.7 "Do not be surprised because I tell you that you must all be born again.
3.8 "The wind blows wherever it wishes; you hear the sound it makes, but you do not know where it comes from or where it is going. It is like that with everyone who is born of the Spirit."
3.9 "How can this be?" asked Nicodemus.
3.10 Jesus answered, "You are a great teacher in Israel, and you don't know this?
3.11 "I am telling you the truth: we speak of what we know and report what we have seen, yet none of you is willing to accept our message.
3.12 "You do not believe me when I tell you about the things of this world; how will you ever believe me, then, when I tell you about the things of heaven?
3.13 "And no one has ever gone up to heaven except the Son of Man, who came down from heaven."
3.14 As Moses lifted up the bronze snake on a pole in the desert, in the same way the Son of Man must be lifted up,
3.15 so that everyone who believes in him may have eternal life.
3.16 For God loved the world so much that he gave his only Son, so

that everyone who believes in him may not die but have eternal life.

<sup>3.17</sup> For God did not send his Son into the world to be its judge, but to be its savior.

<sup>3.18</sup> Those who believe in the Son are not judged; but those who do not believe have already been judged, because they have not believed in God's only Son.

<sup>3.19</sup> This is how the judgment works: the light has come into the world, but people love the darkness rather than the light, because their deeds are evil.

<sup>3.20</sup> Those who do evil things hate the light and will not come to the light, because they do not want their evil deeds to be shown up.

<sup>3.21</sup> But those who do what is true come to the light in order that the light may show that what they did was in obedience to God.

<sup>3.22</sup> After this, Jesus and his disciples went to the province of Judea, where he spent some time with them and baptized.

<sup>3.23</sup> John also was baptizing in Aenon, not far from Salim, because there was plenty of water in that place. People were going to him, and he was baptizing them.

<sup>3.24</sup> (This was before John had been put in prison.)

<sup>3.25</sup> Some of John's disciples began arguing with a Jew about the matter of ritual washing.

<sup>3.26</sup> So they went to John and told him, "Teacher, you remember the man who was with you on the east side of the Jordan, the one you spoke about? Well, he is baptizing now, and everyone is going to him!"

<sup>3.27</sup> John answered, "No one can have anything unless God gives it.

<sup>3.28</sup> "You yourselves are my witnesses that I said, 'I am not the Messiah, but I have been sent ahead of him.'

<sup>3.29</sup> "The bridegroom is the one to whom the bride belongs; but the bridegroom's friend, who stands by and listens, is glad when he hears the bridegroom's voice. This is how my own happiness is made complete.

<sup>3.30</sup> "He must become more important while I become less important."

<sup>3.31</sup> He who comes from above is greater than all. He who is from the earth belongs to the earth and speaks about earthly matters, but he who comes from heaven is above all.

<sup>3.32</sup> He tells what he has seen and heard, yet no one accepts his message.

<sup>3.33</sup> But whoever accepts his message confirms by this that God is truthful.

<sup>3.34</sup> The one whom God has sent speaks God's words, because God

gives him the fullness of his Spirit. <sup>3.35</sup> The Father loves his Son and has put everything in his power. <sup>3.36</sup> Whoever believes in the Son has eternal life; whoever disobeys the Son will not have life, but will remain under God's punishment.

# 4

<sup>4.1</sup> The Pharisees heard that Jesus was winning and baptizing more disciples than John. <sup>4.2</sup> (Actually, Jesus himself did not baptize anyone; only his disciples did.) <sup>4.3</sup> So when Jesus heard what was being said, he left Judea and went back to Galilee; <sup>4.4</sup> on his way there he had to go through Samaria. <sup>4.5</sup> In Samaria he came to a town named Sychar, which was not far from the field that Jacob had given to his son Joseph. <sup>4.6</sup> Jacob's well was there, and Jesus, tired out by the trip, sat down by the well. It was about noon.

<sup>4.7</sup> A Samaritan woman came to draw some water, and Jesus said to her, "Give me a drink of water." <sup>4.8</sup> (His disciples had gone into town to buy food.) <sup>4.9</sup> The woman answered, "You are a Jew, and I am a Samaritan — so how can you ask me for a drink?" (Jews will not use the same cups and bowls that Samaritans use.)

<sup>4.10</sup> Jesus answered, "If you only knew what God gives and who it is that is asking you for a drink, you would ask him, and he would give you life-giving water."

<sup>4.11</sup> "Sir," the woman said, "you don't have a bucket, and the well is deep. Where would you get that life-giving water? <sup>4.12</sup> "It was our ancestor Jacob who gave us this well; he and his sons and his flocks all drank from it. You don't claim to be greater than Jacob, do you?"

<sup>4.13</sup> Jesus answered, "Whoever drinks this water will get thirsty again, <sup>4.14</sup> "but whoever drinks the water that I will give them will never be thirsty again. The water that I will give them will become in them a spring which will provide them with life-giving water and give them eternal life."

<sup>4.15</sup> "Sir," the woman said, "give me that water! Then I will never be thirsty again, nor will I have to come here to draw water."

<sup>4.16</sup> "Go and call your husband," Jesus told her, "and come back."

<sup>4.17</sup> "I don't have a husband," she answered. Jesus replied, "You are

right when you say you don't have a husband.

4.18 "You have been married to five men, and the man you live with now is not really your husband. You have told me the truth."

4.19 "I see you are a prophet, sir," the woman said.

4.20 "My Samaritan ancestors worshiped God on this mountain, but you Jews say that Jerusalem is the place where we should worship God."

4.21 Jesus said to her, "Believe me, woman, the time will come when people will not worship the Father either on this mountain or in Jerusalem.

4.22 "You Samaritans do not really know whom you worship; but we Jews know whom we worship, because it is from the Jews that salvation comes.

4.23 "But the time is coming and is already here, when by the power of God's Spirit people will worship the Father as he really is, offering him the true worship that he wants.

4.24 "God is Spirit, and only by the power of his Spirit can people worship him as he really is."

4.25 The woman said to him, "I know that the Messiah will come, and when he comes, he will tell us everything."

4.26 Jesus answered, "I am he, I who am talking with you."

4.27 At that moment Jesus' disciples returned, and they were greatly surprised to find him talking with a woman. But none of them said to her, "What do you want?" or asked him, "Why are you talking with her?"

4.28 Then the woman left her water jar, went back to the town, and said to the people there,

4.29 "Come and see the man who told me everything I have ever done. Could he be the Messiah?"

4.30 So they left the town and went to Jesus.

4.31 In the meantime the disciples were begging Jesus, "Teacher, have something to eat!"

4.32 But he answered, "I have food to eat that you know nothing about."

4.33 So the disciples started asking among themselves, "Could somebody have brought him food?"

4.34 "My food," Jesus said to them, "is to obey the will of the one who sent me and to finish the work he gave me to do.

4.35 "You have a saying, 'Four more months and then the harvest.' But I tell you, take a good look at the fields; the crops are now ripe and ready to be harvested!

4.36 "The one who reaps the harvest is being paid and gathers the crops for eternal life; so the one who plants and the one who reaps will be glad together.

4.37 "For the saying is true, 'Someone plants, someone else reaps.'

4.38 "I have sent you to reap a harvest in a field where you did not work; others worked there, and you profit from their work."

4.39 Many of the Samaritans in that town believed in Jesus because the woman had said, "He told me everything I have ever done."

4.40 So when the Samaritans came to him, they begged him to stay with them, and Jesus stayed there two days.

4.41 Many more believed because of his message,

4.42 and they told the woman, "We believe now, not because of what you said, but because we ourselves have heard him, and we know that he really is the Savior of the world."

4.43 After spending two days there, Jesus left and went to Galilee.

4.44 For he himself had said, "A prophet is not respected in his own country."

4.45 When he arrived in Galilee, the people there welcomed him, because they had gone to the Passover Festival in Jerusalem and had seen everything that he had done during the festival.

4.46 Then Jesus went back to Cana in Galilee, where he had turned the water into wine. A government official was there whose son was sick in Capernaum.

4.47 When he heard that Jesus had come from Judea to Galilee, he went to him and asked him to go to Capernaum and heal his son, who was about to die.

4.48 Jesus said to him, "None of you will ever believe unless you see miracles and wonders."

4.49 "Sir, " replied the official, "come with me before my child dies."

4.50 Jesus said to him, "Go; your son will live!" The man believed Jesus' words and went.

4.51 On his way home his servants met him with the news, "Your boy is going to live!"

4.52 He asked them what time it was when his son got better, and they answered "It was one o'clock yesterday afternoon when the fever left him."

4.53 Then the father remembered that it was at that very hour when Jesus had told him, "Your son will live." So he and all his family believed.

4.54 This was the second miracle that Jesus performed after coming from Judea to Galilee.

<sup>5.1</sup> After this, Jesus went to Jerusalem for a religious festival. <sup>5.2</sup> Near the Sheep Gate in Jerusalem there is a pool with five porches; in Hebrew it is called Bethzatha. <sup>5.3</sup> A large crowd of sick people were lying on the porches — the blind, the lame, and the paralyzed. <sup>5.4</sup> They were waiting for the water to move, because every now and then an angel of the Lord went down into the pool and stirred up the water. The first sick person to go into the pool after the water was stirred up was healed from whatever disease he had. <sup>5.5</sup> A man was there who had been sick for thirty-eight years. <sup>5.6</sup> Jesus saw him lying there, and he knew that the man had been sick for such a long time; so he asked him, "Do you want to get well?" <sup>5.7</sup> The sick man answered, "Sir, I don't have anyone here to put me in the pool when the water is stirred up; while I am trying to get in, somebody else gets there first." <sup>5.8</sup> Jesus said to him, "Get up, pick up your mat, and walk." <sup>5.9</sup> Immediately the man got well; he picked up his mat and started walking. The day this happened was a Sabbath, <sup>5.10</sup> so the Jewish authorities told the man who had been healed, "This is a Sabbath, and it is against our Law for you to carry your mat." <sup>5.11</sup> He answered, "The man who made me well told me to pick up my mat and walk." <sup>5.12</sup> They asked him, "Who is the man who told you to do this?" <sup>5.13</sup> But the man who had been healed did not know who Jesus was, for there was a crowd in that place, and Jesus had slipped away. <sup>5.14</sup> Afterward, Jesus found him in the Temple and said, "Listen, you are well now; so stop sinning or something worse may happen to you." <sup>5.15</sup> Then the man left and told the Jewish authorities that it was Jesus who had healed him. <sup>5.16</sup> So they began to persecute Jesus, because he had done this healing on a Sabbath. <sup>5.17</sup> Jesus answered them, "My Father is always working, and I too must work." <sup>5.18</sup> This saying made the Jewish authorities all the more determined to kill him; not only had he broken the Sabbath law, but he had said that God was his own Father and in this way had made himself equal with God.

<sup>5.19</sup> So Jesus answered them, "I tell you the truth: the Son can do nothing on his own; he does only what he sees his Father doing. What the Father does, the Son also does.

<sup></sup>5.20 "For the Father loves the Son and shows him all that he himself is doing. He will show him even greater things to do than this, and you will all be amazed.

5.21 "Just as the Father raises the dead and gives them life, in the same way the Son gives life to those he wants to.

5.22 "Nor does the Father himself judge anyone. He has given his Son the full right to judge,

5.23 "so that all will honor the Son in the same way as they honor the Father. Whoever does not honor the Son does not honor the Father who sent him.

5.24 "I am telling you the truth: whoever hears my words and believes in him who sent me have eternal life. They will not be judged, but has already passed from death to life.

5.25 "I am telling you the truth: the time is coming — the time has already come — when the dead will hear the voice of the Son of God, and those who hear it will come to life.

5.26 "Just as the Father is himself the source of life, in the same way he has made his Son to be the source of life.

5.27 "And he has given the Son the right to judge, because he is the Son of Man.

5.28 "Do not be surprised at this; the time is coming when all the dead will hear his voice

5.29 "and come out of their graves: those who have done good will rise and live, and those who have done evil will rise and be condemned.

5.30 "I can do nothing on my own authority; I judge only as God tells me, so my judgment is right, because I am not trying to do what I want, but only what he who sent me wants.

5.31 "If I testify on my own behalf, what I say is not to be accepted as real proof.

5.32 "But there is someone else who testifies on my behalf, and I know that what he says about me is true.

5.33 "John is the one to whom you sent your messengers, and he spoke on behalf of the truth.

5.34 "It is not that I must have a human witness; I say this only in order that you may be saved.

5.35 "John was like a lamp, burning and shining, and you were willing for a while to enjoy his light.

5.36 "But I have a witness on my behalf which is even greater than the witness that John gave: what I do, that is, the deeds my Father gave me to do, these speak on my behalf and show that the Father has sent me.

5.37 "And the Father, who sent me, also testifies on my behalf. You have never heard his voice or seen his face,

5.38 "and you do not keep his message in your hearts, for you do not believe in the one whom he sent.

5.39 "You study the Scriptures, because you think that in them you will find eternal life. And these very Scriptures speak about me!

5.40 "Yet you are not willing to come to me in order to have life.

5.41 "I am not looking for human praise.

5.42 "But I know what kind of people you are, and I know that you have no love for God in your hearts.

5.43 "I have come with my Father's authority, but you have not received me; when, however, someone comes with his own authority, you will receive him.

5.44 "You like to receive praise from one another, but you do not try to win praise from the one who alone is God; how, then, can you believe me?

5.45 "Do not think, however, that I am the one who will accuse you to my Father. Moses, in whom you have put your hope, is the very one who will accuse you.

5.46 "If you had really believed Moses, you would have believed me, because he wrote about me.

5.47 "But since you do not believe what he wrote, how can you believe what I say?"

# 6

6.1 After this, Jesus went across Lake Galilee (or, Lake Tiberias, as it is also called).

6.2 A large crowd followed him, because they had seen his miracles of healing the sick.

6.3 Jesus went up a hill and sat down with his disciples.

6.4 The time for the Passover Festival was near.

6.5 Jesus looked around and saw that a large crowd was coming to him, so he asked Philip, "Where can we buy enough food to feed all these people?"

6.6 (He said this to test Philip; actually he already knew what he would do.)

6.7 Philip answered, "For everyone to have even a little, it would take more than two hundred silver coins to buy enough bread."

6.8 Another one of his disciples, Andrew, who was Simon Peter's brother, said,

6.9 "There is a boy here who has five loaves of barley bread and two fish. But they will certainly not be enough for all these people."

6.10 "Make the people sit down," Jesus told them. (There was a lot of grass there.) So all the people sat down; there were about five thousand men.

6.11 Jesus took the bread, gave thanks to God, and distributed it to the people who were sitting there. He did the same with the fish, and they all had as much as they wanted.

6.12 When they were all full, he said to his disciples, "Gather the pieces left over; let us not waste a bit."

6.13 So they gathered them all and filled twelve baskets with the pieces left over from the five barley loaves which the people had eaten.

6.14 Seeing this miracle that Jesus had performed, the people there said, "Surely this is the Prophet who was to come into the world!"

6.15 Jesus knew that they were about to come and seize him in order to make him king by force; so he went off again to the hills by himself.

6.16 When evening came, Jesus' disciples went down to the lake,

6.17 got into a boat, and went back across the lake toward Capernaum. Night came on, and Jesus still had not come to them.

6.18 By then a strong wind was blowing and stirring up the water.

6.19 The disciples had rowed about three or four miles when they saw Jesus walking on the water, coming near the boat, and they were terrified.

6.20 "Don't be afraid," Jesus told them, "it is I!"

6.21 Then they willingly took him into the boat, and immediately the boat reached land at the place they were heading for.

6.22 Next day the crowd which had stayed on the other side of the lake realized that there had been only one boat there. They knew that Jesus had not gone in it with his disciples, but that they had left without him.

6.23 Other boats, which were from Tiberias, came to shore near the place where the crowd had eaten the bread after the Lord had given thanks.

6.24 When the crowd saw that Jesus was not there, nor his disciples, they got into those boats and went to Capernaum, looking for him.

6.25 When the people found Jesus on the other side of the lake, they said to him, "Teacher, when did you get here?"

6.26 Jesus answered, "I am telling you the truth: you are looking for me because you ate the bread and had all you wanted, not because you understood my miracles.

6.27 "Do not work for food that spoils; instead, work for the food that lasts for eternal life. This is the food which the Son of Man will give you, because God, the Father, has put his mark of approval on him."

6.28 So they asked him, "What can we do in order to do what God wants us to do?"

6.29 Jesus answered, "What God wants you to do is to believe in the one he sent."

6.30 They replied, "What miracle will you perform so that we may see it and believe you? What will you do?

6.31 "Our ancestors ate manna in the desert, just as the scripture says, 'He gave them bread from heaven to eat.'"

6.32 "I am telling you the truth," Jesus said. "What Moses gave you was not the bread from heaven; it is my Father who gives you the real bread from heaven.

6.33 "For the bread that God gives is he who comes down from heaven and gives life to the world."

6.34 "Sir," they asked him, "give us this bread always."

6.35 "I am the bread of life," Jesus told them. "Those who come to me will never be hungry; those who believe in me will never be thirsty.

6.36 "Now, I told you that you have seen me but will not believe.

6.37 "Everyone whom my Father gives me will come to me. I will never turn away anyone who comes to me,

6.38 "because I have come down from heaven to do not my own will but the will of him who sent me.

6.39 "And it is the will of him who sent me that I should not lose any of all those he has given me, but that I should raise them all to life on the last day.

6.40 "For what my Father wants is that all who see the Son and believe in him should have eternal life. And I will raise them to life on the last day."

6.41 The people started grumbling about him, because he said, "I am the bread that came down from heaven."

6.42 So they said, "This man is Jesus son of Joseph, isn't he? We know his father and mother. How, then, does he now say he came down from heaven?"

6.43 Jesus answered, "Stop grumbling among yourselves.

6.44 "People cannot come to me unless the Father who sent me draws them to me; and I will raise them to life on the last day.

6.45 "The prophets wrote, 'Everyone will be taught by God.' Anyone who hears the Father and learns from him comes to me.

6.46 "This does not mean that anyone has seen the Father; he who is from God is the only one who has seen the Father.

<sup>6.47</sup> "I am telling you the truth: he who believes has eternal life.

<sup>6.48</sup> "I am the bread of life.

<sup>6.49</sup> "Your ancestors ate manna in the desert, but they died.

<sup>6.50</sup> "But the bread that comes down from heaven is of such a kind that whoever eats it will not die.

<sup>6.51</sup> "I am the living bread that came down from heaven. If you eat this bread, you will live forever. The bread that I will give you is my flesh, which I give so that the world may live."

<sup>6.52</sup> This started an angry argument among them. "How can this man give us his flesh to eat?" they asked.

<sup>6.53</sup> Jesus said to them, "I am telling you the truth: if you do not eat the flesh of the Son of Man and drink his blood, you will not have life in yourselves.

<sup>6.54</sup> "Those who eat my flesh and drink my blood have eternal life, and I will raise them to life on the last day.

<sup>6.55</sup> "For my flesh is the real food; my blood is the real drink.

<sup>6.56</sup> "Those who eat my flesh and drink my blood live in me, and I live in them.

<sup>6.57</sup> "The living Father sent me, and because of him I live also. In the same way whoever eats me will live because of me.

<sup>6.58</sup> "This, then, is the bread that came down from heaven; it is not like the bread that your ancestors ate, but then later died. Those who eat this bread will live forever."

<sup>6.59</sup> Jesus said this as he taught in the synagogue in Capernaum.

<sup>6.60</sup> Many of his followers heard this and said, "This teaching is too hard. Who can listen to it?"

<sup>6.61</sup> Without being told, Jesus knew that they were grumbling about this, so he said to them, "Does this make you want to give up?

<sup>6.62</sup> "Suppose, then, that you should see the Son of Man go back up to the place where he was before?

<sup>6.63</sup> "What gives life is God's Spirit; human power is of no use at all. The words I have spoken to you bring God's life-giving Spirit.

<sup>6.64</sup> "Yet some of you do not believe." (Jesus knew from the very beginning who were the ones that would not believe and which one would betray him.)

<sup>6.65</sup> And he added, "This is the very reason I told you that no people can come to me unless the Father makes it possible for them to do so."

<sup>6.66</sup> Because of this, many of Jesus' followers turned back and would not go with him any more.

<sup>6.67</sup> So he asked the twelve disciples, "And you — would you also like

to leave?"

6.68 Simon Peter answered him, "Lord, to whom would we go? You have the words that give eternal life.

6.69 "And now we believe and know that you are the Holy One who has come from God."

6.70 Jesus replied, "I chose the twelve of you, didn't I? Yet one of you is a devil!"

6.71 He was talking about Judas, the son of Simon Iscariot. For Judas, even though he was one of the twelve disciples, was going to betray him.

# 7

7.1 After this, Jesus traveled in Galilee; he did not want to travel in Judea, because the Jewish authorities there were wanting to kill him.

7.2 The time for the Festival of Shelters was near,

7.3 so Jesus' brothers said to him, "Leave this place and go to Judea, so that your followers will see the things that you are doing.

7.4 "People don't hide what they are doing if they want to be well known. Since you are doing these things, let the whole world know about you!"

7.5 (Not even his brothers believed in him.)

7.6 Jesus said to them, "The right time for me has not yet come. Any time is right for you.

7.7 "The world cannot hate you, but it hates me, because I keep telling it that its ways are bad.

7.8 "You go on to the festival. I am not going to this festival, because the right time has not come for me."

7.9 He said this and then stayed on in Galilee.

7.10 After his brothers had gone to the festival, Jesus also went; however, he did not go openly, but secretly.

7.11 The Jewish authorities were looking for him at the festival. "Where is he?" they asked.

7.12 There was much whispering about him in the crowd. "He is a good man," some people said. "No," others said, "he fools the people."

7.13 But no one talked about him openly, because they were afraid of the Jewish authorities.

7.14 The festival was nearly half over when Jesus went to the Temple and began teaching.

7.15 The Jewish authorities were greatly surprised and said, "How does this man know so much when he has never been to school?"

7.16 Jesus answered, "What I teach is not my own teaching, but it comes from God, who sent me.

7.17 "Whoever is willing to do what God wants will know whether what I teach comes from God or whether I speak on my own authority.

7.18 "Those who speak on their own authority are trying to gain glory for themselves. But he who wants glory for the one who sent him is honest, and there is nothing false in him.

7.19 "Moses gave you the Law, didn't he? But not one of you obeys the Law. Why are you trying to kill me?"

7.20 "You have a demon in you!" the crowd answered. "Who is trying to kill you?"

7.21 Jesus answered, "I performed one miracle, and you were all surprised.

7.22 "Moses ordered you to circumcise your sons (although it was not Moses but your ancestors who started it), and so you circumcise a boy on the Sabbath.

7.23 "If a boy is circumcised on the Sabbath so that Moses' Law is not broken, why are you angry with me because I made a man completely well on the Sabbath?

7.24 "Stop judging by external standards, and judge by true standards."

7.25 Some of the people of Jerusalem said, "Isn't this the man the authorities are trying to kill?

7.26 "Look! He is talking in public, and they say nothing against him! Can it be that they really know that he is the Messiah?

7.27 "But when the Messiah comes, no one will know where he is from. And we all know where this man comes from."

7.28 As Jesus taught in the Temple, he said in a loud voice, "Do you really know me and know where I am from? I have not come on my own authority. He who sent me, however, is truthful. You do not know him,

7.29 "but I know him, because I come from him and he sent me."

7.30 Then they tried to seize him, but no one laid a hand on him, because his hour had not yet come.

7.31 But many in the crowd believed in him and said, "When the Messiah comes, will he perform more miracles than this man has?"

7.32 The Pharisees heard the crowd whispering these things about Jesus, so they and the chief priests sent some guards to arrest him.

7.33 Jesus said, "I shall be with you a little while longer, and then I shall go away to him who sent me.

7.34 "You will look for me, but you will not find me, because you cannot go where I will be."

7.35 The Jewish authorities said among themselves, "Where is he about to go so that we shall not find him? Will he go to the Greek cities where our people live, and teach the Greeks?

7.36 "He says that we will look for him but will not find him, and that we cannot go where he will be. What does he mean?"

7.37 On the last and most important day of the festival Jesus stood up and said in a loud voice, "Whoever is thirsty should come to me, and 7.38 "whoever believes in me should drink. As the scripture says, 'Streams of life-giving water will pour out from his side.'"

7.39 Jesus said this about the Spirit, which those who believed in him were going to receive. At that time the Spirit had not yet been given, because Jesus had not been raised to glory.

7.40 Some of the people in the crowd heard him say this and said, "This man is really the Prophet!"

7.41 Others said, "He is the Messiah!" But others said, "The Messiah will not come from Galilee!

7.42 "The scripture says that the Messiah will be a descendant of King David and will be born in Bethlehem, the town where David lived."

7.43 So there was a division in the crowd because of Jesus.

7.44 Some wanted to seize him, but no one laid a hand on him.

7.45 When the guards went back, the chief priests and Pharisees asked them, "Why did you not bring him?"

7.46 The guards answered, "Nobody has ever talked the way this man does!"

7.47 "Did he fool you, too?" the Pharisees asked them.

7.48 "Have you ever known one of the authorities or one Pharisee to believe in him?

7.49 "This crowd does not know the Law of Moses, so they are under God's curse!"

7.50 One of the Pharisees there was Nicodemus, the man who had gone to see Jesus before. He said to the others,

7.51 "According to our Law we cannot condemn people before hearing them and finding out what they have done."

7.52 "Well," they answered, "are you also from Galilee? Study the Scriptures and you will learn that no prophet ever comes from Galilee."

**8** <sup>8.1</sup> Then everyone went home, but Jesus went to the Mount of Olives. <sup>8.2</sup> Early the next morning he went back to the Temple. All the people gathered around him, and he sat down and began to teach them. <sup>8.3</sup> The teachers of the Law and the Pharisees brought in a woman who had been caught committing adultery, and they made her stand before them all. <sup>8.4</sup> "Teacher," they said to Jesus, "this woman was caught in the very act of committing adultery. <sup>8.5</sup> "In our Law Moses commanded that such a woman must be stoned to death. Now, what do you say?" <sup>8.6</sup> They said this to trap Jesus, so that they could accuse him. But he bent over and wrote on the ground with his finger. <sup>8.7</sup> As they stood there asking him questions, he straightened up and said to them, "Whichever one of you has committed no sin may throw the first stone at her." <sup>8.8</sup> Then he bent over again and wrote on the ground. <sup>8.9</sup> When they heard this, they all left, one by one, the older ones first. Jesus was left alone, with the woman still standing there. <sup>8.10</sup> He straightened up and said to her, "Where are they? Is there no one left to condemn you?" <sup>8.11</sup> "No one, sir," she answered. "Well, then," Jesus said, "I do not condemn you either. Go, but do not sin again." <sup>8.12</sup> Jesus spoke to the Pharisees again. "I am the light of the world," he said. "Whoever follows me will have the light of life and will never walk in darkness." <sup>8.13</sup> The Pharisees said to him, "Now you are testifying on your own behalf; what you say proves nothing." <sup>8.14</sup> "No," Jesus answered, "even though I do testify on my own behalf, what I say is true, because I know where I came from and where I am going. You do not know where I came from or where I am going. <sup>8.15</sup> "You make judgments in a purely human way; I pass judgment on no one. <sup>8.16</sup> "But if I were to do so, my judgment would be true, because I am not alone in this; the Father who sent me is with me. <sup>8.17</sup> "It is written in your Law that when two witnesses agree, what they say is true. <sup>8.18</sup> "I testify on my own behalf, and the Father who sent me also testifies on my behalf." <sup>8.19</sup> "Where is your father?" they asked him. "You know neither me nor my Father," Jesus answered. "If you knew me, you would know my Father also."

8.20 Jesus said all this as he taught in the Temple, in the room where the offering boxes were placed. And no one arrested him, because his hour had not come.

8.21 Again Jesus said to them, "I will go away; you will look for me, but you will die in your sins. You cannot go where I am going."

8.22 So the Jewish authorities said, "He says that we cannot go where he is going. Does this mean that he will kill himself?"

8.23 Jesus answered, "You belong to this world here below, but I come from above. You are from this world, but I am not from this world.

8.24 "That is why I told you that you will die in your sins. And you will die in your sins if you do not believe that 'I Am Who I Am'."

8.25 "Who are you?" they asked him. Jesus answered, "What I have told you from the very beginning.

8.26 "I have much to say about you, much to condemn you for. The one who sent me, however, is truthful, and I tell the world only what I have heard from him."

8.27 They did not understand that Jesus was talking to them about the Father.

8.28 So he said to them, "When you lift up the Son of Man, you will know that 'I Am Who I Am'; then you will know that I do nothing on my own authority, but I say only what the Father has instructed me to say.

8.29 "And he who sent me is with me; he has not left me alone, because I always do what pleases him."

8.30 Many who heard Jesus say these things believed in him.

8.31 So Jesus said to those who believed in him, "If you obey my teaching, you are really my disciples;

8.32 "you will know the truth, and the truth will set you free."

8.33 "We are the descendants of Abraham," they answered, "and we have never been anybody's slaves. What do you mean, then, by saying, 'You will be free'?"

8.34 Jesus said to them, "I am telling you the truth: everyone who sins is a slave of sin.

8.35 "A slave does not belong to a family permanently, but a son belongs there forever.

8.36 "If the Son sets you free, then you will be really free.

8.37 "I know you are Abraham's descendants. Yet you are trying to kill me, because you will not accept my teaching.

8.38 "I talk about what my Father has shown me, but you do what your father has told you."

8.39 They answered him, "Our father is Abraham." "If you really were

Abraham's children," Jesus replied, "you would do the same things that he did.

8.40 "All I have ever done is to tell you the truth I heard <u>from God</u>, yet you are trying to kill me. Abraham did nothing <u>like this</u>!

8.41 "You are doing what your father did." "God himself is the only Father we have," they answered, "and we are his true children."

8.42 Jesus said <u>to them</u>, "If God really were your Father, you would love me, because I came <u>from God</u> and now I am here. I did not come <u>on my own authority</u>, but he sent me.

8.43 "Why do you not understand what I say? It is because you cannot bear to listen <u>to my message</u>.

8.44 "You are the children <u>of your father</u>, the Devil, and you want to follow your father's desires. <u>From the very beginning</u> he was a murderer and has never been <u>on the side</u> <u>of truth</u>, because there is no truth <u>in him</u>. When he tells a lie, he is only doing what is natural <u>to him</u>, because he is a liar and the father <u>of all lies</u>.

8.45 "But I tell the truth, and that is why you do not believe me.

8.46 "Which one <u>of you</u> can prove that I am guilty <u>of sin</u>? If I tell the truth, then why do you not believe me?

8.47 "He who comes <u>from God</u> listens <u>to God's words</u>. You, however, are not <u>from God</u>, and that is why you will not listen."

8.48 They asked Jesus, "Were we not right <u>in saying</u> that you are a Samaritan and have a demon <u>in you</u>?"

8.49 "I have no demon," Jesus answered. "I honor my Father, but you dishonor me.

8.50 "I am not seeking honor <u>for myself</u>. But there is one who is seeking it and who judges <u>in my favor</u>.

8.51 "I am telling you the truth: whoever obeys my teaching will never die."

8.52 They said <u>to him</u>, "Now we know <u>for sure</u> that you have a demon! Abraham died, and the prophets died, yet you say that whoever obeys your teaching will never die.

8.53 "Our father Abraham died; you do not claim to be greater <u>than Abraham</u>, do you? And the prophets also died. Who do you think you are?"

8.54 Jesus answered, "If I were to honor myself, that honor would be worth nothing. The one who honors me is my Father — the very one you say is your God.

8.55 "You have never known him, but I know him. If I were to say that I do not know him, I would be a liar <u>like you</u>. But I do know him, and I obey his word.

8.56 "Your father Abraham rejoiced that he was to see the time of my coming; he saw it and was glad."

8.57 They said to him, "You are not even fifty years old — and you have seen Abraham?"

8.58 "I am telling you the truth," Jesus replied. "Before Abraham was born, 'I Am'."

8.59 Then they picked up stones to throw at him, but Jesus hid himself and left the Temple.

# 9

9.1 As Jesus was walking along, he saw a man who had been born blind.

9.2 His disciples asked him, "Teacher, whose sin caused him to be born blind? Was it his own or his parents' sin?"

9.3 Jesus answered, "His blindness has nothing to do with his sins or his parents' sins. He is blind so that God's power might be seen at work in him.

9.4 "As long as it is day, we must do the work of him who sent me; night is coming when no one can work.

9.5 "While I am in the world, I am the light for the world."

9.6 After he said this, Jesus spat on the ground and made some mud with the spittle; he rubbed the mud on the man's eyes

9.7 and told him, "Go and wash your face in the Pool of Siloam." (This name means "Sent.") So the man went, washed his face, and came back seeing.

9.8 His neighbors, then, and the people who had seen him begging before this, asked, "Isn't this the man who used to sit and beg?"

9.9 Some said, "He is the one," but others said, "No he isn't; he just looks like him." So the man himself said, "I am the man."

9.10 "How is it that you can now see?" they asked him.

9.11 He answered, "The man called Jesus made some mud, rubbed it on my eyes, and told me to go to Siloam and wash my face. So I went, and as soon as I washed, I could see."

9.12 "Where is he?" they asked. "I don't know," he answered.

9.13 Then they took to the Pharisees the man who had been blind.

9.14 The day that Jesus made the mud and cured him of his blindness was a Sabbath.

9.15 The Pharisees, then, asked the man again how he had received his sight. He told them, "He put some mud on my eyes; I washed my face, and now I can see."

9.16 Some of the Pharisees said, "The man who did this cannot be from God, for he does not obey the Sabbath law." Others, however, said, "How could a man who is a sinner perform such miracles as these?" And there was a division among them.

9.17 So the Pharisees asked the man once more, "You say he cured you of your blindness — well, what do you say about him?" "He is a prophet," the man answered.

9.18 The Jewish authorities, however, were not willing to believe that he had been blind and could now see, until they called his parents 9.19 and asked them, "Is this your son? You say that he was born blind; how is it, then, that he can now see?"

9.20 His parents answered, "We know that he is our son, and we know that he was born blind.

9.21 "But we do not know how it is that he is now able to see, nor do we know who cured him of his blindness. Ask him; he is old enough, and he can answer for himself!"

9.22 His parents said this because they were afraid of the Jewish authorities, who had already agreed that anyone who said he believed that Jesus was the Messiah would be expelled from the synagogue.

9.23 That is why his parents said, "He is old enough; ask him!"

9.24 A second time they called back the man who had been born blind, and said to him, "Promise before God that you will tell the truth! We know that this man who cured you is a sinner."

9.25 "I do not know if he is a sinner or not," the man replied. "One thing I do know: I was blind, and now I see."

9.26 "What did he do to you?" they asked. "How did he cure you of your blindness?"

9.27 "I have already told you," he answered, "and you would not listen. Why do you want to hear it again? Maybe you, too, would like to be his disciples?"

9.28 They insulted him and said, "You are that fellow's disciple; but we are Moses' disciples.

9.29 "We know that God spoke to Moses; as for that fellow, however, we do not even know where he comes from!"

9.30 The man answered, "What a strange thing that is! You do not know where he comes from, but he cured me of my blindness!

9.31 "We know that God does not listen to sinners; he does listen to people who respect him and do what he wants them to do.

9.32 "Since the beginning of the world nobody has ever heard ever heard of anyone giving sight to a person born blind.

9.33 "Unless this man came from God, he would not be able to do a thing."

<sup>9.34</sup> They answered, "You were born and brought up in sin — and you are trying to teach us?" And they expelled him from the synagogue.

<sup>9.35</sup> When Jesus heard what had happened, he found the man and asked him, "Do you believe in the Son of Man?"

<sup>9.36</sup> The man answered, "Tell me who he is, sir, so that I can believe in him!"

<sup>9.37</sup> Jesus said to him, "You have already seen him, and he is the one who is talking with you now."

<sup>9.38</sup> "I believe, Lord!" the man said, and knelt down before Jesus.

<sup>9.39</sup> Jesus said, "I came to this world to judge, so that the blind should see and those who see should become blind."

<sup>9.40</sup> Some Pharisees who were there with him heard him say this and asked him, "Surely you don't mean that we are blind, too?"

<sup>9.41</sup> Jesus answered, "If you were blind, then you would not be guilty; but since you claim that you can see, this means that you are still guilty."

# 10

<sup>10.1</sup> Jesus said, "I am telling you the truth: the man who does not enter the sheep pen by the gate, but climbs in some other way, is a thief and a robber.

<sup>10.2</sup> "The man who goes in through the gate is the shepherd of the sheep.

<sup>10.3</sup> "The gatekeeper opens the gate for him; the sheep hear his voice as he calls his own sheep by name, and he leads them out.

<sup>10.4</sup> "When he has brought them out, he goes ahead of them, and the sheep follow him, because they know his voice.

<sup>10.5</sup> "They will not follow someone else; instead, they will run away from such a person, because they do not know his voice."

<sup>10.6</sup> Jesus told them this parable, but they did not understand what he meant.

<sup>10.7</sup> So Jesus said again, "I am telling you the truth: I am the gate for the sheep.

<sup>10.8</sup> "All others who came before me are thieves and robbers, but the sheep did not listen to them.

<sup>10.9</sup> "I am the gate. Those who come in by me will be saved; they will come in and go out and find pasture.

<sup>10.10</sup> "The thief comes only in order to steal, kill, and destroy. I have come in order that you might have life — life in all its fullness.

<sup>10.11</sup> "I am the good shepherd, who is willing to die for the sheep.

<sup>10.12</sup> "When the hired man, who is not a shepherd and does not own

the sheep, sees a wolf coming, he leaves the sheep and runs away; so the wolf snatches the sheep and scatters them.

10.13 "The hired man runs away because he is only a hired man and does not care about the sheep.

10.14-15 "I am the good shepherd. As the Father knows me and I know the Father, in the same way I know my sheep and they know me. And I am willing to die for them.

10.16 "There are other sheep which belong to me that are not in this sheep pen. I must bring them, too; they will listen to my voice, and they will become one flock with one shepherd.

10.17 "The Father loves me because I am willing to give up my life, in order that I may receive it back again.

10.18 "No one takes my life away from me. I give it up of my own free will. I have the right to give it up, and I have the right to take it back. This is what my Father has commanded me to do."

10.19 Again there was a division among the people because of these words.

10.20 Many of them were saying, "He has a demon! He is crazy! Why do you listen to him?"

10.21 But others were saying, "A man with a demon could not talk like this! How could a demon give sight to blind people?"

10.22 It was winter, and the Festival of the Dedication of the Temple was being celebrated in Jerusalem.

10.23 Jesus was walking in Solomon's Porch in the Temple,

10.24 when the people gathered around him and asked, "How long are you going to keep us in suspense? Tell us the plain truth: are you the Messiah?"

10.25 Jesus answered, "I have already told you, but you would not believe me. The deeds I do by my Father's authority speak on my behalf;

10.26 "but you will not believe, for you are not my sheep.

10.27 "My sheep listen to my voice; I know them, and they follow me.

10.28 "I give them eternal life, and they shall never die. No one can snatch them away from me.

10.29 "What my Father has given me is greater than everything, and no one can snatch them away from the Father's care.

10.30 "The Father and I are one."

10.31 Then the people again picked up stones to throw at him.

10.32 Jesus said to them, "I have done many good deeds in your presence which the Father gave me to do; for which one of these do you want to stone me?"

<sup>10.33</sup> They answered, "We do not want to stone you because of any good deeds, but because of your blasphemy! You are only a man, but you are trying to make yourself God!"

<sup>10.34</sup> Jesus answered, "It is written in your own Law that God said, 'You are gods.'

<sup>10.35</sup> "We know that what the scripture says is true forever; and God called those people gods, the people to whom his message was given.

<sup>10.36</sup> "As for me, the Father chose me and sent me into the world. How, then, can you say that I blaspheme because I said that I am the Son of God?

<sup>10.37</sup> "Do not believe me, then, if I am not doing the things my Father wants me to do.

<sup>10.38</sup> "But if I do them, even though you do not believe me, you should at least believe my deeds, in order that you may know once and for all that the Father is in me and that I am in the Father."

<sup>10.39</sup> Once more they tried to seize Jesus, but he slipped out of their hands.

<sup>10.40</sup> Jesus then went back again across the Jordan River to the place where John had been baptizing, and he stayed there.

<sup>10.41</sup> Many people came to him. "John performed no miracles," they said, "but everything he said about this man was true."

<sup>10.42</sup> And many people there believed in him.

# 11

<sup>11.1</sup> A man named Lazarus, who lived in Bethany, became sick. Bethany was the town where Mary and her sister Martha lived.

<sup>11.2</sup> (This Mary was the one who poured the perfume on the Lord's feet and wiped them with her hair; it was her brother Lazarus who was sick.)

<sup>11.3</sup> The sisters sent Jesus a message: "Lord, your dear friend is sick."

<sup>11.4</sup> When Jesus heard it, he said, "The final result of this sickness will not be the death of Lazarus; this has happened in order to bring glory to God, and it will be the means by which the Son of God will receive glory."

<sup>11.5</sup> Jesus loved Martha and her sister and Lazarus.

<sup>11.6</sup> Yet when he received the news that Lazarus was sick, he stayed where he was for two more days.

<sup>11.7</sup> Then he said to the disciples, "Let us go back to Judea."

<sup>11.8</sup> "Teacher," the disciples answered, "just a short time ago the people there wanted to stone you; and are you planning to go back?"

<sup>11.9</sup> Jesus said, "A day has twelve hours, doesn't it? So those who walk

in broad daylight do not stumble, for they see the light of this world. <sup>11.10</sup> "But if they walk during the night they stumble, because they have no light."

<sup>11.11</sup> Jesus said this and then added, "Our friend Lazarus has fallen asleep, but I will go and wake him up."

<sup>11.12</sup> The disciples answered, "If he is asleep, Lord, he will get well."

<sup>11.13</sup> Jesus meant that Lazarus had died, but they thought he meant natural sleep.

<sup>11.14</sup> So Jesus told them plainly, "Lazarus is dead,

<sup>11.15</sup> "but for your sake I am glad that I was not with him, so that you will believe. Let us go to him."

<sup>11.16</sup> Thomas (called the Twin) said to his fellow disciples, "Let us all go along with the Teacher, so that we may die with him!"

<sup>11.17</sup> When Jesus arrived, he found that Lazarus had been buried four days before.

<sup>11.18</sup> Bethany was less than two miles from Jerusalem,

<sup>11.19</sup> and many Judeans had come to see Martha and Mary to comfort them about their brother's death.

<sup>11.20</sup> When Martha heard that Jesus was coming, she went out to meet him, but Mary stayed in the house.

<sup>11.21</sup> Martha said to Jesus, "If you had been here, Lord, my brother would not have died!

<sup>11.22</sup> "But I know that even now God will give you whatever you ask him for."

<sup>11.23</sup> "Your brother will rise to life," Jesus told her.

<sup>11.24</sup> "I know," she replied, "that he will rise to life on the last day."

<sup>11.25</sup> Jesus said to her, "I am the resurrection and the life. Those who believe in me will live, even though they die;

<sup>11.26</sup> "and those who live and believe in me will never die. Do you believe this?"

<sup>11.27</sup> "Yes, Lord!" she answered. "I do believe that you are the Messiah, the Son of God, who was to come into the world."

<sup>11.28</sup> After Martha said this, she went back and called her sister Mary privately. "The Teacher is here," she told her, "and is asking for you."

<sup>11.29</sup> When Mary heard this, she got up and hurried out to meet him.

<sup>11.30</sup> (Jesus had not yet arrived in the village, but was still in the place where Martha had met him.)

<sup>11.31</sup> The people who were in the house with Mary comforting her followed her when they saw her get up and hurry out. They thought that she was going to the grave to weep there.

<sup>11.32</sup> Mary arrived where Jesus was, and as soon as she saw him, she

fell at his feet. "Lord," she said, "if you had been here, my brother would not have died!"

[11.33] Jesus saw her weeping, and he saw how the people with her were weeping also; his heart was touched, and he was deeply moved.

[11.34] "Where have you buried him?" he asked them. "Come and see, Lord," they answered.

[11.35] Jesus wept.

[11.36] "See how much he loved him!" the people said.

[11.37] But some of them said, "He gave sight to the blind man, didn't he? Could he not have kept Lazarus from dying?"

[11.38] Deeply moved once more, Jesus went to the tomb, which was a cave with a stone placed at the entrance.

[11.39] "Take the stone away!" Jesus ordered. Martha, the dead man's sister, answered, "There will be a bad smell, Lord. He has been buried four days!"

[11.40] Jesus said to her, "Didn't I tell you that you would see God's glory if you believed?"

[11.41] They took the stone away. Jesus looked up and said, "I thank you, Father, that you listen to me.

[11.42] "I know that you always listen to me, but I say this for the sake of the people here, so that they will believe that you sent me."

[11.43] After he had said this, he called out in a loud voice, "Lazarus, come out!"

[11.44] He came out, his hands and feet wrapped in grave cloths, and with a cloth around his face. "Untie him," Jesus told them, "and let him go."

[11.45] Many of the people who had come to visit Mary saw what Jesus did, and they believed in him.

[11.46] But some of them returned to the Pharisees and told them what Jesus had done.

[11.47] So the Pharisees and the chief priests met with the Council and said, "What shall we do? Look at all the miracles this man is performing!

[11.48] "If we let him go on in this way, everyone will believe in him, and the Roman authorities will take action and destroy our Temple and our nation!"

[11.49] One of them, named Caiaphas, who was High Priest that year, said, "What fools you are!

[11.50] "Don't you realize that it is better for you to have one man die for the people, instead of having the whole nation destroyed?"

[11.51] Actually, he did not say this of his own accord; rather, as he was

High Priest that year, he was prophesying that Jesus was going to die for the Jewish people,

<sup>11.52</sup> and not only for them, but also to bring together into one body all the scattered people of God.

<sup>11.53</sup> From that day on the Jewish authorities made plans to kill Jesus.

<sup>11.54</sup> So Jesus did not travel openly in Judea, but left and went to a place near the desert, to a town named Ephraim, where he stayed with the disciples.

<sup>11 55</sup> The time for the Passover Festival was near, and many people went up from the country to Jerusalem to perform the ritual of purification before the festival.

<sup>11.56</sup> They were looking for Jesus, and as they gathered in the Temple, they asked one another, "What do you think? Surely he will not come to the festival, will he?"

<sup>11.57</sup> The chief priests and the Pharisees had given orders that if anyone knew where Jesus was, he must report it, so that they could arrest him.

# 12

<sup>12.1</sup> Six days before the Passover, Jesus went to Bethany, the home of Lazarus, the man he had raised from death.

<sup>12.2</sup> They prepared a dinner for him there, which Martha helped serve; Lazarus was one of those who were sitting at the table with Jesus.

<sup>12.3</sup> Then Mary took a whole pint of a very expensive perfume made of pure nard, poured it on Jesus' feet, and wiped them with her hair. The sweet smell of the perfume filled the whole house.

<sup>12.4</sup> One of Jesus' disciples, Judas Iscariot — the one who was going to betray him — said,

<sup>12.5</sup> "Why wasn't this perfume sold for three hundred silver coins and the money given to the poor?"

<sup>12.6</sup> He said this, not because he cared about the poor, but because he was a thief. He carried the money bag and would help himself from it.

<sup>12.7</sup> But Jesus said, "Leave her alone! Let her keep what she has for the day of my burial.

<sup>12.8</sup> "You will always have poor people with you, but you will not always have me."

<sup>12.9</sup> A large number of people heard that Jesus was in Bethany, so they went there, not only because of Jesus but also to see Lazarus,

whom Jesus had raised from death.

<sup>12.10</sup> So the chief priests made plans to kill Lazarus too,
<sup>12.11</sup> because on his account many Jews were rejecting them and believing in Jesus.

<sup>12.12</sup> The next day the large crowd that had come to the Passover Festival heard that Jesus was coming to Jerusalem.
<sup>12.13</sup> So they took branches of palm trees and went out to meet him, shouting, "Praise God! God bless him who comes in the name of the Lord! God bless the King of Israel!"

<sup>12.14</sup> Jesus found a donkey and rode on it, just as the scripture says,
<sup>12.15</sup> "Do not be afraid, city of Zion! Here comes your king, riding on a young donkey."

<sup>12.16</sup> His disciples did not understand this at the time; but when Jesus had been raised to glory, they remembered that the scripture said this about him and that they had done this for him.

<sup>12.17</sup> The people who had been with Jesus when he called Lazarus out of the grave and raised him from death had reported what had happened.
<sup>12.18</sup> That was why the crowd met him — because they heard that he had performed this miracle.
<sup>12.19</sup> The Pharisees then said to one another, "You see, we are not succeeding at all! Look, the whole world is following him!"

<sup>12.20</sup> Some Greeks were among those who had gone to Jerusalem to worship during the festival.
<sup>12.21</sup> They went to Philip (he was from Bethsaida in Galilee) and said, "Sir, we want to see Jesus."
<sup>12.22</sup> Philip went and told Andrew, and the two of them went and told Jesus.
<sup>12.23</sup> Jesus answered them, "The hour has now come for the Son of Man to receive great glory.
<sup>12.24</sup> "I am telling you the truth: a grain of wheat remains no more than a single grain unless it is dropped into the ground and dies. If it does die, then it produces many grains.
<sup>12.25</sup> "Those who love their own life will lose it; those who hate their own life in this world will keep it for life eternal.
<sup>12.26</sup> "Whoever wants to serve me must follow me, so that my servant will be with me where I am. And my Father will honor anyone who serves me.
<sup>12.27</sup> "Now my heart is troubled — and what shall I say? Shall I say, 'Father, do not let this hour come upon me'? But that is why I came — so that I might go through this hour of suffering.

¹²·²⁸ "Father, bring glory to your name!" Then a voice spoke from heaven, "I have brought glory to it, and I will do so again."

¹²·²⁹ The crowd standing there heard the voice, and some of them said it was thunder, while others said, "An angel spoke to him!"

¹²·³⁰ But Jesus said to them, "It was not for my sake that this voice spoke, but for yours.

¹²·³¹ "Now is the time for this world to be judged; now the ruler of this world will be overthrown.

¹²·³² "When I am lifted up from the earth, I will draw everyone to me."

¹²·³³ (In saying this he indicated the kind of death he was going to suffer.)

¹²·³⁴ The crowd answered, "Our Law tells us that the Messiah will live forever. How, then, can you say that the Son of Man must be lifted up? Who is this Son of Man?"

¹²·³⁵ Jesus answered, "The light will be among you a little longer. Continue on your way while you have the light, so that the darkness will not come upon you; for the one who walks in the dark does not know where he is going.

¹²·³⁶ "Believe in the light, then, while you have it, so that you will be the people of the light." After Jesus said this, he went off and hid himself from them.

¹²·³⁷ Even though he had performed all these miracles in their presence, they did not believe in him,

¹²·³⁸ so that what the prophet Isaiah had said might come true: "Lord, who believed the message we told? To whom did the Lord reveal his power?"

¹²·³⁹ And so they were not able to believe, because Isaiah also said,

¹²·⁴⁰ "God has blinded their eyes and closed their minds, so that their eyes would not see, and their minds would not understand, and they would not turn to me, says God, for me to heal them."

¹²·⁴¹ Isaiah said this because he saw Jesus' glory and spoke about him.

¹²·⁴² Even then, many Jewish authorities believed in Jesus; but because of the Pharisees they did not talk about it openly, so as not to be expelled from the synagogue.

¹²·⁴³ They loved human approval rather than the approval of God.

¹²·⁴⁴ Jesus said in a loud voice, "Whoever believes in me believes not only in me but also in him who sent me.

¹²·⁴⁵ "Whoever sees me sees also him who sent me.

¹²·⁴⁶ "I have come into the world as light, so that everyone who be-

lieves in me should not remain in the darkness.

<sup>12.47</sup> "If people hear my message and do not obey it, I will not judge them. I came, not to judge the world, but to save it.

<sup>12.48</sup> "Those who reject me and do not accept my message have one who will judge them. The words I have spoken will be their judge on the last day!

<sup>12.49</sup> "This is true, because I have not spoken on my own authority, but the Father who sent me has commanded me what I must say and speak.

<sup>12.50</sup> "And I know that his command brings eternal life. What I say, then, is what the Father has told me to say."

# 13

<sup>13.1</sup> It was now the day before the Passover Festival. Jesus knew that the hour had come for him to leave this world and go to the Father. He had always loved those in the world who were his own, and he loved them to the very end.

<sup>13.2</sup> Jesus and his disciples were at supper. The Devil had already put into the heart of Judas, the son of Simon Iscariot, the thought of betraying Jesus.

<sup>13.3</sup> Jesus knew that the Father had given him complete power; he knew that he had come from God and was going to God.

<sup>13.4</sup> So he rose from the table, took off his outer garment, and tied a towel around his waist.

<sup>13.5</sup> Then he poured some water into a washbasin and began to wash the disciples' feet and dry them with the towel around his waist.

<sup>13.6</sup> He came to Simon Peter, who said to him, "Are you going to wash my feet, Lord?"

<sup>13.7</sup> Jesus answered him, "You do not understand now what I am doing, but you will understand later."

<sup>13.8</sup> Peter declared, "Never at any time will you wash my feet!" "If I do not wash your feet," Jesus answered, "you will no longer be my disciple."

<sup>13.9</sup> Simon Peter answered, "Lord, do not wash only my feet, then! Wash my hands and head, too!"

<sup>13.10</sup> Jesus said, "Those who have taken a bath are completely clean and do not have to wash themselves, except for their feet. All of you are clean — all except one."

<sup>13.11</sup> (Jesus already knew who was going to betray him; that is why he said, "All of you, except one, are clean.")

<sup>13.12</sup> After Jesus had washed their feet, he put his outer garment back

on and returned to his place at the table. "Do you understand what I have just done to you?" he asked.

13.13 "You call me Teacher and Lord, and it is right that you do so, because that is what I am.

13.14 "I, your Lord and Teacher, have just washed your feet. You, then, should wash one another's feet.

13.15 "I have set an example for you, so that you will do just what I have done for you.

13.16 "I am telling you the truth: no slaves are greater than their master, and no messengers are greater than the one who sent them.

13.17 "Now that you know this truth, how happy you will be if you put it into practice!

13.18 "I am not talking about all of you; I know those I have chosen. But the scripture must come true that says, 'The man who shared my food turned against me.'

13.19 "I tell you this now before it happens, so that when it does happen, you will believe that 'I Am Who I Am.'

13.20 "I am telling you the truth: whoever receives anyone I send receives me also; and whoever receives me receives him who sent me."

13.21 After Jesus had said this, he was deeply troubled and declared openly, "I am telling you the truth: one of you is going to betray me."

13.22 The disciples looked at one another, completely puzzled about whom he meant.

13.23 One of the disciples, the one whom Jesus loved, was sitting next to Jesus.

13.24 Simon Peter motioned to him and said, "Ask him whom he is talking about."

13.25 So that disciple moved closer to Jesus' side and asked, "Who is it, Lord?"

13.26 Jesus answered, "I will dip some bread in the sauce and give it to him; he is the man." So he took a piece of bread, dipped it, and gave it to Judas, the son of Simon Iscariot.

13.27 As soon as Judas took the bread, Satan entered into him. Jesus said to him, "Hurry and do what you must!"

13.28 None of the others at the table understood why Jesus said this to him.

13.29 Since Judas was in charge of the money bag, some of the disciples thought that Jesus had told him to go and buy what they needed for the festival, or to give something to the poor.

13.30 Judas accepted the bread and went out at once. It was night.

13.31 After Judas had left, Jesus said, "Now the Son of Man's glory is revealed; now God's glory is revealed through him.

¹³·³² "And if God's glory is revealed through him, then God will reveal the glory of the Son of Man in himself, and he will do so at once.

¹³·³³ "My children, I shall not be with you very much longer. You will look for me; but I tell you now what I told the Jewish authorities, 'You cannot go where I am going.'

¹³·³⁴ "And now I give you a new commandment: love one another. As I have loved you, so you must love one another.

¹³·³⁵ "If you have love for one another, then everyone will know that you are my disciples."

¹³·³⁶ "Where are you going, Lord?" Simon Peter asked him. "You cannot follow me now where I am going," answered Jesus; "but later you will follow me."

¹³·³⁷ "Lord, why can't I follow you now?" asked Peter. "I am ready to die for you!"

¹³·³⁸ Jesus answered, "Are you really ready to die for me? I am telling you the truth: before the rooster crows you will say three times that you do not know me.

# 14

¹⁴·¹ "Do not be worried and upset," Jesus told them. "Believe in God and believe also in me.

¹⁴·² "There are many rooms in my Father's house, and I am going to prepare a place for you. I would not tell you this if it were not so.

¹⁴·³ "And after I go and prepare a place for you, I will come back and take you to myself, so that you will be where I am.

¹⁴·⁴ "You know the way that leads to the place where I am going."

¹⁴·⁵ Thomas said to him, "Lord, we do not know where you are going; so how can we know the way to get there?"

¹⁴·⁶ Jesus answered him, "I am the way, the truth, and the life; no one goes to the Father except by me.

¹⁴·⁷ "Now that you have known me," he said to them, "you will know my Father also, and from now on you do know him and you have seen him."

¹⁴·⁸ Philip said to him, "Lord, show us the Father; that is all we need."

¹⁴·⁹ Jesus answered, "For a long time I have been with you all; yet you do not know me, Philip? Whoever has seen me has seen the Father. Why, then, do you say, 'Show us the Father'?

¹⁴·¹⁰ "Do you not believe, Philip, that I am in the Father and the Father is in me? The words that I have spoken to you," Jesus said to

his disciples, "do not come from me. The Father, who remains in me, does his own work.

14.11 "Believe me when I say that I am in the Father and the Father is in me. If not, believe because of the things I do.

14.12 "I am telling you the truth: those who believe in me will do what I do — yes, they will do even greater things, because I am going to the Father.

14.13 "And I will do whatever you ask for in my name, so that the Father's glory will be shown through the Son.

14.14 "If you ask me for anything in my name, I will do it.

14.15 "If you love me, you will obey my commandments.

14.16 "I will ask the Father, and he will give you another Helper, who will stay with you forever.

14.17 "He is the Spirit, who reveals the truth about God. The world cannot receive him, because it cannot see him or know him. But you know him, because he remains with you and is in you.

14.18 "When I go, you will not be left all alone; I will come back to you.

14.19 "In a little while the world will see me no more, but you will see me; and because I live, you also will live.

14.20 "When that day comes, you will know that I am in my Father and that you are in me, just as I am in you.

14.21 "Those who accept my commandments and obey them are the ones who love me. My Father will love those who love me; I too will love them and reveal myself to them."

14.22 Judas (not Judas Iscariot) said, "Lord, how can it be that you will reveal yourself to us and not to the world?"

14.23 Jesus answered him, "Those who love me will obey my teaching. My Father will love them, and my Father and I will come to them and live with them.

14.24 "Those who do not love me do not obey my teaching. And the teaching you have heard is not mine, but comes from the Father, who sent me.

14.25 "I have told you this while I am still with you.

14.26 "The Helper, the Holy Spirit, whom the Father will send in my name, will teach you everything and make you remember all that I have told you.

14.27 "Peace is what I leave with you; it is my own peace that I give you. I do not give it as the world does. Do not be worried and upset; do not be afraid.

14.28 "You heard me say to you, 'I am leaving, but I will come back to you.' If you loved me, you would be glad that I am going to the Father; for he is greater than I. <sup>14.29</sup> "I have told you this now before it all happens, so that when it does happen, you will believe.

<sup>14.30</sup> "I cannot talk with you much longer, because the ruler of this world is coming. He has no power over me,

<sup>14.31</sup> "but the world must know that I love the Father; that is why I do everything as he commands me. Come, let us go from this place.

# 15

<sup>15.1</sup> "I am the real vine, and my Father is the gardener.

<sup>15.2</sup> "He breaks off every branch in me that does not bear fruit, and he prunes every branch that does bear fruit, so that it will be clean and bear more fruit.

<sup>15.3</sup> "You have been made clean already by the teaching I have given you.

<sup>15.4</sup> "Remain united to me, and I will remain united to you. A branch cannot bear fruit by itself; it can do so only if it remains in the vine. In the same way you cannot bear fruit unless you remain in me.

<sup>15.5</sup> "I am the vine, and you are the branches. Those who remain in me, and I in them, will bear much fruit; for you can do nothing without me.

<sup>15.6</sup> "Those who do not remain in me are thrown out like a branch and dry up; such branches are gathered up and thrown into the fire, where they are burned.

<sup>15.7</sup> "If you remain in me and my words remain in you, then you will ask for anything you wish, and you shall have it.

<sup>15.8</sup> "My Father's glory is shown by your bearing much fruit; and in this way you become my disciples.

<sup>15.9</sup> "I love you just as the Father loves me; remain in my love.

<sup>15.10</sup> "If you obey my commands, you will remain in my love, just as I have obeyed my Father's commands and remain in his love.

<sup>15.11</sup> "I have told you this so that my joy may be in you and that your joy may be complete.

<sup>15.12</sup> "My commandment is this: love one another, just as I love you.

<sup>15.13</sup> "The greatest love you can have for your friends is to give your life for them.

<sup>15.14</sup> "And you are my friends if you do what I command you.

<sup>15.15</sup> "I do not call you servants any longer, because servants do not know what their master is doing. Instead, I call you friends, because I have told you everything I heard from my Father.

<sup>15.16</sup> "You did not choose me; I chose you and appointed you to go and

bear much fruit, the kind of fruit that endures. And so the Father will give you whatever you ask of him in my name.

15.17 "This, then, is what I command you: love one another.

15.18 "If the world hates you, just remember that it has hated me first.

15.19 "If you belonged to the world, then the world would love you as its own. But I chose you from this world, and you do not belong to it; that is why the world hates you.

15.20 "Remember what I told you: 'Slaves are not greater than their master.' If people persecuted me, they will persecute you too; if they obeyed my teaching, they will obey yours too.

15.21 "But they will do all this to you because you are mine; for they do not know the one who sent me.

15.22 "They would not have been guilty of sin if I had not come and spoken to them; as it is, they no longer have any excuse for their sin.

15.23 "Whoever hates me hates my Father also.

15.24 "They would not have been guilty of sin if I had not done among them the things that no one else ever did; as it is, they have seen what I did, and they hate both me and my Father.

15.25 "This, however, was bound to happen so that what is written in their Law may come true: 'They hated me for no reason at all.'

15.26 "The Helper will come — the Spirit, who reveals the truth about God and who comes from the Father. I will send him to you from the Father, and he will speak about me.

15.27 "And you, too, will speak about me, because you have been with me from the very beginning.

# 16

16.1 "I have told you this, so that you will not give up your faith.

16.2 "You will be expelled from the synagogues, and the time will come when those who kill you will think that by doing this they are serving God.

16.3 "People will do these things to you because they have not known either the Father or me.

16.4 "But I have told you this, so that when the time comes for them to do these things, you will remember what I told you. I did not tell you these things at the beginning, for I was with you.

16.5 "But now I am going to him who sent me, yet none of you asks me where I am going.

16.6 "And now that I have told you, your hearts are full of sadness.

16.7 "But I am telling you the truth: it is better for you that I go away, because if I do not go, the Helper will not come to you. But if I do go away, then I will send him to you.

16.8 "And when he comes, he will prove to the people of the world that they are wrong about sin and about what is right and about God's judgment.

16.9 "They are wrong about sin, because they do not believe in me;

16.10 "they are wrong about what is right, because I am going to the Father and you will not see me any more;

16.11 "and they are wrong about judgment, because the ruler of this world has already been judged.

16.12 "I have much more to tell you, but now it would be too much for you to bear.

16.13 "When, however, the Spirit comes, who reveals the truth about God, he will lead you into all the truth. He will not speak on his own authority, but he will speak of what he hears and will tell you of things to come.

16.14 "He will give me glory, because he will take what I say and tell it to you.

16.15 "All that my Father has is mine; that is why I said that the Spirit will take what I give him and tell it to you.

16.16 "In a little while you will not see me any more, and then a little while later you will see me."

16.17 Some of his disciples asked among themselves, "What does this mean? He tells us that in a little while we will not see him, and then a little while later we will see him; and he also says, 'It is because I am going to the Father.'

16.18 "What does this 'a little while' mean? We don't know what he is talking about!"

16.19 Jesus knew that they wanted to question him, so he said to them, "I said, 'In a little while you will not see me, and then a little while later you will see me.' Is this what you are asking about among yourselves?

16.20 "I am telling you the truth: you will cry and weep, but the world will be glad; you will be sad, but your sadness will turn into gladness.

16.21 "When a woman is about to give birth, she is sad because her hour of suffering has come; but when the baby is born, she forgets her suffering, because she is happy that a baby has been born into the world.

16.22 "That is how it is with you: now you are sad, but I will see you again, and your hearts will be filled with gladness, the kind of gladness that no one can take away from you.

<sup>16.23</sup> "When that day comes, you will not ask me for anything. I am telling you the truth: the Father will give you whatever you ask of him in my name.

<sup>16.24</sup> "Until now you have not asked for anything in my name; ask and you will receive, so that your happiness may be complete.

<sup>16.25</sup> "I have used figures of speech to tell you these things. But the time will come when I will not use figures of speech, but will speak to you plainly about the Father.

<sup>16.26</sup> "When that day comes, you will ask him in my name; and I do not say that I will ask him on your behalf,

<sup>16.27</sup> "for the Father himself loves you. He loves you because you love me and have believed that I came from God.

<sup>16.28</sup> "I did come from the Father, and I came into the world; and now I am leaving the world and going to the Father."

<sup>16.29</sup> Then his disciples said to him, "Now you are speaking plainly, without using figures of speech.

<sup>16.30</sup> "We know now that you know everything; you do not need to have someone ask you questions. This makes us believe that you came from God."

<sup>16.31</sup> Jesus answered them, "Do you believe now?

<sup>16.32</sup> "The time is coming, and is already here, when all of you will be scattered, each of you to your own home, and I will be left all alone. But I am not really alone, because the Father is with me.

<sup>16.33</sup> "I have told you this so that you will have peace by being united to me. The world will make you suffer. But be brave! I have defeated the world!"

# 17

<sup>17.1</sup> After Jesus finished saying this, he looked up to heaven and said, "Father, the hour has come. Give glory to your Son, so that the Son may give glory to you.

<sup>17.2</sup> "For you gave him authority over all people, so that he might give eternal life to all those you gave him.

<sup>17.3</sup> "And eternal life means to know you, the only true God, and to know Jesus Christ, whom you sent.

<sup>17.4</sup> "I have shown your glory on earth; I have finished the work you gave me to do.

<sup>17.5</sup> "Father! Give me glory in your presence now, the same glory I had with you before the world was made.

<sup>17.6</sup> "I have made you known to those you gave me out of the world. They belonged to you, and you gave them to me. They have obeyed

your word,

<sup>17.7</sup> "and now they **know** that everything you gave me comes from you. <sup>17.8</sup> "I **gave** them the message that you gave me, and they **received** it; they **know** that it is true that I came from you, and they **believe** that you sent me.

<sup>17.9</sup> "I **pray** for them. I do not **pray** for the world but for those you gave me, for they **belong** to you.

<sup>17.10</sup> "All I have is yours, and all you have is mine; and my glory is shown through them.

<sup>17.11</sup> "And now I **am** coming to you; I **am** no longer in the world, but they **are** in the world. Holy Father! **Keep** them safe by the power of your name, the name you gave me, so that they may be one just as you and I are one.

<sup>17.12</sup> "While I was with them, I **kept** them safe by the power of your name, the name you gave me. I **protected** them, and not one of them **was** lost, except the man who was bound to be lost — so that the scripture might come true.

<sup>17.13</sup> "And now I **am** coming to you, and I **say** these things in the world so that they might have my joy in their hearts in all its fullness.

<sup>17.14</sup> "I **gave** them your message, and the world **hated** them, because they do not belong to the world, just as I do not belong to the world.

<sup>17.15</sup> "I do not **ask** you to take them out of the world, but I do **ask** you to keep them safe from the Evil One.

<sup>17.16</sup> "Just as I do not belong to the world, they do not **belong** to the world.

<sup>17.17</sup> "**Dedicate** them to yourself by means of the truth; your word is truth.

<sup>17.18</sup> "I **sent** them into the world, just as you sent me into the world.

<sup>17.19</sup> "And for their sake I **dedicate** myself to you, in order that they, too, may be truly dedicated to you.

<sup>17.20</sup> "I **pray** not only for them, but also for those who believe in me because of their message.

<sup>17.21</sup> "I **pray** that they may all be one. Father! May they be in us, just as you are in me and I am in you. May they be one, so that the world will believe that you sent me.

<sup>17.22</sup> "I **gave** them the same glory you gave me, so that they may be one, just as you and I are one:

<sup>17.23</sup> "I in them and you in me, so that they may be completely one, in order that the world may know that you sent me and that you love them as you love me.

<sup>17.24</sup> "Father! You have given them to me, and I **want** them to be with

me where I am, so that they may see my glory, the glory you gave me; for you loved me before the world was made.

17.25 "Righteous Father! The world does not know you, but I know you, and these know that you sent me.

17.26 "I made you known to them, and I will continue to do so, in order that the love you have for me may be in them, and so that I also may be in them."

# 18

18.1 After Jesus had said this prayer, he left with his disciples and went across Kidron Brook. There was a garden in that place, and Jesus and his disciples went in.

18.2 Judas, the traitor, knew where it was, because many times Jesus had met there with his disciples.

18.3 So Judas went to the garden, taking with him a group of Roman soldiers, and some Temple guards sent by the chief priests and the Pharisees; they were armed and carried lanterns and torches.

18.4 Jesus knew everything that was going to happen to him, so he stepped forward and asked them, "Who is it you are looking for?"

18.5 "Jesus of Nazareth," they answered. "I am he," he said. Judas, the traitor, was standing there with them.

18.6 When Jesus said to them, "I am he," they moved back and fell to the ground.

18.7 Again Jesus asked them, "Who is it you are looking for?" "Jesus of Nazareth," they said.

18.8 "I have already told you that I am he," Jesus said. "If, then, you are looking for me, let these others go."

18.9 (He said this so that what he had said might come true: "Father, I have not lost even one of those you gave me.")

18.10 Simon Peter, who had a sword, drew it and struck the High Priest's slave, cutting off his right ear. The name of the slave was Malchus.

18.11 Jesus said to Peter, "Put your sword back in its place! Do you think that I will not drink the cup of suffering which my Father has given me?"

18.12 Then the Roman soldiers with their commanding officer and the Jewish guards arrested Jesus, tied him up,

18.13 and took him first to Annas. He was the father-in-law of Caiaphas, who was High Priest that year.

18.14 It was Caiaphas who had advised the Jewish authorities that it was better that one man should die for all the people.

<sup>18.15</sup> Simon Peter and another disciple followed Jesus. That other disciple was well known to the High Priest, so he went with Jesus into the courtyard of the High Priest's house,

<sup>18.16</sup> while Peter stayed outside by the gate. Then the other disciple went back out, spoke to the girl at the gate, and brought Peter inside. <sup>18.17</sup> The girl at the gate said to Peter, "Aren't you also one of the disciples of that man?" "No, I am not," answered Peter.

<sup>18.18</sup> It was cold, so the servants and guards had built a charcoal fire and were standing around it, warming themselves. So Peter went over and stood with them, warming himself.

<sup>18.19</sup> The High Priest questioned Jesus about his disciples and about his teaching.

<sup>18.20</sup> Jesus answered, "I have always spoken publicly to everyone; all my teaching was done in the synagogues and in the Temple, where all the people come together. I have never said anything in secret.

<sup>18.21</sup> "Why, then, do you question me? Question the people who heard me. Ask them what I told them — they know what I said."

<sup>18.22</sup> When Jesus said this, one of the guards there slapped him and said, "How dare you talk like that to the High Priest!"

<sup>18.23</sup> Jesus answered him, "If I have said anything wrong, tell everyone here what it was. But if I am right in what I have said, why do you hit me?"

<sup>18.24</sup> Then Annas sent him, still tied up, to Caiaphas the High Priest.

<sup>18.25</sup> Peter was still standing there keeping himself warm. So the others said to him, "Aren't you also one of the disciples of that man?" But Peter denied it. "No, I am not," he said.

<sup>18.26</sup> One of the High Priest's slaves, a relative of the man whose ear Peter had cut off, spoke up. "Didn't I see you with him in the garden?" he asked.

<sup>18.27</sup> Again Peter said "No" — and at once a rooster crowed.

<sup>18.28</sup> Early in the morning Jesus was taken from Caiaphas' house to the governor's palace. The Jewish authorities did not go inside the palace, for they wanted to keep themselves ritually clean, in order to be able to eat the Passover meal.

<sup>18.29</sup> So Pilate went outside to them and asked, "What do you accuse this man of?"

<sup>18.30</sup> Their answer was, "We would not have brought him to you if he had not committed a crime."

<sup>18.31</sup> Pilate said to them, "Then you yourselves take him and try him according to your own law." They replied, "We are not allowed to put anyone to death."

<sup>18.32</sup> (This happened in order to make come true what Jesus had said when he indicated the kind of death he would die.)
<sup>18.33</sup> Pilate went back into the palace and called Jesus. "Are you the king of the Jews?" he asked him.
<sup>18.34</sup> Jesus answered, "Does this question come from you or have others told you about me?"
<sup>18.35</sup> Pilate replied, "Do you think I am a Jew? It was your own people and the chief priests who handed you over to me. What have you done?"
<sup>18.36</sup> Jesus said, "My kingdom does not belong to this world; if my kingdom belonged to this world, my followers would fight to keep me from being handed over to the Jewish authorities. No, my kingdom does not belong here!"
<sup>18.37</sup> So Pilate asked him, "Are you a king, then?" Jesus answered, "You say that I am a king. I was born and came into the world for this one purpose, to speak about the truth. Whoever belongs to the truth listens to me."
<sup>18.38</sup> "And what is truth?" Pilate asked. Then Pilate went back outside to the people and said to them, "I cannot find any reason to condemn him.
<sup>18.39</sup> "But according to the custom you have, I always set free a prisoner for you during the Passover. Do you want me to set free for you the king of the Jews?"
<sup>18.40</sup> They answered him with a shout, "No, not him! We want Barabbas!" (Barabbas was a bandit.)

# 19

<sup>19.1</sup> Then Pilate took Jesus and had him whipped.
<sup>19.2</sup> The soldiers made a crown out of thorny branches and put it on his head; then they put a purple robe on him
<sup>19.3</sup> and came to him and said, "Long live the King of the Jews!" And they went up and slapped him.
<sup>19.4</sup> Pilate went back out once more and said to the crowd, "Look, I will bring him out here to you to let you see that I cannot find any reason to condemn him."
<sup>19.5</sup> So Jesus came out, wearing the crown of thorns and the purple robe. Pilate said to them, "Look! Here is the man!"
<sup>19.6</sup> When the chief priests and the Temple guards saw him, they shouted, "Crucify him! Crucify him!" Pilate said to them, "You take him, then, and crucify him. I find no reason to condemn him."
<sup>19.7</sup> The crowd answered back, "We have a law that says he ought to

die, because he claimed to be the Son of God."

<sup>19.8</sup> When Pilate heard this, he was even more afraid.

<sup>19.9</sup> He went back into the palace and asked Jesus, "Where do you come from?" But Jesus did not answer.

<sup>19.10</sup> Pilate said to him, "You will not speak to me? Remember, I have the authority to set you free and also to have you crucified."

<sup>19.11</sup> Jesus answered, "You have authority over me only because it was given to you by God. So the man who handed me over to you is guilty of a worse sin."

<sup>19.12</sup> When Pilate heard this, he tried to find a way to set Jesus free. But the crowd shouted back, "If you set him free, that means that you are not the Emperor's friend! Anyone who claims to be a king is a rebel against the Emperor!"

<sup>19.13</sup> When Pilate heard these words, he took Jesus outside and sat down on the judge's seat in the place called "The Stone Pavement." (In Hebrew the name is "Gabbatha.")

<sup>19.14</sup> It was then almost noon of the day before the Passover. Pilate said to the people, "Here is your king!"

<sup>19.15</sup> They shouted back, "Kill him! Kill him! Crucify him!" Pilate asked them, "Do you want me to crucify your king?" The chief priests answered, "The only king we have is the Emperor!"

<sup>19.16</sup> Then Pilate handed Jesus over to them to be crucified. So they took charge of Jesus.

<sup>19.17</sup> He went out, carrying his cross, and came to "The Place of the Skull," as it is called. (In Hebrew it is called "Golgotha.")

<sup>19.18</sup> There they crucified him; and they also crucified two other men, one on each side, with Jesus between them.

<sup>19.19</sup> Pilate wrote a notice and had it put on the cross. "Jesus of Nazareth, the King of the Jews," is what he wrote.

<sup>19.20</sup> Many people read it, because the place where Jesus was crucified was not far from the city. The notice was written in Hebrew, Latin, and Greek.

<sup>19.21</sup> The chief priests said to Pilate, "Do not write 'The King of the Jews,' but rather, 'This man said, I am the King of the Jews.'"

<sup>19.22</sup> Pilate answered, "What I have written stays written."

<sup>19.23</sup> After the soldiers had crucified Jesus, they took his clothes and divided them into four parts, one part for each soldier. They also took the robe, which was made of one piece of woven cloth without any seams in it.

<sup>19.24</sup> The soldiers said to one another, "Let's not tear it; let's throw dice to see who will get it." This happened in order to make the

scripture come true: "They divided my clothes among themselves and gambled for my robe." And this is what the soldiers did.

<sup>19.25</sup> Standing close to Jesus' cross were his mother, his mother's sister, Mary the wife of Clopas, and Mary Magdalene.

<sup>19.26</sup> Jesus saw his mother and the disciple he loved standing there; so he said to his mother, "He is your son."

<sup>19.27</sup> Then he said to the disciple, "She is your mother." From that time the disciple took her to live in his home.

<sup>19.28</sup> Jesus knew that by now everything had been completed; and in order to make the scripture come true, he said, "I am thirsty."

<sup>19.29</sup> A bowl was there, full of cheap wine; so a sponge was soaked in the wine, put on a stalk of hyssop, and lifted up to his lips.

<sup>19.30</sup> Jesus drank the wine and said, "It is finished!" Then he bowed his head and gave up his spirit.

<sup>19.31</sup> Then the Jewish authorities asked Pilate to allow them to break the legs of the men who had been crucified, and to take the bodies down from the crosses. They requested this because it was Friday, and they did not want the bodies to stay on the crosses on the Sabbath, since the coming Sabbath was especially holy.

<sup>19.32</sup> So the soldiers went and broke the legs of the first man and then of the other man who had been crucified with Jesus.

<sup>19.33</sup> But when they came to Jesus, they saw that he was already dead, so they did not break his legs.

<sup>19.34</sup> One of the soldiers, however, plunged his spear into Jesus' side, and at once blood and water poured out.

<sup>19.35</sup> (The one who saw this happen has spoken of it, so that you also may believe. What he said is true, and he knows that he speaks the truth.)

<sup>19.36</sup> This was done to make the scripture come true: "Not one of his bones will be broken."

<sup>19.37</sup> And there is another scripture that says, "People will look at him whom they pierced."

<sup>19.38</sup> After this, Joseph, who was from the town of Arimathea, asked Pilate if he could take Jesus' body. (Joseph was a follower of Jesus, but in secret, because he was afraid of the Jewish authorities.) Pilate told him he could have the body, so Joseph went and took it away.

<sup>19.39</sup> Nicodemus, who at first had gone to see Jesus at night, went with Joseph, taking with him about one hundred pounds of spices, a mixture of myrrh and aloes.

<sup>19.40</sup> The two men took Jesus' body and wrapped it in linen cloths with the spices according to the Jewish custom of preparing a body

for burial.

<sup>19.41</sup> There was a garden in the place where Jesus had been put to death, and in it there was a new tomb where no one had ever been buried.

<sup>19.42</sup> Since it was the day before the Sabbath and because the tomb was close by, they placed Jesus' body there.

# 20

<sup>20.1</sup> Early on Sunday morning, while it was still dark, Mary Magdalene went to the tomb and saw that the stone had been taken away from the entrance.

<sup>20.2</sup> She went running to Simon Peter and the other disciple, whom Jesus loved, and told them, "They have taken the Lord from the tomb, and we don't know where they have put him!"

<sup>20.3</sup> Then Peter and the other disciple went to the tomb.

<sup>20.4</sup> The two of them were running, but the other disciple ran faster than Peter and reached the tomb first.

<sup>20.5</sup> He bent over and saw the linen cloths, but he did not go in.

<sup>20.6</sup> Behind him came Simon Peter, and he went straight into the tomb. He saw the linen cloths lying there

<sup>20.7</sup> and the cloth which had been around Jesus' head. It was not lying with the linen cloths but was rolled up by itself.

<sup>20.8</sup> Then the other disciple, who had reached the tomb first, also went in; he saw and believed.

<sup>20.9</sup> (They still did not understand the scripture which said that he must rise from death.)

<sup>20.10</sup> Then the disciples went back home.

<sup>20.11</sup> Mary stood crying outside the tomb. While she was still crying, she bent over and looked in the tomb

<sup>20.12</sup> and saw two angels there dressed in white, sitting where the body of Jesus had been, one at the head and the other at the feet.

<sup>20.13</sup> "Woman, why are you crying?" they asked her. She answered, "They have taken my Lord away, and I do not know where they have put him!"

<sup>20.14</sup> Then she turned around and saw Jesus standing there; but she did not know that it was Jesus.

<sup>20.15</sup> "Woman, why are you crying?" Jesus asked her. "Who is it that you are looking for?" She thought he was the gardener, so she said to him, "If you took him away, sir, tell me where you have put him, and I will go and get him."

<sup>20.16</sup> Jesus said to her, "Mary!" She turned toward him and said in

Hebrew, "Rabboni!" (This means "Teacher.")

<sup>20.17</sup> "Do not hold on to me," Jesus told her, "because I have not yet gone back up to the Father. But go to my brothers and tell them that I am returning to him who is my Father and their Father, my God and their God."

<sup>20.18</sup> So Mary Magdalene went and told the disciples that she had seen the Lord and related to them what he had told her.

<sup>20.19</sup> It was late that Sunday evening, and the disciples were gathered together behind locked doors, because they were afraid of the Jewish authorities. Then Jesus came and stood among them. "Peace be with you," he said.

<sup>20.20</sup> After saying this, he showed them his hands and his side. The disciples were filled with joy at seeing the Lord.

<sup>20.21</sup> Jesus said to them again, "Peace be with you. As the Father sent me, so I send you."

<sup>20.22</sup> Then he breathed on them and said, "Receive the Holy Spirit.

<sup>20.23</sup> "If you forgive people's sins, they are forgiven; if you do not forgive them, they are not forgiven."

<sup>20.24</sup> One of the twelve disciples, Thomas (called the Twin), was not with them when Jesus came.

<sup>20.25</sup> So the other disciples told him, "We have seen the Lord!" Thomas said to them, "Unless I see the scars of the nails in his hands and put my finger on those scars and my hand in his side, I will not believe."

<sup>20.26</sup> A week later the disciples were together again indoors, and Thomas was with them. The doors were locked, but Jesus came and stood among them and said, "Peace be with you."

<sup>20.27</sup> Then he said to Thomas, "Put your finger here, and look at my hands; then reach out your hand and put it in my side. Stop your doubting, and believe!"

<sup>20.28</sup> Thomas answered him, "My Lord and my God!"

<sup>20.29</sup> Jesus said to him, "Do you believe because you see me? How happy are those who believe without seeing me!"

<sup>20.30</sup> In his disciples' presence Jesus performed many other miracles which are not written down in this book.

<sup>20.31</sup> But these have been written in order that you may believe that Jesus is the Messiah, the Son of God, and that through your faith in him you may have life.

# 21

<sup>21.1</sup> After this, Jesus appeared once more to his disciples at Lake Ti-

berias. This is how it happened.

<sup>21.2</sup> Simon Peter, Thomas (called the Twin), Nathanael (the one from Cana in Galilee), the sons of Zebedee, and two other disciples of Jesus were all together.

<sup>21.3</sup> Simon Peter said to the others, "I am going fishing." "We will come with you," they told him. So they went out in a boat, but all that night they did not catch a thing.

<sup>21.4</sup> As the sun was rising, Jesus stood at the water's edge, but the disciples did not know that it was Jesus.

<sup>21.5</sup> Then he asked them, "Young men, haven't you caught anything?" "Not a thing," they answered.

<sup>21.6</sup> He said to them, "Throw your net out on the right side of the boat, and you will catch some." So they threw the net out and could not pull it back in, because they had caught so many fish.

<sup>21.7</sup> The disciple whom Jesus loved said to Peter, "It is the Lord!" When Peter heard that it was the Lord, he wrapped his outer garment around him (for he had taken his clothes off) and jumped into the water.

<sup>21.8</sup> The other disciples came to shore in the boat, pulling the net full of fish. They were not very far from land, about a hundred yards away.

<sup>21.9</sup> When they stepped ashore, they saw a charcoal fire there with fish on it and some bread.

<sup>21.10</sup> Then Jesus said to them, "Bring some of the fish you have just caught."

<sup>21.11</sup> Simon Peter went aboard and dragged the net ashore full of big fish, a hundred and fifty-three in all; even though there were so many, still the net did not tear.

<sup>21.12</sup> Jesus said to them, "Come and eat." None of the disciples dared ask him, "Who are you?" because they knew it was the Lord.

<sup>21.13</sup> So Jesus went over, took the bread, and gave it to them; he did the same with the fish.

<sup>21.14</sup> This, then, was the third time Jesus appeared to the disciples after he was raised from death.

<sup>21.15</sup> After they had eaten, Jesus said to Simon Peter, "Simon son of John, do you love me more than these others do?" "Yes, Lord," he answered, "you know that I love you." Jesus said to him, "Take care of my lambs."

<sup>21.16</sup> A second time Jesus said to him, "Simon son of John, do you love me?" "Yes, Lord," he answered, "you know that I love you." Jesus said to him, "Take care of my sheep."

<sup>21.17</sup> A third time Jesus said, "Simon son of John, do you love me?" Peter became sad because Jesus asked him the third time, "Do you love me?" and so he said to him, "Lord, you know everything; you know that I love you!" Jesus said to him, "Take care of my sheep.

<sup>21.18</sup> "I am telling you the truth: when you were young, you used to get ready and go anywhere you wanted to; but when you are old, you will stretch out your hands and someone else will tie you up and take you where you don't want to go."

<sup>21.19</sup> (In saying this, Jesus was indicating the way in which Peter would die and bring glory to God.) Then Jesus said to him, "Follow me!"

<sup>21.20</sup> Peter turned around and saw behind him that other disciple, whom Jesus loved — the one who had leaned close to Jesus at the meal and had asked, "Lord, who is going to betray you?"

<sup>21.21</sup> When Peter saw him, he asked Jesus, "Lord, what about this man?"

<sup>21.22</sup> Jesus answered him, "If I want him to live until I come, what is that to you? Follow me!"

<sup>21.23</sup> So a report spread among the followers of Jesus that this disciple would not die. But Jesus did not say he would not die; he said, "If I want him to live until I come, what is that to you?"

<sup>21.24</sup> He is the disciple who spoke of these things, the one who also wrote them down; and we know that what he said is true.

<sup>21.25</sup> Now, there are many other things that Jesus did. If they were all written down one by one, I suppose that the whole world could not hold the books that would be written.

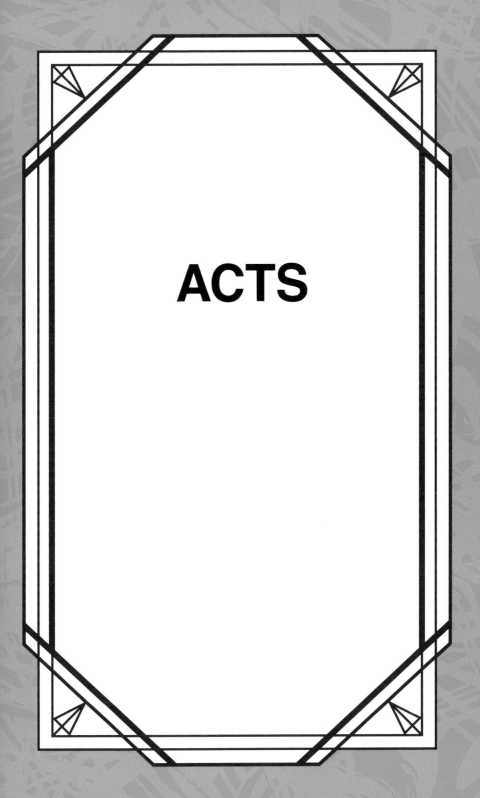

# ACTS

# Acts

# 1

1.1 Dear Theophilus:

In my first book I wrote about all the things that Jesus did and taught from the time he began his work 1.2 until the day he was taken up to heaven. Before he was taken up, he gave instructions by the power of the Holy Spirit to the men he had chosen as his apostles.

1.3 For forty days after his death he appeared to them many times in ways that proved beyond doubt that he was alive. They saw him, and he talked with them about the Kingdom of God.

1.4 And when they came together, he gave them this order: "Do not leave Jerusalem, but wait for the gift I told you about, the gift my Father promised.

1.5 "John baptized with water, but in a few days you will be baptized with the Holy Spirit."

1.6 When the apostles met together with Jesus, they asked him, "Lord, will you at this time give the Kingdom back to Israel?"

1.7 Jesus said to them, "The times and occasions are set by my Father's own authority, and it is not for you to know when they will be.

1.8 "But when the Holy Spirit comes upon you, you will be filled with power, and you will be witnesses for me in Jerusalem, in all of Judea and Samaria, and to the ends of the earth."

1.9 After saying this, he was taken up to heaven as they watched him, and a cloud hid him from their sight.

1.10 They still had their eyes fixed on the sky as he went away, when two men dressed in white suddenly stood beside them

1.11 and said, "Galileans, why are you standing there looking up at the sky? This Jesus, who was taken from you into heaven, will come back in the same way that you saw him go to heaven."

1.12 Then the apostles went back to Jerusalem from the Mount of Olives, which is about half a mile away from the city.

1.13 They entered the city and went up to the room where they were staying: Peter, John, James and Andrew, Philip and Thomas, Bartholomew and Matthew, James son of Alphaeus, Simon the Patriot, and Judas son of James.

1.14 They gathered frequently to pray as a group, together with the women and with Mary the mother of Jesus and with his brothers.

1.15 A few days later there was a meeting of the believers, about a hundred and twenty in all, and Peter stood up to speak.

1.16 "My friends," he said, "the scripture had to come true in which the Holy Spirit, speaking through David, made a prediction about Judas, who was the guide for those who arrested Jesus.

1.17 Judas was a member of our group, for he had been chosen to have a part in our work."

1.18 (With the money that Judas got for his evil act he bought a field, where he fell to his death; he burst open and all his insides spilled out.

1.19 All the people living in Jerusalem heard about it, and so in their own language they call that field Akeldama, which means "Field of Blood.")

1.20 "For it is written in the book of Psalms, 'May his house become empty; may no one live in it.' It is also written, 'May someone else take his place of service.'

1.21-22 "So then, someone must join us as a witness to the resurrection of the Lord Jesus. He must be one of the men who were in our group during the whole time that the Lord Jesus traveled about with us, beginning from the time John preached his message of baptism until the day Jesus was taken up from us to heaven."

1.23 So they proposed two men: Joseph, who was called Barsabbas (also known as Justus), and Matthias.

1.24 Then they prayed, "Lord, you know the thoughts of everyone, so show us which of these two you have chosen

1.25 "to serve as an apostle in the place of Judas, who left to go to the place where he belongs."

1.26 Then they drew lots to choose between the two men, and the one chosen was Matthias, who was added to the group of eleven apostles.

# 2

2.1 When the day of Pentecost came, all the believers were gathered together in one place.

2.2 Suddenly there was a noise from the sky which sounded like a strong wind blowing, and it filled the whole house where they were sitting.

2.3 Then they saw what looked like tongues of fire which spread out and touched each person there.

2.4 They were all filled with the Holy Spirit and began to talk in other languages, as the Spirit enabled them to speak.

2.5 There were Jews living in Jerusalem, religious people who had come from every country in the world.

2.6 When they heard this noise, a large crowd gathered. They were all excited, because all of them heard the believers talking in their own languages.

2.7 In amazement and wonder they exclaimed, "These people who are talking like this are Galileans!

2.8 "How is it, then, that all of us hear them speaking in our own native languages?

2.9 "We are from Parthia, Media, and Elam; from Mesopotamia, Judea, and Cappadocia; from Pontus and Asia,

2.10 "from Phrygia and Pamphylia, from Egypt and the regions of Libya near Cyrene. Some of us are from Rome,

2.11 "both Jews and Gentiles converted to Judaism, and some of us are from Crete and Arabia — yet all of us hear them speaking in our own languages about the great things that God has done!"

2.12 Amazed and confused, they kept asking each other, "What does this mean?"

2.13 But others made fun of the believers, saying, "These people are drunk!"

2.14 Then Peter stood up with the other eleven apostles and in a loud voice began to speak to the crowd: "Fellow Jews and all of you who live in Jerusalem, listen to me and let me tell you what this means.

2.15 "These people are not drunk, as you suppose; it is only nine o'clock in the morning.

2.16 "Instead, this is what the prophet Joel spoke about:

2.17 " 'This is what I will do in the last days, God says: I will pour out my Spirit on everyone. Your sons and daughters will proclaim my message; your young men will see visions, and your old men will have dreams.

2.18 " 'Yes, even on my servants, both men and women, I will pour out my Spirit in those days, and they will proclaim my message.

2.19 " 'I will perform miracles in the sky above and wonders on the earth below. There will be blood, fire, and thick smoke;

2.20 " 'the sun will be darkened, and the moon will turn red as blood, before the great and glorious Day of the Lord comes.

2.21 " 'And then, whoever calls out to the Lord for help will be saved.' "

2.22 "Listen to these words, fellow Israelites! Jesus of Nazareth was a man whose divine authority was clearly proven to you by all the miracles and wonders which God performed through him. You yourselves know this, for it happened here among you.

2.23 "In accordance with his own plan God had already decided that Jesus would be handed over to you; and you killed him by letting sinful men crucify him. 

2.24 "But God raised him from death, setting him free from its power, because it was impossible that death should hold him prisoner. 

2.25 "For David said about him, 'I saw the Lord before me at all times; he is near me, and I will not be troubled. 

2.26 " 'And so I am filled with gladness, and my words are full of joy. And I, mortal though I am, will rest assured in hope, 

2.27 " 'because you will not abandon me in the world of the dead; you will not allow your faithful servant to rot in the grave. 

2.28 " 'You have shown me the paths that lead to life, and your presence will fill me with joy.' " 

2.29 "My friends, I must speak to you plainly about our famous ancestor King David. He died and was buried, and his grave is here with us to this very day. 

2.30 "He was a prophet, and he knew what God had promised him: God had made a vow that he would make one of David's descendants a king, just as David was. 

2.31 "David saw what God was going to do in the future, and so he spoke about the resurrection of the Messiah when he said, 'He was not abandoned in the world of the dead; his body did not rot in the grave.' 

2.32 "God has raised this very Jesus from death, and we are all witnesses to this fact. 

2.33 "He has been raised to the right side of God, his Father, and has received from him the Holy Spirit, as he had promised. What you now see and hear is his gift that he has poured out on us. 

2.34 "For it was not David who went up into heaven; rather he said, 'The Lord said to my Lord: Sit here at my right side 

2.35 " 'until I put your enemies as a footstool under your feet.' " 

2.36 "All the people of Israel, then, are to know for sure that this Jesus, whom you crucified, is the one that God has made Lord and Messiah!" 

2.37 When the people heard this, they were deeply troubled and said to Peter and the other apostles, "What shall we do, brothers?" 

2.38 Peter said to them, "Each one of you must turn away from your sins and be baptized in the name of Jesus Christ, so that your sins will be forgiven; and you will receive God's gift, the Holy Spirit. 

2.39 "For God's promise was made to you and your children, and to all who are far away — all whom the Lord our God calls to himself." 

2.40 Peter made his appeal to them and with many other words he urged them, saying, "Save yourselves from the punishment coming on this wicked people!"

<sup>2.41</sup> Many of them believed his message and were baptized, and about three thousand people were added to the group that day.

<sup>2.42</sup> They spent their time in learning from the apostles, taking part in the fellowship, and sharing in the fellowship meals and the prayers.

<sup>2.43</sup> Many miracles and wonders were being done through the apostles, and everyone was filled with awe.

<sup>2.44</sup> All the believers continued together in close fellowship and shared their belongings with one another.

<sup>2.45</sup> They would sell their property and possessions, and distribute the money among all, according to what each one needed.

<sup>2.46</sup> Day after day they met as a group in the Temple, and they had their meals together in their homes, eating with glad and humble hearts,

<sup>2.47</sup> praising God, and enjoying the good will of all the people. And every day the Lord added to their group those who were being saved.

# 3

<sup>3.1</sup> One day Peter and John went to the Temple at three o'clock in the afternoon, the hour for prayer.

<sup>3.2</sup> There at the Beautiful Gate, as it was called, was a man who had been lame all his life. Every day he was carried to the gate to beg for money from the people who were going into the Temple.

<sup>3.3</sup> When he saw Peter and John going in, he begged them to give him something.

<sup>3.4</sup> They looked straight at him, and Peter said, "Look at us!"

<sup>3.5</sup> So he looked at them, expecting to get something from them.

<sup>3.6</sup> But Peter said to him, "I have no money at all, but I give you what I have: in the name of Jesus Christ of Nazareth I order you to get up and walk!"

<sup>3.7</sup> Then he took him by his right hand and helped him up. At once the man's feet and ankles became strong;

<sup>3.8</sup> he jumped up, stood on his feet, and started walking around. Then he went into the Temple with them, walking and jumping and praising God.

<sup>3.9</sup> The people there saw him walking and praising God,

<sup>3.10</sup> and when they recognized him as the beggar who had sat at the Beautiful Gate, they were all surprised and amazed at what had happened to him.

<sup>3.11</sup> As the man held on to Peter and John in Solomon's Porch, as it

was called, the people were amazed and ran to them.

3.12 When Peter saw the people, he said to them, "Fellow Israelites, why are you surprised at this, and why do you stare at us? Do you think that it was by means of our own power or godliness that we made this man walk?

3.13 "The God of Abraham, Isaac, and Jacob, the God of our ancestors, has given divine glory to his Servant Jesus. But you handed him over to the authorities, and you rejected him in Pilate's presence, even after Pilate had decided to set him free.

3.14 "He was holy and good, but you rejected him, and instead you asked Pilate to do you the favor of turning loose a murderer.

3.15 "You killed the one who leads to life, but God raised him from death — and we are witnesses to this.

3.16 "It was the power of his name that gave strength to this lame man. What you see and know was done by faith in his name; it was faith in Jesus that has made him well, as you can all see.

3.17 "And now, my friends, I know that what you and your leaders did to Jesus was due to your ignorance.

3.18 "God announced long ago through all the prophets that his Messiah had to suffer; and he made it come true in this way.

3.19 "Repent, then, and turn to God, so that he will forgive your sins. If you do,

3.20 "times of spiritual strength will come from the Lord, and he will send Jesus, who is the Messiah he has already chosen for you.

3.21 "He must remain in heaven until the time comes for all things to be made new, as God announced through his holy prophets of long ago.

3.22 "For Moses said, 'The Lord your God will send you a prophet, just as he sent me, and he will be one of your own people. You are to obey everything that he tells you to do.

3.23 " 'Anyone who does not obey that prophet shall be separated from God's people and destroyed.' "

3.24 "And all the prophets who had a message, including Samuel and those who came after him, also announced what has been happening these days.

3.25 "The promises of God through his prophets are for you, and you share in the covenant which God made with your ancestors. As he said to Abraham, 'Through your descendants I will bless all the people on earth.'"

3.26 "And so God chose his Servant and sent him to you first, to bless you by making every one of you turn away from your wicked ways."

**4** <sup>4.1</sup> Peter and John were still speaking to the people when some priests, the officer in charge of the Temple guards, and some Sadducees arrived. <sup>4.2</sup> They were annoyed because the two apostles were teaching the people that Jesus had risen from death, which proved that the dead will rise to life. <sup>4.3</sup> So they arrested them and put them in jail until the next day, since it was already late. <sup>4.4</sup> But many who heard the message believed; and the number grew to about five thousand.

<sup>4.5</sup> The next day the Jewish leaders, the elders, and the teachers of the Law gathered in Jerusalem. <sup>4.6</sup> They met with the High Priest Annas and with Caiaphas, John, Alexander, and the others who belonged to the High Priest's family. <sup>4.7</sup> They made the apostles stand before them and asked them, "How did you do this? What power do you have or whose name did you use?"

<sup>4.8</sup> Peter, full of the Holy Spirit, answered them, "Leaders of the people and elders: <sup>4.9</sup> "if we are being questioned today about the good deed done to the lame man and how he was healed, <sup>4.10</sup> "then you should all know, and all the people of Israel should know, that this man stands here before you completely well through the power of the name of Jesus Christ of Nazareth — whom you crucified and whom God raised from death. <sup>4.11</sup> "Jesus is the one of whom the scripture says, 'The stone that you the builders despised turned out to be the most important of all.' <sup>4.12</sup> "Salvation is to be found through him alone; in all the world there is no one else whom God has given who can save us."

<sup>4.13</sup> The members of the Council were amazed to see how bold Peter and John were and to learn that they were ordinary men of no education. They realized then that they had been companions of Jesus. <sup>4.14</sup> But there was nothing that they could say, because they saw the man who had been healed standing there with Peter and John. <sup>4.15</sup> So they told them to leave the Council room, and then they started discussing among themselves. <sup>4.16</sup> "What shall we do with these men?" they asked. "Everyone in Jerusalem knows that this extraordinary miracle has been performed by them, and we cannot deny it. <sup>4.17</sup> "But to keep this matter from spreading any further among the people, let us warn these men never again to speak to anyone in the

name of Jesus."

4.18 So they called them back in and told them that under no condition were they to speak or to teach in the name of Jesus.

4.19 But Peter and John answered them, "You yourselves judge which is right in God's sight — to obey you or to obey God.

4.20 "For we cannot stop speaking of what we ourselves have seen and heard."

4.21 So the Council warned them even more strongly and then set them free. They saw that it was impossible to punish them, because the people were all praising God for what had happened.

4.22 The man on whom this miracle of healing had been performed was over forty years old.

4.23 As soon as Peter and John were set free, they returned to their group and told them what the chief priests and the elders had said.

4.24 When the believers heard it, they all joined together in prayer to God: "Master and Creator of heaven, earth, and sea, and all that is in them!

4.25 "By means of the Holy Spirit you spoke through our ancestor David, your servant, when he said, 'Why were the Gentiles furious; why did people make their useless plots?

4.26 " 'The kings of the earth prepared themselves, and the rulers met together against the Lord and his Messiah.'

4.27 "For indeed Herod and Pontius Pilate met together in this city with the Gentiles and the people of Israel against Jesus, your holy Servant, whom you made Messiah.

4.28 "They gathered to do everything that you by your power and will had already decided would happen.

4.29 "And now, Lord, take notice of the threats they have made, and allow us, your servants, to speak your message with all boldness.

4.30 "Reach out your hand to heal, and grant that wonders and miracles may be performed through the name of your holy Servant Jesus."

4.31 When they finished praying, the place where they were meeting was shaken. They were all filled with the Holy Spirit and began to proclaim God's message with boldness.

4.32 The group of believers was one in mind and heart. None of them said that any of their belongings were their own, but they all shared with one another everything they had.

4.33 With great power the apostles gave witness to the resurrection of the Lord Jesus, and God poured rich blessings on them all.

4.34 There was no one in the group who was in need. Those who owned fields or houses would sell them, bring the money received from the sale,

<sup>4.35</sup> and turn it over to the apostles; and the money was distributed according to the needs of the people.

<sup>4.36</sup> And so it was that Joseph, a Levite born in Cyprus, whom the apostles called Barnabas (which means "One who Encourages"),

<sup>4.37</sup> sold a field he owned, brought the money, and turned it over to the apostles.

# 5

<sup>5.1</sup> But there was a man named Ananias, who with his wife Sapphira sold some property that belonged to them.

<sup>5.2</sup> But with his wife's agreement he kept part of the money for himself and turned the rest over to the apostles.

<sup>5.3</sup> Peter said to him, "Ananias, why did you let Satan take control of you and make you lie to the Holy Spirit by keeping part of the money you received for the property?

<sup>5.4</sup> "Before you sold the property, it belonged to you; and after you sold it, the money was yours. Why, then, did you decide to do such a thing? You have not lied to people — you have lied to God!"

<sup>5.5</sup> As soon as Ananias heard this, he fell down dead; and all who heard about it were terrified.

<sup>5.6</sup> The young men came in, wrapped up his body, carried him out, and buried him.

<sup>5.7</sup> About three hours later his wife, not knowing what had happened, came in.

<sup>5.8</sup> Peter asked her, "Tell me, was this the full amount you and your husband received for your property?" "Yes," she answered, "the full amount."

<sup>5.9</sup> So Peter said to her, "Why did you and your husband decide to put the Lord's Spirit to the test? The men who buried your husband are at the door right now, and they will carry you out too!"

<sup>5.10</sup> At once she fell down at his feet and died. The young men came in and saw that she was dead, so they carried her out and buried her beside her husband.

<sup>5.11</sup> The whole church and all the others who heard of this were terrified.

<sup>5.12</sup> Many miracles and wonders were being performed among the people by the apostles. All the believers met together in Solomon's Porch.

<sup>5.13</sup> Nobody outside the group dared join them, even though the peo-

ple spoke highly of them.

5.14 But more and more people were added to the group — a crowd of men and women who believed in the Lord.

5.15 As a result of what the apostles were doing, sick people were carried out into the streets and placed on beds and mats so that at least Peter's shadow might fall on some of them as he passed by.

5.16 And crowds of people came in from the towns around Jerusalem, bringing those who were sick or who had evil spirits in them; and they were all healed.

5.17 Then the High Priest and all his companions, members of the local party of the Sadducees, became extremely jealous of the apostles; so they decided to take action.

5.18 They arrested the apostles and put them in the public jail.

5.19 But that night an angel of the Lord opened the prison gates, led the apostles out, and said to them,

5.20 "Go and stand in the Temple, and tell the people all about this new life."

5.21 The apostles obeyed, and at dawn they entered the Temple and started teaching. The High Priest and his companions called together all the Jewish elders for a full meeting of the Council; then they sent orders to the prison to have the apostles brought before them.

5.22 But when the officials arrived, they did not find the apostles in prison, so they returned to the Council and reported,

5.23 "When we arrived at the jail, we found it locked up tight and all the guards on watch at the gates; but when we opened the gates, we found no one inside!"

5.24 When the chief priests and the officer in charge of the Temple guards heard this, they wondered what had happened to the apostles.

5.25 Then a man came in and said to them, "Listen! The men you put in prison are in the Temple teaching the people!"

5.26 So the officer went off with his men and brought the apostles back. They did not use force, however, because they were afraid that the people might stone them.

5.27 They brought the apostles in, made them stand before the Council, and the High Priest questioned them.

5.28 "We gave you strict orders not to teach in the name of this man," he said; "but see what you have done! You have spread your teaching all over Jerusalem, and you want to make us responsible for his death!"

5.29 Peter and the other apostles answered, "We must obey God, not men.

5.30 "The God of our ancestors raised Jesus from death, after you had killed him by nailing him to a cross.

5.31 "God raised him to his right side as Leader and Savior, to give the people of Israel the opportunity to repent and have their sins forgiven.

5.32 "We are witnesses to these things — we and the Holy Spirit, who is God's gift to those who obey him."

5.33 When the members of the Council heard this, they were so furious that they wanted to have the apostles put to death.

5.34 But one of them, a Pharisee named Gamaliel, who was a teacher of the Law and was highly respected by all the people, stood up in the Council. He ordered the apostles to be taken out for a while,

5.35 and then he said to the Council, "Fellow Israelites, be careful what you do to these men.

5.36 "You remember that Theudas appeared some time ago, claiming to be somebody great, and about four hundred men joined him. But he was killed, all his followers were scattered, and his movement died out.

5.37 "After that, Judas the Galilean appeared during the time of the census; he drew a crowd after him, but he also was killed, and all his followers were scattered.

5.38 "And so in this case, I tell you, do not take any action against these men. Leave them alone! If what they have planned and done is of human origin, it will disappear,

5.39 "but if it comes from God, you cannot possibly defeat them. You could find yourselves fighting against God!" The Council followed Gamaliel's advice.

5.40 They called the apostles in, had them whipped, and ordered them never again to speak in the name of Jesus; and then they set them free.

5.41 As the apostles left the Council, they were happy, because God had considered them worthy to suffer disgrace for the sake of Jesus.

5.42 And every day in the Temple and in people's homes they continued to teach and preach the Good News about Jesus the Messiah.

# 6

6.1 Some time later, as the number of disciples kept growing, there was a quarrel between the Greek-speaking Jews and the native Jews. The Greek-speaking Jews claimed that their widows were being neglected in the daily distribution of funds.

<sup>6.2</sup> So the twelve apostles called the whole group of believers together and said, "It is not right for us to neglect the preaching of God's word in order to handle finances.

<sup>6.3</sup> "So then, friends, choose seven men among you who are known to be full of the Holy Spirit and wisdom, and we will put them in charge of this matter.

<sup>6.4</sup> "We ourselves, then, will give our full time to prayer and the work of preaching."

<sup>6.5</sup> The whole group was pleased with the apostles' proposal, so they chose Stephen, a man full of faith and the Holy Spirit, and Philip, Prochorus, Nicanor, Timon, Parmenas, and Nicolaus, a Gentile from Antioch who had earlier been converted to Judaism.

<sup>6.6</sup> The group presented them to the apostles, who prayed and placed their hands on them.

<sup>6.7</sup> And so the word of God continued to spread. The number of disciples in Jerusalem grew larger and larger, and a great number of priests accepted the faith.

<sup>6.8</sup> Stephen, a man richly blessed by God and full of power, performed great miracles and wonders among the people.

<sup>6.9</sup> But he was opposed by some men who were members of the synagogue of the Freedmen (as it was called), which had Jews from Cyrene and Alexandria. They and other Jews from the provinces of Cilicia and Asia started arguing with Stephen.

<sup>6.10</sup> But the Spirit gave Stephen such wisdom that when he spoke, they could not refute him.

<sup>6.11</sup> So they bribed some men to say, "We heard him speaking against Moses and against God!"

<sup>6.12</sup> In this way they stirred up the people, the elders, and the teachers of the Law. They seized Stephen and took him before the Council.

<sup>6.13</sup> Then they brought in some men to tell lies about him. "This man," they said, "is always talking against our sacred Temple and the Law of Moses.

<sup>6.14</sup> "We heard him say that this Jesus of Nazareth will tear down the Temple and change all the customs which have come down to us from Moses!"

<sup>6.15</sup> All those sitting in the Council fixed their eyes on Stephen and saw that his face looked like the face of an angel.

# 7

<sup>7.1</sup> The High Priest asked Stephen, "Is this true?"

<sup>7.2</sup> Stephen answered, "Brothers and fathers, listen to me! Before our ancestor Abraham had gone to live in Haran, the God of glory appeared to him in Mesopotamia <sup>7.3</sup> "and said to him, 'Leave your family and country and go to the land that I will show you.'
<sup>7.4</sup> "And so he left his country and went to live in Haran. After Abraham's father died, God made him move to this land where you now live.
<sup>7.5</sup> "God did not then give Abraham any part of it as his own, not even a square foot of ground, but God promised to give it to him, and that it would belong to him and to his descendants. At the time God made this promise, Abraham had no children.
<sup>7.6</sup> "This is what God said to him: 'Your descendants will live in a foreign country, where they will be slaves and will be badly treated for four hundred years.
<sup>7.7</sup> " 'But I will pass judgment on the people that they will serve, and afterward your descendants will come out of that country and will worship me in this place.'
<sup>7.8</sup> "Then God gave to Abraham the ceremony of circumcision as a sign of the covenant. So Abraham circumcised Isaac a week after he was born; Isaac circumcised his son Jacob, and Jacob circumcised his twelve sons, the famous ancestors of our race.
<sup>7.9</sup> "Jacob's sons became jealous of their brother Joseph and sold him to be a slave in Egypt. But God was with him
<sup>7.10</sup> "and brought him safely through all his troubles. When Joseph appeared before the king of Egypt, God gave him a pleasing manner and wisdom, and the king made Joseph governor over the country and the royal household.
<sup>7.11</sup> "Then there was a famine all over Egypt and Canaan, which caused much suffering. Our ancestors could not find any food,
<sup>7.12</sup> "and when Jacob heard that there was grain in Egypt, he sent his sons, our ancestors, on their first visit there.
<sup>7.13</sup> "On the second visit Joseph made himself known to his brothers, and the king of Egypt came to know about Joseph's family.
<sup>7.14</sup> "So Joseph sent a message to his father Jacob, telling him and the whole family, seventy-five people in all, to come to Egypt.
<sup>7.15</sup> "Then Jacob went to Egypt, where he and his sons died.
<sup>7.16</sup> "Their bodies were taken to Shechem, where they were buried in the grave which Abraham had bought from the clan of Hamor for a sum of money.
<sup>7.17</sup> "When the time drew near for God to keep the promise he had

made to Abraham, the number of our people in Egypt had grown much larger.

7.18 "At last a king who did not know about Joseph began to rule in Egypt.

7.19 "He tricked our ancestors and was cruel to them, forcing them to put their babies out of their homes, so that they would die.

7.20 "It was at this time that Moses was born, a very beautiful child. He was cared for at home for three months,

7.21 "and when he was put out of his home, the king's daughter adopted him and brought him up as her own son.

7.22 "He was taught all the wisdom of the Egyptians and became a great man in words and deeds.

7.23 "When Moses was forty years old, he decided to find out how his fellow Israelites were being treated.

7.24 "He saw one of them being mistreated by an Egyptian, so he went to his help and took revenge on the Egyptian by killing him.

7.25 (He thought that his own people would understand that God was going to use him to set them free, but they did not understand.)

7.26 "The next day he saw two Israelites fighting, and he tried to make peace between them. 'Listen, men,' he said, 'you are fellow Israelites; why are you fighting like this?'

7.27 "But the one who was mistreating the other pushed Moses aside. 'Who made you ruler and judge over us?' he asked.

7.28 " 'Do you want to kill me, just as you killed that Egyptian yesterday?'

7.29 "When Moses heard this, he fled from Egypt and went to live in the land of Midian. There he had two sons.

7.30 "After forty years had passed, an angel appeared to Moses in the flames of a burning bush in the desert near Mount Sinai.

7.31 "Moses was amazed by what he saw, and went near the bush to get a better look. But he heard the Lord's voice:

7.32 " 'I am the God of your ancestors, the God of Abraham, Isaac, and Jacob.' Moses trembled with fear and dared not look.

7.33 "The Lord said to him, 'Take your sandals off, for the place where you are standing is holy ground.

7.34 " 'I have seen the cruel suffering of my people in Egypt. I have heard their groans, and I have come down to set them free. Come now; I will send you to Egypt.'

7.35 "Moses is the one who was rejected by the people of Israel. 'Who made you ruler and judge over us?' they asked. He is the one whom God sent to rule the people and set them free with the help of the angel who appeared to him in the burning bush.

<sup>7.36</sup> "He led the people out of Egypt, performing miracles and wonders in Egypt and at the Red Sea and for forty years in the desert.

<sup>7.37</sup> "Moses is the one who said to the people of Israel, 'God will send you a prophet, just as he sent me, and he will be one of your own people.'

<sup>7.38</sup> "He is the one who was with the people of Israel assembled in the desert; he was there with our ancestors and with the angel who spoke to him on Mount Sinai, and he received God's living messages to pass on to us.

<sup>7.39</sup> "But our ancestors refused to obey him; they pushed him aside and wished that they could go back to Egypt.

<sup>7.40</sup> "So they said to Aaron, 'Make us some gods who will lead us. We do not know what has happened to that man Moses, who brought us out of Egypt.'

<sup>7.41</sup> "It was then that they made an idol in the shape of a bull, offered sacrifice to it, and had a feast in honor of what they themselves had made.

<sup>7.42</sup> "So God turned away from them and gave them over to worship the stars of heaven, as it is written in the book of the prophets: 'People of Israel! It was not to me that you slaughtered and sacrificed animals for forty years in the desert.

<sup>7.43</sup> " 'It was the tent of the god Molech that you carried, and the image of Rephan, your star god; they were idols that you had made to worship. And so I will send you into exile beyond Babylon.'

<sup>7.44</sup> "Our ancestors had the Tent of God's presence with them in the desert. It had been made as God had told Moses to make it, according to the pattern that Moses had been shown.

<sup>7.45</sup> "Later on, our ancestors who received the tent from their fathers carried it with them when they went with Joshua and took over the land from the nations that God drove out as they advanced. And it stayed there until the time of David.

<sup>7.46</sup> "He won God's favor and asked God to allow him to provide a dwelling place for the God of Jacob.

<sup>7.47</sup> "But it was Solomon who built him a house.

<sup>7.48</sup> "But the Most High God does not live in houses built by human hands; as the prophet says,

<sup>7.49</sup> " 'Heaven is my throne, says the Lord, and the earth is my footstool. What kind of house would you build for me? Where is the place for me to live in?

<sup>7.50</sup> " 'Did not I myself make all these things?'

<sup>7.51</sup> "How stubborn you are!" Stephen went on to say. "How heathen your hearts, how deaf you are to God's message! You are just like your ancestors: you too have always resisted the Holy Spirit!
<sup>7.52</sup> "Was there any prophet that your ancestors did not persecute? They killed God's messengers, who long ago announced the coming of his righteous Servant. And now you have betrayed and murdered him.
<sup>7.53</sup> "You are the ones who received God's law, that was handed down by angels — yet you have not obeyed it!"
<sup>7.54</sup> As the members of the Council listened to Stephen, they became furious and ground their teeth at him in anger.
<sup>7.55</sup> But Stephen, full of the Holy Spirit, looked up to heaven and saw God's glory and Jesus standing at the right side of God.
<sup>7.56</sup> "Look!" he said. "I see heaven opened and the Son of Man standing at the right side of God!"
<sup>7.57</sup> With a loud cry the Council members covered their ears with their hands. Then they all rushed at him at once,
<sup>7.58</sup> threw him out of the city, and stoned him. The witnesses left their cloaks in the care of a young man named Saul.
<sup>7.59</sup> They kept on stoning Stephen as he called out to the Lord, "Lord Jesus, receive my spirit!"
<sup>7.60</sup> He knelt down and cried out in a loud voice, "Lord! Do not remember this sin against them!" He said this and died.

# 8

<sup>8.1</sup> And Saul approved of his murder. That very day the church in Jerusalem began to suffer cruel persecution. All the believers, except the apostles, were scattered throughout the provinces of Judea and Samaria.
<sup>8.2</sup> Some devout men buried Stephen, mourning for him with loud cries.
<sup>8.3</sup> But Saul tried to destroy the church; going from house to house, he dragged out the believers, both men and women, and threw them into jail.
<sup>8.4</sup> The believers who were scattered went everywhere, preaching the message.
<sup>8.5</sup> Philip went to the principal city in Samaria and preached the Messiah to the people there.
<sup>8.6</sup> The crowds paid close attention to what Philip said, as they listened to him and saw the miracles that he performed.
<sup>8.7</sup> Evil spirits came out from many people with a loud cry, and many

paralyzed and lame people were healed.

8.8 So there was great joy in that city.

8.9 A man named Simon lived there, who for some time had astounded the Samaritans with his magic. He claimed that he was someone great,

8.10 and everyone in the city, from all classes of society, paid close attention to him. "He is that power of God known as 'The Great Power,'" they said.

8.11 They paid this attention to him because for such a long time he had astonished them with his magic.

8.12 But when they believed Philip's message about the good news of the Kingdom of God and about Jesus Christ, they were baptized, both men and women.

8.13 Simon himself also believed; and after being baptized, he stayed close to Philip and was astounded when he saw the great wonders and miracles that were being performed.

8.14 The apostles in Jerusalem heard that the people of Samaria had received the word of God, so they sent Peter and John to them.

8.15 When they arrived, they prayed for the believers that they might receive the Holy Spirit.

8.16 For the Holy Spirit had not yet come down on any of them; they had only been baptized in the name of the Lord Jesus.

8.17 Then Peter and John placed their hands on them, and they received the Holy Spirit.

8.18 Simon saw that the Spirit had been given to the believers when the apostles placed their hands on them. So he offered money to Peter and John,

8.19 and said, "Give this power to me too, so that anyone I place my hands on will receive the Holy Spirit."

8.20 But Peter answered him, "May you and your money go to hell, for thinking that you can buy God's gift with money!

8.21 "You have no part or share in our work, because your heart is not right in God's sight.

8.22 "Repent, then, of this evil plan of yours, and pray to the Lord that he will forgive you for thinking such a thing as this.

8.23 "For I see that you are full of bitter envy and are a prisoner of sin."

8.24 Simon said to Peter and John, "Please pray to the Lord for me, so that none of these things you spoke of will happen to me."

8.25 After they had given their testimony and proclaimed the Lord's message, Peter and John went back to Jerusalem. On their way they preached the Good News in many villages of Samaria.

8.26 An angel of the Lord said to Philip, "Get ready and go south to the road that goes from Jerusalem to Gaza." (This road is not used nowadays.)

8.27-28 So Philip got ready and went. Now an Ethiopian eunuch, who was an important official in charge of the treasury of the queen of Ethiopia, was on his way home. He had been to Jerusalem to worship God and was going back home in his carriage. As he rode along, he was reading from the book of the prophet Isaiah.

8.29 The Holy Spirit said to Philip, "Go over to that carriage and stay close to it."

8.30 Philip ran over and heard him reading from the book of the prophet Isaiah. He asked him, "Do you understand what you are reading?"

8.31 The official replied, "How can I understand unless someone explains it to me?" And he invited Philip to climb up and sit in the carriage with him.

8.32 The passage of scripture which he was reading was this: "He was like a sheep that is taken to be slaughtered, like a lamb that makes no sound when its wool is cut off. He did not say a word.

8.33 "He was humiliated, and justice was denied him. No one will be able to tell about his descendants, because his life on earth has come to an end."

8.34 The official asked Philip, "Tell me, of whom is the prophet saying this? Of himself or of someone else?"

8.35 Then Philip began to speak; starting from this passage of scripture, he told him the Good News about Jesus.

8.36 As they traveled down the road, they came to a place where there was some water, and the official said, "Here is some water. What is to keep me from being baptized?"

8.37 (Philip said to him, "You may be baptized if you believe with all your heart." "I do," he answered; "I believe that Jesus Christ is the Son of God.")

8.38 The official ordered the carriage to stop, and both Philip and the official went down into the water, and Philip baptized him.

8.39 When they came up out of the water, the Spirit of the Lord took Philip away. The official did not see him again, but continued on his way, full of joy.

8.40 Philip found himself in Azotus; he went on to Caesarea, and on the way he preached the Good News in every town.

**9** ⁹·¹ In the meantime Saul kept up his violent threats of murder against the followers of the Lord. He went to the High Priest ⁹·² and asked for letters of introduction to the synagogues in Damascus, so that if he should find there any followers of the Way of the Lord, he would be able to arrest them, both men and women, and bring them back to Jerusalem.

⁹·³ As Saul was coming near the city of Damascus, suddenly a light from the sky flashed around him.

⁹·⁴ He fell to the ground and heard a voice saying to him, "Saul, Saul! Why do you persecute me?"

⁹·⁵ "Who are you, Lord?" he asked. "I am Jesus, whom you persecute," the voice said.

⁹·⁶ "But get up and go into the city, where you will be told what you must do."

⁹·⁷ The men who were traveling with Saul had stopped, not saying a word; they heard the voice but could not see anyone.

⁹·⁸ Saul got up from the ground and opened his eyes, but could not see a thing. So they took him by the hand and led him into Damascus.

⁹·⁹ For three days he was not able to see, and during that time he did not eat or drink anything.

⁹·¹⁰ There was a believer in Damascus named Ananias. He had a vision, in which the Lord said to him, "Ananias!" "Here I am, Lord," he answered.

⁹·¹¹ The Lord said to him, "Get ready and go to Straight Street, and at the house of Judas ask for a man from Tarsus named Saul. He is praying,

⁹·¹² "and in a vision he has seen a man named Ananias come in and place his hands on him so that he might see again."

⁹·¹³ Ananias answered, "Lord, many people have told me about this man and about all the terrible things he has done to your people in Jerusalem.

⁹·¹⁴ "And he has come to Damascus with authority from the chief priests to arrest all who worship you."

⁹·¹⁵ The Lord said to him, "Go, because I have chosen him to serve me, to make my name known to Gentiles and kings and to the people of Israel.

⁹·¹⁶ "And I myself will show him all that he must suffer for my sake."

⁹·¹⁷ So Ananias went, entered the house where Saul was, and placed his hands on him. "Brother Saul," he said, "the Lord has sent me — Jesus himself, who appeared to you on the road as you were coming

here. He sent me so that you might see again and be filled with the Holy Spirit."

9.18 At once something like fish scales fell from Saul's eyes, and he was able to see again. He stood up and was baptized;

9.19 and after he had eaten, his strength came back. Saul stayed for a few days with the believers in Damascus.

9.20 He went straight to the synagogues and began to preach that Jesus was the Son of God.

9.21 All who heard him were amazed and asked, "Isn't he the one who in Jerusalem was killing those who worship that man Jesus? And didn't he come here for the very purpose of arresting those people and taking them back to the chief priests?"

9.22 But Saul's preaching became even more powerful, and his proofs that Jesus was the Messiah were so convincing that the Jews who lived in Damascus could not answer him.

9.23 After many days had gone by, the Jews met together and made plans to kill Saul,

9.24 but he was told of their plan. Day and night they watched the city gates in order to kill him.

9.25 But one night Saul's followers took him and let him down through an opening in the wall, lowering him in a basket.

9.26 Saul went to Jerusalem and tried to join the disciples. But they would not believe that he was a disciple, and they were all afraid of him.

9.27 Then Barnabas came to his help and took him to the apostles. He explained to them how Saul had seen the Lord on the road and that the Lord had spoken to him. He also told them how boldly Saul had preached in the name of Jesus in Damascus.

9.28 And so Saul stayed with them and went all over Jerusalem, preaching boldly in the name of the Lord.

9.29 He also talked and disputed with the Greek-speaking Jews, but they tried to kill him.

9.30 When the believers found out about this, they took Saul to Caesarea and sent him away to Tarsus.

9.31 And so it was that the church throughout Judea, Galilee, and Samaria had a time of peace. Through the help of the Holy Spirit it was strengthened and grew in numbers, as it lived in reverence for the Lord.

9.32 Peter traveled everywhere, and on one occasion he went to visit God's people who lived in Lydda.

9.33 There he met a man named Aeneas, who was paralyzed and had not been able to get out of bed for eight years.

⁹·³⁴ "Aeneas," Peter said to him, "Jesus Christ makes you well. Get up and make your bed." At once Aeneas got up.

⁹·³⁵ All the people living in Lydda and Sharon saw him, and they turned to the Lord.

⁹·³⁶ In Joppa there was a woman named Tabitha, who was a believer. (Her name in Greek is Dorcas, meaning "a deer.") She spent all her time doing good and helping the poor.

⁹·³⁷ At that time she got sick and died. Her body was washed and laid in a room upstairs.

⁹·³⁸ Joppa was not very far from Lydda, and when the believers in Joppa heard that Peter was in Lydda, they sent two men to him with the message, "Please hurry and come to us."

⁹·³⁹ So Peter got ready and went with them. When he arrived, he was taken to the room upstairs, where all the widows crowded around him, crying and showing him all the shirts and coats that Dorcas had made while she was alive.

⁹·⁴⁰ Peter put them all out of the room, and knelt down and prayed; then he turned to the body and said, "Tabitha, get up!" She opened her eyes, and when she saw Peter, she sat up.

⁹·⁴¹ Peter reached over and helped her get up. Then he called all the believers, including the widows, and presented her alive to them.

⁹·⁴² The news about this spread all over Joppa, and many people believed in the Lord.

⁹·⁴³ Peter stayed on in Joppa for many days with a tanner of leather named Simon.

# 10

¹⁰·¹ There was a man in Caesarea named Cornelius, who was a captain in the Roman army regiment called "The Italian Regiment."

¹⁰·² He was a religious man; he and his whole family worshiped God. He also did much to help the Jewish poor people and was constantly praying to God.

¹⁰·³ It was about three o'clock one afternoon when he had a vision, in which he clearly saw an angel of God come in and say to him, "Cornelius!"

¹⁰·⁴ He stared at the angel in fear and said, "What is it, sir?" The angel answered, "God is pleased with your prayers and works of charity, and is ready to answer you.

¹⁰·⁵ "And now send some men to Joppa for a certain man whose full name is Simon Peter.

<sup>10.6</sup> "He is a guest in the home of a tanner of leather named Simon, who lives by the sea."

<sup>10.7</sup> Then the angel went away, and Cornelius called two of his house servants and a soldier, a religious man who was one of his personal attendants.

<sup>10.8</sup> He told them what had happened and sent them off to Joppa.

<sup>10.9</sup> The next day, as they were on their way and coming near Joppa, Peter went up on the roof of the house about noon in order to pray.

<sup>10.10</sup> He became hungry and wanted something to eat; while the food was being prepared, he had a vision.

<sup>10.11</sup> He saw heaven opened and something coming down that looked like a large sheet being lowered by its four corners to the earth.

<sup>10.12</sup> In it were all kinds of animals, reptiles, and wild birds.

<sup>10.13</sup> A voice said to him, "Get up, Peter; kill and eat!"

<sup>10.14</sup> But Peter said, "Certainly not, Lord! I have never eaten anything ritually unclean or defiled."

<sup>10.15</sup> The voice spoke to him again, "Do not consider anything unclean that God has declared clean."

<sup>10.16</sup> This happened three times, and then the thing was taken back up into heaven.

<sup>10.17</sup> While Peter was wondering about the meaning of this vision, the men sent by Cornelius had learned where Simon's house was, and they were now standing in front of the gate.

<sup>10.18</sup> They called out and asked, "Is there a guest here by the name of Simon Peter?"

<sup>10.19</sup> Peter was still trying to understand what the vision meant, when the Spirit said, "Listen! Three men are here looking for you.

<sup>10.20</sup> "So get ready and go down, and do not hesitate to go with them, for I have sent them."

<sup>10.21</sup> So Peter went down and said to the men, "I am the man you are looking for. Why have you come?"

<sup>10.22</sup> "Captain Cornelius sent us," they answered. "He is a good man who worships God and is highly respected by all the Jewish people. An angel of God told him to invite you to his house, so that he could hear what you have to say."

<sup>10.23</sup> Peter invited the men in and had them spend the night there. The next day he got ready and went with them; and some of the believers from Joppa went along with him.

<sup>10.24</sup> The following day he arrived in Caesarea, where Cornelius was waiting for him, together with relatives and close friends that he had invited.

10.25 As Peter was about to go in, Cornelius met him, fell at his feet, and bowed down before him.

10.26 But Peter made him rise. "Stand up," he said, "I myself am only a man."

10.27 Peter kept on talking to Cornelius as he went into the house, where he found many people gathered.

10.28 He said to them, "You yourselves know very well that a Jew is not allowed by his religion to visit or associate with Gentiles. But God has shown me that I must not consider any person ritually unclean or defiled.

10.29 "And so when you sent for me, I came without any objection. I ask you, then, why did you send for me?"

10.30 Cornelius said, "It was about this time three days ago that I was praying in my house at three o'clock in the afternoon. Suddenly a man dressed in shining clothes stood in front of me

10.31 "and said: 'Cornelius! God has heard your prayer and has taken notice of your works of charity.

10.32 " 'Send someone to Joppa for a man whose full name is Simon Peter. He is a guest in the home of Simon the tanner of leather, who lives by the sea.'

10.33 "And so I sent for you at once, and you have been good enough to come. Now we are all here in the presence of God, waiting to hear anything that the Lord has instructed you to say."

10.34 Peter began to speak: "I now realize that it is true that God treats everyone on the same basis.

10.35 "Those who fear him and do what is right are acceptable to him, no matter what race they belong to.

10.36 "You know the message he sent to the people of Israel, proclaiming the Good News of peace through Jesus Christ, who is Lord of all.

10.37 "You know of the great event that took place throughout the land of Israel, beginning in Galilee after John preached his message of baptism.

10.38 "You know about Jesus of Nazareth and how God poured out on him the Holy Spirit and power. He went everywhere, doing good and healing all who were under the power of the Devil, for God was with him.

10.39 "We are witnesses of everything that he did in the land of Israel and in Jerusalem. Then they put him to death by nailing him to a cross.

10.40 "But God raised him from death three days later and caused him to appear,

<sup>10.41</sup> "not to everyone, but only to the witnesses that God had already chosen, that is, to us who ate and drank with him after he rose from death.

<sup>10.42</sup> "And he commanded us to preach the gospel to the people and to testify that he is the one whom God has appointed judge of the living and the dead.

<sup>10.43</sup> "All the prophets spoke about him, saying that all who believe in him will have their sins forgiven through the power of his name."

<sup>10.44</sup> While Peter was still speaking, the Holy Spirit came down on all those who were listening to his message.

<sup>10.45</sup> The Jewish believers who had come from Joppa with Peter were amazed that God had poured out his gift of the Holy Spirit on the Gentiles also.

<sup>10.46</sup> For they heard them speaking in strange tongues and praising God's greatness. Peter spoke up:

<sup>10.47</sup> "These people have received the Holy Spirit, just as we also did. Can anyone, then, stop them from being baptized with water?"

<sup>10.48</sup> So he ordered them to be baptized in the name of Jesus Christ. Then they asked him to stay with them for a few days.

# 11

<sup>11.1</sup> The apostles and the other believers throughout Judea heard that the Gentiles also had received the word of God.

<sup>11.2</sup> When Peter went to Jerusalem, those who were in favor of circumcising Gentiles criticized him, saying,

<sup>11.3</sup> "You were a guest in the home of uncircumcised Gentiles, and you even ate with them!"

<sup>11.4</sup> So Peter gave them a complete account of what had happened from the very beginning:

<sup>11.5</sup> "While I was praying in the city of Joppa, I had a vision. I saw something coming down that looked like a large sheet being lowered by its four corners from heaven, and it stopped next to me.

<sup>11.6</sup> "I looked closely inside and saw domesticated and wild animals, reptiles, and wild birds.

<sup>11.7</sup> "Then I heard a voice saying to me, 'Get up, Peter; kill and eat!'

<sup>11.8</sup> "But I said, 'Certainly not, Lord! No ritually unclean or defiled food has ever entered my mouth.'

<sup>11.9</sup> "The voice spoke again from heaven, 'Do not consider anything unclean that God has declared clean.'

<sup>11.10</sup> "This happened three times, and finally the whole thing was drawn back up into heaven.

<sup>11.11</sup> "At that very moment three men who had been sent to me from Caesarea arrived at the house where I was staying.

<sup>11.12</sup> "The Spirit told me to go with them without hesitation. These six fellow believers from Joppa accompanied me to Caesarea, and we all went into the house of Cornelius.

<sup>11.13</sup> "He told us how he had seen an angel standing in his house, who said to him, 'Send someone to Joppa for a man whose full name is Simon Peter.

<sup>11.14</sup> "He will speak words to you by which you and all your family will be saved.'

<sup>11.15</sup> "And when I began to speak, the Holy Spirit came down on them just as on us at the beginning.

<sup>11.16</sup> "Then I remembered what the Lord had said: 'John baptized with water, but you will be baptized with the Holy Spirit.'

<sup>11.17</sup> "It is clear that God gave those Gentiles the same gift that he gave us when we believed in the Lord Jesus Christ; who was I, then, to try to stop God!"

<sup>11.18</sup> When they heard this, they stopped their criticism and praised God, saying, "Then God has given to the Gentiles also the opportunity to repent and live!"

<sup>11.19</sup> Some of the believers who were scattered by the persecution which took place when Stephen was killed went as far as Phoenicia, Cyprus, and Antioch, telling the message to Jews only.

<sup>11.20</sup> But other believers, who were from Cyprus and Cyrene, went to Antioch and proclaimed the message to Gentiles also, telling them the Good News about the Lord Jesus.

<sup>11.21</sup> The Lord's power was with them, and a great number of people believed and turned to the Lord.

<sup>11.22</sup> The news about this reached the church in Jerusalem, so they sent Barnabas to Antioch.

<sup>11.23</sup> When he arrived and saw how God had blessed the people, he was glad and urged them all to be faithful and true to the Lord with all their hearts.

<sup>11.24</sup> Barnabas was a good man, full of the Holy Spirit and faith, and many people were brought to the Lord.

<sup>11.25</sup> Then Barnabas went to Tarsus to look for Saul.

<sup>11.26</sup> When he found him, he took him to Antioch, and for a whole year the two met with the people of the church and taught a large group. It was at Antioch that the believers were first called Christians.

<sup>11.27</sup> About that time some prophets went from Jerusalem to Antioch.

[11.28] One of them, named Agabus, stood up and by the power of the Spirit predicted that a severe famine was about to come over all the earth. (It came when Claudius was emperor.)

[11.29] The disciples decided that they each would send as much as they could to help their fellow believers who lived in Judea.

[11.30] They did this, then, and sent the money to the church elders by Barnabas and Saul.

# 12

[12.1] About this time King Herod began to persecute some members of the church.

[12.2] He had James, the brother of John, put to death by the sword.

[12.3] When he saw that this pleased the Jews, he went ahead and had Peter arrested. (This happened during the time of the Festival of Unleavened Bread.)

[12.4] After his arrest Peter was put in jail, where he was handed over to be guarded by four groups of four soldiers each. Herod planned to put him on trial in public after Passover.

[12.5] So Peter was kept in jail, but the people of the church were praying earnestly to God for him.

[12.6] The night before Herod was going to bring him out to the people, Peter was sleeping between two guards. He was tied with two chains, and there were guards on duty at the prison gate.

[12.7] Suddenly an angel of the Lord stood there, and a light shone in the cell. The angel shook Peter by the shoulder, woke him up, and said, "Hurry! Get up!" At once the chains fell off Peter's hands.

[12.8] Then the angel said, "Tighten your belt and put on your sandals." Peter did so, and the angel said, "Put your cloak around you and come with me."

[12.9] Peter followed him out of the prison, not knowing, however, if what the angel, was doing was real; he thought he was seeing a vision.

[12.10] They passed by the first guard station and then the second, and came at last to the iron gate that opens into the city. The gate opened for them by itself, and they went out. They walked down a street, and suddenly the angel left Peter.

[12.11] Then Peter realized what had happened to him, and said, "Now I know that it is really true! The Lord sent his angel to rescue me from Herod's power and from everything the Jewish people expected to happen."

[12.12] Aware of his situation, he went to the home of Mary, the mother of John Mark, where many people had gathered and were praying. <sup>12.13</sup> Peter knocked at the outside door, and a servant named Rhoda came to answer it.

<sup>12.14</sup> She recognized Peter's voice and was so happy that she ran back in without opening the door, and announced that Peter was standing outside.

<sup>12.15</sup> "You are crazy!" they told her. But she insisted that it was true. So they answered, "It is his angel."

<sup>12.16</sup> Meanwhile Peter kept on knocking. At last they opened the door, and when they saw him, they were amazed.

<sup>12.17</sup> He motioned with his hand for them to be quiet, and he explained to them how the Lord had brought him out of prison. "Tell this to James and the rest of the believers," he said; then he left and went somewhere else.

<sup>12.18</sup> When morning came, there was a tremendous confusion among the guards — what had happened to Peter?

<sup>12.19</sup> Herod gave orders to search for him, but they could not find him. So he had the guards questioned and ordered them put to death. After this, Herod left Judea and spent some time in Caesarea.

<sup>12.20</sup> Herod was very angry with the people of Tyre and Sidon, so they went in a group to see him. First they convinced Blastus, the man in charge of the palace, that he should help them. Then they went to Herod and asked him for peace, because their country got its food supplies from the king's country.

<sup>12.21</sup> On a chosen day Herod put on his royal robes, sat on his throne, and made a speech to the people.

<sup>12.22</sup> "It isn't a man speaking, but a god!" they shouted.

<sup>12.23</sup> At once the angel of the Lord struck Herod down, because he did not give honor to God. He was eaten by worms and died.

<sup>12.24</sup> Meanwhile the word of God continued to spread and grow.

<sup>12.25</sup> Barnabas and Saul finished their mission and returned from Jerusalem, taking John Mark with them.

# 13

<sup>13.1</sup> In the church at Antioch there were some prophets and teachers: Barnabas, Simeon (called the Black), Lucius (from Cyrene), Manaen (who had been brought up with Governor Herod), and Saul.

<sup>13.2</sup> While they were serving the Lord and fasting, the Holy Spirit said to them, "Set apart for me Barnabas and Saul, to do the work to which I have called them."

<sup>13.3</sup> They fasted and prayed, placed their hands on them, and sent

them off.

<sup>13.4</sup> Having been sent by the Holy Spirit, Barnabas and Saul went to Seleucia and sailed from there to the island of Cyprus.

<sup>13.5</sup> When they arrived at Salamis, they preached the word of God in the synagogues. They had John Mark with them to help in the work.

<sup>13.6</sup> They went all the way across the island to Paphos, where they met a certain magician named Bar-Jesus, a Jew who claimed to be a prophet.

<sup>13.7</sup> He was a friend of the governor of the island, Sergius Paulus, who was an intelligent man. The governor called Barnabas and Saul before him because he wanted to hear the word of God.

<sup>13.8</sup> But they were opposed by the magician Elymas (that is his name in Greek), who tried to turn the governor away from the faith.

<sup>13.9</sup> Then Saul - also known as Paul — was filled with the Holy Spirit; he looked straight at the magician

<sup>13.10</sup> and said, "You son of the Devil! You are the enemy of everything that is good. You are full of all kinds of evil tricks, and you always keep trying to turn the Lord's truths into lies!

<sup>13.11</sup> "The Lord's hand will come down on you now; you will be blind and will not see the light of day for a time." At once Elymas felt a dark mist cover his eyes, and he walked around trying to find someone to lead him by the hand.

<sup>13.12</sup> When the governor saw what had happened, he believed; for he was greatly amazed at the teaching about the Lord.

<sup>13.13</sup> Paul and his companions sailed from Paphos and came to Perga, a city in Pamphylia, where John Mark left them and went back to Jerusalem.

<sup>13.14</sup> They went on from Perga and arrived in Antioch in Pisidia, and on the Sabbath they went into the synagogue and sat down.

<sup>13.15</sup> After the reading from the Law of Moses and from the writings of the prophets, the officials of the synagogue sent them a message: "Friends, we want you to speak to the people if you have a message of encouragement for them."

<sup>13.16</sup> Paul stood up, motioned with his hand, and began to speak: "Fellow Israelites and all Gentiles here who worship God: hear me!

<sup>13.17</sup> "The God of the people of Israel chose our ancestors and made the people a great nation during the time they lived as foreigners in Egypt. God brought them out of Egypt by his great power,

<sup>13.18</sup> "and for forty years he endured them in the desert.

<sup>13.19</sup> "He destroyed seven nations in the land of Canaan and made his people the owners of the land.

$^{13.20}$ "All of this took about 450 years. After this he gave them judges until the time of the prophet Samuel.

$^{13.21}$ "And when they asked for a king, God gave them Saul son of Kish from the tribe of Benjamin, to be their king for forty years.

$^{13.22}$ "After removing him, God made David their king. This is what God said about him: 'I have found that David son of Jesse is the kind of man I like, a man who will do all I want him to do.'

$^{13.23}$ "It was Jesus, a descendant of David, whom God made the Savior of the people of Israel, as he had promised.

$^{13.24}$ "Before Jesus began his work, John preached to all the people of Israel that they should turn from their sins and be baptized.

$^{13.25}$ "And as John was about to finish his mission, he said to the people, 'Who do you think I am? I am not the one you are waiting for. But listen! He is coming after me, and I am not good enough to take his sandals off his feet.'

$^{13.26}$ "My fellow Israelites, descendants of Abraham, and all Gentiles here who worship God: it is to us that this message of salvation has been sent!

$^{13.27}$ "For the people who live in Jerusalem and their leaders did not know that he is the Savior, nor did they understand the words of the prophets that are read every Sabbath. Yet they made the prophets' words come true by condemning Jesus.

$^{13.28}$ "And even though they could find no reason to pass the death sentence on him, they asked Pilate to have him put to death.

$^{13.29}$ "And after they had done everything that the Scriptures say about him, they took him down from the cross and placed him in a tomb.

$^{13.30}$ "But God raised him from death,

$^{13.31}$ "and for many days he appeared to those who had traveled with him from Galilee to Jerusalem. They are now witnesses for him to the people of Israel.

$^{13.32-33}$ "And we are here to bring the Good News to you: what God promised our ancestors he would do, he has now done for us, who are their descendants, by raising Jesus to life. As it is written in the second Psalm, 'You are my Son; today I have become your Father.'

$^{13.34}$ "And this is what God said about raising him from death, never to rot away in the grave: 'I will give you the sacred and sure blessings that I promised to David.'

$^{13.35}$ "As indeed he says in another passage, 'You will not allow your faithful servant to rot in the grave.'

$^{13.36}$ "For David served God's purposes in his own time, and then he died, was buried with his ancestors, and his body rotted in the grave. ¹³·³⁷ "But this did not happen to the one whom God raised from death. ¹³·³⁸⁻³⁹ "All of you, my fellow Israelites, are to know for sure that it is through Jesus that the message about forgiveness of sins is preached to you; you are to know that everyone who believes in him is set free from all the sins from which the Law of Moses could not set you free. ¹³·⁴⁰ "Take care, then, so that what the prophets said may not happen to you:

¹³·⁴¹ " 'Look, you scoffers! Be astonished and die! For what I am doing today is something that you will not believe, even when someone explains it to you!' "

¹³·⁴² As Paul and Barnabas were leaving the synagogue, the people invited them to come back the next Sabbath and tell them more about these things. ¹³·⁴³ After the people had left the meeting, Paul and Barnabas were followed by many Jews and by many Gentiles who had been converted to Judaism. The apostles spoke to them and encouraged them to keep on living in the grace of God.

¹³·⁴⁴ The next Sabbath nearly everyone in the town came to hear the word of the Lord. ¹³·⁴⁵ When the Jews saw the crowds, they were filled with jealousy; they disputed what Paul was saying and insulted him. ¹³·⁴⁶ But Paul and Barnabas spoke out even more boldly: "It was necessary that the word of God should be spoken first to you. But since you reject it and do not consider yourselves worthy of eternal life, we will leave you and go to the Gentiles. ¹³·⁴⁷ "For this is the commandment that the Lord has given us: 'I have made you a light for the Gentiles, so that all the world may be saved.'"

¹³·⁴⁸ When the Gentiles heard this, they were glad and praised the Lord's message; and those who had been chosen for eternal life became believers. ¹³·⁴⁹ The word of the Lord spread everywhere in that region. ¹³·⁵⁰ But the Jews stirred up the leading men of the city and the Gentile women of high social standing who worshiped God. They started a persecution against Paul and Barnabas and threw them out of their region. ¹³·⁵¹ The apostles shook the dust off their feet in protest against them and went on to Iconium.

13.52 The believers in Antioch were full of joy and the Holy Spirit.

# 14

14.1 The same thing happened in Iconium: Paul and Barnabas went to the synagogue and spoke in such a way that a great number of Jews and Gentiles became believers.

14.2 But the Jews who would not believe stirred up the Gentiles and turned them against the believers.

14.3 The apostles stayed there for a long time, speaking boldly about the Lord, who proved that their message about his grace was true by giving them the power to perform miracles and wonders.

14.4 The people of the city were divided: some were for the Jews, others for the apostles.

14.5 Then some Gentiles and Jews, together with their leaders, decided to mistreat the apostles and stone them.

14.6 When the apostles learned about it, they fled to the cities of Lystra and Derbe in Lycaonia and to the surrounding territory.

14.7 There they preached the Good News.

14.8 In Lystra there was a crippled man who had been lame from birth and had never been able to walk.

14.9 He sat there and listened to Paul's words. Paul saw that he believed and could be healed, so he looked straight at him

14.10 and said in a loud voice, "Stand up straight on your feet!" The man jumped up and started walking around.

14.11 When the crowds saw what Paul had done, they started shouting in their own Lycaonian language, "The gods have become like men and have come down to us!"

14.12 They gave Barnabas the name Zeus, and Paul the name Hermes, because he was the chief speaker.

14.13 The priest of the god Zeus, whose temple stood just outside the town, brought bulls and flowers to the gate, for he and the crowds wanted to offer sacrifice to the apostles.

14.14 When Barnabas and Paul heard what they were about to do, they tore their clothes and ran into the middle of the crowd, shouting,

14.15 "Why are you doing this? We ourselves are only human beings like you! We are here to announce the Good News, to turn you away from these worthless things to the living God, who made heaven, earth, sea, and all that is in them.

14.16 "In the past he allowed all people to go their own way.

14.17 "But he has always given evidence of his existence by the good things he does: he gives you rain from heaven and crops at the right times; he gives you food and fills your hearts with happiness."

14.18 Even with these words the apostles could hardly keep the crowd from offering a sacrifice to them.

14.19 Some Jews came from Antioch in Pisidia and from Iconium; they won the crowds over to their side, stoned Paul and dragged him out of the town, thinking that he was dead.

14.20 But when the believers gathered around him, he got up and went back into the town. The next day he and Barnabas went to Derbe.

14.21 Paul and Barnabas preached the Good News in Derbe and won many disciples. Then they went back to Lystra, to Iconium, and on to Antioch in Pisidia.

14.22 They strengthened the believers and encouraged them to remain true to the faith. "We must pass through many troubles to enter the Kingdom of God," they taught.

14.23 In each church they appointed elders, and with prayers and fasting they commended them to the Lord, in whom they had put their trust.

14.24 After going through the territory of Pisidia, they came to Pamphylia.

14.25 There they preached the message in Perga and then went to Attalia,

14.26 and from there they sailed back to Antioch, the place where they had been commended to the care of God's grace for the work they had now completed.

14.27 When they arrived in Antioch, they gathered the people of the church together and told them about all that God had done with them and how he had opened the way for the Gentiles to believe.

14.28 And they stayed a long time there with the believers.

# 15

15.1 Some men came from Judea to Antioch and started teaching the believers, "You cannot be saved unless you are circumcised as the Law of Moses requires."

15.2 Paul and Barnabas got into a fierce argument with them about this, so it was decided that Paul and Barnabas and some of the others in Antioch should go to Jerusalem and see the apostles and elders about this matter.

15.3 They were sent on their way by the church; and as they went through Phoenicia and Samaria, they reported how the Gentiles had turned to God; this news brought great joy to all the believers.

<sup>15.4</sup> When they arrived in Jerusalem, they were welcomed by the church, the apostles, and the elders, to whom they told all that God had done through them.

<sup>15.5</sup> But some of the believers who belonged to the party of the Pharisees stood up and said, "The Gentiles must be circumcised and told to obey the Law of Moses."

<sup>15.6</sup> " 'The apostles and the elders met together to consider this question.

<sup>15.7</sup> " 'After a long debate Peter stood up and said, "My friends, you know that a long time ago God chose me from among you to preach the Good News to the Gentiles, so that they could hear and believe.

<sup>15.8</sup> " 'And God, who knows the thoughts of everyone, showed his approval of the Gentiles by giving the Holy Spirit to them, just as he had to us.

<sup>15.9</sup> "He made no difference between us and them; he forgave their sins because they believed.

<sup>15.10</sup> "So then, why do you now want to put God to the test by laying a load on the backs of the believers which neither our ancestors nor we ourselves were able to carry?

<sup>15.11</sup> "No! We believe and are saved by the grace of the Lord Jesus, just as they are."

<sup>15.12</sup> The whole group was silent as they heard Barnabas and Paul report all the miracles and wonders that God had performed through them among the Gentiles.

<sup>15.13</sup> When they had finished speaking, James spoke up: "Listen to me, my friends!

<sup>15.14</sup> "Simon has just explained how God first showed his care for the Gentiles by taking from among them a people to belong to him.

<sup>15.15</sup> "The words of the prophets agree completely with this. As the scripture says,

<sup>15.16</sup> " 'After this I will return, says the Lord, and restore the kingdom of David. I will rebuild its ruins and make it strong again.

<sup>15.17</sup> " 'And so all the rest of the human race will come to me, all the Gentiles whom I have called to be my own.

<sup>15.18</sup> " 'So says the Lord, who made this known long ago.' "

<sup>15.19</sup> "It is my opinion," James went on, "that we should not trouble the Gentiles who are turning to God.

<sup>15.20</sup> "Instead, we should write a letter telling them not to eat any food that is ritually unclean because it has been offered to idols; to keep themselves from sexual immorality; and not to eat any animal that has been strangled, or any blood.

15.21 "For the Law of Moses has been read for a very long time in the synagogues every Sabbath, and his words are preached in every town."

15.22 Then the apostles and the elders, together with the whole church, decided to choose some men from the group and send them to Antioch with Paul and Barnabas. They chose two men who were highly respected by the believers, Judas, called Barsabbas, and Silas,

15.23 and they sent the following letter by them: "We, the apostles and the elders, your brothers, send greetings to all our brothers of Gentile birth who live in Antioch, Syria, and Cilicia.

15.24 "We have heard that some who went from our group have troubled and upset you by what they said; they had not, however, received any instruction from us.

15.25 "And so we have met together and have all agreed to choose some messengers and send them to you. They will go with our dear friends Barnabas and Paul,

15.26 "who have risked their lives in the service of our Lord Jesus Christ.

15.27 "We send you, then, Judas and Silas, who will tell you in person the same things we are writing.

15.28 "The Holy Spirit and we have agreed not to put any other burden on you besides these necessary rules:

15.29 "eat no food that has been offered to idols; eat no blood; eat no animal that has been strangled; and keep yourselves from sexual immorality. You will do well if you take care not to do these things. With our best wishes."

15.30 The messengers were sent off and went to Antioch, where they gathered the whole group of believers and gave them the letter.

15.31 When the people read it, they were filled with joy by the message of encouragement.

15.32 Judas and Silas, who were themselves prophets, spoke a long time with them, giving them courage and strength.

15.33 After spending some time there, they were sent off in peace by the believers and went back to those who had sent them.

15.34 (But Silas decided to stay there.)

15.35 Paul and Barnabas spent some time in Antioch, and together with many others they taught and preached the word of the Lord.

15.36 Some time later Paul said to Barnabas, "Let us go back and visit the believers in every town where we preached the word of the Lord, and let us find out how they are getting along."

15.37 Barnabas wanted to take John Mark with them,

15.38 but Paul did not think it was right to take him, because he had not stayed with them to the end of their mission, but had turned back and left them in Pamphylia.

15.39 There was a sharp argument, and they separated: Barnabas took Mark and sailed off for Cyprus,

15.40 while Paul chose Silas and left, commended by the believers to the care of the Lord's grace.

15.41 He went through Syria and Cilicia, strengthening the churches.

# 16

16.1 Paul traveled on to Derbe and Lystra, where a Christian named Timothy lived. His mother, who was also a Christian, was Jewish, but his father was a Greek.

16.2 All the believers in Lystra and Iconium spoke well of Timothy.

16.3 Paul wanted to take Timothy along with him, so he circumcised him. He did so because all the Jews who lived in those places knew that Timothy's father was Greek.

16.4 As they went through the towns, they delivered to the believers the rules decided upon by the apostles and elders in Jerusalem, and they told them to obey those rules.

16.5 So the churches were made stronger in the faith and grew in numbers every day.

16.6 They traveled through the region of Phrygia and Galatia because the Holy Spirit did not let them preach the message in the province of Asia.

16.7 When they reached the border of Mysia, they tried to go into the province of Bithynia, but the Spirit of Jesus did not allow them.

16.8 So they traveled right on through Mysia and went to Troas.

16.9 That night Paul had a vision in which he saw a Macedonian standing and begging him, "Come over to Macedonia and help us!"

16.10 As soon as Paul had this vision, we got ready to leave for Macedonia, because we decided that God had called us to preach the Good News to the people there.

16.11 We left by ship from Troas and sailed straight across to Samothrace, and the next day to Neapolis.

16.12 From there we went inland to Philippi, a city of the first district of Macedonia; it is also a Roman colony. We spent several days there.

16.13 On the Sabbath we went out of the city to the riverside, where we thought there would be a place where Jews gathered for prayer. We sat down and talked to the women who gathered there.

16.14 One of those who heard us was Lydia from Thyatira, who was a dealer in purple cloth. She was a woman who worshiped God, and the Lord opened her mind to pay attention to what Paul was saying.

16.15 After she and the people of her house had been baptized, she invited us, "Come and stay in my house if you have decided that I am a true believer in the Lord." And she persuaded us to go.

16.16 One day as we were going to the place of prayer, we were met by a young servant woman who had an evil spirit that enabled her to predict the future. She earned a lot of money for her owners by telling fortunes.

16.17 She followed Paul and us, shouting, "These men are servants of the Most High God! They announce to you how you can be saved!"

16.18 She did this for many days, until Paul became so upset that he turned around and said to the spirit, "In the name of Jesus Christ I order you to come out of her!" The spirit went out of her that very moment.

16.19 When her owners realized that their chance of making money was gone, they seized Paul and Silas and dragged them to the authorities in the public square.

16.20 They brought them before the Roman officials and said, "These men are Jews, and they are causing trouble in our city.

16.21 "They are teaching customs that are against our law; we are Roman citizens, and we cannot accept these customs or practice them."

16.22 And the crowd joined in the attack against Paul and Silas. Then the officials tore the clothes off Paul and Silas and ordered them to be whipped.

16.23 After a severe beating, they were thrown into jail, and the jailer was ordered to lock them up tight.

16.24 Upon receiving this order, the jailer threw them into the inner cell and fastened their feet between heavy blocks of wood.

16.25 About midnight Paul and Silas were praying and singing hymns to God, and the other prisoners were listening to them.

16.26 Suddenly there was a violent earthquake, which shook the prison to its foundations. At once all the doors opened, and the chains fell off all the prisoners.

16.27 The jailer woke up, and when he saw the prison doors open, he thought that the prisoners had escaped; so he pulled out his sword and was about to kill himself.

16.28 But Paul shouted at the top of his voice, "Don't harm yourself! We are all here!"

16.29 The jailer called for a light, rushed in, and fell trembling at the feet of Paul and Silas.

<sup>16.30</sup> Then he led them out and asked, "Sirs, what must I do to be saved?"

<sup>16.31</sup> They answered, "Believe in the Lord Jesus, and you will be saved — you and your family."

<sup>16.32</sup> Then they preached the word of the Lord to him and to all the others in the house.

<sup>16.33</sup> At that very hour of the night the jailer took them and washed their wounds; and he and all his family were baptized at once.

<sup>16.34</sup> Then he took Paul and Silas up into his house and gave them some food to eat. He and his family were filled with joy, because they now believed in God.

<sup>16.35</sup> The next morning the Roman authorities sent police officers with the order, "Let those men go."

<sup>16.36</sup> So the jailer told Paul, "The officials have sent an order for you and Silas to be released. You may leave, then, and go in peace."

<sup>16.37</sup> But Paul said to the police officers, "We were not found guilty of any crime, yet they whipped us in public — and we are Roman citizens! Then they threw us in prison. And now they want to send us away secretly? Not at all! The Roman officials themselves must come here and let us out."

<sup>16.38</sup> The police officers reported these words to the Roman officials; and when they heard that Paul and Silas were Roman citizens, they were afraid.

<sup>16.39</sup> So they went and apologized to them; then they led them out of the prison and asked them to leave the city.

<sup>16.40</sup> Paul and Silas left the prison and went to Lydia's house. There they met the believers, spoke words of encouragement to them, and left.

# 17

<sup>17.1</sup> Paul and Silas traveled on through Amphipolis and Apollonia and came to Thessalonica, where there was a synagogue.

<sup>17.2</sup> According to his usual habit Paul went to the synagogue. There during three Sabbaths he held discussions with the people, quoting <sup>17.3</sup> and explaining the Scriptures, and proving from them that the Messiah had to suffer and rise from death. "This Jesus whom I announce to you," Paul said, "is the Messiah."

<sup>17.4</sup> Some of them were convinced and joined Paul and Silas; so did many of the leading women and a large group of Greeks who worshiped God.

<sup>17.5</sup> But some Jews were jealous and gathered worthless loafers from

the streets and formed a mob. They set the whole city in an uproar and attacked the home of a man named Jason, in an attempt to find Paul and Silas and bring them out to the people.

<sup>17.6</sup> But when they did not find them, they dragged Jason and some other believers before the city authorities and shouted, "These men have caused trouble everywhere! Now they have come to our city,

<sup>17.7</sup> "and Jason has kept them in his house. They are all breaking the laws of the Emperor, saying that there is another king, whose name is Jesus."

<sup>17.8</sup> With these words they threw the crowd and the city authorities in an uproar.

<sup>17.9</sup> The authorities made Jason and the others pay the required amount of money to be released, and then let them go.

<sup>17.10</sup> As soon as night came, the believers sent Paul and Silas to Berea. When they arrived, they went to the synagogue.

<sup>17.11</sup> The people there were more open-minded than the people in Thessalonica. They listened to the message with great eagerness, and every day they studied the Scriptures to see if what Paul said was really true.

<sup>17.12</sup> Many of them believed; and many Greek women of high social standing and many Greek men also believed.

<sup>17.13</sup> But when the Jews in Thessalonica heard that Paul had preached the word of God in Berea also, they came there and started exciting and stirring up the mobs.

<sup>17.14</sup> At once the believers sent Paul away to the coast; but both Silas and Timothy stayed in Berea.

<sup>17.15</sup> The men who were taking Paul went with him as far as Athens and then returned to Berea with instructions from Paul that Silas and Timothy should join him as soon as possible.

<sup>17.16</sup> While Paul was waiting in Athens for Silas and Timothy, he was greatly upset when he noticed how full of idols the city was.

<sup>17.17</sup> So he held discussions in the synagogue with the Jews and with the Gentiles who worshiped God, and also in the public square every day with the people who happened to come by.

<sup>17.18</sup> Certain Epicurean and Stoic teachers also debated with him. Some of them asked, "What is this ignorant show-off trying to say?" Others answered, "He seems to be talking about foreign gods." They said this because Paul was preaching about Jesus and the resurrection.

<sup>17.19</sup> So they took Paul, brought him before the city council, the Areopagus, and said, "We would like to know what this new teaching is

that you are talking about.

<sup></sup>17.20 "Some of the things we hear you say sound strange to us, and we would like to know what they mean."

17.21 (For all the citizens of Athens and the foreigners who lived there liked to spend all their time telling and hearing the latest new thing.)

17.22 Paul stood up in front of the city council and said, "I see that in every way you Athenians are very religious.

17.23 "For as I walked through your city and looked at the places where you worship, I found an altar on which is written, 'To an Unknown God.' That which you worship, then, even though you do not know it, is what I now proclaim to you.

17.24 "God, who made the world and everything in it, is Lord of heaven and earth and does not live in temples made by human hands.

17.25 "Nor does he need anything that we can supply by working for him, since it is he himself who gives life and breath and everything else to everyone.

17.26 "From one human being he created all races of people and made them live throughout the whole earth. He himself fixed beforehand the exact times and the limits of the places where they would live.

17.27 "He did this so that they would look for him, and perhaps find him as they felt around for him. Yet God is actually not far from any one of us;

17.28 "as someone has said, 'In him we live and move and exist.' It is as some of your poets have said, 'We too are his children.'

17.29 "Since we are God's children, we should not suppose that his nature is anything like an image of gold or silver or stone, shaped by human art and skill.

17.30 "God has overlooked the times when people did not know him, but now he commands all of them everywhere to turn away from their evil ways.

17.31 "For he has fixed a day in which he will judge the whole world with justice by means of a man he has chosen. He has given proof of this to everyone by raising that man from death!"

17.32 When they heard Paul speak about a raising from death, some of them made fun of him, but others said, "We want to hear you speak about this again."

17.33 And so Paul left the meeting.

17.34 Some men joined him and believed, among whom was Dionysius, a member of the council; there was also a woman named Damaris, and some other people.

<sup>18.1</sup> After this, Paul left Athens and went on to Corinth. **18**
<sup>18.2</sup> There he met a Jew named Aquila, born in Pontus, who had recently come from Italy with his wife Priscilla, for Emperor Claudius had ordered all the Jews to leave Rome. Paul went to see them, <sup>18.3</sup> and stayed and worked with them, because he earned his living by making tents, just as they did.
<sup>18.4</sup> He held discussions in the synagogue every Sabbath, trying to convince both Jews and Greeks.
<sup>18.5</sup> When Silas and Timothy arrived from Macedonia, Paul gave his whole time to preaching the message, testifying to the Jews that Jesus is the Messiah.
<sup>18.6</sup> When they opposed him and said evil things about him, he protested by shaking the dust from his clothes and saying to them, "If you are lost, you yourselves must take the blame for it! I am not responsible. From now on I will go to the Gentiles."
<sup>18.7</sup> So he left them and went to live in the house of a Gentile named Titius Justus, who worshiped God; his house was next to the synagogue.
<sup>18.8</sup> Crispus, who was the leader of the synagogue, believed in the Lord, together with all his family; and many other people in Corinth heard the message, believed, and were baptized.
<sup>18.9</sup> One night Paul had a vision in which the Lord said to him, "Do not be afraid, but keep on speaking and do not give up, <sup>18.10</sup> "for I am with you. No one will be able to harm you, for many in this city are my people."
<sup>18.11</sup> So Paul stayed there for a year and a half, teaching the people the word of God.
<sup>18.12</sup> When Gallio was made the Roman governor of Achaia, Jews there got together, seized Paul, and took him into court.
<sup>18.13</sup> "This man," they said, "is trying to persuade people to worship God in a way that is against the law!"
<sup>18.14</sup> Paul was about to speak when Gallio said to the Jews, "If this were a matter of some evil crime or wrong that has been committed, it would be reasonable for me to be patient with you Jews.
<sup>18.15</sup> "But since it is an argument about words and names and your own law, you yourselves must settle it. I will not be the judge of such things!"
<sup>18.16</sup> And he drove them out of the court.
<sup>18.17</sup> They all grabbed Sosthenes, the leader of the synagogue, and beat him in front of the court. But that did not bother Gallio a bit.
<sup>18.18</sup> Paul stayed on with the believers in Corinth for many days, then

left them and sailed off with Priscilla and Aquila for Syria. Before sailing from Cenchreae he had his head shaved because of a vow he had taken.

<sup>18.19</sup> They arrived in Ephesus, where Paul left Priscilla and Aquila. He went into the synagogue and held discussions with the Jews.

<sup>18.20</sup> The people asked him to stay longer, but he would not consent.

<sup>18.21</sup> Instead, he told them as he left, "If it is the will of God, I will come back to you." And so he sailed from Ephesus.

<sup>18.22</sup> When he arrived at Caesarea, he went to Jerusalem and greeted the church, and then went to Antioch.

<sup>18.23</sup> After spending some time there, he left and went through the region of Galatia and Phrygia, strengthening all the believers.

<sup>18.24</sup> At that time a Jew named Apollos, who had been born in Alexandria, came to Ephesus. He was an eloquent speaker and had a thorough knowledge of the Scriptures.

<sup>18.25</sup> He had been instructed in the Way of the Lord, and with great enthusiasm he proclaimed and taught correctly the facts about Jesus. However, he knew only the baptism of John.

<sup>18.26</sup> He began to speak boldly in the synagogue. When Priscilla and Aquila heard him, they took him home with them and explained to him more correctly the Way of God.

<sup>18.27</sup> Apollos then decided to go to Achaia, so the believers in Ephesus helped him by writing to the believers in Achaia, urging them to welcome him. When he arrived, he was a great help to those who through God's grace had become believers.

<sup>18.28</sup> For with his strong arguments he defeated the Jews in public debates by proving from the Scriptures that Jesus is the Messiah.

# 19

<sup>19.1</sup> While Apollos was in Corinth, Paul traveled through the interior of the province and arrived in Ephesus. There he found some disciples

<sup>19.2</sup> and asked them, "Did you receive the Holy Spirit when you became believers?" "We have not even heard that there is a Holy Spirit," they answered.

<sup>19.3</sup> "Well, then, what kind of baptism did you receive?" Paul asked. "The baptism of John," they answered.

<sup>19.4</sup> Paul said, "The baptism of John was for those who turned from their sins; and he told the people of Israel to believe in the one who was coming after him — that is, in Jesus."

<sup>19.5</sup> When they heard this, they were baptized in the name of the

Lord Jesus.

<sup>19.6</sup> Paul placed his hands on them, and the Holy Spirit came upon them; they spoke in strange tongues and also proclaimed God's message.

<sup>19.7</sup> They were about twelve men in all.

<sup>19.8</sup> Paul went into the synagogue and for three months spoke boldly with the people, holding discussions with them and trying to convince them about the Kingdom of God.

<sup>19.9</sup> But some of them were stubborn and would not believe, and before the whole group they said evil things about the Way of the Lord. So Paul left them and took the believers with him, and every day he held discussions in the lecture hall of Tyrannus.

<sup>19.10</sup> This went on for two years, so that all the people who lived in the province of Asia, both Jews and Gentiles, heard the word of the Lord.

<sup>19.11</sup> God was performing unusual miracles through Paul.

<sup>19.12</sup> Even handkerchiefs and aprons he had used were taken to the sick, and their diseases were driven away, and the evil spirits would go out of them.

<sup>19.13</sup> Some Jews who traveled around and drove out evil spirits also tried to use the name of the Lord Jesus to do this. They said to the evil spirits, "I command you in the name of Jesus, whom Paul preaches."

<sup>19.14</sup> Seven brothers, who were the sons of a Jewish High Priest named Sceva, were doing this.

<sup>19.15</sup> But the evil spirit said to them, "I know Jesus, and I know about Paul; but you — who are you?"

<sup>19.16</sup> The man who had the evil spirit in him attacked them with such violence that he overpowered them all. They ran away from his house, wounded and with their clothes torn off.

<sup>19.17</sup> All the Jews and Gentiles who lived in Ephesus heard about this; they were all filled with fear, and the name of the Lord Jesus was given greater honor.

<sup>19.18</sup> Many of the believers came, publicly admitting and revealing what they had done.

<sup>19.19</sup> Many of those who had practiced magic brought their books together and burned them in public. They added up the price of the books, and the total came to fifty thousand silver coins.

<sup>19.20</sup> In this powerful way the word of the Lord kept spreading and growing stronger.

<sup>19.21</sup> After these things had happened, Paul made up his mind to

travel through Macedonia and Achaia and go on to Jerusalem. "After I go there," he said, "I must also see Rome."

<sup>19.22</sup> So he sent Timothy and Erastus, two of his helpers, to Macedonia, while he spent more time in the province of Asia.

<sup>19.23</sup> It was at this time that there was serious trouble in Ephesus because of the Way of the Lord.

<sup>19.24</sup> A certain silversmith named Demetrius made silver models of the temple of the goddess Artemis, and his business brought a great deal of profit to the workers.

<sup>19.25</sup> So he called them all together with others whose work was like theirs and said to them, "Men, you know that our prosperity comes from this work.

<sup>19.26</sup> "Now, you can see and hear for yourselves what this fellow Paul is doing. He says that hand-made gods are not gods at all, and he has succeeded in convincing many people, both here in Ephesus and in nearly the whole province of Asia.

<sup>19.27</sup> "There is the danger, then, that this business of ours will get a bad name. Not only that, but there is also the danger that the temple of the great goddess Artemis will come to mean nothing and that her greatness will be destroyed — the goddess worshiped by everyone in Asia and in all the world!"

<sup>19.28</sup> As the crowd heard these words, they became furious and started shouting, "Great is Artemis of Ephesus!"

<sup>19.29</sup> The uproar spread throughout the whole city. The mob grabbed Gaius and Aristarchus, two Macedonians who were traveling with Paul, and rushed with them to the theater.

<sup>19.30</sup> Paul himself wanted to go before the crowd, but the believers would not let him.

<sup>19.31</sup> Some of the provincial authorities, who were his friends, also sent him a message begging him not to show himself in the theater.

<sup>19.32</sup> Meanwhile the whole meeting was in an uproar: some people were shouting one thing, others were shouting something else, because most of them did not even know why they had come together.

<sup>19.33</sup> Some of the people concluded that Alexander was responsible, since the Jews made him go up to the front. Then Alexander motioned with his hand for the people to be silent, and he tried to make a speech of defense.

<sup>19.34</sup> But when they recognized that he was a Jew, they all shouted together the same thing for two hours: "Great is Artemis of Ephesus!"

<sup>19.35</sup> At last the city clerk was able to calm the crowd. "Fellow Ephesians!" he said. "Everyone knows that the city of Ephesus is the

keeper of the temple of the great Artemis and of the sacred stone that fell down from heaven.

<sup>19.36</sup> "Nobody can deny these things. So then, you must calm down and not do anything reckless.

<sup>19.37</sup> "You have brought these men here even though they have not robbed temples or said evil things about our goddess.

<sup>19.38</sup> "If Demetrius and his workers have an accusation against anyone, we have the authorities and the regular days for court; charges can be made there.

<sup>19.39</sup> "But if there is something more that you want, it will have to be settled in a legal meeting of citizens.

<sup>19.40</sup> "For after what has happened today, there is the danger that we will be accused of a riot. There is no excuse for all this uproar, and we would not be able to give a good reason for it."

<sup>19.41</sup> After saying this, he dismissed the meeting.

# 20

<sup>20.1</sup> After the uproar died down, Paul called together the believers and with words of encouragement said good-bye to them. Then he left and went on to Macedonia.

<sup>20.2</sup> He went through those regions and encouraged the people with many messages. Then he came to Achaia,

<sup>20.3</sup> where he stayed three months. He was getting ready to go to Syria when he discovered that there were Jews plotting against him; so he decided to go back through Macedonia.

<sup>20.4</sup> Sopater son of Pyrrhus, from Berea, went with him; so did Aristarchus and Secundus, from Thessalonica; Gaius, from Derbe; Tychicus and Trophimus, from the province of Asia; and Timothy.

<sup>20.5</sup> They went ahead and waited for us in Troas.

<sup>20.6</sup> We sailed from Philippi after the Festival of Unleavened Bread, and five days later we joined them in Troas, where we spent a week.

<sup>20.7</sup> On Saturday evening we gathered together for the fellowship meal. Paul spoke to the people and kept on speaking until midnight, since he was going to leave the next day.

<sup>20.8</sup> Many lamps were burning in the upstairs room where we were meeting.

<sup>20.9</sup> A young man named Eutychus was sitting in the window, and as Paul kept on talking, Eutychus got sleepier and sleepier, until he finally went sound asleep and fell from the third story to the ground. When they picked him up, he was dead.

<sup>20.10</sup> But Paul went down and threw himself on him and hugged him.

"Don't worry," he said, "he is still alive!"

20.11 Then he went back upstairs, broke bread, and ate. After talking with them for a long time, even until sunrise, Paul left.

20.12 They took the young man home alive and were greatly comforted.

20.13 We went on ahead to the ship and sailed off to Assos, where we were going to take Paul aboard. He had told us to do this, because he was going there by land.

20.14 When he met us in Assos, we took him aboard and went on to Mitylene.

20.15 We sailed from there and arrived off Chios the next day. A day later we came to Samos, and the following day we reached Miletus.

20.16 Paul had decided to sail on by Ephesus, so as not to lose any time in the province of Asia. He was in a hurry to arrive in Jerusalem by the day of Pentecost, if at all possible.

20.17 From Miletus Paul sent a message to Ephesus, asking the elders of the church to meet him.

20.18 When they arrived, he said to them, "You know how I spent the whole time I was with you, from the first day I arrived in the province of Asia.

20.19 "With all humility and many tears I did my work as the Lord's servant during the hard times that came to me because of the plots of some Jews.

20.20 "You know that I did not hold back anything that would be of help to you as I preached and taught in public and in your homes.

20.21 "To Jews and Gentiles alike I gave solemn warning that they should turn from their sins to God and believe in our Lord Jesus.

20.22 "And now, in obedience to the Holy Spirit I am going to Jerusalem, not knowing what will happen to me there.

20.23 "I only know that in every city the Holy Spirit has warned me that prison and troubles wait for me.

20.24 "But I reckon my own life to be worth nothing to me; I only want to complete my mission and finish the work that the Lord Jesus gave me to do, which is to declare the Good News about the grace of God.

20.25 "I have gone about among all of you, preaching the Kingdom of God. And now I know that none of you will ever see me again.

20.26 "So I solemnly declare to you this very day: if any of you should be lost, I am not responsible.

20.27 "For I have not held back from announcing to you the whole purpose of God.

20.28 "So keep watch over yourselves and over all the flock which the

Holy Spirit has placed in your care. Be shepherds of the church of God, which he made his own through the blood of his Son.

20.29 "I know that after I leave, fierce wolves will come among you, and they will not spare the flock.

20.30 "The time will come when some men from your own group will tell lies to lead the believers away after them.

20.31 "Watch, then, and remember that with many tears, day and night, I taught every one of you for three years.

20.32 "And now I commend you to the care of God and to the message of his grace, which is able to build you up and give you the blessings God has for all his people.

20.33 "I have not wanted anyone's silver or gold or clothing.

20.34 "You yourselves know that I have worked with these hands of mine to provide everything that my companions and I have needed.

20.35 "I have shown you in all things that by working hard in this way we must help the weak, remembering the words that the Lord Jesus himself said, 'There is more happiness in giving than in receiving.'"

20.36 When Paul finished, he knelt down with them and prayed.

20.37 They were all crying as they hugged him and kissed him good-bye.

20.38 They were especially sad because he had said that they would never see him again. And so they went with him to the ship.

# 21

21.1 We said good-bye to them and left. After sailing straight across, we came to Cos; the next day we reached Rhodes, and from there we went on to Patara.

21.2 There we found a ship that was going to Phoenicia, so we went aboard and sailed away.

21.3 We came to where we could see Cyprus, and then sailed south of it on to Syria. We went ashore at Tyre, where the ship was going to unload its cargo.

21.4 There we found some believers and stayed with them a week. By the power of the Spirit they told Paul not to go to Jerusalem.

21.5 But when our time with them was over, we left and went on our way. All of them, together with their wives and children, went with us out of the city to the beach, where we all knelt and prayed.

21.6 Then we said good-bye to one another, and we went on board the ship while they went back home.

21.7 We continued our voyage, sailing from Tyre to Ptolemais, where we greeted the believers and stayed with them for a day.

21.8 On the following day we left and arrived in Caesarea. There we stayed at the house of Philip the evangelist, one of the seven men who had been chosen as helpers in Jerusalem.

21.9 He had four unmarried daughters who proclaimed God's message.

21.10 We had been there for several days when a prophet named Agabus arrived from Judea.

21.11 He came to us, took Paul's belt, tied up his own feet and hands with it, and said, "This is what the Holy Spirit says: The owner of this belt will be tied up in this way by the Jews in Jerusalem, and they will hand him over to the Gentiles."

21.12 When we heard this, we and the others there begged Paul not to go to Jerusalem.

21.13 But he answered, "What are you doing, crying like this and breaking my heart? I am ready not only to be tied up in Jerusalem but even to die there for the sake of the Lord Jesus."

21.14 We could not convince him, so we gave up and said, "May the Lord's will be done."

21.15 After spending some time there, we got our things ready and left for Jerusalem.

21.16 Some of the disciples from Caesarea also went with us and took us to the house of the man we were going to stay with — Mnason, from Cyprus, who had been a believer since the early days.

21.17 When we arrived in Jerusalem, the believers welcomed us warmly.

21.18 The next day Paul went with us to see James; and all the church elders were present.

21.19 Paul greeted them and gave a complete report of everything that God had done among the Gentiles through his work.

21.20 After hearing him, they all praised God. Then they said, "Brother Paul, you can see how many thousands of Jews have become believers, and how devoted they all are to the Law.

21.21 "They have been told that you have been teaching all the Jews who live in Gentile countries to abandon the Law of Moses, telling them not to circumcise their children or follow the Jewish customs.

21.22 "They are sure to hear that you have arrived. What should be done, then?

21.23 "This is what we want you to do. There are four men here who have taken a vow.

21.24 "Go along with them and join them in the ceremony of purification and pay their expenses; then they will be able to shave their heads. In this way everyone will know that there is no truth in any of the things that they have been told about you, but that you yourself live in accordance with the Law of Moses.

<sup>21.25</sup> "But as for the Gentiles who have become believers, we have sent them a letter telling them we decided that they must not eat any food that has been offered to idols, or any blood, or any animal that has been strangled, and that they must keep themselves from sexual immorality."

<sup>21.26</sup> So Paul took the men and the next day performed the ceremony of purification with them. Then he went into the Temple and gave notice of how many days it would be until the end of the period of purification, when a sacrifice would be offered for each one of them.

<sup>21.27</sup> But just when the seven days were about to come to an end, some Jews from the province of Asia saw Paul in the Temple. They stirred up the whole crowd and grabbed Paul.

<sup>21.28</sup> "People of Israel!" they shouted. "Help! This is the man who goes everywhere teaching everyone against the people of Israel, the Law of Moses, and this Temple. And now he has even brought some Gentiles into the Temple and defiled this holy place!"

<sup>21.29</sup> (They said this because they had seen Trophimus from Ephesus with Paul in the city, and they thought that Paul had taken him into the Temple.)

<sup>21.30</sup> Confusion spread through the whole city, and the people all ran together, grabbed Paul, and dragged him out of the Temple. At once the Temple doors were closed.

<sup>21.31</sup> The mob was trying to kill Paul, when a report was sent up to the commander of the Roman troops that all of Jerusalem was rioting.

<sup>21.32</sup> At once the commander took some officers and soldiers and rushed down to the crowd. When the people saw him with the soldiers, they stopped beating Paul.

<sup>21.33</sup> The commander went over to Paul, arrested him, and ordered him to be bound with two chains. Then he asked, "Who is this man, and what has he done?"

<sup>21.34</sup> Some in the crowd shouted one thing, others something else. There was such confusion that the commander could not find out exactly what had happened, so he ordered his men to take Paul up into the fort.

<sup>21.35</sup> They got as far as the steps with him, and then the soldiers had to carry him because the mob was so wild.

<sup>21.36</sup> They were all coming after him and screaming, "Kill him!"

<sup>21.37</sup> As the soldiers were about to take Paul into the fort, he spoke to the commander: "May I say something to you?" "You speak Greek, do you?" the commander asked.

<sup>21.38</sup> "Then you are not that Egyptian fellow who some time ago started a revolution and led four thousand armed terrorists out into the desert?"

<sup>21.39</sup> Paul answered, "I am a Jew, born in Tarsus in Cilicia, a citizen of an important city. Please let me speak to the people."

<sup>21.40</sup> The commander gave him permission, so Paul stood on the steps and motioned with his hand for the people to be silent. When they were quiet, Paul spoke to them in Hebrew:

# 22

<sup>22.1</sup> "My fellow Jews, listen to me as I make my defense before you!"

<sup>22.2</sup> When they heard him speaking to them in Hebrew, they became even quieter; and Paul went on:

<sup>22.3</sup> "I am a Jew, born in Tarsus in Cilicia, but brought up here in Jerusalem as a student of Gamaliel. I received strict instruction in the Law of our ancestors and was just as dedicated to God as are all of you who are here today.

<sup>22.4</sup> "I persecuted to the death the people who followed this Way. I arrested men and women and threw them into prison.

<sup>22.5</sup> "The High Priest and the whole Council can prove that I am telling the truth. I received from them letters written to fellow Jews in Damascus, so I went there to arrest these people and bring them back in chains to Jerusalem to be punished.

<sup>22.6</sup> "As I was traveling and coming near Damascus, about midday a bright light from the sky flashed suddenly around me.

<sup>22.7</sup> "I fell to the ground and heard a voice saying to me, 'Saul, Saul! Why do you persecute me?'

<sup>22.8</sup> "'Who are you, Lord?' I asked. 'I am Jesus of Nazareth, whom you persecute,' he said to me.

<sup>22.9</sup> "The men with me saw the light, but did not hear the voice of the one who was speaking to me.

<sup>22.10</sup> "I asked, 'What shall I do, Lord?' and the Lord said to me, 'Get up and go into Damascus, and there you will be told everything that God has determined for you to do.'

<sup>22.11</sup> "I was blind because of the bright light, and so my companions took me by the hand and led me into Damascus.

<sup>22.12</sup> "In that city was a man named Ananias, a religious man who obeyed our Law and was highly respected by all the Jews living

there.

²²·¹³ "He came to me, stood by me, and said, 'Brother Saul, see again!' At that very moment I saw again and looked at him.

²²·¹⁴ "He said, 'The God of our ancestors has chosen you to know his will, to see his righteous Servant, and to hear him speaking with his own voice.

²²·¹⁵ " 'For you will be a witness for him to tell everyone what you have seen and heard.

²²·¹⁶ " 'And now, why wait any longer? Get up and be baptized and have your sins washed away by praying to him.'

²²·¹⁷ "I went back to Jerusalem, and while I was praying in the Temple, I had a vision,

²²·¹⁸ "in which I saw the Lord, as he said to me, 'Hurry and leave Jerusalem quickly, because the people here will not accept your witness about me.'

²²·¹⁹ " 'Lord,' I answered, 'they know very well that I went to the synagogues and arrested and beat those who believe in you.

²²·²⁰ " 'And when your witness Stephen was put to death, I myself was there, approving of his murder and taking care of the cloaks of his murderers.'

²²·²¹ " 'Go,' the Lord said to me, 'for I will send you far away to the Gentiles.' "

²²·²² The people listened to Paul until he said this; but then they started shouting at the top of their voices, "Away with him! Kill him! He's not fit to live!"

²²·²³ They were screaming, waving their clothes, and throwing dust up in the air.

²²·²⁴ The Roman commander ordered his men to take Paul into the fort, and he told them to whip him in order to find out why the Jews were screaming like this against him.

²²·²⁵ But when they had tied him up to be whipped, Paul said to the officer standing there, "Is it lawful for you to whip a Roman citizen who hasn't even been tried for any crime?"

²²·²⁶ When the officer heard this, he went to the commander and asked him, "What are you doing? That man is a Roman citizen!"

²²·²⁷ So the commander went to Paul and asked him, "Tell me, are you a Roman citizen?" "Yes," answered Paul.

²²·²⁸ The commander said, "I became one by paying a large amount of money." "But I am one by birth," Paul answered.

²²·²⁹ At once the men who were going to question Paul drew back from him; and the commander was frightened when he realized that

Paul was a Roman citizen and that he had put him in chains.
²²·³⁰ The commander wanted to find out for sure what the Jews were accusing Paul of; so the next day he had Paul's chains taken off and ordered the chief priests and the whole Council to meet. Then he took Paul and made him stand before them.

# 23

²³·¹ Paul looked straight at the Council and said, "My fellow Israelites! My conscience is perfectly clear about the way in which I have lived before God to this very day."
²³·² The High Priest Ananias ordered those who were standing close to Paul to strike him on the mouth.
²³·³ Paul said to him, "God will certainly strike you — you whitewashed wall! You sit there to judge me according to the Law, yet you break the Law by ordering them to strike me!"
²³·⁴ The men close to Paul said to him, "You are insulting God's High Priest!"
²³·⁵ Paul answered, "My fellow Israelites, I did not know that he was the High Priest. The scripture says, 'You must not speak evil of the ruler of your people.'"
²³·⁶ When Paul saw that some of the group were Sadducees and the others were Pharisees, he called out in the Council, "Fellow Israelites! I am a Pharisee, the son of Pharisees. I am on trial here because of the hope I have that the dead will rise to life!"
²³·⁷ As soon as he said this, the Pharisees and Sadducees started to quarrel, and the group was divided.
²³·⁸ (For the Sadducees say that people will not rise from death and that there are no angels or spirits; but the Pharisees believe in all three.)
²³·⁹ The shouting became louder, and some of the teachers of the Law who belonged to the party of the Pharisees stood up and protested strongly: "We cannot find a thing wrong with this man! Perhaps a spirit or an angel really did speak to him!"
²³·¹⁰ The argument became so violent that the commander was afraid that Paul would be torn to pieces. So he ordered his soldiers to go down into the group, get Paul away from them, and take him into the fort.
²³·¹¹ That night the Lord stood by Paul and said, "Don't be afraid! You have given your witness for me here in Jerusalem, and you must also do the same in Rome."
²³·¹² The next morning some Jews met together and made a plan.

They took a vow that they would not eat or drink anything until they had killed Paul.

<sup>23.13</sup> There were more than forty who planned this together.

<sup>23.14</sup> Then they went to the chief priests and elders and said, "We have taken a solemn vow together not to eat a thing until we have killed Paul.

<sup>23.15</sup> "Now then, you and the Council send word to the Roman commander to bring Paul down to you, pretending that you want to get more accurate information about him. But we will be ready to kill him before he ever gets here."

<sup>23.16</sup> But the son of Paul's sister heard about the plot; so he went to the fort and told Paul.

<sup>23.17</sup> Then Paul called one of the officers and said to him, "Take this young man to the commander; he has something to tell him."

<sup>23.18</sup> The officer took him, led him to the commander, and said, "The prisoner Paul called me and asked me to bring this young man to you, because he has something to say to you."

<sup>23.19</sup> The commander took him by the hand, led him off by himself, and asked him, "What do you have to tell me?

<sup>23. 20</sup> He said, "The Jewish authorities have agreed to ask you tomorrow to take Paul down to the Council, pretending that the Council wants to get more accurate information about him.

<sup>23.21</sup> "But don't listen to them, because there are more than forty men who will be hiding and waiting for him. They have taken a vow not to eat or drink until they have killed him. They are now ready to do it and are waiting for your decision."

<sup>23.22</sup> The commander said, "Don't tell anyone that you have reported this to me." And he sent the young man away.

<sup>23.23</sup> Then the commander called two of his officers and said, "Get two hundred soldiers ready to go to Caesarea, together with seventy horsemen and two hundred spearmen, and be ready to leave by nine o'clock tonight.

<sup>23.24</sup> "Provide some horses for Paul to ride and get him safely through to Governor Felix."

<sup>23.25</sup> Then the commander wrote a letter that went like this:

<sup>23.26</sup> "Claudius Lysias to His Excellency, Governor Felix: Greetings.

<sup>23.27</sup> "The Jews seized this man and were about to kill him. I learned that he is a Roman citizen, so I went with my soldiers and rescued him.

<sup>23.28</sup> "I wanted to know what they were accusing him of, so I took him down to their Council.

<sup>23.29</sup> "I found out that he had not done a thing for which he deserved to die or be put in prison; the accusation against him had to do with questions about their own law.

<sup>23.30</sup> "And when I was informed that there was a plot against him, at once I decided to send him to you. I have told his accusers to make their charges against him before you."

<sup>23.31</sup> The soldiers carried out their orders. They got Paul and took him that night as far as Antipatris.

<sup>23.32</sup> The next day the foot soldiers returned to the fort and left the horsemen to go on with him.

<sup>23.33</sup> They took him to Caesarea, delivered the letter to the governor, and turned Paul over to him.

<sup>23.34</sup> The governor read the letter and asked Paul what province he was from. When he found out that he was from Cilicia,

<sup>23.35</sup> he said, "I will hear you when your accusers arrive." Then he gave orders for Paul to be kept under guard in the governor's headquarters.

# 24

<sup>24.1</sup> Five days later the High Priest Ananias went to Caesarea with some elders and a lawyer named Tertullus. They appeared before Governor Felix and made their charges against Paul.

<sup>24.2</sup> Then Paul was called in, and Tertullus began to make his accusation, as follows: "Your Excellency! Your wise leadership has brought us a long period of peace, and many necessary reforms are being made for the good of our country.

<sup>24.3</sup> "We welcome this everywhere and at all times, and we are deeply grateful to you.

<sup>24.4</sup> "I do not want to take up too much of your time, however, so I beg you to be kind and listen to our brief account.

<sup>24.5</sup> "We found this man to be a dangerous nuisance; he starts riots among Jews all over the world and is a leader of the party of the Nazarenes.

<sup>24.6a</sup> "He also tried to defile the Temple, and we arrested him.

<sup>24.6b</sup> ("We planned to judge him according to our own law,)

<sup>24.7</sup> ("but the commander Lysias came, and with great violence took him from us.)

<sup>24.8a</sup> ("Then Lysias gave orders that his accusers should come before you.)

<sup>24.8b</sup> "If you question this man, you yourself will be able to learn from him all the things that we are accusing him of."

<sup>24.9</sup> The Jews joined in the accusation and said that all this was true.

<sup>24.10</sup> The governor then motioned to Paul to speak, and Paul said, "I know that you have been a judge over this nation for many years, and so I am happy to defend myself before you.

<sup>24.11</sup> "As you can find out for yourself, it was no more than twelve days ago that I went to Jerusalem to worship.

<sup>24.12</sup> "The Jews did not find me arguing with anyone in the Temple, nor did they find me stirring up the people, either in the synagogues or anywhere else in the city.

<sup>24.13</sup> "Nor can they give you proof of the accusations they now bring against me.

<sup>24.14</sup> "I do admit this to you: I worship the God of our ancestors by following that Way which they say is false. But I also believe in everything written in the Law of Moses and the books of the prophets.

<sup>24.15</sup> "I have the same hope in God that these themselves have, namely, that all people, both the good and the bad, will rise from death.

<sup>24.16</sup> "And so I do my best always to have a clear conscience before God and people.

<sup>24.17</sup> "After being away from Jerusalem for several years, I went there to take some money to my own people and to offer sacrifices.

<sup>24.18</sup> "It was while I was doing this that they found me in the Temple after I had completed the ceremony of purification. There was no crowd with me and no disorder.

<sup>24.19</sup> "But some Jews from the province of Asia were there; they themselves ought to come before you and make their accusations if they have anything against me.

<sup>24.20</sup> "Or let these who are here tell what crime they found me guilty of when I stood before the Council —

<sup>24.21</sup> "except for the one thing I called out when I stood before them: 'I am being tried by you today for believing that the dead will rise to life.'"

<sup>24.22</sup> Then Felix, who was well informed about the Way, brought the hearing to a close. "When the commander Lysias arrives," he told them, "I will decide your case."

<sup>24.23</sup> He ordered the officer in charge of Paul to keep him under guard, but to give him some freedom and allow his friends to provide for his needs.

<sup>24.24</sup> After some days Felix came with his wife Drusilla, who was Jewish. He sent for Paul and listened to him as he talked about faith in Christ Jesus.

<sup>24.25</sup> But as Paul went on discussing about goodness, self-control, and

the coming Day of Judgment, Felix was afraid and said, "You may leave now. I will call you again when I get the chance."

24.26 At the same time he was hoping that Paul would give him some money; and for this reason he would call for him often and talk with him.

24.27 After two years had passed, Porcius Festus succeeded Felix as governor. Felix wanted to gain favor with the Jews so he left Paul in prison.

# 25

25.1 Three days after Festus arrived in the province, he went from Caesarea to Jerusalem,

25.2 where the chief priests and the Jewish leaders brought their charges against Paul. They begged Festus

25.3 to do them the favor of having Paul come to Jerusalem, for they had made a plot to kill him on the way.

25.4 Festus answered, "Paul is being kept a prisoner in Caesarea, and I myself will be going back there soon.

25.5 "Let your leaders go to Caesarea with me and accuse the man if he has done anything wrong."

25.6 Festus spent another eight or ten days with them and then went to Caesarea. On the next day he sat down in the judgment court and ordered Paul to be brought in.

25.7 When Paul arrived, the Jews who had come from Jerusalem stood around him and started making many serious charges against him, which they were not able to prove.

25.8 But Paul defended himself: "I have done nothing wrong against the Law of the Jews or against the Temple or against the Roman Emperor."

25.9 But Festus wanted to gain favor with the Jews, so he asked Paul, "Would you be willing to go to Jerusalem and be tried on these charges before me there?"

25.10 Paul said, "I am standing before the Emperor's own judgment court, where I should be tried. I have done no wrong to the Jews, as you yourself well know.

25.11 "If I have broken the law and done something for which I deserve the death penalty, I do not ask to escape it. But if there is no truth in the charges they bring against me, no one can hand me over to them. I appeal to the Emperor."

25.12 Then Festus, after conferring with his advisers, answered, "You have appealed to the Emperor, so to the Emperor you will go."

<sup>25.13</sup> Some time later King Agrippa and Bernice came to Caesarea to pay a visit of welcome to Festus.

<sup>25.14</sup> After they had been there several days, Festus explained Paul's situation to the king: "There is a man here who was left a prisoner by Felix;

<sup>25.15</sup> "and when I went to Jerusalem, the Jewish chief priests and elders brought charges against him and asked me to condemn him.

<sup>25.16</sup> "But I told them that we Romans are not in the habit of handing over any who are accused of a crime before they have met their accusers face-to-face and have had the chance of defending themselves against the accusation.

<sup>25.17</sup> "When they came here, then, I lost no time, but on the very next day I sat in the judgment court and ordered the man to be brought in.

<sup>25.18</sup> "His opponents stood up, but they did not accuse him of any of the evil crimes that I thought they would.

<sup>25.19</sup> "All they had were some arguments with him about their own religion and about a man named Jesus, who has died; but Paul claims that he is alive.

<sup>25.20</sup> "I was undecided about how I could get information on these matters, so I asked Paul if he would be willing to go to Jerusalem and be tried there on these charges.

<sup>25.21</sup> "But Paul appealed; he asked to be kept under guard and to let the Emperor decide his case. So I gave orders for him to be kept under guard until I could send him to the Emperor."

<sup>25.22</sup> Agrippa said to Festus, "I would like to hear this man myself." "You will hear him tomorrow," Festus answered.

<sup>25.23</sup> The next day Agrippa and Bernice came with great pomp and ceremony and entered the audience hall with the military chiefs and the leading men of the city. Festus gave the order, and Paul was brought in.

<sup>25.24</sup> Festus said, "King Agrippa and all who are here with us: You see this man against whom all the Jewish people, both here and in Jerusalem, have brought complaints to me. They scream that he should not live any longer.

<sup>25.25</sup> "But I could not find that he had done anything for which he deserved the death sentence. And since he himself made an appeal to the Emperor, I have decided to send him.

<sup>25.26</sup> "But I have nothing definite about him to write to the Emperor. So I have brought him here before you — and especially before you, King Agrippa! — so that, after investigating his case, I may have

something to write. <sup></sup>25.27 "For it seems unreasonable to me to send a prisoner without clearly indicating the charges against him."

# 26

26.1 Agrippa said to Paul, "You have permission to speak on your own behalf." Paul stretched out his hand and defended himself as follows:
26.2 "King Agrippa! I consider myself fortunate that today I am to defend myself before you from all the things these Jews accuse me of,
26.3 "particularly since you know so well all the Jewish customs and disputes. I ask you, then, to listen to me with patience.
26.4 "All the Jews know how I have lived ever since I was young. They know how I have spent my whole life, at first in my own country and then in Jerusalem.
26.5 "They have always known, if they are willing to testify, that from the very first I have lived as a member of the strictest party of our religion, the Pharisees.
26.6 "And now I stand here to be tried because of the hope I have in the promise that God made to our ancestors —
26.7 "the very thing that the twelve tribes of our people hope to receive, as they worship God day and night. And it is because of this hope, Your Majesty, that I am being accused by these Jews!
26.8 "Why do you who are here find it impossible to believe that God raises the dead?
26.9 "I myself thought that I should do everything I could against the cause of Jesus of Nazareth.
26.10 "That is what I did in Jerusalem. I received authority from the chief priests and put many of God's people in prison; and when they were sentenced to death, I also voted against them.
26.11 "Many times I had them punished in the synagogues and tried to make them deny their faith. I was so furious with them that I even went to foreign cities to persecute them.
26.12 "It was for this purpose that I went to Damascus with authority and orders from the chief priests.
26.13 "It was on the road at midday, Your Majesty, that I saw a light much brighter than the sun, coming from the sky and shining around me and the men traveling with me.
26.14 "All of us fell to the ground, and I heard a voice say to me in Hebrew, 'Saul, Saul! Why are you persecuting me? You are hurting yourself by hitting back, like an ox kicking against its owner's stick.'
26.15 " 'Who are you, Lord?' I asked. And the Lord answered, 'I am Je-

sus, whom you persecute.

<sup>26.16</sup> " 'But get up and stand <u>on your feet</u>. I have appeared <u>to you</u> to appoint you <u>as my servant</u>. You are to tell others what you have seen <u>of me</u> today and what I will show you <u>in the future</u>.

<sup>26.17</sup> " 'I will rescue you <u>from the people</u> of Israel and <u>from the Gentiles</u> <u>to whom</u> I will send you.

<sup>26.18</sup> " 'You are to open their eyes and turn them <u>from the darkness</u> <u>to</u> <u>the light</u> and <u>from the power</u> <u>of Satan</u> <u>to God</u>, so that <u>through their</u> <u>faith</u> <u>in me</u> they will have their sins forgiven and receive their place <u>among God's chosen people</u>.'

<sup>26.19</sup> "And so, King Agrippa, I did not disobey the vision I had <u>from</u> <u>heaven</u>.

<sup>26.20</sup> "First <u>in Damascus</u> and <u>in Jerusalem</u> and then <u>in the whole</u> <u>country</u> <u>of Israel</u> and <u>among the Gentiles</u>, I preached that they must repent <u>of their sins</u> and turn <u>to God</u> and do the things that would show they had repented.

<sup>26.21</sup> "It was <u>for this reason</u> that these Jews seized me while I was <u>in</u> <u>the Temple</u>, and they tried to kill me.

<sup>26.22</sup> "But <u>to this very day</u> I have been helped <u>by God</u>, and so I stand here giving my witness <u>to all</u>, <u>to small and great</u> alike. What I say is the very same thing which the prophets and Moses said was going to happen:

<sup>26.23</sup> "that the Messiah must suffer and be the first one to rise <u>from</u> <u>death</u>, to announce the light <u>of salvation</u> <u>to the Jews</u> and <u>to the Gentiles</u>."

<sup>26.24</sup> As Paul defended himself <u>in this way</u>, Festus shouted <u>at him</u>, "You are mad, Paul! Your great learning is driving you mad!"

<sup>26.25</sup> Paul answered, "I am not mad, Your Excellency! I am speaking the sober truth.

<sup>26.26</sup> "King Agrippa! I can speak <u>to you</u> <u>with all boldness</u>, because you know <u>about these things</u>. I am sure that you have taken notice <u>of</u> <u>every one</u> <u>of them</u>, for this thing has not happened hidden away <u>in a</u> <u>corner</u>.

<sup>26.27</sup> "King Agrippa, do you believe the prophets? I know that you do!"

<sup>26.28</sup> Agrippa said <u>to Paul</u>, "<u>In this short time</u> do you think you will make me a Christian?"

<sup>26.29</sup> "Whether a short time or a long time," Paul answered, "my prayer <u>to God</u> is that you and all the rest <u>of you</u> who are listening <u>to me</u> today might become what I am — except, of course, <u>for these</u> <u>chains</u>!"

<sup>26.30</sup> Then the king, the governor, Bernice, and all the others got up,

<sup>26.31</sup> and after leaving they said to each other, "This man has not done anything for which he should die or be put in prison."
<sup>26.32</sup> And Agrippa said to Festus, "This man could have been released if he had not appealed to the Emperor."

# 27

<sup>27.1</sup> When it was decided that we should sail to Italy, they handed Paul and some other prisoners over to Julius, an officer in the Roman army regiment called "The Emperor's Regiment."
<sup>27.2</sup> We went aboard a ship from Adramyttium, which was ready to leave for the seaports of the province of Asia, and we sailed away. Aristarchus, a Macedonian from Thessalonica, was with us.
<sup>27.3</sup> The next day we arrived at Sidon. Julius was kind to Paul and allowed him to go and see his friends, to be given what he needed.
<sup>27.4</sup> We went on from there, and because the winds were blowing against us, we sailed on the sheltered side of the island of Cyprus.
<sup>27.5</sup> We crossed over the sea off Cilicia and Pamphylia and came to Myra in Lycia.
<sup>27.6</sup> There the officer found a ship from Alexandria that was going to sail for Italy, so he put us aboard.
<sup>27.7</sup> We sailed slowly for several days and with great difficulty finally arrived off the town of Cnidus. The wind would not let us go any farther in that direction, so we sailed down the sheltered side of the island of Crete, passing by Cape Salmone.
<sup>27.8</sup> We kept close to the coast and with great difficulty came to a place called Safe Harbors, not far from the town of Lasea.
<sup>27.9</sup> We spent a long time there, until it became dangerous to continue the voyage, for by now the Day of Atonement was already past. So Paul gave them this advice:
<sup>27.10</sup> "Men, I see that our voyage from here on will be dangerous; there will be great damage to the cargo and to the ship, and loss of life as well."
<sup>27.11</sup> But the army officer was convinced by what the captain and the owner of the ship said, and not by what Paul said.
<sup>27.12</sup> The harbor was not a good one to spend the winter in; so almost everyone was in favor of putting out to sea and trying to reach Phoenix, if possible, in order to spend the winter there. Phoenix is a harbor in Crete that faces southwest and northwest.
<sup>27.13</sup> A soft wind from the south began to blow, and the men thought that they could carry out their plan, so they pulled up the anchor and sailed as close as possible along the coast of Crete.

<sup>27.14</sup> But soon a very strong wind — the one called "Northeaster" — blew down from the island.

<sup>27.15</sup> It hit the ship, and since it was impossible to keep the ship headed into the wind, we gave up trying and let it be carried along by the wind.

<sup>27.16</sup> We got some shelter when we passed to the south of the little island of Cauda. There, with some difficulty we managed to make the ship's boat secure.

<sup>27.17</sup> They pulled it aboard and then fastened some ropes tight around the ship. They were afraid that they might run into the sandbanks off the coast of Libya, so they lowered the sail and let the ship be carried by the wind.

<sup>27.18</sup> The violent storm continued, so on the next day they began to throw some of the ship's cargo overboard,

<sup>27.19</sup> and on the following day they threw part of the ship's equipment overboard.

<sup>27.20</sup> For many days we could not see the sun or the stars, and the wind kept on blowing very hard. We finally gave up all hope of being saved.

<sup>27.21</sup> After everyone had gone a long time without food, Paul stood before them and said, "You should have listened to me and not have sailed from Crete; then we would have avoided all this damage and loss.

<sup>27.22</sup> "But now I beg you, take courage! Not one of you will lose your life; only the ship will be lost.

<sup>27.23</sup> "For last night an angel of the God to whom I belong and whom I worship came to me

<sup>27.24</sup> "and said, 'Don't be afraid, Paul! You must stand before the Emperor. And God in his goodness to you has spared the lives of all those who are sailing with you.'

<sup>27.25</sup> "So take courage, men! For I trust in God that it will be just as I was told.

<sup>27.26</sup> "But we will be driven ashore on some island."

<sup>27.27</sup> It was the fourteenth night, and we were being driven in the Mediterranean by the storm. About midnight the sailors suspected that we were getting close to land.

<sup>27.28</sup> So they dropped a line with a weight tied to it and found that the water was one hundred and twenty feet deep; a little later they did the same and found that it was ninety feet deep.

<sup>27.29</sup> They were afraid that the ship would go on the rocks, so they lowered four anchors from the back of the ship and prayed for day-

light.
²⁷·³⁰ Then the sailors tried to escape from the ship; they lowered the boat into the water and pretended that they were going to put out some anchors from the front of the ship.
²⁷·³¹ But Paul said to the army officer and soldiers, "If the sailors don't stay on board, you have no hope of being saved."
²⁷·³² So the soldiers cut the ropes that held the boat and let it go.
²⁷·³³ Just before dawn, Paul begged them all to eat some food: "You have been waiting for fourteen days now, and all this time you have not eaten a thing.
²⁷·³⁴ "I beg you, then, eat some food; you need it in order to survive. Not even a hair of your heads will be lost."
²⁷·³⁵ After saying this, Paul took some bread, gave thanks to God before them all, broke it, and began to eat.
²⁷·³⁶ They took courage, and every one of them also ate some food.
²⁷·³⁷ There was a total of 276 of us on board.
²⁷·³⁸ After everyone had eaten enough, they lightened the ship by throwing all the wheat into the sea.
²⁷·³⁹ When day came, the sailors did not recognize the coast, but they noticed a bay with a beach and decided that, if possible, they would run the ship aground there.
²⁷·⁴⁰ So they cut off the anchors and let them sink in the sea, and at the same time they untied the ropes that held the steering oars. Then they raised the sail at the front of the ship so that the wind would blow the ship forward, and we headed for shore.
²⁷·⁴¹ But the ship hit a sandbank and went aground; the front part of the ship got stuck and could not move, while the back part was being broken to pieces by the violence of the waves.
²⁷·⁴² The soldiers made a plan to kill all the prisoners, in order to keep them from swimming ashore and escaping.
²⁷·⁴³ But the army officer wanted to save Paul, so he stopped them from doing this. Instead, he ordered everyone who could swim to jump overboard first and swim ashore;
²⁷·⁴⁴ the rest were to follow, holding on to the planks or to some broken pieces of the ship. And this was how we all got safely ashore.

# 28

²⁸·¹ When we were safely ashore, we learned that the island was called Malta.
²⁸·² The natives there were very friendly to us. It had started to rain and was cold, so they built a fire and made us all welcome.

<sup>28.3</sup> Paul gathered up a bundle of sticks and was putting them on the fire when a snake came out on account of the heat and fastened itself to his hand.

<sup>28.4</sup> The natives saw the snake hanging on Paul's hand and said to one another, "This man must be a murderer, but Fate will not let him live, even though he escaped from the sea."

<sup>28.5</sup> But Paul shook the snake off into the fire without being harmed at all.

<sup>28.6</sup> They were waiting for him to swell up or suddenly fall down dead. But after waiting for a long time and not seeing anything unusual happening to him, they changed their minds and said, "He is a god!"

<sup>28.7</sup> Not far from that place were some fields that belonged to Publius, the chief of the island. He welcomed us kindly and for three days we were his guests.

<sup>28.8</sup> Publius' father was in bed, sick with fever and dysentery. Paul went into his room, prayed, placed his hands on him, and healed him.

<sup>28.9</sup> When this happened, all the other sick people on the island came and were healed.

<sup>28.10</sup> They gave us many gifts, and when we sailed, they put on board what we needed for the voyage.

<sup>28.11</sup> After three months we sailed away on a ship from Alexandria, called "The Twin Gods," which had spent the winter in the island.

<sup>28.12</sup> We arrived in the city of Syracuse and stayed there for three days.

<sup>28.13</sup> From there we sailed on and arrived in the city of Rhegium. The next day a wind began to blow from the south, and in two days we came to the town of Puteoli.

<sup>28.14</sup> We found some believers there who asked us to stay with them a week. And so we came to Rome.

<sup>28.15</sup> The believers in Rome heard about us and came as far as the towns of Market of Appius and Three Inns to meet us. When Paul saw them, he thanked God and was greatly encouraged.

<sup>28.16</sup> When we arrived in Rome, Paul was allowed to live by himself with a soldier guarding him.

<sup>28.17</sup> After three days Paul called the local Jewish leaders to a meeting. When they had gathered, he said to them, "My fellow Israelites, even though I did nothing against our people or the customs that we received from our ancestors, I was made a prisoner in Jerusalem and handed over to the Romans.

<sup>28.18</sup> "After questioning me, the Romans wanted to release me, be-

cause they found that I had done nothing for which I deserved to die. 
²⁸·¹⁹ "But when the Jews opposed this, I was forced to appeal to the Emperor, even though I had no accusation to make against my own people.
²⁸·²⁰ "That is why I asked to see you and talk with you. As a matter of fact, I am bound in chains like this for the sake of him for whom the people of Israel hope."
²⁸·²¹ They said to him, "We have not received any letters from Judea about you, nor have any of our people come from there with any news or anything bad to say about you.
²⁸·²² "But we would like to hear your ideas, because we know that everywhere people speak against this party to which you belong."
²⁸·²³ So they set a date with Paul, and a large number of them came that day to the place where Paul was staying. From morning till night he explained to them his message about the Kingdom of God, and he tried to convince them about Jesus by quoting from the Law of Moses and the writings of the prophets.
²⁸·²⁴ Some of them were convinced by his words, but others would not believe.
²⁸·²⁵ So they left, disagreeing among themselves, after Paul had said this one thing: "How well the Holy Spirit spoke through the prophet Isaiah to your ancestors!
²⁸·²⁶ "For he said, 'Go and say to this people: You will listen and listen, but not understand; you will look and look, but not see,
²⁸·²⁷ " 'because this people's minds are dull, and they have stopped up their ears and closed their eyes. Otherwise, their eyes would see, their ears would hear, their minds would understand, and they would turn to me, says God, and I would heal them.'"
²⁸·²⁸ And Paul concluded: "You are to know, then, that God's message of salvation has been sent to the Gentiles. They will listen!"
²⁸·²⁹ (After Paul said this, the Jews left, arguing violently among themselves.)
²⁸·³⁰ For two years Paul lived in a place he rented for himself, and there he welcomed all who came to see him.
²⁸·³¹ He preached about the Kingdom of God and taught about the Lord Jesus Christ, speaking with all boldness and freedom.

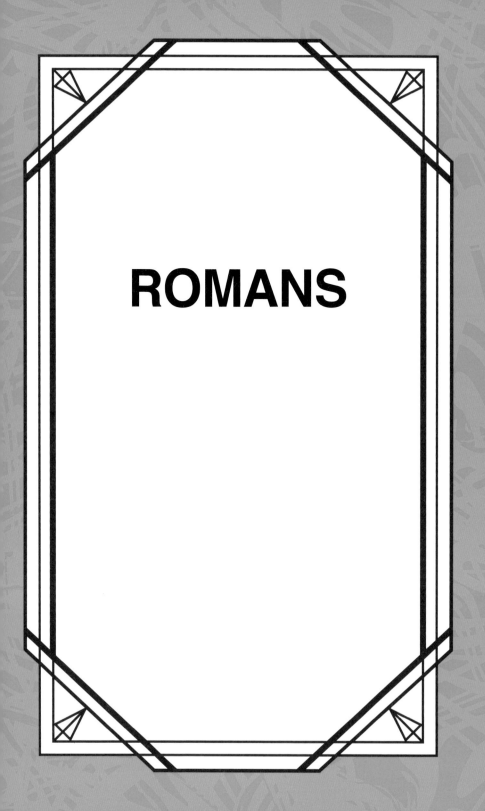

# ROMANS

# Romans

## 1

<sup>1.1</sup> From Paul, a servant of Christ Jesus and an apostle chosen and called by God to preach his Good News.

<sup>1.2</sup> The Good News was promised long ago by God through his prophets, as written in the Holy Scriptures.

<sup>1.3</sup> It is about his Son, our Lord Jesus Christ: as to his humanity, he was born a descendant of David;

<sup>1.4</sup> as to his divine holiness, he was shown with great power to be the Son of God by being raised from death.

<sup>1.5</sup> Through him God gave me the privilege of being an apostle for the sake of Christ, in order to lead people of all nations to believe and obey.

<sup>1.6</sup> This also includes you who are in Rome, whom God has called to belong to Jesus Christ.

<sup>1.7</sup> And so I write to all of you in Rome whom God loves and has called to be his own people: May God our Father and the Lord Jesus Christ give you grace and peace.

<sup>1.8</sup> First, I thank my God through Jesus Christ for all of you, because the whole world is hearing about your faith.

<sup>1.9</sup> God is my witness that what I say is true — the God whom I serve with all my heart by preaching the Good News about his Son. God knows that I remember you

<sup>1.10</sup> every time I pray. I ask that God in his good will may at last make it possible for me to visit you now.

<sup>1.11</sup> For I want very much to see you, in order to share a spiritual blessing with you to make you strong.

<sup>1.12</sup> What I mean is that both you and I will be helped at the same time, you by my faith and I by yours.

<sup>1.13</sup> You must remember, my friends, that many times I have planned to visit you, but something has always kept me from doing so. I want to win converts among you also, as I have among other Gentiles.

<sup>1.14</sup> For I have an obligation to all peoples, to the civilized and to the savage, to the educated and to the ignorant.

<sup>1.15</sup> So then, I am eager to preach the Good News to you also who live in Rome.

<sup>1.16</sup> I have complete confidence in the gospel; it is God's power to save all who believe, first the Jews and also the Gentiles.

<sup>1.17</sup> For the gospel reveals how God puts people right with himself: it

is through faith from beginning to end. As the scripture says, "The person who is put right with God through faith shall live."

1.18 God's anger is revealed from heaven against all the sin and evil of the people whose evil ways prevent the truth from being known. 1.19 God punishes them, because what can be known about God is plain to them, for God himself made it plain. 1.20 Ever since God created the world, his invisible qualities, both his eternal power and his divine nature, have been clearly seen; they are perceived in the things that God has made. So those people have no excuse at all!

1.21 They know God, but they do not give him the honor that belongs to him, nor do they thank him. Instead, their thoughts have become complete nonsense, and their empty minds are filled with darkness. 1.22 They say they are wise, but they are fools; 1.23 instead of worshiping the immortal God, they worship images made to look like mortals or birds or animals or reptiles.

1.24 And so God has given those people over to do the filthy things their hearts desire, and they do shameful things with each other. 1.25 They exchange the truth about God for a lie; they worship and serve what God has created instead of the Creator himself, who is to be praised forever! Amen.

1.26 Because they do this, God has given them over to shameful passions. Even the women pervert the natural use of their sex by unnatural acts. 1.27 In the same way the men give up natural sexual relations with women and burn with passion for each other. Men do shameful things with each other, and as a result they bring upon themselves the punishment they deserve for their wrongdoing.

1.28 Because those people refuse to keep in mind the true knowledge about God, he has given them over to corrupted minds, so that they do the things that they should not do. 1.29 They are filled with all kinds of wickedness, evil, greed, and vice; they are full of jealousy, murder, fighting, deceit, and malice. They gossip 1.30 and speak evil of one another; they are hateful to God, insolent, proud, and boastful; they think of more ways to do evil; they disobey their parents; 1.31 they have no conscience; they do not keep their promises, and they show no kindness or pity for others. 1.32 They know that God's law says that people who live in this way deserve death. Yet, not only do they continue to do these very things, but they even approve of others who do them.

**2** $^{2.1}$ Do you, my friend, pass judgment on others? You have no excuse at all, whoever you are. For when you judge others and then do the same things which they do, you condemn yourself. $^{2.2}$ We know that God is right when he judges the people who do such things as these. $^{2.3}$ But you, my friend, do those very things for which you pass judgment on others! Do you think you will escape God's judgment? $^{2.4}$ Or perhaps you despise his great kindness, tolerance, and patience. Surely you know that God is kind, because he is trying to lead you to repent. $^{2.5}$ But you have a hard and stubborn heart, and so you are making your own punishment even greater on the Day when God's anger and righteous judgments will be revealed. $^{2.6}$ For God will reward each of us according to what we have done. $^{2.7}$ Some people keep on doing good, and seek glory, honor, and immortal life; to them God will give eternal life. $^{2.8}$ Other people are selfish and reject what is right, in order to follow what is wrong; on them God will pour out his anger and fury. $^{2.9}$ There will be suffering and pain for all those who do what is evil, for the Jews first and also for the Gentiles. $^{2.10}$ But God will give glory, honor, and peace to all who do what is good, to the Jews first and also to the Gentiles. $^{2.11}$ For God judges everyone by the same standard. $^{2.12}$ The Gentiles do not have the Law of Moses; they sin and are lost apart from the Law. The Jews have the Law; they sin and are judged by the Law. $^{2.13}$ For it is not by hearing the Law that people are put right with God, but by doing what the Law commands. $^{2.14}$ The Gentiles do not have the Law; but whenever they do by instinct what the Law commands, they are their own law, even though they do not have the Law. $^{2.15}$ Their conduct shows that what the Law commands is written in their hearts. Their consciences also show that this is true, since their thoughts sometimes accuse them and sometimes defend them. $^{2.16}$ And so, according to the Good News I preach, this is how it will be on that Day when God through Jesus Christ will judge the secret thoughts of all. $^{2.17}$ What about you? You call yourself a Jew; you depend on the Law and boast about God; $^{2.18}$ you know what God wants you to do, and you have learned from the Law to choose what is right;

2.19 you are sure that you are a guide for the blind, a light for those who are in darkness,

2.20 an instructor for the foolish, and a teacher for the ignorant. You are certain that in the Law you have the full content of knowledge and of truth.

2.21 You teach others — why don't you teach yourself? You preach, "Do not steal" — but do you yourself steal?

2.22 You say, "Do not commit adultery" — but do you commit adultery? You detest idols — but do you rob temples?

2.23 You boast about having God's law — but do you bring shame on God by breaking his law?

2.24 The scripture says, "Because of you Jews, the Gentiles speak evil of God."

2.25 If you obey the Law, your circumcision is of value; but if you disobey the Law, you might as well never have been circumcised.

2.26 If the Gentile, who is not circumcised, obeys the commands of the Law, will not God regard him as though he were circumcised?

2.27 And so you Jews will be condemned by the Gentiles because you break the Law, even though you have it written down and are circumcised; but they obey the Law, even though they are not physically circumcised.

2.28 After all, who is a real Jew, truly circumcised? It is not the man who is a Jew on the outside, whose circumcision is a physical thing.

2.29 Rather, the real Jew is the person who is a Jew on the inside, that is, whose heart has been circumcised, and this is the work of God's Spirit, not of the written Law. Such a person receives praise from God, not from human beings.

# 3

3.1 Do the Jews then have any advantage over the Gentiles? Or is there any value in being circumcised?

3.2 Much, indeed, in every way! In the first place, God trusted his message to the Jews.

3.3 But what if some of them were not faithful? Does this mean that God will not be faithful?

3.4 Certainly not! God must be true, even though all human beings are liars. As the scripture says, "You must be shown to be right when you speak; you must win your case when you are being tried."

3.5 But what if our doing wrong serves to show up more clearly God's doing right? Can we say that God does wrong when he punishes us? (This would be the natural question to ask.)

<sup>3.6</sup> By no means! If God is not just, how can he judge the world?
<sup>3.7</sup> But what if my untruth serves God's glory by making his truth stand out more clearly? Why should I still be condemned as a sinner?
<sup>3.8</sup> Why not say, then, "Let us do evil so that good may come"? Some people, indeed, have insulted me by accusing me of saying this very thing! They will be condemned, as they should be.

<sup>3.9</sup> Well then, are we Jews in any better condition than the Gentiles? Not at all! I have already shown that Jews and Gentiles alike are all under the power of sin.
<sup>3.10</sup> As the Scriptures say: "There is no one who is righteous,
<sup>3.11</sup> "no one who is wise or who worships God.
<sup>3.12</sup> "All have turned away from God; they have all gone wrong; no one does what is right, not even one.
<sup>3.13</sup> "Their words are full of deadly deceit; wicked lies roll off their tongues, and dangerous threats, like snake's poison, from their lips;
<sup>3.14</sup> "their speech is filled with bitter curses.
<sup>3.15</sup> "They are quick to hurt and kill;
<sup>3.16</sup> "they leave ruin and destruction wherever they go.
<sup>3.17</sup> "They have not known the path of peace,
<sup>3.18</sup> "nor have they learned reverence for God."
<sup>3.19</sup> Now we know that everything in the Law applies to those who live under the Law, in order to stop all human excuses and bring the whole world under God's judgment.
<sup>3.20</sup> For no one is put right in God's sight by doing what the Law requires; what the Law does is to make us know that we have sinned.
<sup>3.21</sup> But now God's way of putting people right with himself has been revealed. It has nothing to do with law, even though the Law of Moses and the prophets gave their witness to it.
<sup>3.22</sup> God puts people right through their faith in Jesus Christ. God does this to all who believe in Christ, because there is no difference at all:
<sup>3.23</sup> everyone has sinned and is far away from God's saving presence.
<sup>3.24</sup> But by the free gift of God's grace all are put right with him through Christ Jesus, who sets them free.
<sup>3.25-26</sup> God offered him, so that by his blood he should become the means by which people's sins are forgiven through their faith in him. God did this in order to demonstrate that he is righteous. In the past he was patient and overlooked people's sins; but in the present time he deals with their sins, in order to demonstrate his righteousness. In this way God shows that he himself is righteous and that he puts right everyone who believes in Jesus.

<sup>3.27</sup> What, then, can we boast about? Nothing! And what is the reason for this? Is it that we obey the Law? No, but that we believe.
<sup>3.28</sup> For we conclude that a person is put right with God only through faith, and not by doing what the Law commands.
<sup>3.29</sup> Or is God the God of the Jews only? Is he not the God of the Gentiles also? Of course, he is.
<sup>3.30</sup> God is one, and he will put the Jews right with himself on the basis of their faith, and will put the Gentiles right through their faith.
<sup>3.31</sup> Does this mean that by this faith we do away with the Law? No, not at all; instead, we uphold the Law.

# 4

<sup>4.1</sup> What shall we say, then, of Abraham, the father of our race? What was his experience?
<sup>4.2</sup> If he was put right with God by the things he did, he would have something to boast about — but not in God's sight.
<sup>4.3</sup> The scripture says, "Abraham believed God, and because of his faith God accepted him as righteous."
<sup>4.4</sup> A person who works is paid wages, but they are not regarded as a gift; they are something that has been earned.
<sup>4.5</sup> But those who depend on faith, not on deeds, and who believe in the God who declares the guilty to be innocent, it is this faith that God takes into account in order to put them right with himself.
<sup>4.6</sup> This is what David meant when he spoke of the happiness of the person whom God accepts as righteous, apart from anything that person does:
<sup>4.7</sup> "Happy are those whose wrongs are forgiven, whose sins are pardoned!
<sup>4.8</sup> "Happy is the person whose sins the Lord will not keep account of!"
<sup>4.9</sup> Does this happiness that David spoke of belong only to those who are circumcised? No indeed! It belongs also to those who are not circumcised. For we have quoted the scripture, "Abraham believed God, and because of his faith God accepted him as righteous."
<sup>4.10</sup> When did this take place? Was it before or after Abraham was circumcised? It was before, not after.
<sup>4.11</sup> He was circumcised later, and his circumcision was a sign to show that because of his faith God had accepted him as righteous before he had been circumcised. And so Abraham is the spiritual father of all who believe in God and are accepted as righteous by him, even though they are not circumcised.
<sup>4.12</sup> He is also the father of those who are circumcised, that is, of

those who, in addition to being circumcised, also live the same life of faith that our father Abraham lived before he was circumcised. <sup>4.13</sup> When God promised Abraham and his descendants that the world would belong to him, he did so, not because Abraham obeyed the Law, but because he believed and was accepted as righteous by God.

<sup>4.14</sup> For if what God promises is to be given to those who obey the Law, then faith means nothing and God's promise is worthless.

<sup>4.15</sup> The Law brings down God's anger; but where there is no law, there is no disobeying of the law.

<sup>4.16</sup> And so the promise was based on faith, in order that the promise should be guaranteed as God's free gift to all of Abraham's descendants — not just to those who obey the Law, but also to those who believe as Abraham did. For Abraham is the spiritual father of us all; <sup>4.17</sup> as the scripture says, "I have made you father of many nations." So the promise is good in the sight of God, in whom Abraham believed — the God who brings the dead to life and whose command brings into being what did not exist.

<sup>4.18</sup> Abraham believed and hoped, even when there was no reason for hoping, and so became "the father of many nations." Just as the scripture says, "Your descendants will be as many as the stars."

<sup>4.19</sup> He was then almost one hundred years old; but his faith did not weaken when he thought of his body, which was already practically dead, or of the fact that Sarah could not have children.

<sup>4.20</sup> His faith did not leave him, and he did not doubt God's promise; his faith filled him with power, and he gave praise to God.

<sup>4.21</sup> He was absolutely sure that God would be able to do what he had promised.

<sup>4.22</sup> That is why Abraham, through faith, "was accepted as righteous by God."

<sup>4.23</sup> The words "he was accepted as righteous" were not written for him alone.

<sup>4.24</sup> They were written also for us who are to be accepted as righteous, who believe in him who raised Jesus our Lord from death.

<sup>4.25</sup> Because of our sins he was given over to die, and he was raised to life in order to put us right with God.

# 5

<sup>5.1</sup> Now that we have been put right with God through faith, we have peace with God through our Lord Jesus Christ. <sup>5.2</sup> He has brought us by faith into this experience of God's grace, in

which we now live. And so we boast of the hope we have of sharing God's glory!

5.3 We also boast of our troubles, because we know that trouble produces endurance,

5.4 endurance brings God's approval, and his approval creates hope.

5.5 This hope does not disappoint us, for God has poured out his love into our hearts by means of the Holy Spirit, who is God's gift to us.

5.6 For when we were still helpless, Christ died for the wicked at the time that God chose.

5.7 It is a difficult thing for someone to die for a righteous person. It may even be that someone might dare to die for a good person.

5.8 But God has shown us how much he loves us — it was while we were still sinners that Christ died for us!

5.9 By his blood we are now put right with God; how much more, then, will we be saved by him from God's anger!

5.10 We were God's enemies, but he made us his friends through the death of his Son. Now that we are God's friends, how much more will we be saved by Christ's life!

5.11 But that is not all; we rejoice because of what God has done through our Lord Jesus Christ, who has now made us God's friends.

5.12 Sin came into the world through one man, and his sin brought death with it. As a result, death has spread to the whole human race because everyone has sinned.

5.13 There was sin in the world before the Law was given; but where there is no law, no account is kept of sins.

5.14 But from the time of Adam to the time of Moses, death ruled over all human beings, even over those who did not sin in the same way that Adam did when he disobeyed God's command. Adam was a figure of the one who was to come.

5.15 But the two are not the same, because God's free gift is not like Adam's sin. It is true that many people died because of the sin of that one man. But God's grace is much greater, and so is his free gift to so many people through the grace of the one man, Jesus Christ.

5.16 And there is a difference between God's gift and the sin of one man. After the one sin, came the judgment of "Guilty"; but after so many sins, comes the undeserved gift of "Not guilty!"

5.17 It is true that through the sin of one man death began to rule because of that one man. But how much greater is the result of what was done by the one man, Jesus Christ! All who receive God's abundant grace and are freely put right with him will rule in life through Christ.

<sup></sup> So then, as the one sin condemned all people, in the same way the one righteous act sets all people free and gives them life.

5.19 And just as all people were made sinners as the result of the disobedience of one man, in the same way they will all be put right with God as the result of the obedience of the one man.

5.20 Law was introduced in order to increase wrongdoing; but where sin increased, God's grace increased much more.

5.21 So then, just as sin ruled by means of death, so also God's grace rules by means of righteousness, leading us to eternal life through Jesus Christ our Lord.

# 6

6.1 What shall we say, then? Should we continue to live in sin so that God's grace will increase?

6.2 Certainly not! We have died to sin — how then can we go on living in it?

6.3 For surely you know that when we were baptized into union with Christ Jesus, we were baptized into union with his death.

6.4 By our baptism, then, we were buried with him and shared his death, in order that, just as Christ was raised from death by the glorious power of the Father, so also we might live a new life.

6.5 For since we have become one with him in dying as he did, in the same way we shall be one with him by being raised to life as he was.

6.6 And we know that our old being has been put to death with Christ on his cross, in order that the power of the sinful self might be destroyed, so that we should no longer be the slaves of sin.

6.7 For when we die, we are set free from the power of sin.

6.8 Since we have died with Christ, we believe that we will also live with him.

6.9 For we know that Christ has been raised from death and will never die again — death will no longer rule over him.

6.10 And so, because he died, sin has no power over him; and now he lives his life in fellowship with God.

6.11 In the same way you are to think of yourselves as dead, so far as sin is concerned, but living in fellowship with God through Christ Jesus.

6.12 Sin must no longer rule in your mortal bodies, so that you obey the desires of your natural self.

6.13 Nor must you surrender any part of yourselves to sin to be used for wicked purposes. Instead, give yourselves to God, as those who have been brought from death to life, and surrender your whole being to him to be used for righteous purposes.

6.14 Sin must not be your master; for you do not live under law but under God's grace.

6.15 What, then? Shall we sin, because we are not under law but under God's grace? By no means!

6.16 Surely you know that when you surrender yourselves as slaves to obey someone, you are in fact the slaves of the master you obey — either of sin, which results in death, or of obedience, which results in being put right with God.

6.17 But thanks be to God! For though at one time you were slaves to sin, you have obeyed with all your heart the truths found in the teaching you received.

6.18 You were set free from sin and became the slaves of righteousness.

6.19 (I use everyday language because of the weakness of your natural selves.) At one time you surrendered yourselves entirely as slaves to impurity and wickedness for wicked purposes. In the same way you must now surrender yourselves entirely as slaves of righteousness for holy purposes.

6.20 When you were the slaves of sin, you were free from righteousness.

6.21 What did you gain from doing the things that you are now ashamed of? The result of those things is death!

6.22 But now you have been set free from sin and are the slaves of God. Your gain is a life fully dedicated to him, and the result is eternal life.

6.23 For sin pays its wage — death; but God's free gift is eternal life in union with Christ Jesus our Lord.

# 7

7.1 Certainly you will understand what I am about to say, my friends, because all of you know about law. The law rules over people only as long as they live.

7.2 A married woman, for example, is bound by the law to her husband as long as he lives; but if he dies, then she is free from the law that bound her to him.

7.3 So then, if she lives with another man while her husband is alive, she will be called an adulteress; but if her husband dies, she is legally a free woman and does not commit adultery if she marries another man.

7.4 That is how it is with you, my friends. As far as the Law is concerned, you also have died because you are part of the body of Christ; and now you belong to him who was raised from death in order that we might be useful in the service of God.

[7.5] For when we lived according to our human nature, the sinful desires stirred up by the Law were at work in our bodies, and all we did ended in death.

[7.6] Now, however, we are free from the Law, because we died to that which once held us prisoners. No longer do we serve in the old way of a written law, but in the new way of the Spirit.

[7.7] Shall we say, then, that the Law itself is sinful? Of course not! But it was the Law that made me know what sin is. If the Law had not said, "Do not desire what belongs to someone else," I would not have known such a desire.

[7.8] But by means of that commandment sin found its chance to stir up all kinds of selfish desires in me. Apart from law, sin is a dead thing.

[7.9] I myself was once alive apart from law; but when the commandment came, sin sprang to life,

[7.10] and I died. And the commandment which was meant to bring life, in my case brought death.

[7.11] Sin found its chance, and by means of the commandment it deceived me and killed me.

[7.12] So then, the Law itself is holy, and the commandment is holy, right, and good.

[7.13] But does this mean that what is good caused my death? By no means! It was sin that did it; by using what is good, sin brought death to me, in order that its true nature as sin might be revealed. And so, by means of the commandment sin is shown to be even more terribly sinful.

[7.14] We know that the Law is spiritual; but I am a mortal, sold as a slave to sin.

[7.15] I do not understand what I do; for I don't do what I would like to do, but instead I do what I hate.

[7.16] Since what I do is what I don't want to do, this shows that I agree that the Law is right.

[7.17] So I am not really the one who does this thing; rather it is the sin that lives in me.

[7.18] I know that good does not live in me — that is, in my human nature. For even though the desire to do good is in me, I am not able to do it.

[7.19] I don't do the good I want to do; instead, I do the evil that I do not want to do.

7.20 If I do what I don't want to do, this means that I am no longer the one who does it; instead, it is the sin that lives in me.

7.21 So I find that this law is at work: when I want to do what is good, what is evil is the only choice I have.

7.22 My inner being delights in the law of God.

7.23 But I see a different law at work in my body — a law that fights against the law which my mind approves of. It makes me a prisoner to the law of sin which is at work in my body.

7.24 What an unhappy man I am! Who will rescue me from this body that is taking me to death?

7.25 Thanks be to God, who does this through our Lord Jesus Christ! This, then, is my condition: on my own I can serve God's law only with my mind, while my human nature serves the law of sin.

# 8

8.1 There is no condemnation now for those who live in union with Christ Jesus.

8.2 For the law of the Spirit, which brings us life in union with Christ Jesus, has set me free from the law of sin and death.

8.3 What the Law could not do, because human nature was weak, God did. He condemned sin in human nature by sending his own Son, who came with a nature like our sinful nature, to do away with sin.

8.4 God did this so that the righteous demands of the Law might be fully satisfied in us who live according to the Spirit, and not according to human nature.

8.5 Those who live as their human nature tells them to, have their minds controlled by what human nature wants. Those who live as the Spirit tells them to, have their minds controlled by what the Spirit wants.

8.6 To be controlled by human nature results in death; to be controlled by the Spirit results in life and peace.

8.7 And so people become enemies of God when they are controlled by their human nature; for they do not obey God's law, and in fact they cannot obey it.

8.8 Those who obey their human nature cannot please God.

8.9 But you do not live as your human nature tells you to; instead, you live as the Spirit tells you to — if, in fact, God's Spirit lives in you. Whoever does not have the Spirit of Christ does not belong to him.

<sup>8.10</sup> But if Christ lives in you, the Spirit is life for you because you have been put right with God, even though your bodies are going to die because of sin.

<sup>8.11</sup> If the Spirit of God, who raised Jesus from death, lives in you, then he who raised Christ from death will also give life to your mortal bodies by the presence of his Spirit in you.

<sup>8.12</sup> So then, my friends, we have an obligation, but it is not to live as our human nature wants us to.

<sup>8.13</sup> For if you live according to your human nature, you are going to die; but if by the Spirit you put to death your sinful actions, you will live.

<sup>8.14</sup> Those who are led by God's Spirit are God's children.

<sup>8.15</sup> For the Spirit that God has given you does not make you slaves and cause you to be afraid; instead, the Spirit makes you God's children, and by the Spirit's power we cry out to God, "Father! my Father!"

<sup>8.16</sup> God's Spirit joins himself to our spirits to declare that we are God's children.

<sup>8.17</sup> Since we are his children, we will possess the blessings he keeps for his people, and we will also possess with Christ what God has kept for him; for if we share Christ's suffering, we will also share his glory.

<sup>8.18</sup> I consider that what we suffer at this present time cannot be compared at all with the glory that is going to be revealed to us.

<sup>8.19</sup> All of creation waits with eager longing for God to reveal his children.

<sup>8.20</sup> For creation was condemned to lose its purpose, not of its own will, but because God willed it to be so. Yet there was the hope

<sup>8.21</sup> that creation itself would one day be set free from its slavery to decay and would share the glorious freedom of the children of God.

<sup>8.22</sup> For we know that up to the present time all of creation groans with pain, like the pain of childbirth.

<sup>8.23</sup> But it is not just creation alone which groans; we who have the Spirit as the first of God's gifts also groan within ourselves as we wait for God to make us his children and set our whole being free.

<sup>8.24</sup> For it was by hope that we were saved; but if we see what we hope for, then it is not really hope. For who of us hopes for something we see?

<sup>8.25</sup> But if we hope for what we do not see, we wait for it with patience.

<sup>8.26</sup> In the same way the Spirit also comes to help us, weak as we are.

For we do not know how we ought to pray; the Spirit himself pleads with God for us in groans that words cannot express.

8.27 And God, who sees into our hearts, knows what the thought of the Spirit is; because the Spirit pleads with God on behalf of his people and in accordance with his will.

8.28 We know that in all things God works for good with those who love him, those whom he has called according to his purpose.

8.29 Those whom God had already chosen he also set apart to become like his Son, so that the Son would be the first among many believers.

8.30 And so those whom God set apart, he called; and those he called, he put right with himself, and he shared his glory with them.

8.31 In view of all this, what can we say? If God is for us, who can be against us?

8.32 Certainly not God, who did not even keep back his own Son, but offered him for us all! He gave us his Son — will he not also freely give us all things?

8.33 Who will accuse God's chosen people? God himself declares them not guilty!

8.34 Who, then, will condemn them? Not Christ Jesus, who died, or rather, who was raised to life and is at the right side of God, pleading with him for us!

8.35 Who, then, can separate us from the love of Christ? Can trouble do it, or hardship or persecution or hunger or poverty or danger or death?

8.36 As the scripture says, "For your sake we are in danger of death at all times; we are treated like sheep that are going to be slaughtered."

8.37 No, in all these things we have complete victory through him who loved us!

8.38 For I am certain that nothing can separate us from his love: neither death nor life, neither angels nor other heavenly rulers or powers, neither the present nor the future,

8.39 neither the world above nor the world below — there is nothing in all creation that will ever be able to separate us from the love of God which is ours through Christ Jesus our Lord.

# 9

9.1 I am speaking the truth; I belong to Christ and I do not lie. My conscience, ruled by the Holy Spirit, also assures me that I am not lying

9.2 when I say how great is my sorrow, how endless the pain in my heart
9.3 for my people, my own flesh and blood! For their sake I could wish that I myself were under God's curse and separated from Christ.
9.4 They are God's people; he made them his children and revealed his glory to them; he made his covenants with them and gave them the Law; they have the true worship; they have received God's promises;
9.5 they are descended from the famous Hebrew ancestors; and Christ, as a human being, belongs to their race. May God, who rules over all, be praised forever! Amen.
9.6 I am not saying that the promise of God has failed; for not all the people of Israel are the people of God.
9.7 Nor are all of Abraham's descendants the children of God. God said to Abraham, "It is through Isaac that you will have the descendants I promised you."
9.8 This means that the children born in the usual way are not the children of God; instead, the children born as a result of God's promise are regarded as the true descendants.
9.9 For God's promise was made in these words: "At the right time I will come back, and Sarah will have a son."
9.10 And this is not all. For Rebecca's two sons had the same father, our ancestor Isaac.
9.11-12 But in order that the choice of one son might be completely the result of God's own purpose, God said to her, "The older will serve the younger." He said this before they were born, before they had done anything either good or bad; so God's choice was based on his call, and not on anything they had done.
9.13 As the scripture says, "I loved Jacob, but I hated Esau."
9.14 Shall we say, then, that God is unjust? Not at all.
9.15 For he said to Moses, "I will have mercy on anyone I wish; I will take pity on anyone I wish."
9.16 So then, everything depends, not on what we humans want or do, but only on God's mercy.
9.17 For the scripture says to the king of Egypt, "I made you king in order to use you to show my power and to spread my fame over the whole world."
9.18 So then, God has mercy on anyone he wishes, and he makes stubborn anyone he wishes.
9.19 But one of you will say to me, "If this is so, how can God find fault with anyone? Who can resist God's will?"

<sup>9.20</sup> But who are you, my friend, to talk back to God? A clay pot does not ask the man who made it, "Why did you make me like this?"

<sup>9.21</sup> After all, the man who makes the pots has the right to use the clay as he wishes, and to make two pots from the same lump of clay, one for special occasions and the other for ordinary use.

<sup>9.22</sup> And the same is true of what God has done. He wanted to show his anger and to make his power known. But he was very patient in enduring those who were the objects of his anger, who were doomed to destruction.

<sup>9.23</sup> And he also wanted to reveal his abundant glory, which was poured out on us who are the objects of his mercy, those of us whom he has prepared to receive his glory.

<sup>9.24</sup> For we are the people he called, not only from among the Jews but also from among the Gentiles.

<sup>9.25</sup> This is what he says in the book of Hosea: "The people who were not mine I will call 'My People.' The nation that I did not love I will call 'My Beloved.'

<sup>9.26</sup> "And in the very place where they were told, 'You are not my people,' there they will be called the children of the living God."

<sup>9.27</sup> And Isaiah exclaims about Israel: "Even if the people of Israel are as many as the grains of sand by the sea, yet only a few of them will be saved;

<sup>9.28</sup> "for the Lord will quickly settle his full account with the world."

<sup>9.29</sup> It is as Isaiah had said before, "If the Lord Almighty had not left us some descendants, we would have become like Sodom, we would have been like Gomorrah."

<sup>9.30</sup> So we say that the Gentiles, who were not trying to put themselves right with God, were put right with him through faith;

<sup>9.31</sup> while God's people, who were seeking a law that would put them right with God, did not find it.

<sup>9.32</sup> And why not? Because they did not depend on faith but on what they did. And so they stumbled over the "stumbling stone"

<sup>9.33</sup> that the scripture speaks of: "Look, I place in Zion a stone that will make people stumble, a rock that will make them fall. But whoever believes in him will not be disappointed."

# 10

<sup>10.1</sup> My friends, how I wish with all my heart that my own people might be saved! How I pray to God for them!

<sup>10.2</sup> I can assure you that they are deeply devoted to God; but their devotion is not based on true knowledge.

**10.3** They have not known the way in which God puts people right with himself, and instead, they have tried to set up their own way; and so they did not submit themselves to God's way of putting people right.

**10.4** For Christ has brought the Law to an end, so that everyone who believes is put right with God.

**10.5** Moses wrote this about being put right with God by obeying the Law: "Whoever obeys the commands of the Law will live."

**10.6** But what the scripture says about being put right with God through faith is this: "You are not to ask yourself, Who will go up into heaven?" (that is, to bring Christ down).

**10.7** "Nor are you to ask, Who will go down into the world below?" (that is, to bring Christ up from death).

**10.8** What it says is this: "God's message is near you, on your lips and in your heart" — that is, the message of faith that we preach.

**10.9** If you confess that Jesus is Lord and believe that God raised him from death, you will be saved.

**10.10** For it is by our faith that we are put right with God; it is by our confession that we are saved.

**10.11** The scripture says, "Whoever believes in him will not be disappointed."

**10.12** This includes everyone, because there is no difference between Jews and Gentiles; God is the same Lord of all and richly blesses all who call to him.

**10.13** As the scripture says, "Everyone who calls out to the Lord for help will be saved."

**10.14** But how can they call to him for help if they have not believed? And how can they believe if they have not heard the message? And how can they hear if the message is not proclaimed?

**10.15** And how can the message be proclaimed if the messengers are not sent out? As the scripture says, "How wonderful is the coming of messengers who bring good news!"

**10.16** But not all have accepted the Good News. Isaiah himself said, "Lord, who believed our message?"

**10.17** So then, faith comes from hearing the message, and the message comes through preaching Christ.

**10.18** But I ask: Is it true that they did not hear the message? Of course, they did — for as the scripture says: "The sound of their voice went out to all the world; their words reached the ends of the earth."

**10.19** Again I ask: Did the people of Israel not understand? Moses himself is the first one to answer: "I will use a so-called nation to make my people jealous; and by means of a nation of fools I will make my people angry."

<sup>10.20</sup> And Isaiah is even bolder when he says, "I was found by those who were not looking for me; I appeared to those who were not asking for me."

<sup>10.21</sup> But concerning Israel he says, "All day long I held out my hands to welcome a disobedient and rebellious people."

# 11

<sup>11.1</sup> I ask, then: Did God reject his own people? Certainly not! I myself am an Israelite, a descendant of Abraham, a member of the tribe of Benjamin.

<sup>11.2</sup> God has not rejected his people, whom he chose from the beginning. You know what the scripture says in the passage where Elijah pleads with God against Israel:

<sup>11.3</sup> "Lord, they have killed your prophets and torn down your altars; I am the only one left, and they are trying to kill me."

<sup>11.4</sup> What answer did God give him? "I have kept for myself seven thousand men who have not worshiped the false god Baal."

<sup>11.5</sup> It is the same way now: there is a small number left of those whom God has chosen because of his grace.

<sup>11.6</sup> His choice is based on his grace, not on what they have done. For if God's choice were based on what people do, then his grace would not be real grace.

<sup>11.7</sup> What then? The people of Israel did not find what they were looking for. It was only the small group that God chose who found it; the rest grew deaf to God's call.

<sup>11.8</sup> As the scripture says, "God made their minds and hearts dull; to this very day they cannot see or hear."

<sup>11.9</sup> And David says, "May they be caught and trapped at their feasts; may they fall, may they be punished!

<sup>11.10</sup> "May their eyes be blinded so that they cannot see; and make them bend under their troubles at all times."

<sup>11.11</sup> I ask, then: When the Jews stumbled, did they fall to their ruin? By no means! Because they sinned, salvation has come to the Gentiles, to make the Jews jealous of them.

<sup>11.12</sup> The sin of the Jews brought rich blessings to the world, and their spiritual poverty brought rich blessings to the Gentiles. Then, how much greater the blessings will be when the complete number of Jews is included!

<sup>11.13</sup> I am speaking now to you Gentiles: As long as I am an apostle to

the Gentiles, I will take pride in my work.

<sup>11.14</sup> Perhaps I can make the people of my own race jealous, and so be able to save some of them.

<sup>11.15</sup> For when they were rejected, all other people were changed from God's enemies into his friends. What will it be, then, when they are accepted? It will be life for the dead!

<sup>11.16</sup> If the first piece of bread is given to God, then the whole loaf is his also; and if the roots of a tree are offered to God, the branches are his also.

<sup>11.17</sup> Some of the branches of the cultivated olive tree have been broken off, and a branch of a wild olive tree has been joined to it. You Gentiles are like that wild olive tree, and now you share the strong spiritual life of the Jews.

<sup>11.18</sup> So then, you must not despise those who were broken off like branches. How can you be proud? You are just a branch; you don't support the roots — the roots support you.

<sup>11.19</sup> But you will say, "Yes, but the branches were broken off to make room for me."

<sup>11.20</sup> That is true. They were broken off because they did not believe, while you remain in place because you do believe. But do not be proud of it; instead, be afraid.

<sup>11.21</sup> God did not spare the Jews, who are like natural branches; do you think he will spare you?

<sup>11.22</sup> Here we see how kind and how severe God is. He is severe toward those who have fallen, but kind to you — if you continue in his kindness. But if you do not, you too will be broken off.

<sup>11.23</sup> And if the Jews abandon their unbelief, they will be put back in the place where they were; for God is able to do that.

<sup>11.24</sup> You Gentiles are like the branch of a wild olive tree that is broken off and then, contrary to nature, is joined to a cultivated olive tree. The Jews are like this cultivated tree; and it will be much easier for God to join these broken-off branches to their own tree again.

<sup>11.25</sup> There is a secret truth, my friends, which I want you to know, for it will keep you from thinking how wise you are. It is that the stubbornness of the people of Israel is not permanent, but will last only until the complete number of Gentiles comes to God.

<sup>11.26</sup> And this is how all Israel will be saved. As the scripture says,"The Savior will come from Zion and remove all wickedness from the descendants of Jacob.

<sup>11.27</sup> "I will make this covenant with them when I take away their sins."

<sup>11.28</sup> Because they reject the Good News, the Jews are God's enemies for the sake of you Gentiles. But because of God's choice, they are his friends because of their ancestors.

<sup>11.29</sup> For God does not change his mind about whom he chooses and blesses.

<sup>11.30</sup> As for you Gentiles, you disobeyed God in the past; but now you have received God's mercy because the Jews were disobedient.

<sup>11.31</sup> In the same way, because of the mercy that you have received, the Jews now disobey God, in order that they also may now receive God's mercy.

<sup>11.32</sup> For God has made all people prisoners of disobedience, so that he might show mercy to them all.

<sup>11.33</sup> How great are God's riches! How deep are his wisdom and knowledge! Who can explain his decisions? Who can understand his ways?

<sup>11.34</sup> As the scripture says, "Who knows the mind of the Lord? Who is able to give him advice?

<sup>11.35</sup> "Who has ever given him anything, so that he had to pay it back?"

<sup>11.36</sup> For all things were created by him, and all things exist through him and for him. To God be the glory forever! Amen.

# 12

<sup>12.1</sup> So then, my friends, because of God's great mercy to us I appeal to you: Offer yourselves as a living sacrifice to God, dedicated to his service and pleasing to him. This is the true worship that you should offer.

<sup>12.2</sup> Do not conform yourselves to the standards of this world, but let God transform you inwardly by a complete change of your mind. Then you will be able to know the will of God — what is good and is pleasing to him and is perfect.

<sup>12.3</sup> And because of God's gracious gift to me I say to every one of you: Do not think of yourself more highly than you should. Instead, be modest in your thinking, and judge yourself according to the amount of faith that God has given you.

<sup>12.4</sup> We have many parts in the one body, and all these parts have different functions.

<sup>12.5</sup> In the same way, though we are many, we are one body in union with Christ, and we are all joined to each other as different parts of one body.

<sup>12.6</sup> So we are to use our different gifts in accordance with the grace that God has given us. If our gift is to speak God's message, we

should do it according to the faith that we have;
<sup>12.7</sup> if it is to serve, we should serve; if it is to teach, we should teach;
<sup>12.8</sup> if it is to encourage others, we should do so. Whoever shares with others should do it generously; whoever has authority should work hard; whoever shows kindness to others should do it cheerfully.
<sup>12.9</sup> Love must be completely sincere. Hate what is evil, hold on to what is good.
<sup>12.10</sup> Love one another warmly as Christians, and be eager to show respect for one another.
<sup>12.11</sup> Work hard and do not be lazy. Serve the Lord with a heart full of devotion.
<sup>12.12</sup> Let your hope keep you joyful, be patient in your troubles, and pray at all times.
<sup>12.13</sup> Share your belongings with your needy fellow Christians, and open your homes to strangers.
<sup>12.14</sup> Ask God to bless those who persecute you — yes, ask him to bless, not to curse.
<sup>12.15</sup> Be happy with those who are happy, weep with those who weep.
<sup>12.16</sup> Have the same concern for everyone. Do not be proud, but accept humble duties. Do not think of yourselves as wise.
<sup>12.17</sup> If someone has done you wrong, do not repay him with a wrong. Try to do what everyone considers to be good.
<sup>12.18</sup> Do everything possible on your part to live in peace with everybody.
<sup>12.19</sup> Never take revenge, my friends, but instead let God's anger do it. For the scripture says, "I will take revenge, I will pay back, says the Lord."
<sup>12.20</sup> Instead, as the scripture says: "If your enemies are hungry, feed them; if they are thirsty, give them a drink; for by doing this you will make them burn with shame."
<sup>12.21</sup> Do not let evil defeat you; instead, conquer evil with good.

# 13

<sup>13.1</sup> Everyone must obey state authorities, because no authority exists without God's permission, and the existing authorities have been put there by God.
<sup>13.2</sup> Whoever opposes the existing authority opposes what God has ordered; and anyone who does so will bring judgment on himself.
<sup>13.3</sup> For rulers are not to be feared by those who do good, but by those who do evil. Would you like to be unafraid of those in authority? Then do what is good, and they will praise you,

<sup>13.4</sup> because they are God's servants working for your own good. But if you do evil, then be afraid of them, because their power to punish is real. They are God's servants and carry out God's punishment on those who do evil.

<sup>13.5</sup> For this reason you must obey the authorities — not just because of God's punishment, but also as a matter of conscience.

<sup>13.6</sup> That is also why you pay taxes, because the authorities are working for God when they fulfill their duties.

<sup>13.7</sup> Pay, then, what you owe them; pay them your personal and property taxes, and show respect and honor for them all.

<sup>13.8</sup> Be under obligation to no one — the only obligation you have is to love one another. Whoever does this has obeyed the Law.

<sup>13.9</sup> The commandments, "Do not commit adultery; do not commit murder; do not steal; do not desire what belongs to someone else" — all these, and any others besides, are summed up in the one command, "Love your neighbor as you love yourself."

<sup>13.10</sup> If you love others, you will never do them wrong; to love, then, is to obey the whole Law.

<sup>13.11</sup> You must do this, because you know that the time has come for you to wake up from your sleep. For the moment when we will be saved is closer now than it was when we first believed.

<sup>13.12</sup> The night is nearly over, day is almost here. Let us stop doing the things that belong to the dark, and let us take up weapons for fighting in the light.

<sup>13.13</sup> Let us conduct ourselves properly, as people who live in the light of day — no orgies or drunkenness, no immorality or indecency, no fighting or jealousy.

<sup>13.14</sup> But take up the weapons of the Lord Jesus Christ, and stop paying attention to your sinful nature and satisfying its desires.

# 14

<sup>14.1</sup> Welcome those who are weak in faith, but do not argue with them about their personal opinions.

<sup>14.2</sup> Some people's faith allows them to eat anything, but the person who is weak in the faith eats only vegetables.

<sup>14.3</sup> The person who will eat anything is not to despise the one who doesn't; while the one who eats only vegetables is not to pass judgment on the one who will eat anything; for God has accepted that person.

<sup>14.4</sup> Who are you to judge the servants of someone else? It is their own Master who will decide whether they succeed or fail. And they will

succeed, because the Lord is able to make them succeed.

14.5 Some people think that a certain day is more important than other days, while others think that all days are the same. We each should firmly make up our own minds.

14.6 Those who think highly of a certain day do so in honor of the Lord; those who will eat anything do so in honor of the Lord, because they give thanks to God for the food. Those who refuse to eat certain things do so in honor of the Lord, and they give thanks to God.

14.7 We do not live for ourselves only, and we do not die for ourselves only.

14.8 If we live, it is for the Lord that we live, and if we die, it is for the Lord that we die. So whether we live or die, we belong to the Lord.

14.9 For Christ died and rose to life in order to be the Lord of the living and of the dead.

14.10 You then, who eat only vegetables — why do you pass judgment on others? And you who eat anything — why do you despise other believers? All of us will stand before God to be judged by him.

14.11 For the scripture says, "As surely as I am the living God, says the Lord, everyone will kneel before me, and everyone will confess that I am God."

14.12 Every one of us, then, will have to give an account to God.

14.13 So then, let us stop judging one another. Instead, you should decide never to do anything that would make others stumble or fall into sin.

14.14 My union with the Lord Jesus makes me certain that no food is of itself ritually unclean; but if you believe that some food is unclean, then it becomes unclean for you.

14.15 If you hurt others because of something you eat, then you are no longer acting from love. Do not let the food that you eat ruin the person for whom Christ died!

14.16 Do not let what you regard as good get a bad name.

14.17 For God's Kingdom is not a matter of eating and drinking, but of the righteousness, peace, and joy which the Holy Spirit gives.

14.18 And when you serve Christ in this way, you please God and are approved by others.

14.19 So then, we must always aim at those things that bring peace and that help strengthen one another.

14.20 Do not, because of food, destroy what God has done. All foods may be eaten, but it is wrong to eat anything that will cause someone else to fall into sin.

14.21 The right thing to do is to keep from eating meat, drinking wine, or doing anything else that will make other believers fall.

<sup>14.22</sup> Keep what you believe about this matter, then, between yourself and God. Happy are those who do not feel guilty when they do something they judge is right!

<sup>14.23</sup> But if they have doubts about what they eat, God condemns them when they eat it, because their action is not based on faith. And anything that is not based on faith is sin.

# 15

<sup>15.1</sup> We who are strong in the faith ought to help the weak to carry their burdens. We should not please ourselves.

<sup>15.2</sup> Instead, we should all please other believers for their own good, in order to build them up in the faith.

<sup>15.3</sup> For Christ did not please himself. Instead, as the scripture says, "The insults which are hurled at you have fallen on me."

<sup>15.4</sup> Everything written in the Scriptures was written to teach us, in order that we might have hope through the patience and encouragement which the Scriptures give us.

<sup>15.5</sup> And may God, the source of patience and encouragement, enable you to have the same point of view among yourselves by following the example of Christ Jesus,

<sup>15.6</sup> so that all of you together may praise with one voice the God and Father of our Lord Jesus Christ.

<sup>15.7</sup> Accept one another, then, for the glory of God, as Christ has accepted you.

<sup>15.8</sup> For I tell you that Christ's life of service was on behalf of the Jews, to show that God is faithful, to make his promises to their ancestors come true,

<sup>15.9</sup> and to enable even the Gentiles to praise God for his mercy. As the scripture says, "And so I will praise you among the Gentiles; I will sing praises to you."

<sup>15.10</sup> Again it says, "Rejoice, Gentiles, with God's people!"

<sup>15.11</sup> And again, "Praise the Lord, all Gentiles; praise him, all peoples!"

<sup>15.12</sup> And again, Isaiah says, "A descendant of Jesse will appear; he will come to rule the Gentiles, and they will put their hope in him."

<sup>15.13</sup> May God, the source of hope, fill you with all joy and peace by means of your faith in him, so that your hope will continue to grow by the power of the Holy Spirit.

<sup>15.14</sup> My friends: I myself feel sure that you are full of goodness, that

you have all knowledge, and that you are able to teach one another. ¹⁵·¹⁵ But in this letter I have been quite bold about certain subjects of which I have reminded you. I have been bold because of the privilege God has given me

¹⁵·¹⁶ of being a servant of Christ Jesus to work for the Gentiles. I serve like a priest in preaching the Good News from God, in order that the Gentiles may be an offering acceptable to God, dedicated to him by the Holy Spirit.

¹⁵·¹⁷ In union with Christ Jesus, then, I can be proud of my service for God.

¹⁵·¹⁸ I will be bold and speak only about what Christ has done through me to lead the Gentiles to obey God. He has done this by means of words and deeds,

¹⁵·¹⁹ by the power of miracles and wonders, and by the power of the Spirit of God. And so, in traveling all the way from Jerusalem to Illyricum, I have proclaimed fully the Good News about Christ.

¹⁵·²⁰ My ambition has always been to proclaim the Good News in places where Christ has not been heard of, so as not to build on a foundation laid by someone else.

¹⁵·²¹ As the scripture says, "Those who were not told about him will see, and those who have not heard will understand."

¹⁵·²² And so I have been prevented many times from coming to you.

¹⁵·²³ But now that I have finished my work in these regions and since I have been wanting for so many years to come to see you,

¹⁵·²⁴ I hope to do so now. I would like to see you on my way to Spain, and be helped by you to go there, after I have enjoyed visiting you for a while.

¹⁵·²⁵ Right now, however, I am going to Jerusalem in the service of God's people there.

¹⁵·²⁶ For the churches in Macedonia and Achaia have freely decided to give an offering to help the poor among God's people in Jerusalem.

¹⁵·²⁷ That decision was their own; but, as a matter of fact, they have an obligation to help them. Since the Jews shared their spiritual blessings with the Gentiles, the Gentiles ought to use their material blessings to help the Jews.

¹⁵·²⁸ When I have finished this task and have turned over to them all the money that has been raised for them, I shall leave for Spain and visit you on my way there.

¹⁵·²⁹ When I come to you, I know that I shall come with a full measure of the blessing of Christ.

<sup>15.30</sup> I urge you, friends, by our Lord Jesus Christ and by the love that the Spirit gives: join me in praying fervently to God for me.
<sup>15.31</sup> Pray that I may be kept safe from the unbelievers in Judea and that my service in Jerusalem may be acceptable to God's people there.
<sup>15.32</sup> And so I will come to you full of joy, if it is God's will, and enjoy a refreshing visit with you.
<sup>15.33</sup> May God, our source of peace, be with all of you. Amen.

# 16

<sup>16.1</sup> I recommend to you our sister Phoebe, who serves the church at Cenchreae.
<sup>16.2</sup> Receive her in the Lord's name, as God's people should, and give her any help she may need from you; for she herself has been a good friend to many people and also to me.
<sup>16.3</sup> I send greetings to Priscilla and Aquila, my fellow workers in the service of Christ Jesus;
<sup>16.4</sup> they risked their lives for me. I am grateful to them — not only I, but all the Gentile churches as well.
<sup>16.5</sup> Greetings also to the church that meets in their house. Greetings to my dear friend Epaenetus, who was the first in the province of Asia to believe in Christ.
<sup>16.6</sup> Greetings to Mary, who has worked so hard for you.
<sup>16.7</sup> Greetings also to Andronicus and Junia, fellow Jews who were in prison with me; they are well known among the apostles, and they became Christians before I did.
<sup>16.8</sup> My greetings to Ampliatus, my dear friend in the fellowship of the Lord.
<sup>16.9</sup> Greetings also to Urbanus, our fellow worker in Christ's service, and to Stachys, my dear friend.
<sup>16.10</sup> Greetings to Apelles, whose loyalty to Christ has been proved. Greetings to those who belong to the family of Aristobulus.
<sup>16.11</sup> Greetings to Herodion, a fellow Jew, and to the Christians in the family of Narcissus.
<sup>16.12</sup> My greetings to Tryphaena and Tryphosa, who work in the Lord's service, and to my dear friend Persis, who has done so much work for the Lord.
<sup>16.13</sup> I send greetings to Rufus, that outstanding worker in the Lord's service, and to his mother, who has always treated me like a son.
<sup>16.14</sup> My greetings to Asyncritus, Phlegon, Hermes, Patrobas, Hermas, and all the other Christians with them.

<sup>16.15</sup> Greetings to Philologus and Julia, to Nereus and his sister, to Olympas and to all of God's people who are with them.
<sup>16.16</sup> Greet one another with the kiss of peace. All the churches of Christ send you their greetings.

<sup>16.17</sup> I urge you, my friends: watch out for those who cause divisions and upset people's faith and go against the teaching which you have received. Keep away from them!
<sup>16.18</sup> For those who do such things are not serving Christ our Lord, but their own appetites. By their fine words and flattering speech they deceive innocent people.
<sup>16.19</sup> Everyone has heard of your loyalty to the gospel, and for this reason I am happy about you. I want you to be wise about what is good, but innocent in what is evil.
<sup>16.20</sup> And God, our source of peace, will soon crush Satan under your feet. The grace of our Lord Jesus be with you.

<sup>16.21</sup> Timothy, my fellow worker, sends you his greetings; and so do Lucius, Jason, and Sosipater, fellow Jews.
<sup>16.22</sup> I, Tertius, the writer of this letter, send you Christian greetings.
<sup>16.23</sup> My host Gaius, in whose house the church meets, sends you his greetings; Erastus, the city treasurer, and our brother Quartus send you their greetings.
<sup>16.24</sup> (The grace of our Lord Jesus Christ be with you all.)

<sup>16.25</sup> Let us give glory to God! He is able to make you stand firm in your faith, according to the Good News I preach about Jesus Christ and according to the revelation of the secret truth which was hidden for long ages in the past.
<sup>16.26</sup> Now, however, that truth has been brought out into the open through the writings of the prophets; and by the command of the eternal God it is made known to all nations, so that all may believe and obey.
<sup>16.27</sup> To the only God, who alone is all-wise, be glory through Jesus Christ forever! Amen.

# 1 CORINTHIANS

# 1 Corinthians

**1**

<sup>1.1</sup> From Paul, who was called by the will of God to be an apostle of Christ Jesus, and from our brother Sosthenes —
<sup>1.2</sup> To the church of God which is in Corinth, to all who are called to be God's holy people, who belong to him in union with Christ Jesus, together with all people everywhere who worship our Lord Jesus Christ, their Lord and ours:
<sup>1.3</sup> May God our Father and the Lord Jesus Christ give you grace and peace.
<sup>1.4</sup> I always give thanks to my God for you because of the grace he has given you through Christ Jesus.
<sup>1.5</sup> For in union with Christ you have become rich in all things, including all speech and all knowledge.
<sup>1.6</sup> The message about Christ has become so firmly established in you
<sup>1.7</sup> that you have not failed to receive a single blessing, as you wait for our Lord Jesus Christ to be revealed.
<sup>1.8</sup> He will also keep you firm to the end, so that you will be faultless on the Day of our Lord Jesus Christ.
<sup>1.9</sup> God is to be trusted, the God who called you to have fellowship with his Son Jesus Christ, our Lord.
<sup>1.10</sup> By the authority of our Lord Jesus Christ I appeal to all of you, my friends, to agree in what you say, so that there will be no divisions among you. Be completely united, with only one thought and one purpose.
<sup>1.11</sup> For some people from Chloe's family have told me quite plainly, my friends, that there are quarrels among you.
<sup>1.12</sup> Let me put it this way: each one of you says something different. One says, "I follow Paul"; another, "I follow Apollos"; another, "I follow Peter"; and another, "I follow Christ."
<sup>1.13</sup> Christ has been divided into groups! Was it Paul who died on the cross for you? Were you baptized as Paul's disciples?
<sup>1.14</sup> I thank God that I did not baptize any of you except Crispus and Gaius.
<sup>1.15</sup> No one can say, then, that you were baptized as my disciples.
<sup>1.16</sup> (Oh yes, I also baptized Stephanas and his family; but I can't remember whether I baptized anyone else.)
<sup>1.17</sup> Christ did not send me to baptize. He sent me to tell the Good News, and to tell it without using the language of human wisdom, in

order to make sure that Christ's death on the cross is not robbed of its power.

1.18 For the message about Christ's death on the cross is nonsense to those who are being lost; but for us who are being saved it is God's power.

1.19 The scripture says, "I will destroy the wisdom of the wise and set aside the understanding of the scholars."

1.20 So then, where does that leave the wise? or the scholars? or the skillful debaters of this world? God has shown that this world's wisdom is foolishness!

1.21 For God in his wisdom made it impossible for people to know him by means of their own wisdom. Instead, by means of the so-called "foolish" message we preach, God decided to save those who believe.

1.22 Jews want miracles for proof, and Greeks look for wisdom.

1.23 As for us, we proclaim the crucified Christ, a message that is offensive to the Jews and nonsense to the Gentiles;

1.24 but for those whom God has called, both Jews and Gentiles, this message is Christ, who is the power of God and the wisdom of God.

1.25 For what seems to be God's foolishness is wiser than human wisdom, and what seems to be God's weakness is stronger than human strength.

1.26 Now remember what you were, my friends, when God called you. From the human point of view few of you were wise or powerful or of high social standing.

1.27 God purposely chose what the world considers nonsense in order to shame the wise, and he chose what the world considers weak in order to shame the powerful.

1.28 He chose what the world looks down on and despises and thinks is nothing, in order to destroy what the world thinks is important.

1.29 This means that no one can boast in God's presence.

1.30 But God has brought you into union with Christ Jesus, and God has made Christ to be our wisdom. By him we are put right with God; we become God's holy people and are set free.

1.31 So then, as the scripture says, "Whoever wants to boast must boast of what the Lord has done."

# 2

2.1 When I came to you, my friends, to preach God's secret truth, I did not use big words and great learning.

2.2 For while I was with you, I made up my mind to forget everything except Jesus Christ and especially his death on the cross.

<sup>2.3</sup> So when I came to you, I was weak and trembled all over with fear,
<sup>2.4</sup> and my teaching and message were not delivered with skillful words of human wisdom, but with convincing proof of the power of God's Spirit.
<sup>2.5</sup> Your faith, then, does not rest on human wisdom but on God's power.
<sup>2.6</sup> Yet I do proclaim a message of wisdom to those who are spiritually mature. But it is not the wisdom that belongs to this world or to the powers that rule this world — powers that are losing their power.
<sup>2.7</sup> The wisdom I proclaim is God's secret wisdom, which is hidden from human beings, but which he had already chosen for our glory even before the world was made.
<sup>2.8</sup> None of the rulers of this world knew this wisdom. If they had known it, they would not have crucified the Lord of glory.
<sup>2.9</sup> However, as the scripture says, "What no one ever saw or heard, what no one ever thought could happen, is the very thing God prepared for those who love him."
<sup>2.10</sup> But it was to us that God made known his secret by means of his Spirit. The Spirit searches everything, even the hidden depths of God's purposes.
<sup>2.11</sup> It is only our own spirit within us that knows all about us; in the same way, only God's Spirit knows all about God.
<sup>2.12</sup> We have not received this world's spirit; instead, we have received the Spirit sent by God, so that we may know all that God has given us.
<sup>2.13</sup> So then, we do not speak in words taught by human wisdom, but in words taught by the Spirit, as we explain spiritual truths to those who have the Spirit.
<sup>2.14</sup> Whoever does not have the Spirit cannot receive the gifts that come from God's Spirit. Such a person really does not understand them, and they seem to be nonsense, because their value can be judged only on a spiritual basis.
<sup>2.15</sup> Whoever has the Spirit, however, is able to judge the value of everything, but no one is able to judge him.
<sup>2.16</sup> As the scripture says, "Who knows the mind of the Lord? Who is able to give him advice?" We, however, have the mind of Christ.

# 3

<sup>3.1</sup> As a matter of fact, my friends, I could not talk to you as I talk to people who have the Spirit; I had to talk to you as though you be-

longed to this world, as children in the Christian faith.

3.2 I had to feed you milk, not solid food, because you were not ready for it. And even now you are not ready for it,

3.3 because you still live as the people of this world live. When there is jealousy among you and you quarrel with one another, doesn't this prove that you belong to this world, living by its standards?

3.4 When one of you says, "I follow Paul," and another, "I follow Apollos" — aren't you acting like worldly people?

3.5 After all, who is Apollos? And who is Paul? We are simply God's servants, by whom you were led to believe. Each one of us does the work which the Lord gave him to do:

3.6 I planted the seed, Apollos watered the plant, but it was God who made the plant grow.

3.7 The one who plants and the one who waters really do not matter. It is God who matters, because he makes the plant grow.

3.8 There is no difference between the one who plants and the one who waters; God will reward each one according to the work each has done.

3.9 For we are partners working together for God, and you are God's field. You are also God's building.

3.10 Using the gift that God gave me, I did the work of an expert builder and laid the foundation, and someone else is building on it. But each of you must be careful how you build.

3.11 For God has already placed Jesus Christ as the one and only foundation, and no other foundation can be laid.

3.12 Some will use gold or silver or precious stones in building on the foundation; others will use wood or grass or straw.

3.13 And the quality of each person's work will be seen when the Day of Christ exposes it. For on that Day fire will reveal everyone's work; the fire will test it and show its real quality.

3.14 If what was built on the foundation survives the fire, the builder will receive a reward.

3.15 But if your work is burnt up, then you will lose it; but you yourself will be saved, as if you had escaped through the fire.

3.16 Surely you know that you are God's temple and that God's Spirit lives in you!

3.17 God will destroy anyone who destroys God's temple. For God's temple is holy, and you yourselves are his temple.

3.18 You should not fool yourself. If any of you think that you are wise by this world's standards, you should become a fool, in order to be really wise.

<sup>3.19</sup> For what this world considers to be wisdom is nonsense in God's sight. As the scripture says, "God traps the wise in their cleverness"; <sup>3.20</sup> and another scripture says, "The Lord knows that the thoughts of the wise are worthless."

<sup>3.21</sup> No one, then, should boast about what human beings can do. Actually everything belongs to you: <sup>3.22</sup> Paul, Apollos, and Peter; this world, life and death, the present and the future — all these are yours, <sup>3.23</sup> and you belong to Christ, and Christ belongs to God.

# 4

<sup>4.1</sup> You should think of us as Christ's servants, who have been put in charge of God's secret truths. <sup>4.2</sup> The one thing required of such servants is that they be faithful to their master. <sup>4.3</sup> Now, I am not at all concerned about being judged by you or by any human standard; I don't even pass judgment on myself. <sup>4.4</sup> My conscience is clear, but that does not prove that I am really innocent. The Lord is the one who passes judgment on me. <sup>4.5</sup> So you should not pass judgment on anyone before the right time comes. Final judgment must wait until the Lord comes; he will bring to light the dark secrets and expose the hidden purposes of people's minds. And then all will receive from God the praise they deserve.

<sup>4.6</sup> For your sake, my friends, I have applied all this to Apollos and me, using the two of us as an example, so that you may learn what the saying means, "Observe the proper rules." None of you should be proud of one person and despise another. <sup>4.7</sup> Who made you superior to others? Didn't God give you everything you have? Well, then, how can you boast, as if what you have were not a gift?

<sup>4.8</sup> Do you already have everything you need? Are you already rich? Have you become kings, even though we are not? Well, I wish you really were kings, so that we could be kings together with you. <sup>4.9</sup> For it seems to me that God has given the very last place to us apostles, like people condemned to die in public as a spectacle for the whole world of angels and of human beings.

<sup>4.10</sup> For Christ's sake we are fools; but you are wise in union with Christ! We are weak, but you are strong! We are despised, but you are honored! <sup>4.11</sup> To this very moment we go hungry and thirsty; we are clothed in rags; we are beaten; we wander from place to place;

<sup>4.12</sup> we wear ourselves out <u>with hard work</u>. When we are cursed, we bless; when we are persecuted, we endure;
<sup>4.13</sup> when we are insulted, we answer back <u>with kind words</u>. We are no more <u>than this world's garbage</u>; we are the scum <u>of the earth to this very moment</u>!
<sup>4.14</sup> I write this <u>to you</u>, not because I want to make you feel ashamed, but to instruct you <u>as my own dear children</u>.
<sup>4.15</sup> For even if you have ten thousand guardians <u>in your Christian life</u>, you have only one father. For <u>in your life in union with Christ Jesus</u> I have become your father <u>by</u> bringing the Good News <u>to you</u>.
<sup>4.16</sup> I beg you, then, to follow my example.
<sup>4.17</sup> <u>For this purpose</u> I am sending <u>to you</u> Timothy, who is my own dear and faithful son <u>in the Christian life</u>. He will remind you <u>of the principles</u> which I follow <u>in the new life in union with Christ Jesus</u> and which I teach <u>in all the churches</u> everywhere.
<sup>4.18</sup> Some <u>of you</u> have become proud because you have thought that I would not be coming to visit you.
<sup>4.19</sup> If the Lord is willing, however, I will come <u>to you</u> soon, and then I will find out <u>for myself</u> the power which these proud people have, and not just what they say.
<sup>4.20</sup> For the Kingdom <u>of God</u> is not a matter <u>of words</u> but <u>of power</u>.
<sup>4.21</sup> Which do you prefer? Shall I come <u>to you with a whip</u>, or <u>in a spirit of love and gentleness</u>?

# 5

<sup>5.1</sup> Now, it is actually being said that there is sexual immorality <u>among you</u> so terrible that not even the heathen would be guilty <u>of it</u>. I am told that a man is sleeping <u>with his stepmother</u>!
<sup>5.2</sup> How, then, can you be proud? <u>On the contrary</u>, you should be filled <u>with sadness</u>, and the man who has done such a thing should be expelled <u>from your fellowship</u>.
<sup>5.3-4</sup> And even though I am far away <u>from you in body</u>, still I am there <u>with you in spirit</u>; and as though I were there <u>with you</u>, I have <u>in the name of our Lord Jesus</u> already passed judgment <u>on the man</u> who has done this terrible thing. As you meet together, and I meet <u>with you in my spirit</u>, <u>by the power</u> of our Lord Jesus present <u>with us</u>,
<sup>5.5</sup> you are to hand this man over <u>to Satan for his body</u> to be destroyed, so that his spirit may be saved <u>in the Day of the Lord</u>.
<sup>5.6</sup> It is not right <u>for you</u> to be proud! You know the saying, "A little bit <u>of yeast</u> makes the whole batch <u>of dough</u> rise."
<sup>5.7</sup> You must remove the old yeast <u>of sin</u> so that you will be entirely

pure. Then you will be like a new batch of dough without any yeast, as indeed I know you actually are. For our Passover Festival is ready, now that Christ, our Passover lamb, has been sacrificed.

⁵·⁸ Let us celebrate our Passover, then, not with bread having the old yeast of sin and wickedness, but with the bread that has no yeast, the bread of purity and truth.

⁵·⁹ In the letter that I wrote you I told you not to associate with immoral people.

⁵·¹⁰ Now I did not mean pagans who are immoral or greedy or are thieves, or who worship idols. To avoid them you would have to get out of the world completely.

⁵·¹¹ What I meant was that you should not associate with a person who calls himself a believer but is immoral or greedy or worships idols or is a slanderer or a drunkard or a thief. Don't even sit down to eat with such a person.

⁵·¹²⁻¹³ After all, it is none of my business to judge outsiders. God will judge them. But should you not judge the members of your own fellowship? As the scripture says, "Remove the evil person from your group."

# 6

⁶·¹ If any of you have a dispute with another Christian, how dare you go before heathen judges instead of letting God's people settle the matter?

⁶·² Don't you know that God's people will judge the world? Well, then, if you are to judge the world, aren't you capable of judging small matters?

⁶·³ Do you not know that we shall judge the angels? How much more, then, the things of this life!

⁶·⁴ If such matters come up, are you going to take them to be settled by people who have no standing in the church?

⁶·⁵ Shame on you! Surely there is at least one wise person in your fellowship who can settle a dispute between fellow Christians.

⁶·⁶ Instead, one Christian goes to court against another and lets unbelievers judge the case!

⁶·⁷ The very fact that you have legal disputes among yourselves shows that you have failed completely. Would it not be better for you to be wronged? Would it not be better for you to be robbed?

⁶·⁸ Instead, you yourselves wrong one another and rob one another, even other believers!

⁶·⁹ Surely you know that the wicked will not possess God's Kingdom.

Do not fool yourselves; people who are immoral or who worship idols or are adulterers or homosexual perverts

6.10 or who steal or are greedy or are drunkards or who slander others or are thieves — none of these will possess God's Kingdom.

6.11 Some of you were like that. But you have been purified from sin; you have been dedicated to God; you have been put right with God by the Lord Jesus Christ and by the Spirit of our God.

6.12 Someone will say, "I am allowed to do anything." Yes; but not everything is good for you. I could say that I am allowed to do anything, but I am not going to let anything make me its slave.

6.13 Someone else will say, "Food is for the stomach, and the stomach is for food." Yes; but God will put an end to both. The body is not to be used for sexual immorality, but to serve the Lord; and the Lord provides for the body.

6.14 God raised the Lord from death, and he will also raise us by his power.

6.15 You know that your bodies are parts of the body of Christ. Shall I take a part of Christ's body and make it part of the body of a prostitute? Impossible!

6.16 Or perhaps you don't know that the man who joins his body to a prostitute becomes physically one with her? The scripture says quite plainly, "The two will become one body."

6.17 But he who joins himself to the Lord becomes spiritually one with him.

6.18 Avoid immorality. Any other sin a man commits does not affect his body; but the man who is guilty of sexual immorality sins against his own body.

6.19 Don't you know that your body is the temple of the Holy Spirit, who lives in you and who was given to you by God? You do not belong to yourselves but to God;

6.20 he bought you for a price. So use your bodies for God's glory.

7

7.1 Now, to deal with the matters you wrote about. A man does well not to marry.

7.2 But because there is so much immorality, every man should have his own wife, and every woman should have her own husband.

7.3 A man should fulfill his duty as a husband, and a woman should fulfill her duty as a wife, and each should satisfy the other's needs.

7.4 A wife is not the master of her own body, but her husband is; in the same way a husband is not the master of his own body, but his wife is.

<sup>7.5</sup> Do not deny yourselves to each other, unless you first agree to do so for a while in order to spend your time in prayer; but then resume normal marital relations. In this way you will be kept from giving in to Satan's temptation because of your lack of self-control.

<sup>7.6</sup> I tell you this not as an order, but simply as a permission.

<sup>7.7</sup> Actually I would prefer that all of you were as I am; but each one has a special gift from God, one person this gift, another one that gift.

<sup>7.8</sup> Now, to the unmarried and to the widows I say that it would be better for you to continue to live alone as I do.

<sup>7.9</sup> But if you cannot restrain your desires, go ahead and marry — it is better to marry than to burn with passion.

<sup>7.10</sup> For married people I have a command which is not my own but the Lord's: a wife must not leave her husband;

<sup>7.11</sup> but if she does, she must remain single or else be reconciled to her husband; and a husband must not divorce his wife.

<sup>7.12</sup> To the others I say (I, myself, not the Lord): if a Christian man has a wife who is an unbeliever and she agrees to go on living with him, he must not divorce her.

<sup>7.13</sup> And if a Christian woman is married to a man who is an unbeliever and he agrees to go on living with her, she must not divorce him.

<sup>7.14</sup> For the unbelieving husband is made acceptable to God by being united to his wife, and the unbelieving wife is made acceptable to God by being united to her Christian husband. If this were not so, their children would be like pagan children; but as it is, they are acceptable to God.

<sup>7.15</sup> However, if the one who is not a believer wishes to leave the Christian partner, let it be so. In such cases the Christian partner, whether husband or wife, is free to act. God has called you to live in peace.

<sup>7.16</sup> How can you be sure, Christian wife, that you will not save your husband? Or how can you be sure, Christian husband, that you will not save your wife?

<sup>7.17</sup> Each of you should go on living according to the Lord's gift to you, and as you were when God called you. This is the rule I teach in all the churches.

<sup>7.18</sup> If a circumcised man has accepted God's call, he should not try to remove the marks of circumcision; if an uncircumcised man has accepted God's call, he should not get circumcised.

<sup>7.19</sup> For whether or not a man is circumcised means nothing; what matters is to obey God's commandments.

<sup>7.20</sup> Each of you should remain as you were when you accepted God's call.

<sup>7.21</sup> Were you a slave when God called you? Well, never mind; but if you have a chance to become free, use it.

<sup>7.22</sup> For a slave who has been called by the Lord is the Lord's free person; in the same way a free person who has been called by Christ is his slave.

<sup>7.23</sup> God bought you for a price; so do not become slaves of people.

<sup>7.24</sup> My friends, each of you should remain in fellowship with God in the same condition that you were when you were called.

<sup>7.25</sup> Now, concerning what you wrote about unmarried people: I do not have a command from the Lord, but I give my opinion as one who by the Lord's mercy is worthy of trust.

<sup>7.26</sup> Considering the present distress, I think it is better for a man to stay as he is.

<sup>7.27</sup> Do you have a wife? Then don't try to get rid of her. Are you unmarried? Then don't look for a wife.

<sup>7.28</sup> But if you do marry, you haven't committed a sin; and if an unmarried woman marries, she hasn't committed a sin. But I would rather spare you the everyday troubles that married people will have.

<sup>7.29</sup> What I mean, my friends, is this: there is not much time left, and from now on married people should live as though they were not married;

<sup>7.30</sup> those who weep, as though they were not sad; those who laugh, as though they were not happy; those who buy, as though they did not own what they bought;

<sup>7.31</sup> those who deal in material goods, as though they were not fully occupied with them. For this world, as it is now, will not last much longer.

<sup>7.32</sup> I would like you to be free from worry. An unmarried man concerns himself with the Lord's work, because he is trying to please the Lord.

<sup>7.33</sup> But a married man concerns himself with worldly matters, because he wants to please his wife;

<sup>7.34</sup> and so he is pulled in two directions. An unmarried woman or a virgin concerns herself with the Lord's work, because she wants to be dedicated both in body and spirit; but a married woman concerns herself with worldly matters, because she wants to please her hus-

band.

7.35 I am saying this because I want to help you. I am not trying to put restrictions on you. Instead, I want you to do what is right and proper, and to give yourselves completely to the Lord's service without any reservation.

7.36 In the case of an engaged couple who have decided not to marry: if the man feels that he is not acting properly toward the young woman and if his passions are too strong and he feels that they ought to marry, then they should get married, as he wants to. There is no sin in this.

7.37 But if a man, without being forced to do so, has firmly made up his mind not to marry, and if he has his will under complete control and has already decided in his own mind what to do — then he does well not to marry the young woman.

7.38 So the man who marries does well, but the one who doesn't marry does even better.

7.39 A married woman is not free as long as her husband lives; but if her husband dies, then she is free to be married to any man she wishes, but only if he is a Christian.

7.40 She will be happier, however, if she stays as she is. That is my opinion, and I think that I too have God's Spirit.

# 8

8.1 Now, concerning what you wrote about food offered to idols. It is true, of course, that "all of us have knowledge," as they say. Such knowledge, however, puffs a person up with pride; but love builds up.

8.2 Those who think they know something really don't know as they ought to know.

8.3 But the person who loves God is known by him.

8.4 So then, about eating the food offered to idols: we know that an idol stands for something that does not really exist; we know that there is only the one God.

8.5 Even if there are so-called "gods," whether in heaven or on earth, and even though there are many of these "gods" and "lords,"

8.6 yet there is for us only one God, the Father, who is the Creator of all things and for whom we live; and there is only one Lord, Jesus Christ, through whom all things were created and through whom we live.

8.7 But not everyone knows this truth. Some people have been so used to idols that to this day when they eat such food they still think of it as food that belongs to an idol; their conscience is weak, and they feel they are defiled by the food.

<sup></sup>8.8 Food, however, will not improve our relation with God; we shall not lose anything if we do not eat, nor shall we gain anything if we do eat.

8.9 Be careful, however, not to let your freedom of action make those who are weak in the faith fall into sin.

8.10 Suppose a person whose conscience is weak in this matter sees you, who have so-called "knowledge," eating in the temple of an idol; will not this encourage him to eat food offered to idols?

8.11 And so this weak person, your brother for whom Christ died, will perish because of your "knowledge"!

8.12 And in this way you will be sinning against Christ by sinning against other Christians and wounding their weak conscience.

8.13 So then, if food makes a believer sin, I will never eat meat again, so as not to make a believer fall into sin.

# 9

9.1 Am I not a free man? Am I not an apostle? Haven't I seen Jesus our Lord? And aren't you the result of my work for the Lord?

9.2 Even if others do not accept me as an apostle, surely you do! Because of your life in union with the Lord you yourselves are proof of the fact that I am an apostle.

9.3 When people criticize me, this is how I defend myself:

9.4 Don't I have the right to be given food and drink for my work?

9.5 Don't I have the right to follow the example of the other apostles and the Lord's brothers and Peter, by taking a Christian wife with me on my trips?

9.6 Or are Barnabas and I the only ones who have to work for our living?

9.7 What soldiers ever have to pay their own expenses in the army? What farmers do not eat the grapes from their own vineyard? What shepherds do not use the milk from their own sheep?

9.8 I don't have to limit myself to these everyday examples, because the Law says the same thing.

9.9 We read in the Law of Moses, "Do not muzzle an ox when you are using it to thresh grain." Now, is God concerned about oxen?

9.10 Didn't he really mean us when he said that? Of course, that was written for us. Anyone who plows and anyone who reaps should do their work in the hope of getting a share of the crop.

9.11 We have sown spiritual seed among you. Is it too much if we reap material benefits from you?

<sup>9.12</sup> If others have the right to expect this from you, don't we have an even greater right? But we haven't made use of this right. Instead, we have endured everything in order not to put any obstacle in the way of the Good News about Christ.

<sup>9.13</sup> Surely you know that the men who work in the Temple get their food from the Temple and that those who offer the sacrifices on the altar get a share of the sacrifices.

<sup>9.14</sup> In the same way, the Lord has ordered that those who preach the gospel should get their living from it.

<sup>9.15</sup> But I haven't made use of any of these rights, nor am I writing this now in order to claim such rights for myself. I would rather die first! Nobody is going to turn my rightful boast into empty words!

<sup>9.16</sup> I have no right to boast just because I preach the gospel. After all, I am under orders to do so. And how terrible it would be for me if I did not preach the gospel!

<sup>9.17</sup> If I did my work as a matter of free choice, then I could expect to be paid; but I do it as a matter of duty, because God has entrusted me with this task.

<sup>9.18</sup> What pay do I get, then? It is the privilege of preaching the Good News without charging for it, without claiming my rights in my work for the gospel.

<sup>9.19</sup> I am a free man, nobody's slave; but I make myself everybody's slave in order to win as many people as possible.

<sup>9.20</sup> While working with the Jews, I live like a Jew in order to win them; and even though I myself am not subject to the Law of Moses, I live as though I were when working with those who are, in order to win them.

<sup>9.21</sup> In the same way, when working with Gentiles, I live like a Gentile, outside the Jewish Law, in order to win Gentiles. This does not mean that I don't obey God's law; I am really under Christ's law.

<sup>9.22</sup> Among the weak in faith I become weak like one of them, in order to win them. So I become all things to all people, that I may save some of them by whatever means are possible.

<sup>9.23</sup> All this I do for the gospel's sake, in order to share in its blessings.

<sup>9.24</sup> Surely you know that many runners take part in a race, but only one of them wins the prize. Run, then, in such a way as to win the prize.

<sup>9.25</sup> Every athlete in training submits to strict discipline, in order to be crowned with a wreath that will not last; but we do it for one that will last forever.

<sup>9.26</sup> That is why I run straight for the finish line; that is why I am like a boxer who does not waste his punches.

<sup>9.27</sup> I harden my body with blows and bring it under complete control, to keep myself from being disqualified after having called others to the contest.

# 10

<sup>10.1</sup> I want you to remember, my friends, what happened to our ancestors who followed Moses. They were all under the protection of the cloud, and all passed safely through the Red Sea.

<sup>10.2</sup> In the cloud and in the sea they were all baptized as followers of Moses.

<sup>10.3</sup> All ate the same spiritual bread

<sup>10.4</sup> and drank the same spiritual drink. They drank from the spiritual rock that went with them; and that rock was Christ himself.

<sup>10.5</sup> But even then God was not pleased with most of them, and so their dead bodies were scattered over the desert.

<sup>10.6</sup> Now, all of this is an example for us, to warn us not to desire evil things, as they did,

<sup>10.7</sup> nor to worship idols, as some of them did. As the scripture says, "The people sat down to a feast which turned into an orgy of drinking and sex."

<sup>10.8</sup> We must not be guilty of sexual immorality, as some of them were — and in one day twenty-three thousand of them fell dead.

<sup>10.9</sup> We must not put the Lord to the test, as some of them did — and they were killed by snakes.

<sup>10.10</sup> We must not complain, as some of them did — and they were destroyed by the Angel of Death.

<sup>10.11</sup> All these things happened to them as examples for others, and they were written down as a warning for us. For we live at a time when the end is about to come.

<sup>10.12</sup> If you think you are standing firm you had better be careful that you do not fall.

<sup>10.13</sup> Every test that you have experienced is the kind that normally comes to people. But God keeps his promise, and he will not allow you to be tested beyond your power to remain firm; at the time you are put to the test, he will give you the strength to endure it, and so provide you with a way out.

<sup>10.14</sup> So then, my dear friends, keep away from the worship of idols.

<sup>10.15</sup> I speak to you as sensible people; judge for yourselves what I say.

<sup>10.16</sup> The cup we use in the Lord's Supper and for which we give

thanks to God: when we drink from it, we are sharing in the blood of Christ. And the bread we break: when we eat it, we are sharing in the body of Christ.

<sup></sup>¹⁰·¹⁷ Because there is the one loaf of bread, all of us, though many, are one body, for we all share the same loaf.

¹⁰·¹⁸ Consider the people of Israel; those who eat what is offered in sacrifice share in the altar's service to God.

¹⁰·¹⁹ Do I imply, then, that an idol or the food offered to it really amounts to anything?

¹⁰·²⁰ No! What I am saying is that what is sacrificed on pagan altars is offered to demons, not to God. And I do not want you to be partners with demons.

¹⁰·²¹ You cannot drink from the Lord's cup and also from the cup of demons; you cannot eat at the Lord's table and also at the table of demons.

¹⁰·²² Or do we want to make the Lord jealous? Do we think that we are stronger than he?

¹⁰·²³ "We are allowed to do anything," so they say. That is true, but not everything is good. "We are allowed to do anything" — but not everything is helpful.

¹⁰·²⁴ None of you should be looking out for your own interests, but for the interests of others.

¹⁰·²⁵ You are free to eat anything sold in the meat market, without asking any questions because of your conscience.

¹⁰·²⁶ For, as the scripture says, "The earth and everything in it belong to the Lord."

¹⁰·²⁷ If an unbeliever invites you to a meal and you decide to go, eat what is set before you, without asking any questions because of your conscience.

¹⁰·²⁸ But if someone tells you, "This food was offered to idols," then do not eat that food, for the sake of the one who told you and for conscience' sake —

¹⁰·²⁹ that is, not your own conscience, but the other person's conscience. "Well, then," someone asks, "why should my freedom to act be limited by another person's conscience?

¹⁰·³⁰ "If I thank God for my food, why should anyone criticize me about food for which I give thanks?"

¹⁰·³¹ Well, whatever you do, whether you eat or drink, do it all for God's glory.

¹⁰·³² Live in such a way as to cause no trouble either to Jews or Gentiles or to the church of God.

<sup>10.33</sup> Just do as I do; I try to please everyone in all that I do, not thinking of my own good, but of the good of all, so that they might be saved.

# 11

<sup>11.1</sup> Imitate me, then, just as I imitate Christ.

<sup>11.2</sup> I praise you because you always remember me and follow the teachings that I have handed on to you.

<sup>11.3</sup> But I want you to understand that Christ is supreme over every man, the husband is supreme over his wife, and God is supreme over Christ.

<sup>11.4</sup> So a man who prays or proclaims God's message in public worship with his head covered disgraces Christ.

<sup>11.5</sup> And any woman who prays or proclaims God's message in public worship with nothing on her head disgraces her husband; there is no difference between her and a woman whose head has been shaved.

<sup>11.6</sup> If the woman does not cover her head, she might as well cut her hair. And since it is a shameful thing for a woman to shave her head or cut her hair, she should cover her head.

<sup>11.7</sup> A man has no need to cover his head, because he reflects the image and glory of God. But woman reflects the glory of man;

<sup>11.8</sup> for man was not created from woman, but woman from man.

<sup>11.9</sup> Nor was man created for woman's sake, but woman was created for man's sake.

<sup>11.10</sup> On account of the angels, then, a woman should have a covering over her head to show that she is under her husband's authority.

<sup>11.11</sup> In our life in the Lord, however, woman is not independent of man, nor is man independent of woman.

<sup>11.12</sup> For as woman was made from man, in the same way man is born of woman; and it is God who brings everything into existence.

<sup>11.13</sup> Judge for yourselves whether it is proper for a woman to pray to God in public worship with nothing on her head.

<sup>11.14</sup> Why, nature itself teaches you that long hair on a man is a disgrace,

<sup>11.15</sup> but on a woman it is a thing of beauty. Her long hair has been given her to serve as a covering.

<sup>11.16</sup> But if anyone wants to argue about it, all I have to say is that neither we nor the churches of God have any other custom in worship.

<sup>11.17</sup> In the following instructions, however, I do not praise you, because your meetings for worship actually do more harm than good.

<sup>11.18</sup> In the first place, I have been told that there are opposing groups in your meetings; and this I believe is partly true.

<sup>11.19</sup> (No doubt there must be divisions among you so that the ones who are in the right may be clearly seen.)

<sup>11.20</sup> When you meet together as a group, it is not the Lord's Supper that you eat.

<sup>11.21</sup> For as you eat, you each go ahead with your own meal, so that some are hungry while others get drunk.

<sup>11.22</sup> Don't you have your own homes in which to eat and drink? Or would you rather despise the church of God and put to shame the people who are in need? What do you expect me to say to you about this? Shall I praise you? Of course, I don't!

<sup>11.23</sup> For I received from the Lord the teaching that I passed on to you: that the Lord Jesus, on the night he was betrayed, took a piece of bread,

<sup>11.24</sup> gave thanks to God, broke it, and said, "This is my body, which is for you. Do this in memory of me."

<sup>11.25</sup> In the same way, after the supper he took the cup and said, "This cup is God's new covenant, sealed with my blood. Whenever you drink it, do so in memory of me."

<sup>11.26</sup> This means that every time you eat this bread and drink from this cup you proclaim the Lord's death until he comes.

<sup>11.27</sup> It follows that if one of you eats the Lord's bread or drinks from his cup in a way that dishonors him, you are guilty of sin against the Lord's body and blood.

<sup>11.28</sup> So then, you should each examine yourself first, and then eat the bread and drink from the cup.

<sup>11.29</sup> For if you do not recognize the meaning of the Lord's body when you eat the bread and drink from the cup, you bring judgment on yourself as you eat and drink.

<sup>11.30</sup> That is why many of you are sick and weak, and several have died.

<sup>11.31</sup> If we would examine ourselves first, we would not come under God's judgment.

<sup>11.32</sup> But we are judged and punished by the Lord, so that we shall not be condemned together with the world.

<sup>11.33</sup> So then, my friends, when you gather together to eat the Lord's Supper, wait for one another.

<sup>11.34</sup> And if any of you are hungry, you should eat at home, so that you will not come under God's judgment as you meet together. As for the other matters, I will settle them when I come.

<sup>12.1</sup> Now, concerning what you wrote about the gifts from the Holy Spirit. I want you to know the truth about them, my friends.

<sup>12.2</sup> You know that while you were still heathen, you were led astray in many ways to the worship of lifeless idols.

<sup>12.3</sup> I want you to know that no one who is led by God's Spirit can say "A curse on Jesus!" and no one can confess "Jesus is Lord," without being guided by the Holy Spirit.

<sup>12.4</sup> There are different kinds of spiritual gifts, but the same Spirit gives them.

<sup>12.5</sup> There are different ways of serving, but the same Lord is served.

<sup>12.6</sup> There are different abilities to perform service, but the same God gives ability to all for their particular service.

<sup>12.7</sup> The Spirit's presence is shown in some way in each person for the good of all.

<sup>12.8</sup> The Spirit gives one person a message full of wisdom, while to another person the same Spirit gives a message full of knowledge.

<sup>12.9</sup> One and the same Spirit gives faith to one person, while to another person he gives the power to heal.

<sup>12.10</sup> The Spirit gives one person the power to work miracles; to another, the gift of speaking God's message; and to yet another, the ability to tell the difference between gifts that come from the Spirit and those that do not. To one person he gives the ability to speak in strange tongues, and to another he gives the ability to explain what is said.

<sup>12.11</sup> But it is one and the same Spirit who does all this; as he wishes, he gives a different gift to each person.

<sup>12.12</sup> Christ is like a single body, which has many parts; it is still one body, even though it is made up of different parts.

<sup>12.13</sup> In the same way, all of us, whether Jews or Gentiles, whether slaves or free, have been baptized into the one body by the same Spirit, and we have all been given the one Spirit to drink.

<sup>12.14</sup> For the body itself is not made up of only one part, but of many parts.

<sup>12.15</sup> If the foot were to say, "Because I am not a hand, I don't belong to the body," that would not keep it from being a part of the body.

<sup>12.16</sup> And if the ear were to say, "Because I am not an eye, I don't belong to the body," that would not keep it from being a part of the body.

<sup>12.17</sup> If the whole body were just an eye, how could it hear? And if it were only an ear, how could it smell?

<sup>12.18</sup> As it is, however, God put every different part in the body just as

he wanted it to be.

<sup>12.19</sup> There would not be a body if it were all only one part!

<sup>12.20</sup> As it is, there are many parts but one body.

<sup>12.21</sup> So then, the eye cannot say to the hand, "I don't need you!" Nor can the head say to the feet, "Well, I don't need you!"

<sup>12.22</sup> On the contrary, we cannot do without the parts of the body that seem to be weaker;

<sup>12.23</sup> and those parts that we think aren't worth very much are the ones which we treat with greater care; while the parts of the body which don't look very nice are treated with special modesty,

<sup>12.24</sup> which the more beautiful parts do not need. God himself has put the body together in such a way as to give greater honor to those parts that need it.

<sup>12.25</sup> And so there is no division in the body, but all its different parts have the same concern for one another.

<sup>12.26</sup> If one part of the body suffers, all the other parts suffer with it; if one part is praised, all the other parts share its happiness.

<sup>12.27</sup> All of you are Christ's body, and each one is a part of it.

<sup>12.28</sup> In the church God has put all in place: in the first place apostles, in the second place prophets, and in the third place teachers; then those who perform miracles, followed by those who are given the power to heal or to help others or to direct them or to speak in strange tongues.

<sup>12.29</sup> They are not all apostles or prophets or teachers. Not everyone has the power to work miracles

<sup>12.30</sup> or to heal diseases or to speak in strange tongues or to explain what is said.

<sup>12.31</sup> Set your hearts, then, on the more important gifts. Best of all, however, is the following way.

# 13

<sup>13.1</sup> I may be able to speak the languages of human beings and even of angels, but if I have no love, my speech is no more than a noisy gong or a clanging bell.

<sup>13.2</sup> I may have the gift of inspired preaching; I may have all knowledge and understand all secrets; I may have all the faith needed to move mountains — but if I have no love, I am nothing.

<sup>13.3</sup> I may give away everything I have, and even give up my body to be burned — but if I have no love, this does me no good.

<sup>13.4</sup> Love is patient and kind; it is not jealous or conceited or proud;

<sup>13.5</sup> love is not ill-mannered or selfish or irritable; love does not keep

a record of wrongs;

<sup>13.6</sup> love is not happy with evil, but is happy with the truth.

<sup>13.7</sup> Love never gives up; and its faith, hope, and patience never fail.

<sup>13.8</sup> Love is eternal. There are inspired messages, but they are temporary; there are gifts of speaking in strange tongues, but they will cease; there is knowledge, but it will pass.

<sup>13.9</sup> For our gifts of knowledge and of inspired messages are only partial;

<sup>13.10</sup> but when what is perfect comes, then what is partial will disappear.

<sup>13.11</sup> When I was a child, my speech, feelings, and thinking were all those of a child; now that I am an adult, I have no more use for childish ways.

<sup>13.12</sup> What we see now is like a dim image in a mirror; then we shall see face-to-face. What I know now is only partial; then it will be complete —as complete as God's knowledge of me.

<sup>13.13</sup> Meanwhile these three remain: faith, hope, and love; and the greatest of these is love.

# 14

<sup>14.1</sup> It is love, then, that you should strive for. Set your hearts on spiritual gifts, especially the gift of proclaiming God's message.

<sup>14.2</sup> Those who speak in strange tongues do not speak to others but to God, because no one understands them. They are speaking secret truths by the power of the Spirit.

<sup>14.3</sup> But those who proclaim God's message speak to people and give them help, encouragement, and comfort.

<sup>14.4</sup> Those who speak in strange tongues help only themselves, but those who proclaim God's message help the whole church.

<sup>14.5</sup> I would like for all of you to speak in strange tongues; but I would rather that you had the gift of proclaiming God's message. For the person who proclaims God's message is of greater value than the one who speaks in strange tongues — unless there is someone present who can explain what is said, so that the whole church may be helped.

<sup>14.6</sup> So when I come to you, my friends, what use will I be to you if I speak in strange tongues? Not a bit, unless I bring you some revelation from God or some knowledge or some inspired message or some teaching.

<sup>14.7</sup> Take such lifeless musical instruments as the flute or the harp — how will anyone know the tune that is being played unless the notes

are sounded distinctly?

<sup>14.8</sup> And if the one who plays the bugle does not sound a clear call, who will prepare for battle?

<sup>14.9</sup> In the same way, how will anyone understand what you are talking about if your message given in strange tongues is not clear? Your words will vanish in the air!

<sup>14.10</sup> There are many different languages in the world, yet none of them is without meaning.

<sup>14.11</sup> But if I do not know the language being spoken, those who use it will be foreigners to me and I will be a foreigner to them.

<sup>14.12</sup> Since you are eager to have the gifts of the Spirit, you must try above everything else to make greater use of those which help to build up the church.

<sup>14.13</sup> The person who speaks in strange tongues, then, must pray for the gift to explain what is said.

<sup>14.14</sup> For if I pray in this way, my spirit prays indeed, but my mind has no part in it.

<sup>14.15</sup> What should I do, then? I will pray with my spirit, but I will pray also with my mind; I will sing with my spirit, but I will sing also with my mind.

<sup>14.16</sup> When you give thanks to God in spirit only, how can ordinary people taking part in the meeting say "Amen" to your prayer of thanksgiving? They have no way of knowing what you are saying.

<sup>14.17</sup> Even if your prayer of thanks to God is quite good, other people are not helped at all.

<sup>14.18</sup> I thank God that I speak in strange tongues much more than any of you.

<sup>14.19</sup> But in church worship I would rather speak five words that can be understood, in order to teach others, than speak thousands of words in strange tongues.

<sup>14.20</sup> Do not be like children in your thinking, my friends; be children so far as evil is concerned, but be grown up in your thinking.

<sup>14.21</sup> In the Scriptures it is written, "By means of people speaking strange languages I will speak to my people, says the Lord. I will speak through lips of foreigners, but even then my people will not listen to me."

<sup>14.22</sup> So then, the gift of speaking in strange tongues is proof for unbelievers, not for believers, while the gift of proclaiming God's message is proof for believers, not for unbelievers.

<sup>14.23</sup> If, then, the whole church meets together and everyone starts speaking in strange tongues — and if some ordinary people or unbe-

lievers come in, won't they say that you are all crazy?

<sup>14.24</sup> But if everyone is proclaiming God's message when some unbelievers or ordinary people come in, they will be convinced of their sin by what they hear. They will be judged by all they hear,

<sup>14.25</sup> their secret thoughts will be brought into the open, and they will bow down and worship God, confessing, "Truly God is here among you!"

<sup>14.26</sup> This is what I mean, my friends. When you meet for worship, one person has a hymn, another a teaching, another a revelation from God, another a message in strange tongues, and still another the explanation of what is said. Everything must be of help to the church.

<sup>14.27</sup> If someone is going to speak in strange tongues, two or three at the most should speak, one after the other, and someone else must explain what is being said.

<sup>14.28</sup> But if no one is there who can explain, then the one who speaks in strange tongues must be quiet and speak only to himself and to God.

<sup>14.29</sup> Two or three who are given God's message should speak, while the others are to judge what they say.

<sup>14.30</sup> But if someone sitting in the meeting receives a message from God, the one who is speaking should stop.

<sup>14.31</sup> All of you may proclaim God's message, one by one, so that everyone will learn and be encouraged.

<sup>14.32</sup> The gift of proclaiming God's message should be under the speaker's control,

<sup>14.33</sup> because God does not want us to be in disorder but in harmony and peace. As in all the churches of God's people,

<sup>14.34</sup> the women should keep quiet in the meetings. They are not allowed to speak; as the Jewish Law says, they must not be in charge.

<sup>14.35</sup> If they want to find out about something, they should ask their husbands at home. It is a disgraceful thing for a woman to speak in a church meeting.

<sup>14.36</sup> Or could it be that the word of God came from you? Or are you the only ones to whom it came?

<sup>14.37</sup> If anyone supposes he is God's messenger or has a spiritual gift, he must realize that what I am writing to you is the Lord's command.

<sup>14.38</sup> But if he does not pay attention to this, pay no attention to him.

<sup>14.39</sup> So then, my friends, set your heart on proclaiming God's message, but do not forbid the speaking in strange tongues.

<sup>14.40</sup> Everything must be done in a proper and orderly way.

# 15

<sup>15.1</sup> And now I want to remind you, my friends, of the Good News which I preached to you, which you received, and on which your faith stands firm.

<sup>15.2</sup> That is the gospel, the message that I preached to you. You are saved by the gospel if you hold firmly to it — unless it was for nothing that you believed.

<sup>15.3</sup> I passed on to you what I received, which is of the greatest importance: that Christ died for our sins, as written in the Scriptures;

<sup>15.4</sup> that he was buried and that he was raised to life three days later, as written in the Scriptures;

<sup>15.5</sup> that he appeared to Peter and then to all twelve apostles.

<sup>15.6</sup> Then he appeared to more than five hundred of his followers at once, most of whom are still alive, although some have died.

<sup>15.7</sup> Then he appeared to James, and afterward to all the apostles.

<sup>15.8</sup> Last of all he appeared also to me — even though I am like someone whose birth was abnormal.

<sup>15.9</sup> For I am the least of all the apostles — I do not even deserve to be called an apostle, because I persecuted God's church.

<sup>15.10</sup> But by God's grace I am what I am, and the grace that he gave me was not without effect. On the contrary, I have worked harder than any of the other apostles, although it was not really my own doing, but God's grace working with me.

<sup>15.11</sup> So then, whether it came from me or from them, this is what we all preach, and this is what you believe.

<sup>15.12</sup> Now, since our message is that Christ has been raised from death, how can some of you say that the dead will not be raised to life?

<sup>15.13</sup> If that is true, it means that Christ was not raised;

<sup>15.14</sup> and if Christ has not been raised from death, then we have nothing to preach and you have nothing to believe.

<sup>15.15</sup> More than that, we are shown to be lying about God, because we said that he raised Christ from death — but if it is true that the dead are not raised to life, then he did not raise Christ.

<sup>15.16</sup> For if the dead are not raised, neither has Christ been raised.

<sup>15.17</sup> And if Christ has not been raised, then your faith is a delusion and you are still lost in your sins.

<sup>15.18</sup> It would also mean that the believers in Christ who have died are lost.

<sup>15.19</sup> If our hope in Christ is good for this life only and no more, then we deserve more pity than anyone else in all the world.

<sup>15.20</sup> But the truth is that Christ has been raised from death, as the

guarantee that those who sleep in death will also be raised.

<sup></sup>15.21 For just as death came by means of a man, in the same way the rising from death comes by means of a man.

15.22 For just as all people die because of their union with Adam, in the same way all will be raised to life because of their union with Christ.

15.23 But each one will be raised in proper order: Christ, first of all; then, at the time of his coming, those who belong to him.

15.24 Then the end will come; Christ will overcome all spiritual rulers, authorities, and powers, and will hand over the Kingdom to God the Father.

15.25 For Christ must rule until God defeats all enemies and puts them under his feet.

15.26 The last enemy to be defeated will be death.

15.27 For the scripture says, "God put [all] things under his feet." It is clear, of course, that the words "all things" do not include God himself, who puts all things under Christ.

15.28 But when all things have been placed under Christ's rule, then he himself, the Son, will place himself under God, who placed all things under him; and God will rule completely over all.

15.29 Now, what about those people who are baptized for the dead? What do they hope to accomplish? If it is true, as some claim, that the dead are not raised to life, why are those people being baptized for the dead?

15.30 And as for us — why would we run the risk of danger every hour?

15.31 My friends, I face death every day! The pride I have in you, in our life in union with Christ Jesus our Lord, makes me declare this.

15.32 If I have, as it were, fought "wild beasts" here in Ephesus simply from human motives, what have I gained? But if the dead are not raised to life, then, as the saying goes, "Let us eat and drink, for tomorrow we will die."

15.33 Do not be fooled. "Bad companions ruin good character."

15.34 Come back to your right senses and stop your sinful ways. I declare to your shame that some of you do not know God.

15.35 Someone will ask, "How can the dead be raised to life? What kind of body will they have?"

15.36 You fool! When you plant a seed in the ground, it does not sprout to life unless it dies.

15.37 And what you plant is a bare seed, perhaps a grain of wheat or some other grain, not the full-bodied plant that will later grow up.

15.38 God provides that seed with the body he wishes; he gives each seed its own proper body.

<sup>15.39</sup> And the flesh of living beings is not all the same kind of flesh; human beings have one kind of flesh, animals another, birds another, and fish another.

<sup>15.40</sup> And there are heavenly bodies and earthly bodies; the beauty that belongs to heavenly bodies is different from the beauty that belongs to earthly bodies.

<sup>15.41</sup> The sun has its own beauty, the moon another beauty, and the stars a different beauty; and even among stars there are different kinds of beauty.

<sup>15.42</sup> This is how it will be when the dead are raised to life. When the body is buried, it is mortal; when raised, it will be immortal.

<sup>15.43</sup> When buried, it is ugly and weak; when raised, it will be beautiful and strong.

<sup>15.44</sup> When buried, it is a physical body; when raised, it will be a spiritual body. There is, of course, a physical body, so there has to be a spiritual body.

<sup>15.45</sup> For the scripture says, "The first man, Adam, was created a living being"; but the last Adam is the life-giving Spirit.

<sup>15.46</sup> It is not the spiritual that comes first, but the physical, and then the spiritual.

<sup>15.47</sup> The first Adam, made of earth, came from the earth; the second Adam came from heaven.

<sup>15.48</sup> Those who belong to the earth are like the one who was made of earth; those who are of heaven are like the one who came from heaven.

<sup>15.49</sup> Just as we wear the likeness of the man made of earth, so we will wear the likeness of the Man from heaven.

<sup>15.50</sup> What I mean, friends, is that what is made of flesh and blood cannot share in God's Kingdom, and what is mortal cannot possess immortality.

<sup>15.51-52</sup> Listen to this secret truth: we shall not all die, but when the last trumpet sounds, we shall all be changed in an instant, as quickly as the blinking of an eye. For when the trumpet sounds, the dead will be raised, never to die again, and we shall all be changed.

<sup>15.53</sup> For what is mortal must be changed into what is immortal; what will die must be changed into what cannot die.

<sup>15.54</sup> So when this takes place, and the mortal has been changed into the immortal, then the scripture will come true: "Death is destroyed; victory is complete!"

<sup>15.55</sup> "Where, Death, is your victory? Where, Death, is your power to

hurt?"

<sup>15.56</sup> Death gets its power to hurt from sin, and sin gets its power from the Law.

<sup>15.57</sup> But thanks be to God who gives us the victory through our Lord Jesus Christ!

<sup>15.58</sup> So then, my dear friends, stand firm and steady. Keep busy always in your work for the Lord, since you know that nothing you do in the Lord's service is ever useless.

# 16

<sup>16.1</sup> Now, concerning what you wrote about the money to be raised to help God's people in Judea. You must do what I told the churches in Galatia to do.

<sup>16.2</sup> Every Sunday each of you must put aside some money, in proportion to what you have earned, and save it up, so that there will be no need to collect money when I come.

<sup>16.3</sup> After I come, I shall give letters of introduction to those you have approved, and send them to take your gift to Jerusalem.

<sup>16.4</sup> If it seems worthwhile for me to go, then they can go along with me.

<sup>16.5</sup> I shall come to you after I have gone through Macedonia — for I have to go through Macedonia.

<sup>16.6</sup> I shall probably spend some time with you, perhaps the whole winter, and then you can help me to continue my trip, wherever it is I shall go next.

<sup>16.7</sup> I want to see you more than just briefly in passing; I hope to spend quite a long time with you, if the Lord allows.

<sup>16.8</sup> I will stay here in Ephesus until the day of Pentecost.

<sup>16.9</sup> There is a real opportunity here for great and worthwhile work, even though there are many opponents.

<sup>16.10</sup> If Timothy comes your way, be sure to make him feel welcome among you, because he is working for the Lord, just as I am.

<sup>16.11</sup> No one should look down on him, but you must help him continue his trip in peace, so that he will come back to me; for I am expecting him back with the believers.

<sup>16.12</sup> Now, about brother Apollos. I have often encouraged him to visit you with the other believers, but he is not completely convinced that he should go at this time. When he gets the chance, however, he will go.

<sup>16.13</sup> Be alert, stand firm in the faith, be brave, be strong.

<sup>16.14</sup> Do all your work in love.

<sup>16.15</sup> You know about Stephanas and his family; they are the first Christian converts in Achaia and have given themselves to the service of God's people. I beg you, my friends,
<sup>16.16</sup> to follow the leadership of such people as these, and of anyone else who works and serves with them.
<sup>16.17</sup> I am happy about the coming of Stephanas, Fortunatus, and Achaicus; they have made up for your absence
<sup>16.18</sup> and have cheered me up, just as they cheered you up. Such men as these deserve notice.
<sup>16.19</sup> The churches in the province of Asia send you their greetings; Aquila and Priscilla and the church that meets in their house send warm Christian greetings.
<sup>16.20</sup> All the believers here send greetings. Greet one another with the kiss of peace.
<sup>16.21</sup> With my own hand I write this: Greetings from Paul.
<sup>16.22</sup> Whoever does not love the Lord — a curse on him! Marana tha — Our Lord, come!
<sup>16.23</sup> The grace of the Lord Jesus be with you.
<sup>16.24</sup> My love be with you all in Christ Jesus.

# 2 CORINTHIANS

# 2 Corinthians

1

<sup>1.1</sup> From Paul, an apostle of Christ Jesus by God's will, and from our brother Timothy — To the church of God in Corinth, and to all God's people throughout Achaia:

<sup>1.2</sup> May God our Father and the Lord Jesus Christ give you grace and peace.

<sup>1.3</sup> Let us give thanks to the God and Father of our Lord Jesus Christ, the merciful Father, the God from whom all help comes!

<sup>1.4</sup> He helps us in all our troubles, so that we are able to help others who have all kinds of troubles, using the same help that we ourselves have received from God.

<sup>1.5</sup> Just as we have a share in Christ's many sufferings, so also through Christ we share in God's great help.

<sup>1.6</sup> If we suffer, it is for your help and salvation; if we are helped, then you too are helped and given the strength to endure with patience the same sufferings that we also endure.

<sup>1.7</sup> So our hope in you is never shaken; we know that just as you share in our sufferings, you also share in the help we receive.

<sup>1.8</sup> We want to remind you, friends, of the trouble we had in the province of Asia. The burdens laid upon us were so great and so heavy that we gave up all hope of staying alive.

<sup>1.9</sup> We felt that the death sentence had been passed on us. But this happened so that we should rely, not on ourselves, but only on God, who raises the dead.

<sup>1.10</sup> From such terrible dangers of death he saved us, and will save us; and we have placed our hope in him that he will save us again,

<sup>1.11</sup> as you help us by means of your prayers for us. So it will be that the many prayers for us will be answered, and God will bless us; and many will raise their voices to him in thanksgiving for us.

<sup>1.12</sup> We are proud that our conscience assures us that our lives in this world, and especially our relations with you, have been ruled by God-given frankness and sincerity, by the power of God's grace and not by human wisdom.

<sup>1.13-14</sup> We write to you only what you can read and understand. But even though you now understand us only in part, I hope that you will come to understand us completely, so that in the Day of our Lord Jesus you can be as proud of us as we shall be of you.

<sup>1.15</sup> I was so sure of all this that I made plans at first to visit you, in

order that you might be blessed twice.

<sup>1.16</sup> For I planned to visit you on my way to Macedonia and again on my way back, in order to get help from you for my trip to Judea.

<sup>1.17</sup> In planning this, did I appear fickle? When I make my plans, do I make them from selfish motives, ready to say "Yes, yes" and "No, no" at the same time?

<sup>1.18</sup> As surely as God speaks the truth, my promise to you was not a "Yes" and a "No."

<sup>1.19</sup> For Jesus Christ, the Son of God, who was preached among you by Silas, Timothy, and myself, is not one who is "Yes" and "No." On the contrary, he is God's "Yes";

<sup>1.20</sup> for it is he who is the "Yes" to all of God's promises. This is why through Jesus Christ our "Amen" is said to the glory of God.

<sup>1.21</sup> It is God himself who makes us, together with you, sure of our life in union with Christ; it is God himself who has set us apart,

<sup>1.22</sup> who has placed his mark of ownership upon us, and who has given us the Holy Spirit in our hearts as the guarantee of all that he has in store for us.

<sup>1.23</sup> I call God as my witness — he knows my heart! It was in order to spare you that I decided not to go to Corinth.

<sup>1.24</sup> We are not trying to dictate to you what you must believe; we know that you stand firm in the faith. Instead, we are working with you for your own happiness.

# 2

<sup>2.1</sup> So I made up my mind not to come to you again to make you sad.

<sup>2.2</sup> For if I were to make you sad, who would be left to cheer me up? Only the very persons I had made sad.

<sup>2.3</sup> That is why I wrote that letter to you — I did not want to come to you and be made sad by the very people who should make me glad. For I am convinced that when I am happy, then all of you are happy too.

<sup>2.4</sup> I wrote you with a greatly troubled and distressed heart and with many tears; my purpose was not to make you sad, but to make you realize how much I love you all.

<sup>2.5</sup> Now, if anyone has made somebody sad, he has not done it to me but to all of you — in part, at least. (I say this because I do not want to be too hard on him.)

<sup>2.6</sup> It is enough that this person has been punished in this way by most of you.

<sup>2.7</sup> Now, however, you should forgive him and encourage him, in order

to keep him from becoming so sad as to give up completely.

2.8 And so I beg you to let him know that you really do love him.

2.9 I wrote you that letter because I wanted to find out how well you had stood the test and whether you are always ready to obey my instructions.

2.10 When you forgive people for what they have done, I forgive them too. For when I forgive — if, indeed, I need to forgive anything - I do it in Christ's presence because of you,

2.11 in order to keep Satan from getting the upper hand over us; for we know what his plans are.

2.12 When I arrived in Troas to preach the Good News about Christ, I found that the Lord had opened the way for the work there.

2.13 But I was deeply worried, because I could not find our brother Titus. So I said good-bye to the people there and went on to Macedonia.

2.14 But thanks be to God! For in union with Christ we are always led by God as prisoners in Christ's victory procession. God uses us to make the knowledge about Christ spread everywhere like a sweet fragrance.

2.15 For we are like a sweet-smelling incense offered by Christ to God, which spreads among those who are being saved and those who are being lost.

2.16 For those who are being lost, it is a deadly stench that kills; but for those who are being saved, it is a fragrance that brings life. Who, then, is capable for such a task?

2.17 We are not like so many others, who handle God's message as if it were cheap merchandise; but because God has sent us, we speak with sincerity in his presence, as servants of Christ.

# 3

3.1 Does this sound as if we were again boasting about ourselves? Could it be that, like some other people, we need letters of recommendation to you or from you?

3.2 You yourselves are the letter we have, written on our hearts for everyone to know and read.

3.3 It is clear that Christ himself wrote this letter and sent it by us. It is written, not with ink but with the Spirit of the living God, and not on stone tablets but on human hearts.

3.4 We say this because we have confidence in God through Christ.

3.5 There is nothing in us that allows us to claim that we are capable of doing this work. The capacity we have comes from God;

3.6 it is he who made us capable of serving the new covenant, which consists not of a written law but of the Spirit. The written law brings death, but the Spirit gives life.

3.7 The Law was carved in letters on stone tablets, and God's glory appeared when it was given. Even though the brightness on Moses' face was fading, it was so strong that the people of Israel could not keep their eyes fixed on him. If the Law, which brings death when it is in force, came with such glory,

3.8 how much greater is the glory that belongs to the activity of the Spirit!

3.9 The system which brings condemnation was glorious; how much more glorious is the activity which brings salvation!

3.10 We may say that because of the far brighter glory now the glory that was so bright in the past is gone.

3.11 For if there was glory in that which lasted for a while, how much more glory is there in that which lasts forever!

3.12 Because we have this hope, we are very bold.

3.13 We are not like Moses, who had to put a veil over his face so that the people of Israel would not see the brightness fade and disappear.

3.14 Their minds, indeed, were closed; and to this very day their minds are covered with the same veil as they read the books of the old covenant. The veil is removed only when a person is joined to Christ.

3.15 Even today, whenever they read the Law of Moses, the veil still covers their minds.

3.16 But it can be removed, as the scripture says about Moses: "His veil was removed when he turned to the Lord."

3.17 Now, "the Lord" in this passage is the Spirit; and where the Spirit of the Lord is present, there is freedom.

3.18 All of us, then, reflect the glory of the Lord with uncovered faces; and that same glory, coming from the Lord, who is the Spirit, transforms us into his likeness in an ever greater degree of glory.

4

4.1 God in his mercy has given us this work to do, and so we do not become discouraged.

4.2 We put aside all secret and shameful deeds; we do not act with deceit, nor do we falsify the word of God. In the full light of truth we live in God's sight and try to commend ourselves to everyone's good conscience.

4.3 For if the gospel we preach is hidden, it is hidden only from those who are being lost.

<sup>4.4</sup> They do not believe, because their minds have been kept in the dark by the evil god of this world. He keeps them from seeing the light shining on them, the light that comes from the Good News about the glory of Christ, who is the exact likeness of God. <sup>4.5</sup> For it is not ourselves that we preach; we preach Jesus Christ as Lord, and ourselves as your servants for Jesus' sake. <sup>4.6</sup> The God who said, "Out of darkness the light shall shine!" is the same God who made his light shine in our hearts, to bring us the knowledge of God's glory shining in the face of Christ.

<sup>4.7</sup> Yet we who have this spiritual treasure are like common clay pots, in order to show that the supreme power belongs to God, not to us. <sup>4.8</sup> We are often troubled, but not crushed; sometimes in doubt, but never in despair; <sup>4.9</sup> there are many enemies, but we are never without a friend; and though badly hurt at times, we are not destroyed. <sup>4.10</sup> At all times we carry in our mortal bodies the death of Jesus, so that his life also may be seen in our bodies. <sup>4.11</sup> Throughout our lives we are always in danger of death for Jesus' sake, in order that his life may be seen in this mortal body of ours. <sup>4.12</sup> This means that death is at work in us, but life is at work in you.

<sup>4.13</sup> The scripture says, "I spoke because I believed." In the same spirit of faith we also speak because we believe. <sup>4.14</sup> We know that God, who raised the Lord Jesus to life, will also raise us up with Jesus and take us, together with you, into his presence. <sup>4.15</sup> All this is for your sake; and as God's grace reaches more and more people, they will offer to the glory of God more prayers of thanksgiving.

<sup>4.16</sup> For this reason we never become discouraged. Even though our physical being is gradually decaying, yet our spiritual being is renewed day after day. <sup>4.17</sup> And this small and temporary trouble we suffer will bring us a tremendous and eternal glory, much greater than the trouble. <sup>4.18</sup> For we fix our attention, not on things that are seen, but on things that are unseen. What can be seen lasts only for a time, but what cannot be seen lasts forever.

# 5

<sup>5.1</sup> For we know that when this tent we live in — our body here on earth — is torn down, God will have a house in heaven for us to live in, a home he himself has made, which will last forever.

5.2 And now we sigh, so great is our desire that our home which comes from heaven should be put on over us;

5.3 by being clothed with it we shall not be without a body.

5.4 While we live in this earthly tent, we groan with a feeling of oppression; it is not that we want to get rid of our earthly body, but that we want to have the heavenly one put on over us, so that what is mortal will be transformed by life.

5.5 God is the one who has prepared us for this change, and he gave us his Spirit as the guarantee of all that he has in store for us.

5.6 So we are always full of courage. We know that as long as we are at home in the body we are away from the Lord's home.

5.7 For our life is a matter of faith, not of sight.

5.8 We are full of courage and would much prefer to leave our home in the body and be at home with the Lord.

5.9 More than anything else, however, we want to please him, whether in our home here or there.

5.10 For all of us must appear before Christ, to be judged by him. We will each receive what we deserve, according to everything we have done, good or bad, in our bodily life.

5.11 We know what it means to fear the Lord, and so we try to persuade others. God knows us completely, and I hope that in your hearts you know me as well.

5.12 We are not trying again to recommend ourselves to you; rather, we are trying to give you a good reason to be proud of us, so that you will be able to answer those who boast about people's appearance and not about their character.

5.13 Are we really insane? It is for God's sake. Or are we sane? Then it is for your sake.

5.14 We are ruled by the love of Christ, now that we recognize that one man died for everyone, which means that they all share in his death.

5.15 He died for all, so that those who live should no longer live for themselves, but only for him who died and was raised to life for their sake.

5.16 No longer, then, do we judge anyone by human standards. Even if at one time we judged Christ according to human standards, we no longer do so.

5.17 Anyone who is joined to Christ is a new being; the old is gone, the new has come.

5.18 All this is done by God, who through Christ changed us from enemies into his friends and gave us the task of making others his friends also.

<sup></sup>5.19 Our message is that God was making all human beings his friends through Christ. God did not keep an account of their sins, and he has given us the message which tells how he makes them his friends.

5.20 Here we are, then, speaking for Christ, as though God himself were making his appeal through us. We plead on Christ's behalf: let God change you from enemies into his friends!

5.21 Christ was without sin, but for our sake God made him share our sin in order that in union with him we might share the righteousness of God.

# 6

6.1 In our work together with God, then, we beg you who have received God's grace not to let it be wasted.

6.2 Hear what God says: "When the time came for me to show you favor, I heard you; when the day arrived for me to save you, I helped you."

Listen! This is the hour to receive God's favor; today is the day to be saved!

6.3 We do not want anyone to find fault with our work, so we try not to put obstacles in anyone's way.

6.4 Instead, in everything we do we show that we are God's servants by patiently enduring troubles, hardships, and difficulties.

6.5 We have been beaten, jailed, and mobbed; we have been overworked and have gone without sleep or food.

6.6 By our purity, knowledge, patience, and kindness we have shown ourselves to be God's servants — by the Holy Spirit, by our true love,

6.7 by our message of truth, and by the power of God. We have righteousness as our weapon, both to attack and to defend ourselves.

6.8 We are honored and disgraced; we are insulted and praised. We are treated as liars, yet we speak the truth;

6.9 as unknown, yet we are known by all; as though we were dead, but, as you see, we live on. Although punished, we are not killed;

6.10 although saddened, we are always glad; we seem poor, but we make many people rich; we seem to have nothing, yet we really possess everything.

6.11 Dear friends in Corinth! We have spoken frankly to you; we have opened our hearts wide.

6.12 It is not we who have closed our hearts to you; it is you who have closed your hearts to us.

<sup>6.13</sup> I speak now as though you were my children: show us the same feelings that we have for you. Open your hearts wide!

<sup>6.14</sup> Do not try to work together as equals with unbelievers, for it cannot be done. How can right and wrong be partners? How can light and darkness live together?

<sup>6.15</sup> How can Christ and the Devil agree? What does a believer have in common with an unbeliever?

<sup>6.16</sup> How can God's temple come to terms with pagan idols? For we are the temple of the living God! As God himself has said, "I will make my home with my people and live among them; I will be their God, and they shall be my people."

<sup>6.17</sup> And so the Lord says, "You must leave them and separate yourselves from them. Have nothing to do with what is unclean, and I will accept you.

<sup>6.18</sup> I will be your father, and you shall be my sons and daughters, says the Lord Almighty."

# 7

<sup>7.1</sup> All these promises are made to us, my dear friends. So then, let us purify ourselves from everything that makes body or soul unclean, and let us be completely holy by living in awe of God.

<sup>7.2</sup> Make room for us in your hearts. We have wronged no one; we have ruined no one, nor tried to take advantage of anyone.

<sup>7.3</sup> I do not say this to condemn you; for, as I have said before, you are so dear to us that we are always together, whether we live or die.

<sup>7.4</sup> I am so sure of you; I take such pride in you! In all our troubles I am still full of courage; I am running over with joy.

<sup>7.5</sup> Even after we arrived in Macedonia, we did not have any rest. There were troubles everywhere, quarrels with others, fears in our hearts.

<sup>7.6</sup> But God, who encourages the downhearted, encouraged us with the coming of Titus.

<sup>7.7</sup> It was not only his coming that cheered us, but also his report of how you encouraged him. He told us how much you want to see me, how sorry you are, how ready you are to defend me; and so I am even happier now.

<sup>7.8</sup> For even if that letter of mine made you sad, I am not sorry I wrote it. I could have been sorry when I saw that it made you sad for a while.

<sup>7.9</sup> But now I am happy — not because I made you sad, but because your sadness made you change your ways. That sadness was used by

God, and so we caused you no harm.

7.10 For the sadness that is used by God brings a change of heart that leads to salvation — and there is no regret in that! But sadness that is merely human causes death.

7.11 See what God did with this sadness of yours: how earnest it has made you, how eager to prove your innocence! Such indignation, such alarm, such feelings, such devotion, such readiness to punish wrongdoing! You have shown yourselves to be without fault in the whole matter.

7.12 So, even though I wrote that letter, it was not because of the one who did wrong or the one who was wronged. Instead, I wrote it to make plain to you, in God's sight, how deep your devotion to us really is.

7.13 That is why we were encouraged. Not only were we encouraged; how happy Titus made us with his happiness over the way in which all of you helped to cheer him up!

7.14 I did boast of you to him, and you have not disappointed me. We have always spoken the truth to you, and in the same way the boast we made to Titus has proved true.

7.15 And so his love for you grows stronger, as he remembers how all of you were ready to obey his instructions, how you welcomed him with fear and trembling.

7.16 How happy I am that I can depend on you completely!

# 8

8.1 Our friends, we want you to know what God's grace has accomplished in the churches in Macedonia.

8.2 They have been severely tested by the troubles they went through; but their joy was so great that they were extremely generous in their giving, even though they are very poor.

8.3 I can assure you that they gave as much as they could, and even more than they could. Of their own free will

8.4 they begged us and pleaded for the privilege of having a part in helping God's people in Judea.

8.5 It was more than we could have hoped for! First they gave themselves to the Lord; and then, by God's will they gave themselves to us as well.

8.6 So we urged Titus, who began this work, to continue it and help you complete this special service of love.

8.7 You are so rich in all you have: in faith, speech, and knowledge, in your eagerness to help and in your love for us. And so we want you to be generous also in this service of love.

8.8 I am not laying down any rules. But by showing how eager others are to help, I am trying to find out how real your own love is.

8.9 You know the grace of our Lord Jesus Christ; rich as he was, he made himself poor for your sake, in order to make you rich by means of his poverty.

8.10 My opinion is that it is better for you to finish now what you began last year. You were the first, not only to act, but also to be willing to act.

8.11 On with it, then, and finish the job! Be as eager to finish it as you were to plan it, and do it with what you now have.

8.12 If you are eager to give, God will accept your gift on the basis of what you have to give, not on what you don't have.

8.13-14 I am not trying to relieve others by putting a burden on you; but since you have plenty at this time, it is only fair that you should help those who are in need. Then, when you are in need and they have plenty, they will help you. In this way both are treated equally.

8.15 As the scripture says, "The one who gathered much did not have too much, and the one who gathered little did not have too little."

8.16 How we thank God for making Titus as eager as we are to help you!

8.17 Not only did he welcome our request; he was so eager to help that of his own free will he decided to go to you.

8.18 With him we are sending the brother who is highly respected in all the churches for his work in preaching the gospel.

8.19 And besides that, he has been chosen and appointed by the churches to travel with us as we carry out this service of love for the sake of the Lord's glory and in order to show that we want to help.

8.20 We are being careful not to stir up any complaints about the way we handle this generous gift.

8.21 Our purpose is to do what is right, not only in the sight of the Lord, but also in the sight of others.

8.22 So we are sending our brother with them; we have tested him many times and found him always very eager to help. And now that he has so much confidence in you, he is all the more eager to help.

8.23 As for Titus, he is my partner and works with me to help you; as for the other brothers who are going with him, they represent the churches and bring glory to Christ.

8.24 Show your love to them, so that all the churches will be sure of it and know that we are right in boasting about you.

# 9

⁹·¹ There is really no need for me to write you about the help being sent to God's people in Judea.

⁹·² I know that you are willing to help, and I have boasted of you to the people in Macedonia. "The believers in Achaia," I said, "have been ready to help since last year." Your eagerness has stirred up most of them.

⁹·³ Now I am sending these believers, so that our boasting about you in this matter may not turn out to be empty words. But, just as I said, you will be ready with your help.

⁹·⁴ However, if the people from Macedonia should come with me and find out that you are not ready, how ashamed we would be — not to speak of your shame — for feeling so sure of you!

⁹·⁵ So I thought it was necessary to urge these believers to go to you ahead of me and get ready in advance the gift you promised to make. Then it will be ready when I arrive, and it will show that you give because you want to, not because you have to.

⁹·⁶ Remember that the person who plants few seeds will have a small crop; the one who plants many seeds will have a large crop.

⁹·⁷ You should each give, then, as you have decided, not with regret or out of a sense of duty; for God loves the one who gives gladly.

⁹·⁸ And God is able to give you more than you need, so that you will always have all you need for yourselves and more than enough for every good cause.

⁹·⁹ As the scripture says, "He gives generously to the needy; his kindness lasts forever."

⁹·¹⁰ And God, who supplies seed for the sower and bread to eat, will also supply you with all the seed you need and will make it grow and produce a rich harvest from your generosity.

⁹·¹¹ He will always make you rich enough to be generous at all times, so that many will thank God for your gifts which they receive from us.

⁹·¹² For this service you perform not only meets the needs of God's people, but also produces an outpouring of gratitude to God.

⁹·¹³ And because of the proof which this service of yours brings, many will give glory to God for your loyalty to the gospel of Christ, which you profess, and for your generosity in sharing with them and everyone else.

⁹·¹⁴ And so with deep affection they will pray for you because of the extraordinary grace God has shown you.

⁹·¹⁵ Let us thank God for his priceless gift!

<sup>10.1</sup> I, Paul, make a personal appeal to you — I who am said to be meek and mild when I am with you, but harsh with you when I am away. By the gentleness and kindness of Christ **10**

<sup>10.2</sup> I beg you not to force me to be harsh when I come; for I am sure I can deal harshly with those who say that we act from worldly motives.

<sup>10.3</sup> It is true that we live in the world, but we do not fight from worldly motives.

<sup>10.4</sup> The weapons we use in our fight are not the world's weapons but God's powerful weapons, which we use to destroy strongholds. We destroy false arguments;

<sup>10.5</sup> we pull down every proud obstacle that is raised against the knowledge of God; we take every thought captive and make it obey Christ.

<sup>10.6</sup> And after you have proved your complete loyalty, we will be ready to punish any act of disloyalty.

<sup>10.7</sup> You are looking at the outward appearance of things. Are there some there who reckon themselves to belong to Christ? Well, let them think again about themselves, because we belong to Christ just as much as they do.

<sup>10.8</sup> For I am not ashamed, even if I have boasted somewhat too much about the authority that the Lord has given us — authority to build you up, not to tear you down.

<sup>10.9</sup> I do not want it to appear that I am trying to frighten you with my letters.

<sup>10.10</sup> Someone will say, "Paul's letters are severe and strong, but when he is with us in person, he is weak, and his words are nothing!"

<sup>10.11</sup> Such a person must understand that there is no difference between what we write in our letters when we are away and what we will do when we are there with you.

<sup>10.12</sup> Of course we would not dare classify ourselves or compare ourselves with those who rate themselves so highly. How stupid they are! They make up their own standards to measure themselves by, and they judge themselves by their own standards!

<sup>10.13</sup> As for us, however, our boasting will not go beyond certain limits; it will stay within the limits of the work which God has set for us, and this includes our work among you.

<sup>10.14</sup> And since you are within those limits, we were not going beyond them when we came to you, bringing the Good News about Christ.

<sup>10.15</sup> So we do not boast about the work that others have done beyond the limits God set for us. Instead, we hope that your faith may grow

and that we may be able to do a much greater work among you, always within the limits that God has set.

<sup>10.16</sup> Then we can preach the Good News in other countries beyond you and shall not have to boast about work already done in someone else's field.

<sup>10.17</sup> But as the scripture says, "Whoever wants to boast must boast about what the Lord has done."

<sup>10.18</sup> For it is when the Lord thinks well of us that we are really approved, and not when we think well of ourselves.

# 11

<sup>11.1</sup> I wish you would tolerate me, even when I am a bit foolish. Please do!

<sup>11.2</sup> I am jealous for you, just as God is; you are like a pure virgin whom I have promised in marriage to one man only, Christ himself.

<sup>11.3</sup> I am afraid that your minds will be corrupted and that you will abandon your full and pure devotion to Christ — in the same way that Eve was deceived by the snake's clever lies.

<sup>11.4</sup> For you gladly tolerate anyone who comes to you and preaches a different Jesus, not the one we preached; and you accept a spirit and a gospel completely different from the Spirit and the gospel you received from us!

<sup>11.5</sup> I do not think that I am the least bit inferior to those very special so-called "apostles" of yours!

<sup>11.6</sup> Perhaps I am an amateur in speaking, but certainly not in knowledge; we have made this clear to you at all times and in all conditions.

<sup>11.7</sup> I did not charge you a thing when I preached the Good News of God to you; I humbled myself in order to make you important. Was that wrong of me?

<sup>11.8</sup> While I was working among you, I was paid by other churches. I was robbing them, so to speak, in order to help you.

<sup>11.9</sup> And during the time I was with you I did not bother you for help when I needed money; the believers who came from Macedonia brought me everything I needed. As in the past, so in the future: I will never be a burden to you!

<sup>11.10</sup> By Christ's truth in me, I promise that this boast of mine will not be silenced anywhere in all of Achaia.

<sup>11.11</sup> Do I say this because I don't love you? God knows I love you!

<sup>11.12</sup> I will go on doing what I am doing now, in order to keep those other "apostles" from having any reason for boasting and saying that

they work in the same way that we do.

¹¹·¹³ Those men are not true apostles — they are false apostles, who lie about their work and disguise themselves to look like real apostles of Christ.

¹¹·¹⁴ Well, no wonder! Even Satan can disguise himself to look like an angel of light!

¹¹·¹⁵ So it is no great thing if his servants disguise themselves to look like servants of righteousness. In the end they will get exactly what their actions deserve.

¹¹·¹⁶ I repeat: no one should think that I am a fool. But if you do, at least accept me as a fool, just so I will have a little to boast of.

¹¹·¹⁷ Of course what I am saying now is not what the Lord would have me say; in this matter of boasting I am really talking like a fool.

¹¹·¹⁸ But since there are so many who boast for merely human reasons, I will do the same.

¹¹·¹⁹ You yourselves are so wise, and so you gladly tolerate fools!

¹¹·²⁰ You tolerate anyone who orders you around or takes advantage of you or traps you or looks down on you or slaps you in the face.

¹¹·²¹ I am ashamed to admit that we were too timid to do those things! But if anyone dares to boast about something — I am talking like a fool - I will be just as daring.

¹¹·²² Are they Hebrews? So am I. Are they Israelites? So am I. Are they Abraham's descendants? So am I.

¹¹·²³ Are they Christ's servants? I sound like a madman — but I am a better servant than they are! I have worked much harder, I have been in prison more times, I have been whipped much more, and I have been near death more often.

¹¹·²⁴ Five times I was given the thirty-nine lashes by the Jews;

¹¹·²⁵ three times I was whipped by the Romans; and once I was stoned. I have been in three shipwrecks, and once I spent twenty-four hours in the water.

¹¹·²⁶ In my many travels I have been in danger from floods and from robbers, in danger from my own people and from Gentiles; there have been dangers in the cities, dangers in the wilds, dangers on the high seas, and dangers from false friends.

¹¹·²⁷ There has been work and toil; often I have gone without sleep; I have been hungry and thirsty; I have often been without enough food, shelter, or clothing.

¹¹·²⁸ And not to mention other things, every day I am under the pressure of my concern for all the churches.

¹¹·²⁹ When someone is weak, then I feel weak too; when someone is

led into sin, I am filled with distress.

<sup>11.30</sup> If I must boast, I will boast about things that show how weak I am.

<sup>11.31</sup> The God and Father of the Lord Jesus — blessed be his name forever! — knows that I am not lying.

<sup>11.32</sup> When I was in Damascus, the governor under King Aretas placed guards at the city gates to arrest me.

<sup>11.33</sup> But I was let down in a basket through an opening in the wall and escaped from him.

# 12

<sup>12.1</sup> I have to boast, even though it doesn't do any good. But I will now talk about visions and revelations given me by the Lord.

<sup>12.2</sup> I know a certain Christian man who fourteen years ago was snatched up to the highest heaven (I do not know whether this actually happened or whether he had a vision — only God knows).

<sup>12.3-4</sup> I repeat, I know that this man was snatched to Paradise (again, I do not know whether this actually happened or whether it was a vision — only God knows), and there he heard things which cannot be put into words, things that human lips may not speak.

<sup>12.5</sup> So I will boast about this man — but I will not boast about myself, except the things that show how weak I am.

<sup>12.6</sup> If I wanted to boast, I would not be a fool, because I would be telling the truth. But I will not boast, because I do not want any of you to have a higher opinion of me than you have as a result of what you have seen me do and heard me say.

<sup>12.7</sup> But to keep me from being puffed up with pride because of the many wonderful things I saw, I was given a painful physical ailment, which acts as Satan's messenger to beat me and keep me from being proud.

<sup>12.8</sup> Three times I prayed to the Lord about this and asked him to take it away.

<sup>12.9</sup> But his answer was: "My grace is all you need, for my power is greatest when you are weak." I am most happy, then, to be proud of my weaknesses, in order to feel the protection of Christ's power over me.

<sup>12.10</sup> I am content with weaknesses, insults, hardships, persecutions, and difficulties for Christ's sake. For when I am weak, then I am strong.

<sup>12.11</sup> I am acting like a fool — but you have made me do it. You are the ones who ought to show your approval of me. For even if I am

nothing, I am in no way inferior to those very special "apostles" of yours.

12.12 The many miracles and wonders that prove that I am an apostle were performed among you with much patience.

12.13 How were you treated any worse than the other churches, except that I did not bother you for financial help? Please forgive me for being so unfair!

12.14 This is now the third time that I am ready to come to visit you —and I will not make any demands on you. It is you I want, not your money. After all, children should not have to provide for their parents, but parents should provide for their children.

12.15 I will be glad to spend all I have, and myself as well, in order to help you. Will you love me less because I love you so much?

12.16 You will agree, then, that I was not a burden to you. But someone will say that I was tricky, and trapped you with lies.

12.17 How? Did I take advantage of you through any of the messengers I sent?

12.18 I begged Titus to go, and I sent the other believer with him. Would you say that Titus took advantage of you? Do not he and I act from the very same motives and behave in the same way?

12.19 Perhaps you think that all along we have been trying to defend ourselves before you. No! We speak as Christ would have us speak in the presence of God, and everything we do, dear friends, is done to help you.

12.20 I am afraid that when I get there I will find you different from what I would like you to be and you will find me different from what you would like me to be. I am afraid that I will find quarreling and jealousy, hot tempers and selfishness, insults and gossip, pride and disorder.

12.21 I am afraid that the next time I come my God will humiliate me in your presence, and I shall weep over many who sinned in the past and have not repented of the immoral things they have done — their lust and their sexual sins.

# 13

13.1 This is now the third time that I am coming to visit you. "Any accusation must be upheld by the evidence of two or more witnesses" —as the scripture says.

13.2 I want to tell those of you who have sinned in the past, and all the others; I said it before during my second visit to you, but I will say it again now that I am away: the next time I come nobody will escape punishment.

¹³·³ You will have all the proof you want that Christ speaks through me. When he deals with you, he is not weak; instead, he shows his power among you.

¹³·⁴ For even though it was in weakness that he was put to death on the cross, it is by God's power that he lives. In union with him we also are weak; but in our relations with you we shall share God's power in his life.

¹³·⁵ Put yourselves to the test and judge yourselves, to find out whether you are living in faith. Surely you know that Christ Jesus is in you? — unless you have completely failed.

¹³·⁶ I trust you will know that we are not failures.

¹³·⁷ We pray to God that you will do no wrong — not in order to show that we are a success, but so that you may do what is right, even though we may seem to be failures.

¹³·⁸ For we cannot do a thing against the truth, but only for it.

¹³·⁹ We are glad when we are weak but you are strong. And so we also pray that you will become perfect.

¹³·¹⁰ That is why I write this while I am away from you; it is so that when I arrive I will not have to deal harshly with you in using the authority that the Lord has given me — authority to build you up, not to tear you down.

¹³·¹¹ And now, my friends, good-bye! Strive for perfection; listen to my appeals; agree with one another; live in peace. And the God of love and peace will be with you.

¹³·¹² Greet one another with the kiss of peace. All of God's people send you their greetings.

¹³·¹³ The grace of the Lord Jesus Christ, the love of God, and the fellowship of the Holy Spirit be with you all.

# GALATIANS

# Galatians

# 1

<sup>1.1</sup> From Paul, whose call to be an apostle did not come from human beings or by human means, but from Jesus Christ and God the Father, who raised him from death.

<sup>1.2</sup> All the believers who are here join me in sending greetings to the churches of Galatia:

<sup>1.3</sup> May God our Father and the Lord Jesus Christ give you grace and peace.

<sup>1.4</sup> In order to set us free from this present evil age, Christ gave himself for our sins, in obedience to the will of our God and Father.

<sup>1.5</sup> To God be the glory forever and ever! Amen.

<sup>1.6</sup> I am surprised at you! In no time at all you are deserting the one who called you by the grace of Christ, and are accepting another gospel.

<sup>1.7</sup> Actually, there is no "other gospel," but I say this because there are some people who are upsetting you and trying to change the gospel of Christ.

<sup>1.8</sup> But even if we or an angel from heaven should preach to you a gospel that is different from the one we preached to you, may he be condemned to hell!

<sup>1.9</sup> We have said it before, and now I say it again: if anyone preaches to you a gospel that is different from the one you accepted, may he be condemned to hell!

<sup>1.10</sup> Does this sound as if I am trying to win human approval? No indeed! What I want is God's approval! Am I trying to be popular with people? If I were still trying to do so, I would not be a servant of Christ.

<sup>1.11</sup> Let me tell you, my friends, that the gospel I preach is not of human origin.

<sup>1.12</sup> I did not receive it from any human being, nor did anyone teach it to me. It was Jesus Christ himself who revealed it to me.

<sup>1.13</sup> You have been told how I used to live when I was devoted to the Jewish religion, how I persecuted without mercy the church of God and did my best to destroy it.

<sup>1.14</sup> I was ahead of most other Jews of my age in my practice of the Jewish religion, and was much more devoted to the traditions of our ancestors.

<sup>1.15</sup> But God in his grace chose me even before I was born, and called

me to serve him. And when he decided

<sup>1.16</sup> to reveal his Son <u>to me</u>, so that I might preach the Good News about <u>him</u> <u>to the Gentiles</u>, I did not go <u>to anyone</u> <u>for advice</u>,

<sup>1.17</sup> nor did I go <u>to Jerusalem</u> to see those who were apostles <u>before</u> <u>me</u>. Instead, I went <u>at once</u> <u>to Arabia</u>, and then I returned <u>to Damascus</u>.

<sup>1.18</sup> It was three years later that I went <u>to Jerusalem</u> to obtain information <u>from Peter</u>, and I stayed <u>with him</u> <u>for two weeks</u>.

<sup>1.19</sup> I did not see any other apostle <u>except James</u>, the Lord's brother.

<sup>1.20</sup> What I write is true. God knows that I am not lying!

<sup>1.21</sup> Afterward I went <u>to places</u> <u>in Syria and Cilicia</u>.

<sup>1.22</sup> <u>At that time</u> the members <u>of the churches</u> <u>in Judea</u> did not know me personally.

<sup>1.23</sup> They knew only what others were saying: "The man who used to persecute us is now preaching the faith that he once tried to destroy!"

<sup>1.24</sup> And so they praised God <u>because of me</u>.

# 2

<sup>2.1</sup> Fourteen years later I went back <u>to Jerusalem</u> <u>with Barnabas</u>, taking Titus along <u>with me</u>.

<sup>2.2</sup> I went because God revealed <u>to me</u> that I should go. <u>In a private meeting</u> <u>with the leaders</u> I explained the gospel message that I preach <u>to the Gentiles</u>. I did not want my work <u>in the past</u> or <u>in the present</u> to be a failure.

<sup>2.3</sup> My companion Titus, even though he is Greek, was not forced to be circumcised,

<sup>2.4</sup> although some wanted it done. Pretending to be believers, these men slipped <u>into our group</u> <u>as spies</u>, <u>in order</u> to find out <u>about the freedom</u> we have <u>through our union</u> <u>with Christ Jesus</u>. They wanted to make slaves <u>of us</u>,

<sup>2.5</sup> but <u>in order</u> to keep the truth <u>of the gospel</u> safe <u>for you</u>, we did not give in <u>to them</u> <u>for a minute</u>.

<sup>2.6</sup> But those who seemed to be the leaders — I say this because it makes no difference <u>to me</u> what they were; God does not judge <u>by outward appearances</u> — those leaders, I say, made no new suggestions <u>to me</u>.

<sup>2.7</sup> <u>On the contrary</u>, they saw that God had given me the task <u>of</u> preaching the gospel <u>to the Gentiles</u>, just as he had given Peter the task <u>of</u> preaching the gospel <u>to the Jews</u>.

<sup>2.8</sup> For <u>by God's power</u> I was made an apostle <u>to the Gentiles</u>, just as

Peter was made an apostle to the Jews.

2.9 James, Peter, and John, who seemed to be the leaders, recognized that God had given me this special task; so they shook hands with Barnabas and me, as a sign that we were all partners. We agreed that Barnabas and I would work among the Gentiles and they among the Jews.

2.10 All they asked was that we should remember the needy in their group, which is the very thing I have been eager to do.

2.11 But when Peter came to Antioch, I opposed him in public, because he was clearly wrong.

2.12 Before some men who had been sent by James arrived there, Peter had been eating with the Gentile believers. But after these men arrived, he drew back and would not eat with the Gentiles, because he was afraid of those who were in favor of circumcising them.

2.13 The other Jewish believers also started acting like cowards along with Peter; and even Barnabas was swept along by their cowardly action.

2.14 When I saw that they were not walking a straight path in line with the truth of the gospel, I said to Peter in front of them all, "You are a Jew, yet you have been living like a Gentile, not like a Jew. How, then, can you try to force Gentiles to live like Jews?"

2.15 Indeed, we are Jews by birth and not "Gentile sinners," as they are called.

2.16 Yet we know that a person is put right with God only through faith in Jesus Christ, never by doing what the Law requires. We, too, have believed in Christ Jesus in order to be put right with God through our faith in Christ, and not by doing what the Law requires. For no one is put right with God by doing what the Law requires.

2.17 If, then, as we try to be put right with God by our union with Christ, we are found to be sinners, as much as the Gentiles are — does this mean that Christ is serving the cause of sin? By no means!

2.18 If I start to rebuild the system of Law that I tore down, then I show myself to be someone who breaks the Law.

2.19 So far as the Law is concerned, however, I am dead — killed by the Law itself — in order that I might live for God. I have been put to death with Christ on his cross,

2.20 so that it is no longer I who live, but it is Christ who lives in me. This life that I live now, I live by faith in the Son of God, who loved me and gave his life for me.

2.21 I refuse to reject the grace of God. But if a person is put right with God through the Law, it means that Christ died for nothing!

<sup>3.1</sup> You foolish Galatians! Who put a spell on you? Before your very eyes you had a clear description of the death of Jesus Christ on the cross!

<sup>3.2</sup> Tell me this one thing: did you receive God's Spirit by doing what the Law requires or by hearing the gospel and believing it?

<sup>3.3</sup> How can you be so foolish! You began by God's Spirit; do you now want to finish by your own power?

<sup>3.4</sup> Did all your experience mean nothing at all? Surely it meant something!

<sup>3.5</sup> Does God give you the Spirit and work miracles among you because you do what the Law requires or because you hear the gospel and believe it?

<sup>3.6</sup> Consider the experience of Abraham; as the scripture says, "He believed God, and because of his faith God accepted him as righteous."

<sup>3.7</sup> You should realize, then, that the real descendants of Abraham are the people who have faith.

<sup>3.8</sup> The scripture predicted that God would put the Gentiles right with himself through faith. And so the scripture announced the Good News to Abraham: "Through you God will bless all people."

<sup>3.9</sup> Abraham believed and was blessed; so all who believe are blessed as he was.

<sup>3.10</sup> Those who depend on obeying the Law live under a curse. For the scripture says, "Whoever does not always obey everything that is written in the book of the Law is under God's curse!"

<sup>3.11</sup> Now, it is clear that no one is put right with God by means of the Law, because the scripture says, "Only the person who is put right with God through faith shall live."

<sup>3.12</sup> But the Law has nothing to do with faith. Instead, as the scripture says, "Whoever does everything the Law requires will live."

<sup>3.13</sup> But by becoming a curse for us Christ has redeemed us from the curse that the Law brings; for the scripture says, "Anyone who is hanged on a tree is under God's curse."

<sup>3.14</sup> Christ did this in order that the blessing which God promised to Abraham might be given to the Gentiles by means of Christ Jesus, so that through faith we might receive the Spirit promised by God.

<sup>3.15</sup> My friends, I am going to use an everyday example: when two people agree on a matter and sign an agreement, no one can break it or add anything to it.

<sup>3.16</sup> Now, God made his promises to Abraham and to his descendant. The scripture does not use the plural "descendants," meaning many

people, but the singular "descendant," meaning one person only, namely, Christ.

<sup>3.17</sup> What I mean is that God made a covenant with Abraham and promised to keep it. The Law, which was given four hundred and thirty years later, cannot break that covenant and cancel God's promise.

<sup>3.18</sup> For if God's gift depends on the Law, then it no longer depends on his promise. However, it was because of his promise that God gave that gift to Abraham.

<sup>3.19</sup> What, then, was the purpose of the Law? It was added in order to show what wrongdoing is, and it was meant to last until the coming of Abraham's descendant, to whom the promise was made. The Law was handed down by angels, with a man acting as a go-between.

<sup>3.20</sup> But a go-between is not needed when only one person is involved; and God is one.

<sup>3.21</sup> Does this mean that the Law is against God's promises? No, not at all! For if human beings had received a law that could bring life, then everyone could be put right with God by obeying it.

<sup>3.22</sup> But the scripture says that the whole world is under the power of sin; and so the gift which is promised on the basis of faith in Jesus Christ is given to those who believe.

<sup>3.23</sup> But before the time for faith came, the Law kept us all locked up as prisoners until this coming faith should be revealed.

<sup>3.24</sup> And so the Law was in charge of us until Christ came, in order that we might then be put right with God through faith.

<sup>3.25</sup> Now that the time for faith is here, the Law is no longer in charge of us.

<sup>3.26</sup> It is through faith that all of you are God's children in union with Christ Jesus.

<sup>3.27</sup> You were baptized into union with Christ, and now you are clothed, so to speak, with the life of Christ himself.

<sup>3.28</sup> So there is no difference between Jews and Gentiles, between slaves and free people, between men and women; you are all one in union with Christ Jesus.

<sup>3.29</sup> If you belong to Christ, then you are the descendants of Abraham and will receive what God has promised.

# 4

<sup>4.1</sup> But now to continue — the son who will receive his father's property is treated just like a slave while he is young, even though he really owns everything.

<sup>4.2</sup> While he is young, there are men who take care of him and manage his affairs until the time set by his father.

<sup>4.3</sup> In the same way, we too were slaves of the ruling spirits of the universe before we reached spiritual maturity.

<sup>4.4</sup> But when the right time finally came, God sent his own Son. He came as the son of a human mother and lived under the Jewish Law, <sup>4.5</sup> to redeem those who were under the Law, so that we might become God's children.

<sup>4.6</sup> To show that you are his children, God sent the Spirit of his Son into our hearts, the Spirit who cries out, "Father, my Father."

<sup>4.7</sup> So then, you are no longer a slave but a child. And since you are his child, God will give you all that he has for his children.

<sup>4.8</sup> In the past you did not know God, and so you were slaves of beings who are not gods.

<sup>4.9</sup> But now that you know God — or, I should say, now that God knows you — how is it that you want to turn back to those weak and pitiful ruling spirits? Why do you want to become their slaves all over again?

<sup>4.10</sup> You pay special attention to certain days, months, seasons, and years.

<sup>4.11</sup> I am worried about you! Can it be that all my work for you has been for nothing?

<sup>4.12</sup> I beg you, my friends, be like me. After all, I am like you. You have not done me any wrong.

<sup>4.13</sup> You remember why I preached the gospel to you the first time; it was because I was sick.

<sup>4.14</sup> But even though my physical condition was a great trial to you, you did not despise or reject me. Instead, you received me as you would an angel from heaven; you received me as you would Christ Jesus.

<sup>4.15</sup> You were so happy! What has happened? I myself can say that you would have taken out your own eyes, if you could, and given them to me.

<sup>4.16</sup> Have I now become your enemy by telling you the truth?

<sup>4.17</sup> Those other people show a deep interest in you, but their intentions are not good. All they want is to separate you from me, so that you will have the same interest in them as they have in you.

<sup>4.18</sup> Now, it is good to have such a deep interest if the purpose is good — this is true always, and not merely when I am with you.

<sup>4.19</sup> My dear children! Once again, just like a mother in childbirth, I feel the same kind of pain for you until Christ's nature is formed in

you.

4.20 How I wish I were **with you** now, so that I could take a different attitude **toward you**. I am so worried **about you!**

4.21 Let me ask those **of you** who want to be subject **to the Law**: do you not hear what the Law says?

4.22 It says that Abraham had two sons, one **by a slave woman**, the other **by a free woman**.

4.23 His son **by the slave woman** was born **in the usual way**, but his son **by the free woman** was born **as a result** of God's promise.

4.24 These things can be understood **as a figure**: the two women represent two covenants. The one whose children are born **in slavery** is Hagar, and she represents the covenant made **at Mount Sinai**.

4.25 Hagar, who stands **for Mount Sinai in Arabia**, is a figure **of the present city** of Jerusalem, **in slavery with all its people**.

4.26 But the heavenly Jerusalem is free, and she is our mother.

4.27 For the scripture says, "Be happy, you childless woman! Shout and cry **with joy**, you who never felt the pains **of childbirth!** For the woman who was deserted will have more children **than the woman** whose husband never left her."

4.28 Now, you, my friends, are God's children **as a result of his promise**, just as Isaac was.

4.29 **At that time** the son who was born **in the usual way** persecuted the one who was born **because of God's Spirit**; and it is the same now.

4.30 But what does the scripture say? It says, "Send the slave woman and her son away; for the son **of the slave woman** will not have a part **of the father's property** along **with the son** of the free woman."

4.31 So then, my friends, we are not the children **of a slave woman** but **of a free woman**.

# 5

5.1 Freedom is what we have — Christ has set us free! Stand, then, **as free people**, and do not allow yourselves to become slaves again.

5.2 Listen! I, Paul, tell you that if you allow yourselves to be circumcised, it means that Christ is **of no use to you at all**.

5.3 Once more I warn any man who allows himself to be circumcised that he is obliged to obey the whole Law.

5.4 Those **of you** who try to be put right **with God by** obeying the Law have cut yourselves off **from Christ**. You are **outside God's grace**.

5.5 **As for us**, our hope is that God will put us right **with him**; and this is what we wait for by **the power** of God's Spirit working **through our faith**.

5.6 For when we are in union with Christ Jesus, neither circumcision nor the lack of it makes any difference at all; what matters is faith that works through love.

5.7 You were doing so well! Who made you stop obeying the truth? How did he persuade you?

5.8 It was not done by God, who calls you.

5.9 "It takes only a little yeast to make the whole batch of dough rise," as they say.

5.10 But I still feel confident about you. Our life in union with the Lord makes me confident that you will not take a different view and that whoever is upsetting you will be punished by God.

5.11 But as for me, my friends, if I continue to preach that circumcision is necessary, why am I still being persecuted? If that were true, then my preaching about the cross of Christ would cause no trouble.

5.12 I wish that the people who are upsetting you would go all the way; let them go on and castrate themselves!

5.13 As for you, my friends, you were called to be free. But do not let this freedom become an excuse for letting your physical desires control you. Instead, let love make you serve one another.

5.14 For the whole Law is summed up in one commandment: "Love your neighbor as you love yourself."

5.15 But if you act like wild animals, hurting and harming each other, then watch out, or you will completely destroy one another.

5.16 What I say is this: let the Spirit direct your lives, and you will not satisfy the desires of the human nature.

5.17 For what our human nature wants is opposed to what the Spirit wants, and what the Spirit wants is opposed to what our human nature wants. These two are enemies, and this means that you cannot do what you want to do.

5.18 If the Spirit leads you, then you are not subject to the Law.

5.19 What human nature does is quite plain. It shows itself in immoral, filthy, and indecent actions;

5.20 in worship of idols and witchcraft. People become enemies and they fight; they become jealous, angry, and ambitious. They separate into parties and groups;

5.21 they are envious, get drunk, have orgies, and do other things like these. I warn you now as I have before: those who do these things will not possess the Kingdom of God.

5.22 But the Spirit produces love, joy, peace, patience, kindness, goodness, faithfulness,

5.23 humility, and self-control. There is no law against such things as these.

<sup>5.24</sup> And those who belong to Christ Jesus have put to death their human nature with all its passions and desires.

<sup>5.25</sup> The Spirit has given us life; he must also control our lives.

<sup>5.26</sup> We must not be proud or irritate one another or be jealous of one another.

# 6

<sup>6.1</sup> My friends, if someone is caught in any kind of wrongdoing, those of you who are spiritual should set him right; but you must do it in a gentle way. And keep an eye on yourselves, so that you will not be tempted, too.

<sup>6.2</sup> Help carry one another's burdens, and in this way you will obey the law of Christ.

<sup>6.3</sup> If you think you are something when you really are nothing, you are only deceiving yourself.

<sup>6.4</sup> You should each judge your own conduct. If it is good, then you can be proud of what you yourself have done, without having to compare it with what someone else has done.

<sup>6.5</sup> For each of you have to carry your own load.

<sup>6.6</sup> If you are being taught the Christian message, you should share all the good things you have with your teacher.

<sup>6.7</sup> Do not deceive yourselves; no one makes a fool of God. You will reap exactly what you plant.

<sup>6.8</sup> If you plant in the field of your natural desires, from it you will gather the harvest of death; if you plant in the field of the Spirit, from the Spirit you will gather the harvest of eternal life.

<sup>6.9</sup> So let us not become tired of doing good; for if we do not give up, the time will come when we will reap the harvest.

<sup>6.10</sup> So then, as often as we have the chance, we should do good to everyone, and especially to those who belong to our family in the faith.

<sup>6.11</sup> See what big letters I make as I write to you now with my own hand!

<sup>6.12</sup> The people who are trying to force you to be circumcised are the ones who want to show off and boast about external matters. They do it, however, only so that they may not be persecuted for the cross of Christ.

<sup>6.13</sup> Even those who practice circumcision do not obey the Law; they want you to be circumcised so that they can boast that you submitted to this physical ceremony.

<sup>6.14</sup> As for me, however, I will boast only about the cross of our Lord

Jesus Christ; for by means of his cross the world is dead to me, and I am dead to the world.

⁶·¹⁵ It does not matter at all whether or not one is circumcised; what does matter is being a new creature.

⁶·¹⁶ As for those who follow this rule in their lives, may peace and mercy be with them — with them and with all of God's people!

⁶·¹⁷ To conclude: let no one give me any more trouble, because the scars I have on my body show that I am the slave of Jesus.

⁶·¹⁸ May the grace of our Lord Jesus Christ be with you all, my friends. Amen.

# EPHESIANS

# Ephesians

1

<sup>1.1</sup> From Paul, who by God's will is an apostle of Christ Jesus –
To God's people in Ephesus, who are faithful in their life in union with Christ Jesus:
<sup>1.2</sup> May God our Father and the Lord Jesus Christ give you grace and peace.

<sup>1.3</sup> Let us give thanks to the God and Father of our Lord Jesus Christ! For in our union with Christ he has blessed us by giving us every spiritual blessing in the heavenly world.
<sup>1.4</sup> Even before the world was made, God had already chosen us to be his through our union with Christ, so that we would be holy and without fault before him. Because of his love
<sup>1.5</sup> God had already decided that through Jesus Christ he would make us his children — this was his pleasure and purpose.
<sup>1.6</sup> Let us praise God for his glorious grace, for the free gift he gave us in his dear Son!
<sup>1.7</sup> For by the blood of Christ we are set free, that is, our sins are forgiven. How great is the grace of God,
<sup>1.8</sup> which he gave to us in such large measure! In all his wisdom and insight
<sup>1.9</sup> God did what he had purposed, and made known to us the secret plan he had already decided to complete by means of Christ.
<sup>1.10</sup> This plan, which God will complete when the time is right, is to bring all creation together, everything in heaven and on earth, with Christ as head.
<sup>1.11</sup> All things are done according to God's plan and decision; and God chose us to be his own people in union with Christ because of his own purpose, based on what he had decided from the very beginning.
<sup>1.12</sup> Let us, then, who were the first to hope in Christ, praise God's glory!
<sup>1.13</sup> And you also became God's people when you heard the true message, the Good News that brought you salvation. You believed in Christ, and God put his stamp of ownership on you by giving you the Holy Spirit he had promised.
<sup>1.14</sup> The Spirit is the guarantee that we shall receive what God has promised his people, and this assures us that God will give complete freedom to those who are his. Let us praise his glory!

<sup>1.15</sup> For this reason, ever since I heard of your faith in the Lord Jesus and your love for all of God's people,

<sup>1.16</sup> I have not stopped giving thanks to God for you. I remember you in my prayers

<sup>1.17</sup> and ask the God of our Lord Jesus Christ, the glorious Father, to give you the Spirit, who will make you wise and reveal God to you, so that you will know him.

<sup>1.18</sup> I ask that your minds may be opened to see his light, so that you will know what is the hope to which he has called you, how rich are the wonderful blessings he promises his people,

<sup>1.19</sup> and how very great is his power at work in us who believe. This power working in us is the same as the mighty strength

<sup>1.20</sup> which he used when he raised Christ from death and seated him at his right side in the heavenly world.

<sup>1.21</sup> Christ rules there above all heavenly rulers, authorities, powers, and lords; he has a title superior to all titles of authority in this world and in the next.

<sup>1.22</sup> God put all things under Christ's feet and gave him to the church as supreme Lord over all things.

<sup>1.23</sup> The church is Christ's body, the completion of him who himself completes all things everywhere.

# 2

<sup>2.1</sup> In the past you were spiritually dead because of your disobedience and sins.

<sup>2.2</sup> At that time you followed the world's evil way; you obeyed the ruler of the spiritual powers in space, the spirit who now controls the people who disobey God.

<sup>2.3</sup> Actually all of us were like them and lived according to our natural desires, doing whatever suited the wishes of our own bodies and minds. In our natural condition we, like everyone else, were destined to suffer God's anger.

<sup>2.4</sup> But God's mercy is so abundant, and his love for us is so great,

<sup>2.5</sup> that while we were spiritually dead in our disobedience he brought us to life with Christ. It is by God's grace that you have been saved.

<sup>2.6</sup> In our union with Christ Jesus he raised us up with him to rule with him in the heavenly world.

<sup>2.7</sup> He did this to demonstrate for all time to come the extraordinary greatness of his grace in the love he showed us in Christ Jesus.

<sup>2.8</sup> For it is by God's grace that you have been saved through faith. It is not the result of your own efforts,

2.9 but God's gift, so that no one can boast about it.

2.10 God has made us what we are, and in our union with Christ Jesus he has created us for a life of good deeds, which he has already prepared for us to do.

2.11 You Gentiles by birth — called "the uncircumcised" by the Jews, who call themselves the circumcised (which refers to what men do to their bodies) — remember what you were in the past.

2.12 At that time you were apart from Christ. You were foreigners and did not belong to God's chosen people. You had no part in the covenants, which were based on God's promises to his people, and you lived in this world without hope and without God.

2.13 But now, in union with Christ Jesus you, who used to be far away, have been brought near by the blood of Christ.

2.14 For Christ himself has brought us peace by making Jews and Gentiles one people. With his own body he broke down the wall that separated them and kept them enemies.

2.15 He abolished the Jewish Law with its commandments and rules, in order to create out of the two races one new people in union with himself, in this way making peace.

2.16 By his death on the cross Christ destroyed their enmity; by means of the cross he united both races into one body and brought them back to God.

2.17 So Christ came and preached the Good News of peace to all — to you Gentiles, who were far away from God, and to the Jews, who were near to him.

2.18 It is through Christ that all of us, Jews and Gentiles, are able to come in the one Spirit into the presence of the Father.

2.19 So then, you Gentiles are not foreigners or strangers any longer; you are now citizens together with God's people and members of the family of God.

2.20 You, too, are built upon the foundation laid by the apostles and prophets, the cornerstone being Christ Jesus himself.

2.21 He is the one who holds the whole building together and makes it grow into a sacred temple dedicated to the Lord.

2.22 In union with him you too are being built together with all the others into a place where God lives through his Spirit.

# 3

3.1 For this reason I, Paul, the prisoner of Christ Jesus for the sake of you Gentiles, pray to God.

3.2 Surely you have heard that God in his grace has given me this work to do for your good.

<sup>3.3</sup> God revealed his secret plan and made it known to me. (I have written briefly about this,

<sup>3.4</sup> and if you will read what I have written, you can learn about my understanding of the secret of Christ.)

<sup>3.5</sup> In past times human beings were not told this secret, but God has revealed it now by the Spirit to his holy apostles and prophets.

<sup>3.6</sup> The secret is that by means of the gospel the Gentiles have a part with the Jews in God's blessings; they are members of the same body and share in the promise that God made through Christ Jesus.

<sup>3.7</sup> I was made a servant of the gospel by God's special gift, which he gave me through the working of his power.

<sup>3.8</sup> I am less than the least of all God's people; yet God gave me this privilege of taking to the Gentiles the Good News about the infinite riches of Christ,

<sup>3.9</sup> and of making all people see how God's secret plan is to be put into effect. God, who is the Creator of all things, kept his secret hidden through all the past ages,

<sup>3.10</sup> in order that at the present time, by means of the church, the angelic rulers and powers in the heavenly world might learn of his wisdom in all its different forms.

<sup>3.11</sup> God did this according to his eternal purpose, which he achieved through Christ Jesus our Lord.

<sup>3.12</sup> In union with Christ and through our faith in him we have the boldness to go into God's presence with all confidence.

<sup>3.13</sup> I beg you, then, not to be discouraged because I am suffering for you; it is all for your benefit.

<sup>3.14</sup> For this reason I fall on my knees before the Father,

<sup>3.15</sup> from whom every family in heaven and on earth receives its true name.

<sup>3.16</sup> I ask God from the wealth of his glory to give you power through his Spirit to be strong in your inner selves,

<sup>3.17</sup> and I pray that Christ will make his home in your hearts through faith. I pray that you may have your roots and foundation in love,

<sup>3.18</sup> so that you, together with all God's people, may have the power to understand how broad and long, how high and deep, is Christ's love.

<sup>3.19</sup> Yes, may you come to know his love — although it can never be fully known — and so be completely filled with the very nature of God.

<sup>3.20</sup> To him who by means of his power working in us is able to do so much more than we can ever ask for, or even think of:

<sup></sup>$^{3.21}$ to God be the glory in the church and in Christ Jesus for all time, forever and ever! Amen.

# 4

$^{4.1}$ I urge you, then — I who am a prisoner because I serve the Lord: live a life that measures up to the standard God set when he called you.

$^{4.2}$ Be always humble, gentle, and patient. Show your love by being tolerant with one another.

$^{4.3}$ Do your best to preserve the unity which the Spirit gives by means of the peace that binds you together.

$^{4.4}$ There is one body and one Spirit, just as there is one hope to which God has called you.

$^{4.5}$ There is one Lord, one faith, one baptism;

$^{4.6}$ there is one God and Father of all people, who is Lord of all, works through all, and is in all.

$^{4.7}$ Each one of us has received a special gift in proportion to what Christ has given.

$^{4.8}$ As the scripture says, "When he went up to the very heights, he took many captives with him; he gave gifts to people."

$^{4.9}$ Now, what does "he went up" mean? It means that first he came down to the lowest depths of the earth.

$^{4.10}$ So the one who came down is the same one who went up, above and beyond the heavens, to fill the whole universe with his presence.

$^{4.11}$ It was he who "gave gifts to people"; he appointed some to be apostles, others to be prophets, others to be evangelists, others to be pastors and teachers.

$^{4.12}$ He did this to prepare all God's people for the work of Christian service, in order to build up the body of Christ.

$^{4.13}$ And so we shall all come together to that oneness in our faith and in our knowledge of the Son of God; we shall become mature people, reaching to the very height of Christ's full stature.

$^{4.14}$ Then we shall no longer be children, carried by the waves and blown about by every shifting wind of the teaching of deceitful people, who lead others into error by the tricks they invent.

$^{4.15}$ Instead, by speaking the truth in a spirit of love, we must grow up in every way to Christ, who is the head.

$^{4.16}$ Under his control all the different parts of the body fit together, and the whole body is held together by every joint with which it is provided. So, when each separate part works as it should, the whole body grows and builds itself up through love.

$^{4.17}$ In the Lord's name, then, I warn you: do not continue to live like the heathen, whose thoughts are worthless

$^{4.18}$ and whose minds are in the dark. They have no part in the life that God gives, for they are completely ignorant and stubborn.

$^{4.19}$ They have lost all feeling of shame; they give themselves over to vice and do all sorts of indecent things without restraint.

$^{4.20}$ That was not what you learned about Christ!

$^{4.21}$ You certainly heard about him, and as his followers you were taught the truth that is in Jesus.

$^{4.22}$ So get rid of your old self, which made you live as you used to — the old self that was being destroyed by its deceitful desires.

$^{4.23}$ Your hearts and minds must be made completely new,

$^{4.24}$ and you must put on the new self, which is created in God's likeness and reveals itself in the true life that is upright and holy.

$^{4.25}$ No more lying, then! Each of you must tell the truth to the other believer, because we are all members together in the body of Christ.

$^{4.26}$ If you become angry, do not let your anger lead you into sin, and do not stay angry all day.

$^{4.27}$ Don't give the Devil a chance.

$^{4.28}$ If you used to rob, you must stop robbing and start working, in order to earn an honest living for yourself and to be able to help the poor.

$^{4.29}$ Do not use harmful words, but only helpful words, the kind that build up and provide what is needed, so that what you say will do good to those who hear you.

$^{4.30}$ And do not make God's Holy Spirit sad; for the Spirit is God's mark of ownership on you, a guarantee that the Day will come when God will set you free.

$^{4.31}$ Get rid of all bitterness, passion, and anger. No more shouting or insults, no more hateful feelings of any sort.

$^{4.32}$ Instead, be kind and tender-hearted to one another, and forgive one another, as God has forgiven you through Christ.

# 5

$^{5.1}$ Since you are God's dear children, you must try to be like him.

$^{5.2}$ Your life must be controlled by love, just as Christ loved us and gave his life for us as a sweet-smelling offering and sacrifice that pleases God.

$^{5.3}$ Since you are God's people, it is not right that any matters of sexual immorality or indecency or greed should even be mentioned among you.

<sup>5.4</sup> Nor is it fitting for you to use language which is obscene, profane, or vulgar. Rather you should give thanks to God.

<sup>5.5</sup> You may be sure that no one who is immoral, indecent, or greedy (for greed is a form of idolatry) will ever receive a share in the Kingdom of Christ and of God.

<sup>5.6</sup> Do not let anyone deceive you with foolish words; it is because of these very things that God's anger will come upon those who do not obey him.

<sup>5.7</sup> So have nothing at all to do with such people.

<sup>5.8</sup> You yourselves used to be in the darkness, but since you have become the Lord's people, you are in the light. So you must live like people who belong to the light,

<sup>5.9</sup> for it is the light that brings a rich harvest of every kind of goodness, righteousness, and truth.

<sup>5.10</sup> Try to learn what pleases the Lord.

<sup>5.11</sup> Have nothing to do with the worthless things that people do, things that belong to the darkness. Instead, bring them out to the light.

<sup>5.12</sup> (It is really too shameful even to talk about the things they do in secret.)

<sup>5.13</sup> And when all things are brought out to the light, then their true nature is clearly revealed;

<sup>5.14</sup> for anything that is clearly revealed becomes light. That is why it is said, "Wake up, sleeper, and rise from death, and Christ will shine on you."

<sup>5.15</sup> So be careful how you live. Don't live like ignorant people, but like wise people.

<sup>5.16</sup> Make good use of every opportunity you have, because these are evil days.

<sup>5.17</sup> Don't be fools, then, but try to find out what the Lord wants you to do.

<sup>5.18</sup> Do not get drunk with wine, which will only ruin you; instead, be filled with the Spirit.

<sup>5.19</sup> Speak to one another with the words of psalms, hymns, and sacred songs; sing hymns and psalms to the Lord with praise in your hearts.

<sup>5.20</sup> In the name of our Lord Jesus Christ, always give thanks for everything to God the Father.

<sup>5.21</sup> Submit yourselves to one another because of your reverence for Christ.

<sup>5.22</sup> Wives, submit yourselves to your husbands as to the Lord.

<sup>5.23</sup> For a husband has authority over his wife just as Christ has authority over the church; and Christ is himself the Savior of the church, his body.

<sup>5.24</sup> And so wives must submit themselves completely to their husbands just as the church submits itself to Christ.

<sup>5.25</sup> Husbands, love your wives just as Christ loved the church and gave his life for it.

<sup>5.26</sup> He did this to dedicate the church to God by his word, after making it clean by washing it in water,

<sup>5.27</sup> in order to present the church to himself in all its beauty — pure and faultless, without spot or wrinkle or any other imperfection.

<sup>5.28</sup> Men ought to love their wives just as they love their own bodies. A man who loves his wife loves himself.

<sup>5.29</sup> (None of us ever hate our own bodies. Instead, we feed them, and take care of them, just as Christ does the church;

<sup>5.30</sup> for we are members of his body.)

<sup>5.31</sup> As the scripture says, "For this reason a man will leave his father and mother and unite with his wife, and the two will become one."

<sup>5.32</sup> There is a deep secret truth revealed in this scripture, which I understand as applying to Christ and the church.

<sup>5.33</sup> But it also applies to you: every husband must love his wife as himself, and every wife must respect her husband.

# 6

<sup>6.1</sup> Children, it is your Christian duty to obey your parents, for this is the right thing to do.

<sup>6.2</sup> "Respect your father and mother" is the first commandment that has a promise added:

<sup>6.3</sup> "so that all may go well with you, and you may live a long time in the land."

<sup>6.4</sup> Parents, do not treat your children in such a way as to make them angry. Instead, raise them with Christian discipline and instruction.

<sup>6.5</sup> Slaves, obey your human masters with fear and trembling; and do it with a sincere heart, as though you were serving Christ.

<sup>6.6</sup> Do this not only when they are watching you, because you want to gain their approval; but with all your heart do what God wants, as slaves of Christ.

<sup>6.7</sup> Do your work as slaves cheerfully, as though you served the Lord, and not merely human beings.

<sup>6.8</sup> Remember that the Lord will reward each of us, whether slave or free, for the good work we do.

<sup>6.9</sup> Masters, behave in the same way toward your slaves and stop using threats. Remember that you and your slaves belong to the same Master in heaven, who judges everyone by the same standard.

<sup>6.10</sup> Finally, build up your strength in union with the Lord and by means of his mighty power.

<sup>6.11</sup> Put on all the armor that God gives you, so that you will be able to stand up against the Devil's evil tricks.

<sup>6.12</sup> For we are not fighting against human beings but against the wicked spiritual forces in the heavenly world, the rulers, authorities, and cosmic powers of this dark age.

<sup>6.13</sup> So put on God's armor now! Then when the evil day comes, you will be able to resist the enemy's attacks; and after fighting to the end, you will still hold your ground.

<sup>6.14</sup> So stand ready, with truth as a belt tight around your waist, with righteousness as your breastplate,

<sup>6.15</sup> and as your shoes the readiness to announce the Good News of peace.

<sup>6.16</sup> At all times carry faith as a shield; for with it you will be able to put out all the burning arrows shot by the Evil One.

<sup>6.17</sup> And accept salvation as a helmet, and the word of God as the sword which the Spirit gives you.

<sup>6.18</sup> Do all this in prayer, asking for God's help. Pray on every occasion, as the Spirit leads. For this reason keep alert and never give up; pray always for all God's people.

<sup>6.19</sup> And pray also for me, that God will give me a message when I am ready to speak, so that I may speak boldly and make known the gospel's secret.

<sup>6.20</sup> For the sake of this gospel I am an ambassador, though now I am in prison. Pray that I may be bold in speaking about the gospel as I should.

<sup>6.21</sup> Tychicus, our dear brother and faithful servant in the Lord's work, will give you all the news about me, so that you may know how I am getting along.

<sup>6.22</sup> That is why I am sending him to you — to tell you how all of us are getting along and to encourage you.

<sup>6.23</sup> May God the Father and the Lord Jesus Christ give to all Christians peace and love with faith.

<sup>6.24</sup> May God's grace be with all those who love our Lord Jesus Christ with undying love.

# PHILIPPIANS

# Philippians

1

<sup>1.1</sup> From Paul and Timothy, servants of Christ Jesus – To all God's people in Philippi who are in union with Christ Jesus, including the church leaders and helpers:
<sup>1.2</sup> May God our Father and the Lord Jesus Christ give you grace and peace.
<sup>1.3</sup> I thank my God for you every time I think of you;
<sup>1.4</sup> and every time I pray for you all, I pray with joy
<sup>1.5</sup> because of the way in which you have helped me in the work of the gospel from the very first day until now.
<sup>1.6</sup> And so I am sure that God, who began this good work in you, will carry it on until it is finished on the Day of Christ Jesus.
<sup>1.7</sup> You are always in my heart! And so it is only right for me to feel as I do about you. For you have all shared with me in this privilege that God has given me, both now that I am in prison and also while I was free to defend the gospel and establish it firmly.
<sup>1.8</sup> God is my witness that I tell the truth when I say that my deep feeling for you all comes from the heart of Christ Jesus himself.
<sup>1.9</sup> I pray that your love will keep on growing more and more, together with true knowledge and perfect judgment,
<sup>1.10</sup> so that you will be able to choose what is best. Then you will be free from all impurity and blame on the Day of Christ.
<sup>1.11</sup> Your lives will be filled with the truly good qualities which only Jesus Christ can produce, for the glory and praise of God.
<sup>1.12</sup> I want you to know, my friends, that the things that have happened to me have really helped the progress of the gospel.
<sup>1.13</sup> As a result, the whole palace guard and all the others here know that I am in prison because I am a servant of Christ.
<sup>1.14</sup> And my being in prison has given most of the believers more confidence in the Lord, so that they grow bolder all the time to preach the message fearlessly.
<sup>1.15</sup> Of course some of them preach Christ because they are jealous and quarrelsome, but others from genuine good will.
<sup>1.16</sup> These do so from love, because they know that God has given me the work of defending the gospel.
<sup>1.17</sup> The others do not proclaim Christ sincerely, but from a spirit of selfish ambition; they think that they will make more trouble for me while I am in prison.

$^{1.18}$ It does not matter! I am happy about it — just so Christ is preached in every way possible, whether from wrong or right motives. And I will continue to be happy,

$^{1.19}$ because I know that by means of your prayers and the help which comes from the Spirit of Jesus Christ I shall be set free.

$^{1.20}$ My deep desire and hope is that I shall never fail in my duty, but that at all times, and especially right now, I shall be full of courage, so that with my whole being I shall bring honor to Christ, whether I live or die.

$^{1.21}$ For what is life? To me, it is Christ. Death, then, will bring more.

$^{1.22}$ But if by continuing to live I can do more worthwhile work, then I am not sure which I should choose.

$^{1.23}$ I am pulled in two directions. I want very much to leave this life and be with Christ, which is a far better thing;

$^{1.24}$ but for your sake it is much more important that I remain alive.

$^{1.25}$ I am sure of this, and so I know that I will stay. I will stay on with you all, to add to your progress and joy in the faith,

$^{1.26}$ so that when I am with you again, you will have even more reason to be proud of me in your life in union with Christ Jesus.

$^{1.27}$ Now, the important thing is that your way of life should be as the gospel of Christ requires, so that, whether or not I am able to go and see you, I will hear that you are standing firm with one common purpose and that with only one desire you are fighting together for the faith of the gospel.

$^{1.28}$ Don't be afraid of your enemies; always be courageous, and this will prove to them that they will lose and that you will win, because it is God who gives you the victory.

$^{1.29}$ For you have been given the privilege of serving Christ, not only by believing in him, but also by suffering for him.

$^{1.30}$ Now you can take part with me in the battle. It is the same battle you saw me fighting in the past, and as you hear, the one I am fighting still.

# 2

$^{2.1}$ Your life in Christ makes you strong, and his love comforts you. You have fellowship with the Spirit, and you have kindness and compassion for one another.

$^{2.2}$ I urge you, then, to make me completely happy by having the same thoughts, sharing the same love, and being one in soul and mind.

$^{2.3}$ Don't do anything from selfish ambition or from a cheap desire to boast, but be humble toward one another, always considering others better than yourselves.

<sup>2.4</sup> And look out for one another's interests, not just for your own.

<sup>2.5</sup> The attitude you should have is the one that Christ Jesus had:

<sup>2.6</sup> He always had the nature of God, but he did not think that by force he should try to remain equal with God.

<sup>2.7</sup> Instead of this, of his own free will he gave up all he had, and took the nature of a servant. He became like a human being and appeared in human likeness.

<sup>2.8</sup> He was humble and walked the path of obedience all the way to death — his death on the cross.

<sup>2.9</sup> For this reason God raised him to the highest place above and gave him the name that is greater than any other name.

<sup>2.10</sup> And so, in honor of the name of Jesus all beings in heaven, on earth, and in the world below will fall on their knees,

<sup>2.11</sup> and all will openly proclaim that Jesus Christ is Lord, to the glory of God the Father.

<sup>2.12</sup> So then, dear friends, as you always obeyed me when I was with you, it is even more important that you obey me now while I am away from you. Keep on working with fear and trembling to complete your salvation,

<sup>2.13</sup> because God is always at work in you to make you willing and able to obey his own purpose.

<sup>2.14</sup> Do everything without complaining or arguing,

<sup>2.15</sup> so that you may be innocent and pure as God's perfect children, who live in a world of corrupt and sinful people. You must shine among them like stars lighting up the sky,

<sup>2.16</sup> as you offer them the message of life. If you do so, I shall have reason to be proud of you on the Day of Christ, because it will show that all my effort and work have not been wasted.

<sup>2.17</sup> Perhaps my life's blood is to be poured out like an offering on the sacrifice that your faith offers to God. If that is so, I am glad and share my joy with you all.

<sup>2.18</sup> In the same way, you too must be glad and share your joy with me.

<sup>2.19</sup> If it is the Lord's will, I hope that I will be able to send Timothy to you soon, so that I may be encouraged by news about you.

<sup>2.20</sup> He is the only one who shares my feelings and who really cares about you.

<sup>2.21</sup> Everyone else is concerned only with their own affairs, not with the cause of Jesus Christ.

<sup>2.22</sup> And you yourselves know how he has proved his worth, how he and I, <u>like a son and his father</u>, have worked together <u>for the sake</u> of <u>the gospel</u>.

<sup>2.23</sup> So I hope to send him <u>to you</u> as soon as I know how things are going to turn out <u>for me</u>.

<sup>2.24</sup> And I trust <u>in the Lord</u> that I myself will be able to come <u>to you</u> soon.

<sup>2.25</sup> I have thought it necessary to send <u>to you</u> our brother Epaphroditus, who has worked and fought <u>by my side</u> and who has served <u>as your messenger</u> in helping me.

<sup>2.26</sup> He is anxious to see you all and is very upset because you had heard that he was sick.

<sup>2.27</sup> Indeed he was sick and almost died. But God had pity <u>on him</u>, and not only <u>on him</u> but <u>on me</u>, too, and spared me an even greater sorrow.

<sup>2.28</sup> I am all the more eager, then, to send him <u>to you</u>, so that you will be glad again when you see him, and my own sorrow will disappear.

<sup>2.29</sup> Receive him, then, <u>with joy</u>, <u>as a believer</u> <u>in the Lord</u>. Show respect <u>to all such people</u> <u>as he</u>,

<sup>2.30</sup> because he risked his life and nearly died <u>for the sake</u> of the work of Christ, <u>in order</u> to give me the help that you yourselves could not give.

# 3

<sup>3.1</sup> <u>In conclusion</u>, my friends, be joyful <u>in your union</u> <u>with the Lord</u>. I don't mind repeating what I have written before, and you will be safer if I do so.

<sup>3.2</sup> Watch out <u>for those</u> who do evil things, those dogs, those who insist <u>on cutting</u> the body.

<sup>3.3</sup> It is we, not they, who have received the true circumcision, for we worship God <u>by means</u> <u>of his Spirit</u> and rejoice <u>in our life</u> <u>in union</u> <u>with Christ Jesus</u>. We do not put any trust <u>in external ceremonies</u>.

<sup>3.4</sup> I could, <u>of course</u>, put my trust <u>in such things</u>. If any <u>of you</u> think you can trust <u>in external ceremonies</u>, I have even more reason to feel that way.

<sup>3.5</sup> I was circumcised when I was a week old. I am an Israelite <u>by birth</u>, <u>of the tribe</u> <u>of Benjamin</u>, a pure-blooded Hebrew. As far as keeping the Jewish Law is concerned, I was a Pharisee,

<sup>3.6</sup> and I was so zealous that I persecuted the church. As far as a person can be righteous by obeying the commands <u>of the Law</u>, I was <u>without fault</u>.

<sup>3.7</sup> But all those things that I might count as profit I now reckon as loss for Christ's sake.

<sup>3.8</sup> Not only those things; I reckon everything as complete loss for the sake of what is so much more valuable, the knowledge of Christ Jesus my Lord. For his sake I have thrown everything away; I consider it all as mere garbage, so that I may gain Christ

<sup>3.9</sup> and be completely united with him. I no longer have a righteousness of my own, the kind that is gained by obeying the Law. I now have the righteousness that is given through faith in Christ, the righteousness that comes from God and is based on faith.

<sup>3.10</sup> All I want is to know Christ and to experience the power of his resurrection, to share in his sufferings and become like him in his death,

<sup>3.11</sup> in the hope that I myself will be raised from death to life.

<sup>3.12</sup> I do not claim that I have already succeeded or have already become perfect. I keep striving to win the prize for which Christ Jesus has already won me to himself.

<sup>3.13</sup> Of course, my friends, I really do not think that I have already won it; the one thing I do, however, is to forget what is behind me and do my best to reach what is ahead.

<sup>3.14</sup> So I run straight toward the goal in order to win the prize, which is God's call through Christ Jesus to the life above.

<sup>3.15</sup> All of us who are spiritually mature should have this same attitude. But if some of you have a different attitude, God will make this clear to you.

<sup>3.16</sup> However that may be, let us go forward according to the same rules we have followed until now.

<sup>3.17</sup> Keep on imitating me, my friends. Pay attention to those who follow the right example that we have set for you.

<sup>3.18</sup> I have told you this many times before, and now I repeat it with tears: there are many whose lives make them enemies of Christ's death on the cross.

<sup>3.19</sup> They are going to end up in hell, because their god is their bodily desires. They are proud of what they should be ashamed of, and they think only of things that belong to this world.

<sup>3.20</sup> We, however, are citizens of heaven, and we eagerly wait for our Savior, the Lord Jesus Christ, to come from heaven.

<sup>3.21</sup> He will change our weak mortal bodies and make them like his own glorious body, using that power by which he is able to bring all things under his rule.

<sup>4.1</sup> So then, my friends, how dear you are to me and how I miss you! How happy you make me, and how proud I am of you! — this, dear friends, is how you should stand firm in your life in the Lord.
<sup>4.2</sup> Euodia and Syntyche, please, I beg you, try to agree as sisters in the Lord.
<sup>4.3</sup> And you too, my faithful partner, I want you to help these women; for they have worked hard with me to spread the gospel, together with Clement and all my other fellow workers, whose names are in God's book of the living.
<sup>4.4</sup> May you always be joyful in your union with the Lord. I say it again: rejoice!
<sup>4.5</sup> Show a gentle attitude toward everyone. The Lord is coming soon.
<sup>4.6</sup> Don't worry about anything, but in all your prayers ask God for what you need, always asking him with a thankful heart.
<sup>4.7</sup> And God's peace, which is far beyond human understanding, will keep your hearts and minds safe in union with Christ Jesus.
<sup>4.8</sup> In conclusion, my friends, fill your minds with those things that are good and that deserve praise: things that are true, noble, right, pure, lovely, and honorable.
<sup>4.9</sup> Put into practice what you learned and received from me, both from my words and from my actions. And the God who gives us peace will be with you.
<sup>4.10</sup> In my life in union with the Lord it is a great joy to me that after so long a time you once more had the chance of showing that you care for me. I don't mean that you had stopped caring for me — you just had no chance to show it.
<sup>4.11</sup> And I am not saying this because I feel neglected, for I have learned to be satisfied with what I have.
<sup>4.12</sup> I know what it is to be in need and what it is to have more than enough. I have learned this secret, so that anywhere, at any time, I am content, whether I am full or hungry, whether I have too much or too little.
<sup>4.13</sup> I have the strength to face all conditions by the power that Christ gives me.
<sup>4.14</sup> But it was very good of you to help me in my troubles.
<sup>4.15</sup> You Philippians know very well that when I left Macedonia in the early days of preaching the Good News, you were the only church to help me; you were the only ones who shared my profits and losses.
<sup>4.16</sup> More than once when I needed help in Thessalonica, you sent it to me.
<sup>4.17</sup> It is not that I just want to receive gifts; rather, I want to see

profit added to your account.

<sup></sup>⁴·¹⁸ Here, then, is my receipt for everything you have given me — and it has been more than enough! I have all I need now that Epaphroditus has brought me all your gifts. They are like a sweet-smelling offering to God, a sacrifice which is acceptable and pleasing to him.

⁴·¹⁹ And with all his abundant wealth through Christ Jesus, my God will supply all your needs.

⁴·²⁰ To our God and Father be the glory forever and ever! Amen.

⁴·²¹ Greetings to each one of God's people who belong to Christ Jesus. The believers here with me send you their greetings.

⁴·²² All God's people here send greetings, especially those who belong to the Emperor's palace.

⁴·²³ May the grace of the Lord Jesus Christ be with you all.

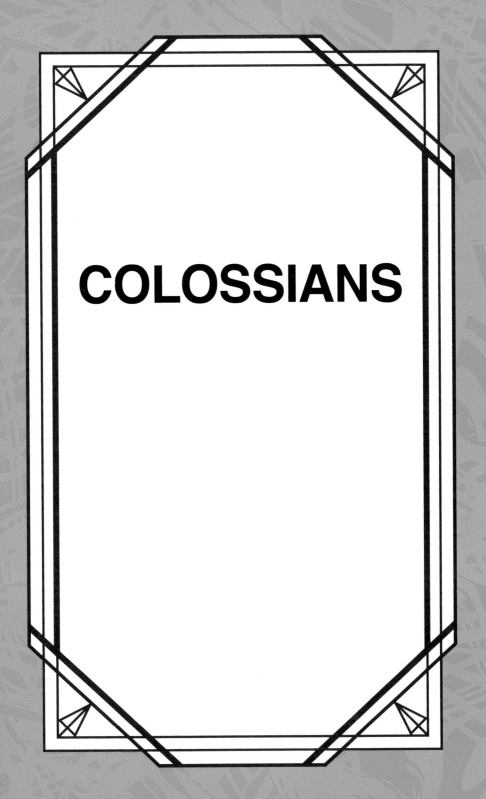

# COLOSSIANS

# Colossians

1

<sup>1.1</sup> From Paul, who by God's will is an apostle of Christ Jesus, and from our brother Timothy —

<sup>1.2</sup> To God's people in Colossae, who are our faithful friends in union with Christ: May God our Father give you grace and peace.

<sup>1.3</sup> We always give thanks to God, the Father of our Lord Jesus Christ, when we pray for you.

<sup>1.4</sup> For we have heard of your faith in Christ Jesus and of your love for all God's people.

<sup>1.5</sup> When the true message, the Good News, first came to you, you heard about the hope it offers. So your faith and love are based on what you hope for, which is kept safe for you in heaven.

<sup>1.6</sup> The gospel keeps bringing blessings and is spreading throughout the world, just as it has among you ever since the day you first heard about the grace of God and came to know it as it really is.

<sup>1.7</sup> You learned of God's grace from Epaphras, our dear fellow servant, who is Christ's faithful worker on our behalf.

<sup>1.8</sup> He has told us of the love that the Spirit has given you.

<sup>1.9</sup> For this reason we have always prayed for you, ever since we heard about you. We ask God to fill you with the knowledge of his will, with all the wisdom and understanding that his Spirit gives.

<sup>1.10</sup> Then you will be able to live as the Lord wants and will always do what pleases him. Your lives will produce all kinds of good deeds, and you will grow in your knowledge of God.

<sup>1.11-12</sup> May you be made strong with all the strength which comes from his glorious power, so that you may be able to endure everything with patience. And with joy give thanks to the Father, who was made you fit to have your share of what God has reserved for his people in the kingdom of light.

<sup>1.13</sup> He rescued us from the power of darkness and brought us safe into the kingdom of his dear Son,

<sup>1.14</sup> by whom we are set free, that is, our sins are forgiven.

<sup>1.15</sup> Christ is the visible likeness of the invisible God. He is the firstborn Son, superior to all created things.

<sup>1.16</sup> For through him God created everything in heaven and on earth, the seen and the unseen things, including spiritual powers, lords, rulers, and authorities. God created the whole universe through him and for him.

1.17 Christ existed before all things, and in union with him all things have their proper place.

1.18 He is the head of his body, the church; he is the source of the body's life. He is the first-born Son, who was raised from death, in order that he alone might have the first place in all things.

1.19 For it was by God's own decision that the Son has in himself the full nature of God.

1.20 Through the Son, then, God decided to bring the whole universe back to himself. God made peace through his Son's blood on the cross and so brought back to himself all things, both on earth and in heaven.

1.21 At one time you were far away from God and were his enemies because of the evil things you did and thought.

1.22 But now, by means of the physical death of his Son, God has made you his friends, in order to bring you, holy, pure, and faultless, into his presence.

1.23 You must, of course, continue faithful on a firm and sure foundation, and must not allow yourselves to be shaken from the hope you gained when you heard the gospel. It is of this gospel that I, Paul, became a servant — this gospel which has been preached to everybody in the world.

1.24 And now I am happy about my sufferings for you, for by means of my physical sufferings I am helping to complete what still remains of Christ's sufferings on behalf of his body, the church.

1.25 And I have been made a servant of the church by God, who gave me this task to perform for your good. It is the task of fully proclaiming his message,

1.26 which is the secret he hid through all past ages from all human beings but has now revealed to his people.

1.27 God's plan is to make known his secret to his people, this rich and glorious secret which he has for all peoples. And the secret is that Christ is in you, which means that you will share in the glory of God.

1.28 So we preach Christ to everyone. With all possible wisdom we warn and teach them in order to bring each one into God's presence as a mature individual in union with Christ.

1.29 To get this done I toil and struggle, using the mighty strength which Christ supplies and which is at work in me.

2

2.1 Let me tell you how hard I have worked for you and for the people

in Laodicea and for all others who do not know me personally.
<sup>2.2</sup> I do this in order that they may be filled with courage and may be drawn together in love, and so have the full wealth of assurance which true understanding brings. In this way they will know God's secret, which is Christ himself. <sup>2.3</sup> He is the key that opens all the hidden treasures of God's wisdom and knowledge.

<sup>2.4</sup> I tell you, then, do not let anyone deceive you with false arguments, no matter how good they seem to be. <sup>2.5</sup> For even though I am absent in body, yet I am with you in spirit, and I am glad as I see the resolute firmness with which you stand together in your faith in Christ.

<sup>2.6</sup> Since you have accepted Christ Jesus as Lord, live in union with him. <sup>2.7</sup> Keep your roots deep in him, build your lives on him, and become stronger in your faith, as you were taught. And be filled with thanksgiving.

<sup>2.8</sup> See to it, then, that no one enslaves you by means of the worthless deceit of human wisdom, which comes from the teachings handed down by human beings and from the ruling spirits of the universe, and not from Christ. <sup>2.9</sup> For the full content of divine nature lives in Christ, in his humanity, <sup>2.10</sup> and you have been given full life in union with him. He is supreme over every spiritual ruler and authority.

<sup>2.11</sup> In union with Christ you were circumcised, not with the circumcision that is made by human beings, but with the circumcision made by Christ, which consists of being freed from the power of this sinful self. <sup>2.12</sup> For when you were baptized, you were buried with Christ, and in baptism you were also raised with Christ through your faith in the active power of God, who raised him from death. <sup>2.13</sup> You were at one time spiritually dead because of your sins and because you were Gentiles without the Law. But God has now brought you to life with Christ. God forgave us all our sins; <sup>2.14</sup> he canceled the unfavorable record of our debts with its binding rules and did away with it completely by nailing it to the cross. <sup>2.15</sup> And on that cross Christ freed himself from the power of the spiritual rulers and authorities; he made a public spectacle of them by leading them as captives in his victory procession.

<sup>2.16</sup> So let no one make rules about what you eat or drink or about

holy days or the New Moon Festival or the Sabbath.

<sup>2.17</sup> All such things are only a shadow of things in the future; the reality is Christ.

<sup>2.18</sup> Do not allow yourselves to be condemned by anyone who claims to be superior because of special visions and who insists on false humility and the worship of angels. For no reason at all, such people are all puffed up by their human way of thinking

<sup>2.19</sup> and have stopped holding on to Christ, who is the head of the body. Under Christ's control the whole body is nourished and held together by its joints and ligaments, and it grows as God wants it to grow.

<sup>2.20</sup> You have died with Christ and are set free from the ruling spirits of the universe. Why, then, do you live as though you belonged to this world? Why do you obey such rules as

<sup>2.21</sup> "Don't handle this," "Don't taste that," "Don't touch the other"?

<sup>2.22</sup> All these refer to things which become useless once they are used; they are only human rules and teachings.

<sup>2.23</sup> Of course such rules appear to be based on wisdom in their forced worship of angels, and false humility, and severe treatment of the body; but they have no real value in controlling physical passions.

# 3

<sup>3.1</sup> You have been raised to life with Christ, so set your hearts on the things that are in heaven, where Christ sits on his throne at the right side of God.

<sup>3.2</sup> Keep your minds fixed on things there, not on things here on earth.

<sup>3.3</sup> For you have died, and your life is hidden with Christ in God.

<sup>3.4</sup> Your real life is Christ and when he appears, then you too will appear with him and share his glory!

<sup>3.5</sup> You must put to death, then, the earthly desires at work in you, such as sexual immorality, indecency, lust, evil passions, and greed (for greed is a form of idolatry).

<sup>3.6</sup> Because of such things God's anger will come upon those who do not obey him.

<sup>3.7</sup> At one time you yourselves used to live according to such desires, when your life was dominated by them.

<sup>3.8</sup> But now you must get rid of all these things: anger, passion, and hateful feelings. No insults or obscene talk must ever come from your lips.

<sup>3.9</sup> Do not lie to one another, for you have put off the old self with its

habits

<sup>3.10</sup> and have put on the new self. This is the new being which God, its Creator, is constantly renewing in his own image, in order to bring you to a full knowledge of himself.

<sup>3.11</sup> As a result, there is no longer any distinction between Gentiles and Jews, circumcised and uncircumcised, barbarians, savages, slaves, and free, but Christ is all, Christ is in all.

<sup>3.12</sup> You are the people of God; he loved you and chose you for his own. So then, you must clothe yourselves with compassion, kindness, humility, gentleness, and patience.

<sup>3.13</sup> Be tolerant with one another and forgive one another whenever any of you has a complaint against someone else. You must forgive one another just as the Lord has forgiven you.

<sup>3.14</sup> And to all these qualities add love, which binds all things together in perfect unity.

<sup>3.15</sup> The peace that Christ gives is to guide you in the decisions you make; for it is to this peace that God has called you together in the one body. And be thankful.

<sup>3.16</sup> Christ's message in all its richness must live in your hearts. Teach and instruct one another with all wisdom. Sing psalms, hymns, and sacred songs; sing to God with thanksgiving in your hearts.

<sup>3.17</sup> Everything you do or say, then, should be done in the name of the Lord Jesus, as you give thanks through him to God the Father.

<sup>3.18</sup> Wives, submit yourselves to your husbands, for that is what you should do as Christians.

<sup>3.19</sup> Husbands, love your wives and do not be harsh with them.

<sup>3.20</sup> Children, it is your Christian duty to obey your parents always, for that is what pleases God.

<sup>3.21</sup> Parents, do not irritate your children, or they will become discouraged.

<sup>3.22</sup> Slaves, obey your human masters in all things, not only when they are watching you because you want to gain their approval; but do it with a sincere heart because of your reverence for the Lord.

<sup>3.23</sup> Whatever you do, work at it with all your heart, as though you were working for the Lord and not for people.

<sup>3.24</sup> Remember that the Lord will give you as a reward what he has kept for his people. For Christ is the real Master you serve.

<sup>3.25</sup> And all wrongdoers will be repaid for the wrong things they do, because God judges everyone by the same standard.

<sup>4.1</sup> Masters, be fair and just in the way you treat your slaves. Remember that you too have a Master in heaven.

<sup>4.2</sup> Be persistent in prayer, and keep alert as you pray, giving thanks to God.

<sup>4.3</sup> At the same time pray also for us, so that God will give us a good opportunity to preach his message about the secret of Christ. For that is why I am now in prison.

<sup>4.4</sup> Pray, then, that I may speak, as I should, in such a way as to make it clear.

<sup>4.5</sup> Be wise in the way you act toward those who are not believers, making good use of every opportunity you have.

<sup>4.6</sup> Your speech should always be pleasant and interesting, and you should know how to give the right answer to everyone.

<sup>4.7</sup> Our dear friend Tychicus, who is a faithful worker and fellow servant in the Lord's work, will give you all the news about me.

<sup>4.8</sup> That is why I am sending him to you, in order to cheer you up by telling you how all of us are getting along.

<sup>4.9</sup> With him goes Onesimus, that dear and faithful friend, who belongs to your group. They will tell you everything that is happening here.

<sup>4.10</sup> Aristarchus, who is in prison with me, sends you greetings, and so does Mark, the cousin of Barnabas. (You have already received instructions to welcome Mark if he comes your way.)

<sup>4.11</sup> Joshua, also called Justus, sends greetings too. These three are the only Jewish believers who work with me for the Kingdom of God, and they have been a great help to me.

<sup>4.12</sup> Greetings from Epaphras, another member of your group and a servant of Christ Jesus. He always prays fervently for you, asking God to make you stand firm, as mature and fully convinced Christians, in complete obedience to God's will.

<sup>4.13</sup> I can personally testify to his hard work for you and for the people in Laodicea and Hierapolis.

<sup>4.14</sup> Luke, our dear doctor, and Demas send you their greetings.

<sup>4.15</sup> Give our best wishes to the believers in Laodicea and to Nympha and the church that meets in her house.

<sup>4.16</sup> After you read this letter, make sure that it is read also in the church at Laodicea. At the same time, you are to read the letter that the believers in Laodicea will send you.

<sup>4.17</sup> And tell Archippus, "Be sure to finish the task you were given in the Lord's service."

<sup>4.18</sup> With my own hand I write this: Greetings from Paul. Do not forget my chains! May God's grace be with you.

# 1 THESSALONIANS

# 1 Thessalonians

**1**

<sup>1.1</sup> From Paul, Silas, and Timothy – To the people of the church in Thessalonica, who belong to God the Father and the Lord Jesus Christ: May grace and peace be yours.

<sup>1.2</sup> We always thank God for you all and always mention you in our prayers.

<sup>1.3</sup> For we remember before our God and Father how you put your faith into practice, how your love made you work so hard, and how your hope in our Lord Jesus Christ is firm.

<sup>1.4</sup> Our friends, we know that God loves you and has chosen you to be his own.

<sup>1.5</sup> For we brought the Good News to you, not with words only, but also with power and the Holy Spirit, and with complete conviction of its truth. You know how we lived when we were with you; it was for your own good.

<sup>1.6</sup> You imitated us and the Lord; and even though you suffered much, you received the message with the joy that comes from the Holy Spirit.

<sup>1.7</sup> So you became an example to all believers in Macedonia and Achaia.

<sup>1.8</sup> For not only did the message about the Lord go out from you throughout Macedonia and Achaia, but the news about your faith in God has gone everywhere. There is nothing, then, that we need to say.

<sup>1.9</sup> All those people speak about how you received us when we visited you, and how you turned away from idols to God, to serve the true and living God

<sup>1.10</sup> and to wait for his Son to come from heaven — his Son Jesus, whom he raised from death and who rescues us from God's anger that is coming.

**2**

<sup>2.1</sup> Our friends, you yourselves know that our visit to you was not a failure.

<sup>2.2</sup> You know how we had already been mistreated and insulted in Philippi before we came to you in Thessalonica. And even though there was much opposition, our God gave us courage to tell you the Good News that comes from him.

<sup></sup>2.3 Our appeal to you is not based on error or impure motives, nor do we try to trick anyone.

2.4 Instead, we always speak as God wants us to, because he has judged us worthy to be entrusted with the Good News. We do not try to please people, but to please God, who tests our motives.

2.5 You know very well that we did not come to you with flattering talk, nor did we use words to cover up greed — God is our witness!

2.6 We did not try to get praise from anyone, either from you or from others,

2.7 even though as apostles of Christ we could have made demands on you. But we were gentle when we were with you, like a mother taking care of her children.

2.8 Because of our love for you we were ready to share with you not only the Good News from God but even our own lives. You were so dear to us!

2.9 Surely you remember, our friends, how we worked and toiled! We worked day and night so that we would not be any trouble to you as we preached to you the Good News from God.

2.10 You are our witnesses, and so is God, that our conduct toward you who believe was pure, right, and without fault.

2.11 You know that we treated each one of you just as parents treat their own children.

2.12 We encouraged you, we comforted you, and we kept urging you to live the kind of life that pleases God, who calls you to share in his own Kingdom and glory.

2.13 And there is another reason why we always give thanks to God. When we brought you God's message, you heard it and accepted it, not as a message from human beings but as God's message, which indeed it is. For God is at work in you who believe.

2.14 Our friends, the same things happened to you that happened to the churches of God in Judea, to the people there who belong to Christ Jesus. You suffered the same persecutions from your own people that they suffered from the Jews,

2.15 who killed the Lord Jesus and the prophets, and persecuted us. How displeasing they are to God! How hostile they are to everyone!

2.16 They even tried to stop us from preaching to the Gentiles the message that would bring them salvation. In this way they have brought to completion all the sins they have always committed. And now God's anger has at last come down on them!

2.17 As for us, friends, when we were separated from you for a little while — not in our thoughts, of course, but only in body — how we missed you and how hard we tried to see you again!

2.18 We wanted to return to you. I myself tried to go back more than once, but Satan would not let us.

2.19 After all, it is you — you, no less than others! — who are our hope, our joy, and our reason for boasting of our victory in the presence of our Lord Jesus when he comes.

2.20 Indeed, you are our pride and our joy!

# 3

3.1 Finally, we could not bear it any longer. So we decided to stay on alone in Athens

3.2 while we sent Timothy, our brother who works with us for God in preaching the Good News about Christ. We sent him to strengthen you and help your faith,

3.3 so that none of you should turn back because of these persecutions. You yourselves know that such persecutions are part of God's will for us.

3.4 For while we were still with you, we told you ahead of time that we were going to be persecuted; and as you well know, that is exactly what happened.

3.5 That is why I had to send Timothy. I could not bear it any longer, so I sent him to find out about your faith. Surely it could not be that the Devil had tempted you and all our work had been for nothing!

3.6 Now Timothy has come back, and he has brought us the welcome news about your faith and love. He has told us that you always think well of us and that you want to see us just as much as we want to see you.

3.7 So, in all our trouble and suffering we have been encouraged about you, friends. It was your faith that encouraged us,

3.8 because now we really live if you stand firm in your life in union with the Lord.

3.9 Now we can give thanks to our God for you. We thank him for the joy we have in his presence because of you.

3.10 Day and night we ask him with all our heart to let us see you personally and supply what is needed in your faith.

3.11 May our God and Father himself and our Lord Jesus prepare the way for us to come to you!

3.12 May the Lord make your love for one another and for all people grow more and more and become as great as our love for you.

3.13 In this way he will strengthen you, and you will be perfect and holy in the presence of our God and Father when our Lord Jesus comes **with all** who belong **to him**.

4

**4.1** Finally, our friends, you learned <u>from us</u> how you should live **in order** to please God. This is, <u>of course</u>, the way you have been living. And now we beg and urge you <u>in the name</u> of the Lord Jesus to do even more.
**4.2** For you know the instructions we gave you <u>by the authority</u> of the Lord Jesus.
**4.3** God wants you to be holy and completely free <u>from sexual immorality</u>.
**4.4** Each <u>of you</u> should know how to live <u>with your wife</u> in a holy and honorable way,
**4.5** not <u>with a lustful desire</u>, <u>like the heathen</u> who do not know God.
**4.6** <u>In this matter</u>, then, none <u>of you</u> should do wrong <u>to other Christians</u> or take advantage <u>of them</u>. We have told you this before, and we strongly warned you that the Lord will punish those who do that.
**4.7** God did not call us to live <u>in immorality</u>, but <u>in holiness</u>.
**4.8** So then, whoever rejects this teaching is not rejecting a human being, but God, who gives you his Holy Spirit.
**4.9** There is no need to write you <u>about love</u> <u>for each other</u>. You yourselves have been taught <u>by God</u> how you should love one another.
**4.10** And you have, <u>in fact</u>, behaved <u>like this</u> <u>toward all the believers in all</u> of Macedonia. So we beg you, our friends, to do even more.
**4.11** Make it your aim to live a quiet life, to mind your own business, and to earn your own living, just as we told you before.
**4.12** <u>In this way</u> you will win the respect <u>of those</u> who are not believers, and you will not have to depend <u>on anyone</u> <u>for what</u> you need.
**4.13** Our friends, we want you to know the truth <u>about those</u> who have died, so that you will not be sad, as are those who have no hope.
**4.14** We believe that Jesus died and rose again, and so we believe that God will take back <u>with Jesus</u> those who have died believing <u>in him</u>.
**4.15** What we are teaching you now is the Lord's teaching: we who are alive <u>on the day</u> the Lord comes will not go ahead <u>of those</u> who have died.
**4.16** There will be the shout <u>of command</u>, the archangel's voice, the sound <u>of God's trumpet</u>, and the Lord himself will come down <u>from heaven</u>. Those who have died believing <u>in Christ</u> will rise <u>to life</u> first;
**4.17** then we who are living <u>at that time</u> will be gathered up along <u>with them</u> <u>in the clouds</u> to meet the Lord <u>in the air</u>. And so we will

1 THESSALONIANS | 567

always be with the Lord.

4.18 So then, encourage one another with these words.

# 5

5.1 There is no need to write you, friends, about the times and occasions when these things will happen.

5.2 For you yourselves know very well that the Day of the Lord will come as a thief comes at night.

5.3 When people say, "Everything is quiet and safe," then suddenly destruction will hit them! It will come as suddenly as the pains that come upon a woman in labor, and people will not escape.

5.4 But you, friends, are not in the darkness, and the Day should not take you by surprise like a thief.

5.5 All of you are people who belong to the light, who belong to the day. We do not belong to the night or to the darkness.

5.6 So then, we should not be sleeping like the others; we should be awake and sober.

5.7 It is at night when people sleep; it is at night when they get drunk.

5.8 But we belong to the day, and we should be sober. We must wear faith and love as a breastplate, and our hope of salvation as a helmet.

5.9 God did not choose us to suffer his anger, but to possess salvation through our Lord Jesus Christ,

5.10 who died for us in order that we might live together with him, whether we are alive or dead when he comes.

5.11 And so encourage one another and help one another, just as you are now doing.

5.12 We beg you, our friends, to pay proper respect to those who work among you, who guide and instruct you in the Christian life.

5.13 Treat them with the greatest respect and love because of the work they do. Be at peace among yourselves.

5.14 We urge you, our friends, to warn the idle, encourage the timid, help the weak, be patient with everyone.

5.15 See that no one pays back wrong for wrong, but at all times make it your aim to do good to one another and to all people.

5.16 Be joyful always,

5.17 pray at all times,

5.18 be thankful in all circumstances. This is what God wants from you in your life in union with Christ Jesus.

5.19 Do not restrain the Holy Spirit;

5.20 do not despise inspired messages.

5.21 Put all things to the test: keep what is good 5.22 and avoid every kind of evil. 5.23 May the God who gives us peace make you holy in every way and keep your whole being - spirit, soul, and body — free from every fault at the coming of our Lord Jesus Christ. 5.24 He who calls you will do it, because he is faithful. 5.25 Pray also for us, friends. 5.26 Greet all the believers with the kiss of peace. 5.27 I urge you by the authority of the Lord to read this letter to all the believers. 5.28 The grace of our Lord Jesus Christ be with you.

# 2 THESSALONIANS

# 2 Thessalonians

**1**

¹·¹ From Paul, Silas, and Timothy – To the people of the church in Thessalonica, who belong to God our Father and the Lord Jesus Christ:

¹·² May God our Father and the Lord Jesus Christ give you grace and peace.

¹·³ Our friends, we must thank God at all times for you. It is right for us to do so, because your faith is growing so much and the love each of you has for the others is becoming greater.

¹·⁴ That is why we ourselves boast about you in the churches of God. We boast about the way you continue to endure and believe through all the persecutions and sufferings you are experiencing.

¹·⁵ All of this proves that God's judgment is just and as a result you will become worthy of his Kingdom, for which you are suffering.

¹·⁶ God will do what is right: he will bring suffering on those who make you suffer,

¹·⁷ and he will give relief to you who suffer and to us as well. He will do this when the Lord Jesus appears from heaven with his mighty angels,

¹·⁸ with a flaming fire, to punish those who reject God and who do not obey the Good News about our Lord Jesus.

¹·⁹ They will suffer the punishment of eternal destruction, separated from the presence of the Lord and from his glorious might,

¹·¹⁰ when he comes on that Day to receive glory from all his people and honor from all who believe. You too will be among them, because you have believed the message that we told you.

¹·¹¹ That is why we always pray for you. We ask our God to make you worthy of the life he has called you to live. May he fulfill by his power all your desire for goodness and complete your work of faith.

¹·¹² In this way the name of our Lord Jesus will receive glory from you, and you from him, by the grace of our God and of the Lord Jesus Christ.

**2**

²·¹ Concerning the coming of our Lord Jesus Christ and our being gathered together to be with him: I beg you, my friends,

²·² not to be so easily confused in your thinking or upset by the claim that the Day of the Lord has come. Perhaps it is thought that we said

this while prophesying or preaching, or that we wrote it in a letter.

2.3 Do not let anyone deceive you in any way. For the Day will not come until the final Rebellion takes place and the Wicked One appears, who is destined to hell.

2.4 He will oppose every so-called god or object of worship and will put himself above them all. He will even go in and sit down in God's Temple and claim to be God.

2.5 Don't you remember? I told you all this while I was with you.

2.6 Yet there is something that keeps this from happening now, and you know what it is. At the proper time, then, the Wicked One will appear.

2.7 The Mysterious Wickedness is already at work, but what is going to happen will not happen until the one who holds it back is taken out of the way.

2.8 Then the Wicked One will be revealed, but when the Lord Jesus comes, he will kill him with the breath from his mouth and destroy him with his dazzling presence.

2.9 The Wicked One will come with the power of Satan and perform all kinds of false miracles and wonders,

2.10 and use every kind of wicked deceit on those who will perish. They will perish because they did not welcome and love the truth so as to be saved.

2.11 And so God sends the power of error to work in them so that they believe what is false.

2.12 The result is that all who have not believed the truth, but have taken pleasure in sin, will be condemned.

2.13 We must thank God at all times for you, friends, you whom the Lord loves. For God chose you as the first to be saved by the Spirit's power to make you his holy people and by your faith in the truth.

2.14 God called you to this through the Good News we preached to you; he called you to possess your share of the glory of our Lord Jesus Christ.

2.15 So then, our friends, stand firm and hold on to those truths which we taught you, both in our preaching and in our letter.

2.16 May our Lord Jesus Christ himself and God our Father, who loved us and in his grace gave us unfailing courage and a firm hope,

2.17 encourage you and strengthen you to always do and say what is good.

3

3.1 Finally, our friends, pray for us that the Lord's message may continue to spread **rapidly and** be received **with honor,** just as it was **among you.**

<sup>3.2</sup> Pray also that God will rescue us from wicked and evil people; for not everyone believes the message.

<sup>3.3</sup> But the Lord is faithful, and he will strengthen you and keep you safe from the Evil One.

<sup>3.4</sup> And the Lord gives us confidence in you, and we are sure that you are doing and will continue to do what we tell you.

<sup>3.5</sup> May the Lord lead you into a greater understanding of God's love and the endurance that is given by Christ.

<sup>3.6</sup> Our friends, we command you in the name of our Lord Jesus Christ to keep away from all believers who are living a lazy life and who do not follow the instructions that we gave them.

<sup>3.7</sup> You yourselves know very well that you should do just what we did. We were not lazy when we were with you.

<sup>3.8</sup> We did not accept anyone's support without paying for it. Instead, we worked and toiled; we kept working day and night so as not to be an expense to any of you.

<sup>3.9</sup> We did this, not because we do not have the right to demand our support; we did it to be an example for you to follow.

<sup>3.10</sup> While we were with you, we used to tell you, "Whoever refuses to work is not allowed to eat."

<sup>3.11</sup> We say this because we hear that there are some people among you who live lazy lives and who do nothing except meddle in other people's business.

<sup>3.12</sup> In the name of the Lord Jesus Christ we command these people and warn them to lead orderly lives and work to earn their own living.

<sup>3.13</sup> But you, friends, must not become tired of doing good.

<sup>3.14</sup> It may be that some there will not obey the message we send you in this letter. If so, take note of them and have nothing to do with them, so that they will be ashamed.

<sup>3.15</sup> But do not treat them as enemies; instead, warn them as believers.

<sup>3.16</sup> May the Lord himself, who is our source of peace, give you peace at all times and in every way. The Lord be with you all.

<sup>3.17</sup> With my own hand I write this: [Greetings from Paul.] This is the way I sign every letter; this is how I write.

<sup>3.18</sup> May the grace of our Lord Jesus Christ be with you all.

# 1 TIMOTHY

# 1 Timothy

## 1

<sup>1.1</sup> From Paul, an apostle of Christ Jesus by order of God our Savior and Christ Jesus our hope —

<sup>1.2</sup> To Timothy, my true son in the faith: May God the Father and Christ Jesus our Lord give you grace, mercy, and peace.

<sup>1.3</sup> I want you to stay in Ephesus, just as I urged you when I was on my way to Macedonia. Some people there are teaching false doctrines, and you must order them to stop.

<sup>1.4</sup> Tell them to give up those legends and those long lists of ancestors, which only produce arguments; they do not serve God's plan, which is known by faith.

<sup>1.5</sup> The purpose of this order is to arouse the love that comes from a pure heart, a clear conscience, and a genuine faith.

<sup>1.6</sup> Some people have turned away from these and have lost their way in foolish discussions.

<sup>1.7</sup> They want to be teachers of God's law, but they do not understand their own words or the matters about which they speak with so much confidence.

<sup>1.8</sup> We know that the Law is good if it is used as it should be used.

<sup>1.9</sup> It must be remembered, of course, that laws are made, not for good people, but for lawbreakers and criminals, for the godless and sinful, for those who are not religious or spiritual, for those who kill their fathers or mothers, for murderers,

<sup>1.10</sup> for the immoral, for sexual perverts, for kidnappers, for those who lie and give false testimony or who do anything else contrary to sound doctrine.

<sup>1.11</sup> That teaching is found in the gospel that was entrusted to me to announce, the Good News from the glorious and blessed God.

<sup>1.12</sup> I give thanks to Christ Jesus our Lord, who has given me strength for my work. I thank him for considering me worthy and appointing me to serve him,

<sup>1.13</sup> even though in the past I spoke evil of him and persecuted and insulted him. But God was merciful to me because I did not yet have faith and so did not know what I was doing.

<sup>1.14</sup> And our Lord poured out his abundant grace on me and gave me the faith and love which are ours in union with Christ Jesus.

<sup>1.15</sup> This is a true saying, to be completely accepted and believed: Christ Jesus came into the world to save sinners. I am the worst of

them,

<sup>1.16</sup> but God was merciful to me in order that Christ Jesus might show his full patience in dealing with me, the worst of sinners, as an example for all those who would later believe in him and receive eternal life.

<sup>1.17</sup> To the eternal King, immortal and invisible, the only God — to him be honor and glory forever and ever! Amen.

<sup>1.18</sup> Timothy, my child, I entrust to you this command, which is in accordance with the words of prophecy spoken in the past about you. Use those words as weapons in order to fight well,

<sup>1.19</sup> and keep your faith and a clear conscience. Some people have not listened to their conscience and have made a ruin of their faith.

<sup>1.20</sup> Among them are Hymenaeus and Alexander, whom I have punished by handing them over to the power of Satan; this will teach them to stop their blasphemy.

# 2

<sup>2.1</sup> First of all, then, I urge that petitions, prayers, requests, and thanksgivings be offered to God for all people;

<sup>2.2</sup> for kings and all others who are in authority, that we may live a quiet and peaceful life with all reverence toward God and with proper conduct.

<sup>2.3</sup> This is good and it pleases God our Savior,

<sup>2.4</sup> who wants everyone to be saved and to come to know the truth.

<sup>2.5</sup> For there is one God, and there is one who brings God and human beings together, the man Christ Jesus,

<sup>2.6</sup> who gave himself to redeem the whole human race. That was the proof at the right time that God wants everyone to be saved,

<sup>2.7</sup> and that is why I was sent as an apostle and teacher of the Gentiles, to proclaim the message of faith and truth. I am not lying; I am telling the truth!

<sup>2.8</sup> In every church service I want the men to pray, men who are dedicated to God and can lift up their hands in prayer without anger or argument.

<sup>2.9</sup> I also want the women to be modest and sensible about their clothes and to dress properly; not with fancy hair styles or with gold ornaments or pearls or expensive dresses,

<sup>2.10</sup> but with good deeds, as is proper for women who claim to be religious.

<sup>2.11</sup> Women should learn in silence and all humility.

<sup>2.12</sup> I do not allow them to teach or to have authority over men; they

must keep quiet.

2.13 For Adam was created first, and then Eve.

2.14 And it was not Adam who was deceived; it was the woman who was deceived and broke God's law.

2.15 But a woman will be saved through having children, if she perseveres in faith and love and holiness, with modesty.

# 3

3.1 This is a true saying: If a man is eager to be a church leader, he desires an excellent work.

3.2 A church leader must be without fault; he must have only one wife, be sober, self-controlled, and orderly; he must welcome strangers in his home; he must be able to teach;

3.3 he must not be a drunkard or a violent man, but gentle and peaceful; he must not love money;

3.4 he must be able to manage his own family well and make his children obey him with all respect.

3.5 For if a man does not know how to manage his own family, how can he take care of the church of God?

3.6 He must be mature in the faith, so that he will not swell up with pride and be condemned, as the Devil was.

3.7 He should be a man who is respected by the people outside the church, so that he will not be disgraced and fall into the Devil's trap.

3.8 Church helpers must also have a good character and be sincere; they must not drink too much wine or be greedy for money;

3.9 they should hold to the revealed truth of the faith with a clear conscience.

3.10 They should be tested first, and then, if they pass the test, they are to serve.

3.11 Their wives also must be of good character and must not gossip; they must be sober and honest in everything.

3.12 A church helper must have only one wife, and be able to manage his children and family well.

3.13 Those helpers who do their work well win for themselves a good standing and are able to speak boldly about their faith in Christ Jesus.

3.14 As I write this letter to you, I hope to come and see you soon.

3.15 But if I delay, this letter will let you know how we should conduct ourselves in God's household, which is the church of the living God, the pillar and support of the truth.

3.16 No one can deny how great is the secret of our religion: He appeared in human form, was shown to be right by the Spirit, and was seen by angels. He was preached among the nations, was believed in throughout the world, and was taken up to heaven.

# 4

<sup>4.1</sup> The Spirit says clearly that some people will abandon the faith in later times; they will obey lying spirits and follow the teachings of demons.

<sup>4.2</sup> Such teachings are spread by deceitful liars, whose consciences are dead, as if burnt with a hot iron.

<sup>4.3</sup> Such people teach that it is wrong to marry and to eat certain foods. But God created those foods to be eaten, after a prayer of thanks, by those who are believers and have come to know the truth.

<sup>4.4</sup> Everything that God has created is good; nothing is to be rejected, but everything is to be received with a prayer of thanks,

<sup>4.5</sup> because the word of God and the prayer make it acceptable to God.

<sup>4.6</sup> If you give these instructions to the believers, you will be a good servant of Christ Jesus, as you feed yourself spiritually on the words of faith and of the true teaching which you have followed.

<sup>4.7</sup> But keep away from those godless legends, which are not worth telling. Keep yourself in training for a godly life.

<sup>4.8</sup> Physical exercise has some value, but spiritual exercise is valuable in every way, because it promises life both for the present and for the future.

<sup>4.9</sup> This is a true saying, to be completely accepted and believed.

<sup>4.10</sup> We struggle and work hard, because we have placed our hope in the living God, who is the Savior of all and especially of those who believe.

<sup>4.11</sup> Give them these instructions and these teachings.

<sup>4.12</sup> Do not let anyone look down on you because you are young, but be an example for the believers in your speech, your conduct, your love, faith, and purity.

<sup>4.13</sup> Until I come, give your time and effort to the public reading of the Scriptures and to preaching and teaching.

<sup>4.14</sup> Do not neglect the spiritual gift that is in you, which was given to you when the prophets spoke and the elders laid their hands on you.

<sup>4.15</sup> Practice these things and devote yourself to them, in order that your progress may be seen by all.

<sup>4.16</sup> Watch yourself and watch your teaching. Keep on doing these things, because if you do, you will save both yourself and those who hear you.

**5** <sup>5.1</sup> Do not rebuke an older man, but appeal to him as if he were your father. Treat the younger men as your brothers,
<sup>5.2</sup> the older women as mothers, and the younger women as sisters, with all purity.

<sup>5.3</sup> Show respect for widows who really are all alone.
<sup>5.4</sup> But if a widow has children or grandchildren, they should learn first to carry out their religious duties toward their own family and in this way repay their parents and grandparents, because that is what pleases God.
<sup>5.5</sup> A widow who is all alone, with no one to take care of her, has placed her hope in God and continues to pray and ask him for his help night and day.
<sup>5.6</sup> But a widow who gives herself to pleasure has already died, even though she lives.
<sup>5.7</sup> Give them these instructions, so that no one will find fault with them.
<sup>5.8</sup> But if any do not take care of their relatives, especially the members of their own family, they have denied the faith and are worse than an unbeliever.
<sup>5.9</sup> Do not add any widow to the list of widows unless she is over sixty years of age. In addition, she must have been married only once
<sup>5.10</sup> and have a reputation for good deeds: a woman who brought up her children well, received strangers in her home, performed humble duties for other Christians, helped people in trouble, and devoted herself to doing good.
<sup>5.11</sup> But do not include younger widows in the list; because when their desires make them want to marry, they turn away from Christ,
<sup>5.12</sup> and so become guilty of breaking their earlier promise to him.
<sup>5.13</sup> They also learn to waste their time in going around from house to house; but even worse, they learn to be gossips and busybodies, talking of things they should not.
<sup>5.14</sup> So I would prefer that the younger widows get married, have children, and take care of their homes, so as to give our enemies no chance of speaking evil of us.
<sup>5.15</sup> For some widows have already turned away to follow Satan.
<sup>5.16</sup> But if any Christian woman has widows in her family, she must take care of them and not put the burden on the church, so that it may take care of the widows who are all alone.
<sup>5.17</sup> The elders who do good work as leaders should be considered worthy of receiving double pay, especially those who work hard at preaching and teaching.

5.18 For the scripture says, "Do not muzzle an ox when you are using it to thresh grain" and "Workers should be given their pay."

5.19 Do not listen to an accusation against an elder unless it is brought by two or more witnesses.

5.20 Rebuke publicly all those who commit sins, so that the rest may be afraid.

5.21 In the presence of God and of Christ Jesus and of the holy angels I solemnly call upon you to obey these instructions without showing any prejudice or favor to anyone in anything you do.

5.22 Be in no hurry to lay hands on people to dedicate them to the Lord's service. Take no part in the sins of others; keep yourself pure.

5.23 Do not drink water only, but take a little wine to help your digestion, since you are sick so often.

5.24 The sins of some people are plain to see, and their sins go ahead of them to judgment; but the sins of others are seen only later.

5.25 In the same way good deeds are plainly seen, and even those that are not so plain cannot be hidden.

# 6

6.1 Those who are slaves must consider their masters worthy of all respect, so that no one will speak evil of the name of God and of our teaching.

6.2 Slaves belonging to Christian masters must not despise them, for they are believers too. Instead, they are to serve them even better, because those who benefit from their work are believers whom they love. You must teach and preach these things.

6.3 Whoever teaches a different doctrine and does not agree with the true words of our Lord Jesus Christ and with the teaching of our religion

6.4 is swollen with pride and knows nothing. He has an unhealthy desire to argue and quarrel about words, and this brings on jealousy, disputes, insults, evil suspicions,

6.5 and constant arguments from people whose minds do not function and who no longer have the truth. They think that religion is a way to become rich.

6.6 Well, religion does make us very rich, if we are satisfied with what we have.

6.7 What did we bring into the world? Nothing! What can we take out of the world? Nothing!

6.8 So then, if we have food and clothes, that should be enough for us.

6.9 But those who want to get rich fall into temptation and are caught in the trap of many foolish and harmful desires, which pull them down to ruin and destruction.

6.10 For the love of money is a source of all kinds of evil. Some have been so eager to have it that they have wandered away from the faith and have broken their hearts with many sorrows.

6.11 But you, man of God, avoid all these things. Strive for righteousness, godliness, faith, love, endurance, and gentleness.

6.12 Run your best in the race of faith, and win eternal life for yourself; for it was to this life that God called you when you firmly professed your faith before many witnesses.

6.13 Before God, who gives life to all things, and before Christ Jesus, who firmly professed his faith before Pontius Pilate, I command you

6.14 to obey your orders and keep them faithfully until the Day when our Lord Jesus Christ will appear.

6.15 His appearing will be brought about at the right time by God, the blessed and only Ruler, the King of kings and the Lord of lords.

6.16 He alone is immortal; he lives in the light that no one can approach. No one has ever seen him; no one can ever see him. To him be honor and eternal power! Amen.

6.17 Command those who are rich in the things of this life not to be proud, but to place their hope, not in such an uncertain thing as riches, but in God, who generously gives us everything for our enjoyment.

6.18 Command them to do good, to be rich in good works, to be generous and ready to share with others.

6.19 In this way they will store up for themselves a treasure which will be a solid foundation for the future. And then they will be able to win the life which is true life.

6.20 Timothy, keep safe what has been entrusted to your care. Avoid the profane talk and foolish arguments of what some people wrongly call "Knowledge."

6.21 For some have claimed to possess it, and as a result they have lost the way of faith. God's grace be with you all.

# 2 TIMOTHY

# 2 Timothy

1

<sup>1.1</sup> From Paul, an apostle of Christ Jesus by God's will, sent to proclaim the promised life which we have in union with Christ Jesus —
<sup>1.2</sup> To Timothy, my dear son: May God the Father and Christ Jesus our Lord give you grace, mercy, and peace.

<sup>1.3</sup> I give thanks to God, whom I serve with a clear conscience, as my ancestors did. I thank him as I remember you always in my prayers night and day.

<sup>1.4</sup> I remember your tears, and I want to see you very much, so that I may be filled with joy.

<sup>1.5</sup> I remember the sincere faith you have, the kind of faith that your grandmother Lois and your mother Eunice also had. I am sure that you have it also.

<sup>1.6</sup> For this reason I remind you to keep alive the gift that God gave you when I laid my hands on you.

<sup>1.7</sup> For the Spirit that God has given us does not make us timid; instead, his Spirit fills us with power, love, and self-control.

<sup>1.8</sup> Do not be ashamed, then, of witnessing for our Lord; neither be ashamed of me, a prisoner for Christ's sake. Instead, take your part in suffering for the Good News, as God gives you the strength for it.

<sup>1.9</sup> He saved us and called us to be his own people, not because of what we have done, but because of his own purpose and grace. He gave us this grace by means of Christ Jesus before the beginning of time,

<sup>1.10</sup> but now it has been revealed to us through the coming of our Savior, Christ Jesus. He has ended the power of death and through the gospel has revealed immortal life.

<sup>1.11</sup> God has appointed me as an apostle and teacher to proclaim the Good News,

<sup>1.12</sup> and it is for this reason that I suffer these things. But I am still full of confidence, because I know whom I have trusted, and I am sure that he is able to keep safe until that Day what he has entrusted to me.

<sup>1.13</sup> Hold firmly to the true words that I taught you, as the example for you to follow, and remain in the faith and love that are ours in union with Christ Jesus.

<sup>1.14</sup> Through the power of the Holy Spirit, who lives in us, keep the good things that have been entrusted to you.

1.15 You know that everyone in the province of Asia, including Phygelus and Hermogenes, has deserted me.

1.16 May the Lord show mercy to the family of Onesiphorus, because he cheered me up many times. He was not ashamed that I am in prison,

1.17 but as soon as he arrived in Rome, he started looking for me until he found me.

1.18 May the Lord grant him his mercy on that Day! And you know very well how much he did for me in Ephesus.

# 2

2.1 As for you, my son, be strong through the grace that is ours in union with Christ Jesus.

2.2 Take the teachings that you heard me proclaim in the presence of many witnesses, and entrust them to reliable people, who will be able to teach others also.

2.3 Take your part in suffering, as a loyal soldier of Christ Jesus.

2.4 A soldier on active duty wants to please his commanding officer and so does not get mixed up in the affairs of civilian life.

2.5 An athlete who runs in a race cannot win the prize unless he obeys the rules.

2.6 The farmer who has done the hard work should have the first share of the harvest.

2.7 Think about what I am saying, because the Lord will enable you to understand it all.

2.8 Remember Jesus Christ, who was raised from death, who was a descendant of David, as is taught in the Good News I preach.

2.9 Because I preach the Good News, I suffer and I am even chained like a criminal. But the word of God is not in chains,

2.10 and so I endure everything for the sake of God's chosen people, in order that they too may obtain the salvation that comes through Christ Jesus and brings eternal glory.

2.11 This is a true saying: "If we have died with him, we shall also live with him.

2.12 "If we continue to endure, we shall also rule with him. If we deny him, he also will deny us.

2.13 "If we are not faithful, he remains faithful, because he cannot be false to himself."

2.14 Remind your people of this, and give them a solemn warning in God's presence not to fight over words. It does no good, but only ruins the people who listen.

$^{2.15}$ Do your best to win full approval in God's sight, as a worker who is not ashamed of his work, one who correctly teaches the message of God's truth.

$^{2.16}$ Keep away from profane and foolish discussions, which only drive people farther away from God.

$^{2.17}$ Such teaching is like an open sore that eats away the flesh. Two men who have taught such things are Hymenaeus and Philetus.

$^{2.18}$ They have left the way of truth and are upsetting the faith of some believers by saying that our resurrection has already taken place.

$^{2.19}$ But the solid foundation that God has laid cannot be shaken; and on it are written these words: "The Lord knows those who are his" and "Those who say that they belong to the Lord must turn away from wrongdoing."

$^{2.20}$ In a large house there are dishes and bowls of all kinds: some are made of silver and gold, others of wood and clay; some are for special occasions, others for ordinary use.

$^{2.21}$ Those who make themselves clean from all those evil things, will be used for special purposes, because they are dedicated and useful to their Master, ready to be used for every good deed.

$^{2.22}$ Avoid the passions of youth, and strive for righteousness, faith, love, and peace, together with those who with a pure heart call out to the Lord for help.

$^{2.23}$ But keep away from foolish and ignorant arguments; you know that they end up in quarrels.

$^{2.24}$ As the Lord's servant, you must not quarrel. You must be kind toward all, a good and patient teacher,

$^{2.25}$ who is gentle as you correct your opponents, for it may be that God will give them the opportunity to repent and come to know the truth.

$^{2.26}$ And then they will come to their senses and escape from the trap of the Devil, who had caught them and made them obey his will.

# 3

$^{3.1}$ Remember that there will be difficult times in the last days.

$^{3.2}$ People will be selfish, greedy, boastful, and conceited; they will be insulting, disobedient to their parents, ungrateful, and irreligious;

$^{3.3}$ they will be unkind, merciless, slanderers, violent, and fierce; they will hate the good;

$^{3.4}$ they will be treacherous, reckless, and swollen with pride; they will love pleasure rather than God;

<sup>3.5</sup> they will hold to the outward form of our religion, but reject its real power. Keep away from such people.

<sup>3.6</sup> Some of them go into people's houses and gain control over weak women who are burdened by the guilt of their sins and driven by all kinds of desires,

<sup>3.7</sup> women who are always trying to learn but who can never come to know the truth.

<sup>3.8</sup> As Jannes and Jambres were opposed to Moses, so also these people are opposed to the truth — people whose minds do not function and who are failures in the faith.

<sup>3.9</sup> But they will not get very far, because everyone will see how stupid they are. That is just what happened to Jannes and Jambres.

<sup>3.10</sup> But you have followed my teaching, my conduct, and my purpose in life; you have observed my faith, my patience, my love, my endurance,

<sup>3.11</sup> my persecutions, and my sufferings. You know all that happened to me in Antioch, Iconium, and Lystra, the terrible persecutions I endured! But the Lord rescued me from them all.

<sup>3.12</sup> Everyone who wants to live a godly life in union with Christ Jesus will be persecuted;

<sup>3.13</sup> and evil persons and impostors will keep on going from bad to worse, deceiving others and being deceived themselves.

<sup>3.14</sup> But as for you, continue in the truths that you were taught and firmly believe. You know who your teachers were,

<sup>3.15</sup> and you remember that ever since you were a child, you have known the Holy Scriptures, which are able to give you the wisdom that leads to salvation through faith in Christ Jesus.

<sup>3.16</sup> All Scripture is inspired by God and is useful for teaching the truth, rebuking error, correcting faults, and giving instruction for right living,

<sup>3.17</sup> so that the person who serves God may be fully qualified and equipped to do every kind of good deed.

# 4

<sup>4.1</sup> In the presence of God and of Christ Jesus, who will judge the living and the dead, and because he is coming to rule as King, I solemnly urge you

<sup>4.2</sup> to preach the message, to insist upon proclaiming it (whether the time is right or not), to convince, reproach, and encourage, as you teach with all patience.

<sup>4.3</sup> The time will come when people will not listen to sound doctrine,

but will follow their own desires and will collect for themselves more and more teachers who will tell them what they are itching to hear. <sup>4.4</sup> They will turn away from listening to the truth and give their attention to legends.

<sup>4.5</sup> But you must keep control of yourself in all circumstances; endure suffering, do the work of a preacher of the Good News, and perform your whole duty as a servant of God.

<sup>4.6</sup> As for me, the hour has come for me to be sacrificed; the time is here for me to leave this life. <sup>4.7</sup> I have done my best in the race, I have run the full distance, and I have kept the faith. <sup>4.8</sup> And now there is waiting for me the victory prize of being put right with God, which the Lord, the righteous Judge, will give me on that Day — and not only to me, but to all those who wait with love for him to appear.

<sup>4.9</sup> Do your best to come to me soon. <sup>4.10</sup> Demas fell in love with this present world and has deserted me, going off to Thessalonica. Crescens went to Galatia, and Titus to Dalmatia. <sup>4.11</sup> Only Luke is with me. Get Mark and bring him with you, because he can help me in the work. <sup>4.12</sup> I sent Tychicus to Ephesus. <sup>4.13</sup> When you come, bring my coat that I left in Troas with Carpus; bring the books too, and especially the ones made of parchment. <sup>4.14</sup> Alexander the metalworker did me great harm; the Lord will reward him according to what he has done. <sup>4.15</sup> Be on your guard against him yourself, because he was violently opposed to our message.

<sup>4.16</sup> No one stood by me the first time I defended myself; all deserted me. May God not count it against them! <sup>4.17</sup> But the Lord stayed with me and gave me strength, so that I was able to proclaim the full message for all the Gentiles to hear; and I was rescued from being sentenced to death. <sup>4.18</sup> And the Lord will rescue me from all evil and take me safely into his heavenly Kingdom. To him be the glory forever and ever! Amen.

<sup>4.19</sup> I send greetings to Priscilla and Aquila and to the family of Onesiphorus. <sup>4.20</sup> Erastus stayed in Corinth, and I left Trophimus in Miletus, because he was sick. <sup>4.21</sup> Do your best to come before winter. Eubulus, Pudens, Linus, and Claudia send their greetings, and so do all the other Christians.

<sup>4.22</sup> The Lord be with your spirit. God's grace be with you all.

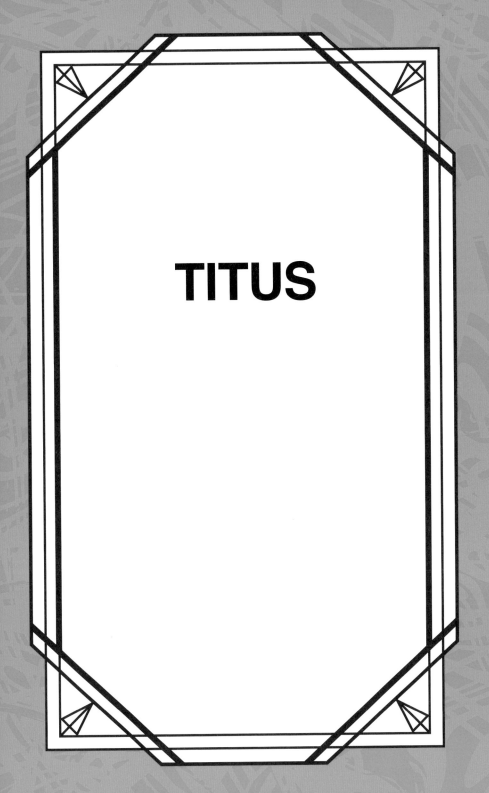

# TITUS

# Titus

## 1

<sup>1.1</sup> From Paul, a servant of God and an apostle of Jesus Christ. I was chosen and sent to help the faith of God's chosen people and to lead them to the truth taught by our religion,
<sup>1.2</sup> which is based on the hope for eternal life. God, who does not lie, promised us this life before the beginning of time,
<sup>1.3</sup> and at the right time he revealed it in his message. This was entrusted to me, and I proclaim it by order of God our Savior.
<sup>1.4</sup> I write to Titus, my true son in the faith that we have in common. May God the Father and Christ Jesus our Savior give you grace and peace.
<sup>1.5</sup> I left you in Crete, so that you could put in order the things that still needed doing and appoint church elders in every town. Remember my instructions:
<sup>1.6</sup> an elder must be without fault; he must have only one wife, and his children must be believers and not have the reputation of being wild or disobedient.
<sup>1.7</sup> For since a church leader is in charge of God's work, he should be without fault. He must not be arrogant or quick-tempered, or a drunkard or violent or greedy for money.
<sup>1.8</sup> He must be hospitable and love what is good. He must be self-controlled, upright, holy, and disciplined.
<sup>1.9</sup> He must hold firmly to the message which can be trusted and which agrees with the doctrine. In this way he will be able to encourage others with the true teaching and also to show the error of those who are opposed to it.
<sup>1.10</sup> For there are many, especially the converts from Judaism, who rebel and deceive others with their nonsense.
<sup>1.11</sup> It is necessary to stop their talk, because they are upsetting whole families by teaching what they should not, and all for the shameful purpose of making money.
<sup>1.12-13</sup> It was a Cretan himself, one of their own prophets, who spoke the truth when he said, "Cretans are always liars, wicked beasts, and lazy gluttons." For this reason you must rebuke them sharply, so that they may have a healthy faith
<sup>1.14</sup> and no longer hold on to Jewish legends and to human commandments which come from people who have rejected the truth.
<sup>1.15</sup> Everything is pure to those who are themselves pure; but nothing

is pure to those who are defiled and unbelieving, for their minds and consciences have been defiled.

<sup>1.16</sup> They claim that they know God, but their actions deny it. They are hateful and disobedient, not fit to do anything good.

# 2

<sup>2.1</sup> But you must teach what agrees with sound doctrine.

<sup>2.2</sup> Instruct the older men to be sober, sensible, and self-controlled; to be sound in their faith, love, and endurance.

<sup>2.3</sup> In the same way instruct the older women to behave as women should who live a holy life. They must not be slanderers or slaves to wine. They must teach what is good,

<sup>2.4</sup> in order to train the younger women to love their husbands and children,

<sup>2.5</sup> to be self-controlled and pure, and to be good housewives who submit themselves to their husbands, so that no one will speak evil of the message that comes from God.

<sup>2.6</sup> In the same way urge the young men to be self-controlled.

<sup>2.7</sup> In all things you yourself must be an example of good behavior. Be sincere and serious in your teaching.

<sup>2.8</sup> Use sound words that cannot be criticized, so that your enemies may be put to shame by not having anything bad to say about us.

<sup>2.9</sup> Slaves are to submit themselves to their masters and please them in all things. They must not talk back to them

<sup>2.10</sup> or steal from them. Instead, they must show that they are always good and faithful, so as to bring credit to the teaching about God our Savior in all they do.

<sup>2.11</sup> For God has revealed his grace for the salvation of all people.

<sup>2.12</sup> That grace instructs us to give up ungodly living and worldly passions, and to live self-controlled, upright, and godly lives in this world,

<sup>2.13</sup> as we wait for the blessed Day we hope for, when the glory of our great God and Savior Jesus Christ will appear.

<sup>2.14</sup> He gave himself for us, to rescue us from all wickedness and to make us a pure people who belong to him alone and are eager to do good.

<sup>2.15</sup> Teach these things and use your full authority as you encourage and rebuke your hearers. Let none of them look down on you.

# 3

<sup>3.1</sup> Remind your people to submit to rulers and authorities, to obey

them, and to be ready to do good in every way. <sup>3.2</sup> Tell them not to speak evil of anyone, but to be peaceful and friendly, and always to show a gentle attitude toward everyone.

<sup>3.3</sup> For we ourselves were once foolish, disobedient, and wrong. We were slaves to passions and pleasures of all kinds. We spent our lives in malice and envy; others hated us and we hated them.

<sup>3.4</sup> But when the kindness and love of God our Savior was revealed, <sup>3.5</sup> he saved us. It was not because of any good deeds that we ourselves had done, but because of his own mercy that he saved us, through the Holy Spirit, who gives us new birth and new life by washing us.

<sup>3.6</sup> God poured out the Holy Spirit abundantly on us through Jesus Christ our Savior, <sup>3.7</sup> so that by his grace we might be put right with God and come into possession of the eternal life we hope for.

<sup>3.8</sup> This is a true saying. I want you to give special emphasis to these matters, so that those who believe in God may be concerned with giving their time to doing good deeds, which are good and useful for everyone.

<sup>3.9</sup> But avoid stupid arguments, long lists of ancestors, quarrels, and fights about the Law. They are useless and worthless.

<sup>3.10</sup> Give at least two warnings to those who cause divisions, and then have nothing more to do with them. <sup>3.11</sup> You know that such people are corrupt, and their sins prove that they are wrong.

<sup>3.12</sup> When I send Artemas or Tychicus to you, do your best to come to me in Nicopolis, because I have decided to spend the winter there. <sup>3.13</sup> Do your best to help Zenas the lawyer and Apollos to get started on their travels, and see to it that they have everything they need. <sup>3.14</sup> Our people must learn to spend their time doing good, in order to provide for real needs; they should not live useless lives.

<sup>3.15</sup> All who are with me send you greetings. Give our greetings to our friends in the faith. God's grace be with you all.

# PHILEMON

# Philemon

# 1

<sup>1.1</sup> From Paul, a prisoner for the sake of Christ Jesus, and from our brother Timothy – To our friend and fellow worker Philemon,
<sup>1.2</sup> and the church that meets in your house, and our sister Apphia, and our fellow soldier Archippus:
<sup>1.3</sup> May God our Father and the Lord Jesus Christ give you grace and peace.
<sup>1.4</sup> Brother Philemon, every time I pray, I mention you and give thanks to my God.
<sup>1.5</sup> For I hear of your love for all of God's people and the faith you have in the Lord Jesus.
<sup>1.6</sup> My prayer is that our fellowship with you as believers will bring about a deeper understanding of every blessing which we have in our life in union with Christ.
<sup>1.7</sup> Your love, dear brother, has brought me great joy and much encouragement! You have cheered the hearts of all of God's people.
<sup>1.8</sup> For this reason I could be bold enough, as your brother in Christ, to order you to do what should be done.
<sup>1.9</sup> But because I love you, I make a request instead. I do this even though I am Paul, the ambassador of Christ Jesus, and at present also a prisoner for his sake.
<sup>1.10</sup> So I make a request to you on behalf of Onesimus, who is my own son in Christ; for while in prison I have become his spiritual father.
<sup>1.11</sup> At one time he was of no use to you, but now he is useful both to you and to me.
<sup>1.12</sup> I am sending him back to you now, and with him goes my heart.
<sup>1.13</sup> I would like to keep him here with me, while I am in prison for the gospel's sake, so that he could help me in your place.
<sup>1.14</sup> However, I do not want to force you to help me; rather, I would like for you to do it of your own free will. So I will not do anything unless you agree.
<sup>1.15</sup> It may be that Onesimus was away from you for a short time so that you might have him back for all time.
<sup>1.16</sup> And now he is not just a slave, but much more than a slave: he is a dear brother in Christ. How much he means to me! And how much more he will mean to you, both as a slave and as a brother in the Lord!
<sup>1.17</sup> So, if you think of me as your partner, welcome him back just as

you would welcome me.

¹·¹⁸ If he has done you any wrong or owes you anything, charge it to my account.

¹·¹⁹ Here, I will write this with my own hand: I, Paul, will pay you back. (I should not have to remind you, of course, that you owe your very self to me.)

¹·²⁰ So, my brother, please do me this favor for the Lord's sake; as a brother in Christ, cheer me up!

¹·²¹ I am sure, as I write this, that you will do what I ask — in fact I know that you will do even more.

¹·²² At the same time, get a room ready for me, because I hope that God will answer the prayers of all of you and give me back to you.

¹·²³ Epaphras, who is in prison with me for the sake of Christ Jesus, sends you his greetings,

¹·²⁴ and so do my co-workers Mark, Aristarchus, Demas, and Luke.

¹·²⁵ May the grace of the Lord Jesus Christ be with you all.

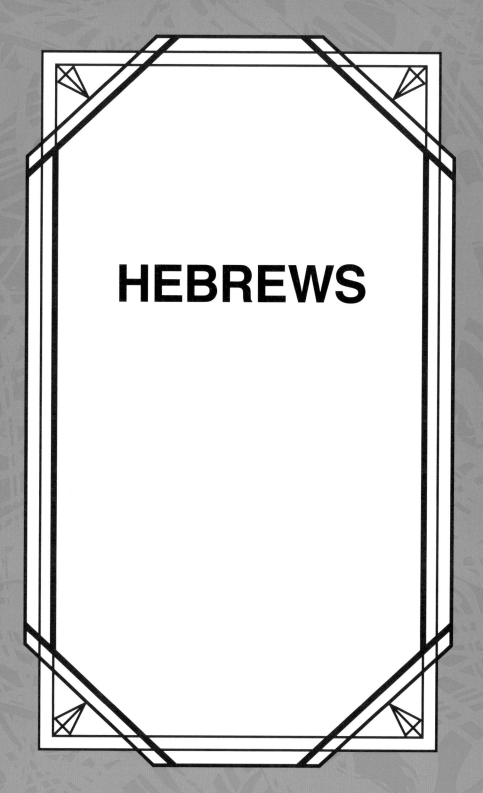

# HEBREWS

# Hebrews

## 1

<sup></sup>

¹·¹ In the past God spoke to our ancestors many times and in many ways through the prophets,

¹·² but in these last days he has spoken to us through his Son. He is the one through whom God created the universe, the one whom God has chosen to possess all things at the end.

¹·³ He reflects the brightness of God's glory and is the exact likeness of God's own being, sustaining the universe with his powerful word. After achieving forgiveness for the sins of all human beings, he sat down in heaven at the right side of God, the Supreme Power.

¹·⁴ The Son was made greater than the angels, just as the name that God gave him is greater than theirs.

¹·⁵ For God never said to any of his angels, "You are my Son; today I have become your Father." Nor did God say about any angel, "I will be his Father, and he will be my Son."

¹·⁶ But when God was about to send his first-born Son into the world, he said, "All of God's angels must worship him."

¹·⁷ But about the angels God said, "God makes his angels winds, and his servants flames of fire."

¹·⁸ About the Son, however, God said: "Your kingdom, O God, will last forever and ever! You rule over your people with justice.

¹·⁹ "You love what is right and hate what is wrong. That is why God, your God, has chosen you and has given you the joy of an honor far greater than he gave to your companions."

¹·¹⁰ He also said, "You, Lord, in the beginning created the earth, and with your own hands you made the heavens.

¹·¹¹ "They will disappear, but you will remain; they will all wear out like clothes.

¹·¹² "You will fold them up like a coat, and they will be changed like clothes. But you are always the same, and your life never ends."

¹·¹³ God never said to any of his angels: "Sit here at my right side until I put your enemies as a footstool under your feet."

¹·¹⁴ What are the angels, then? They are spirits who serve God and are sent by him to help those who are to receive salvation.

## 2

²·¹ That is why we must hold on all the more firmly to the truths we have heard, so that we will not be carried away.

<sup>2.2</sup> The message given to our ancestors by the angels was shown to be true, and those who did not follow it or obey it received the punishment they deserved.

<sup>2.3</sup> How, then, shall we escape if we pay no attention to such a great salvation? The Lord himself first announced this salvation, and those who heard him proved to us that it is true.

<sup>2.4</sup> At the same time God added his witness to theirs by performing all kinds of miracles and wonders and by distributing the gifts of the Holy Spirit according to his will.

<sup>2.5</sup> God has not placed the angels as rulers over the new world to come — the world of which we speak.

<sup>2.6</sup> Instead, as it is said somewhere in the Scriptures: "What are human beings, O God, that you should think of them; mere human beings, that you should care for them?

<sup>2.7</sup> "You made them for a little while lower than the angels; you crowned them with glory and honor,

<sup>2.8</sup> "and made them rulers over all things." It says that God made them "rulers over all things"; this clearly includes everything. We do not, however, see human beings ruling over all things now.

<sup>2.9</sup> But we do see Jesus, who for a little while was made lower than the angels, so that through God's grace he should die for everyone. We see him now crowned with glory and honor because of the death he suffered.

<sup>2.10</sup> It was only right that God, who creates and preserves all things, should make Jesus perfect through suffering, in order to bring many children to share his glory. For Jesus is the one who leads them to salvation.

<sup>2.11</sup> He purifies people from their sins, and both he and those who are made pure all have the same Father. That is why Jesus is not ashamed to call them his family.

<sup>2.12</sup> He says to God, "I will tell my people what you have done; I will praise you in their meeting."

<sup>2.13</sup> He also says, "I will put my trust in God." And he also says, "Here I am with the children that God has given me."

<sup>2.14</sup> Since the children, as he calls them, are people of flesh and blood, Jesus himself became like them and shared their human nature. He did this so that through his death he might destroy the Devil, who has the power over death,

<sup>2.15</sup> and in this way set free those who were slaves all their lives because of their fear of death.

<sup>2.16</sup> For it is clear that it is not the angels that he helps. Instead, he

helps the descendants of Abraham.

<sup>2.17</sup> This means that he had to become like his people in every way, in order to be their faithful and merciful High Priest in his service to God, so that the people's sins would be forgiven.

<sup>2.18</sup> And now he can help those who are tempted, because he himself was tempted and suffered.

# 3

<sup>3.1</sup> My Christian friends, who also have been called by God! Think of Jesus, whom God sent to be the High Priest of the faith we profess.

<sup>3.2</sup> He was faithful to God, who chose him to do this work, just as Moses was faithful in his work in God's house.

<sup>3.3</sup> A man who builds a house receives more honor than the house itself. In the same way Jesus is worthy of much greater honor than Moses.

<sup>3.4</sup> Every house, of course, is built by someone — and God is the one who has built all things.

<sup>3.5</sup> Moses was faithful in God's house as a servant, and he spoke of the things that God would say in the future.

<sup>3.6</sup> But Christ is faithful as the Son in charge of God's house. We are his house if we keep up our courage and our confidence in what we hope for.

<sup>3.7</sup> So then, as the Holy Spirit says, "If you hear God's voice today,

<sup>3.8</sup> do not be stubborn, as your ancestors were when they rebelled against God, as they were that day in the desert when they put him to the test.

<sup>3.9</sup> "There they put me to the test and tried me, says God, although they had seen what I did for forty years.

<sup>3.10</sup> "And so I was angry with those people and said, 'They are always disloyal and refuse to obey my commands.'

<sup>3.11</sup> "I was angry and made a solemn promise: 'They will never enter the land where I would have given them rest!'"

<sup>3.12</sup> My friends, be careful that none of you have a heart so evil and unbelieving that you will turn away from the living God.

<sup>3.13</sup> Instead, in order that none of you be deceived by sin and become stubborn, you must help one another every day, as long as the word "Today" in the scripture applies to us.

<sup>3.14</sup> For we are all partners with Christ if we hold firmly to the end the confidence we had at the beginning.

<sup>3.15</sup> This is what the scripture says: "If you hear God's voice today, do not be stubborn, as your ancestors were when they rebelled against

God."

<sup>3.16</sup> Who were the people who heard God's voice and rebelled against him? All those who were led out of Egypt by Moses.

<sup>3.17</sup> With whom was God angry for forty years? With the people who sinned, who fell down dead in the desert.

<sup>3.18</sup> When God made his solemn promise, "They will never enter the land where I would have given them rest" — of whom was he speaking? Of those who rebelled.

<sup>3.19</sup> We see, then, that they were not able to enter the land, because they did not believe.

# 4

<sup>4.1</sup> Now, God has offered us the promise that we may receive that rest he spoke about. Let us take care, then, that none of you will be found to have failed to receive that promised rest.

<sup>4.2</sup> For we have heard the Good News, just as they did. They heard the message, but it did them no good, because when they heard it, they did not accept it with faith.

<sup>4.3</sup> We who believe, then, do receive that rest which God promised. It is just as he said, "I was angry and made a solemn promise: 'They will never enter the land where I would have given them rest!'" He said this even though his work had been finished from the time he created the world.

<sup>4.4</sup> For somewhere in the Scriptures this is said about the seventh day: "God rested on the seventh day from all his work."

<sup>4.5</sup> This same matter is spoken of again: "They will never enter that land where I would have given them rest."

<sup>4.6</sup> Those who first heard the Good News did not receive that rest, because they did not believe. There are, then, others who are allowed to receive it.

<sup>4.7</sup> This is shown by the fact that God sets another day, which is called "Today." Many years later he spoke of it through David in the scripture already quoted: "If you hear God's voice today, do not be stubborn."

<sup>4.8</sup> If Joshua had given the people the rest that God had promised, God would not have spoken later about another day.

<sup>4.9</sup> As it is, however, there still remains for God's people a rest like God's resting on the seventh day.

<sup>4.10</sup> For those who receive that rest which God promised will rest from their own work, just as God rested from his.

<sup>4.11</sup> Let us, then, do our best to receive that rest, so that no one of us

will fail as they did because of their lack of faith.

<sup>4.12</sup> The word of God is alive and active, sharper than any double-edged sword. It cuts all the way through, to where soul and spirit meet, to where joints and marrow come together. It judges the desires and thoughts of the heart.

<sup>4.13</sup> There is nothing that can be hid from God; everything in all creation is exposed and lies open before his eyes. And it is to him that we must all give an account of ourselves.

<sup>4.14</sup> Let us, then, hold firmly to the faith we profess. For we have a great High Priest who has gone into the very presence of God — Jesus, the Son of God.

<sup>4.15</sup> Our High Priest is not one who cannot feel sympathy for our weaknesses. On the contrary, we have a High Priest who was tempted in every way that we are, but did not sin.

<sup>4.16</sup> Let us have confidence, then, and approach God's throne, where there is grace. There we will receive mercy and find grace to help us just when we need it.

# 5

<sup>5.1</sup> Every high priest is chosen from his fellow-men and appointed to serve God on their behalf, to offer sacrifices and offerings for sins.

<sup>5.2</sup> Since he himself is weak in many ways, he is able to be gentle with those who are ignorant and make mistakes.

<sup>5.3</sup> And because he is himself weak, he must offer sacrifices not only for the sins of the people but also for his own sins.

<sup>5.4</sup> No one chooses for himself the honor of being a high priest. It is only by God's call that a man is made a high priest — just as Aaron was.

<sup>5.5</sup> In the same way, Christ did not take upon himself the honor of being a high priest. Instead, God said to him, "You are my Son; today I have become your Father."

<sup>5.6</sup> He also said in another place, "You will be a priest forever, in the priestly order of Melchizedek."

<sup>5.7</sup> In his life on earth Jesus made his prayers and requests with loud cries and tears to God, who could save him from death. Because he was humble and devoted, God heard him.

<sup>5.8</sup> But even though he was God's Son, he learned through his sufferings to be obedient.

<sup>5.9</sup> When he was made perfect, he became the source of eternal salvation for all those who obey him,

<sup>5.10</sup> and God declared him to be high priest, in the priestly order of

Melchizedek.

<sup>5.11</sup> There is much we have to say about this matter, but it is hard to explain to you, because you are so slow to understand.

<sup>5.12</sup> There has been enough time for you to be teachers — yet you still need someone to teach you the first lessons of God's message. Instead of eating solid food, you still have to drink milk.

<sup>5.13</sup> Anyone who has to drink milk is still a child, without any experience in the matter of right and wrong.

<sup>5.14</sup> Solid food, on the other hand, is for adults, who through practice are able to distinguish between good and evil.

# 6

<sup>6.1</sup> Let us go forward, then, to mature teaching and leave behind us the first lessons of the Christian message. We should not lay again the foundation of turning away from useless works and believing in God;

<sup>6.2</sup> of the teaching about baptisms and the laying on of hands; of the resurrection of the dead and the eternal judgment.

<sup>6.3</sup> Let us go forward! And this is what we will do, if God allows.

<sup>6.4</sup> For how can those who abandon their faith be brought back to repent again? They were once in God's light; they tasted heaven's gift and received their share of the Holy Spirit;

<sup>6.5</sup> they knew from experience that God's word is good, and they had felt the powers of the coming age.

<sup>6.6</sup> And then they abandoned their faith! It is impossible to bring them back to repent again, because they are again crucifying the Son of God and exposing him to public shame.

<sup>6.7</sup> God blesses the soil which drinks in the rain that often falls on it and which grows plants that are useful to those for whom it is cultivated.

<sup>6.8</sup> But if it grows thorns and weeds, it is worth nothing; it is in danger of being cursed by God and will be destroyed by fire.

<sup>6.9</sup> But even if we speak like this, dear friends, we feel sure about you. We know that you have the better blessings that belong to your salvation.

<sup>6.10</sup> God is not unfair. He will not forget the work you did or the love you showed for him in the help you gave and are still giving to other Christians.

<sup>6.11</sup> Our great desire is that each of you keep up your eagerness to the end, so that the things you hope for will come true.

<sup>6.12</sup> We do not want you to become lazy, but to be like those who be-

lieve and are patient, and so receive what God has promised.

6.13 When God made his promise to Abraham, he made a vow to do what he had promised. Since there was no one greater than himself, he used his own name when he made his vow.

6.14 He said, "I promise you that I will bless you and give you many descendants."

6.15 Abraham was patient, and so he received what God had promised.

6.16 When we make a vow, we use the name of someone greater than ourselves, and the vow settles all arguments.

6.17 To those who were to receive what he promised, God wanted to make it very clear that he would never change his purpose; so he added his vow to the promise.

6.18 There are these two things, then, that cannot change and about which God cannot lie. So we who have found safety with him are greatly encouraged to hold firmly to the hope placed before us.

6.19 We have this hope as an anchor for our lives. It is safe and sure, and goes through the curtain of the heavenly temple into the inner sanctuary.

6.20 On our behalf Jesus has gone in there before us and has become a high priest forever, in the priestly order of Melchizedek.

# 7

7.1 This Melchizedek was king of Salem and a priest of the Most High God. As Abraham was coming back from the battle in which he defeated the four kings, Melchizedek met him and blessed him,

7.2 and Abraham gave him one tenth of all he had taken. (The first meaning of Melchizedek's name is "King of Righteousness"; and because he was king of Salem, his name also means "King of Peace.")

7.3 There is no record of Melchizedek's father or mother or of any of his ancestors; no record of his birth or of his death. He is like the Son of God; he remains a priest forever.

7.4 You see, then, how great he was. Abraham, our famous ancestor, gave him one tenth of all he got in the battle.

7.5 And those descendants of Levi who are priests are commanded by the Law to collect one tenth from the people of Israel, that is, from their own people, even though they are also descendants of Abraham.

7.6 Melchizedek was not descended from Levi, but he collected one tenth from Abraham and blessed him, the man who received God's promises.

<sup>7.7</sup> There is no doubt that the one who blesses is greater than the one who is blessed.

<sup>7.8</sup> In the case of the priests the tenth is collected by men who die; but as for Melchizedek the tenth was collected by one who lives, as the scripture says.

<sup>7.9</sup> And, so to speak, when Abraham paid the tenth, Levi (whose descendants collect the tenth) also paid it.

<sup>7.10</sup> For Levi had not yet been born, but was, so to speak, in the body of his ancestor Abraham when Melchizedek met him.

<sup>7.11</sup> It was on the basis of the levitical priesthood that the Law was given to the people of Israel. Now, if the work of the levitical priests had been perfect, there would have been no need for a different kind of priest to appear, one who is in the priestly order of Melchizedek, not of Aaron.

<sup>7.12</sup> For when the priesthood is changed, there also has to be a change in the law.

<sup>7.13</sup> And our Lord, of whom these things are said, belonged to a different tribe, and no member of his tribe ever served as a priest.

<sup>7.14</sup> It is well known that he was born a member of the tribe of Judah; and Moses did not mention this tribe when he spoke of priests.

<sup>7.15</sup> The matter becomes even plainer; a different priest has appeared, who is like Melchizedek.

<sup>7.16</sup> He was made a priest, not by human rules and regulations, but through the power of a life which has no end.

<sup>7.17</sup> For the scripture says, "You will be a priest forever, in the priestly order of Melchizedek."

<sup>7.18</sup> The old rule, then, is set aside, because it was weak and useless.

<sup>7.19</sup> For the Law of Moses could not make anything perfect. And now a better hope has been provided through which we come near to God.

<sup>7.20</sup> In addition, there is also God's vow. There was no such vow when the others were made priests.

<sup>7.21</sup> But Jesus became a priest by means of a vow when God said to him, "The Lord has made a solemn promise and will not take it back: 'You will be a priest forever.'"

<sup>7.22</sup> This difference, then, also makes Jesus the guarantee of a better covenant.

<sup>7.23</sup> There is another difference: there were many of those other priests, because they died and could not continue their work.

<sup>7.24</sup> But Jesus lives on forever, and his work as priest does not pass on to someone else.

<sup>7.25</sup> And so he is able, now and always, to save those who come to God through him, because he lives forever to plead with God for them.

<sup>7.26</sup> Jesus, then, is the High Priest that meets our needs. He is holy; he has no fault or sin in him; he has been set apart from sinners and raised above the heavens.

<sup>7.27</sup> He is not like other high priests; he does not need to offer sacrifices every day for his own sins first and then for the sins of the people. He offered one sacrifice, once and for all, when he offered himself.

<sup>7.28</sup> The Law of Moses appoints men who are imperfect to be high priests; but God's promise made with the vow, which came later than the Law, appoints the Son, who has been made perfect forever.

# 8

<sup>8.1</sup> The whole point of what we are saying is that we have such a High Priest, who sits at the right of the throne of the Divine Majesty in heaven.

<sup>8.2</sup> He serves as high priest in the Most Holy Place, that is, in the real tent which was put up by the Lord, not by human hands.

<sup>8.3</sup> Every high priest is appointed to present offerings and animal sacrifices to God, and so our High Priest must also have something to offer.

<sup>8.4</sup> If he were on earth, he would not be a priest at all, since there are priests who offer the gifts required by the Jewish Law.

<sup>8.5</sup> The work they do as priests is really only a copy and a shadow of what is in heaven. It is the same as it was with Moses. When he was about to build the Sacred Tent, God told him, "Be sure to make everything according to the pattern you were shown on the mountain."

<sup>8.6</sup> But now, Jesus has been given priestly work which is superior to theirs, just as the covenant which he arranged between God and his people is a better one, because it is based on promises of better things.

<sup>8.7</sup> If there had been nothing wrong with the first covenant, there would have been no need for a second one.

<sup>8.8</sup> But God finds fault with his people when he says, "The days are coming, says the Lord, when I will draw up a new covenant with the people of Israel and with the people of Judah.

<sup>8.9</sup> "It will not be like the covenant that I made with their ancestors on the day I took them by the hand and led them out of Egypt. They were not faithful to the covenant I made with them, and so I paid no attention to them.

<sup>8.10</sup> "Now, this is the covenant that I will make with the people of

Israel in the days to come, says the Lord: I will put my laws in their minds and write them on their hearts. I will be their God, and they will be my people.

8.11 "None of them will have to teach their friends or tell their neighbors, 'Know the Lord.' For they will all know me, from the least to the greatest.

8.12 "I will forgive their sins and will no longer remember their wrongs."

8.13 By speaking of a new covenant, God has made the first one old; and anything that becomes old and worn out will soon disappear.

# 9

9.1 The first covenant had rules for worship and a place made for worship as well.

9.2 A tent was put up, the outer one, which was called the Holy Place. In it were the lampstand and the table with the bread offered to God.

9.3 Behind the second curtain was the tent called the Most Holy Place.

9.4 In it were the gold altar for the burning of incense and the Covenant Box all covered with gold and containing the gold jar with the manna in it, Aaron's stick that had sprouted leaves, and the two stone tablets with the commandments written on them.

9.5 Above the Box were the winged creatures representing God's presence, with their wings spread over the place where sins were forgiven. But now is not the time to explain everything in detail.

9.6 This is how those things have been arranged. The priests go into the outer tent every day to perform their duties,

9.7 but only the high priest goes into the inner tent, and he does so only once a year. He takes with him blood which he offers to God on behalf of himself and for the sins which the people have committed without knowing they were sinning.

9.8 The Holy Spirit clearly teaches from all these arrangements that the way into the Most Holy Place has not yet been opened as long as the outer tent still stands.

9.9 This is a symbol which points to the present time. It means that the offerings and animal sacrifices presented to God cannot make the worshiper's heart perfect,

9.10 since they have to do only with food, drink, and various purification ceremonies. These are all outward rules, which apply only until the time when God will establish the new order.

<sup>9.11</sup> But Christ has already come as the High Priest of the good things that are already here. The tent in which he serves is greater and more perfect; it is not a tent made by human hands, that is, it is not a part of this created world.

<sup>9.12</sup> When Christ went through the tent and entered once and for all into the Most Holy Place, he did not take the blood of goats and bulls to offer as a sacrifice; rather, he took his own blood and obtained eternal salvation for us.

<sup>9.13</sup> The blood of goats and bulls and the ashes of a burnt calf are sprinkled on the people who are ritually unclean, and this purifies them by taking away their ritual impurity.

<sup>9.14</sup> Since this is true, how much more is accomplished by the blood of Christ! Through the eternal Spirit he offered himself as a perfect sacrifice to God. His blood will purify our consciences from useless rituals, so that we may serve the living God.

<sup>9.15</sup> For this reason Christ is the one who arranges a new covenant, so that those who have been called by God may receive the eternal blessings that God has promised. This can be done because there has been a death which sets people free from the wrongs they did while the first covenant was in effect.

<sup>9.16</sup> In the case of a will it is necessary to prove that the person who made it has died,

<sup>9.17</sup> for a will means nothing while the person who made it is alive; it goes into effect only after his death.

<sup>9.18</sup> That is why even the first covenant went into effect only with the use of blood.

<sup>9.19</sup> First, Moses proclaimed to the people all the commandments as set forth in the Law. Then he took the blood of bulls and goats, mixed it with water, and sprinkled it on the book of the Law and all the people, using a sprig of hyssop and some red wool.

<sup>9.20</sup> He said, "This is the blood which seals the covenant that God has commanded you to obey."

<sup>9.21</sup> In the same way Moses also sprinkled the blood on the Sacred Tent and over all the things used in worship.

<sup>9.22</sup> Indeed, according to the Law almost everything is purified by blood, and sins are forgiven only if blood is poured out.

<sup>9.23</sup> Those things, which are copies of the heavenly originals, had to be purified in that way. But the heavenly things themselves require much better sacrifices.

<sup>9.24</sup> For Christ did not go into a Holy Place made by human hands, which was a copy of the real one. He went into heaven itself, where

he now appears on our behalf in the presence of God.

<sup>9.25</sup> The Jewish high priest goes into the Most Holy Place every year with the blood of an animal. But Christ did not go in to offer himself many times,

<sup>9.26</sup> for then he would have had to suffer many times ever since the creation of the world. Instead, now when all ages of time are nearing the end, he has appeared once and for all, to remove sin through the sacrifice of himself.

<sup>9.27</sup> Everyone must die once, and after that be judged by God.

<sup>9.28</sup> In the same manner Christ also was offered in sacrifice once to take away the sins of many. He will appear a second time, not to deal with sin, but to save those who are waiting for him.

# 10

<sup>10.1</sup> The Jewish Law is not a full and faithful model of the real things; it is only a faint outline of the good things to come. The same sacrifices are offered forever, year after year. How can the Law, then, by means of these sacrifices make perfect the people who come to God?

<sup>10.2</sup> If the people worshiping God had really been purified from their sins, they would not feel guilty of sin any more, and all sacrifices would stop.

<sup>10.3</sup> As it is, however, the sacrifices serve year after year to remind people of their sins.

<sup>10.4</sup> For the blood of bulls and goats can never take away sins.

<sup>10.5</sup> For this reason, when Christ was about to come into the world, he said to God: "You do not want sacrifices and offerings, but you have prepared a body for me.

<sup>10.6</sup> "You are not pleased with animals burned whole on the altar or with sacrifices to take away sins.

<sup>10.7</sup> "Then I said, 'Here I am, to do your will, O God, just as it is written of me in the book of the Law.'"

<sup>10.8</sup> First he said, "You neither want nor are you pleased with sacrifices and offerings or with animals burned on the altar and the sacrifices to take away sins." He said this even though all these sacrifices are offered according to the Law.

<sup>10.9</sup> Then he said, "Here I am, O God, to do your will." So God does away with all the old sacrifices and puts the sacrifice of Christ in their place.

<sup>10.10</sup> Because Jesus Christ did what God wanted him to do, we are all purified from sin by the offering that he made of his own body once and for all.

<sup></sup> Every Jewish priest performs his services every day and offers the same sacrifices many times; but these sacrifices can never take away sins.

10.12 Christ, however, offered one sacrifice for sins, an offering that is effective forever, and then he sat down at the right side of God.

10.13 There he now waits until God puts his enemies as a footstool under his feet.

10.14 With one sacrifice, then, he has made perfect forever those who are purified from sin.

10.15 And the Holy Spirit also gives us his witness. First he says,

10.16 "This is the covenant that I will make with them in the days to come, says the Lord: I will put my laws in their hearts and write them on their minds."

10.17 And then he says, "I will not remember their sins and evil deeds any longer."

10.18 So when these have been forgiven, an offering to take away sins is no longer needed.

10.19 We have, then, my friends, complete freedom to go into the Most Holy Place by means of the death of Jesus.

10.20 He opened for us a new way, a living way, through the curtain — that is, through his own body.

10.21 We have a great priest in charge of the house of God.

10.22 So let us come near to God with a sincere heart and a sure faith, with hearts that have been purified from a guilty conscience and with bodies washed with clean water.

10.23 Let us hold on firmly to the hope we profess, because we can trust God to keep his promise.

10.24 Let us be concerned for one another, to help one another to show love and to do good.

10.25 Let us not give up the habit of meeting together, as some are doing. Instead, let us encourage one another all the more, since you see that the Day of the Lord is coming nearer.

10.26 For there is no longer any sacrifice that will take away sins if we purposely go on sinning after the truth has been made known to us.

10.27 Instead, all that is left is to wait in fear for the coming Judgment and the fierce fire which will destroy those who oppose God!

10.28 Anyone who disobeys the Law of Moses is put to death without any mercy when judged guilty from the evidence of two or more witnesses.

10.29 What, then, of those who despise the Son of God? who treat as a cheap thing the blood of God's covenant which purified them from sin? who insult the Spirit of grace? Just think how much worse is the punishment they will deserve!

<sup>10.30</sup> For we know who said, "I will take revenge, I will repay"; and who also said, "The Lord will judge his people."

<sup>10.31</sup> It is a terrifying thing to fall into the hands of the living God!

<sup>10.32</sup> Remember how it was with you in the past. In those days, after God's light had shone on you, you suffered many things, yet were not defeated by the struggle.

<sup>10.33</sup> You were at times publicly insulted and mistreated, and at other times you were ready to join those who were being treated in this way.

<sup>10.34</sup> You shared the sufferings of prisoners, and when all your belongings were seized, you endured your loss gladly, because you knew that you still possessed something much better, which would last forever.

<sup>10.35</sup> Do not lose your courage, then, because it brings with it a great reward.

<sup>10.36</sup> You need to be patient, in order to do the will of God and receive what he promises.

<sup>10.37</sup> For, as the scripture says, "Just a little while longer, and he who is coming will come; he will not delay.

<sup>10.38</sup> "My righteous people, however, will believe and live; but if any of them turns back, I will not be pleased with them."

<sup>10.39</sup> We are not people who turn back and are lost. Instead, we have faith and are saved.

# 11

<sup>11.1</sup> To have faith is to be sure of the things we hope for, to be certain of the things we cannot see.

<sup>11.2</sup> It was by their faith that people of ancient times won God's approval.

<sup>11.3</sup> It is by faith that we understand that the universe was created by God's word, so that what can be seen was made out of what cannot be seen.

<sup>11.4</sup> It was faith that made Abel offer to God a better sacrifice than Cain's. Through his faith he won God's approval as a righteous man, because God himself approved of his gifts. By means of his faith Abel still speaks, even though he is dead.

<sup>11.5</sup> It was faith that kept Enoch from dying. Instead, he was taken up to God, and nobody could find him, because God had taken him up. The scripture says that before Enoch was taken up, he had

pleased God.

<sup>11.6</sup> No one can please God without faith, for whoever comes to God must have faith that God exists and rewards those who seek him.

<sup>11.7</sup> It was faith that made Noah hear God's warnings about things in the future that he could not see. He obeyed God and built a boat in which he and his family were saved. As a result, the world was condemned, and Noah received from God the righteousness that comes by faith.

<sup>11.8</sup> It was faith that made Abraham obey when God called him to go out to a country which God had promised to give him. He left his own country without knowing where he was going.

<sup>11.9</sup> By faith he lived as a foreigner in the country that God had promised him. He lived in tents, as did Isaac and Jacob, who received the same promise from God.

<sup>11.10</sup> For Abraham was waiting for the city which God has designed and built, the city with permanent foundations.

<sup>11.11</sup> It was faith that made Abraham able to become a father, even though he was too old and Sarah herself could not have children. He trusted God to keep his promise.

<sup>11.12</sup> Though Abraham was practically dead, from this one man came as many descendants as there are stars in the sky, as many as the numberless grains of sand on the seashore.

<sup>11.13</sup> It was in faith that all these persons died. They did not receive the things God had promised, but from a long way off they saw them and welcomed them, and admitted openly that they were foreigners and refugees on earth.

<sup>11.14</sup> Those who say such things make it clear that they are looking for a country of their own.

<sup>11.15</sup> They did not keep thinking about the country they had left; if they had, they would have had the chance to return.

<sup>11.16</sup> Instead, it was a better country they longed for, the heavenly country. And so God is not ashamed for them to call him their God, because he has prepared a city for them.

<sup>11.17</sup> It was faith that made Abraham offer his son Isaac as a sacrifice when God put Abraham to the test. Abraham was the one to whom God had made the promise, yet he was ready to offer his only son as a sacrifice.

<sup>11.18</sup> God had said to him, "It is through Isaac that you will have the descendants I promised."

<sup>11.19</sup> Abraham reckoned that God was able to raise Isaac from death — and, so to speak, Abraham did receive Isaac back from death.

<sup>11.20</sup> It was faith that made Isaac promise blessings for the future to Jacob and Esau.

<sup>11.21</sup> It was faith that made Jacob bless each of the sons of Joseph just before he died. He leaned on the top of his walking stick and worshiped God.

<sup>11.22</sup> It was faith that made Joseph, when he was about to die, speak of the departure of the Israelites from Egypt, and leave instructions about what should be done with his body.

<sup>11.23</sup> It was faith that made the parents of Moses hide him for three months after he was born. They saw that he was a beautiful child, and they were not afraid to disobey the king's order.

<sup>11.24</sup> It was faith that made Moses, when he had grown up, refuse to be called the son of the king's daughter.

<sup>11.25</sup> He preferred to suffer with God's people rather than to enjoy sin for a little while.

<sup>11.26</sup> He reckoned that to suffer scorn for the Messiah was worth far more than all the treasures of Egypt, for he kept his eyes on the future reward.

<sup>11.27</sup> It was faith that made Moses leave Egypt without being afraid of the king's anger. As though he saw the invisible God, he refused to turn back.

<sup>11.28</sup> It was faith that made him establish the Passover and order the blood to be sprinkled on the doors, so that the Angel of Death would not kill the first-born sons of the Israelites.

<sup>11.29</sup> It was faith that made the Israelites able to cross the Red Sea as if on dry land; when the Egyptians tried to do it, the water swallowed them up.

<sup>11.30</sup> It was faith that made the walls of Jericho fall down after the Israelites had marched around them for seven days.

<sup>11.31</sup> It was faith that kept the prostitute Rahab from being killed with those who disobeyed God, for she gave the Israelite spies a friendly welcome.

<sup>11.32</sup> Should I go on? There isn't enough time for me to speak of Gideon, Barak, Samson, Jephthah, David, Samuel, and the prophets.

<sup>11.33</sup> Through faith they fought whole countries and won. They did what was right and received what God had promised. They shut the mouths of lions,

<sup>11.34</sup> put out fierce fires, escaped being killed by the sword. They were weak, but became strong; they were mighty in battle and defeated the armies of foreigners.

<sup>11.35</sup> Through faith women received their dead relatives raised back to

life. Others, refusing to accept freedom, died under torture in order to be raised to a better life.

<sup>11.36</sup> Some were mocked and whipped, and others were put in chains and taken off to prison.

<sup>11.37</sup> They were stoned, they were sawed in two, they were killed by the sword. They went around clothed in skins of sheep or goats — poor, persecuted, and mistreated.

<sup>11.38</sup> The world was not good enough for them! They wandered like refugees in the deserts and hills, living in caves and holes in the ground.

<sup>11.39</sup> What a record all of these have won by their faith! Yet they did not receive what God had promised,

<sup>11.40</sup> because God had decided on an even better plan for us. His purpose was that only in company with us would they be made perfect.

# 12

<sup>12.1</sup> As for us, we have this large crowd of witnesses around us. So then, let us rid ourselves of everything that gets in the way, and of the sin which holds on to us so tightly, and let us run with determination the race that lies before us.

<sup>12.2</sup> Let us keep our eyes fixed on Jesus, on whom our faith depends from beginning to end. He did not give up because of the cross! On the contrary, because of the joy that was waiting for him, he thought nothing of the disgrace of dying on the cross, and he is now seated at the right side of God's throne.

<sup>12.3</sup> Think of what he went through; how he put up with so much hatred from sinners! So do not let yourselves become discouraged and give up.

<sup>12.4</sup> For in your struggle against sin you have not yet had to resist to the point of being killed.

<sup>12.5</sup> Have you forgotten the encouraging words which God speaks to you as his children? "My child, pay attention when the Lord corrects you, and do not be discouraged when he rebukes you.

<sup>12.6</sup> "Because the Lord corrects everyone he loves, and punishes everyone he accepts as a child."

<sup>12.7</sup> Endure what you suffer as being a father's punishment; your suffering shows that God is treating you as his children. Was there ever a child who was not punished by his father?

<sup>12.8</sup> If you are not punished, as all his children are, it means you are not real children, but bastards.

<sup>12.9</sup> In the case of our human fathers, they punished us and we re-

spected them. How much more, then, should we submit to our spiritual Father and live!

¹²·¹⁰ Our human fathers punished us for a short time, as it seemed right to them; but God does it for our own good, so that we may share his holiness.

¹²·¹¹ When we are punished, it seems to us at the time something to make us sad, not glad. Later, however, those who have been disciplined by such punishment reap the peaceful reward of a righteous life.

¹²·¹² Lift up your tired hands, then, and strengthen your trembling knees!

¹²·¹³ Keep walking on straight paths, so that the lame foot may not be disabled, but instead be healed.

¹²·¹⁴ Try to be at peace with everyone, and try to live a holy life, because no one will see the Lord without it.

¹²·¹⁵ Guard against turning back from the grace of God. Let no one become like a bitter plant that grows up and causes many troubles with its poison.

¹²·¹⁶ Let no one become immoral or unspiritual like Esau, who for a single meal sold his rights as the older son.

¹²·¹⁷ Afterward, you know, he wanted to receive his father's blessing; but he was turned back, because he could not find any way to change what he had done, even though in tears he looked for it.

¹²·¹⁸ You have not come, as the people of Israel came, to what you can feel, to Mount Sinai with its blazing fire, the darkness and the gloom, the storm,

¹²·¹⁹ the blast of a trumpet, and the sound of a voice. When the people heard the voice, they begged not to hear another word,

¹²·²⁰ because they could not bear the order which said, "If even an animal touches the mountain, it must be stoned to death."

¹²·²¹ The sight was so terrifying that Moses said, "I am trembling and afraid!"

¹²·²² Instead, you have come to Mount Zion and to the city of the living God, the heavenly Jerusalem, with its thousands of angels.

¹²·²³ You have come to the joyful gathering of God's first-born, whose names are written in heaven. You have come to God, who is the judge of all people, and to the spirits of good people made perfect.

¹²·²⁴ You have come to Jesus, who arranged the new covenant, and to the sprinkled blood that promises much better things than does the blood of Abel.

¹²·²⁵ Be careful, then, and do not refuse to hear him who speaks.

Those who refused to hear the one who gave the divine message on earth did not escape. How much less shall we escape, then, if we turn away from the one who speaks from heaven!

<sup></sup>12.26 His voice shook the earth at that time, but now he has promised, "I will once more shake not only the earth but heaven as well."

12.27 The words "once more" plainly show that the created things will be shaken and removed, so that the things that cannot be shaken will remain.

12.28 Let us be thankful, then, because we receive a kingdom that cannot be shaken. Let us be grateful and worship God in a way that will please him, with reverence and awe;

12.29 because our God is indeed a destroying fire.

# 13

13.1 Keep on loving one another as Christians.

13.2 Remember to welcome strangers in your homes. There were some who did that and welcomed angels without knowing it.

13.3 Remember those who are in prison, as though you were in prison with them. Remember those who are suffering, as though you were suffering as they are.

13.4 Marriage is to be honored by all, and husbands and wives must be faithful to each other. God will judge those who are immoral and those who commit adultery.

13.5 Keep your lives free from the love of money, and be satisfied with what you have. For God has said, "I will never leave you; I will never abandon you."

13.6 Let us be bold, then, and say, "The Lord is my helper, I will not be afraid. What can anyone do to me?"

13.7 Remember your former leaders, who spoke God's message to you. Think back on how they lived and died, and imitate their faith.

13.8 Jesus Christ is the same yesterday, today, and forever.

13.9 Do not let all kinds of strange teachings lead you from the right way. It is good to receive inner strength from God's grace, and not by obeying rules about foods; those who obey these rules have not been helped by them.

13.10 The priests who serve in the Jewish place of worship have no right to eat any of the sacrifice on our altar.

13.11 The Jewish high priest brings the blood of the animals into the Most Holy Place to offer it as a sacrifice for sins; but the bodies of the animals are burned outside the camp.

13.12 For this reason Jesus also died outside the city, in order to purify the people from sin with his own blood.

<sup>13.13</sup> Let us, then, go to him outside the camp and share his shame.

<sup>13.14</sup> For there is no permanent city for us here on earth; we are looking for the city which is to come.

<sup>13.15</sup> Let us, then, always offer praise to God as our sacrifice through Jesus, which is the offering presented by lips that confess him as Lord.

<sup>13.16</sup> Do not forget to do good and to help one another, because these are the sacrifices that please God.

<sup>13.17</sup> Obey your leaders and follow their orders. They watch over your souls without resting, since they must give to God an account of their service. If you obey them, they will do their work gladly; if not, they will do it with sadness, and that would be of no help to you.

<sup>13.18</sup> Keep on praying for us. We are sure we have a clear conscience, because we want to do the right thing at all times.

<sup>13.19</sup> And I beg you even more earnestly to pray that God will send me back to you soon.

<sup>13.20-21</sup> God has raised from death our Lord Jesus, who is the Great Shepherd of the sheep as the result of his blood, by which the eternal covenant is sealed. May the God of peace provide you with every good thing you need in order to do his will, and may he, through Jesus Christ, do in us what pleases him. And to Christ be the glory forever and ever! Amen.

<sup>13.22</sup> I beg you, my friends, to listen patiently to this message of encouragement; for this letter I have written you is not very long.

<sup>13.23</sup> I want you to know that our brother Timothy has been let out of prison. If he comes soon enough, I will have him with me when I see you.

<sup>13.24</sup> Give our greetings to all your leaders and to all God's people. The believers from Italy send you their greetings.

<sup>13.25</sup> May God's grace be with you all.

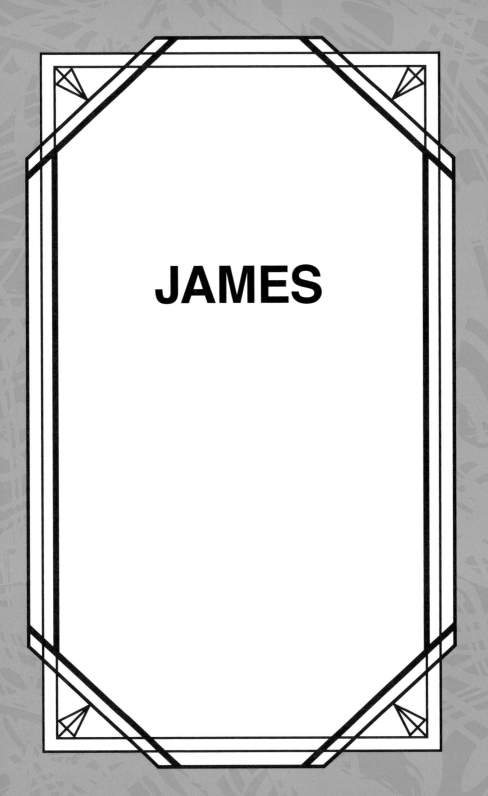

# JAMES

# James

**1**

<sup>1.1</sup> From James, a servant of God and of the Lord Jesus Christ: Greetings to all God's people scattered over the whole world.

<sup>1.2</sup> My friends, consider yourselves fortunate when all kinds of trials come your way,

<sup>1.3</sup> for you know that when your faith succeeds in facing such trials, the result is the ability to endure.

<sup>1.4</sup> Make sure that your endurance carries you all the way without failing, so that you may be perfect and complete, lacking nothing.

<sup>1.5</sup> But if any of you lack wisdom, you should pray to God, who will give it to you; because God gives generously and graciously to all.

<sup>1.6</sup> But when you pray, you must believe and not doubt at all. Whoever doubts is like a wave in the sea that is driven and blown about by the wind.

<sup>1.7-8</sup> If you are like that, unable to make up your mind and undecided in all you do, you must not think that you will receive anything from the Lord.

<sup>1.9</sup> Those Christians who are poor must be glad when God lifts them up,

<sup>1.10</sup> and the rich Christians must be glad when God brings them down. For the rich will pass away like the flower of a wild plant.

<sup>1.11</sup> The sun rises with its blazing heat and burns the plant; its flower falls off, and its beauty is destroyed. In the same way the rich will be destroyed while they go about their business.

<sup>1.12</sup> Happy are those who remain faithful under trials, because when they succeed in passing such a test, they will receive as their reward the life which God has promised to those who love him.

<sup>1.13</sup> If we are tempted by such trials, we must not say, "This temptation comes from God." For God cannot be tempted by evil, and he himself tempts no one.

<sup>1.14</sup> But we are tempted when we are drawn away and trapped by our own evil desires.

<sup>1.15</sup> Then our evil desires conceive and give birth to sin; and sin, when it is full-grown, gives birth to death.

<sup>1.16</sup> Do not be deceived, my dear friends!

<sup>1.17</sup> Every good gift and every perfect present comes from heaven; it comes down from God, the Creator of the heavenly lights, who does not change or cause darkness by turning.

1.18 By his own will he brought us into being through the word of truth, so that we should have first place among all his creatures.

1.19 Remember this, my dear friends! Everyone must be quick to listen, but slow to speak and slow to become angry.

1.20 Human anger does not achieve God's righteous purpose.

1.21 So get rid of every filthy habit and all wicked conduct. Submit to God and accept the word that he plants in your hearts, which is able to save you.

1.22 Do not deceive yourselves by just listening to his word; instead, put it into practice.

1.23 If you listen to the word, but do not put it into practice you are like people who look in a mirror and see themselves as they are.

1.24 They take a good look at themselves and then go away and at once forget what they look like.

1.25 But if you look closely into the perfect law that sets people free, and keep on paying attention to it and do not simply listen and then forget it, but put it into practice — you will be blessed by God in what you do.

1.26 Do any of you think you are religious? If you do not control your tongue, your religion is worthless and you deceive yourself.

1.27 What God the Father considers to be pure and genuine religion is this: to take care of orphans and widows in their suffering and to keep oneself from being corrupted by the world.

# 2

2.1 My friends, as believers in our Lord Jesus Christ, the Lord of glory, you must never treat people in different ways according to their outward appearance.

2.2 Suppose a rich man wearing a gold ring and fine clothes comes to your meeting, and a poor man in ragged clothes also comes.

2.3 If you show more respect to the well-dressed man and say to him, "Have this best seat here," but say to the poor man, "Stand over there, or sit here on the floor by my feet,"

2.4 then you are guilty of creating distinctions among yourselves and of making judgments based on evil motives.

2.5 Listen, my dear friends! God chose the poor people of this world to be rich in faith and to possess the kingdom which he promised to those who love him.

2.6 But you dishonor the poor! Who are the ones who oppress you and drag you before the judges? The rich!

2.7 They are the ones who speak evil of that good name which has been given to you.

2.8 You will be doing the right thing if you obey the law of the Kingdom, which is found in the scripture, "Love your neighbor as you love yourself."

2.9 But if you treat people according to their outward appearance, you are guilty of sin, and the Law condemns you as a lawbreaker.

2.10 Whoever breaks one commandment is guilty of breaking them all.

2.11 For the same one who said, "Do not commit adultery," also said, "Do not commit murder." Even if you do not commit adultery, you have become a lawbreaker if you commit murder.

2.12 Speak and act as people who will be judged by the law that sets us free.

2.13 For God will not show mercy when he judges the person who has not been merciful; but mercy triumphs over judgment.

2.14 My friends, what good is it for one of you to say that you have faith if your actions do not prove it? Can that faith save you?

2.15 Suppose there are brothers or sisters who need clothes and don't have enough to eat.

2.16 What good is there in your saying to them, "God bless you! Keep warm and eat well!" — if you don't give them the necessities of life?

2.17 So it is with faith: if it is alone and includes no actions, then it is dead.

2.18 But someone will say, "One person has faith, another has actions." My answer is, "Show me how anyone can have faith without actions. I will show you my faith by my actions."

2.19 Do you believe that there is only one God? Good! The demons also believe — and tremble with fear.

2.20 You fool! Do you want to be shown that faith without actions is useless?

2.21 How was our ancestor Abraham put right with God? It was through his actions, when he offered his son Isaac on the altar.

2.22 Can't you see? His faith and his actions worked together; his faith was made perfect through his actions.

2.23 And the scripture came true that said, "Abraham believed God, and because of his faith God accepted him as righteous." And so Abraham was called God's friend.

2.24 You see, then, that it is by our actions that we are put right with God, and not by our faith alone.

2.25 It was the same with the prostitute Rahab. She was put right with God through her actions, by welcoming the Israelite spies and helping them to escape by a different road.

<sup>2.26</sup> So then, as the body without the spirit is dead, also faith without actions is dead.

# 3

<sup>3.1</sup> My friends, not many of you should become teachers. As you know, we teachers will be judged with greater strictness than others.

<sup>3.2</sup> All of us often make mistakes. But if a person never makes a mistake in what he says, he is perfect and is also able to control his whole being.

<sup>3.3</sup> We put a bit into the mouth of a horse to make it obey us, and we are able to make it go where we want.

<sup>3.4</sup> Or think of a ship: big as it is and driven by such strong winds, it can be steered by a very small rudder, and it goes wherever the pilot wants it to go.

<sup>3.5</sup> So it is with the tongue: small as it is, it can boast about great things. Just think how large a forest can be set on fire by a tiny flame!

<sup>3.6</sup> And the tongue is like a fire. It is a world of wrong, occupying its place in our bodies and spreading evil through our whole being. It sets on fire the entire course of our existence with the fire that comes to it from hell itself.

<sup>3.7</sup> We humans are able to tame and have tamed all other creatures — wild animals and birds, reptiles and fish.

<sup>3.8</sup> But no one has ever been able to tame the tongue. It is evil and uncontrollable, full of deadly poison.

<sup>3.9</sup> We use it to give thanks to our Lord and Father and also to curse other people, who are created in the likeness of God.

<sup>3.10</sup> Words of thanksgiving and cursing pour out from the same mouth. My friends, this should not happen!

<sup>3.11</sup> No spring of water pours out sweet water and bitter water from the same opening.

<sup>3.12</sup> A fig tree, my friends, cannot bear olives; a grapevine cannot bear figs, nor can a salty spring produce sweet water.

<sup>3.13</sup> Are there any of you who are wise and understanding? You are to prove it by your good life, by your good deeds performed with humility and wisdom.

<sup>3.14</sup> But if in your heart you are jealous, bitter, and selfish, don't sin against the truth by boasting of your wisdom.

<sup>3.15</sup> Such wisdom does not come down from heaven; it belongs to the world, it is unspiritual and demonic.

<sup>3.16</sup> Where there is jealousy and selfishness, there is also disorder and every kind of evil.

<sup>3.17</sup> But the wisdom from above is pure first of all; it is also peaceful, gentle, and friendly; it is full of compassion and produces a harvest of good deeds; it is free from prejudice and hypocrisy.

<sup>3.18</sup> And goodness is the harvest that is produced from the seeds the peacemakers plant in peace.

# 4

<sup>4.1</sup> Where do all the fights and quarrels among you come from? They come from your desires for pleasure, which are constantly fighting within you.

<sup>4.2</sup> You want things, but you cannot have them, so you are ready to kill; you strongly desire things, but you cannot get them, so you quarrel and fight. You do not have what you want because you do not ask God for it.

<sup>4.3</sup> And when you ask, you do not receive it, because your motives are bad; you ask for things to use for your own pleasures.

<sup>4.4</sup> Unfaithful people! Don't you know that to be the world's friend means to be God's enemy? If you want to be the world's friend, you make yourself God's enemy.

<sup>4.5</sup> Don't think that there is no truth in the scripture that says, "The spirit that God placed in us is filled with fierce desires."

<sup>4.6</sup> But the grace that God gives is even stronger. As the scripture says, "God resists the proud, but gives grace to the humble."

<sup>4.7</sup> So then, submit yourselves to God. Resist the Devil, and he will run away from you.

<sup>4.8</sup> Come near to God, and he will come near to you. Wash your hands, you sinners! Purify your hearts, you hypocrites!

<sup>4.9</sup> Be sorrowful, cry, and weep; change your laughter into crying, your joy into gloom!

<sup>4.10</sup> Humble yourselves before the Lord, and he will lift you up.

<sup>4.11</sup> Do not criticize one another, my friends. If you criticize or judge another Christian, you criticize and judge the Law. If you judge the Law, then you are no longer one who obeys the Law, but one who judges it.

<sup>4.12</sup> God is the only lawgiver and judge. He alone can save and destroy. Who do you think you are, to judge someone else?

<sup>4.13</sup> Now listen to me, you that say, "Today or tomorrow we will travel to a certain city, where we will stay a year and go into business and make a lot of money."

<sup></sup>4.14 You don't even know what your life tomorrow will be! You are like a puff of smoke, which appears for a moment and then disappears.
4.15 What you should say is this: "If the Lord is willing, we will live and do this or that."
4.16 But now you are proud, and you boast; all such boasting is wrong.
4.17 So then, if we do not do the good we know we should do, we are guilty of sin.

# 5

5.1 And now, you rich people, listen to me! Weep and wail over the miseries that are coming upon you!
5.2 Your riches have rotted away, and your clothes have been eaten by moths.
5.3 Your gold and silver are covered with rust, and this rust will be a witness against you and will eat up your flesh like fire. You have piled up riches in these last days.
5.4 You have not paid any wages to those who work in your fields. Listen to their complaints! The cries of those who gather in your crops have reached the ears of God, the Lord Almighty.
5.5 Your life here on earth has been full of luxury and pleasure. You have made yourselves fat for the day of slaughter.
5.6 You have condemned and murdered innocent people, and they do not resist you.
5.7 Be patient, then, my friends, until the Lord comes. See how patient farmers are as they wait for their land to produce precious crops. They wait patiently for the autumn and spring rains.
5.8 You also must be patient. Keep your hopes high, for the day of the Lord's coming is near.
5.9 Do not complain against one another, my friends, so that God will not judge you. The Judge is near, ready to appear.
5.10 My friends, remember the prophets who spoke in the name of the Lord. Take them as examples of patient endurance under suffering.
5.11 We call them happy because they endured. You have heard of Job's patience, and you know how the Lord provided for him in the end. For the Lord is full of mercy and compassion.
5.12 Above all, my friends, do not use an oath when you make a promise. Do not swear by heaven or by earth or by anything else. Say only "Yes" when you mean yes, and "No" when you mean no, and then you will not come under God's judgment.
5.13 Are any among you in trouble? They should pray. Are any among you happy? They should sing praises.

5.14 Are any among you sick? They should send for the church elders, who will pray for them and rub olive oil on them in the name of the Lord.

5.15 This prayer made in faith will heal the sick; the Lord will restore them to health, and the sins they have committed will be forgiven.

5.16 So then, confess your sins to one another and pray for one another, so that you will be healed. The prayer of a good person has a powerful effect.

5.17 Elijah was the same kind of person as we are. He prayed earnestly that there would be no rain, and no rain fell on the land for three and a half years.

5.18 Once again he prayed, and the sky poured out its rain and the earth produced its crops.

5.19 My friends, if any of you wander away from the truth and another one brings you back again,

5.20 remember this: whoever turns a sinner back from the wrong way will save that sinner's soul from death and bring about the forgiveness of many sins.

# 1 PETER

# 1 Peter

1

<sup>1.1</sup> From Peter, apostle of Jesus Christ – To God's chosen people who live as refugees scattered throughout the provinces of Pontus, Galatia, Cappadocia, Asia, and Bithynia.

<sup>1.2</sup> You were chosen according to the purpose of God the Father and were made a holy people by his Spirit, to obey Jesus Christ and be purified by his blood. May grace and peace be yours in full measure.

<sup>1.3</sup> Let us give thanks to the God and Father of our Lord Jesus Christ! Because of his great mercy he gave us new life by raising Jesus Christ from death. This fills us with a living hope,

<sup>1.4</sup> and so we look forward to possessing the rich blessings that God keeps for his people. He keeps them for you in heaven, where they cannot decay or spoil or fade away.

<sup>1.5</sup> They are for you, who through faith are kept safe by God's power for the salvation which is ready to be revealed at the end of time.

<sup>1.6</sup> Be glad about this, even though it may now be necessary for you to be sad for a while because of the many kinds of trials you suffer.

<sup>1.7</sup> Their purpose is to prove that your faith is genuine. Even gold, which can be destroyed, is tested by fire; and so your faith, which is much more precious than gold, must also be tested, so that it may endure. Then you will receive praise and glory and honor on the Day when Jesus Christ is revealed.

<sup>1.8</sup> You love him, although you have not seen him, and you believe in him, although you do not now see him. So you rejoice with a great and glorious joy which words cannot express,

<sup>1.9</sup> because you are receiving the salvation of your souls, which is the purpose of your faith in him.

<sup>1.10</sup> It was concerning this salvation that the prophets made careful search and investigation, and they prophesied about this gift which God would give you.

<sup>1.11</sup> They tried to find out when the time would be and how it would come. This was the time to which Christ's Spirit in them was pointing, in predicting the sufferings that Christ would have to endure and the glory that would follow.

<sup>1.12</sup> God revealed to these prophets that their work was not for their own benefit, but for yours, as they spoke about those things which you have now heard from the messengers who announced the Good News by the power of the Holy Spirit sent from heaven. These are things which even the angels would like to understand.

<sup>1.13</sup> So then, have your minds ready for action. Keep alert and set your hope completely on the blessing which will be given you when Jesus Christ is revealed.

<sup>1.14</sup> Be obedient to God, and do not allow your lives to be shaped by those desires you had when you were still ignorant.

<sup>1.15</sup> Instead, be holy in all that you do, just as God who called you is holy.

<sup>1.16</sup> The scripture says, "Be holy because I am holy."

<sup>1.17</sup> You call him Father, when you pray to God, who judges all people by the same standard, according to what each one has done; so then, spend the rest of your lives here on earth in reverence for him.

<sup>1.18</sup> For you know what was paid to set you free from the worthless manner of life handed down by your ancestors. It was not something that can be destroyed, such as silver or gold;

<sup>1.19</sup> it was the costly sacrifice of Christ, who was like a lamb without defect or flaw.

<sup>1.20</sup> He had been chosen by God before the creation of the world and was revealed in these last days for your sake.

<sup>1.21</sup> Through him you believe in God, who raised him from death and gave him glory; and so your faith and hope are fixed on God.

<sup>1.22</sup> Now that by your obedience to the truth you have purified yourselves and have come to have a sincere love for other believers, love one another earnestly with all your heart.

<sup>1.23</sup> For through the living and eternal word of God you have been born again as the children of a parent who is immortal, not mortal.

<sup>1.24</sup> As the scripture says, "All human beings are like grass, and all their glory is like wild flowers. The grass withers, and the flowers fall,

<sup>1.25</sup> but the word of the Lord remains forever." This word is the Good News that was proclaimed to you.

# 2

<sup>2.1</sup> Rid yourselves, then, of all evil; no more lying or hypocrisy or jealousy or insulting language.

<sup>2.2</sup> Be like newborn babies, always thirsty for the pure spiritual milk, so that by drinking it you may grow up and be saved.

<sup>2.3</sup> As the scripture says, "You have found out for yourselves how kind the Lord is."

<sup>2.4</sup> Come to the Lord, the living stone rejected by people as worthless but chosen by God as valuable.

<sup>2.5</sup> Come as living stones, and let yourselves be used in building the

spiritual temple, where you will serve as holy priests to offer spiritual and acceptable sacrifices to God through Jesus Christ.

2.6 For the scripture says, "I chose a valuable stone, which I am placing as the cornerstone in Zion; and whoever believes in him will never be disappointed."

2.7 This stone is of great value for you that believe; but for those who do not believe: "The stone which the builders rejected as worthless turned out to be the most important of all."

2.8 And another scripture says, "This is the stone that will make people stumble, the rock that will make them fall." They stumbled because they did not believe in the word; such was God's will for them.

2.9 But you are the chosen race, the King's priests, the holy nation, God's own people, chosen to proclaim the wonderful acts of God, who called you out of darkness into his own marvelous light.

2.10 At one time you were not God's people, but now you are his people; at one time you did not know God's mercy, but now you have received his mercy.

2.11 I appeal to you, my friends, as strangers and refugees in this world! Do not give in to bodily passions, which are always at war against the soul.

2.12 Your conduct among the heathen should be so good that when they accuse you of being evildoers, they will have to recognize your good deeds and so praise God on the Day of his coming.

2.13 For the sake of the Lord submit yourselves to every human authority: to the Emperor, who is the supreme authority,

2.14 and to the governors, who have been appointed by him to punish the evildoers and to praise those who do good.

2.15 For God wants you to silence the ignorant talk of foolish people by the good things you do.

2.16 Live as free people; do not, however, use your freedom to cover up any evil, but live as God's slaves.

2.17 Respect everyone, love other believers, honor God, and respect the Emperor.

2.18 You servants must submit yourselves to your masters and show them complete respect, not only to those who are kind and considerate, but also to those who are harsh.

2.19 God will bless you for this, if you endure the pain of undeserved suffering because you are conscious of his will.

2.20 For what credit is there if you endure the beatings you deserve for having done wrong? But if you endure suffering even when you have done right, God will bless you for it.

2.21 It was to this that God called you, for Christ himself suffered for you and left you an example, so that you would follow in his steps.

2.22 He committed no sin, and no one ever heard a lie come from his lips.

2.23 When he was insulted, he did not answer back with an insult; when he suffered, he did not threaten, but placed his hopes in God, the righteous Judge.

2.24 Christ himself carried our sins in his body to the cross, so that we might die to sin and live for righteousness. It is by his wounds that you have been healed.

2.25 You were like sheep that had lost their way, but now you have been brought back to follow the Shepherd and Keeper of your souls.

3

3.1 In the same way you wives must submit yourselves to your husbands, so that if any of them do not believe God's word, your conduct will win them over to believe. It will not be necessary for you to say a word,

3.2 because they will see how pure and reverent your conduct is.

3.3 You should not use outward aids to make yourselves beautiful, such as the way you fix your hair, or the jewelry you put on, or the dresses you wear.

3.4 Instead, your beauty should consist of your true inner self, the ageless beauty of a gentle and quiet spirit, which is of the greatest value in God's sight.

3.5 For the devout women of the past who placed their hope in God used to make themselves beautiful by submitting themselves to their husbands.

3.6 Sarah was like that; she obeyed Abraham and called him her master. You are now her daughters if you do good and are not afraid of anything.

3.7 In the same way you husbands must live with your wives with the proper understanding that they are more delicate than you. Treat them with respect, because they also will receive, together with you, God's gift of life. Do this so that nothing will interfere with your prayers.

3.8 To conclude: you must all have the same attitude and the same feelings; love one another, and be kind and humble with one another.

3.9 Do not pay back evil with evil or cursing with cursing; instead, pay back with a blessing, because a blessing is what God promised to give you when he called you.

<sup></sup>3.10 As the scripture says, "If you want to enjoy life and wish to see good times, you must keep from speaking evil and stop telling lies.
3.11 "You must turn away from evil and do good; you must strive for peace with all your heart.
3.12 "For the Lord watches over the righteous and listens to their prayers; but he opposes those who do evil."
3.13 Who will harm you if you are eager to do what is good?
3.14 But even if you should suffer for doing what is right, how happy you are! Do not be afraid of anyone, and do not worry.
3.15 But have reverence for Christ in your hearts, and honor him as Lord. Be ready at all times to answer anyone who asks you to explain the hope you have in you,
3.16 but do it with gentleness and respect. Keep your conscience clear, so that when you are insulted, those who speak evil of your good conduct as followers of Christ will become ashamed of what they say.
3.17 For it is better to suffer for doing good, if this should be God's will, than for doing evil.
3.18 For Christ died for sins once and for all, a good man on behalf of sinners, in order to lead you to God. He was put to death physically, but made alive spiritually,
3.19 and in his spiritual existence he went and preached to the imprisoned spirits.
3.20 These were the spirits of those who had not obeyed God when he waited patiently during the days that Noah was building his boat. The few people in the boat — eight in all — were saved by the water,
3.21 which was a symbol pointing to baptism, which now saves you. It is not the washing off of bodily dirt, but the promise made to God from a good conscience. It saves you through the resurrection of Jesus Christ,
3.22 who has gone to heaven and is at the right side of God, ruling over all angels and heavenly authorities and powers.

# 4

4.1 Since Christ suffered physically, you too must strengthen yourselves with the same way of thinking that he had; because whoever suffers physically is no longer involved with sin.
4.2 From now on, then, you must live the rest of your earthly lives controlled by God's will and not by human desires.
4.3 You have spent enough time in the past doing what the heathen like to do. Your lives were spent in indecency, lust, drunkenness, orgies, drinking parties, and the disgusting worship of idols.

<sup>4.4</sup> And now the heathen are surprised when you do not join them in the same wild and reckless living, and so they insult you.

<sup>4.5</sup> But they will have to give an account of themselves to God, who is ready to judge the living and the dead.

<sup>4.6</sup> That is why the Good News was preached also to the dead, to those who had been judged in their physical existence as everyone is judged; it was preached to them so that in their spiritual existence they may live as God lives.

<sup>4.7</sup> The end of all things is near. You must be self-controlled and alert, to be able to pray.

<sup>4.8</sup> Above everything, love one another earnestly, because love covers over many sins.

<sup>4.9</sup> Open your homes to each other without complaining.

<sup>4.10</sup> Each one, as a good manager of God's different gifts, must use for the good of others the special gift he has received from God.

<sup>4.11</sup> Those who preach must preach God's messages; those who serve must serve with the strength that God gives them, so that in all things praise may be given to God through Jesus Christ, to whom belong glory and power forever and ever. Amen.

<sup>4.12</sup> My dear friends, do not be surprised at the painful test you are suffering, as though something unusual were happening to you.

<sup>4.13</sup> Rather be glad that you are sharing Christ's sufferings, so that you may be full of joy when his glory is revealed.

<sup>4.14</sup> Happy are you if you are insulted because you are Christ's followers; this means that the glorious Spirit, the Spirit of God, is resting on you.

<sup>4.15</sup> If you suffer, it must not be because you are a murderer or a thief or a criminal or a meddler in other people's affairs.

<sup>4.16</sup> However, if you suffer because you are a Christian, don't be ashamed of it, but thank God that you bear Christ's name.

<sup>4.17</sup> The time has come for judgment to begin, and God's own people are the first to be judged. If it starts with us, how will it end with those who do not believe the Good News from God?

<sup>4.18</sup> As the scripture says, "It is difficult for good people to be saved; what, then, will become of godless sinners?"

<sup>4.19</sup> So then, those who suffer because it is God's will for them, should by their good actions trust themselves completely to their Creator, who always keeps his promise.

# 5

<sup>5.1</sup> I, who am an elder myself, appeal to the church elders among you.

I am a witness of Christ's sufferings, and I will share in the glory that will be revealed. I appeal to you

5.2 to be shepherds of the flock that God gave you and to take care of it willingly, as God wants you to, and not unwillingly. Do your work, not for mere pay, but from a real desire to serve.

5.3 Do not try to rule over those who have been put in your care, but be examples to the flock.

5.4 And when the Chief Shepherd appears, you will receive the glorious crown which will never lose its brightness.

5.5 In the same way you younger people must submit yourselves to your elders. And all of you must put on the apron of humility, to serve one another; for the scripture says, "God resists the proud, but shows favor to the humble."

5.6 Humble yourselves, then, under God's mighty hand, so that he will lift you up in his own good time.

5.7 Leave all your worries with him, because he cares for you.

5.8 Be alert, be on watch! Your enemy, the Devil, roams around like a roaring lion, looking for someone to devour.

5.9 Be firm in your faith and resist him, because you know that other believers in all the world are going through the same kind of sufferings.

5.10 But after you have suffered for a little while, the God of all grace, who calls you to share his eternal glory in union with Christ, will himself perfect you and give you firmness, strength, and a sure foundation.

5.11 To him be the power forever! Amen.

5.12 I write you this brief letter with the help of Silas, whom I regard as a faithful Christian. I want to encourage you and give my testimony that this is the true grace of God. Stand firm in it.

5.13 Your sister church in Babylon, also chosen by God, sends you greetings, and so does my son Mark.

5.14 Greet one another with the kiss of Christian love. May peace be with all of you who belong to Christ.

# 2 PETER

# 2 Peter

1

<sup>1.1</sup> From Simon Peter, a servant and apostle of Jesus Christ – To those who through the righteousness of our God and Savior Jesus Christ have been given a faith as precious as ours:

<sup>1.2</sup> May grace and peace be yours in full measure through your knowledge of God and of Jesus our Lord.

<sup>1.3</sup> God's divine power has given us everything we need to live a truly religious life through our knowledge of the one who called us to share in his own glory and goodness.

<sup>1.4</sup> In this way he has given us the very great and precious gifts he promised, so that by means of these gifts you may escape from the destructive lust that is in the world, and may come to share the divine nature.

<sup>1.5</sup> For this very reason do your best to add goodness to your faith; to your goodness add knowledge;

<sup>1.6</sup> to your knowledge add self-control; to your self-control add endurance; to your endurance add godliness;

<sup>1.7</sup> to your godliness add Christian affection; and to your Christian affection add love.

<sup>1.8</sup> These are the qualities you need, and if you have them in abundance, they will make you active and effective in your knowledge of our Lord Jesus Christ.

<sup>1.9</sup> But if you do not have them, you are so shortsighted that you cannot see and have forgotten that you have been purified from your past sins.

<sup>1.10</sup> So then, my friends, try even harder to make God's call and his choice of you a permanent experience; if you do so, you will never abandon your faith.

<sup>1.11</sup> In this way you will be given the full right to enter the eternal Kingdom of our Lord and Savior Jesus Christ.

<sup>1.12</sup> And so I will always remind you of these matters, even though you already know them and are firmly grounded in the truth you have received.

<sup>1.13</sup> I think it only right for me to stir up your memory of these matters as long as I am still alive.

<sup>1.14</sup> I know that I shall soon put off this mortal body, as our Lord Jesus Christ plainly told me.

<sup>1.15</sup> I will do my best, then, to provide a way for you to remember

these matters at all times after my death.

<sup>1.16</sup> We have not depended on made-up stories in making known to you the mighty coming of our Lord Jesus Christ. With our own eyes we saw his greatness.

<sup>1.17</sup> We were there when he was given honor and glory by God the Father, when the voice came to him from the Supreme Glory, saying, "This is my own dear Son, with whom I am pleased!"

<sup>1.18</sup> We ourselves heard this voice coming from heaven, when we were with him on the holy mountain.

<sup>1.19</sup> So we are even more confident of the message proclaimed by the prophets. You will do well to pay attention to it, because it is like a lamp shining in a dark place until the Day dawns and the light of the morning star shines in your hearts.

<sup>1.20</sup> Above all else, however, remember that none of us can explain by ourselves a prophecy in the Scriptures.

<sup>1.21</sup> For no prophetic message ever came just from the human will, but people were under the control of the Holy Spirit as they spoke the message that came from God.

# 2

<sup>2.1</sup> False prophets appeared in the past among the people, and in the same way false teachers will appear among you. They will bring in destructive, untrue doctrines, and will deny the Master who redeemed them, and so they will bring upon themselves sudden destruction.

<sup>2.2</sup> Even so, many will follow their immoral ways; and because of what they do, others will speak evil of the Way of truth.

<sup>2.3</sup> In their greed these false teachers will make a profit out of telling you made-up stories. For a long time now their Judge has been ready, and their Destroyer has been wide awake!

<sup>2.4</sup> God did not spare the angels who sinned, but threw them into hell, where they are kept chained in darkness, waiting for the Day of Judgment.

<sup>2.5</sup> God did not spare the ancient world, but brought the flood on the world of godless people; the only ones he saved were Noah, who preached righteousness, and seven other people.

<sup>2.6</sup> God condemned the cities of Sodom and Gomorrah, destroying them with fire, and made them an example of what will happen to the godless.

<sup>2.7</sup> He rescued Lot, a good man, who was distressed by the immoral conduct of lawless people.

<sup>2.8</sup> That good man lived <u>among them</u>, and day <u>after day</u> he suffered agony as he saw and heard their evil actions.

<sup>2.9</sup> And so the Lord knows how to rescue godly people <u>from their trials</u> and how to keep the wicked <u>under punishment</u> <u>for the Day of Judgment</u>,

<sup>2.10</sup> especially those who follow their filthy bodily lusts and despise God's authority. These false teachers are bold and arrogant, and show no respect <u>for the glorious beings</u> above; instead, they insult them.

<sup>2.11</sup> Even the angels, who are so much stronger and mightier <u>than these false teachers</u>, do not accuse them <u>with insults</u> <u>in the presence of the Lord</u>.

<sup>2.12</sup> But these people act <u>by instinct</u>, <u>like wild animals</u> born to be captured and killed; they attack <u>with insults</u> anything they do not understand. They will be destroyed <u>like wild animals</u>,

<sup>2.13</sup> and they will be paid <u>with suffering for the suffering</u> they have caused. Pleasure <u>for them</u> is to do anything <u>in broad daylight</u> that will satisfy their bodily appetites; they are a shame and a disgrace as they join you <u>in your meals</u>, all the while enjoying their deceitful ways!

<sup>2.14</sup> They want to look <u>for nothing</u> <u>but the chance</u> to commit adultery; their appetite <u>for sin</u> is never satisfied. They lead weak people <u>into a trap</u>. Their hearts are trained to be greedy. They are <u>under God's curse</u>!

<sup>2.15</sup> They have left the straight path and have lost their way; they have followed the path taken <u>by Balaam</u> son <u>of Beor</u>, who loved the money he would get <u>for doing</u> wrong

<sup>2.16</sup> and was rebuked <u>for his sin</u>. His donkey spoke <u>with a human voice</u> and stopped the prophet's insane action.

<sup>2.17</sup> These people are <u>like dried-up springs</u>, <u>like clouds</u> blown along <u>by a storm</u>; God has reserved a place <u>for them</u> <u>in the deepest darkness</u>.

<sup>2.18</sup> They make proud and stupid statements, and use immoral bodily lusts to trap those who are just beginning to escape <u>from among people</u> who live <u>in error</u>.

<sup>2.19</sup> They promise them freedom while they themselves are slaves <u>of destructive habits</u> — for we are slaves <u>of anything</u> that has conquered us.

<sup>2.20</sup> If people have escaped <u>from the corrupting forces</u> <u>of the world</u> <u>through their knowledge</u> <u>of our Lord and Savior Jesus Christ</u>, and then are again caught and conquered <u>by them</u>, such people are <u>in worse condition</u> <u>at the end</u> than they were <u>at the beginning</u>.

<sup>2.21</sup> It would have been much better for them never to have known the way of righteousness than to know it and then turn away from the sacred command that was given them.
<sup>2.22</sup> What happened to them shows that the proverbs are true: "A dog goes back to what it has vomited" and "A pig that has been washed goes back to roll in the mud."

3

<sup>3.1</sup> My dear friends, this is now the second letter I have written you. In both letters I have tried to arouse pure thoughts in your minds by reminding you of these things.
<sup>3.2</sup> I want you to remember the words that were spoken long ago by the holy prophets, and the command from the Lord and Savior which was given you by your apostles.
<sup>3.3</sup> First of all, you must understand that in the last days some people will appear whose lives are controlled by their own lusts. They will make fun of you
<sup>3.4</sup> and will ask, "He promised to come, didn't he? Where is he? Our ancestors have already died, but everything is still the same as it was since the creation of the world!"
<sup>3.5</sup> They purposely ignore the fact that long ago God gave a command, and the heavens and earth were created. The earth was formed out of water and by water,
<sup>3.6</sup> and it was also by water, the water of the flood, that the old world was destroyed.
<sup>3.7</sup> But the heavens and the earth that now exist are being preserved by the same command of God, in order to be destroyed by fire. They are being kept for the day when godless people will be judged and destroyed.
<sup>3.8</sup> But do not forget one thing, my dear friends! There is no difference in the Lord's sight between one day and a thousand years; to him the two are the same.
<sup>3.9</sup> The Lord is not slow to do what he has promised, as some think. Instead, he is patient with you, because he does not want anyone to be destroyed, but wants all to turn away from their sins.
<sup>3.10</sup> But the Day of the Lord will come like a thief. On that Day the heavens will disappear with a shrill noise, the heavenly bodies will burn up and be destroyed, and the earth with everything in it will vanish.
<sup>3.11</sup> Since all these things will be destroyed in this way, what kind of people should you be? Your lives should be holy and dedicated to

God,

<sup>3.12</sup> as you wait for the Day of God and do your best to make it come soon — the Day when the heavens will burn up and be destroyed, and the heavenly bodies will be melted by the heat.

<sup>3.13</sup> But we wait for what God has promised: new heavens and a new earth, where righteousness will be at home.

<sup>3.14</sup> And so, my friends, as you wait for that Day, do your best to be pure and faultless in God's sight and to be at peace with him.

<sup>3.15</sup> Look on our Lord's patience as the opportunity he is giving you to be saved, just as our dear friend Paul wrote to you, using the wisdom that God gave him.

<sup>3.16</sup> This is what he says in all his letters when he writes on the subject. There are some difficult things in his letters which ignorant and unstable people explain falsely, as they do with other passages of the Scriptures. So they bring on their own destruction.

<sup>3.17</sup> But you, my friends, already know this. Be on your guard, then, so that you will not be led away by the errors of lawless people and fall from your safe position.

<sup>3.18</sup> But continue to grow in the grace and knowledge of our Lord and Savior Jesus Christ. To him be the glory, now and forever! Amen.

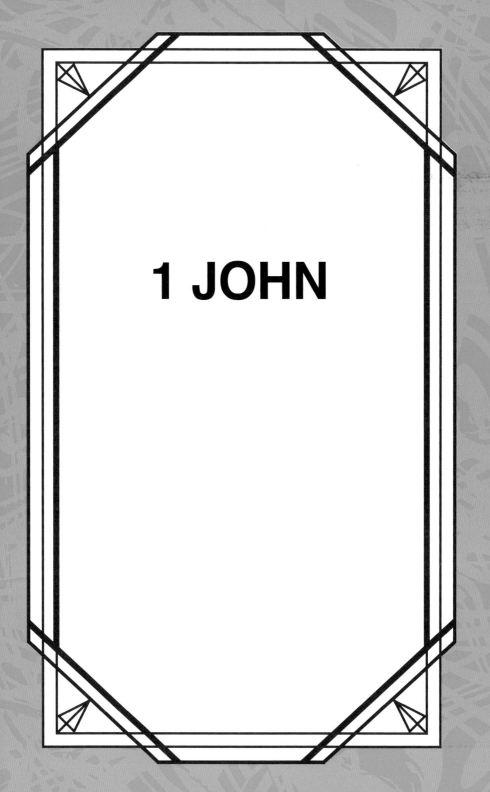

# 1 JOHN

# 1 John

## 1

<sup>1.1</sup> We write to you about the Word of life, which has existed from the very beginning. We have heard it, and we have seen it with our eyes; yes, we have seen it, and our hands have touched it.

<sup>1.2</sup> When this life became visible, we saw it; so we speak of it and tell you about the eternal life which was with the Father and was made known to us.

<sup>1.3</sup> What we have seen and heard we announce to you also, so that you will join with us in the fellowship that we have with the Father and with his Son Jesus Christ.

<sup>1.4</sup> We write this in order that our joy may be complete.

<sup>1.5</sup> Now the message that we have heard from his Son and announce is this: God is light, and there is no darkness at all in him.

<sup>1.6</sup> If, then, we say that we have fellowship with him, yet at the same time live in the darkness, we are lying both in our words and in our actions.

<sup>1.7</sup> But if we live in the light — just as he is in the light — then we have fellowship with one another, and the blood of Jesus, his Son, purifies us from every sin.

<sup>1.8</sup> If we say that we have no sin, we deceive ourselves, and there is no truth in us.

<sup>1.9</sup> But if we confess our sins to God, he will keep his promise and do what is right: he will forgive us our sins and purify us from all our wrongdoing.

<sup>1.10</sup> If we say that we have not sinned, we make a liar out of God, and his word is not in us.

## 2

<sup>2.1</sup> I am writing this to you, my children, so that you will not sin; but if anyone does sin, we have someone who pleads with the Father on our behalf — Jesus Christ, the righteous one.

<sup>2.2</sup> And Christ himself is the means by which our sins are forgiven, and not our sins only, but also the sins of everyone.

<sup>2.3</sup> If we obey God's commands, then we are sure that we know him.

<sup>2.4</sup> If we say that we know him, but do not obey his commands, we are liars and there is no truth in us.

<sup>2.5</sup> But if we obey his word, we are the ones whose love for God has really been made perfect. This is how we can be sure that we are in

union with God:

<sup>2.6</sup> if we say that we remain in union with God, we should live just as Jesus Christ did.

<sup>2.7</sup> My dear friends, this command I am writing you is not new; it is the old command, the one you have had from the very beginning. The old command is the message you have already heard.

<sup>2.8</sup> However, the command I now write you is new, because its truth is seen in Christ and also in you. For the darkness is passing away, and the real light is already shining.

<sup>2.9</sup> If we say that we are in the light, yet hate others, we are in the darkness to this very hour.

<sup>2.10</sup> If we love others, we live in the light, and so there is nothing in us that will cause someone else to sin.

<sup>2.11</sup> But if we hate others, we are in the darkness; we walk in it and do not know where we are going, because the darkness has made us blind.

<sup>2.12</sup> I write to you, my children, because your sins are forgiven for the sake of Christ.

<sup>2.13</sup> I write to you, fathers, because you know him who has existed from the beginning. I write to you, young people, because you have defeated the Evil One.

<sup>2.14</sup> I write to you, my children, because you know the Father. I write to you, fathers, because you know him who has existed from the beginning. I write to you, young people, because you are strong; the word of God lives in you, and you have defeated the Evil One.

<sup>2.15</sup> Do not love the world or anything that belongs to the world. If you love the world, you do not love the Father.

<sup>2.16</sup> Everything that belongs to the world — what the sinful self desires, what people see and want, and everything in this world that people are so proud of — none of this comes from the Father; it all comes from the world.

<sup>2.17</sup> The world and everything in it that people desire is passing away; but those who do the will of God live forever.

<sup>2.18</sup> My children, the end is near! You were told that the Enemy of Christ would come; and now many enemies of Christ have already appeared, and so we know that the end is near.

<sup>2.19</sup> These people really did not belong to our fellowship, and that is why they left us; if they had belonged to our fellowship, they would have stayed with us. But they left so that it might be clear that none of them really belonged to us.

<sup>2.20</sup> But you have had the Holy Spirit poured out on you by Christ,

and so all of you know the truth.

<sup>2.21</sup> I write you, then, not because you do not know the truth; instead, it is because you do know it, and you also know that no lie ever comes from the truth.

<sup>2.22</sup> Who, then, is the liar? It is those who say that Jesus is not the Messiah. Such people are the Enemy of Christ — they reject both the Father and the Son.

<sup>2.23</sup> For those who reject the Son reject also the Father; those who accept the Son have the Father also.

<sup>2.24</sup> Be sure, then, to keep in your hearts the message you heard from the beginning. If you keep that message, then you will always live in union with the Son and the Father.

<sup>2.25</sup> And this is what Christ himself promised to give us — eternal life.

<sup>2.26</sup> I am writing this to you about those who are trying to deceive you.

<sup>2.27</sup> But as for you, Christ has poured out his Spirit on you. As long as his Spirit remains in you, you do not need anyone to teach you. For his Spirit teaches you about everything, and what he teaches is true, not false. Obey the Spirit's teaching, then, and remain in union with Christ.

<sup>2.28</sup> Yes, my children, remain in union with him, so that when he appears we may be full of courage and need not hide in shame from him on the Day he comes.

<sup>2.29</sup> You know that Christ is righteous; you should know, then, that everyone who does what is right is God's child.

# 3

<sup>3.1</sup> See how much the Father has loved us! His love is so great that we are called God's children — and so, in fact, we are. This is why the world does not know us: it has not known God.

<sup>3.2</sup> My dear friends, we are now God's children, but it is not yet clear what we shall become. But we know that when Christ appears, we shall be like him, because we shall see him as he really is.

<sup>3.3</sup> Everyone who has this hope in Christ keeps himself pure, just as Christ is pure.

<sup>3.4</sup> Whoever sins is guilty of breaking God's law, because sin is a breaking of the law.

<sup>3.5</sup> You know that Christ appeared in order to take away sins, and that there is no sin in him.

<sup>3.6</sup> So everyone who lives in union with Christ does not continue to sin; but whoever continues to sin has never seen him or known him.

<sup></sup>3.7 Let no one deceive you, my children! Whoever does what is right is righteous, just as Christ is righteous.

3.8 Whoever continues to sin belongs to the Devil, because the Devil has sinned from the very beginning. The Son of God appeared for this very reason, to destroy what the Devil had done.

3.9 Those who are children of God do not continue to sin, for God's very nature is in them; and because God is their Father, they cannot continue to sin.

3.10 Here is the clear difference between God's children and the Devil's children: those who do not do what is right or do not love others are not God's children.

3.11 The message you heard from the very beginning is this: we must love one another.

3.12 We must not be like Cain; he belonged to the Evil One and murdered his own brother Abel. Why did Cain murder him? Because the things he himself did were wrong, and the things his brother did were right.

3.13 So do not be surprised, my friends, if the people of the world hate you.

3.14 We know that we have left death and come over into life; we know it because we love others. Those who do not love are still under the power of death.

3.15 Those who hate others are murderers, and you know that murderers do not have eternal life in them.

3.16 This is how we know what love is: Christ gave his life for us. We too, then, ought to give our lives for others!

3.17 If we are rich and see others in need, yet close our hearts against them, how can we claim that we love God?

3.18 My children, our love should not be just words and talk; it must be true love, which shows itself in action.

3.19 This, then, is how we will know that we belong to the truth; this is how we will be confident in God's presence.

3.20 If our conscience condemns us, we know that God is greater than our conscience and that he knows everything.

3.21 And so, my dear friends, if our conscience does not condemn us, we have courage in God's presence.

3.22 We receive from him whatever we ask, because we obey his commands and do what pleases him.

3.23 What he commands is that we believe in his Son Jesus Christ and love one another, just as Christ commanded us.

3.24 Those who obey God's commands live in union with God and God lives in union with them. And because of the Spirit that God has given us we know that God lives in union with us.

# 4

4.1 My dear friends, do not believe all who claim to have the Spirit, but test them to find out if the spirit they have comes from God. For many false prophets have gone out everywhere.

4.2 This is how you will be able to know whether it is God's Spirit: anyone who acknowledges that Jesus Christ came as a human being has the Spirit who comes from God.

4.3 But anyone who denies this about Jesus does not have the Spirit from God. The spirit that he has is from the Enemy of Christ; you heard that it would come, and now it is here in the world already.

4.4 But you belong to God, my children, and have defeated the false prophets, because the Spirit who is in you is more powerful than the spirit in those who belong to the world.

4.5 Those false prophets speak about matters of the world, and the world listens to them because they belong to the world.

4.6 But we belong to God. Whoever knows God listens to us; whoever does not belong to God does not listen to us. This, then, is how we can tell the difference between the Spirit of truth and the spirit of error.

4.7 Dear friends, let us love one another, because love comes from God. Whoever loves is a child of God and knows God.

4.8 Whoever does not love does not know God, for God is love.

4.9 And God showed his love for us by sending his only Son into the world, so that we might have life through him.

4.10 This is what love is: it is not that we have loved God, but that he loved us and sent his Son to be the means by which our sins are forgiven.

4.11 Dear friends, if this is how God loved us, then we should love one another.

4.12 No one has ever seen God, but if we love one another, God lives in union with us, and his love is made perfect in us.

4.13 We are sure that we live in union with God and that he lives in union with us, because he has given us his Spirit.

4.14 And we have seen and tell others that the Father sent his Son to be the Savior of the world.

4.15 If we declare that Jesus is the Son of God, we live in union with God and God lives in union with us.

4.16 And we ourselves know and believe the love which God has for us. God is love, and those who live in love live in union with God and God lives in union with them.

[4.17] Love is made perfect in us in order that we may have courage on the Judgment Day; and we will have it because our life in this world is the same as Christ's.

[4.18] There is no fear in love; perfect love drives out all fear. So then, love has not been made perfect in anyone who is afraid, because fear has to do with punishment.

[4.19] We love because God first loved us.

[4.20] If we say we love God, but hate others, we are liars. For we cannot love God, whom we have not seen, if we do not love others, whom we have seen.

[4.21] The command that Christ has given us is this: whoever loves God must love others also.

# 5

[5.1] Whoever believes that Jesus is the Messiah is a child of God; and whoever loves a father loves his child also.

[5.2] This is how we know that we love God's children: it is by loving God and obeying his commands.

[5.3] For our love for God means that we obey his commands. And his commands are not too hard for us,

[5.4] because every child of God is able to defeat the world. And we win the victory over the world by means of our faith.

[5.5] Who can defeat the world? Only the person who believes that Jesus is the Son of God.

[5.6] Jesus Christ is the one who came with the water of his baptism and the blood of his death. He came not only with the water, but with both the water and the blood. And the Spirit himself testifies that this is true, because the Spirit is truth.

[5.7] There are three witnesses:

[5.8] the Spirit, the water, and the blood; and all three give the same testimony.

[5.9] We believe human testimony; but God's testimony is much stronger, and he has given this testimony about his Son.

[5.10] So those who believe in the Son of God have this testimony in their own heart; but those who do not believe God, have made a liar of him, because they have not believed what God has said about his Son.

[5.11] The testimony is this: God has given us eternal life, and this life has its source in his Son.

5.12 Whoever has the Son has this life; whoever does not have the Son of God does not have life.

5.13 I am writing this to you so that you may know that you have eternal life — you that believe in the Son of God.

5.14 We have courage in God's presence, because we are sure that he hears us if we ask him for anything that is according to his will.

5.15 He hears us whenever we ask him; and since we know this is true, we know also that he gives us what we ask from him.

5.16 If you see a believer commit a sin that does not lead to death, you should pray to God, who will give that person life. This applies to those whose sins do not lead to death. But there is sin which leads to death, and I do not say that you should pray to God about that.

5.17 All wrongdoing is sin, but there is sin which does not lead to death.

5.18 We know that no children of God keep on sinning, for the Son of God keeps them safe, and the Evil One cannot harm them.

5.19 We know that we belong to God even though the whole world is under the rule of the Evil One.

5.20 We know that the Son of God has come and has given us understanding, so that we know the true God. We live in union with the true God — in union with his Son Jesus Christ. This is the true God, and this is eternal life.

5.21 My children, keep yourselves safe from false gods!

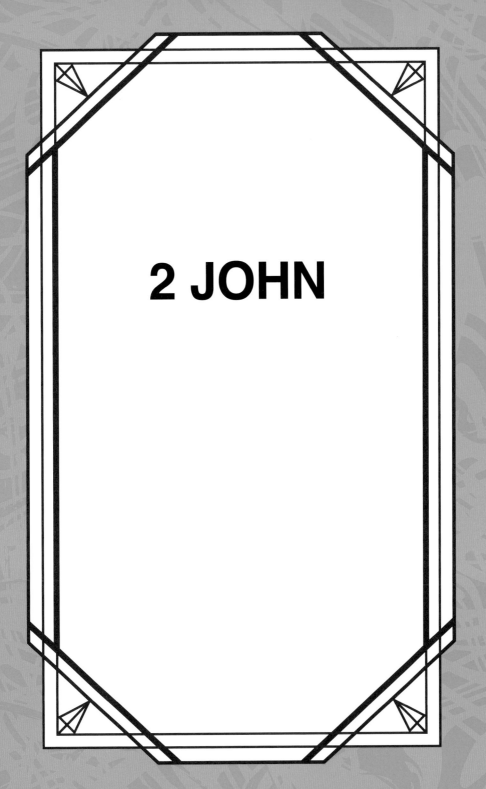

# 2 JOHN

# 2 John

## 1

<sup>1.1</sup> From the Elder — To the dear Lady and to her children, whom I truly love. And I am not the only one, but all who know the truth love you,
<sup>1.2</sup> because the truth remains in us and will be with us forever.
<sup>1.3</sup> May God the Father and Jesus Christ, the Father's Son, give us grace, mercy, and peace; may they be ours in truth and love.
<sup>1.4</sup> How happy I was to find that some of your children live in the truth, just as the Father commanded us.
<sup>1.5</sup> And so I ask you, dear Lady: let us all love one another. This is no new command I am writing you; it is the command which we have had from the beginning.
<sup>1.6</sup> This love I speak of means that we must live in obedience to God's commands. The command, as you have all heard from the beginning, is that you must all live in love.
<sup>1.7</sup> Many deceivers have gone out over the world, people who do not acknowledge that Jesus Christ came as a human being. Such a person is a deceiver and the Enemy of Christ.
<sup>1.8</sup> Be on your guard, then, so that you will not lose what we have worked for, but will receive your reward in full.
<sup>1.9</sup> Anyone who does not stay with the teaching of Christ, but goes beyond it, does not have God. Whoever does stay with the teaching has both the Father and the Son.
<sup>1.10</sup> So then, if some come to you who do not bring this teaching, do not welcome them in your homes; do not even say, "Peace be with you."
<sup>1.11</sup> For anyone who wishes them peace becomes their partner in the evil things they do.
<sup>1.12</sup> I have so much to tell you, but I would rather not do it with paper and ink; instead, I hope to visit you and talk with you personally, so that we shall be completely happy.
<sup>1.13</sup> The children of your dear Sister send you their greetings.

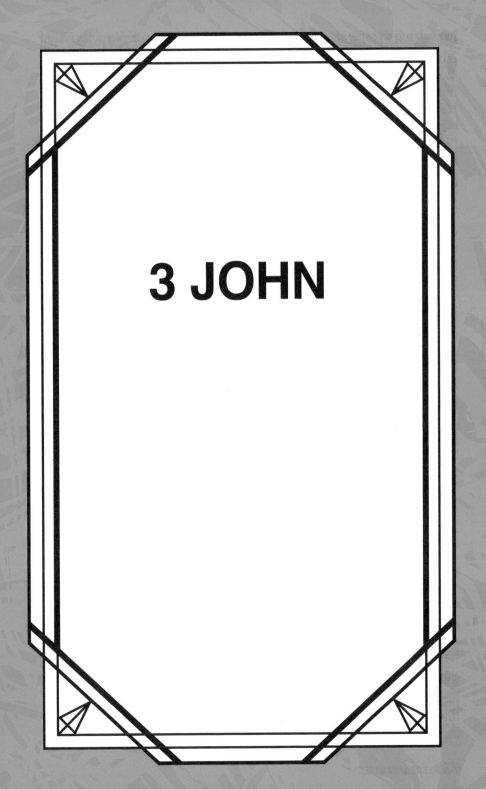

# 3 JOHN

# 3 John

## 1

<sup>1.1</sup> From the Elder — To my dear Gaius, whom I truly love.

<sup>1.2</sup> My dear friend, I pray that everything may go well with you and that you may be in good health — as I know you are well in spirit.

<sup>1.3</sup> I was so happy when some Christians arrived and told me how faithful you are to the truth — just as you always live in the truth.

<sup>1.4</sup> Nothing makes me happier than to hear that my children live in the truth.

<sup>1.5</sup> My dear friend, you are so faithful in the work you do for other Christians, even when they are strangers.

<sup>1.6</sup> They have spoken to the church here about your love. Please help them to continue their trip in a way that will please God.

<sup>1.7</sup> For they set out on their trip in the service of Christ without accepting any help from unbelievers.

<sup>1.8</sup> We Christians, then, must help these people, so that we may share in their work for the truth.

<sup>1.9</sup> I wrote a short letter to the church; but Diotrephes, who likes to be their leader, will not pay any attention to what I say.

<sup>1.10</sup> When I come, then, I will bring up everything he has done: the terrible things he says about us and the lies he tells! But that is not enough for him; he will not receive the Christians when they come, and even stops those who want to receive them and tries to drive them out of the church!

<sup>1.11</sup> My dear friend, do not imitate what is bad, but imitate what is good. Whoever does good belongs to God; whoever does what is bad has not seen God.

<sup>1.12</sup> Everyone speaks well of Demetrius; truth itself speaks well of him. And we add our testimony, and you know that what we say is true.

<sup>1.13</sup> I have so much to tell you, but I do not want to do it with pen and ink.

<sup>1.14</sup> I hope to see you soon, and then we will talk personally.

<sup>1.15</sup> Peace be with you. All your friends send greetings. Greet all our friends personally.

# JUDE

# Jude

## 1

<sup>1.1</sup> From Jude, servant of Jesus Christ, and brother of James – To those who have been called by God, who live in the love of God the Father and the protection of Jesus Christ:

<sup>1.2</sup> May mercy, peace, and love be yours in full measure.

<sup>1.3</sup> My dear friends, I was doing my best to write to you about the salvation we share in common, when I felt the need of writing at once to encourage you to fight on for the faith which once and for all God has given to his people.

<sup>1.4</sup> For some godless people have slipped in unnoticed among us, persons who distort the message about the grace of our God in order to excuse their immoral ways, and who reject Jesus Christ, our only Master and Lord. Long ago the Scriptures predicted the condemnation they have received.

<sup>1.5</sup> For even though you know all this, I want to remind you of how the Lord once rescued the people of Israel from Egypt, but afterward destroyed those who did not believe.

<sup>1.6</sup> Remember the angels who did not stay within the limits of their proper authority, but abandoned their own dwelling place: they are bound with eternal chains in the darkness below, where God is keeping them for that great Day on which they will be condemned.

<sup>1.7</sup> Remember Sodom and Gomorrah, and the nearby towns, whose people acted as those angels did and indulged in sexual immorality and perversion: they suffer the punishment of eternal fire as a plain warning to all.

<sup>1.8</sup> In the same way also, these people have visions which make them sin against their own bodies; they despise God's authority and insult the glorious beings above.

<sup>1.9</sup> Not even the chief angel Michael did this. In his quarrel with the Devil, when they argued about who would have the body of Moses, Michael did not dare condemn the Devil with insulting words, but said, "The Lord rebuke you!"

<sup>1.10</sup> But these people attack with insults anything they do not understand; and those things that they know by instinct, like wild animals, are the very things that destroy them.

<sup>1.11</sup> How terrible for them! They have followed the way that Cain took. For the sake of money they have given themselves over to the error that Balaam committed. They have rebelled as Korah rebelled,

and like him they are destroyed.

<sup></sup>1.12 With their shameless carousing they are like dirty spots in your fellowship meals. They take care only of themselves. They are like clouds carried along by the wind, but bringing no rain. They are like trees that bear no fruit, even in autumn, trees that have been pulled up by the roots and are completely dead.

1.13 They are like wild waves of the sea, with their shameful deeds showing up like foam. They are like wandering stars, for whom God has reserved a place forever in the deepest darkness.

1.14 It was Enoch, the seventh direct descendant from Adam, who long ago prophesied this about them: "The Lord will come with many thousands of his holy angels

1.15 "to bring judgment on all, to condemn them all for the godless deeds they have performed and for all the terrible words that godless sinners have spoken against him!"

1.16 These people are always grumbling and blaming others; they follow their own evil desires; they brag about themselves and flatter others in order to get their own way.

1.17 But remember, my friends, what you were told in the past by the apostles of our Lord Jesus Christ.

1.18 They said to you, "When the last days come, people will appear who will make fun of you, people who follow their own godless desires."

1.19 These are the people who cause divisions, who are controlled by their natural desires, who do not have the Spirit.

1.20 But you, my friends, keep on building yourselves up on your most sacred faith. Pray in the power of the Holy Spirit,

1.21 and keep yourselves in the love of God, as you wait for our Lord Jesus Christ in his mercy to give you eternal life.

1.22 Show mercy toward those who have doubts;

1.23 save others by snatching them out of the fire; and to others show mercy mixed with fear, but hate their very clothes, stained by their sinful lusts.

1.24 To him who is able to keep you from falling and to bring you faultless and joyful before his glorious presence —

1.25 to the only God our Savior, through Jesus Christ our Lord, be glory, majesty, might, and authority, from all ages past, and now, and forever and ever! Amen.

# REVELATION

# Revelation

1

<sup>1.1</sup> This book is the record of the events that Jesus Christ revealed. God gave him this revelation in order to show to his servants what must happen very soon. Christ made these things known to his servant John by sending his angel to him,

<sup>1.2</sup> and John has told all that he has seen. This is his report concerning the message from God and the truth revealed by Jesus Christ.

<sup>1.3</sup> Happy is the one who reads this book, and happy are those who listen to the words of this prophetic message and obey what is written in this book! For the time is near when all these things will happen.

<sup>1.4</sup> From John to the seven churches in the province of Asia: Grace and peace be yours from God, who is, who was, and who is to come, and from the seven spirits in front of his throne,

<sup>1.5</sup> and from Jesus Christ, the faithful witness, the first to be raised from death and who is also the ruler of the kings of the world. He loves us, and by his sacrificial death he has freed us from our sins

<sup>1.6</sup> and made us a kingdom of priests to serve his God and Father. To Jesus Christ be the glory and power forever and ever! Amen.

<sup>1.7</sup> Look, he is coming on the clouds! Everyone will see him, including those who pierced him. All peoples on earth will mourn over him. So shall it be!

<sup>1.8</sup> "I am the first and the last," says the Lord God Almighty, who is, who was, and who is to come.

<sup>1.9</sup> I am John, your brother, and as a follower of Jesus I am your partner in patiently enduring the suffering that comes to those who belong to his Kingdom. I was put on the island of Patmos because I had proclaimed God's word and the truth that Jesus revealed.

<sup>1.10</sup> On the Lord's day the Spirit took control of me, and I heard a loud voice, that sounded like a trumpet, speaking behind me.

<sup>1.11</sup> It said, "Write down what you see, and send the book to the churches in these seven cities: Ephesus, Smyrna, Pergamum, Thyatira, Sardis, Philadelphia, and Laodicea."

<sup>1.12</sup> I turned around to see who was talking to me, and I saw seven gold lampstands,

<sup>1.13</sup> and among them there was what looked like a human being, wearing a robe that reached to his feet, and a gold band around his chest.

<sup>1.14</sup> His hair was white as wool, or as snow, and his eyes blazed like fire;

<sup>1.15</sup> his feet shone like brass that has been refined and polished, and his voice sounded like a roaring waterfall.

<sup>1.16</sup> He held seven stars in his right hand, and a sharp two-edged sword came out of his mouth. His face was as bright as the midday sun.

<sup>1.17</sup> When I saw him, I fell down at his feet like a dead man. He placed his right hand on me and said, "Don't be afraid! I am the first and the last.

<sup>1.18</sup> "I am the living one! I was dead, but now I am alive forever and ever. I have authority over death and the world of the dead.

<sup>1.19</sup> Write, then, the things you see, both the things that are now and the things that will happen afterward.

<sup>1.20</sup> Here is the secret meaning of the seven stars that you see in my right hand, and of the seven gold lampstands: the seven stars are the angels of the seven churches, and the seven lampstands are the seven churches.

# 2

<sup>2.1</sup> "To the angel of the church in Ephesus write: "This is the message from the one who holds the seven stars in his right hand and who walks among the seven gold lampstands.

<sup>2.2</sup> "I know what you have done; I know how hard you have worked and how patient you have been. I know that you cannot tolerate evil people and that you have tested those who say they are apostles but are not, and have found out that they are liars.

<sup>2.3</sup> "You are patient, you have suffered for my sake, and you have not given up.

<sup>2.4</sup> "But this is what I have against you: you do not love me now as you did at first.

<sup>2.5</sup> "Think how far you have fallen! Turn from your sins and do what you did at first. If you don't turn from your sins, I will come to you and take your lampstand from its place.

<sup>2.6</sup> "But this is what you have in your favor: you hate what the Nicolaitans do, as much as I do.

<sup>2.7</sup> "If you have ears, then, listen to what the Spirit says to the churches!

"To those who win the victory I will give the right to eat the fruit of the tree of life that grows in the Garden of God.

<sup>2.8</sup> "To the angel of the church in Smyrna write:

"This is the message from the one who is the first and the last, who died and lived again.

2.9 "I know your troubles; I know that you are poor — but really you are rich! I know the evil things said against you by those who claim to be Jews but are not; they are a group that belongs to Satan!

2.10 "Don't be afraid of anything you are about to suffer. Listen! The Devil will put you to the test by having some of you thrown into prison, and your troubles will last ten days. Be faithful to me, even if it means death, and I will give you life as your prize of victory.

2.11 "If you have ears, then, listen to what the Spirit says to the churches!

"Those who win the victory will not be hurt by the second death.

2.12 "To the angel of the church in Pergamum write:

"This is the message from the one who has the sharp two-edged sword.

2.13 "I know where you live, there where Satan has his throne. You are true to me, and you did not abandon your faith in me even during the time when Antipas, my faithful witness, was killed there where Satan lives.

2.14 "But there are a few things I have against you: there are some among you who follow the teaching of Balaam, who taught Balak how to lead the people of Israel into sin by persuading them to eat food that had been offered to idols and to practice sexual immorality.

2.15 "In the same way you have people among you who follow the teaching of the Nicolaitans.

2.16 "Now turn from your sins! If you don't, I will come to you soon and fight against those people with the sword that comes out of my mouth.

2.17 "If you have ears, then, listen to what the Spirit says to the churches!

"To those who win the victory I will give some of the hidden manna. I will also give each of them a white stone on which is written a new name that no one knows except the one who receives it.

2.18 "To the angel of the church in Thyatira write:

"This is the message from the Son of God, whose eyes blaze like fire, whose feet shine like polished brass.

2.19 "I know what you do. I know your love, your faithfulness, your service, and your patience. I know that you are doing more now than you did at first.

2.20 "But this is what I have against you: you tolerate that woman Jezebel, who calls herself a messenger of God. By her teaching she misleads my servants into practicing sexual immorality and eating food that has been offered to idols.

2.21 "I have given her time to repent of her sins, but she does not want to turn from her immorality.

2.22 "And so I will throw her on a bed where she and those who committed adultery with her will suffer terribly. I will do this now unless they repent of the wicked things they did with her.

2.23 "I will also kill her followers, and then all the churches will know that I am the one who knows everyone's thoughts and wishes. I will repay each of you according to what you have done.

2.24 "But the rest of you in Thyatira have not followed this evil teaching; you have not learned what the others call 'the deep secrets of Satan.' I say to you that I will not put any other burden on you.

2.25 "But until I come, you must hold firmly to what you have.

2.26-28 "To those who win the victory, who continue to the end to do what I want, I will give the same authority that I received from my Father: I will give them authority over the nations, to rule them with an iron rod and to break them to pieces like clay pots. I will also give them the morning star.

2.29 "If you have ears, then, listen to what the Spirit says to the churches!

3

3.1 "To the angel of the church in Sardis write:

"This is the message from the one who has the seven spirits of God and the seven stars. I know what you are doing; I know that you have the reputation of being alive, even though you are dead!

3.2 "So wake up, and strengthen what you still have before it dies completely. For I find that what you have done is not yet perfect in the sight of my God.

3.3 "Remember, then, what you were taught and what you heard; obey it and turn from your sins. If you do not wake up, I will come upon you like a thief, and you will not even know the time when I will come.

3.4 "But a few of you there in Sardis have kept your clothes clean. You will walk with me, clothed in white, because you are worthy to do so.

3.5 "Those who win the victory will be clothed like this in white, and I will not remove their names from the book of the living. In the presence of my Father and of his angels I will declare openly that they belong to me.

3.6 "If you have ears, then, listen to what the Spirit says to the churches!

<sup>3.7</sup> "To the angel of the church in Philadelphia write:

"This is the message from the one who is holy and true. He has the key that belonged to David, and when he opens a door, no one can close it, and when he closes it, no one can open it.

<sup>3.8</sup> "I know what you do; I know that you have a little power; you have followed my teaching and have been faithful to me. I have opened a door in front of you, which no one can close.

<sup>3.9</sup> "Listen! As for that group that belongs to Satan, those liars who claim that they are Jews but are not, I will make them come and bow down at your feet. They will all know that I love you.

<sup>3.10</sup> "Because you have kept my command to endure, I will also keep you safe from the time of trouble which is coming upon the world to test all the people on earth.

<sup>3.11</sup> "I am coming soon. Keep safe what you have, so that no one will rob you of your victory prize.

<sup>3.12</sup> "I will make those who are victorious pillars in the temple of my God, and they will never leave it. I will write on them the name of my God and the name of the city of my God, the new Jerusalem, which will come down out of heaven from my God. I will also write on them my new name.

<sup>3.13</sup> "If you have ears, then, listen to what the Spirit says to the churches!

<sup>3.14</sup> "To the angel of the church in Laodicea write:

"This is the message from the Amen, the faithful and true witness, who is the origin of all that God has created.

<sup>3.15</sup> "I know what you have done; I know that you are neither cold nor hot. How I wish you were either one or the other!

<sup>3.16</sup> "But because you are lukewarm, neither hot nor cold, I am going to spit you out of my mouth!

<sup>3.17</sup> "You say, 'I am rich and well off; I have all I need.' But you do not know how miserable and pitiful you are! You are poor, naked, and blind.

<sup>3.18</sup> "I advise you, then, to buy gold from me, pure gold, in order to be rich. Buy also white clothing to dress yourself and cover up your shameful nakedness. Buy also some ointment to put on your eyes, so that you may see.

<sup>3.19</sup> "I rebuke and punish all whom I love. Be in earnest, then, and turn from your sins.

<sup>3.20</sup> "Listen! I stand at the door and knock; if any hear my voice and open the door, I will come into their house and eat with them, and

they will eat with me.

<sup>3.21</sup> "To those who win the victory I will give the right to sit beside me on my throne, just as I have been victorious and now sit by my Father on his throne.

<sup>3.22</sup> "If you have ears, then, listen to what the Spirit says to the churches!"

# 4

<sup>4.1</sup> At this point I had another vision and saw an open door in heaven. And the voice that sounded like a trumpet, which I had heard speaking to me before, said, "Come up here, and I will show you what must happen after this."

<sup>4.2</sup> At once the Spirit took control of me. There in heaven was a throne with someone sitting on it.

<sup>4.3</sup> His face gleamed like such precious stones as jasper and carnelian, and all around the throne there was a rainbow the color of an emerald.

<sup>4.4</sup> In a circle around the throne were twenty-four other thrones, on which were seated twenty-four elders dressed in white and wearing crowns of gold.

<sup>4.5</sup> From the throne came flashes of lightning, rumblings, and peals of thunder. In front of the throne seven lighted torches were burning, which are the seven spirits of God.

<sup>4.6</sup> Also in front of the throne there was what looked like a sea of glass, clear as crystal. Surrounding the throne on each of its sides, were four living creatures covered with eyes in front and behind.

<sup>4.7</sup> The first one looked like a lion; the second looked like a bull; the third had a face like a human face; and the fourth looked like an eagle in flight.

<sup>4.8</sup> Each one of the four living creatures had six wings, and they were covered with eyes, inside and out. Day and night they never stop singing: "Holy, holy, holy, is the Lord God Almighty, who was, who is, and who is to come."

<sup>4.9</sup> The four living creatures sing songs of glory and honor and thanks to the one who sits on the throne, who lives forever and ever. When they do so,

<sup>4.10</sup> the twenty-four elders fall down before the one who sits on the throne, and worship him who lives forever and ever. They throw their crowns down in front of the throne and say,

<sup>4.11</sup> "Our Lord and God! You are worthy to receive glory, honor, and power. For you created all things, and by your will they were given existence and life."

**5** ⁵·¹ I saw a scroll in the right hand of the one who sits on the throne; it was covered with writing on both sides and was sealed with seven seals.

⁵·² And I saw a mighty angel, who announced in a loud voice, "Who is worthy to break the seals and open the scroll?"

⁵·³ But there was no one in heaven or on earth or in the world below who could open the scroll and look inside it.

⁵·⁴ I cried bitterly because no one could be found who was worthy to open the scroll or look inside it.

⁵·⁵ Then one of the elders said to me, "Don't cry. Look! The Lion from Judah's tribe, the great descendant of David, has won the victory, and he can break the seven seals and open the scroll."

⁵·⁶ Then I saw a Lamb standing in the center of the throne, surrounded by the four living creatures and the elders. The Lamb appeared to have been killed. It had seven horns and seven eyes, which are the seven spirits of God that have been sent through the whole earth.

⁵·⁷ The Lamb went and took the scroll from the right hand of the one who sits on the throne.

⁵·⁸ As he did so, the four living creatures and the twenty-four elders fell down before the Lamb. Each had a harp and gold bowls filled with incense, which are the prayers of God's people.

⁵·⁹ They sang a new song: "You are worthy to take the scroll and to break open its seals. For you were killed, and by your sacrificial death you bought for God people from every tribe, language, nation, and race.

⁵·¹⁰ "You have made them a kingdom of priests to serve our God, and they shall rule on earth."

⁵·¹¹ Again I looked, and I heard angels, thousands and millions of them! They stood around the throne, the four living creatures, and the elders,

⁵·¹² and sang in a loud voice: "The Lamb who was killed is worthy to receive power, wealth, wisdom, and strength, honor, glory, and praise!"

⁵·¹³ And I heard every creature in heaven, on earth, in the world below, and in the sea — all living beings in the universe — and they were singing: "To him who sits on the throne and to the Lamb, be praise and honor, glory and might, forever and ever!"

⁵·¹⁴ The four living creatures answered, "Amen!" And the elders fell down and worshiped.

<sup>6.1</sup> Then I saw the Lamb break open the first of the seven seals, and I heard one of the four living creatures say in a voice that sounded like thunder, "Come!"

<sup>6.2</sup> I looked, and there was a white horse. Its rider held a bow, and he was given a crown. He rode out as a conqueror to conquer.

<sup>6.3</sup> Then the Lamb broke open the second seal; and I heard the second living creature say, "Come!"

<sup>6.4</sup> Another horse came out, a red one. Its rider was given the power to bring war on the earth, so that people should kill each other. He was given a large sword.

<sup>6.5</sup> Then the Lamb broke open the third seal; and I heard the third living creature say, "Come!" I looked, and there was a black horse. Its rider held a pair of scales in his hand.

<sup>6.6</sup> I heard what sounded like a voice coming from among the four living creatures, which said, "A quart of wheat for a day's wages, and three quarts of barley for a day's wages. But do not damage the olive trees and the vineyards!"

<sup>6.7</sup> Then the Lamb broke open the fourth seal; and I heard the fourth living creature say, "Come!"

<sup>6.8</sup> I looked, and there was a pale-colored horse. Its rider was named Death, and Hades followed close behind. They were given authority over one fourth of the earth, to kill by means of war, famine, disease, and wild animals.

<sup>6.9</sup> Then the Lamb broke open the fifth seal. I saw underneath the altar the souls of those who had been killed because they had proclaimed God's word and had been faithful in their witnessing.

<sup>6.10</sup> They shouted in a loud voice, "Almighty Lord, holy and true! How long will it be until you judge the people on earth and punish them for killing us?"

<sup>6.11</sup> Each of them was given a white robe, and they were told to rest a little while longer, until the complete number of other servants and believers were killed, as they had been.

<sup>6.12</sup> And I saw the Lamb break open the sixth seal. There was a violent earthquake, and the sun became black like coarse black cloth, and the moon turned completely red like blood.

<sup>6.13</sup> The stars fell down to the earth, like unripe figs falling from the tree when a strong wind shakes it.

<sup>6.14</sup> The sky disappeared like a scroll being rolled up, and every mountain and island was moved from its place.

<sup>6.15</sup> Then the kings of the earth, the rulers and the military chiefs, the rich and the powerful, and all other people, slave and free, hid

themselves in caves and under rocks on the mountains.

<sup>6.16</sup> They called out to the mountains and to the rocks, "Fall on us and hide us from the eyes of the one who sits on the throne and from the anger of the Lamb!

<sup>6.17</sup> "The terrible day of their anger is here, and who can stand up against it?"

# 7

<sup>7.1</sup> After this I saw four angels standing at the four corners of the earth, holding back the four winds so that no wind should blow on the earth or the sea or against any tree.

<sup>7.2</sup> And I saw another angel coming up from the east with the seal of the living God. He called out in a loud voice to the four angels to whom God had given the power to damage the earth and the sea.

<sup>7.3</sup> The angel said, "Do not harm the earth, the sea, or the trees, until we mark the servants of our God with a seal on their foreheads."

<sup>7.4</sup> And I was told that the number of those who were marked with God's seal on their foreheads was 144,000. They were from the twelve tribes of Israel,

<sup>7.5-8</sup> twelve thousand from each tribe: Judah, Reuben, Gad, Asher, Naphtali, Manasseh, Simeon, Levi, Issachar, Zebulun, Joseph, and Benjamin.

<sup>7.9</sup> After this I looked, and there was an enormous crowd — no one could count all the people! They were from every race, tribe, nation, and language, and they stood in front of the throne and of the Lamb, dressed in white robes and holding palm branches in their hands.

<sup>7.10</sup> They called out in a loud voice: "Salvation comes from our God, who sits on the throne, and from the Lamb!"

<sup>7.11</sup> All the angels stood around the throne, the elders, and the four living creatures. Then they threw themselves face downward in front of the throne and worshiped God,

<sup>7.12</sup> saying, "Amen! Praise, glory, wisdom, thanksgiving, honor, power, and might belong to our God forever and ever! Amen!"

<sup>7.13</sup> One of the elders asked me, "Who are these people dressed in white robes, and where do they come from?"

<sup>7.14</sup> "I don't know, sir. You do," I answered. He said to me, "These are the people who have come safely through the terrible persecution. They have washed their robes and made them white with the blood of the Lamb.

<sup>7.15</sup> "That is why they stand before God's throne and serve him day and night in his temple. He who sits on the throne will protect them

with his presence.

7.16 "Never again will they hunger or thirst; neither sun nor any scorching heat will burn them,

7.17 "because the Lamb, who is in the center of the throne, will be their shepherd, and he will guide them to springs of life-giving water. And God will wipe away every tear from their eyes."

# 8

8.1 When the Lamb broke open the seventh seal, there was silence in heaven for about half an hour.

8.2 Then I saw the seven angels who stand before God, and they were given seven trumpets.

8.3 Another angel, who had a gold incense container, came and stood at the altar. He was given a lot of incense to add to the prayers of all God's people and to offer it on the gold altar that stands before the throne.

8.4 The smoke of the burning incense went up with the prayers of God's people from the hands of the angel standing before God.

8.5 Then the angel took the incense container, filled it with fire from the altar, and threw it on the earth. There were rumblings and peals of thunder, flashes of lightning, and an earthquake.

8.6 "Then the seven angels with the seven trumpets prepared to blow them.

8.7 "The first angel blew his trumpet. Hail and fire, mixed with blood, came pouring down on the earth. A third of the earth was burned up, a third of the trees, and every blade of green grass.

8.8 "Then the second angel blew his trumpet. Something that looked like a huge mountain on fire was thrown into the sea. A third of the sea was turned into blood,

8.9 a third of the living creatures in the sea died, and a third of the ships were destroyed.

8.10 Then the third angel blew his trumpet. A large star, burning like a torch, dropped from the sky and fell on a third of the rivers and on the springs of water.

8.11 (The name of the star is "Bitterness.") A third of the water turned bitter, and many people died from drinking the water, because it had turned bitter.

8.12 Then the fourth angel blew his trumpet. A third of the sun was struck, and a third of the moon, and a third of the stars, so that their light lost a third of its brightness; there was no light during a third of the day and a third of the night also.

<sup>8.13</sup> Then I looked, and I heard an eagle that was flying high in the air say in a loud voice, "O horror! horror! How horrible it will be for all who live on earth when the sound comes from the trumpets that the other three angels must blow!"

# 9

<sup>9.1</sup> Then the fifth angel blew his trumpet. I saw a star which had fallen down to the earth, and it was given the key to the abyss.
<sup>9.2</sup> The star opened the abyss, and smoke poured out of it, like the smoke from a large furnace; the sunlight and the air were darkened by the smoke from the abyss.
<sup>9.3</sup> Locusts came down out of the smoke upon the earth, and they were given the same kind of power that scorpions have.
<sup>9.4</sup> They were told not to harm the grass or the trees or any other plant; they could harm only the people who did not have the mark of God's seal on their foreheads.
<sup>9.5</sup> The locusts were not allowed to kill these people, but only to torture them for five months. The pain caused by the torture is like the pain caused by a scorpion's sting.
<sup>9.6</sup> During those five months they will seek death, but will not find it; they will want to die, but death will flee from them.
<sup>9.7</sup> The locusts looked like horses ready for battle; on their heads they had what seemed to be crowns of gold, and their faces were like human faces.
<sup>9.8</sup> Their hair was like women's hair, their teeth were like lions' teeth.
<sup>9.9</sup> Their chests were covered with what looked like iron breastplates, and the sound made by their wings was like the noise of many horse-drawn chariots rushing into battle.
<sup>9.10</sup> They have tails and stings like those of a scorpion, and it is with their tails that they have the power to hurt people for five months.
<sup>9.11</sup> They have a king ruling over them, who is the angel in charge of the abyss. His name in Hebrew is Abaddon; in Greek the name is Apollyon (meaning "The Destroyer").
<sup>9.12</sup> The first horror is over; after this there are still two more horrors to come.
<sup>9.13</sup> Then the sixth angel blew his trumpet. I heard a voice coming from the four corners of the gold altar standing before God.
<sup>9.14</sup> The voice said to the sixth angel, "Release the four angels who are bound at the great Euphrates River!"
<sup>9.15</sup> The four angels were released; for this very hour of this very day of this very month and year they had been kept ready to kill a third

of all the human race.

<sup>9.16</sup> I was told the number of the mounted troops: it was two hundred million.

<sup>9.17</sup> And in my vision I saw the horses and their riders: they had breastplates red as fire, blue as sapphire, and yellow as sulfur. The horses' heads were like lions' heads, and from their mouths came out fire, smoke, and sulfur.

<sup>9.18</sup> A third of the human race was killed by those three plagues: the fire, the smoke, and the sulfur coming out of the horses' mouths.

<sup>9.19</sup> For the power of the horses is in their mouths and also in their tails. Their tails are like snakes with heads, and they use them to hurt people.

<sup>9.20</sup> The rest of the human race, all those who had not been killed by these plagues, did not turn away from what they themselves had made. They did not stop worshiping demons, nor the idols of gold, silver, bronze, stone, and wood, which cannot see, hear, or walk.

<sup>9.21</sup> Nor did they repent of their murders, their magic, their sexual immorality, or their stealing.

# 10

<sup>10.1</sup> Then I saw another mighty angel coming down out of heaven. He was wrapped in a cloud and had a rainbow around his head; his face was like the sun, and his legs were like columns of fire.

<sup>10.2</sup> He had a small scroll open in his hand. He put his right foot on the sea and his left foot on the land,

<sup>10.3</sup> and called out in a loud voice that sounded like the roar of lions. After he had called out, the seven thunders answered with a roar.

<sup>10.4</sup> As soon as they spoke, I was about to write. But I heard a voice speak from heaven, "Keep secret what the seven thunders have said; do not write it down!"

<sup>10.5</sup> Then the angel that I saw standing on the sea and on the land raised his right hand to heaven

<sup>10.6</sup> and took a vow in the name of God, who lives forever and ever, who created heaven, earth, and the sea, and everything in them. The angel said, "There will be no more delay!

<sup>10.7</sup> "But when the seventh angel blows his trumpet, then God will accomplish his secret plan, as he announced to his servants, the prophets."

<sup>10.8</sup> Then the voice that I had heard speaking from heaven spoke to me again, saying, "Go and take the open scroll which is in the hand of the angel standing on the sea and on the land."

<sup>10.9</sup> I went to the angel and asked him to give me the little scroll. He said to me, "Take it and eat it; it will turn sour in your stomach, but in your mouth it will be sweet as honey."

<sup>10.10</sup> I took the little scroll from his hand and ate it, and it tasted sweet as honey in my mouth. But after I swallowed it, it turned sour in my stomach.

<sup>10.11</sup> Then I was told, "Once again you must proclaim God's message about many nations, races, languages, and kings."

# 11

<sup>11.1</sup> I was then given a stick that looked like a measuring-rod, and was told, "Go and measure the temple of God and the altar, and count those who are worshiping in the temple.

<sup>11.2</sup> "But do not measure the outer courts, because they have been given to the heathen, who will trample on the Holy City for forty-two months.

<sup>11.3</sup> "I will send my two witnesses dressed in sackcloth, and they will proclaim God's message during those 1,260 days."

<sup>11.4</sup> The two witnesses are the two olive trees and the two lamps that stand before the Lord of the earth.

<sup>11.5</sup> If anyone tries to harm them, fire comes out of their mouths and destroys their enemies; and in this way whoever tries to harm them will be killed.

<sup>11.6</sup> They have authority to shut up the sky so that there will be no rain during the time they proclaim God's message. They have authority also over the springs of water, to turn them into blood; they have authority also to strike the earth with every kind of plague as often as they wish.

<sup>11.7</sup> When they finish proclaiming their message, the beast that comes up out of the abyss will fight against them. He will defeat them and kill them,

<sup>11.8</sup> and their bodies will lie in the street of the great city, where their Lord was crucified. The symbolic name of that city is Sodom, or Egypt.

<sup>11.9</sup> People from all nations, tribes, languages, and races will look at their bodies for three and a half days and will not allow them to be buried.

<sup>11.10</sup> The people of the earth will be happy because of the death of these two. They will celebrate and send presents to each other, because those two prophets brought much suffering upon the whole human race.

<sup>11.11</sup> After three and a half days a life-giving breath came from God and entered them, and they stood up; and all who saw them were terrified.

<sup>11.12</sup> Then the two prophets heard a loud voice say to them from heaven, "Come up here!" As their enemies watched, they went up into heaven in a cloud.

<sup>11.13</sup> At that very moment there was a violent earthquake; a tenth of the city was destroyed, and seven thousand people were killed. The rest of the people were terrified and praised the greatness of the God of heaven.

<sup>11.14</sup> The second horror is over, but the third horror will come soon!

<sup>11.15</sup> Then the seventh angel blew his trumpet, and there were loud voices in heaven, saying, "The power to rule over the world belongs now to our Lord and his Messiah, and he will rule forever and ever!"

<sup>11.16</sup> Then the twenty-four elders who sit on their thrones in front of God threw themselves face downward and worshiped God,

<sup>11.17</sup> saying: "Lord God Almighty, the one who is and who was! We thank you that you have taken your great power and have begun to rule!

<sup>11.18</sup> "Then heathen were filled with rage, because the time for your anger has come, the time for the dead to be judged. The time has come to reward your servants, the prophets, and all your people, all who have reverence for you, great and small alike. The time has come to destroy those who destroy the earth!"

<sup>11.19</sup> God's temple in heaven was opened, and the Covenant Box was seen there. Then there were flashes of lightning, rumblings and peals of thunder, an earthquake, and heavy hail.

# 12

<sup>12.1</sup> Then a great and mysterious sight appeared in the sky. There was a woman, whose dress was the sun and who had the moon under her feet and a crown of twelve stars on her head.

<sup>12.2</sup> She was soon to give birth, and the pains and suffering of childbirth made her cry out.

<sup>12.3</sup> Another mysterious sight appeared in the sky. There was a huge red dragon with seven heads and ten horns and a crown on each of his heads.

<sup>12.4</sup> With his tail he dragged a third of the stars out of the sky and threw them down to the earth. He stood in front of the woman, in order to eat her child as soon as it was born.

<sup>12.5</sup> Then she gave birth to a son, who will rule over all nations with

an iron rod. But the child was snatched away and taken to God and his throne.

<sup>12.6</sup> The woman fled to the desert, to a place God had prepared for her, where she will be taken care of for 1,260 days.

<sup>12.7</sup> Then war broke out in heaven. Michael and his angels fought against the dragon, who fought back with his angels;

<sup>12.8</sup> but the dragon was defeated, and he and his angels were not allowed to stay in heaven any longer.

<sup>12.9</sup> The huge dragon was thrown out — that ancient serpent, named the Devil, or Satan, that deceived the whole world. He was thrown down to earth, and all his angels with him.

<sup>12.10</sup> Then I heard a loud voice in heaven saying, "Now God's salvation has come! Now God has shown his power as King! Now his Messiah has shown his authority! For the one who stood before our God and accused believers day and night has been thrown out of heaven.

<sup>12.11</sup> "They won the victory over him by the blood of the Lamb and by the truth which they proclaimed; and they were willing to give up their lives and die.

<sup>12.12</sup> "And so be glad, you heavens, and all you that live there! But how terrible for the earth and the sea! For the Devil has come down to you, and he is filled with rage, because he knows that he has only a little time left."

<sup>12.13</sup> When the dragon realized that he had been thrown down to the earth, he began to pursue the woman who had given birth to the boy.

<sup>12.14</sup> She was given the two wings of a large eagle in order to fly to her place in the desert, where she will be taken care of for three and a half years, safe from the dragon's attack.

<sup>12.15</sup> And then from his mouth the dragon poured out a flood of water after the woman, so that it would carry her away.

<sup>12.16</sup> But the earth helped the woman; it opened its mouth and swallowed the water that had come from the dragon's mouth.

<sup>12.17</sup> The dragon was furious with the woman and went off to fight against the rest of her descendants, all those who obey God's commandments and are faithful to the truth revealed by Jesus.

<sup>12.18</sup> And the dragon stood on the seashore.

# 13

<sup>13.1</sup> Then I saw a beast coming up out of the sea. It had ten horns and seven heads; on each of its horns there was a crown, and on each of its heads there was a name that was insulting to God.

<sup>13.2</sup> The beast looked like a leopard, with feet like a bear's feet and a

mouth like a lion's mouth. The dragon gave the beast his own power, his throne, and his vast authority.

¹³·³ One of the heads of the beast seemed to have been fatally wounded, but the wound had healed. The whole earth was amazed and followed the beast.

¹³·⁴ Everyone worshiped the dragon because he had given his authority to the beast. They worshiped the beast also, saying, "Who is like the beast? Who can fight against it?"

¹³·⁵ The beast was allowed to make proud claims which were insulting to God, and it was permitted to have authority for forty-two months.

¹³·⁶ It began to curse God, his name, the place where he lives, and all those who live in heaven.

¹³·⁷ It was allowed to fight against God's people and to defeat them, and it was given authority over every tribe, nation, language, and race.

¹³·⁸ All people living on earth will worship it, except those whose names were written before the creation of the world in the book of the living which belongs to the Lamb that was killed.

¹³·⁹ "Listen, then, if you have ears!

¹³·¹⁰ "Whoever is meant to be captured will surely be captured; whoever is meant to be killed by the sword will surely be killed by the sword. This calls for endurance and faith on the part of God's people."

¹³·¹¹ Then I saw another beast, which came up out of the earth. It had two horns like a lamb's horns, and it spoke like a dragon.

¹³·¹² It used the vast authority of the first beast in its presence. It forced the earth and all who live on it to worship the first beast, whose wound had healed.

¹³·¹³ This second beast performed great miracles; it made fire come down out of heaven to earth in the sight of everyone.

¹³·¹⁴ And it deceived all the people living on earth by means of the miracles which it was allowed to perform in the presence of the first beast. The beast told them to build an image in honor of the beast that had been wounded by the sword and yet lived.

¹³·¹⁵ The second beast was allowed to breathe life into the image of the first beast, so that the image could talk and put to death all those who would not worship it.

¹³·¹⁶ The beast forced all the people, small and great, rich and poor, slave and free, to have a mark placed on their right hands or on their foreheads.

<sup>13.17</sup> No one could buy or sell <u>without this mark</u>, that is, the beast's name or the number that stands <u>for the name</u>.

<sup>13.18</sup> This calls <u>for wisdom</u>. Whoever is intelligent can figure out the meaning <u>of the number</u> <u>of the beast</u>, because the number stands <u>for the name</u> of someone. Its number is 666.

# 14

<sup>14.1</sup> Then I looked, and there was the Lamb standing <u>on Mount Zion;</u> <u>with him</u> were 144,000 people who have his name and his Father's name written <u>on their foreheads.</u>

<sup>14.2</sup> And I heard a voice <u>from heaven</u> that sounded <u>like a roaring wa-</u><u>terfall</u>, <u>like a loud peal</u> <u>of thunder.</u> It sounded <u>like the music</u> made <u>by</u> <u>musicians</u> playing their harps.

<sup>14.3</sup> The 144,000 people stood <u>before the throne, the four living crea-</u><u>tures, and the elders;</u> they were singing a new song, which only they could learn. <u>Of the whole human race</u> they are the only ones who have been redeemed.

<sup>14.4</sup> They are the men who have kept themselves pure <u>by not</u> hav-ing sexual relations <u>with women;</u> they are virgins. They follow the Lamb wherever he goes. They have been redeemed <u>from the rest</u> <u>of</u> <u>the human race</u> and are the first ones to be offered <u>to God</u> and <u>to the</u> <u>Lamb.</u>

<sup>14.5</sup> They have never been known to tell lies; they are faultless.

<sup>14.6</sup> Then I saw another angel flying high <u>in the air</u>, <u>with an eternal</u> <u>message</u> of Good News to announce <u>to the peoples</u> <u>of the earth</u>, <u>to</u> <u>every race, tribe, language, and nation.</u>

<sup>14.7</sup> He said <u>in a loud voice</u>, "Honor God and praise his greatness! For the time has come <u>for him</u> to judge all people. Worship him who made heaven, earth, sea, and the springs <u>of water!</u>"

<sup>14.8</sup> A second angel followed the first one, saying, "She has fallen! Great Babylon has fallen! She made all peoples drink her wine — the strong wine <u>of her immoral lust!</u>"

<sup>14.9</sup> A third angel followed the first two, saying <u>in a loud voice</u>, "Those who worship the beast and its image and receive the mark <u>on their</u> <u>forehead</u> or <u>on their hand</u>

<sup>14.10</sup> "will themselves drink God's wine, the wine <u>of his fury</u>, which he has poured <u>at full strength</u> <u>into the cup</u> <u>of his anger!</u> All who do this will be tormented <u>in fire and sulfur</u> <u>before the holy angels and the</u> <u>Lamb.</u>

<sup>14.11</sup> "The smoke <u>of the fire</u> that torments them goes up forever and ever. There is no relief day or night <u>for those</u> who worship the beast

and its image, for anyone who has the mark of its name."

14.12 This calls for endurance on the part of God's people, those who obey God's commandments and are faithful to Jesus.

14.13 Then I heard a voice from heaven saying, "Write this: Happy are those who from now on die in the service of the Lord!" "Yes indeed!" answers the Spirit. "They will enjoy rest from their hard work, because the results of their service go with them."

14.14 Then I looked, and there was a white cloud, and sitting on the cloud was what looked like a human being, with a crown of gold on his head and a sharp sickle in his hand.

14.15 Then another angel came out from the temple and cried out in a loud voice to the one who was sitting on the cloud, "Use your sickle and reap the harvest, because the time has come; the earth is ripe for the harvest!"

14.16 Then the one who sat on the cloud swung his sickle on the earth, and the earth's harvest was reaped.

14.17 Then I saw another angel come out of the temple in heaven, and he also had a sharp sickle.

14.18 Then another angel, who is in charge of the fire, came from the altar. He shouted in a loud voice to the angel who had the sharp sickle, "Use your sickle, and cut the grapes from the vineyard of the earth, because the grapes are ripe!"

14.19 So the angel swung his sickle on the earth, cut the grapes from the vine, and threw them into the wine press of God's furious anger.

14.20 The grapes were squeezed out in the wine press outside the city, and blood came out of the wine press in a flood two hundred miles long and about five feet deep.

# 15

15.1 Then I saw in the sky another mysterious sight, great and amazing. There were seven angels with seven plagues, which are the last ones, because they are the final expression of God's anger.

15.2 Then I saw what looked like a sea of glass mixed with fire. I also saw those who had won the victory over the beast and its image and over the one whose name is represented by a number. They were standing by the sea of glass, holding harps that God had given them

15.3 and singing the song of Moses, the servant of God, and the song of the Lamb: "Lord God Almighty, how great and wonderful are your deeds! King of the nations, how right and true are your ways!

15.4 "Who will not stand in awe of you, Lord? Who will refuse to declare your greatness? You alone are holy. All the nations will come and worship you, because your just actions are seen by all."

<sup>15.5</sup> After this I saw the temple in heaven open, with the Sacred Tent in it.

<sup>15.6</sup> The seven angels who had the seven plagues came out of the temple, dressed in clean shining linen and with gold bands tied around their chests.

<sup>15.7</sup> Then one of the four living creatures gave the seven angels seven gold bowls full of the anger of God, who lives forever and ever.

<sup>15.8</sup> The temple was filled with smoke from the glory and power of God, and no one could go into the temple until the seven plagues brought by the seven angels had come to an end.

# 16

<sup>16.1</sup> Then I heard a loud voice speaking from the temple to the seven angels: "Go and pour out the seven bowls of God's anger on the earth!"

<sup>16.2</sup> The first angel went and poured out his bowl on the earth. Terrible and painful sores appeared on those who had the mark of the beast and on those who had worshiped its image.

<sup>16.3</sup> Then the second angel poured out his bowl on the sea. The water became like the blood of a dead person, and every living creature in the sea died.

<sup>16.4</sup> Then the third angel poured out his bowl on the rivers and the springs of water, and they turned into blood.

<sup>16.5</sup> I heard the angel in charge of the waters say, "The judgments you have made are just, O Holy One, you who are and who were!

<sup>16.6</sup> "They poured out the blood of God's people and of the prophets, and so you have given them blood to drink. They are getting what they deserve!"

<sup>16.7</sup> Then I heard a voice from the altar saying, "Lord God Almighty! True and just indeed are your judgments!"

<sup>16.8</sup> Then the fourth angel poured out his bowl on the sun, and it was allowed to burn people with its fiery heat.

<sup>16.9</sup> They were burned by the fierce heat, and they cursed the name of God, who has authority over these plagues. But they would not turn from their sins and praise his greatness.

<sup>16.10</sup> Then the fifth angel poured out his bowl on the throne of the beast. Darkness fell over the beast's kingdom, and people bit their tongues because of their pain,

<sup>16.11</sup> and they cursed the God of heaven for their pains and sores. But they did not turn from their evil ways.

¹⁶·¹² Then the sixth angel poured out his bowl on the great Euphrates River. The river dried up, to provide a way for the kings who come from the east.

¹⁶·¹³ Then I saw three unclean spirits that looked like frogs. They were coming out of the mouth of the dragon, the mouth of the beast, and the mouth of the false prophet.

¹⁶·¹⁴ They are the spirits of demons that perform miracles. These three spirits go out to all the kings of the world, to bring them together for the battle on the great Day of Almighty God.

¹⁶·¹⁵ "Listen! I am coming like a thief! Happy is he who stays awake and guards his clothes, so that he will not walk around naked and be ashamed in public!"

¹⁶·¹⁶ Then the spirits brought the kings together in the place that in Hebrew is called Armageddon.

¹⁶·¹⁷ Then the seventh angel poured out his bowl in the air. A loud voice came from the throne in the temple, saying, "It is done!"

¹⁶·¹⁸ There were flashes of lightning, rumblings and peals of thunder, and a terrible earthquake. There has never been such an earthquake since the creation of human beings; this was the worst earthquake of all!

¹⁶·¹⁹ The great city was split into three parts, and the cities of all countries were destroyed. God remembered great Babylon and made her drink the wine from his cup — the wine of his furious anger.

¹⁶·²⁰ All the islands disappeared, all the mountains vanished.

¹⁶·²¹ Huge hailstones, each weighing as much as a hundred pounds, fell from the sky on people, who cursed God on account of the plague of hail, because it was such a terrible plague.

# 17

¹⁷·¹ Then one of the seven angels who had the seven bowls came to me and said, "Come, and I will show you how the famous prostitute is to be punished, that great city that is built near many rivers.

¹⁷·² "The kings of the earth practiced sexual immorality with her, and the people of the world became drunk from drinking the wine of her immorality."

¹⁷·³ The Spirit took control of me, and the angel carried me to a desert. There I saw a woman sitting on a red beast that had names insulting to God written all over it; the beast had seven heads and ten horns.

¹⁷·⁴ The woman was dressed in purple and scarlet, and covered with gold ornaments, precious stones, and pearls. In her hand she held a

gold cup full of obscene and filthy things, the result of her immorality.

<sup>17.5</sup> On her forehead was written a name that has a secret meaning: "Great Babylon, the mother of all prostitutes and perverts in the world."

<sup>17.6</sup> And I saw that the woman was drunk with the blood of God's people and the blood of those who were killed because they had been loyal to Jesus. When I saw her, I was completely amazed.

<sup>17.7</sup> "Why are you amazed?" the angel asked me. "I will tell you the secret meaning of the woman and of the beast that carries her, the beast with seven heads and ten horns.

<sup>17.8</sup> "That beast was once alive, but lives no longer; it is about to come up from the abyss and will go off to be destroyed. The people living on earth whose names have not been written before the creation of the world in the book of the living, will all be amazed as they look at the beast. It was once alive; now it no longer lives, but it will reappear.

<sup>17.9</sup> "This calls for wisdom and understanding. The seven heads are seven hills, on which the woman sits. They are also seven kings:

<sup>17.10</sup> "five of them have fallen, one still rules, and the other one has not yet come; when he comes, he must rule only a little while.

<sup>17.11</sup> "And the beast that was once alive, but lives no longer, is itself an eighth king who is one of the seven and is going off to be destroyed.

<sup>17.12</sup> "The ten horns you saw are ten kings who have not yet begun to rule, but who will be given authority to rule as kings for one hour with the beast.

<sup>17.13</sup> "These ten all have the same purpose, and they give their power and authority to the beast.

<sup>17.14</sup> "They will fight against the Lamb; but the Lamb, together with his called, chosen, and faithful followers, will defeat them, because he is Lord of lords and King of kings."

<sup>17.15</sup> The angel also said to me, "The waters you saw, on which the prostitute sits, are nations, peoples, races, and languages.

<sup>17.16</sup> "The ten horns you saw and the beast will hate the prostitute; they will take away everything she has and leave her naked; they will eat her flesh and destroy her with fire.

<sup>17.17</sup> "For God has placed in their hearts the will to carry out his purpose by acting together and giving to the beast their power to rule until God's words come true.

<sup>17.18</sup> "The woman you saw is the great city that rules over the kings of the earth."

<sup>18.1</sup> <u>After this</u> I saw another angel coming down <u>out of heaven</u>. He had great authority, and his splendor brightened the whole earth.

<sup>18.2</sup> He cried out <u>in a loud voice</u>: "She has fallen! Great Babylon has fallen! She is now haunted <u>by demons and unclean spirits</u>; all kinds of filthy and hateful birds live <u>in her</u>.

<sup>18.3</sup> "For all the nations have drunk her wine — the strong wine <u>of her immoral lust</u>. The kings <u>of the earth</u> practiced sexual immorality <u>with her</u>, and the merchants <u>of the world</u> grew rich <u>from her unrestrained lust</u>."

<sup>18.4</sup> Then I heard another voice <u>from heaven</u>, saying, "Come out, my people! Come out <u>from her</u>! You must not take part <u>in her sins</u>; you must not share <u>in her punishment</u>!

<sup>18.5</sup> "For her sins are piled up as high <u>as heaven</u>, and God remembers her wicked ways.

<sup>18.6</sup> "Treat her exactly as she has treated you; pay her back double <u>for all</u> she has done. Fill her cup <u>with a drink</u> twice as strong <u>as the drink</u> she prepared <u>for you</u>.

<sup>18.7</sup> "Give her as much suffering and grief <u>as the glory and luxury</u> she gave herself. For she keeps telling herself: 'Here I sit, a queen! I am no widow, I will never know grief!'

<sup>18.8</sup> "<u>Because of this</u>, <u>in one day</u> she will be struck <u>with plagues</u> — disease, grief, and famine. And she will be burned <u>with fire</u>, because the Lord God, who judges her, is mighty."

<sup>18.9</sup> The kings <u>of the earth</u> who took part <u>in her immorality and lust</u> will cry and weep <u>over the city</u> when they see the smoke <u>from the flames</u> that consume her.

<sup>18.10</sup> They stand a long way off, because they are afraid of sharing <u>in her suffering</u>. They say, "How terrible! How awful! This great and mighty city Babylon! <u>In just one hour</u> you have been punished!"

<sup>18.11</sup> The merchants <u>of the earth</u> also cry and mourn <u>for her</u>, because no one buys their goods any longer;

<sup>18.12</sup> no one buys their gold, silver, precious stones, and pearls; their goods <u>of linen</u>, purple cloth, silk, and scarlet cloth; all kinds <u>of rare woods</u> and all kinds <u>of objects</u> made <u>of ivory</u> and <u>of expensive wood</u>, <u>of bronze, iron, and marble</u>;

<sup>18.13</sup> and cinnamon, spice, incense, myrrh, and frankincense; wine and oil, flour and wheat, cattle and sheep, horses and carriages, slaves, and even human lives.

<sup>18.14</sup> The merchants say <u>to her</u>, "All the good things you longed to own have disappeared, and all your wealth and glamor are gone, and you will never find them again!"

<sup>18.15</sup> The merchants, who became rich from doing business in that city, will stand a long way off, because they are afraid of sharing in her suffering. They will cry and mourn,

<sup>18.16</sup> and say, "How terrible! How awful for the great city! She used to dress herself in linen, purple, and scarlet, and cover herself with gold ornaments, precious stones, and pearls!

<sup>18.17</sup> "And in one hour she has lost all this wealth!" All the ships' captains and passengers, the sailors and all others who earn their living on the sea, stood a long way off,

<sup>18.18</sup> and cried out as they saw the smoke from the flames that consumed her: "There never has been another city like this great city!"

<sup>18.19</sup> They threw dust on their heads, they cried and mourned, saying, "How terrible! How awful for the great city! She is the city where all who have ships sailing the seas became rich on her wealth! And in one hour she has lost everything!"

<sup>18.20</sup> Be glad, heaven, because of her destruction! Be glad, God's people and the apostles and prophets! For God has condemned her for what she did to you!

<sup>18.21</sup> Then a mighty angel picked up a stone the size of a large millstone and threw it into the sea, saying, "This is how the great city Babylon will be violently thrown down and will never be seen again.

<sup>18.22</sup> "The music of harps and of human voices, of players of the flute and the trumpet, will never be heard in you again! No workman in any trade will ever be found in you again; and the sound of the millstone will be heard no more!

<sup>18.23</sup> "Never again will the light of a lamp be seen in you; no more will the voices of brides and grooms be heard in you. Your merchants were the most powerful in all the world, and with your false magic you deceived all the peoples of the world!"

<sup>18.24</sup> Babylon was punished because the blood of prophets and of God's people was found in the city; yes, the blood of all those who have been killed on earth.

# 19

<sup>19.1</sup> After this I heard what sounded like the roar of a large crowd of people in heaven, saying, "Praise God! Salvation, glory, and power belong to our God!

<sup>19.2</sup> "True and just are his judgments! He has condemned the prostitute who was corrupting the earth with her immorality. God has punished her because she killed his servants."

<sup>19.3</sup> Again they shouted, "Praise God! The smoke from the flames

that consume the great city goes up forever and ever!"

¹⁹·⁴ The twenty-four elders and the four living creatures fell down and worshiped God, who was seated on the throne. They said, "Amen! Praise God!"

¹⁹·⁵ Then there came from the throne the sound of a voice, saying, "Praise our God, all his servants and all people, both great and small, who have reverence for him!"

¹⁹·⁶ Then I heard what sounded like a crowd, like the sound of a roaring waterfall, like loud peals of thunder. I heard them say, "Praise God! For the Lord, our Almighty God, is King!

¹⁹·⁷ "Let us rejoice and be glad; let us praise his greatness! For the time has come for the wedding of the Lamb, and his bride has prepared herself for it.

¹⁹·⁸ "She has been given clean shining linen to wear." (The linen is the good deeds of God's people.)

¹⁹·⁹ Then the angel said to me, "Write this: Happy are those who have been invited to the wedding feast of the Lamb." And the angel added, "These are the true words of God."

¹⁹·¹⁰ I fell down at his feet to worship him, but he said to me, "Don't do it! I am a servant together with you and with other believers, all those who hold to the truth that Jesus revealed. Worship God!"
For the truth that Jesus revealed is what inspires the prophets.

¹⁹·¹¹ Then I saw heaven open, and there was a white horse. Its rider is called Faithful and True; it is with justice that he judges and fights his battles.

¹⁹·¹² His eyes were like a flame of fire, and he wore many crowns on his head. He had a name written on him, but no one except himself knows what it is.

¹⁹·¹³ The robe he wore was covered with blood. His name is "The Word of God."

¹⁹·¹⁴ The armies of heaven followed him, riding on white horses and dressed in clean white linen.

¹⁹·¹⁵ Out of his mouth came a sharp sword, with which he will defeat the nations. He will rule over them with a rod of iron, and he will trample out the wine in the wine press of the furious anger of the Almighty God.

¹⁹·¹⁶ On his robe and on his thigh was written the name: "King of kings and Lord of lords."

¹⁹·¹⁷ Then I saw an angel standing on the sun. He shouted in a loud voice to all the birds flying in midair: "Come and gather together for God's great feast!

<sup>19.18</sup> "Come and eat the flesh of kings, generals, and soldiers, the flesh of horses and their riders, the flesh of all people, slave and free, great and small!"

<sup>19.19</sup> Then I saw the beast and the kings of the earth and their armies gathered to fight against the one who was riding the horse and against his army.

<sup>19.20</sup> The beast was taken prisoner, together with the false prophet who had performed miracles in his presence. (It was by those miracles that he had deceived those who had the mark of the beast and those who had worshiped the image of the beast.) The beast and the false prophet were both thrown alive into the lake of fire that burns with sulfur.

<sup>19.21</sup> Their armies were killed by the sword that comes out of the mouth of the one who was riding the horse; and all the birds ate all they could of their flesh.

# 20

<sup>20.1</sup> Then I saw an angel coming down from heaven, holding in his hand the key of the abyss and a heavy chain.

<sup>20.2</sup> He seized the dragon, that ancient serpent — that is, the Devil, or Satan - and chained him up for a thousand years.

<sup>20.3</sup> The angel threw him into the abyss, locked it, and sealed it, so that he could not deceive the nations any more until the thousand years were over. After that he must be set loose for a little while.

<sup>20.4</sup> Then I saw thrones, and those who sat on them were given the power to judge. I also saw the souls of those who had been executed because they had proclaimed the truth that Jesus revealed and the word of God. They had not worshiped the beast or its image, nor had they received the mark of the beast on their foreheads or their hands. They came to life and ruled as kings with Christ for a thousand years.

<sup>20.5</sup> (The rest of the dead did not come to life until the thousand years were over.) This is the first raising of the dead.

<sup>20.6</sup> Happy and greatly blessed are those who are included in this first raising of the dead. The second death has no power over them; they shall be priests of God and of Christ, and they will rule with him for a thousand years.

<sup>20.7</sup> After the thousand years are over, Satan will be set loose from his prison,

<sup>20.8</sup> and he will go out to deceive the nations scattered over the whole world, that is, Gog and Magog. Satan will bring them all together for

battle, as many as the grains of sand on the seashore.

<sup>20.9</sup> They spread out over the earth and surrounded the camp of God's people and the city that he loves. But fire came down from heaven and destroyed them.

<sup>20.10</sup> Then the Devil, who deceived them, was thrown into the lake of fire and sulfur, where the beast and the false prophet had already been thrown; and they will be tormented day and night forever and ever.

<sup>20.11</sup> Then I saw a great white throne and the one who sits on it. Earth and heaven fled from his presence and were seen no more.

<sup>20.12</sup> And I saw the dead, great and small alike, standing before the throne. Books were opened, and then another book was opened, the book of the living. The dead were judged according to what they had done, as recorded in the books.

<sup>20.13</sup> Then the sea gave up its dead. Death and the world of the dead also gave up the dead they held. And all were judged according to what they had done.

<sup>20.14</sup> Then death and the world of the dead were thrown into the lake of fire. (This lake of fire is the second death.)

<sup>20.15</sup> Those who did not have their name written in the book of the living were thrown into the lake of fire.

# 21

<sup>21.1</sup> Then I saw a new heaven and a new earth. The first heaven and the first earth disappeared, and the sea vanished.

<sup>21.2</sup> And I saw the Holy City, the new Jerusalem, coming down out of heaven from God, prepared and ready, like a bride dressed to meet her husband.

<sup>21.3</sup> I heard a loud voice speaking from the throne: "Now God's home is with people! He will live with them, and they shall be his people. God himself will be with them, and he will be their God.

<sup>21.4</sup> "He will wipe away all tears from their eyes. There will be no more death, no more grief or crying or pain. The old things have disappeared."

<sup>21.5</sup> Then the one who sits on the throne said, "And now I make all things new!" He also said to me, "Write this, because these words are true and can be trusted."

<sup>21.6</sup> And he said, "It is done! I am the first and the last, the beginning and the end. To anyone who is thirsty I will give the right to drink from the spring of the water of life without paying for it.

<sup>21.7</sup> "Those who win the victory will receive this from me: I will be

their God, and they will be my children.

<sup>21.8</sup> "But cowards, traitors, perverts, murderers, the immoral, those who practice magic, those who worship idols, and all liars — the place for them is the lake burning with fire and sulfur, which is the second death."

<sup>21.9</sup> One of the seven angels who had the seven bowls full of the seven last plagues came to me and said, "Come, and I will show you the Bride, the wife of the Lamb."

<sup>21.10</sup> The Spirit took control of me, and the angel carried me to the top of a very high mountain. He showed me Jerusalem, the Holy City, coming down out of heaven from God

<sup>21.11</sup> and shining with the glory of God. The city shone like a precious stone, like a jasper, clear as crystal.

<sup>21.12</sup> It had a great, high wall with twelve gates and with twelve angels in charge of the gates. On the gates were written the names of the twelve tribes of the people of Israel.

<sup>21.13</sup> There were three gates on each side: three on the east, three on the south, three on the north, and three on the west.

<sup>21.14</sup> The city's wall was built on twelve foundation stones, on which were written the names of the twelve apostles of the Lamb.

<sup>21.15</sup> The angel who spoke to me had a gold measuring stick to measure the city, its gates, and its wall.

<sup>21.16</sup> The city was perfectly square, as wide as it was long. The angel measured the city with his measuring stick: it was fifteen hundred miles long and was as wide and as high as it was long.

<sup>21.17</sup> The angel also measured the wall, and it was 216 feet high, according to the standard unit of measure which he was using.

<sup>21.18</sup> The wall was made of jasper, and the city itself was made of pure gold, as clear as glass.

<sup>21.19</sup> The foundation stones of the city wall were adorned with all kinds of precious stones. The first foundation stone was jasper, the second sapphire, the third agate, the fourth emerald,

<sup>21.20</sup> the fifth onyx, the sixth carnelian, the seventh yellow quartz, the eighth beryl, the ninth topaz, the tenth chalcedony, the eleventh turquoise, the twelfth amethyst.

<sup>21.21</sup> The twelve gates were twelve pearls; each gate was made from a single pearl. The street of the city was of pure gold, transparent as glass.

<sup>21.22</sup> I did not see a temple in the city, because its temple is the Lord God Almighty and the Lamb.

<sup>21.23</sup> The city has no need of the sun or the moon to shine on it, be-

cause the glory of God shines on it, and the Lamb is its lamp.
²¹·²⁴ The peoples of the world will walk by its light, and the kings of the earth will bring their wealth into it.
²¹·²⁵ The gates of the city will stand open all day; they will never be closed, because there will be no night there.
²¹·²⁶ The greatness and the wealth of the nations will be brought into the city.
²¹·²⁷ But nothing that is impure will enter the city, nor anyone who does shameful things or tells lies. Only those whose names are written in the Lamb's book of the living will enter the city.

# 22

²²·¹ The angel also showed me the river of the water of life, sparkling like crystal, and coming from the throne of God and of the Lamb
²²·² and flowing down the middle of the city's street. On each side of the river was the tree of life, which bears fruit twelve times a year, once each month; and its leaves are for the healing of the nations.
²²·³ Nothing that is under God's curse will be found in the city. The throne of God and of the Lamb will be in the city, and his servants will worship him.
²²·⁴ They will see his face, and his name will be written on their foreheads.
²²·⁵ There shall be no more night, and they will not need lamps or sunlight, because the Lord God will be their light, and they will rule as kings forever and ever.
²²·⁶ Then the angel said to me, "These words are true and can be trusted. And the Lord God, who gives his Spirit to the prophets, has sent his angel to show his servants what must happen very soon."
²²·⁷ "Listen!" says Jesus. "I am coming soon! Happy are those who obey the prophetic words in this book!"
²²·⁸ I, John, have heard and seen all these things. And when I finished hearing and seeing them, I fell down at the feet of the angel who had shown me these things, and I was about to worship him.
²²·⁹ But he said to me, "Don't do it! I am a servant together with you and with your brothers the prophets and of all those who obey the words in this book. Worship God!"
²²·¹⁰ And he said to me, "Do not keep the prophetic words of this book a secret, because the time is near when all this will happen.
²²·¹¹ "Whoever is evil must go on doing evil, and whoever is filthy must go on being filthy; whoever is good must go on doing good, and whoever is holy must go on being holy."

<sup>22.12</sup> "Listen!" says Jesus. "I am coming soon! I will bring my rewards with me, to give to each one according to what he has done.

<sup>22.13</sup> "I am the first and the last, the beginning and the end."

<sup>22.14</sup> Happy are those who wash their robes clean and so have the right to eat the fruit from the tree of life and to go through the gates into the city.

<sup>22.15</sup> But outside the city are the perverts and those who practice magic, the immoral and the murderers, those who worship idols and those who are liars both in words and deeds.

<sup>22.16</sup> "I, Jesus, have sent my angel to announce these things to you in the churches. I am descended from the family of David; I am the bright morning star."

<sup>22.17</sup> The Spirit and the Bride say, "Come!" Everyone who hears this must also say, "Come!" Come, whoever is thirsty; accept the water of life as a gift, whoever wants it.

<sup>22.18</sup> I, John, solemnly warn everyone who hears the prophetic words of this book: if any add anything to them, God will add to their punishment the plagues described in this book.

<sup>22.19</sup> And if any take anything away from the prophetic words of this book, God will take away from them their share of the fruit of the tree of life and of the Holy City, which are described in this book.

<sup>22.20</sup> He who gives his testimony to all this says, "Yes indeed! I am coming soon!" So be it. Come, Lord Jesus!

<sup>22.21</sup> May the grace of the Lord Jesus be with everyone.